T0190363

# Lecture Notes in Computer Science  13957

Founding Editors

Gerhard Goos
Juris Hartmanis

The series Lecture Notes in Computer Science (LNCS), including its subseries Lecture Notes in Artificial Intelligence (LNAI) and Lecture Notes in Bioinformatics (LNBI), has established itself as a medium for the publication of new developments in computer science and information technology research, teaching, and education.

LNCS enjoys close cooperation with the computer science R & D community, the series counts many renowned academics among its volume editors and paper authors, and collaborates with prestigious societies. Its mission is to serve this international community by providing an invaluable service, mainly focused on the publication of conference and workshop proceedings and postproceedings. LNCS commenced publication in 1973.

Osvaldo Gervasi · Beniamino Murgante ·
David Taniar · Bernady O. Apduhan ·
Ana Cristina Braga · Chiara Garau ·
Anastasia Stratigea
Editors

# Computational Science and Its Applications – ICCSA 2023

23rd International Conference
Athens, Greece, July 3–6, 2023
Proceedings, Part II

Springer

*Editors*
Osvaldo Gervasi 🔟
University of Perugia
Perugia, Italy

David Taniar 🔟
Monash University
Clayton, VIC, Australia

Ana Cristina Braga 🔟
University of Minho
Braga, Portugal

Anastasia Stratigea 🔟
National Technical University of Athens
Athens, Greece

Beniamino Murgante 🔟
University of Basilicata
Potenza, Italy

Bernady O. Apduhan
Kyushu Sangyo University
Fukuoka, Japan

Chiara Garau 🔟
University of Cagliari
Cagliari, Italy

ISSN 0302-9743          ISSN 1611-3349 (electronic)
Lecture Notes in Computer Science
ISBN 978-3-031-36807-3          ISBN 978-3-031-36808-0 (eBook)
https://doi.org/10.1007/978-3-031-36808-0

This Springer imprint is published by the registered company Springer Nature Switzerland AG
The registered company address is: Gewerbestrasse 11, 6330 Cham, Switzerland

# Preface

These two volumes (LNCS volumes 13956–13957) consist of the peer-reviewed papers from the 2023 International Conference on Computational Science and Its Applications (ICCSA 2023) which took place during July 3–6, 2023. In addition, the peer-reviewed papers of the 61 Workshops, the Workshops proceedings, are published in a separate set consisting of nine volumes (LNCS 14104–14112).

The conference was finally held in person after the difficult period of the Covid-19 pandemic in the wonderful city of Athens, in the cosy facilities of the National Technical University. Our experience during the pandemic period allowed us to enable virtual participation also this year for those who were unable to attend the event, due to logistical, political and economic problems, by adopting a technological infrastructure based on open source software (jitsi + riot), and a commercial cloud infrastructure.

ICCSA 2023 was another successful event in the International Conference on Computational Science and Its Applications (ICCSA) series, previously held as a hybrid event (with one third of registered authors attending in person) in Malaga, Spain (2022), Cagliari, Italy (hybrid with few participants in person in 2021 and completely online in 2020), whilst earlier editions took place in Saint Petersburg, Russia (2019), Melbourne, Australia (2018), Trieste, Italy (2017), Beijing, China (2016), Banff, Canada (2015), Guimaraes, Portugal (2014), Ho Chi Minh City, Vietnam (2013), Salvador, Brazil (2012), Santander, Spain (2011), Fukuoka, Japan (2010), Suwon, South Korea (2009), Perugia, Italy (2008), Kuala Lumpur, Malaysia (2007), Glasgow, UK (2006), Singapore (2005), Assisi, Italy (2004), Montreal, Canada (2003), and (as ICCS) Amsterdam, The Netherlands (2002) and San Francisco, USA (2001).

Computational Science is the main pillar of most of the present research, industrial and commercial applications, and plays a unique role in exploiting ICT innovative technologies, and the ICCSA series have been providing a venue to researchers and industry practitioners to discuss new ideas, to share complex problems and their solutions, and to shape new trends in Computational Science. As the conference mirrors society from a scientific point of view, this year's undoubtedly dominant theme was the machine learning and artificial intelligence and their applications in the most diverse economic and industrial fields.

The ICCSA 2023 conference is structured in 6 general tracks covering the fields of computational science and its applications: Computational Methods, Algorithms and Scientific Applications – High Performance Computing and Networks – Geometric Modeling, Graphics and Visualization – Advanced and Emerging Applications – Information Systems and Technologies – Urban and Regional Planning. In addition, the conference consisted of 61 workshops, focusing on very topical issues of importance to science, technology and society: from new mathematical approaches for solving complex computational systems, to information and knowledge in the Internet of Things, new statistical and optimization methods, several Artificial Intelligence approaches, sustainability issues, smart cities and related technologies.

We accepted 67 full papers, 13 short papers and 6 PHD Showcase papers from 283 submissions to the General Tracks of the conference (acceptance rate 30%). For the 61 workshops we accepted 350 full papers, 29 short papers and 2 PHD Showcase papers. We would like to express our appreciations for the workshops chairs and co-chairs for their hard work and dedication.

The success of the ICCSA series in general, and of ICCSA 2023 in particular, vitally depends on the support of many people: authors, presenters, participants, keynote speakers, workshop chairs, session chairs, organizing committee members, student volunteers, Program Committee members, Advisory Committee members, International Liaison chairs, reviewers and others in various roles. We take this opportunity to wholehartedly thank them all.

We also wish to thank our publisher, Springer, for their acceptance to publish the proceedings, for sponsoring part of the best papers awards and for their kind assistance and cooperation during the editing process.

We cordially invite you to visit the ICCSA website https://iccsa.org where you can find all the relevant information about this interesting and exciting event.

July 2023

Osvaldo Gervasi
David Taniar
Bernady O. Apduhan

# Welcome Message from Organizers

After the 2021 ICCSA in Cagliari, Italy and the 2022 ICCSA in Malaga, Spain, ICCSA continued its successful scientific endeavours in 2023, hosted again in the Mediterranean neighbourhood. This time, ICCSA 2023 moved a bit more to the east of the Mediterranean Region and was held in the metropolitan city of Athens, the capital of Greece and a vibrant urban environment endowed with a prominent cultural heritage that dates back to the ancient years. As a matter of fact, Athens is one of the oldest cities in the world, and the cradle of democracy. The city has a history of over 3,000 years and, according to the myth, it took its name from Athena, the Goddess of Wisdom and daughter of Zeus.

ICCSA 2023 took place in a secure environment, relieved from the immense stress of the COVID-19 pandemic. This gave us the chance to have a safe and vivid, in-person participation which, combined with the very active engagement of the ICCSA 2023 scientific community, set the ground for highly motivating discussions and interactions as to the latest developments of computer science and its applications in the real world for improving quality of life.

The National Technical University of Athens (NTUA), one of the most prestigious Greek academic institutions, had the honour of hosting ICCSA 2023. The Local Organizing Committee really feels the burden and responsibility of such a demanding task; and puts in all the necessary energy in order to meet participants' expectations and establish a friendly, creative and inspiring, scientific and social/cultural environment that allows for new ideas and perspectives to flourish.

Since all ICCSA participants, either informatics-oriented or application-driven, realize the tremendous steps and evolution of computer science during the last few decades and the huge potential these offer to cope with the enormous challenges of humanity in a globalized, 'wired' and highly competitive world, the expectations from ICCSA 2023 were set high in order for a successful matching between computer science progress and communities' aspirations to be attained, i.e., a progress that serves real, place- and people-based needs and can pave the way towards a visionary, smart, sustainable, resilient and inclusive future for both the current and the next generation.

On behalf of the Local Organizing Committee, I would like to sincerely thank all of you who have contributed to ICCSA 2023 and I cordially welcome you to my 'home', NTUA.

On behalf of the Local Organizing Committee.

Anastasia Stratigea

# Organization

ICCSA 2023 was organized by the National Technical University of Athens (Greece), the University of the Aegean (Greece), the University of Perugia (Italy), the University of Basilicata (Italy), Monash University (Australia), Kyushu Sangyo University (Japan), the University of Minho (Portugal). The conference was supported by two NTUA Schools, namely the School of Rural, Surveying and Geoinformatics Engineering and the School of Electrical and Computer Engineering.

## Honorary General Chairs

Norio Shiratori                    Chuo University, Japan
Kenneth C. J. Tan                  Sardina Systems, UK

## General Chairs

Osvaldo Gervasi                    University of Perugia, Italy
Anastasia Stratigea                National Technical University of Athens, Greece
Bernady O. Apduhan                 Kyushu Sangyo University, Japan

## Program Committee Chairs

Beniamino Murgante                 University of Basilicata, Italy
Dimitris Kavroudakis               University of the Aegean, Greece
Ana Maria A. C. Rocha              University of Minho, Portugal
David Taniar                       Monash University, Australia

## International Advisory Committee

Jemal Abawajy                      Deakin University, Australia
Dharma P. Agarwal                  University of Cincinnati, USA
Rajkumar Buyya                     Melbourne University, Australia
Claudia Bauzer Medeiros            University of Campinas, Brazil
Manfred M. Fisher                  Vienna University of Economics and Business, Austria
Marina L. Gavrilova                University of Calgary, Canada

| Sumi Helal | University of Florida, USA and University of Lancaster, UK |
| Yee Leung | Chinese University of Hong Kong, China |

## International Liaison Chairs

| Ivan Blečić | University of Cagliari, Italy |
| Giuseppe Borruso | University of Trieste, Italy |
| Elise De Donker | Western Michigan University, USA |
| Maria Irene Falcão | University of Minho, Portugal |
| Inmaculada Garcia Fernandez | University of Malaga, Spain |
| Eligius Hendrix | University of Malaga, Spain |
| Robert C. H. Hsu | Chung Hua University, Taiwan |
| Tai-Hoon Kim | Beijing Jaotong University, China |
| Vladimir Korkhov | Saint Petersburg University, Russia |
| Takashi Naka | Kyushu Sangyo University, Japan |
| Rafael D. C. Santos | National Institute for Space Research, Brazil |
| Maribel Yasmina Santos | University of Minho, Portugal |
| Elena Stankova | Saint Petersburg University, Russia |

## Workshop and Session Organizing Chairs

| Beniamino Murgante | University of Basilicata, Italy |
| Chiara Garau | University of Cagliari, Italy |

## Award Chair

| Wenny Rahayu | La Trobe University, Australia |

## Publicity Committee Chairs

| Elmer Dadios | De La Salle University, Philippines |
| Nataliia Kulabukhova | Saint Petersburg University, Russia |
| Daisuke Takahashi | Tsukuba University, Japan |
| Shangwang Wang | Beijing University of Posts and Telecommunications, China |

## Local Organizing Committee Chairs

| | |
|---|---|
| Anastasia Stratigea | National Technical University of Athens, Greece |
| Dimitris Kavroudakis | University of the Aegean, Greece |
| Charalambos Ioannidis | National Technical University of Athens, Greece |
| Nectarios Koziris | National Technical University of Athens, Greece |
| Efthymios Bakogiannis | National Technical University of Athens, Greece |
| Yiota Theodora | National Technical University of Athens, Greece |
| Dimitris Fotakis | National Technical University of Athens, Greece |
| Apostolos Lagarias | National Technical University of Athens, Greece |
| Akrivi Leka | National Technical University of Athens, Greece |
| Dionisia Koutsi | National Technical University of Athens, Greece |
| Alkistis Dalkavouki | National Technical University of Athens, Greece |
| Maria Panagiotopoulou | National Technical University of Athens, Greece |
| Angeliki Papazoglou | National Technical University of Athens, Greece |
| Natalia Tsigarda | National Technical University of Athens, Greece |
| Konstantinos Athanasopoulos | National Technical University of Athens, Greece |
| Ioannis Xatziioannou | National Technical University of Athens, Greece |
| Vasiliki Krommyda | National Technical University of Athens, Greece |
| Panayiotis Patsilinakos | National Technical University of Athens, Greece |
| Sofia Kassiou | National Technical University of Athens, Greece |

## Technology Chair

| | |
|---|---|
| Damiano Perri | University of Florence, Italy |

## Program Committee

| | |
|---|---|
| Vera Afreixo | University of Aveiro, Portugal |
| Filipe Alvelos | University of Minho, Portugal |
| Hartmut Asche | University of Potsdam, Germany |
| Ginevra Balletto | University of Cagliari, Italy |
| Michela Bertolotto | University College Dublin, Ireland |
| Sandro Bimonte | CEMAGREF, TSCF, France |
| Rod Blais | University of Calgary, Canada |
| Ivan Blečić | University of Sassari, Italy |
| Giuseppe Borruso | University of Trieste, Italy |
| Ana Cristina Braga | University of Minho, Portugal |
| Massimo Cafaro | University of Salento, Italy |
| Yves Caniou | Lyon University, France |

Ermanno Cardelli — University of Perugia, Italy
José A. Cardoso e Cunha — Universidade Nova de Lisboa, Portugal
Rui Cardoso — University of Beira Interior, Portugal
Leocadio G. Casado — University of Almeria, Spain
Carlo Cattani — University of Salerno, Italy
Mete Celik — Erciyes University, Turkey
Maria Cerreta — University of Naples "Federico II", Italy
Hyunseung Choo — Sungkyunkwan University, Korea
Rachel Chieng-Sing Lee — Sunway University, Malaysia
Min Young Chung — Sungkyunkwan University, Korea
Florbela Maria da Cruz Domingues Correia — Polytechnic Institute of Viana do Castelo, Portugal
Gilberto Corso Pereira — Federal University of Bahia, Brazil
Alessandro Costantini — INFN, Italy
Carla Dal Sasso Freitas — Universidade Federal do Rio Grande do Sul, Brazil

Pradesh Debba — The Council for Scientific and Industrial Research (CSIR), South Africa

Hendrik Decker — Instituto Tecnológico de Informática, Spain
Robertas Damaševičius — Kausan University of Technology, Lithuania
Frank Devai — London South Bank University, UK
Rodolphe Devillers — Memorial University of Newfoundland, Canada
Joana Matos Dias — University of Coimbra, Portugal
Paolino Di Felice — University of L'Aquila, Italy
Prabu Dorairaj — NetApp, India/USA
Noelia Faginas Lago — University of Perugia, Italy
M. Irene Falcao — University of Minho, Portugal
Cherry Liu Fang — U.S. DOE Ames Laboratory, USA
Florbela P. Fernandes — Polytechnic Institute of Bragança, Portugal
Jose-Jesus Fernandez — National Centre for Biotechnology, CSIS, Spain
Paula Odete Fernandes — Polytechnic Institute of Bragança, Portugal
Adelaide de Fátima Baptista Valente Freitas — University of Aveiro, Portugal
Manuel Carlos Figueiredo — University of Minho, Portugal
Maria Celia Furtado Rocha — PRODEB–PósCultura/UFBA, Brazil
Chiara Garau — University of Cagliari, Italy
Paulino Jose Garcia Nieto — University of Oviedo, Spain
Raffaele Garrisi — Polizia di Stato, Italy
Jerome Gensel — LSR-IMAG, France
Maria Giaoutzi — National Technical University, Athens, Greece
Arminda Manuela Andrade Pereira Gonçalves — University of Minho, Portugal

| | |
|---|---|
| Louiza de Macedo Mourelle | State University of Rio de Janeiro, Brazil |
| Nadia Nedjah | State University of Rio de Janeiro, Brazil |
| Laszlo Neumann | University of Girona, Spain |
| Kok-Leong Ong | Deakin University, Australia |
| Belen Palop | Universidad de Valladolid, Spain |
| Marcin Paprzycki | Polish Academy of Sciences, Poland |
| Eric Pardede | La Trobe University, Australia |
| Kwangjin Park | Wonkwang University, Korea |
| Ana Isabel Pereira | Polytechnic Institute of Bragança, Portugal |
| Massimiliano Petri | University of Pisa, Italy |
| Telmo Pinto | University of Coimbra, Portugal |
| Maurizio Pollino | Italian National Agency for New Technologies, Energy and Sustainable Economic Development, Italy |
| Alenka Poplin | University of Hamburg, Germany |
| Vidyasagar Potdar | Curtin University of Technology, Australia |
| David C. Prosperi | Florida Atlantic University, USA |
| Wenny Rahayu | La Trobe University, Australia |
| Jerzy Respondek | Silesian University of Technology Poland |
| Humberto Rocha | INESC-Coimbra, Portugal |
| Jon Rokne | University of Calgary, Canada |
| Octavio Roncero | CSIC, Spain |
| Maytham Safar | Kuwait University, Kuwait |
| Chiara Saracino | A.O. Ospedale Niguarda Ca' Granda - Milano, Italy |
| Marco Paulo Seabra dos Reis | University of Coimbra, Portugal |
| Jie Shen | University of Michigan, USA |
| Qi Shi | Liverpool John Moores University, UK |
| Dale Shires | U.S. Army Research Laboratory, USA |
| Inês Soares | University of Coimbra, Portugal |
| Elena Stankova | St. Petersburg University, Russia |
| Takuo Suganuma | Tohoku University, Japan |
| Eufemia Tarantino | Polytechnic of Bari, Italy |
| Sergio Tasso | University of Perugia, Italy |
| Ana Paula Teixeira | University of Trás-os-Montes and Alto Douro, Portugal |
| M. Filomena Teodoro | Portuguese Naval Academy and University of Lisbon, Portugal |
| Parimala Thulasiraman | University of Manitoba, Canada |
| Carmelo Torre | Polytechnic of Bari, Italy |
| Javier Martinez Torres | Centro Universitario de la Defensa Zaragoza, Spain |

| Giuseppe A. Trunfio | University of Sassari, Italy |
| Pablo Vanegas | University of Cuenca, Equador |
| Marco Vizzari | University of Perugia, Italy |
| Varun Vohra | Merck Inc., USA |
| Koichi Wada | University of Tsukuba, Japan |
| Krzysztof Walkowiak | Wroclaw University of Technology, Poland |
| Zequn Wang | Intelligent Automation Inc, USA |
| Robert Weibel | University of Zurich, Switzerland |
| Frank Westad | Norwegian University of Science and Technology, Norway |
| Roland Wismüller | Universität Siegen, Germany |
| Mudasser Wyne | SOET National University, USA |
| Chung-Huang Yang | National Kaohsiung Normal University, Taiwan |
| Xin-She Yang | National Physical Laboratory, UK |
| Salim Zabir | France Telecom Japan Co., Japan |
| Haifeng Zhao | University of California, Davis, USA |
| Fabiana Zollo | University of Venice "Cà Foscari", Italy |
| Albert Y. Zomaya | University of Sydney, Australia |

## Workshop Organizers

## Advanced Data Science Techniques with Applications in Industry and Environmental Sustainability (ATELIERS 2023)

| Dario Torregrossa | Goodyear, Luxemburg |
| Antonino Marvuglia | Luxembourg Institute of Science and Technology, Luxemburg |
| Valeria Borodin | École des Mines de Saint-Étienne, Luxemburg |
| Mohamed Laib | Luxembourg Institute of Science and Technology, Luxemburg |

## Advances in Artificial Intelligence Learning Technologies: Blended Learning, STEM, Computational Thinking and Coding (AAILT 2023)

| Alfredo Milani | University of Perugia, Italy |
| Valentina Franzoni | University of Perugia, Italy |
| Sergio Tasso | University of Perugia, Italy |

## Advanced Processes of Mathematics and Computing Models in Complex Computational Systems (ACMC 2023)

| | |
|---|---|
| Yeliz Karaca | University of Massachusetts Chan Medical School and Massachusetts Institute of Technology, USA |
| Dumitru Baleanu | Cankaya University, Turkey |
| Osvaldo Gervasi | University of Perugia, Italy |
| Yudong Zhang | University of Leicester, UK |
| Majaz Moonis | University of Massachusetts Medical School, USA |

## Artificial Intelligence Supported Medical Data Examination (AIM 2023)

| | |
|---|---|
| David Taniar | Monash University, Australia |
| Seifedine Kadry | Noroff University College, Norway |
| Venkatesan Rajinikanth | Saveetha School of Engineering, India |

## Advanced and Innovative Web Apps (AIWA 2023)

| | |
|---|---|
| Damiano Perri | University of Perugia, Italy |
| Osvaldo Gervasi | University of Perugia, Italy |

## Assessing Urban Sustainability (ASUS 2023)

| | |
|---|---|
| Elena Todella | Polytechnic of Turin, Italy |
| Marika Gaballo | Polytechnic of Turin, Italy |
| Beatrice Mecca | Polytechnic of Turin, Italy |

## Advances in Web Based Learning (AWBL 2023)

| | |
|---|---|
| Birol Ciloglugil | Ege University, Turkey |
| Mustafa Inceoglu | Ege University, Turkey |

## Blockchain and Distributed Ledgers: Technologies and Applications (BDLTA 2023)

| | |
|---|---|
| Vladimir Korkhov | Saint Petersburg State University, Russia |
| Elena Stankova | Saint Petersburg State University, Russia |
| Nataliia Kulabukhova | Saint Petersburg State University, Russia |

## Bio and Neuro Inspired Computing and Applications (BIONCA 2023)

| | |
|---|---|
| Nadia Nedjah | State University of Rio De Janeiro, Brazil |
| Luiza De Macedo Mourelle | State University of Rio De Janeiro, Brazil |

## Choices and Actions for Human Scale Cities: Decision Support Systems (CAHSC–DSS 2023)

| | |
|---|---|
| Giovanna Acampa | University of Florence and University of Enna Kore, Italy |
| Fabrizio Finucci | Roma Tre University, Italy |
| Luca S. Dacci | Polytechnic of Turin, Italy |

## Computational and Applied Mathematics (CAM 2023)

| | |
|---|---|
| Maria Irene Falcao | University of Minho, Portugal |
| Fernando Miranda | University of Minho, Portugal |

## Computational and Applied Statistics (CAS 2023)

| | |
|---|---|
| Ana Cristina Braga | University of Minho, Portugal |

## Cyber Intelligence and Applications (CIA 2023)

| | |
|---|---|
| Gianni Dangelo | University of Salerno, Italy |
| Francesco Palmieri | University of Salerno, Italy |
| Massimo Ficco | University of Salerno, Italy |

## Conversations South-North on Climate Change Adaptation Towards Smarter and More Sustainable Cities (CLAPS 2023)

| | |
|---|---|
| Chiara Garau | University of Cagliari, Italy |
| Cristina Trois | University of kwaZulu-Natal, South Africa |
| Claudia Loggia | University of kwaZulu-Natal, South Africa |
| John Östh | Faculty of Technology, Art and Design, Norway |
| Mauro Coni | University of Cagliari, Italy |
| Alessio Satta | MedSea Foundation, Italy |

## Computational Mathematics, Statistics and Information Management (CMSIM 2023)

| | |
|---|---|
| Maria Filomena Teodoro | University of Lisbon and Portuguese Naval Academy, Portugal |
| Marina A. P. Andrade | University Institute of Lisbon, Portugal |

## Computational Optimization and Applications (COA 2023)

| | |
|---|---|
| Ana Maria A. C. Rocha | University of Minho, Portugal |
| Humberto Rocha | University of Coimbra, Portugal |

## Computational Astrochemistry (CompAstro 2023)

| | |
|---|---|
| Marzio Rosi | University of Perugia, Italy |
| Nadia Balucani | University of Perugia, Italy |
| Cecilia Ceccarelli | University of Grenoble Alpes and Institute for Planetary Sciences and Astrophysics, France |
| Stefano Falcinelli | University of Perugia, Italy |

## Computational Methods for Porous Geomaterials (CompPor 2023)

| | |
|---|---|
| Vadim Lisitsa | Russian Academy of Science, Russia |
| Evgeniy Romenski | Russian Academy of Science, Russia |

# Workshop on Computational Science and HPC (CSHPC 2023)

| | |
|---|---|
| Elise De Doncker | Western Michigan University, USA |
| Fukuko Yuasa | High Energy Accelerator Research Organization, Japan |
| Hideo Matsufuru | High Energy Accelerator Research Organization, Japan |

# Cities, Technologies and Planning (CTP 2023)

| | |
|---|---|
| Giuseppe Borruso | University of Trieste, Italy |
| Beniamino Murgante | University of Basilicata, Italy |
| Malgorzata Hanzl | Lodz University of Technology, Poland |
| Anastasia Stratigea | National Technical University of Athens, Greece |
| Ljiljana Zivkovic | Republic Geodetic Authority, Serbia |
| Ginevra Balletto | University of Cagliari, Italy |

# Gender Equity/Equality in Transport and Mobility (DELIA 2023)

| | |
|---|---|
| Tiziana Campisi | University of Enna Kore, Italy |
| Ines Charradi | Sousse University, Tunisia |
| Alexandros Nikitas | University of Huddersfield, UK |
| Kh Md Nahiduzzaman | University of British Columbia, Canada |
| Andreas Nikiforiadis | Aristotle University of Thessaloniki, Greece |
| Socrates Basbas | Aristotle University of Thessaloniki, Greece |

# International Workshop on Defense Technology and Security (DTS 2023)

| | |
|---|---|
| Yeonseung Ryu | Myongji University, South Korea |

# Integrated Methods for the Ecosystem-Services Accounting in Urban Decision Process (Ecourbn 2023)

| | |
|---|---|
| Maria Rosaria Guarini | Sapienza University of Rome, Italy |
| Francesco Sica | Sapienza University of Rome, Italy |
| Francesco Tajani | Sapienza University of Rome, Italy |

| | |
|---|---|
| Carmelo Maria Torre | Polytechnic University of Bari, Italy |
| Pierluigi Morano | Polytechnic University of Bari, Italy |
| Rossana Ranieri | Sapienza Università di Roma, Italy |

## Evaluating Inner Areas Potentials (EIAP 2023)

| | |
|---|---|
| Diana Rolando | Politechnic of Turin, Italy |
| Manuela Rebaudengo | Politechnic of Turin, Italy |
| Alice Barreca | Politechnic of Turin, Italy |
| Giorgia Malavasi | Politechnic of Turin, Italy |
| Umberto Mecca | Politechnic of Turin, Italy |

## Sustainable Mobility Last Mile Logistic (ELLIOT 2023)

| | |
|---|---|
| Tiziana Campisi | University of Enna Kore, Italy |
| Socrates Basbas | Aristotle University of Thessaloniki, Greece |
| Grigorios Fountas | Aristotle University of Thessaloniki, Greece |
| Paraskevas Nikolaou | University of Cyprus, Cyprus |
| Drazenko Glavic | University of Belgrade, Serbia |
| Antonio Russo | University of Enna Kore, Italy |

## Econometrics and Multidimensional Evaluation of Urban Environment (EMEUE 2023)

| | |
|---|---|
| Maria Cerreta | University of Naples Federico II, Italy |
| Carmelo Maria Torre | Politechnic of Bari, Italy |
| Pierluigi Morano | Polytechnic of Bari, Italy |
| Debora Anelli | Polytechnic of Bari, Italy |
| Francesco Tajani | Sapienza University of Rome, Italy |
| Simona Panaro | University of Sussex, UK |

## Ecosystem Services in Spatial Planning for Resilient Urban and Rural Areas (ESSP 2023)

| | |
|---|---|
| Sabrina Lai | University of Cagliari, Italy |
| Francesco Scorza | University of Basilicata, Italy |
| Corrado Zoppi | University of Cagliari, Italy |

| | |
|---|---|
| Gerardo Carpentieri | University of Naples Federico II, Italy |
| Floriana Zucaro | University of Naples Federico II, Italy |
| Ana Clara Mourão Moura | Federal University of Minas Gerais, Brazil |

## Ethical AI Applications for a Human-Centered Cyber Society (EthicAI 2023)

| | |
|---|---|
| Valentina Franzoni | University of Perugia, Italy |
| Alfredo Milani | University of Perugia, Italy |
| Jordi Vallverdu | University Autonoma Barcelona, Spain |
| Roberto Capobianco | Sapienza University of Rome, Italy |

## 13th International Workshop on Future Computing System Technologies and Applications (FiSTA 2023)

| | |
|---|---|
| Bernady Apduhan | Kyushu Sangyo University, Japan |
| Rafael Santos | National Institute for Space Research, Brazil |

## Collaborative Planning and Designing for the Future with Geospatial Applications (GeoCollab 2023)

| | |
|---|---|
| Alenka Poplin | Iowa State University, USA |
| Rosanna Rivero | University of Georgia, USA |
| Michele Campagna | University of Cagliari, Italy |
| Ana Clara Mourão Moura | Federal University of Minas Gerais, Brazil |

## Geomatics in Agriculture and Forestry: New Advances and Perspectives (GeoForAgr 2023)

| | |
|---|---|
| Maurizio Pollino | Italian National Agency for New Technologies, Energy and Sustainable Economic Development, Italy |
| Giuseppe Modica | University of Reggio Calabria, Italy |
| Marco Vizzari | University of Perugia, Italy |
| Salvatore Praticò | University of Reggio Calabria, Italy |

## Geographical Analysis, Urban Modeling, Spatial Statistics (Geog-An-Mod 2023)

| | |
|---|---|
| Giuseppe Borruso | University of Trieste, Italy |
| Beniamino Murgante | University of Basilicata, Italy |
| Harmut Asche | Hasso-Plattner-Institut für Digital Engineering Ggmbh, Germany |

## Geomatics for Resource Monitoring and Management (GRMM 2023)

| | |
|---|---|
| Alessandra Capolupo | Polytechnic of Bari, Italy |
| Eufemia Tarantino | Polytechnic of Bari, Italy |
| Enrico Borgogno Mondino | University of Turin, Italy |

## International Workshop on Information and Knowledge in the Internet of Things (IKIT 2023)

| | |
|---|---|
| Teresa Guarda | Peninsula State University of Santa Elena, Ecuador |
| Modestos Stavrakis | University of the Aegean, Greece |

## International Workshop on Collective, Massive and Evolutionary Systems (IWCES 2023)

| | |
|---|---|
| Alfredo Milani | University of Perugia, Italy |
| Rajdeep Niyogi | Indian Institute of Technology, India |
| Valentina Franzoni | University of Perugia, Italy |

## Multidimensional Evolutionary Evaluations for Transformative Approaches (MEETA 2023)

| | |
|---|---|
| Maria Cerreta | University of Naples Federico II, Italy |
| Giuliano Poli | University of Naples Federico II, Italy |
| Ludovica Larocca | University of Naples Federico II, Italy |
| Chiara Mazzarella | University of Naples Federico II, Italy |

Stefania Regalbuto                 University of Naples Federico II, Italy
Maria Somma                        University of Naples Federico II, Italy

## Building Multi-dimensional Models for Assessing Complex Environmental Systems (MES 2023)

Marta Dell'Ovo                     Politechnic of Milan, Italy
Vanessa Assumma                    University of Bologna, Italy
Caterina Caprioli                  Politechnic of Turin, Italy
Giulia Datola                      Politechnic of Turin, Italy
Federico Dellanna                  Politechnic of Turin, Italy
Marco Rossitti                     Politechnic of Milan, Italy

## Metropolitan City Lab (Metro_City_Lab 2023)

Ginevra Balletto                   University of Cagliari, Italy
Luigi Mundula                      University for Foreigners of Perugia, Italy
Giuseppe Borruso                   University of Trieste, Italy
Jacopo Torriti                     University of Reading, UK
Isabella Ligia                     Metropolitan City of Cagliari, Italy

## Mathematical Methods for Image Processing and Understanding (MMIPU 2023)

Ivan Gerace                        University of Perugia, Italy
Gianluca Vinti                     University of Perugia, Italy
Arianna Travaglini                 University of Florence, Italy

## Models and Indicators for Assessing and Measuring the Urban Settlement Development in the View of ZERO Net Land Take by 2050 (MOVEto0 2023)

Lucia Saganeiti                    University of L'Aquila, Italy
Lorena Fiorini                     University of L'Aquila, Italy
Angela Pilogallo                   University of L'Aquila, Italy
Alessandro Marucci                 University of L'Aquila, Italy
Francesco Zullo                    University of L'Aquila, Italy

## Modelling Post-Covid Cities (MPCC 2023)

| | |
|---|---|
| Giuseppe Borruso | University of Trieste, Italy |
| Beniamino Murgante | University of Basilicata, Italy |
| Ginevra Balletto | University of Cagliari, Italy |
| Lucia Saganeiti | University of L'Aquila, Italy |
| Marco Dettori | University of Sassari, Italy |

## 3rd Workshop on Privacy in the Cloud/Edge/IoT World (PCEIoT 2023)

| | |
|---|---|
| Michele Mastroianni | University of Salerno, Italy |
| Lelio Campanile | University of Campania Luigi Vanvitelli, Italy |
| Mauro Iacono | University of Campania Luigi Vanvitelli, Italy |

## Port City Interface: Land Use, Logistic and Rear Port Area Planning (PORTUNO 2023)

| | |
|---|---|
| Tiziana Campisi | University of Enna Kore, Italy |
| Socrates Basbas | Aristotle University of Thessaloniki, Greece |
| Efstathios Bouhouras | Aristotle University of Thessaloniki, Greece |
| Giovanni Tesoriere | University of Enna Kore, Italy |
| Elena Cocuzza | University of Catania, Italy |
| Gianfranco Fancello | University of Cagliari, Italy |

## Scientific Computing Infrastructure (SCI 2023)

| | |
|---|---|
| Elena Stankova | St. Petersburg State University, Russia |
| Vladimir Korkhov | St. Petersburg University, Russia |

## Supply Chains, IoT, and Smart Technologies (SCIS 2023)

| | |
|---|---|
| Ha Jin Hwang | Sunway University, South Korea |
| Hangkon Kim | Daegu Catholic University, South Korea |
| Jan Seruga | Australian Catholic University, Australia |

## Spatial Cognition in Urban and Regional Planning Under Risk (SCOPUR23)

| | |
|---|---|
| Domenico Camarda | Polytechnic of Bari, Italy |
| Giulia Mastrodonato | Polytechnic of Bari, Italy |
| Stefania Santoro | Polytechnic of Bari, Italy |
| Maria Rosaria Stufano Melone | Polytechnic of Bari, Italy |
| Mauro Patano | Polytechnic of Bari, Italy |

## Socio-Economic and Environmental Models for Land Use Management (SEMLUM 2023)

| | |
|---|---|
| Debora Anelli | Polytechnic of Bari, Italy |
| Pierluigi Morano | Polytechnic of Bari, Italy |
| Benedetto Manganelli | University of Basilicata, Italy |
| Francesco Tajani | Sapienza University of Rome, Italy |
| Marco Locurcio | Polytechnic of Bari, Italy |
| Felicia Di Liddo | Polytechnic of Bari, Italy |

## Ports of the Future - Smartness and Sustainability (SmartPorts 2023)

| | |
|---|---|
| Ginevra Balletto | University of Cagliari, Italy |
| Gianfranco Fancello | University of Cagliari, Italy |
| Patrizia Serra | University of Cagliari, Italy |
| Agostino Bruzzone | University of Genoa, Italy |
| Alberto Camarero | Politechnic of Madrid, Spain |
| Thierry Vanelslander | University of Antwerp, Belgium |

## Smart Transport and Logistics - Smart Supply Chains (SmarTransLog 2023)

| | |
|---|---|
| Giuseppe Borruso | University of Trieste, Italy |
| Marco Mazzarino | University of Venice, Italy |
| Marcello Tadini | University of Eastern Piedmont, Italy |
| Luigi Mundula | University for Foreigners of Perugia, Italy |
| Mara Ladu | University of Cagliari, Italy |
| Maria del Mar Munoz Leonisio | University of Cadiz, Spain |

## Smart Tourism (SmartTourism 2023)

| | |
|---|---|
| Giuseppe Borruso | University of Trieste, Italy |
| Silvia Battino | University of Sassari, Italy |
| Ainhoa Amaro Garcia | University of Alcala and University of Las Palmas, Spain |
| Francesca Krasna | University of Trieste, Italy |
| Ginevra Balletto | University of Cagliari, Italy |
| Maria del Mar Munoz Leonisio | University of Cadiz, Spain |

## Sustainability Performance Assessment: Models, Approaches, and Applications Toward Interdisciplinary and Integrated Solutions (SPA 2023)

| | |
|---|---|
| Sabrina Lai | University of Cagliari, Italy |
| Francesco Scorza | University of Basilicata, Italy |
| Jolanta Dvarioniene | Kaunas University of Technology, Lithuania |
| Valentin Grecu | Lucian Blaga University of Sibiu, Romania |
| Georgia Pozoukidou | Aristotle University of Thessaloniki, Greece |

## Spatial Energy Planning, City and Urban Heritage (Spatial_Energy_City 2023)

| | |
|---|---|
| Ginevra Balletto | University of Cagliari, Italy |
| Mara Ladu | University of Cagliari, Italy |
| Emilio Ghiani | University of Cagliari, Italy |
| Roberto De Lotto | University of Pavia, Italy |
| Roberto Gerundo | University of Salerno, Italy |

## Specifics of Smart Cities Development in Europe (SPEED 2023)

| | |
|---|---|
| Chiara Garau | University of Cagliari, Italy |
| Katarína Vitálišová | Matej Bel University, Slovakia |
| Paolo Nesi | University of Florence, Italy |
| Anna Vaňová | Matej Bel University, Slovakia |
| Kamila Borsekova | Matej Bel University, Slovakia |
| Paola Zamperlin | University of Pisa, Italy |

## Smart, Safe and Health Cities (SSHC 2023)

| | |
|---|---|
| Chiara Garau | University of Cagliari, Italy |
| Gerardo Carpentieri | University of Naples Federico II, Italy |
| Floriana Zucaro | University of Naples Federico II, Italy |
| Aynaz Lotfata | Chicago State University, USA |
| Alfonso Annunziata | University of Basilicata, Italy |
| Diego Altafini | University of Pisa, Italy |

## Smart and Sustainable Island Communities (SSIC_2023)

| | |
|---|---|
| Chiara Garau | University of Cagliari, Italy |
| Anastasia Stratigea | National Technical University of Athens, Greece |
| Yiota Theodora | National Technical University of Athens, Greece |
| Giulia Desogus | University of Cagliari, Italy |

## Theoretical and Computational Chemistry and Its Applications (TCCMA 2023)

| | |
|---|---|
| Noelia Faginas-Lago | University of Perugia, Italy |
| Andrea Lombardi | University of Perugia, Italy |

## Transport Infrastructures for Smart Cities (TISC 2023)

| | |
|---|---|
| Francesca Maltinti | University of Cagliari, Italy |
| Mauro Coni | University of Cagliari, Italy |
| Francesco Pinna | University of Cagliari, Italy |
| Chiara Garau | University of Cagliari, Italy |
| Nicoletta Rassu | University of Cagliari, Italy |
| James Rombi | University of Cagliari, Italy |

## Urban Regeneration: Innovative Tools and Evaluation Model (URITEM 2023)

| | |
|---|---|
| Fabrizio Battisti | University of Florence, Italy |
| Giovanna Acampa | University of Florence and University of Enna Kore, Italy |
| Orazio Campo | La Sapienza University of Rome, Italy |

## Urban Space Accessibility and Mobilities (USAM 2023)

Chiara Garau               University of Cagliari, Italy
Matteo Ignaccolo           University of Catania, Italy
Michela Tiboni             University of Brescia, Italy
Francesco Pinna            Università of Cagliari, Italy
Silvia Rossetti            University of Parma, Italy
Vincenza Torrisi           University of Catania, Italy
Ilaria Delponte            University of Genoa, Italy

## Virtual Reality and Augmented Reality and Applications (VRA 2023)

Osvaldo Gervasi            University of Perugia, Italy
Damiano Perri              University of Florence, Italy
Marco Simonetti            University of Florence, Italy
Sergio Tasso               University of Perugia, Italy

## Workshop on Advanced and Computational Methods for Earth Science Applications (WACM4ES 2023)

Luca Piroddi               University of Malta, Malta
Sebastiano Damico          University of Malta, Malta
Marilena Cozzolino         Università del Molise, Italy
Adam Gauci                 University of Malta, Italy
Giuseppina Vacca           University of Cagliari, Italy
Chiara Garau               University of Cagliari, Italy

## Sponsoring Organizations

ICCSA 2023 would not have been possible without the tremendous support of many organizations and institutions, for which all organizers and participants of ICCSA 2023 express their sincere gratitude:

Springer Nature Switzerland AG, Switzerland
(https://www.springer.com)

Computers Open Access Journal
(https://www.mdpi.com/journal/computers)

National Technical University of Athens, Greece
(https://www.ntua.gr/)

University of the Aegean, Greece
(https://www.aegean.edu/)

University of Perugia, Italy
(https://www.unipg.it)

University of Basilicata, Italy
(http://www.unibas.it)

Monash University, Australia
(https://www.monash.edu/)

Kyushu Sangyo University, Japan
(https://www.kyusan-u.ac.jp/)

University of Minho, Portugal
(https://www.uminho.pt/)

Universidade do Minho
Escola de Engenharia

## Referees

| | |
|---|---|
| Francesca Abastante | Turin Polytechnic, Italy |
| Giovanna Acampa | University of Enna Kore, Italy |
| Adewole Adewumi | Algonquin College, Canada |
| Vera Afreixo | University of Aveiro, Portugal |
| Riad Aggoune | Luxembourg Institute of Science and Technology, Luxembourg |
| Akshat Agrawal | Amity University Haryana, India |
| Waseem Ahmad | National Institute of Technology Karnataka, India |
| Oylum Alatlı | Ege University, Turkey |
| Abraham Alfa | Federal University of Technology Minna, Nigeria |
| Diego Altafini | University of Pisa, Italy |
| Filipe Alvelos | University of Minho, Portugal |
| Marina Alexandra Pedro Andrade | University Institute of Lisbon, Portugal |
| Debora Anelli | Polytechnic University of Bari, Italy |
| Mariarosaria Angrisano | Pegaso University, Italy |
| Alfonso Annunziata | University of Cagliari, Italy |
| Magarò Antonio | Sapienza University of Rome, Italy |
| Bernady Apduhan | Kyushu Sangyo University, Japan |
| Jonathan Apeh | Covenant University, Nigeria |
| Daniela Ascenzi | University of Trento, Italy |
| Vanessa Assumma | University of Bologna, Italy |
| Maria Fernanda Augusto | Bitrum Research Center, Spain |
| Marco Baioletti | University of Perugia, Italy |

| | |
|---|---|
| Ginevra Balletto | University of Cagliari, Italy |
| Carlos Balsa | Polytechnic Institute of Bragança, Portugal |
| Benedetto Barabino | University of Brescia, Italy |
| Simona Barbaro | University of Palermo, Italy |
| Sebastiano Barbieri | Turin Polytechnic, Italy |
| Kousik Barik | University of Alcala, Spain |
| Alice Barreca | Turin Polytechnic, Italy |
| Socrates Basbas | Aristotle University of Thessaloniki, Greece |
| Rosaria Battarra | National Research Council, Italy |
| Silvia Battino | University of Sassari, Italy |
| Fabrizio Battisti | University of Florence, Italy |
| Yaroslav Bazaikin | Jan Evangelista Purkyne University, Czech Republic |
| Ranjan Kumar Behera | Indian Institute of Information Technology, India |
| Simone Belli | Complutense University of Madrid, Spain |
| Oscar Bellini | Polytechnic University of Milan, Italy |
| Giulio Biondi | University of Perugia, Italy |
| Adriano Bisello | Eurac Research, Italy |
| Semen Bochkov | Ulyanovsk State Technical University, Russia |
| Alexander Bogdanov | St. Petersburg State University, Russia |
| Letizia Bollini | Free University of Bozen, Italy |
| Giuseppe Borruso | University of Trieste, Italy |
| Marilisa Botte | University of Naples Federico II, Italy |
| Ana Cristina Braga | University of Minho, Portugal |
| Frederico Branco | University of Trás-os-Montes and Alto Douro, Portugal |
| Jorge Buele | Indoamérica Technological University, Ecuador |
| Datzania Lizeth Burgos | Peninsula State University of Santa Elena, Ecuador |
| Isabel Cacao | University of Aveiro, Portugal |
| Francesco Calabrò | Mediterranea University of Reggio Calabria, Italy |
| Rogerio Calazan | Institute of Sea Studies Almirante Paulo Moreira, Brazil |
| Lelio Campanile | University of Campania Luigi Vanvitelli, Italy |
| Tiziana Campisi | University of Enna Kore, Italy |
| Orazio Campo | University of Rome La Sapienza, Italy |
| Caterina Caprioli | Turin Polytechnic, Italy |
| Gerardo Carpentieri | University of Naples Federico II, Italy |
| Martina Carra | University of Brescia, Italy |
| Barbara Caselli | University of Parma, Italy |
| Danny Casprini | Politechnic of Milan, Italy |

| | |
|---|---|
| Omar Fernando Castellanos Balleteros | Peninsula State University of Santa Elena, Ecuador |
| Arcangelo Castiglione | University of Salerno, Italy |
| Giulio Cavana | Turin Polytechnic, Italy |
| Maria Cerreta | University of Naples Federico II, Italy |
| Sabarathinam Chockalingam | Institute for Energy Technology, Norway |
| Luis Enrique Chuquimarca Jimenez | Peninsula State University of Santa Elena, Ecuador |
| Birol Ciloglugil | Ege University, Turkey |
| Elena Cocuzza | Univesity of Catania, Italy |
| Emanuele Colica | University of Malta, Malta |
| Mauro Coni | University of Cagliari, Italy |
| Simone Corrado | University of Basilicata, Italy |
| Elisete Correia | University of Trás-os-Montes and Alto Douro, Portugal |
| Florbela Correia | Polytechnic Institute Viana do Castelo, Portugal |
| Paulo Cortez | University of Minho, Portugal |
| Martina Corti | Politechnic of Milan, Italy |
| Lino Costa | Universidade do Minho, Portugal |
| Cecília Maria Vasconcelos Costa e Castro | University of Minho, Portugal |
| Alfredo Cuzzocrea | University of Calabria, Italy |
| Sebastiano D'amico | University of Malta, Malta |
| Maria Danese | National Rescarch Council, Italy |
| Gianni Dangelo | University of Salerno, Italy |
| Ana Daniel | Aveiro University, Portugal |
| Giulia Datola | Politechnic of Milan, Italy |
| Regina De Almeida | University of Trás-os-Montes and Alto Douro, Portugal |
| Maria Stella De Biase | University of Campania Luigi Vanvitelli, Italy |
| Elise De Doncker | Western Michigan University, USA |
| Luiza De Macedo Mourelle | State University of Rio de Janeiro, Brazil |
| Itamir De Morais Barroca Filho | Federal University of Rio Grande do Norte, Brazil |
| Pierfrancesco De Paola | University of Naples Federico II, Italy |
| Francesco De Pascale | University of Turin, Italy |
| Manuela De Ruggiero | University of Calabria, Italy |
| Alexander Degtyarev | St. Petersburg State University, Russia |
| Federico Dellanna | Turin Polytechnic, Italy |
| Marta Dellovo | Politechnic of Milan, Italy |
| Bashir Derradji | Sfax University, Tunisia |
| Giulia Desogus | University of Cagliari, Italy |
| Frank Devai | London South Bank University, UK |

| | |
|---|---|
| Piero Di Bonito | University of Campania Luigi Vanvitelli, Italy |
| Chiara Di Dato | University of L'Aquila, Italy |
| Michele Di Giovanni | University of Campania Luigi Vanvitelli, Italy |
| Felicia Di Liddo | Polytechnic University of Bari, Italy |
| Joana Dias | University of Coimbra, Portugal |
| Luigi Dolores | University of Salerno, Italy |
| Marco Donatelli | University of Insubria, Italy |
| Aziz Dursun | Virginia Tech University, USA |
| Jaroslav Dvořak | Klaipeda University, Lithuania |
| Wolfgang Erb | University of Padova, Italy |
| Maurizio Francesco Errigo | University of Enna Kore, Italy |
| Noelia Faginas-Lago | University of Perugia, Italy |
| Maria Irene Falcao | University of Minho, Portugal |
| Stefano Falcinelli | University of Perugia, Italy |
| Grazia Fattoruso | Italian National Agency for New Technologies, Energy and Sustainable Economic Development, Italy |
| Sara Favargiotti | University of Trento, Italy |
| Marcin Feltynowski | University of Lodz, Poland |
| António Fernandes | Polytechnic Institute of Bragança, Portugal |
| Florbela P. Fernandes | Polytechnic Institute of Bragança, Portugal |
| Paula Odete Fernandes | Polytechnic Institute of Bragança, Portugal |
| Luis Fernandez-Sanz | University of Alcala, Spain |
| Maria Eugenia Ferrao | University of Beira Interior and University of Lisbon, Portugal |
| Luís Ferrás | University of Minho, Portugal |
| Angela Ferreira | Polytechnic Institute of Bragança, Portugal |
| Maddalena Ferretti | Politechnic of Marche, Italy |
| Manuel Carlos Figueiredo | University of Minho, Portugal |
| Fabrizio Finucci | Roma Tre University, Italy |
| Ugo Fiore | University Pathenope of Naples, Italy |
| Lorena Fiorini | University of L'Aquila, Italy |
| Valentina Franzoni | Perugia University, Italy |
| Adelaide Freitas | University of Aveiro, Portugal |
| Kirill Gadylshin | Russian Academy of Sciences, Russia |
| Andrea Gallo | University of Trieste, Italy |
| Luciano Galone | University of Malta, Malta |
| Chiara Garau | University of Cagliari, Italy |
| Ernesto Garcia Para | Universidad del País Vasco, Spain |
| Rachele Vanessa Gatto | Università della Basilicata, Italy |
| Marina Gavrilova | University of Calgary, Canada |
| Georgios Georgiadis | Aristotle University of Thessaloniki, Greece |

| | |
|---|---|
| Marcelo Leon | Ecotec University, Ecuador |
| Federica Leone | University of Cagliari, Italy |
| Barbara Lino | University of Palermo, Italy |
| Vadim Lisitsa | Russian Academy of Sciences, Russia |
| Carla Lobo | Portucalense University, Portugal |
| Marco Locurcio | Polytechnic University of Bari, Italy |
| Claudia Loggia | University of KwaZulu-Natal, South Africa |
| Andrea Lombardi | University of Perugia, Italy |
| Isabel Lopes | Polytechnic Institut of Bragança, Portugal |
| Immacolata Lorè | Mediterranean University of Reggio Calabria, Italy |
| Vanda Lourenco | Nova University of Lisbon, Portugal |
| Giorgia Malavasi | Turin Polytechnic, Italy |
| Francesca Maltinti | University of Cagliari, Italy |
| Luca Mancini | University of Perugia, Italy |
| Marcos Mandado | University of Vigo, Spain |
| Benedetto Manganelli | University of Basilicata, Italy |
| Krassimir Markov | Institute of Electric Engineering and Informatics, Bulgaria |
| Enzo Martinelli | University of Salerno, Italy |
| Fiammetta Marulli | University of Campania Luigi Vanvitelli, Italy |
| Antonino Marvuglia | Luxembourg Institute of Science and Technology, Luxembourg |
| Rytis Maskeliunas | Kaunas University of Technology, Lithuania |
| Michele Mastroianni | University of Salerno, Italy |
| Hideo Matsufuru | High Energy Accelerator Research Organization, Japan |
| D'Apuzzo Mauro | University of Cassino and Southern Lazio, Italy |
| Luis Mazon | Bitrum Research Group, Spain |
| Chiara Mazzarella | University Federico II, Naples, Italy |
| Beatrice Mecca | Turin Polytechnic, Italy |
| Umberto Mecca | Turin Polytechnic, Italy |
| Paolo Mengoni | Hong Kong Baptist University, China |
| Gaetano Messina | Mediterranean University of Reggio Calabria, Italy |
| Alfredo Milani | University of Perugia, Italy |
| Alessandra Milesi | University of Cagliari, Italy |
| Richard Millham | Durban University of Technology, South Africa |
| Fernando Miranda | Universidade do Minho, Portugal |
| Biswajeeban Mishra | University of Szeged, Hungary |
| Giuseppe Modica | University of Reggio Calabria, Italy |
| Pierluigi Morano | Polytechnic University of Bari, Italy |

| | |
|---|---|
| Filipe Mota Pinto | Polytechnic Institute of Leiria, Portugal |
| Maria Mourao | Polytechnic Institute of Viana do Castelo, Portugal |
| Eugenio Muccio | University of Naples Federico II, Italy |
| Beniamino Murgante | University of Basilicata, Italy |
| Rocco Murro | Sapienza University of Rome, Italy |
| Giuseppe Musolino | Mediterranean University of Reggio Calabria, Italy |
| Nadia Nedjah | State University of Rio de Janeiro, Brazil |
| Juraj Nemec | Masaryk University, Czech Republic |
| Andreas Nikiforiadis | Aristotle University of Thessaloniki, Greece |
| Silvio Nocera | IUAV University of Venice, Italy |
| Roseline Ogundokun | Kaunas University of Technology, Lithuania |
| Emma Okewu | University of Alcala, Spain |
| Serena Olcuire | Sapienza University of Rome, Italy |
| Irene Oliveira | University Trás-os-Montes and Alto Douro, Portugal |
| Samson Oruma | Ostfold University College, Norway |
| Antonio Pala | University of Cagliari, Italy |
| Maria Panagiotopoulou | National Technical University of Athens, Greece |
| Simona Panaro | University of Sussex Business School, UK |
| Jay Pancham | Durban University of Technology, South Africa |
| Eric Pardede | La Trobe University, Australia |
| Hyun Kyoo Park | Ministry of National Defense, South Korea |
| Damiano Perri | University of Florence, Italy |
| Quoc Trung Pham | Ho Chi Minh City University of Technology, Vietnam |
| Claudio Piferi | University of Florence, Italy |
| Angela Pilogallo | University of L'Aquila, Italy |
| Francesco Pinna | University of Cagliari, Italy |
| Telmo Pinto | University of Coimbra, Portugal |
| Luca Piroddi | University of Malta, Malta |
| Francesco Pittau | Politechnic of Milan, Italy |
| Giuliano Poli | Università Federico II di Napoli, Italy |
| Maurizio Pollino | Italian National Agency for New Technologies, Energy and Sustainable Economic Development, Italy |
| Vijay Prakash | University of Malta, Malta |
| Salvatore Praticò | Mediterranean University of Reggio Calabria, Italy |
| Carlotta Quagliolo | Turin Polytechnic, Italy |
| Garrisi Raffaele | Operations Center for Cyber Security, Italy |
| Mariapia Raimondo | Università della Campania Luigi Vanvitelli, Italy |

| | |
|---|---|
| Bruna Ramos | Universidade Lusíada Norte, Portugal |
| Nicoletta Rassu | University of Cagliari, Italy |
| Roberta Ravanelli | University of Roma La Sapienza, Italy |
| Pier Francesco Recchi | University of Naples Federico II, Italy |
| Stefania Regalbuto | University of Naples Federico II, Italy |
| Rommel Regis | Saint Joseph's University, USA |
| Marco Reis | University of Coimbra, Portugal |
| Jerzy Respondek | Silesian University of Technology, Poland |
| Isabel Ribeiro | Polytechnic Institut of Bragança, Portugal |
| Albert Rimola | Autonomous University of Barcelona, Spain |
| Corrado Rindone | Mediterranean University of Reggio Calabria, Italy |
| Maria Rocco | Roma Tre University, Italy |
| Ana Maria A. C. Rocha | University of Minho, Portugal |
| Fabio Rocha | Universidade Federal de Sergipe, Brazil |
| Humberto Rocha | University of Coimbra, Portugal |
| Maria Clara Rocha | Politechnic Institut of Coimbra, Portual |
| Carlos Rodrigues | Polytechnic Institut of Bragança, Portugal |
| Diana Rolando | Turin Polytechnic, Italy |
| James Rombi | University of Cagliari, Italy |
| Evgeniy Romenskiy | Russian Academy of Sciences, Russia |
| Marzio Rosi | University of Perugia, Italy |
| Silvia Rossetti | University of Parma, Italy |
| Marco Rossitti | Politechnic of Milan, Italy |
| Antonio Russo | University of Enna, Italy |
| Insoo Ryu | MoaSoftware, South Korea |
| Yeonseung Ryu | Myongji University, South Korea |
| Lucia Saganeiti | University of L'Aquila, Italy |
| Valentina Santarsiero | University of Basilicata, Italy |
| Luigi Santopietro | University of Basilicata, Italy |
| Rafael Santos | National Institute for Space Research, Brazil |
| Valentino Santucci | University for Foreigners of Perugia, Italy |
| Alessandra Saponieri | University of Salento, Italy |
| Mattia Scalas | Turin Polytechnic, Italy |
| Francesco Scorza | University of Basilicata, Italy |
| Ester Scotto Di Perta | University of Napoli Federico II, Italy |
| Nicoletta Setola | University of Florence, Italy |
| Ricardo Severino | University of Minho, Portugal |
| Angela Silva | Polytechnic Institut of Viana do Castelo, Portugal |
| Carina Silva | Polytechnic of Lisbon, Portugal |
| Marco Simonetti | University of Florence, Italy |
| Sergey Solovyev | Russian Academy of Sciences, Russia |

| | |
|---|---|
| Maria Somma | University of Naples Federico II, Italy |
| Changgeun Son | Ministry of National Defense, South Korea |
| Alberico Sonnessa | Polytechnic of Bari, Italy |
| Inês Sousa | University of Minho, Portugal |
| Lisete Sousa | University of Lisbon, Portugal |
| Elena Stankova | Saint-Petersburg State University, Russia |
| Modestos Stavrakis | University of the Aegean, Greece |
| Flavio Stochino | University of Cagliari, Italy |
| Anastasia Stratigea | National Technical University of Athens, Greece |
| Yue Sun | European XFEL GmbH, Germany |
| Anthony Suppa | Turin Polytechnic, Italy |
| David Taniar | Monash University, Australia |
| Rodrigo Tapia McClung | Centre for Research in Geospatial Information Sciences, Mexico |
| Tarek Teba | University of Portsmouth, UK |
| Ana Paula Teixeira | University of Trás-os-Montes and Alto Douro, Portugal |
| Tengku Adil Tengku Izhar | Technological University MARA, Malaysia |
| Maria Filomena Teodoro | University of Lisbon and Portuguese Naval Academy, Portugal |
| Yiota Theodora | National Technical University of Athens, Greece |
| Elena Todella | Turin Polytechnic, Italy |
| Graça Tomaz | Polytechnic Institut of Guarda, Portugal |
| Anna Tonazzini | National Research Council, Italy |
| Dario Torregrossa | Goodyear, Luxembourg |
| Francesca Torrieri | University of Naples Federico II, Italy |
| Vincenza Torrisi | University of Catania, Italy |
| Nikola Tosic | Polytechnic University of Catalonia, Spain |
| Vincenzo Totaro | Polytechnic University of Bari, Italy |
| Arianna Travaglini | University of Florence, Italy |
| António Trigo | Polytechnic of Coimbra, Portugal |
| Giuseppe A. Trunfio | University of Sassari, Italy |
| Toshihiro Uchibayashi | Kyushu University, Japan |
| Piero Ugliengo | University of Torino, Italy |
| Jordi Vallverdu | University Autonoma Barcelona, Spain |
| Gianmarco Vanuzzo | University of Perugia, Italy |
| Dmitry Vasyunin | T-Systems, Russia |
| Laura Verde | University of Campania Luigi Vanvitelli, Italy |
| Giulio Vignoli | University of Cagliari, Italy |
| Gianluca Vinti | University of Perugia, Italy |
| Katarína Vitálišová | Matej Bel University, Slovak Republic |
| Daniel Mark Vitiello | University of Cagliari |

# Plenary Lectures

# A Multiscale Planning Concept for Sustainable Metropolitan Development

Pierre Frankhauser

Théma, Université de Franche-Comté, 32, rue Mégevand, 20030 Besançon, France
pierre.frankhauser@univ-fcomte.fr

**Keywords:** Sustainable metropolitan development · Multiscale approach · Urban modelling

Urban sprawl has often been pointed out as having an important negative impact on environment and climate. Residential zones have grown up in what were initially rural areas, located far from employment areas and often lacking shopping opportunities, public services and public transportation. Hence urban sprawl increased car-traffic flows, generating pollution and increasing energy consumption. New road axes consume considerable space and weaken biodiversity by reducing and cutting natural areas. A return to "compact cities" or "dense cities" has often been contemplated as the most efficient way to limit urban sprawl. However, the real impact of density on car use is less clearcut (Daneshpour and Shakibamanesh 2011). Let us emphasize that moreover climate change will increase the risk of heat islands on an intra-urban scale. This prompts a more nuanced reflection on how urban fabrics should be structured.

Moreover, urban planning cannot ignore social demand. Lower land prices in rural areas, often put forward by economists, is not the only reason of urban sprawl. The quality of the residential environment comes into play, too, through features like noise, pollution, landscape quality, density etc. Schwanen et al. (2004) observe for the Netherlands that households preferring a quiet residential environment and individual housing with a garden will not accept densification, which might even lead them to move to lower-density rural areas even farther away from jobs and shopping amenities. Many scholars emphasize the importance of green amenities for residential environments and report the importance of easy access to leisure areas (Guo and Bhat 2002). Vegetation in the residential environment has an important impact on health and well-being (Lafortezza et al. 2009).

We present here the Fractalopolis concept which we developed in the frame of several research projects and which aims reconciling environmental and social issues (Bonin et al., 2020; Frankhauser 2021; Frankhauser et al. 2018). This concept introduces a multiscale approach based on multifractal geometry for conceiving spatial development for metropolitan areas. For taking into account social demand we refer to the fundamental work of Max-Neef et al. (1991) based on Maslow's work about basic human needs. He introduces the concept of satisfiers assigned to meet the basic needs of "Subsistence, Protection, Affection, Understanding, Participation, Idleness, Creation, Identity and Freedom". Satisfiers thus become the link between the needs of everyone and society and may depend on the cultural context. We consider their importance, their location and their accessibility and we rank the needs according to their importance for individuals or households. In order to enjoy a good quality of life and to shorten trips and to reduce automobile use, it seems important for satisfiers of daily needs to be easily accessible. Hence, we consider the purchase rate when reflecting on the implementation of shops which is reminiscent of central place theory.

The second important feature is taking care of environment and biodiversity by avoiding fragmentation of green space (Ekren and Arslan 2022) which must benefit, moreover, of a good accessibility, as pointed out. These areas must, too, ply the role of cooling areas ensuring ventilation of urbanized areas (Kuttler et al. 1998).

For integrating these different objectives, we propose a concept for developing spatial configurations of metropolitan areas designed which is based on multifractal geometry. It allows combining different issues across a large range of scales in a coherent way. These issues include:

- providing easy access to a large array of amenities to meet social demand;
- promoting the use of public transportation and soft modes instead of automobile use;
- preserving biodiversity and improving the local climate.

The concept distinguishes development zones localized in the vicinity of a nested and hierarchized system of public transport axes. The highest ranked center offers all types of amenities, whereas lower ranked centers lack the highest ranked amenities. The lowest ranked centers just offer the amenities for daily needs. A coding system allows distinguishing the centers according to their rank.

Each subset of central places is in some sense autonomous, since they are not linked by transportation axes to subcenters of the same order. This allows to preserve a linked system of green corridors penetrating the development zones across scales avoiding the fragmentation of green areas and ensuring a good accessibility to recreational areas.

The spatial model is completed by a population distribution model which globally follows the same hierarchical logic. However, we weakened the strong fractal order what allows to conceive a more or less polycentric spatial system.

We can adapt the theoretical concept easily to real world situation without changing the underlying multiscale logic. A decision support system has been developed allowing to simulate development scenarios and to evaluate them. The evaluation procedure is based on fuzzy evaluation of distance acceptance for accessing to the different types of amenities according to the ranking of needs. We used for evaluation data issued from a great set of French planning documents like Master plans. We show an example how the software package can be used concretely.

# References

Bonin, O., et al.: Projet SOFT sobriété énergétique par les formes urbaines et le transport (Research Report No. 1717C0003; p. 214). ADEME (2020)

Daneshpour, A., Shakibamanesh, A.: Compact city; dose it create an obligatory context for urban sustainability? Int. J. Archit. Eng. Urban Plann. 21(2), 110–118 (2011)

Ekren, E., Arslan, M.: Functions of greenways as an ecologically-based planning strategy. In: Çakır, M., Tuğluer, M., Fırat Örs, P.: Architectural Sciences and Ecology, pp. 134–156. Iksad Publications (2022)

Frankhauser, P.: Fractalopolis—a fractal concept for the sustainable development of metropolitan areas. In: Sajous, P., Bertelle, C. (eds.) Complex Systems, Smart Territories and Mobility, pp. 15–50. Springer, Cham (2021). https://doi.org/10.1007/978-3-030-59302-5_2

Frankhauser, P., Tannier, C., Vuidel, G., Houot, H.: An integrated multifractal modelling to urban and regional planning. Comput. Environ. Urban Syst. **67**(1), 132–146 (2018). https://doi.org/10.1016/j.compenvurbsys.2017.09.011

Guo, J., Bhat, C.: Residential location modeling: accommodating sociodemographic, school quality and accessibility effects. University of Texas, Austin (2002)

Kuttler, W., Dütemeyer, D., Barlag, A.-B.: Influence of regional and local winds on urban ventilation in Cologne, Germany. Meteorologische Zeitschrift, 77–87 (1998) https://doi.org/10.1127/metz/7/1998/77

Lafortezza, R., Carrus, G., Sanesi, G., Davies, C.: Benefits and well-being perceived by people visiting green spaces in periods of heat stress. Urban For. Urban Green. **8**(2), 97–108 (2009)

Max-Neef, M. A., Elizalde, A., Hopenhayn, M.: Human scale development: conception, application and further reflections. The Apex Press (1991)

Schwanen, T., Dijst, M., Dieleman, F. M.: Policies for urban form and their impact on travel: The Netherlands experience. Urban Stud. **41**(3), 579–603 (2004)

# Graph Drawing and Network Visualization – An Overview – (Keynote Speech)

Giuseppe Liotta

Dipartimento di Ingegneria, Università degli Studi di Perugia, Italy
giuseppe.liotta@unipg.it

**Abstract.** Graph Drawing and Network visualization supports the exploration, analysis, and communication of relational data arising in a variety of application domains: from bioinformatics to software engineering, from social media to cyber-security, from data bases to powergrid systems. Aim of this keynote speech is to introduce this thriving research area, highlighting some of its basic approaches and pointing to some promising research directions.

## 1 Introduction

Graph Drawing and Network Visualization is at the intersection of different disciplines and it combines topics that traditionally belong to theoretical computer science with methods and approaches that characterize more applied disciplines. Namely, it can be related to Graph Algorithms, Geometric Graph Theory and Geometric computing, Combinatorial Optimization, Experimental Analysis, User Studies, System Design and Development, and Human Computer Interaction. This combination of theory and practice is well reflected in the flagship conference of the area, the *International Symposium on Graph Drawing and Network Visualization*, that has two tracks, one focusing on combinatorial and algorithmic aspects and the other on the design of network visualization systems and interfaces. The conference is now at its 31st edition; a full list of the symposia and their proceedings, published by Springer in the LNCS series can be found at the URL: http://www.graphdrawing.org/.

Aim of this short paper is to outline the content of my Keynote Speech at ICCSA 2023, which will be referred to as the "Talk" in the rest of the paper. The talk will introduce the field of Graph Drawing and Network Visualization to a broad audience, with the goal to not only present some key methodological and technological aspects, but also point to some unexplored or partially explored research directions. The rest of this short paper briefly outlines the content of the talk and provides some references that can be a starting point for researchers interested in working on Graph Drawing and Network Visualization.

## 2  Why Visualize Networks?

Back in 1973 the famous statistician Francis Anscombe, gave a convincing example of why visualization is fundamental component of data analysis. The example is known as the *Anscombe's quartet* [3] and it consists of four sets of 11 points each that are almost identical in terms of the basic statistic properties of their $x$– and $y$– coordinates. Namely the mean values and the variance of $x$ and $y$ are exactly the same in the four sets, while the correlation of $x$ and $y$ and the linear regression are the same up to the second decimal. In spite of this statistical similarity, the data look very different when displayed in the Euclidean plane which leads to the conclusion that they correspond to significantly different phenomena. Figure 1 reports the four sets of Anscombe's quartet. After fifty years, with the arrival of AI-based technologies and the need of explaining and interpreting machine-driven suggestions before making strategic decision, the lesson of Anscombe's quartet has not just kept but even increased its relevance.

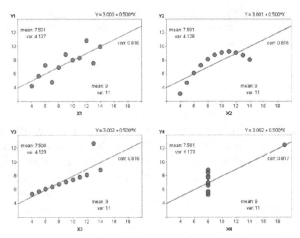

**Fig. 1.** The four point sets in Anscombe's quartet [3]; the figure also reports statistical values of the x and y variables.

As a matter of fact, nowadays the need of visualization systems goes beyond the verification of the accuracy of some statistical analysis on a set of scattered data. Recent technological advances have generated torrents of data that area relational in nature and typically modeled as networks: the nodes of the networks store the features of the data and the edges of the networks describe the semantic relationships between the data features. Such networked data sets (whose algebraic underlying structure is a called graph in discrete mathematics) arise in a variety of application domains including, for example, Systems Biology, Social Network Analysis, Software Engineering, Networking, Data Bases, Homeland Security, and Business Intelligence. In these (and many other) contexts, systems that support the visual analysis of networks and graphs play a central role in critical decision making processes. These are human-in-the-loop processes where the continuous interaction between humans (decision makers) and data mining or optimization algorithms (AI/ML components) supports the data exploration, the development of verifiable theories about the data, and the extraction of new knowledge that is used to make strategic choices. A seminal book by Keim et al. [33] schematically represents the human-in-the-loop approach to making sense of networked data sets as in Fig. 2. See also [46–49].

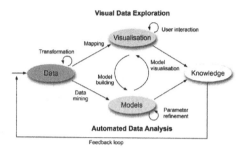

**Fig. 2.** Sense-making/knowledge generation loop. This conceptual interaction model between human analysts and network visualization system is at the basis of network visual analytics system design [33].

To make a concrete application example of the analysis of a network by interacting with its visualization, consider the problem of contrasting financial crimes such as money laundering or tax evasion. These crimes are based on relevant volumes of financial transactions to conceal the identity, the source, or the destination of illegally gained money. Also, the adopted patterns to pursue the illegal goals continuously change to conceal the crimes. Therefore, contrasting them requires special investigation units which must analyze very large and highly dynamic data sets and discover relationships between different subjects to untangle complex fraudulent plots. The investigative cycle begins with data collection and filtering; it is then followed by modeling the data as a social network (also called *financial activity network* in this context) to which different data mining and data analytic methods are applied, including graph pattern matching, social network analysis, machine learning, and information diffusion. By the network visualization system detectives can interactively explore the data, gain insight and make new hypotheses about possible criminal activities, verify the hypotheses by asking the system to provide more details about specific portions of the network, refine previous outputs, and eventually gain new knowledge. Figure 3 illustrates a small financial activity network where, by means of the interaction between an officer of the Italian Revenue Agency and the MALDIVE system described in [10] a fraudulent pattern has been identified. Precisely, the tax officer has encoded a risky relational scheme among taxpayers into a suspicious graph pattern; in response, the system has made a search in the taxpayer network and it has returned one such pattern. See, e.g., [9, 11, 14, 18, 38] for more papers and references about visual analytic applications to contrasting financial crimes.

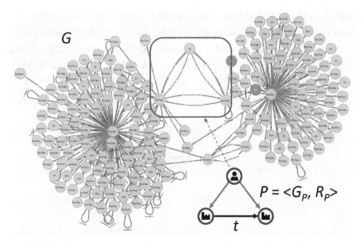

**Fig. 3.** A financial activity network from [10]. The pattern in the figure represents a Sup-pliesFromAssociated scheme, consisting of an economic transaction and two shareholding relationships.

## 3 Facets of Graph Drawing and Network Visualization

The Talk overviews some of the fundamental facets that characterize the research in Graph Drawing and Network Visualization. Namely:

- Graph drawing metaphors: Depending on the application context, different metaphors can be used to represent a relational data set modeled as a graph. The talk will briefly recall the matrix representation, the space filling representation, the contact representation, and the node-link representation which is, by far, the most commonly used (see, e.g., [43]).
- Interaction paradigms: Different interaction paradigms have different impacts on the sense-making process of the user about the visualized network. The Talk will go through the full-view, top-down, bottom-up, incremental, and narrative paradigms. Pros and cons will be highlighted for each approach, also by means of examples and applications. The discussion of the top-down interaction paradigm will also consider the hybrid visualization models (see, e.g., [2, 24, 26, 28, 39]) while the discussion about the incremental paradigm will focus on research about graph storyplans (see, e.g., [4, 6, 7]).
- Graph drawing algorithms: Three main algorithmic approaches will be reviewed, namely the force-directed, the layered), and the planarization-based approach; see, e.g., [5]. We shall also make some remarks about FPT algorithms for graph drawing (see, e.g., [8, 19, 20, 25, 27, 40, 53]) and about how the optimization challenges vary when it is assumed that the input has or does not have a fixed combinatorial embedding (see, e.g., [12, 13, 16, 17, 23]).
- Experimental analysis and user-studies: The Talk will mostly compare two models to define and experimentally validate those optimization goals that define a "readable"

network visualization, i.e. a visualization that in a given application context can easily convey the structure of a relational data set so to guarantee efficiency both in its visual exploration and in the elaboration of new knowledge. Special focus will be given to a set emerging optimization goals related to edge crossings that are currently investigated in the graph drawing and network visualization community unedr the name of "graph drawing beyond planarity" (see, e.g., [1, 15, 29, 35]).

The talk shall also point to some promising research directions, including: (i) Extend the body of papers devoted to user-studies that compare the impact of different graph drawing metaphors on the user perception. (ii) Extend the study of interaction paradigms to extended reality environments (see, e.g., [21, 30, 36, 37]); (iii) Engineer the FPT algorithms for graph drawing and experimentally compare their performances with exact or approximate solutions; and (iv) Develop new algorithmic fameworks in the context of graph drawing beyond planarity.

We conclude this short paper with pointers to publication venues and key references that can be browsed by researchers interested in the fascinating field of Graph Drawing and Network Visualization.

## 4 Pointers to Publication venues and Key References

A limited list of conferences where Graph Drawing and Network Visualization papers are regularly part of the program includes *IEEE VIS, EuroVis, SoCG, ISAAC, ACM-SIAM SODA, WADS,* and *WG.* Among the many journals where several Graph Drawing and Network Visualization papers have appeared during the last three decades we recall *IEEE Transactions on Visualization and Computer Graphs, SIAM Jounal of Computing, Computer Graphics Forum, Journal of Computer and System Sciences, Algorithmica, Journal of Graph Algorithms and Applications, Theoretical Computer Science, Information Sciences, Discrete and Computational Geometry, Computational Geometry: Theory and Applications, ACM Computing Surveys,* and *Computer Science Review.* A limited list of books, surveys, or papers that contain interesting algorithmic challenges on Graph Drawing and Network Visualization include [5, 15, 22, 29, 31–35, 41–45, 50–52].

## References

1. Angelini, P., et al.: Simple k-planar graphs are simple (k+1)-quasiplanar. J. Comb. Theory, Ser. B, **142**, 1–35 (2020)
2. Angori, L., Didimo, W., Montecchiani, F., Pagliuca, D., Tappini, A.: Hybrid graph visualizations with chordlink: Algorithms, experiments, and applications. IEEE Trans. Vis. Comput. Graph. **28**(2), 1288–1300 (2022)
3. Anscombe, F.J.: Graphs in statistical analysis. Am. Stat. **27**(1), 17–21 (1973)
4. Di Battista, G., et al.: Small point-sets supporting graph stories. In: Angelini, P., von Hanxleden, R. (eds.) Graph Drawing and Network Visualization. GD 2022, LNCS, vol. 13764, pp. 289–303. Springer, Cham (2022). https://doi.org/10.1007/978-3-031-22203-0_21

5. Battista, G.D., Eades, P., Tamassia, R., Tollis, I.G.: Graph Drawing: Algorithms for the Visualization of Graphs. Prentice-Hall, Hoboken (1999)
6. Binucci, C., et al.: On the complexity of the storyplan problem. In: Angelini, P., von Hanxleden, R. (eds.) Graph Drawing and Network Visualization. GD 2022. LNCS, vol. 13764, pp. 304–318. Springer, Cham (2023). https://doi.org/10.1007/978-3-031-22203-0_22
7. Borrazzo, M., Lozzo, G.D., Battista, G.D., Frati, F., Patrignani, M.: Graph stories in small area. J. Graph Algorithms Appl. **24**(3), 269–292 (2020)
8. Chaplick, S., Giacomo, E.D., Frati, F., Ganian, R., Raftopoulou, C.N., Simonov, K.: Parameterized algorithms for upward planarity. In: Goaoc, X., Kerber, M. (eds.) 38th International Symposium on Computational Geometry, SoCG 2022, June 7–10, 2022, Berlin, Germany, LIPIcs, vol. 224, pp. 26:1–26:16. Schloss Dagstuhl - Leibniz-Zentrum für Informatik (2022)
9. Didimo, W., Giamminonni, L., Liotta, G., Montecchiani, F., Pagliuca, D.: A visual analytics system to support tax evasion discovery. Decis. Support Syst. **110**, 71–83 (2018)
10. Didimo, W., Grilli, L., Liotta, G., Menconi, L., Montecchiani, F., Pagliuca, D.: Combining network visualization and data mining for tax risk assessment. IEEE Access **8**, 16073–16086 (2020)
11. Didimo, W., Grilli, L., Liotta, G., Montecchiani, F., Pagliuca, D.: Visual querying and analysis of temporal fiscal networks. Inf. Sci. **505**, 406–421 (2019)
12. W. Didimo, M. Kaufmann, G. Liotta, and G. Ortali. Didimo, W., Kaufmann, M., Liotta, G., Ortali, G.: Rectilinear planarity testing of plane series-parallel graphs in linear time. In: Auber, D., Valtr, P. (eds.) Graph Drawing and Network Visualization. GD 2020. LNCS, vol. 12590, pp. 436–449. Springer, Cham (2020). https://doi.org/10.1007/978-3-030-68766-3_34
13. Didimo, W., Kaufmann, M., Liotta, G., Ortali, G.: Rectilinear planarity of partial 2-trees. In: Angelini, P., von Hanxleden, R. (eds.) Graph Drawing and Network Visualization. GD 2022. LNCS, vol. 13764, pp. 157–172. Springer, Cham (2023). https://doi.org/10.1007/978-3-031-22203-0_12
14. Didimo, W., Liotta, G., Montecchiani, F.: Network visualization for financial crime detection. J. Vis. Lang. Comput. **25**(4), 433–451 (2014)
15. Didimo, W., Liotta, G., Montecchiani, F.: A survey on graph drawing beyond planarity. ACM Comput. Surv. **52**(1), 4:1–4:37 (2019)
16. Didimo, W., Liotta, G., Ortali, G., Patrignani, M.: Optimal orthogonal drawings of planar 3-graphs in linear time. In: Chawla, S. (ed.) Proceedings of the 2020 ACM-SIAM Symposium on Discrete Algorithms, SODA 2020, Salt Lake City, UT, USA, January 5–8, 2020, pp. 806–825. SIAM (2020)
17. Didimo, W., Liotta, G., Patrignani, M.: HV-planarity: algorithms and complexity. J. Comput. Syst. Sci. **99**, 72–90 (2019)
18. Dilla, W.N., Raschke, R.L.: Data visualization for fraud detection: practice implications and a call for future research. Int. J. Acc. Inf. Syst. **16**, 1–22 (2015)
19. Dujmovic, V., et al.: A fixed-parameter approach to 2-layer planarization. Algorithmica **45**(2), 159–182 (2006)
20. Dujmovic, V., et al.: On the parameterized complexity of layered graph drawing. Algorithmica **52**(2), 267–292 (2008)

21. Dwyer, T., et al.: Immersive analytics: an introduction. In: Marriott, K., et al. (eds.) Immersive Analytics, LNCS, vol. 11190, pp. 1–23. Springer, Cham (2018)

22. Filipov, V., Arleo, A., Miksch, S.: Are we there yet? a roadmap of network visualization from surveys to task taxonomies. Computer Graphics Forum (2023, on print)

23. Garg, A., Tamassia, R.: On the computational complexity of upward and rectilinear planarity testing. SIAM J. Comput. **31**(2), 601–625 (2001)

24. Di Giacomo, E., Didimo, W., Montecchiani, F., Tappini, A.: A user study on hybrid graph visualizations. In: Purchase, H.C., Rutter, I. (eds.) Graph Drawing and Network Visualization. GD 2021. LNCS, vol. 12868, pp. 21–38. Springer, Cham (2021). https://doi.org/10.1007/978-3-030-92931-2_2

25. Giacomo, E.D., Giordano, F., Liotta, G.: Upward topological book embeddings of dags. SIAM J. Discret. Math. **25**(2), 479–489 (2011)

26. Giacomo, E.D., Lenhart, W.J., Liotta, G., Randolph, T.W., Tappini, A.: (k, p)-planarity: a relaxation of hybrid planarity. Theor. Comput. Sci. **896**, 19–30 (2021)

27. Giacomo, E.D., Liotta, G., Montecchiani, F.: Orthogonal planarity testing of bounded treewidth graphs. J. Comput. Syst. Sci. **125**, 129–148 (2022)

28. Giacomo, E.D., Liotta, G., Patrignani, M., Rutter, I., Tappini, A.: Nodetrix planarity testing with small clusters. Algorithmica **81**(9), 3464–3493 (2019)

29. Hong, S., Tokuyama, T. (eds.) Beyond Planar Graphs. Springer, Singapore (2020). https://doi.org/10.1007/978-981-15-6533-5

30. Joos, L., Jaeger-Honz, S., Schreiber, F., Keim, D.A., Klein, K.: Visual comparison of networks in VR. IEEE Trans. Vis. Comput. Graph. **28**(11), 3651–3661 (2022)

31. Jünger, M., Mutzel, P. (eds.) Graph Drawing Software. Springer, Berlin (2004). https://doi.org/10.1007/978-3-642-18638-7

32. Kaufmann, M., Wagner, D. (eds.): Drawing Graphs, Methods and Models (the book grow out of a Dagstuhl Seminar, April 1999), LNCS, vol. 2025. Springer, Berlin (2001). https://doi.org/10.1007/3-540-44969-8

33. Keim, D.A., Kohlhammer, J., Ellis, G.P., Mansmann, F.: Mastering the Information Age - Solving Problems with Visual Analytics. Eurographics Association, Saarbrücken (2010)

34. Keim, D.A., Mansmann, F., Stoffel, A., Ziegler, H.: Visual analytics. In: Liu, L., Özsu, M.T. (eds.) Encyclopedia of Database Systems, 2nd edn. Springer, Berlin (2018)

35. Kobourov, S.G., Liotta, G., Montecchiani, F.: An annotated bibliography on 1-planarity. Comput. Sci. Rev. **25**, 49–67 (2017)

36. Kraus, M., et al.: Immersive analytics with abstract 3D visualizations: a survey. Comput. Graph. Forum **41**(1), 201–229 (2022)

37. Kwon, O., Muelder, C., Lee, K., Ma, K.: A study of layout, rendering, and interaction methods for immersive graph visualization. IEEE Trans. Vis. Comput. Graph. **22**(7), 1802–1815 (2016)

38. Leite, R.A., Gschwandtner, T., Miksch, S., Gstrein, E., Kuntner, J.: NEVA: visual analytics to identify fraudulent networks. Comput. Graph. Forum **39**(6), 344–359 (2020)

39. Liotta, G., Rutter, I., Tappini, A.: Simultaneous FPQ-ordering and hybrid planarity testing. Theor. Comput. Sci. **874**, 59–79 (2021)
40. Liotta, G., Rutter, I., Tappini, A.: Parameterized complexity of graph planarity with restricted cyclic orders. J. Comput. Syst. Sci. **135**, 125–144 (2023)
41. Ma, K.: Pushing visualization research frontiers: essential topics not addressed by machine learning. IEEE Comput. Graphics Appl. **43**(1), 97–102 (2023)
42. McGee, F., et al.: Visual Analysis of Multilayer Networks. Synthesis Lectures on Visualization. Morgan & Claypool Publishers, San Rafael (2021)
43. Munzner, T.: Visualization Analysis and Design. A.K. Peters visualization series. A K Peters (2014)
44. Nishizeki, T., Rahman, M.S.: Planar Graph Drawing, vol. 12. World Scientific, Singapore (2004)
45. Nobre, C., Meyer, M.D., Streit, M., Lex, A.: The state of the art in visualizing multivariate networks. Comput. Graph. Forum **38**(3), 807–832 (2019)
46. Sacha, D.: Knowledge generation in visual analytics: Integrating human and machine intelligence for exploration of big data. In: Apel, S., et al. (eds.) Ausgezeichnete Informatikdissertationen 2018, LNI, vol. D-19, pp. 211–220. GI (2018)
47. Sacha, D., et al.: What you see is what you can change: human-centered machine learning by interactive visualization. Neurocomputing **268**, 164–175 (2017)
48. Sacha, D., Senaratne, H., Kwon, B.C., Ellis, G.P., Keim, D.A.: The role of uncertainty, awareness, and trust in visual analytics. IEEE Trans. Vis. Comput. Graph. **22**(1), 240–249 (2016)
49. Sacha, D., Stoffel, A., Stoffel, F., Kwon, B.C., Ellis, G.P., Keim, D.A.: Knowledge generation model for visual analytics. IEEE Trans. Vis. Comput. Graph. **20**(12), 1604–1613 (2014)
50. Tamassia, R.: Graph drawing. In: Sack, J., Urrutia, J. (eds.) Handbook of Computational Geometry, pp. 937–971. North Holland/Elsevier, Amsterdam (2000)
51. Tamassia, R. (ed.) Handbook on Graph Drawing and Visualization. Chapman and Hall/CRC, Boca Raton (2013)
52. Tamassia, R., Liotta, G.: Graph drawing. In: Goodman, J.E., O'Rourke, J. (eds.) Handbook of Discrete and Computational Geometry, 2nd edn., pp. 1163–1185. Chapman and Hall/CRC, Boca Raton (2004)
53. Zehavi, M.: Parameterized analysis and crossing minimization problems. Comput. Sci. Rev. **45**, 100490 (2022)

# Understanding Non-Covalent Interactions in Biological Processes through QM/MM-EDA Dynamic Simulations

Marcos Mandado

Department of Physical Chemistry, University of Vigo, Lagoas-Marcosende s/n, 36310 Vigo, Spain
mandado@uvigo.es

Molecular dynamic simulations in biological environments such as proteins, DNA or lipids involves a large number of atoms, so classical models based on widely parametrized force fields are employed instead of more accurate quantum methods, whose high computational requirements preclude their application. The parametrization of appropriate force fields for classical molecular dynamics relies on the precise knowledge of the non-covalent inter and intramolecular interactions responsible for very important aspects, such as macromolecular arrangements, cell membrane permeation, ion solvation, etc. This implies, among other things, knowledge of the nature of the interaction, which may be governed by electrostatic, repulsion or dispersion forces. In order to know the balance between different forces, quantum calculations are frequently performed on simplified molecular models and the data obtained from these calculations are used to parametrize the force fields employed in classical simulations. These parameters are, among others, atomic charges, permanent electric dipole moments and atomic polarizabilities. However, it sometimes happens that the molecular models used for the quantum calculations are too simple and the results obtained can differ greatly from those of the extended system. As an alternative to classical and quantum methods, hybrid quantum/classical schemes (QM/MM) can be introduced, where the extended system is neither truncated nor simplified, but only the most important region is treated quantum mechanically.

In this presentation, molecular dynamic simulations and calculations with hybrid schemes are first introduced in a simple way for a broad and multidisciplinary audience. Then, a method developed in our group to investigate intermolecular interactions using hybrid quantum/classical schemes (QM/MM-EDA) is presented and some applications to the study of dynamic processes of ion solvation and membrane permeation are discussed [1–3]. Special attention is paid to the implementation details of the method in the EDA-NCI software [4].

## References

1. Cárdenas, G., Pérez-Barcia, A., Mandado, M., Nogueira, J.J.: Phys. Chem. Chem. Phys. **23**, 20533 (2021)
2. Pérez-Barcia, A., Cárdenas, G., Nogueira, J.J., Mandado, M.: J. Chem. Inf. Model. **63**, 882 (2023)

3. Alvarado, R., Cárdenas, G., Nogueira, J.J., Ramos-Berdullas, N., Mandado, M.: Membranes **13**, 28 (2023)
4. Mandado, M., Van Alsenoy, C.: EDA-NCI: A program to perform energy decomposition analysis of non-covalent interactions. https://github.com/marcos-mandado/EDA-NCI

# Contents – Part II

## Urban and Regional Planning

## PHD Showcase Papers

## Short Papers

# Contents – Part I

## High Performance Computing and Networks

**Information Systems and Technologies**

# Geometric Modeling, Graphics and Visualization

# Automatic User Testing and Emotion Detection in Interactive Urban Devices

Rui P. Duarte[1,2]([✉]) [iD], Carlos A. Cunha[1,2] [iD], and José C. Cardoso[2]

[1] CISeD - Research Centre in Digital Services, Viseu, Portugal
{pduarte,cacunha}@estgv.ipv.pt
[2] Polytechnic of Viseu, Viseu, Portugal
jcardoso@estgv.ipv.pt

**Abstract.** Automated testing and evaluation of interfaces is a well-established reality supported by many tools that shorten the time to deploy new software versions to the user. However, exploring users' emotions while interacting with interfaces as a tool to further increase the quality of traditional usability evaluation methods is still far from being a reality. This work uses the automatic analysis of users' emotions while interacting with touchable interactive urban devices to detect usability issues. To this end, a coupled approach is implemented: the data is acquired from the interaction, and user emotions are extracted and processed to determine the emotional status during the interaction. This data is integrated into a web application so that designers can further improve the quality of the interface in the presence of negative emotions. Results show that the experimental tests showed that different users manifest similar negative emotions in the same contexts, which is a clear sign of usability issues that are to be corrected by the design team.

**Keywords:** User Testing · Emotion Detection · User Experience · Automation Processes · Evaluation

## 1 Introduction

Interactive urban devices have spread with the evolution of smart cities and become an immersive interaction point that brings cities closer to people who live, work, and travel to them. At the city level, they are a unique way to promote multiple activities and points of interest, such as tourism, culture, local commerce, and public services. At the citizen level, they have to be user-friendly and have a way to interact with the dynamics of a city based on information gathered by it. Inside hospitals, parking lots, and industry, these kiosks have been used as a pertinent medium to deal with services and information. However, some kiosks are not easy to use or understand, and people require specific computer skills to find what they need [1,2]. Smart cities face the challenge of implementing easy-yo-use technologies, infrastructures, and best practices [3]. With the use of interactive urban devices that spread across cities all over the world, there

O. Gervasi et al. (Eds.): ICCSA 2023, LNCS 13957, pp. 3–18, 2023.
https://doi.org/10.1007/978-3-031-36808-0_1

is a need to create user-friendly interfaces, that is, interfaces that are simple, pleasant, and easy to understand but that still maintain all the functions for which they were intended [4,5].

Interaction usability problems can be identified using techniques varying from empirical to analytic methods. While the first focus on the subjective opinion of users and experts [6–9], the second focus on automated testing [10–12], and presents several advantages, when compared to traditional techniques. One of the approaches explored in this paper is identifying usability issues by automatically detecting users' facial expressions while interacting with the interfaces.

This paper proposes an open-source facial recognition application that correlates user emotions and interactions with interactive urban devices. This provides valuable information to identify improvements to introduce in the device interface. The major contribution of this paper is to detect emotions in the interaction with touchscreen devices to determine the problems in the interface. To this end, several requirements were specified:

- Create a facial recognition application to accurately detect emotions
- Analysis on the accuracy of obtained results
- The storage of detected emotions synchronized with the interactions carried out by users during interface tests on the outdoor device database
- Express the interactions correlated with the emotions detected, graphically, in a web application, for possible identification of points of improvement.

The remainder of this paper is organized as follows. Section 2 presents a review of techniques for facial recognition and APIs on emotion detection. Section 3 presents a view of the high-level architecture and the frameworks that support the data visualizer that is presented in Sect. 4. In Sect. 5, user scenarios are created, and the visualizer is applied to real interaction contexts. Finally, Sect. 6 presents the major conclusions and some hints of future work.

## 2   Background

This section reviews the state of the art in two fundamental contexts related to the work presented in this paper: facial recognition and emotion detection API. Moreover, a view of interactive urban devices is also presented.

Using interactive systems to access information or services is a well-known challenge. The first interactive system was based on the Plato Computing System [13]. Since then, these systems have evolved and are used to communicate with citizens in the context of smart cities [14]. Several projects are implemented in real scenarios. The LinkNYC project [15] is a digital Kiosk that contains WiFi hotspots for the city of New York. Citizens can connect their devices for free WiFi access, and provide services in the city. The system has an interactive tablet on its side, and two fifty-five-inch screens on both sides, which display public service announcements and publicity. IKE Smart City [16] is another example of a digital kiosk available in several locations. It aims to create value for municipal customers and the cities it serves through smart city solutions and is similar to a city guide with information about its location. The system has two sides, one interactive and the other aimed at promoting communication and video advertising. The interactive side promotes city information such as where to eat, shop or sleep, events, and fun games. The TOMI [17] interactive urban device can be compared to a city guide with information about the urban region where it is located. TOMI works in a very interactive way between the user and the machine, allowing several actions, such as consulting news, booking events and accommodation, searching for places and means of transport, and even the possibility of creating an animated gif and taking a picture to post on social media. Many other solutions are available in the market (Partteam [18], Moobo [19], and Lamasatech [20], just to cite some). However, they all have one point in common: to bring together the city and the citizen.

For human beings, recognizing a person by his face is an involuntary act, performed naturally that provides information used in communication, and developing interaction between human beings. For a machine, the process is quite different. With the evolution of computer technology came the interest in video and image processing in terms of security and entertainment. A facial recognition system has as its main function to map the human face, using algorithms and programs as a resource, in order to be able to collect information, such as facial expressions [21, 22]. The human face has a composition of common characteristics from person to person, such as eyes, nose, and distance from nose to mouth, among others. The systems can read and map these common points, which are assembled into geometric and/or algorithmic shapes. In a way, face recognition methods act to compare a person's facial features in a certain image with faces already existing in a database [23, 24].

The first stage of facial recognition begins by locating a face in an image or video containing one or more people simultaneously. The second stage consists of collecting and analyzing a face from the image or video. In this situation, the software is responsible for making the geometric reading of the faces, identifying their main characteristics, called nodal points, such as the shape of the lips, the chin, the distance and depth of the eyes, and the length of the face, the latter being the distance between forehead and chin. A grid on the identified face usually marks these features. After collecting and analyzing the collected face, if facial detection aims to collect emotions, the position of the nodal points is analyzed, which depending on the algorithm analyzes the contractions of the facial muscles marked with the nodal points, this recorded information is transformed into data via a mathematical formula, which gives rise to a unique numerical code, which, like a fingerprint, is unique. Finally, the numerical code obtained is compared with others from faces stored in different datasets. Emotions datasets are a kind of collection of data, in this case, emotions are stored in the form of a table, where each column represents a variable and the rows, in this case, correspond to values of emotions.

The performance of machine learning models is deeply dependent on the volume of data available for training models. For that reason, the most accurate models are provided by giants of software that have access to large volumes of data for training models capable of accurately detecting emotions from images. Fortunately, these models are widely available through an Internet-accessible API like the IBM Watson [25], Face API [26], Kairos [27], and Amazon AWSRekognition [28]. In this paper, the API has to be adequate to detect emotions in real-time and is open source. For that purpose, several emotion detection APIs are analyzed, and results are presented in Table 1.

**Table 1.** List of API tested.

| APIs | Cost | JSON Format | Emotion Detection | Emotions detected (anger, fear, surprise..) | Dataset used | Accuracy | Real Time |
|------|------|-------------|-------------------|---------------------------------------------|--------------|----------|-----------|
| Kairos | Freemium | yes | yes | 4 | KairosDB | 0,62 | yes |
| Animetrics | Freemium | yes | yes | 3 | | 0.99 | |
| Lambda Labs | Freemium | yes | no | 1 | | 0.99 | no |
| Google Cloud Vision | Freemium | yes | yes | 8 | local or cloud | | |
| Luxand.cloud | Freemium | yes | yes | 8 | | 0.94 | yes |
| EyeRecognize | Freemium | no | no | | | 0.99 | |
| Face++ | Freemium | yes | yes | 8 | LFW and others | 0,99 | yes |
| Macgyver | Freemium | | | | | 0,74 | |
| Computer Vision | Freemium | yes | no | | local or cloud | 0.96 | yes |
| BetaFace | Freemium | yes | yes | | LFW | 0.81 | yes |
| Deep Face | Free | yes | yes | 7 | LFW | 0.94 | yes |
| EmoVu | Freemium | | yes | 7 | | | yes |
| AWSRekognition | Freemium | yes | yes | 9 | local or cloud | | yes |
| OpenFace | Free | yes | no | | LFW | | yes |
| Keras | Free | yes | yes | 5 | Fer+ and AffectNet | | yes |

Of the APIs presented in Table 1, two were chosen for testing: Keras (with the FER+ and AffectNet datasets, and with the FER2013 dataset), and the DeepFace API. The inclusion criteria were the ability to detect emotions and are free to use in all functionalities present in the API, unlike the others that are only free in a basic plan (real-time detection and free use).

## 3   Materials and Methods

This section presents the process of integrating emotion detection APIs with user interaction in devices to detect negative and positive emotions during the interaction. This can assist the designer of interfaces in improving them based on emotions. It presents a high-level architecture description and a detailed view of its components.

### 3.1   High-Level Architecture

The high-level architecture description provides a general view of integrating separate components that result in the interaction interface. The system must detect emotions in real-time while users interact with an interactive urban device, as illustrated in Fig. 1. The overall view of the architecture can be interpreted in three stages: data gathering, data storage, and the data visualizer.

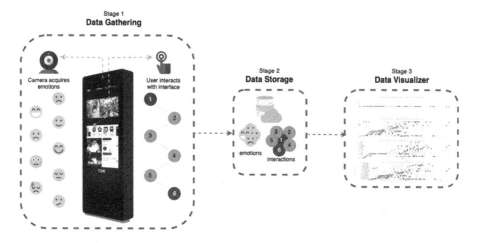

**Fig. 1.** High-level view of the proposed architecture.

Data gathering comprises the acquisition of user emotions while interacting with the touchable device. This stage generates data stored in a database where emotions are associated with each interaction. Next, this data is processed to generate visual representations of the execution of tasks that allow for the determination of negative emotions. These are the most important since they infer usability issues on the interface.

### 3.2   Emotion Detection Framework

There are several parameters associated with emotions returned by facial recognition systems, namely anger $(A_p)$, contempt $(C_p)$, disgust $(D_p)$, fear $(F_p)$, happiness $(H_p)$, neutral $(N_p)$, sadness $(S_p)$ and surprise $(Su_p)$. These emotions are related to positive, negative, and neutral emotions. To determine the weights to consider in each of the emotions, an empirical study was carried out with users that were asked to express several emotions that were compared to the results obtained from the API, to determine the level of accuracy (comparison between 8th and 9th columns of Tables 7, 8, and 9, presented in Appendix A). For the Deepface API, the accuracy of measurements is 68.29%, and typical measurement errors occur when the real emotion is negative, which is detected as neutral, as shown in Table 7 of Appendix A. On the other hand, the accuracy of the Keras API with Fer+ and AffectNet is 70.73%, where more inaccuracy is present on positive emotions, as shown in Table 8 of Appendix A. Finally, considering the Fer2013 dataset, the accuracy increases to 87.80%; however, errors still occur in the detection of negative emotions that are processed as neutral emotions (see Table 9) of Appendix A. These results are summarized in Table 2.

**Table 2.** Accuracy and detection issues in selected APIs for emotion detection.

|  | API - analysis of general values of emotions | | |
|---|---|---|---|
|  | DeepFace | Keras with Fer and AffectNet | Keras with Fer2013 |
| Accuracy | 68.29% | 70.73% | 87.80% |
| Detection issues | Negative as neutral | Positive as neutral | Negative as neutral |

Given the lack of precision of the results presented in the previous section, and considering that this paper aims to measure positive and negative emotions while interacting with an interface, the final classification focuses on these three categories (positive, negative, and neutral). This is carried out in two manners: first, emotions reduce to these categories, where *happy* and *surprise* define a *positive* emotion ($P_i = (H_p)_i + (Su_p)_i$); *sad*, *fear*, *anger* and *disgust* define the *negative* emotion ($NE_i = (S_p)_i + (F_p)_i + (A_p)_i + (D_p)_i$), and *neutral* maintains its definition. This is depicted in columns 10–12 of Tables 7, 8, and 9, while column 13 presents the resulting value based on categories of emotions.

In the second stage, several metrics are applied to refine the values of emotions to obtain a correct reading of the emotion. This approach improved the accuracy of the emotion detection for each API, which is presented in Table 3.

**Table 3.** Refinement on accuracy in three categories: positive, negative, and neutral emotions

|  | API - analysis of three categories | | |
|---|---|---|---|
|  | DeepFace | Keras with Fer and AffectNet | Keras with Fer2013 |
| Accuracy | 90.48% | 92.85% | 100.0% |

From the results, the API Keras with Fer2013 provided the best detection results and is used for emotion detection in the interaction with the interface. After the correct specification of the emotion analysis framework, the next step is to focus on the interaction framework.

### 3.3   Interaction Framework

TOMI [17] are devices for public use, with dimensions that allow them to integrate a touch screen of 47 to 55 in. and that provide various services, of which we highlight the provision of local information and communication functionalities for residents and tourists of the cities where they are located. Due to their characteristics, they classify as Urban Furniture for Information (MUPI). However, in addition to being digital, they are also interactive; that is, the services they provide depend on users' actions through the interface. Users can use all these features through touches on the TOMI touch panel, as shown in Fig. 2.

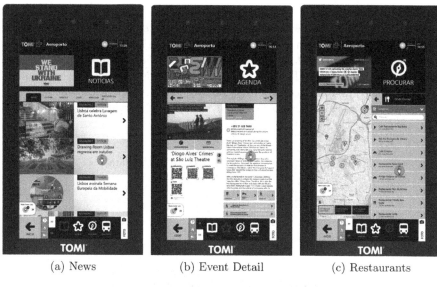

(a) News          (b) Event Detail          (c) Restaurants

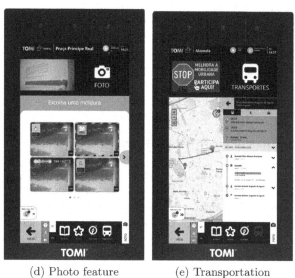

(d) Photo feature          (e) Transportation

**Fig. 2.** TOMI graphic user interface.

With regard to interactions on the TOMI device, each touch on the touch panel identifies a user interaction, which is stored in the device's database (developed in *SQLite*) containing information about where the touch was made in the touch panel. This new entry to the database is automatically generated with several data obtained from the device as illustrated in Table 4. The acquired data vary from interaction coordinates (denoted by $x$ and $y$); *menu_slug* is the category where the touch was carried out; *create_date* corresponds to the date and time of the user touch in the device, and is used to synchronize with the timestamp of emotions; *meta_tag* that marks the touches in objects like buttons, dialogues, or text events. The *objective* is the goal defined by the user and is used for tests in the interface, where users have to carry out tasks. The *objective* is reached when its value matches the concatenation of *menu_slug*, *meta_tag*, and *meta_value*.

**Table 4.** Example of an event inserted in the database.

| id | x | y | menu_slug | create_date | meta_tag | meta_value | objective | Emotion | user |
|------|-----|------|----------------|-------------|-------------------|-----------|------------------------|----------|--------|
| 3358 | 790 | 795 | TRANSPORTATION | 1624460415 | subFilterClick | onde-comer | SEARCH openDirections car | Negative | User 1 |
| 3360 | 495 | 1314 | TRANSPORTATION | 1624460420 | keyPressSearchDialog | V | SEARCH openDirections car | Negative | User 1 |

As an example, if the column *objective* is defined by *Transportation Key-PressSearchDialog V* and the columns *menu_slug*, *meta_tag*, and *meta_value* contain the values *Transportation*, *KeyPressSearchDialog* and *V*, respectively, then the goal is reached in the interaction.

Finally, the columns *emotion* and *user* correspond to the interactions of the test user and the emotion in each interaction (where the emotion detection process is applied, as described in Sect. 3.2).

# 4   Emotion-Interaction Visualizer

This section approaches the web implementation of the emotion-interaction visualizer, which accounts for the overlap of emotions and interaction timelines to detect usability issues. The data is represented in a line chart, using the Chart.js library [29]. The $yy$ axis represents the category of the interaction, and the $xx$ axis is the value of the interaction. In the $(x, y)$ coordinate, the associated emotion is represented (green for the positive emotion, yellow for the neutral, and red for the negative). Finally, the blue color represents the interaction where the user has reached the goal, as shown in Fig. 3.

Data visualization requires a pre-processing stage. To this end, for the accurate representation of the interaction with the TOMI device, the database contains the *menu_slug*, *meta_data*, and *meta_value* columns, as presented in Sect. 3.3. The representation of data from the database requires that these values are synchronized in the chart so that a correct match can be established between the $xx$ and the $yy$ axis. Moreover, it is required that the $yy$ axis does not contain repeated values. With the $yy$ axis prepared, it is necessary to treat the values of each user interaction. In this process, each user interaction will be

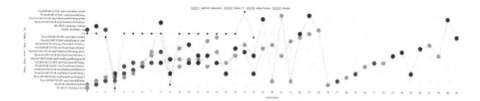

**Fig. 3.** The emotion-interaction visualizer.

compared with the different values of the $yy$ axis where, if applicable, that value will be changed by the integer corresponding to the position of the $y$ value on the axis, as shown in Fig. 4a. Later, this value will be the correct position of the interaction on the chart.

(a) Data                                        (b) Emotion

**Fig. 4.** Data and emotion treatment for axis representation.

Regarding the treatment of emotions obtained from the database, the method is different, since in the chart the data correspond to colors. Instead of collecting integer numbers, there will be a collection of colors corresponding to the emotion, changing the value by the color that represents the emotion, as shown in Fig. 4b.

## 5   Results

In order to verify the existence of usability errors in the interaction with the TOMI device, some tests are created with goals to be achieved. These tests are carried out by test users who do not know or know very little about the device's interface, thus enabling secure data collection regarding the application's usability. During the tests, the emotion detection application was used simultaneously with TOMI to collect the users' facial expressions. The interaction scenario of the tests is presented in Table 5.

After the execution of tasks with users, data is generated to be processed by the web application. A general view of the results is presented in Table 6, which allows an understanding of the number of interactions required for a user to complete their goal and also the percentage of emotions predominant in the interactions.

**Table 5.** Scenarios for the interaction with the TOMI device.

| # | Goal | Tasks |
|---|------|-------|
| 1 | You have just arrived in <city>, hungry, and it is close to lunchtime. You found a TOMI in the middle of the street and heard that it has information on restaurants in the city | 1. Find a restaurant close to you<br>2. Meanwhile, your friend Joana, who is a vegetarian, called and said she would like to have lunch with you. Look for the nearest vegetarian restaurant and calculate the driving distance there<br>3. Share the restaurant location with your friend José through WhatsApp, so that he can join you |
| 2 | Your friend José has told you that you can take photos in a TOMI. Try it | 1. Take a photo in the TOMI device, and send it to your friend José<br>2. Try to make a video, instead of taking a photo<br>3. Since you are a fan of emojis, you use them a lot. Try to add an emoji to your video<br>4. You have created an amazing video. Share it on Instagram |
| 3 | You are going to spend the day in <city> and have three yours available in the afternoon. | 1. Find an event and save the event in the calendar on your phone. Try to find an easy way to do it<br>2. Since you are also staying in <city> to sleep, see if there is a hotel near the event location<br>3. Check if there is any traffic congestion at the event<br>4. Since there is not much traffic, send the location of the event to your phone |

**Table 6.** General view of emotions in user testing.

| User | Interactions | Positive | Negative | Neutral | Goal Reached |
|------|-------------|----------|----------|---------|--------------|
| 1 | 112% | 32.61% | 26.09% | 41.30% | Yes |
| 2 | 129% | 41.51% | 22.64% | 35.85% | Yes |
| 3 | 176% | 5.56% | 37.50% | 56.94% | Yes |
| 4 | 134% | 45.45% | 30.91% | 23.64% | Yes |
| 5 | 80% | 9.09% | 30.30% | 60.61% | Yes |
| 6 | 129% | 30.19% | 30.19% | 39.62% | Yes |
| 7 | 107% | 15.91% | 56.82% | 27.27% | Yes |
| Average | 124% | 25.76% | 33.49% | 40.75% | – |

Results show that it is possible to infer that in relation to the goal, the number of interactions is higher than 100% of the optimal interaction and that all users managed to reach the intended goal. As far as emotions are concerned, on average several negative emotions were detected, which suggests that there is a usability problem, given that users presented negative emotions. By refining the information in the chart format presented in Fig. 5, it is possible to understand the interactions that gave emphasis to the negative emotions and are to be analyzed by the design team. In Fig. 5, several users had negative emotions between interactions 8–19 which were analyzed by the research team and revealed effective problems of interaction.

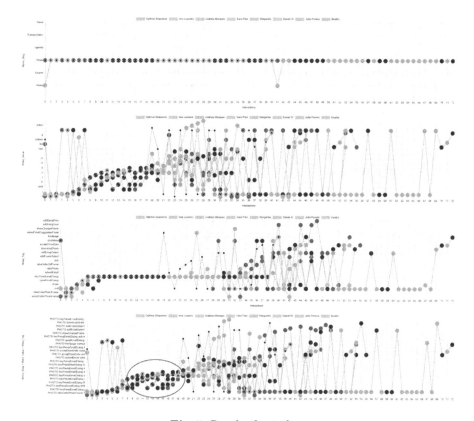

**Fig. 5.** Results for tasks.

# 6    Conclusions

This paper addresses the analysis of emotions to detect usability issues in a touchable user interface. The methodology followed was based on two essential frameworks: the implementation of an emotion detection system based on facial recognition and a recorder of interactions that account for the objects the user has touched in a graphical user interface. These two frameworks are matched in a timeline, which allows the evaluation of both interactions and associated emotions with the interaction. With this, it is possible to measure the state of mind of a user when interacting with an interface.

The overlapping of interactions and emotions is represented in a timeline using a web application for the correct identification of emotions in the interactions with components, following a baseline of the optimal interaction. The relationship between both is presented in a chart format.

Results show that most users reached the goal but exceeded the number of interactions and did not follow the path defined by the optimal interaction for the task. Several negative emotions were detected in the same context of interaction, which were later identified as usability issues of the interface by the design team.

**Acknowledgements.** This work is funded by National Funds through the FCT - Foundation for Science and Technology, I.P., within the scope of the project Ref. UIDB/05583/2020. Furthermore, we would like to thank the Research Centre in Digital Services (CISeD) and the Polytechnic of Viseu under the Special Projects Program (project ref. Don't Stand So Close To Me) for their support.

# A    Tests with APIs

As presented in Sect. 3.2, several tests were carried out with two APIs: Keras (with the FER+ and AffectNet datasets, and with the FER2013 dataset), and the DeepFace API. Differences in emotions when compared to real emotions are represented with a different color.

**Table 7.** Deepface API test.

| Anger $(A_p)$ | Disgust $(D_p)$ | Fear $(F_p)$ | Happiness $(H_p)$ | Neutral $(N_p)$ | Sadness $(S_p)$ | Surprise $(Su_p)$ | Obtained API emotion | Real Emotion | Negative | Positive | Neutral | Emotion Value |
|---|---|---|---|---|---|---|---|---|---|---|---|---|
| 96.5 | 0 | 0.07 | 0 | 2.6 | 0.76 | 0 | Anger | Anger | 97.33 | 0 | 2.6 | Negative |
| 51.6 | 3.1 | 0.8 | 0 | 18.79 | 25.2 | 0.2 | Anger | Anger | 80.7 | 0.2 | 18.79 | Negative |
| 79.8 | 0.12 | 0 | 0 | 7.6 | 11.6 | 0.6 | Anger | Anger | 91.52 | 0.6 | 7.6 | Negative |
| 32 | 0 | 0 | 3.98 | 41.79 | 21.93 | 0.2 | Neutral | Anger | 53.93 | 4.18 | 41.79 | Negative |
| 28 | 0 | 5.5 | 0.93 | 54.95 | 10.2 | 0 | Neutral | Anger | 43.7 | 0.93 | 54.95 | Negative |
| 35.2 | 0 | 7.7 | 3.77 | 45.7 | 5.58 | 1.9 | Neutral | Anger | 48.48 | 5.67 | 45.7 | Negative |
| 4.89 | 0 | 5 | 5.26 | 78.2 | 6.16 | 0.3 | Neutral | Anger | 16.05 | 5.56 | 78.2 | Neutral |
| 0.4 | 0.3 | 45.6 | 1.01 | 18.3 | 34.13 | 0 | Fear | Fear | 80.43 | 1.01 | 18.3 | Negative |
| 0 | 0.1 | 84.42 | 3.87 | 3.63 | 7.89 | 0 | Fear | Fear | 92.41 | 3.87 | 3.63 | Negative |
| 3.6 | 62.4 | 22.24 | 3.82 | 2.12 | 5.7 | 0 | Disgust | Fear | 93.04 | 3.82 | 2.12 | Negative |
| 6 | 13.6 | 28.5 | 4.65 | 39 | 7.85 | 0.15 | Neutral | Fear | 55.95 | 4.8 | 39 | Negative |
| 0.25 | 18.5 | 49.4 | 0.3 | 0.66 | 30.75 | 0 | Fear | Fear | 98.9 | 0.3 | 0.66 | Negative |
| 7.48 | 0 | 39.18 | 29.95 | 15.5 | 2.95 | 4.91 | Fear | Fear | 49.61 | 34.86 | 15.5 | Negative |
| 5.3 | 0 | 15.65 | 31.91 | 12.8 | 33.85 | 0.39 | Sadness | Fear | 54.8 | 32.3 | 12.8 | Negative |
| 0 | 0 | 0 | 99.99 | 0.0099 | 0 | 0 | Happiness | Happiness | 0 | 99.99 | 0.0099 | Positive |
| 0 | 0 | 0 | 99.99 | 0 | 0 | 0 | Happiness | Happiness | 0 | 99.99 | 0 | Positive |
| 0.03 | 0 | 0 | 96.9 | 0.29 | 2.75 | 0 | Happiness | Happiness | 2.78 | 96.9 | 0.29 | Positive |
| 0 | 0 | 0.4 | 86.92 | 0 | 12.66 | 0 | Happiness | Happiness | 13.06 | 86.92 | 0 | Positive |
| 0 | 0 | 0 | 99.43 | 0.54 | 0.02 | 0 | Happiness | Happiness | 0.02 | 99.43 | 0.54 | Positive |
| 0 | 0 | 0 | 49.22 | 50.77 | 0 | 0 | Neutral | Happiness | 0 | 49.22 | 50.77 | Positive |
| 0 | 0 | 0 | 97.63 | 0.01 | 2.35 | 0 | Happiness | Happiness | 2.35 | 97.63 | 0.01 | Positive |
| 3.16 | 1.33 | 0.03 | 1 | 28.17 | 66.23 | 0.04 | Sadness | Sadness | 70.75 | 1.04 | 28.17 | Negative |
| 0 | 0 | 0 | 0 | 0 | 99.99 | 0 | Sadness | Sadness | 99.99 | 0 | 0 | Negative |
| 0.2 | 0.02 | 0 | 35.71 | 16.53 | 47.5 | 0 | Sadness | Sadness | 47.72 | 35.71 | 16.53 | Negative |
| 0 | 0 | 0.02 | 0.02 | 0 | 99.95 | 0 | Sadness | Sadness | 99.97 | 0.02 | 0 | Negative |
| 0.43 | 0.1 | 0.01 | 13.86 | 42.22 | 43.35 | 0 | Sadness | Sadness | 43.89 | 13.86 | 42.22 | Negative |
| 0.96 | 0 | 0.33 | 59.95 | 7.71 | 31.03 | 0 | Happiness | Sadness | 32.32 | 59.95 | 7.71 | Negative |
| 0.35 | 3.37 | 0.32 | 5.08 | 7.07 | 83.77 | 0 | Sadness | Sadness | 87.81 | 5.08 | 7.07 | Negative |
| 10.83 | 0 | 43.86 | 0.33 | 7.17 | 18.22 | 19.55 | Fear | Surprise | 72.91 | 19.88 | 7.17 | Negative |
| 13.63 | 2.69 | 12.8 | 65.34 | 0.54 | 3.54 | 1.42 | Happiness | Surprise | 32.66 | 66.76 | 0.54 | Positive |
| 0.002 | 0 | 5.3 | 0 | 22.43 | 0.03 | 72.22 | Surprise | Surprise | 5.332 | 72.22 | 22.43 | Positive |
| 11.49 | 0 | 29.07 | 0.01 | 2.64 | 0.14 | 56.62 | Surprise | Surprise | 40.7 | 56.63 | 2.64 | Negative |
| 7 | 0.7 | 24.78 | 0.13 | 49.06 | 10.01 | 8.29 | Neutral | Surprise | 42.49 | 8.42 | 49.06 | Negative |
| 3.62 | 10.9 | 61.24 | 0.12 | 1.83 | 19.16 | 3.09 | Fear | Surprise | 94.92 | 3.21 | 1.83 | Negative |
| 0 | 0 | 0.05 | 0 | 80.11 | 16.53 | 3.28 | Neutral | Surprise | 16.58 | 3.28 | 80.11 | Neutral |
| 0.39 | 0 | 0 | 0.17 | 92.82 | 6.6 | 0 | Neutral | Neutral | 6.99 | 0.17 | 92.82 | Neutral |
| 0.6 | 0 | 0 | 0.91 | 80.07 | 18.39 | 0 | Neutral | Neutral | 18.99 | 0.91 | 80.07 | Neutral |
| 0.14 | 0 | 0 | 2.52 | 93.58 | 3.74 | 0 | Neutral | Neutral | 3.88 | 2.52 | 93.58 | Neutral |
| 0.04 | 0 | 0 | 2.39 | 96.23 | 1.32 | 0 | Neutral | Neutral | 1.36 | 2.39 | 96.23 | Neutral |
| 5.59 | 0 | 0.09 | 0 | 54.96 | 39.34 | 0 | Neutral | Neutral | 45.02 | 0 | 54.96 | Neutral |
| 1.29 | 0 | 0.18 | 0 | 78.46 | 20.05 | 0 | Neutral | Neutral | 21.52 | 0 | 78.46 | Neutral |
| 0.35 | 0 | 0 | 0 | 97.43 | 2.2 | 0 | Neutral | Neutral | 2.55 | 0 | 97.43 | Neutral |

**Table 8.** Keras API with Fer+ and AffectNet

| Anger $(A_p)$ | Disgust $(D_p)$ | Fear $(F_p)$ | Happiness $(H_p)$ | Neutral $(N_p)$ | Sadness $(S_p)$ | Surprise $(Su_p)$ | Obtained API emotion | Real Emotion | Negative | Positive | Neutral | Emotion Value |
|---|---|---|---|---|---|---|---|---|---|---|---|---|
| 0.52 | 0.02 | 0.03 | 0.01 | 0.15 | 0.28 | 0.01 | Anger | Angry | 0.85 | 0.02 | 0.15 | Negative |
| 0.18 | 0 | 0.01 | 0 | 0.5 | 0.3 | 0.01 | Neutral | Angry | 0.49 | 0.01 | 0.5 | Negative |
| 0.49 | 0 | 0.11 | 0 | 0.15 | 0.25 | 0.01 | Anger | Angry | 0.85 | 0.01 | 0.15 | Negative |
| 0.81 | 0 | 0 | 0 | 0.03 | 0.14 | 0.01 | Anger | Angry | 0.95 | 0.01 | 0.03 | Negative |
| 0.98 | 0 | 0 | 0 | 0.01 | 0.01 | 0 | Anger | Angry | 0.99 | 0 | 0.01 | Negative |
| 0.41 | 0 | 0.02 | 0.02 | 0.14 | 0.39 | 0.02 | Anger | Angry | 0.82 | 0.04 | 0.14 | Negative |
| 0.7 | 0 | 0.01 | 0.01 | 0.1 | 0.14 | 0.04 | Anger | Angry | 0.85 | 0.05 | 0.1 | Negative |
| 0.09 | 0 | 0.61 | 0.01 | 0.03 | 0.07 | 0.19 | Fear | Fear | 0.77 | 0.2 | 0.03 | Negative |
| 0.09 | 0 | 0.8 | 0.01 | 0 | 0.01 | 0.08 | Fear | Fear | 0.9 | 0.09 | 0 | Negative |
| 0.27 | 0 | 0.66 | 0.01 | 0.01 | 0.02 | 0.03 | Fear | Fear | 0.95 | 0.04 | 0.01 | Negative |
| 0.11 | 0 | 0.78 | 0.01 | 0.01 | 0.02 | 0.07 | Fear | Fear | 0.91 | 0.08 | 0.01 | Negative |
| 0.17 | 0 | 0.51 | 0 | 0.03 | 0.15 | 0.14 | Fear | Fear | 0.83 | 0.14 | 0.03 | Negative |
| 0.1 | 0 | 0.07 | 0.01 | 0.39 | 0.25 | 0.17 | Neutral | Fear | 0.42 | 0.18 | 0.39 | Negative |
| 0.17 | 0 | 0.39 | 0.03 | 0.05 | 0.32 | 0.05 | Fear | Fear | 0.88 | 0.08 | 0.05 | Negative |
| 0.12 | 0 | 0.07 | 0.38 | 0.22 | 0.19 | 0 | Happiness | Happiness | 0.38 | 0.38 | 0.22 | Positive |
| 0.16 | 0 | 0.08 | 0.09 | 0.54 | 0.12 | 0.01 | Neutral | Happiness | 0.36 | 0.1 | 0.54 | Neutral |
| 0.42 | 0 | 0.03 | 0.19 | 0.24 | 0.12 | 0 | Anger | Happiness | 0.57 | 0.19 | 0.24 | Negative |
| 0.17 | 0 | 0.02 | 0.19 | 0.51 | 0.1 | 0 | Neutral | Happiness | 0.29 | 0.19 | 0.51 | Positive |
| 0.07 | 0.02 | 0.04 | 0.83 | 0.01 | 0.03 | 0 | Happiness | Happiness | 0.16 | 0.83 | 0.01 | Positive |
| 0.02 | 0 | 0.01 | 0.75 | 0.15 | 0.07 | 0.01 | Happiness | Happiness | 0.1 | 0.76 | 0.15 | Positive |
| 0.15 | 0.01 | 0.09 | 0.18 | 0.28 | 0.28 | 0.05 | Sadness | Happiness | 0.53 | 0.23 | 0.28 | Positive |
| 0.1 | 0 | 0.03 | 0.01 | 0.39 | 0.48 | 0 | Sadness | Sadness | 0.61 | 0.01 | 0.39 | Negative |
| 0.08 | 0 | 0.02 | 0.02 | 0.55 | 0.32 | 0 | Neutral | Sadness | 0.42 | 0.02 | 0.55 | Negative |
| 0.16 | 0 | 0.21 | 0.02 | 0.23 | 0.38 | 0 | Sadness | Sadness | 0.75 | 0.02 | 0.23 | Negative |
| 0.02 | 0 | 0.01 | 0.01 | 0.29 | 0.67 | 0 | Sadness | Sadness | 0.7 | 0.01 | 0.29 | Negative |
| 0.13 | 0 | 0.2 | 0.01 | 0.24 | 0.4 | 0.02 | Sadness | Sadness | 0.73 | 0.03 | 0.24 | Negative |
| 0.09 | 0 | 0.02 | 0.17 | 0.43 | 0.28 | 0.02 | Neutral | Sadness | 0.39 | 0.19 | 0.43 | Negative |
| 0.23 | 0 | 0.13 | 0.05 | 0.34 | 0.24 | 0.01 | Neutral | Sadness | 0.6 | 0.06 | 0.34 | Negative |
| 0.02 | 0 | 0.59 | 0.01 | 0.1 | 0.07 | 0.21 | Fear | Surprise | 0.68 | 0.22 | 0.1 | Positive |
| 0.05 | 0 | 0.63 | 0.15 | 0.02 | 0.02 | 0.13 | Fear | Surprise | 0.7 | 0.28 | 0.02 | Positive |
| 0.06 | 0 | 0.25 | 0.29 | 0.01 | 0.01 | 0.37 | Surprise | Surprise | 0.32 | 0.66 | 0.01 | Positive |
| 0 | 0 | 0.13 | 0 | 0 | 0 | 0.87 | Surprise | Surprise | 0.13 | 0.87 | 0 | Positive |
| 0 | 0 | 0.4 | 0.01 | 0.06 | 0.04 | 0.49 | Surprise | Surprise | 0.44 | 0.5 | 0.06 | Positive |
| 0 | 0 | 0.15 | 0 | 0 | 0 | 0.85 | Surprise | Surprise | 0.15 | 0.85 | 0.0 | Positive |
| 0.06 | 0 | 0.16 | 0.03 | 0.29 | 0.3 | 0.16 | Sadness | Surprise | 0.52 | 0.19 | 0.29 | Negative |
| 0.1 | 0 | 0.02 | 0.04 | 0.61 | 0.22 | 0 | Neutral | Neutral | 0.34 | 0.04 | 0.61 | Neutral |
| 0.01 | 0 | 0.02 | 0 | 0.79 | 0.18 | 0.01 | Neutral | Neutral | 0.21 | 0.01 | 0.79 | Neutral |
| 0.05 | 0 | 0.01 | 0.07 | 0.71 | 0.13 | 0.02 | Neutral | Neutral | 0.19 | 0.09 | 0.71 | Neutral |
| 0.01 | 0 | 0.01 | 0.25 | 0.52 | 0.19 | 0.01 | Neutral | Neutral | 0.21 | 0.26 | 0.52 | Neutral |
| 0.01 | 0 | 0.01 | 0.31 | 0.4 | 0.31 | 0.01 | Neutral | Neutral | 0.33 | 0.32 | 0.4 | Positive |
| 0.03 | 0 | 0.01 | 0.27 | 0.59 | 0.27 | 0.03 | Neutral | Neutral | 0.31 | 0.3 | 0.59 | Neutral |
| 0.01 | 0 | 0.01 | 0.16 | 0.73 | 0.16 | 0.03 | Neutral | Neutral | 0.18 | 0.19 | 0.73 | Neutral |

**Table 9.** Keras API with Fer2013.

| Anger $(A_p)$ | Disgust $(D_p)$ | Fear $(F_p)$ | Happiness $(H_p)$ | Neutral $(N_p)$ | Sadness $(S_p)$ | Surprise $(Su_p)$ | Obtained API emotion | Real Emotion | Negative | Positive | Neutral | Emotion Value |
|---|---|---|---|---|---|---|---|---|---|---|---|---|
| 29.06 | 0.4 | 19.99 | 23.95 | 15.79 | 8.43 | 2.32 | Anger | Anger | 57.88 | 26.27 | 15.79 | Negative |
| 41.11 | 0.1 | 25.66 | 1.6 | 24.34 | 5.05 | 2.08 | Anger | Anger | 71.92 | 3.68 | 24.34 | Negative |
| 37.53 | 0.3 | 29.49 | 4.22 | 17.35 | 10.03 | 0.9 | Anger | Anger | 77.35 | 5.12 | 17.35 | Negative |
| 35.16 | 0.1 | 23.1 | 7.3 | 23.51 | 10.14 | 0.6 | Anger | Anger | 68.5 | 7.9 | 23.51 | Negative |
| 37.09 | 0.3 | 34.07 | 8.52 | 12.55 | 6.38 | 1.04 | Anger | Anger | 77.84 | 9.56 | 12.55 | Negative |
| 27.09 | 0.3 | 51.54 | 5.87 | 0.52 | 2.02 | 7.92 | Fear | Anger | 80.95 | 13.79 | 0.52 | Negative |
| 27.09 | 0.2 | 32.31 | 12.87 | 19.31 | 3.2 | 0.49 | Fear | Anger | 62.8 | 13.36 | 19.31 | Negative |
| 7.57 | 0.1 | 51.65 | 4.56 | 18.43 | 12.03 | 5.62 | Fear | Fear | 71.35 | 10.18 | 18.43 | Negative |
| 6.99 | 0 | 49.96 | 7.12 | 20.01 | 11.4 | 4.43 | Fear | Fear | 68.35 | 11.55 | 20.01 | Negative |
| 13.43 | 0 | 31.94 | 17.84 | 22.97 | 10.7 | 3.03 | Fear | Fear | 56.07 | 20.87 | 22.97 | Negative |
| 27.92 | 0.1 | 28.43 | 6.02 | 23.59 | 13.57 | 0.3 | Fear | Fear | 70.02 | 6.32 | 23.59 | Negative |
| 13.36 | 0 | 48.14 | 8.77 | 19.52 | 8.05 | 2.05 | Fear | Fear | 69.55 | 10.82 | 19.52 | Negative |
| 8.92 | 0.1 | 58.82 | 12.31 | 4.68 | 10.1 | 4.99 | Fear | Fear | 77.94 | 17.3 | 4.68 | Negative |
| 27.93 | 0.1 | 48.56 | 5.67 | 10.11 | 6.96 | 0.5 | Fear | Fear | 83.55 | 6.17 | 10.11 | Negative |
| 7.27 | 1.08 | 10.07 | 58.26 | 14.2 | 7.74 | 1.34 | Happiness | Happiness | 26.16 | 59.6 | 14.2 | Positive |
| 3.77 | 0.5 | 16.19 | 55.68 | 11.96 | 10.98 | 0.8 | Happiness | Happiness | 31.44 | 56.48 | 11.96 | Positive |
| 4.86 | 0.1 | 32.63 | 35.28 | 3.73 | 11.03 | 12.32 | Happiness | Happiness | 48.62 | 47.6 | 3.73 | Positive |
| 2.43 | 0.1 | 24.83 | 47.37 | 7.37 | 8.7 | 9.16 | Happiness | Happiness | 36.06 | 56.53 | 7.37 | Positive |
| 3.17 | 0 | 21.81 | 51.04 | 8.69 | 4.27 | 10.91 | Happiness | Happiness | 29.25 | 61.95 | 8.69 | Positive |
| 15.76 | 0 | 16.95 | 40.81 | 13.96 | 4.39 | 8.05 | Happiness | Happiness | 37.1 | 48.86 | 13.96 | Positive |
| 11.82 | 0 | 10.3 | 34.08 | 26.99 | 9.31 | 7.42 | Happiness | Happiness | 31.43 | 41.5 | 26.99 | Positive |
| 8.71 | 0 | 17.61 | 11.68 | 25.74 | 28.45 | 7.75 | Sadness | Sadness | 54.77 | 19.43 | 25.74 | Negative |
| 10.38 | 0 | 23.39 | 3.36 | 29.45 | 32.81 | 0.52 | Sadness | Sadness | 66.58 | 3.88 | 29.45 | Negative |
| 12.91 | 0.11 | 17.61 | 7.59 | 35.26 | 25.51 | 0.99 | Neutral | Sadness | 56.14 | 8.58 | 35.26 | Negative |
| 11.44 | 0 | 19.63 | 5.29 | 34.49 | 28.08 | 0.97 | Neutral | Sadness | 59.15 | 6.26 | 34.49 | Negative |
| 12.61 | 0.12 | 19.68 | 6.05 | 30.9 | 29.99 | 0.62 | Neutral | Sadness | 62.4 | 6.67 | 30.9 | Negative |
| 12.46 | 0 | 18.07 | 3.49 | 32.71 | 32.91 | 0.29 | Sadness | Sadness | 63.44 | 3.78 | 32.71 | Negative |
| 9.39 | 0 | 32.23 | 2.1 | 22.24 | 33.8 | 0.16 | Sadness | Sadness | 75.42 | 2.26 | 22.24 | Negative |
| 4.61 | 0 | 33.94 | 6.66 | 7.14 | 2.15 | 45.42 | Surprise | Surprise | 40.7 | 52.08 | 7.14 | Positive |
| 5.65 | 0 | 30.97 | 1.73 | 23.08 | 3.68 | 34.83 | Surprise | Surprise | 40.3 | 36.56 | 23.08 | Positive |
| 7.28 | 0 | 27.49 | 3.7 | 7.02 | 3.49 | 50.98 | Surprise | Surprise | 38.26 | 54.68 | 7.02 | Positive |
| 5.21 | 0 | 22.72 | 1.56 | 1.64 | 1.18 | 67.67 | Surprise | Surprise | 29.11 | 69.23 | 1.64 | Positive |
| 3.15 | 0 | 26 | 1.91 | 5.05 | 1.86 | 61.99 | Surprise | Surprise | 31.01 | 63.9 | 5.05 | Positive |
| 2.31 | 0 | 24.79 | 1.9 | 1.66 | 0.78 | 68.53 | Surprise | Surprise | 27.88 | 70.43 | 1.66 | Positive |
| 2.34 | 0 | 29.1 | 0.66 | 0.89 | 0.75 | 66.24 | Surprise | Surprise | 32.19 | 66.9 | 0.89 | Positive |
| 9.08 | 0 | 25.79 | 0.23 | 49.71 | 15.16 | 0.01 | Neutral | Neutral | 50.03 | 0.24 | 49.71 | Neutral |
| 11.65 | 0 | 16.75 | 0.71 | 57.07 | 13.75 | 0 | Neutral | Neutral | 42.15 | 0.71 | 57.07 | Neutral |
| 14.78 | 0 | 17.67 | 0.3 | 55.1 | 12.1 | 0.02 | Neutral | Neutral | 44.55 | 0.32 | 55.1 | Neutral |
| 15.23 | 0 | 16.56 | 0.39 | 55.58 | 12.17 | 0 | Neutral | Neutral | 43.96 | 0.39 | 55.58 | Neutral |
| 14.83 | 0 | 13.57 | 0.32 | 59.9 | 11.33 | 0.02 | Neutral | Neutral | 39.73 | 0.34 | 59.9 | Neutral |
| 13.89 | 0 | 16.07 | 0.24 | 57.85 | 11.9 | 0.01 | Neutral | Neutral | 41.86 | 0.25 | 57.85 | Neutral |
| 15.58 | 0 | 14.25 | 0.29 | 57.33 | 12.5 | 0.03 | Neutral | Neutral | 42.33 | 0.32 | 57.33 | Neutral |

# References

1. Mäkinen, E., Patomäki, S., Raisamo, R.: Experiences on a multimodal information kiosk with an interactive agent. In: Proceedings of the Second Nordic Conference on Human-Computer Interaction, pp. 275–278. NordiCHI 2002, Association for Computing Machinery, New York, NY, USA (2002). https://doi.org/10.1145/572020.572064

2. Johnston, M., Bangalore, S.: Matchkiosk: a multimodal interactive city guide. In: Proceedings of the ACL 2004 on Interactive Poster and Demonstration Sessions, pp. 33–es. ACLdemo 2004, Association for Computational Linguistics, USA (2004). https://doi.org/10.3115/1219044.1219077

3. Albino, V., Berardi, U., Dangelico, R.M.: Smart cities: definitions, dimensions, performance, and initiatives. J. Urban Technol. **22**(1), 3–21 (2015). https://doi.org/10.1080/10630732.2014.942092
4. Ganov, S.R., Killmar, C., Khurshid, S., Perry, D.E.: Test generation for graphical user interfaces based on symbolic execution. In: Proceedings of the 3rd International Workshop on Automation of Software Test, pp. 33–40. AST 2008, Association for Computing Machinery, New York, NY, USA (2008). https://doi.org/10.1145/1370042.1370050
5. Memon, A.M.: A comprehensive framework for testing graphical user interfaces. Ph.D., University of Pittsburgh (2001), advisors: Mary Lou Soffa and Martha Pollack; Committee members: Prof. Rajiv Gupta (University of Arizona), Prof. Adele E. Howe (Colorado State University), Prof. Lori Pollock (University of Delaware)
6. Callahan, E., Koenemann, J.: A comparative usability evaluation of user interfaces for online product catalog. In: Proceedings of the 2nd ACM Conference on Electronic Commerce, pp. 197–206. EC 2000, Association for Computing Machinery, New York, NY, USA (2000). https://doi.org/10.1145/352871.352893
7. Paz, F., Paz, F.A., Pow-Sang, J.A.: Evaluation of usability heuristics for transactional web sites: a comparative study. In: Information Technology: New Generations. AISC, vol. 448, pp. 1063–1073. Springer, Cham (2016). https://doi.org/10.1007/978-3-319-32467-8_92
8. Paz, F., Paz, F.A., Villanueva, D., Pow-Sang, J.A.: Heuristic evaluation as a complement to usability testing: a case study in web domain, pp. 546–551. ITNG 2015, IEEE Computer Society, USA (2015). https://doi.org/10.1109/ITNG.2015.92
9. Yushiana, M., Rani, W.A.: Heuristic evaluation of interface usability for a web-based OPAC. Library Hi Tech. **25**, 538–549 (2007). https://doi.org/10.1108/07378830710840491
10. Fernandez, A., Insfran, E., Abrahão, S.: Usability evaluation methods for the web: a systematic mapping study. Inf. Softw. Technol. **53**(8), 789–817 (2011). https://doi.org/10.1016/j.infsof.2011.02.007
11. Bakaev, M., Mamysheva, T., Gaedke, M.: Current trends in automating usability evaluation of websites: can you manage what you can't measure? In: 2016 11th International Forum on Strategic Technology (IFOST), pp. 510–514 (2016). https://doi.org/10.1109/IFOST.2016.7884307
12. Cunha, D., Duarte, R.P., Cunha, C.A.: KLM-GOMS detection of interaction patterns through the execution of unplanned tasks. In: Gervasi, O., et al. (eds.) ICCSA 2021. LNCS, vol. 12950, pp. 203–219. Springer, Cham (2021). https://doi.org/10.1007/978-3-030-86960-1_15
13. Smith, S.G., Sherwood, B.A.: Educational uses of the Plato computer system. Science. **192**(4237), 344–352 (1976). https://www.science.org/doi/abs/10.1126/science.769165
14. Lehofer, M., et al.: Platforms for smart cities - connecting humans, infrastructure and industrial it. In: 2016 1st International Workshop on Science of Smart City Operations and Platforms Engineering (SCOPE) in Partnership with Global City Teams Challenge (GCTC) (SCOPE - GCTC), pp. 1–6 (2016)
15. Linknyc project. https://www.link.nyc/. Accessed 10 Apr 2023
16. Ike smart city. https://www.ikesmartcity.com/. Accessed 10 Apr 2023
17. Tomi interactive urban device (2023). http://tomiworld.com/meet-tomi/. Accessed 7 Apr 2023
18. Partteam & oemkiosks (2023). https://partteams.com/?page=digital_billboards_stand_up. Accessed 7 Apr 2023

19. Moobo (2023). https://moobo.pt/. Accessed 7 Apr 2023
20. Lamasatech (2023). https://www.lamasatech.com/products/standing-kiosks/outdoor-kiosks/. Accessed 7 Apr 2023
21. Zhang, X., Gao, Y.: Face recognition across pose: a review. Pattern Recogn. **42**(11), 2876–2896 (2009). https://www.sciencedirect.com/science/article/pii/S0031320309001538
22. Li, L., Mu, X., Li, S., Peng, H.: A review of face recognition technology. IEEE Access **8**, 139110–139120 (2020)
23. Celiktutan, O., Ulukaya, S., Sankur, B.: A comparative study of face landmarking techniques. EURASIP J. Image Video Process. **2013**(1), 13 (2013)
24. Johnston, B., de Chazal, P.: A review of image-based automatic facial landmark identification techniques. EURASIP J. Image Video Process. **2018**(1), 86 (2018)
25. Ibm watson - visual recognition. https://www.ibm.com/watson/services/visual-recognition/. Accessed 10 Nov 2023
26. Microsoft cognitive services: Face API (2019). https://azure.microsoft.com/en-us/services/cognitive-services/face/. Accessed 10 Nov 2023
27. Kairos APIS and SDKS (2019). https://www.kairos.com/. Accessed 10 Nov 2023
28. Amazon rekognition - video and image. https://aws.amazon.com/rekognition. Accessed 10 Nov 2023
29. Chart.js open source html5 charts (2023). https://www.chartjs.org/. Accessed 7 Apr 2023

# Robust Seeded Image Segmentation Using Adaptive Label Propagation and Deep Learning-Based Contour Orientation

Aldimir José Bruzadin[1], Marilaine Colnago[2], Rogério Galante Negri[3], and Wallace Casaca[1(✉)]

[1] IBILCE, São Paulo State University, São José do Rio Preto - SP, Brazil
{aldimir.j.bruzadin,wallace.casaca}@unesp.br
[2] IQ - São Paulo State University, Araraquara - SP, Brazil
marilaine.colnago@unesp.br
[3] ICT, São Paulo State University, São José dos Campos - SP, Brazil
rogerio.negri@unesp.br

**Abstract.** Deep Learning has become a popular tool for addressing complex tasks in many computer vision applications. Label diffusion methods have also been a very effective technique for getting accurate segmentations of real-world images, as they combine user autonomy, versatility and accurateness through a user-friendly interface. In this paper, we propose a seeded segmentation framework for partitioning real-world images by combining deep contour learning and graph-based label propagation models. More precisely, our approach takes a CNN-type contour detection network to learn graph edge weights, which are used as input to solve a coupled energy minimization problem that diffuses the user-selected annotations to the desired targets. To accurately extract deep features from image contours while generating diffusion maps, we train a deep learning architecture that integrates a hierarchical neural network, a graph-based label propagation model and a loss function, allowing the coupled training mechanism to refine the results until convergence. We attest to the effectiveness and accuracy of the proposed approach by conducting both quantitative and qualitative assessments with existing seeded image segmentation methods.

**Keywords:** Seeded Segmentation · Contour Learning

## 1 Introduction

Image Segmentation refers to the process of splitting an image into disjointed partitions [7]. This task is a critical and mandatory step in many Computer

This research has been funded by the São Paulo Research Foundation (FAPESP – grants 2013/07375-0, #2021/03328-3 and #2021/01305-6), the Coordination for the Improvement of Higher Education Personnel (CAPES - Funding Code 001), and the National Council for Scientific and Technological Development (CNPq – grants #316228/2021-4 and #305220/2022-5).

Vision applications, including image classification [24], object detection [13] and pattern recognition [22]. In this context, a very effective approach for clustering digital images is the seeded segmentation application, which consists of manually selecting a small set of user-labaled pixels to initialize the segmentation process [27]. In fact, seeded segmentation methods have proved to be effective and robust in obtaining precise image partitions, as it offers users autonomy, adaptability, and user-friendliness while capturing the marked targets among numerous objects in the image [6].

Some of the most widely recognized seed-based segmentation methods are *Random Walker* (RW) [14] and *Watershed* (WS) [9], as they are formulated in terms of the solid theory of energy minimization on graphs [19,26]. The RW solves a graph-based quadratic optimization problem to proceed with the image label propagation, and it has still served as inspiration for the development of current segmentation approaches [1,11,17], while the WS method stands out as a valuable technique devoted to capturing objects that overlap on the image.

Deep learning (DL) is another consolidated and powerful approach to partition images, which achieves very accurate segmentations for a variety of image-driven domains such as image registration [4] and remote sensing [25]. Indeed, the advance promoted by DL can be attributed to its ability to extract relevant features from large datasets of training images, allowing the trained models to continuously learn and improve over time. Popular deep learning architectures such as Convolutional Neural Networks (CNNs) can be successfully used to extract high-level features from images, hence improving the segmentation task significantly.

In the past few years, there has been growing interest in integrating deep learning techniques with graph-based label propagation strategies to improve the segmentation task in an intuitive and user-friendly way. For example, Kucharski et al. [20] utilize a CNN-based methodology to predict markers, which are used in conjunction with a WS transform to segment corneal endothelium. Hu et al. [18] take a seed-guided segmentation algorithm together with two parallel CNN-type networks to reduce the user intervention. Despite the satisfactory results, their methodology relies on specific sets of clicks rather than brushed pixels. Roth et al. [28] propose a weakly supervised approach that applies the RW model to generate pseudo-masks based on extreme points, so that these pseudo-masks are then used to train a network to produce the final masks. While their method is flexible enough to process medical data, it is not suitable to partition real-world digital images. Can et al. [5] also utilize the RW model as part of their advances, to obtain semi-automated segmentations of prostate and cardiac data by applying a Fully Convolutional Network (FCN). Similarly, Cerrone et al. [8] present a learning architecture that unifies a CNN-type network and the RW model for segmenting Electron Microscopy (EM) data, while Wolf et al. [32] focus on addressing the same segmentation problem (i.e., EM data), but by taking shape priors via a WS-driven framework coupled with a CNN instead of an RW-based one.

As previously discussed, a prevalent trait present in most seeded segmentation methods based on DL is that they are designed to be effective for very particular imaging modalities (e.g., medical data). Also, the requirement for specific data sources for training is another challenge difficult to overcome in practical application scenarios. Lastly, most purely DL-based segmentation approaches do not allow the user to interact and customize the segmentation process according to their needs and preferences, thus setting aside the autonomy and flexibility offered by different interactive segmentation tools.

In this paper, we introduce a new DL-based seeded segmentation framework for partitioning real-world images that is capable of tackling most of the aforementioned issues. The proposed approach combines the precision of deep contour learning with the high adaptability of seeded image segmentation towards delivering a fully learning approach that takes the so-called Convolutional Oriented Boundaries (COB) [21] network, to learn graph edge weights, whose values are inputted to the RW label propagation method to generate diffusion maps. In our approach, we also employ a gradient computation scheme to accelerate the training process, while still ensuring an appropriate balance between segmentation precision and computational efficiency.

## 2 Learning Label Propagation from Deep Oriented Boundaries and Seeded Maps

In this section, we present the main steps of our learning architecture for segmenting real-world images (see Fig. 1). First, we apply the COB network to recursively learn a set of edge weights from image contour maps. This set is then inputted together with the seed mask into the RW model to propagate the prior labeled data to the image targets, producing diffusion maps. Next, a cost function evaluates the diffusion maps so as to provide updated parameters to the COB network. Such a procedure is repeated until convergence to build the final segmentation model.

### 2.1 Deep Contour Orientation Mapping

To properly capture different types of contours from the target image, we utilize the *Convolutional Oriented Boundaries* (COB) network [21]. COB is a robust CNN-type network that enables deep learning of multiscale boundary representations of the image. The network builds upon the ResNet [16], but with the fully connected layers removed. Instead, it employs a series of convolutional layers paired that are combined with ReLU activation functions, arranged into five stages, where each stage extracts feature maps of similar sizes so as to obtain specific scales. The fine-scale mappings capture high-level contours, while the coarse ones detect lower-level boundaries, thus resulting in a multi-scale segmentation of the image.

Furthermore, COB enables for the extraction of multiple oriented contours representations of the image. To train our model, we utilize both horizontal- and

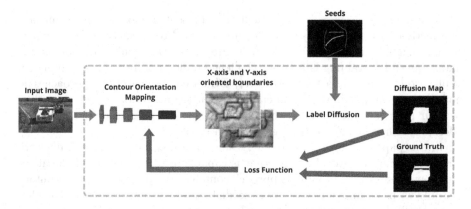

**Fig. 1.** Top: Initially, the input image is processed by a Convolutional Neural Network, generating deep contour orientation maps, which are taken to guide the label propagation step. The diffusion map is then obtained for the image targets by using a label propagation model. Bottom: The loss function is calculated from the diffusion map, while the backpropagation algorithm is applied to refine the network parameters.

vertical-oriented contour maps. The edge weights learned from the boundary maps are then assigned to the label diffusion graph, as described in Sect. 2.2. For additional information regarding the COB network, we refer to [16,21].

## 2.2  Weighted Graph Construction

After obtaining the contour orientation maps from the COB network [21], we build a weighted graph $G = (V, E, W_E)$, where the set $V$ consists of image pixels, i.e., each node $k \in V$ corresponds to a single pixel $P_k$ from the image. The set $E$ is defined as the collection of edges connecting adjacent pixels by means of a 4-neighborhood stencil. The weight of each edge $w_{kj}$ changes as the learning process advances, as it is obtained from the contour orientation maps. Specifically, for edges in the x-direction, we designate weight $w_{kj}$ to correspond to the leftmost pixel value between $P_k$ and $P_j$ concerning the horizontal contour map. Similarly, for edges in the y-direction, we designate weight $w_{kj}$ to denote the value of the topmost pixel between $P_k$ and $P_j$ in relation to the vertical contour map.

## 2.3  Label Propagation Model

Given a node $k \in V$, we can define its local neighborhood set $N(k)$ as the set of vertices $j$ that are connected to $k$, i.e., $N(k) = j : (k, j) \in E$. The weighted valency of node $k$, represented by $d_k$, is calculated as the sum of the weights of all edges that are incident to $k$, which can be expressed as $d_k = \sum_{j \in N(k)} w_{kj}$.

We denote the *graph Laplacian matrix* by $\mathbf{L} = (L_{kj})$, which is computed as:

$$L_{kj} = \begin{cases} -w_{kj}, \text{ if } \quad j \in N(k) \\ \quad d_k, \text{ if } \quad k = j \\ \quad 0, \text{ otherwise} \end{cases} . \tag{1}$$

Laplacian matrix $\mathbf{L}$ (1) can be decomposed in terms of the diagonal matrix $\mathbf{D}$, $D_{kk} = d_k$, and the weighted adjacency matrix $\mathbf{W}$, $W_{kj} = w_{kj}, (k, j) \in E$, and 0 otherwise: $\mathbf{L} = \mathbf{D} - \mathbf{W}$.

Define the set of seeded nodes by $S \subset V$, thus $U = V \backslash S$ gives the subset of unseeded nodes. We permute the columns and rows of matrix $\mathbf{L}$ in order to separate the labeled from the unseeded nodes:

$$\mathbf{P}_\pi \mathbf{L} \mathbf{P}_\pi^{\mathrm{T}} = \left[ \begin{array}{c|c} \mathbf{L}_S & \mathbf{R} \\ \hline \mathbf{R}^{\mathrm{T}} & \mathbf{L}_U \end{array} \right], \tag{2}$$

where $\mathbf{P}_\pi$ is the permutation matrix. Submatrices $\mathbf{L}_S$ and $\mathbf{L}_U$ are symmetric due to the symmetry of matrix $\mathbf{L}$, while $\mathbf{R}$ defines the weighted adjacency matrix that encompasses both seeded and unseeded nodes in its rows and columns, respectively.

By taking Eq. (2), one can formulate a suitable graph-based energy minimization problem, and subsequently solve it. In our learning scheme, we choose the Random Walker (RW) method as the label propagation method.

In order to segment the image into binary segments, we partition the set S into disjoint subsets of the foreground ($F$) pixels and background ($B$) ones, i.e., $S = F \cup B$. Thus, the use of the RW-based label diffusion method leads to the minimization problem of the following energy equation [14]:

$$E(\mathbf{x}) = \begin{bmatrix} \mathbf{x}_S^{\mathrm{T}} & \mathbf{x}_U^{\mathrm{T}} \end{bmatrix} \left[ \begin{array}{c|c} \mathbf{L}_S & \mathbf{R} \\ \hline \mathbf{R}^{\mathrm{T}} & \mathbf{L}_U \end{array} \right] \begin{bmatrix} \mathbf{x}_S \\ \mathbf{x}_U \end{bmatrix}, \tag{3}$$

where $\mathbf{x} = \begin{bmatrix} \mathbf{x}_S \\ \mathbf{x}_U \end{bmatrix} \in \mathbb{R}^{|V|}$ is a vector with real entries where each $x_k$, $k \in U$, determines the probability that a random walker starting at an unlabeled node to reach a foreground node in $S$. Scalars $x_F$ and $x_B$ in $\mathbf{x}_S = [(x_F)_{1 \times |F|} \ (x_B)_{1 \times |B|}]^T$ match the foreground and background tags in Eq. (3).

Since Eq. (3) is a quadratic form, its global minimum can be obtained by solving the following system of linear equations. This is achieved by differentiating $E(\mathbf{x})$ w.r.t. $\mathbf{x}_U$ and setting the resulting expression equal to zero:

$$\mathbf{L}_U \mathbf{x}_U = -\mathbf{R}^{\mathrm{T}} \mathbf{x}_S. \tag{4}$$

The existence of a unique solution in $\mathbf{x}_U$ for Equation (4) is guaranteed only if the corresponding affinity graph $G$ is connected and $S \neq \emptyset$ [14]. In our approach, we assume $x_F = 1$ and $x_B = 0$ in Equation (4) to obtain $\mathbf{x}_U$ as a genuine diffusion map.

## 2.4   Loss Function Minimization

Our methodology is recursively trained by solving Eq. (4) and minimizing the discrepancy between the diffusion map $\mathbf{x}_U = (x_i)$ and the ground-truth map $\mathbf{x}_U^* = (x_i^*) \in \{0, 1\}$. We take as cost function the *Cross-Entropy Error*, which takes into account the *softmax* $q_i$ of $\mathbf{x}_U$:

$$l(\mathbf{x}_U^*, \mathbf{x}_U) = -\frac{1}{|U|} \sum_{k \in U} \left[ x_k^* \log(q_k) + (1 - x_k^*) \log(1 - q_k) \right]. \tag{5}$$

When the loss value is high, the model's estimate deviates significantly from the ground-truth data. Conversely, a low loss value corresponds to diffusion maps that are closer to the desired segmentation.

## 2.5   Implementation Aspects, Gradient Simplification and Training

In order to computationally apply the Gradient Descent (GD) method while training our model, we adopt the approach outlined in [8] to obtain a formula for the partial derivatives that can be used to calculate the partial derivatives of the term $l(\mathbf{x}_U^*, \mathbf{x}_U)$.

From Eq. (4), $l(\mathbf{x}_U^*, \mathbf{x}_U) = l(\mathbf{x}_U^*, -\mathbf{L}_U^{-1}\mathbf{R}^T\mathbf{x}_S)$, where $\mathbf{L}_U = \mathbf{L}_U(\mathbf{w}(\varTheta))$ and $\mathbf{R} = \mathbf{R}(\mathbf{w}(\varTheta))$ are given in terms of the edge weights $\mathbf{w} = (w_1, w_2, \ldots, w_{|W_E|})$, $w_k \in W_E$, and the neural network parameters, $\varTheta$. While the chain rule allows us to get the derivative of the cost function w.r.t. $\varTheta$, it also introduces the term $\partial \mathbf{x}_U / \partial \mathbf{w} \in \mathbb{R}^{|U| \times |E|}$, which requires specific manipulations to determine an explicit computation formula. By differentiating Equation (4) w.r.t. $\mathbf{w}$ and rearranging the output, the following linear system is generated:

$$\mathbf{L}_U \frac{\partial \mathbf{x}_U}{\partial \mathbf{w}} = -\left( \frac{\partial \mathbf{L}_U}{\partial \mathbf{w}} \mathbf{x}_U + \frac{\partial \mathbf{R}^T}{\partial \mathbf{w}} \mathbf{x}_S \right). \tag{6}$$

The system of equations (6) incurs significant computational cost, as it demands solving $|E|$ linear systems during every GD iteration to obtain $\partial \mathbf{x}_U / \partial \mathbf{w}$. To deal with this issue, instead of solving (6) for all edges, we pick a random subset of representative edges $\tilde{E} \subset E$, $|\tilde{E}| \ll |E|$, and only solve the linear systems that correspond to $\tilde{E}$, keeping the gradients as zero for the remaining edges. In particular, we select the subset $\tilde{E}$ so that the following heuristics are satisfied:

1. Edges $(k, l)$ can not have any seeded node, i.e., $k \notin N(l)$, $\forall l \in S$.
2. Edges in $\tilde{E}$ must be placed as close as feasible to the object area, i.e., within the pixel portion delimited by the background seeds enclosing the object.

By applying such a simplification scheme, the gradient dimension $\partial \mathbf{x}_U / \partial \mathbf{w}$ can be reduced from $|U| \times |E|$ to $|U| \times |\tilde{E}|$, which means that only sparse linear systems of size $|\tilde{E}|$ have to be solved. Figure 2 shows the described gradient simplification scheme.

Lastly, regarding our training design, the COB network integrated with the RW model was trained on the *Geostar Dataset* [15] by taking a total of 100

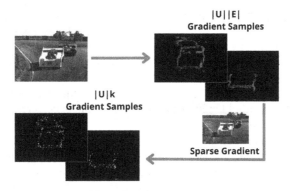

**Fig. 2.** Gradient simplification scheme.

epochs. This benchmark consists of 152 real-world images, each of which is paired with its corresponding ground-truth and seeded mask.

## 2.6   Segmentation

After the model is trained to propagate labels on regular images, the segmentation process is then accomplished by implementing a standard binarization technique like *Otsu* or any other suitable thresholding method on diffusion map $\mathbf{x}_U$. Our approach assigns the labels $y_k \in \{x_B, x_F\} = \{0, 1\}$, where $k \in U$, based on the following cutting scheme:

$$y_k = \begin{cases} 1, \text{if} & x_k \geq 1/2 \\ 0, \text{otherwise} \end{cases} . \tag{7}$$

# 3   Results and Discussion

In this section, we provide a comprehensive evaluation of the proposed framework by comparing it to a range of existing state-of-the-art seed-based segmentation methods. More specifically, we perform both qualitative and quantitative experiments involving the following seeded segmentation methods: Laplacian Coordinates (LC) [6], Normalized Lazy Random Walker (NLRW) [3], One Cut (ONE) [30], and the classic Random Walker (RW) [14] method.

To assess the segmentation results, we take the popular *Grab-Cut Dataset* [29], which gathers a variety of real-world images with their counterparts of ground-truth segmentations, as well as several digital images taken from the well-known *Berkeley Image Segmentation Benchmark Database* [2]. Concerning the seeded maps used in our experimental assessments, we take the challenge set of *Grab-Cut sparse seeds* comprising small portions of foreground and background pixels of the images. Lastly, we use publicly available versions of the segmentation algorithms and made adjustments to their parameters based on the specific recommendations provided by the authors.

## 3.1 Quantitative Evaluation

To numerically gauge the quality of the resulting segmentations, we apply four traditional evaluation metrics used in the computer vision literature: *F1-Score* (F1) [10], *Rand Index* (RI) [31], *Variation of Information* (VOI) [23], and *Boundary Displacement Error* (BDE) [12]. To facilitate a comprehension of the metrics quantification, the symbol (↑) indicates a higher value is better, while (↓) implies that a lower score is better.

We start by numerically assessing the segmentation outputs in Table 1. From the tabulated measurements (mean and standard deviation values) in Table 1, one can see that the proposed framework achieves the best average scores for the evaluation metrics F1, RI, and BDE, while maintaining superior or competitive across all assessments in terms of std. Regarding the VOI metric, our approach achieves the second-lowest error rate, with only a slight difference compared to the best performer as determined by the ONE method.

**Table 1.** F1, RI, VOI and BDE metrics calculated for the segmentation methods. Bold values indicate the best scores.

| Metrics | Methods | | | | |
|---|---|---|---|---|---|
| | **Proposed** | **LC** | **NLRW** | **ONE** | **RW** |
| (↑) F1 | **0.915** ± 0.080 | 0.907 ± 0.066 | 0.897 ± 0.088 | 0.866 ± 0.197 | 0.867 ± 0.095 |
| (↑) RI | **0.941** ± 0.051 | 0.933 ± 0.071 | 0.920 ± 0.079 | 0.928 ± 0.095 | 0.898 ± 0.087 |
| (↓) VOI | 0.328 ± 0.210 | 0.381 ± 0.264 | 0.393 ± 0.289 | **0.312** ± 0.250 | 0.468 ± 0.304 |
| (↓) BDE | **5.985** ± 4.372 | 6.677 ± 6.343 | 6.894 ± 6.328 | 8.353 ± 13.931 | 9.117 ± 7.651 |

We also compare, in Fig. 3, the capability of the segmentation techniques in clustering the category of photographic images.

While the proposed framework remains highly accurate and stable, with very few instances of large variations in scores, the NLRW, ONE, and RW methods encounter challenges in dealing with many images. Although the LC method was competitive in most cases, it was still outperformed by the proposed framework in most of these cases. This is also observed in the VOI plot, which shows that although the ONE method performed better for most images, the proposed framework remained competitive in the majority of the cases.

## 3.2 Qualitative Evaluation

Aiming at assessing the qualitative performance of the segmentation algorithms, we provide in Fig. 4 the segmentations of a few real-world images. To enhance the visual inspection, we highlight the ground-truth segments (in green) and the outputs generated by each method (in red).

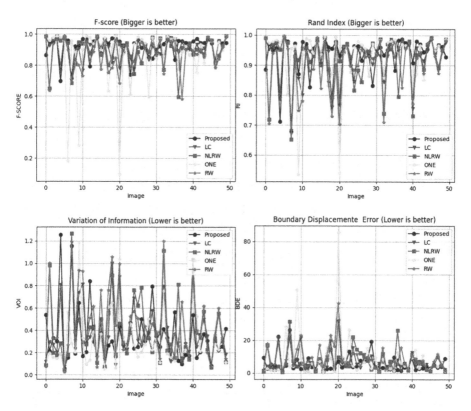

**Fig. 3.** Evaluation metrics calculated for several digital images. Segmentations produced by the proposed framework (dark blue), LC (green), NLRW (red), ONE (light blue), and RW (lilac). (Color figure online)

By visually examining the segmentation results, one can check that the outputs produced by our approach present smooth boundaries, leading to a better quality in terms of contour adherence and accurate object detection. In contrast, accurately capturing the targets within the images can pose obstacles for other segmentation algorithms.

From a more detailed visual inspection, one can observe that in the first three cases, the NLRW, ONE, and RW methods failed to accurately fit the targets, either by missing the object boundaries or propagating the seeds incorrectly. While our approach and LC method achieved better segmentations, the weak edges present in the first and the last images were not properly segmented by the LC method, as well as the narrow regions in the second image.

Overall, our approach delivers smoother partitions not only in terms of adherent contours but also in identifying small details of object edges.

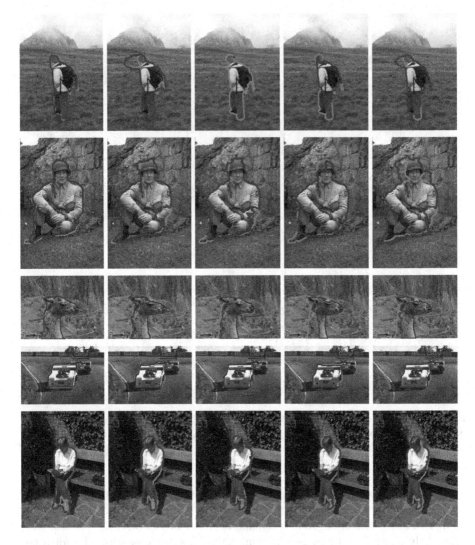

**Fig. 4.** Qualitative results. From left to right: segmentations produced by the proposed framework, LC, NLRW, ONE and RW.

## 4   Conclusion

We proposed in this paper a deep learning-based seeded image segmentation framework for real-world images that integrates a deep contour learning network with a label propagation method in a recursive and effective manner. The proposed framework enables the customized learning of the label propagation task for a variety of real-world scenes and photographic images, as shown and discussed in the experiments.

We compared the assertiveness and the fitting capability of our approach against existing segmentation methods from a battery of verification tests and metrics. As shown in the experiments, the trained model can robustly learn the graph edge weights so that the threshold between the foreground and the background segments can be accurately detected, resulting in smooth boundaries and high-quality segmentations concerning contour adherence and object detection.

As future work, we intend to extend our framework to deal with both the segmentation and classification tasks simultaneously. Furthermore, we aim to evaluate the accuracy of other label propagation models and alternative contour learning networks in an effort to improve the ability of the segmentation model to distinguish objects in complex scenarios, including the particular application of remote sensing.

**Acknowledgment.** The authors would like to thank the São Paulo Research Foundation (FAPESP – grants #2013/07375-0, #2021/03328-3 and #2021/01305-6), the Coordination for the Improvement of Higher Education Personnel (CAPES - Funding Code 001), and the National Council for Scientific and Technological Development (CNPq – grants #316228/2021-4 and #305220/2022-5) for providing resources that greatly contributed to the development of this research.

# References

1. Aletti, G., Benfenati, A., Naldi, G.: A semiautomatic multi-label color image segmentation coupling dirichlet problem and colour distances. J. Imaging. **7**(10) (2021)
2. Arbeláez, P., Maire, M., Fowlkes, C., Malik, J.: Contour detection and hierarchical image segmentation. IEEE Trans. Pattern Anal. Mach. Intell. **33**(5), 898–916 (2011)
3. Bampis, C.G., Maragos, P., Bovik, A.C.: Graph-driven diffusion and random walk schemes for image segmentation. IEEE Trans. Image Process. **26**(1), 35–50 (2017)
4. Benvenuto, G.A., Colnago, M., Dias, M.A., Negri, R.G., Silva, E.A., Casaca, W.: A fully unsupervised deep learning framework for non-rigid fundus image registration. Bioengineering **9**(8), 369 (2022)
5. Can, Y.B., Chaitanya, K., Mustafa, B., Koch, L.M., Konukoglu, E., Baumgartner, C.F.: Learning to segment medical images with scribble-supervision alone. In: Stoyanov, D., et al. (eds.) DLMIA/ML-CDS -2018. LNCS, vol. 11045, pp. 236–244. Springer, Cham (2018). https://doi.org/10.1007/978-3-030-00889-5_27
6. Casaca, W., Gois, J.P., Batagelo, H.C., Taubin, G., Nonato, L.G.: Laplacian coordinates: theory and methods for seeded image segmentation. IEEE Trans. Pattern Anal. Mach. Intell. **43**(8), 2665–2681 (2021)
7. Casaca, W., Nonato, L.G., Taubin, G.: Laplacian coordinates for seeded image segmentation. In: IEEE Conference on Computer Vision and Pattern Recognition (CVPR), pp. 384–391 (2014)
8. Cerrone, L., Zeilmann, A., Hamprecht, F.A.: End-to-end learned random walker for seeded image segmentation. In: Proceedings of the IEEE/CVF Conference on Computer Vision and Pattern Recognition, pp. 12559–12568 (2019)
9. Cousty, J., Bertrand, G., Najman, L., Couprie, M.: Watershed cuts: minimum spanning forests and the drop of water principle. IEEE Trans. Pattern Anal. Mach. Intell. **31**(8), 1362–1374 (2009)

10. Estrada, F.J., Jepson, A.D.: Benchmarking image segmentation algorithms. Int. J. Comput. Vision **85**(2), 167–181 (2009)
11. Fischer, M., Hepp, T., Gatidis, S., Yang, B.: Self-supervised contrastive learning with random walks for medical image segmentation with limited annotations. Computerized Medical Imaging and Graphics, p. 102174 (2023)
12. Freixenet, J., Muñoz, X., Raba, D., Martí, J., Cufí, X.: Yet another survey on image segmentation: region and boundary information integration. In: Heyden, A., Sparr, G., Nielsen, M., Johansen, P. (eds.) ECCV 2002. LNCS, vol. 2352, pp. 408–422. Springer, Heidelberg (2002). https://doi.org/10.1007/3-540-47977-5_27
13. Gao, G., Xu, G., Yu, Y., Xie, J., Yang, J., Yue, D.: MSCFNet: a lightweight network with multi-scale context fusion for real-time semantic segmentation. IEEE Trans. Intell. Transp. Syst. **23**(12), 25489–25499 (2021)
14. Grady, L.: Random walks for image segmentation. IEEE Trans. Pattern Anal. Mach. Intell. **28**(11), 1768–1783 (2006)
15. Gulshan, V., Rother, C., Criminisi, A., Blake, A., Zisserman, A.: Geodesic star convexity for interactive image segmentation. In: 2010 IEEE Computer Society Conference on Computer Vision and Pattern Recognition, pp. 3129–3136 (2010)
16. He, K., Zhang, X., Ren, S., Sun, J.: Deep residual learning for image recognition. In: IEEE Conference on Computer Vision and Pattern Recognition (CVPR), pp. 770–778 (2016)
17. Hu, J., Chen, Z., Zhang, R., Yang, M., Zhang, S.: Robust random walk for leaf segmentation. IET Image Proc. **14**(6), 1180–1186 (2020)
18. Hu, Y., Soltoggio, A., Lock, R., Carter, S.: A fully convolutional two-stream fusion network for interactive image segmentation. Neural Netw. **109**, 31–42 (2019)
19. Kim, K.I., Tompkin, J., Pfister, H., Theobalt, C.: Context-guided diffusion for label propagation on graphs. In: Proceedings of the IEEE International Conference on Computer Vision, pp. 2776–2784 (2015)
20. Kucharski, A., Fabijańska, A.: CNN-watershed: a watershed transform with predicted markers for corneal endothelium image segmentation. Biomed. Signal Process. Control **68**, 102805 (2021)
21. Maninis, K.K., Pont-Tuset, J., Arbeláez, P., Gool, L.V.: Convolutional oriented boundaries: from image segmentation to high-level tasks. IEEE Trans. Pattern Anal. Mach. Intell. **40**(4), 819–833 (2018)
22. Markovic, M., Malehmir, R., Malehmir, A.: Diffraction pattern recognition using deep semantic segmentation. Near Surface Geophys. **20**(5), 507–518 (2022)
23. Meilă, M.: Comparing clusterings: an axiomatic view. In: Proceedings of the 22nd International Conference on Machine Learning, p. 577–584 (2005)
24. Negri, R.G., da Silva, E.A., Casaca, W.: Inducing contextual classifications with kernel functions into support vector machines. IEEE Geosci. Remote Sens. Lett. **15**(6), 962–966 (2018)
25. Neupane, B., Horanont, T., Aryal, J.: Deep learning-based semantic segmentation of urban features in satellite images: a review and meta-analysis. Rem. Sens. **13**(4), 808 (2021)
26. Tai, X.-C., Bae, E., Chan, T.F., Lysaker, M. (eds.): Energy Minimization Methods in Computer Vision and Pattern Recognition, EMMCVPR 2015. LNCS, vol. 8932. Springer, Cham (2015). https://doi.org/10.1007/978-3-319-14612-6
27. Ramadan, H., Lachqar, C., Tairi, H.: A survey of recent interactive image segmentation methods. Comput. Visual Med. **6**, 355–384 (2020)
28. Roth, H.R., Yang, D., Xu, Z., Wang, X., Xu, D.: Going to extremes: weakly supervised medical image segmentation. Mach. Learn. Knowl. Extract. **3**(2), 507–524 (2021)

29. Rother, C., Kolmogorov, V., Boykov, Y., Blake, A.: Interactive foreground extraction using graph cut. In: Advances in Markov Random Fields for Vision and Image Processing (2011)
30. Tang, M., Gorelick, L., Veksler, O., Boykov, Y.: Grabcut in one cut. In: 2013 IEEE International Conference on Computer Vision, pp. 1769–1776 (2013)
31. Warrens, M.J., van der Hoef, H.: Understanding the rand index. In: Imaizumi, T., Okada, A., Miyamoto, S., Sakaori, F., Yamamoto, Y., Vichi, M. (eds.) Advanced Studies in Classification and Data Science, pp. 301–313 (2020)
32. Wolf, S., Schott, L., Kothe, U., Hamprecht, F.: Learned watershed: End-to-end learning of seeded segmentation. In: Proceedings of the IEEE International Conference on Computer Vision, pp. 2011–2019 (2017)

# Siamese Network with Gabor Filter for Recognizing Handwritten Digits

Rauzan Sumara[1]([✉]) [iD] and Ivan Luthfi Ihwani[2,3] [iD]

[1] Faculty of Mathematics and Information Science, Warsaw University of Technology, Warsaw 00661, Poland
rauzan.sumara.dokt@pw.edu.pl
[2] Department of Mathematics, Universitas Gadjah Mada, Yogyakarta 55281, Indonesia
[3] Department of Mathematics, National Central University, Taoyuan City 32001, Taiwan

**Abstract.** Even though significant progress has been made in the field of pattern recognition in recent years, handwritten digit recognition remains an exciting challenge. Due to its widely possible application, this issue has attracted much attention. Nowadays, different methods are available for handwritten digit recognition. The current demand is for researchers to find new techniques for better performing handwritten digit recognition problems. Therefore, this paper aims to propose a new approach, the Siamese network with Gabor filter, for handwritten digit recognition. Inspired by several studies on the Siamese network and Gabor filter separately, which have already achieved superb performances, this research will bring out the best qualities of their fusion. The computational experiments have been conducted on a handwritten digit image of the MNIST dataset. Empirically, the results implied that the proposed Siamese network with the Gabor filter algorithm outperformed the classical Siamese network and other existing methods in terms of accuracy.

**Keywords:** Gabor Filter · Handwritten Digit · Recognition · Siamese Network

## 1 Introduction

Recently, handwritten digit recognition has been one of the most challenging issues. Many researchers have looked into this extensively in recent years. In empirical practice, high recognition accuracy and reliability are of the essence in handwritten digit recognition systems. The recognition system is even more complex because each person's writing pattern and style are unique. Handwritten digit recognition remains an ongoing issue. The current demand is for how researchers can find new techniques for handwritten digit recognition problems. The methods are to improve the performance in terms of accuracy.

Multiple algorithms have been developed for handwritten recognitions. Several of them used various techniques, including k-nearest neighbor (kNN) [1],

O. Gervasi et al. (Eds.): ICCSA 2023, LNCS 13957, pp. 32–47, 2023.
https://doi.org/10.1007/978-3-031-36808-0_3

support vector machines (SVM) [2], neural networks (NN) [3], and convolutional neural networks (CNN) [4]. In [5], a new approach to identifying handwritten digits was presented. The writer suggested an ensemble classification strategy that employs bagging to enhance accuracy. A hybrid system incorporating bagged-radial basis function (RBF), bagged-SVM, and RBF-SVM was developed and assessed using various standard datasets. The authors in [6] suggested a NN and extreme learning machine (ELM) based method for handwritten digit recognition. The convolutional recurrent neural network (CRNN) introduced by the authors in [7] effectively merged the benefits of deep convolutional neural networks (CNN) and recurrent neural networks (RNN). Moreover, this approach proved to be valuable for the task of categorizing text within scenes.

Numerous classification algorithms were introduced in [8], such as naive Bayes, multilayer perception (MLP), Bayes-net, J48, SVM, random trees, and random forest (RF). The results showed that MLP exceeds other classifiers in handwritten recognition performance. A unique method for feature computation, as described in reference [9], employed structural and statistical approaches. The initial step involved preprocessing the input data through binarization, cropping, and normalization. Subsequently, four distinct sets of features were computed using methods such as a cavity, zoning, profile projection, and Freeman chain coding (FFC). Finally, kNN was utilized for key point classification. However, it is important to note that all these previous techniques require extensive computations.

In this study, we formulated a new approach using a Siamese network with a Gabor filter for handwritten digit recognition to overcome the challenge. Several studies on the Gabor filter, such as that conducted by [10], showed that using the Gabor filter can improve the accuracy rate of the CNN architecture in the case of vision-based vehicle recognition. Other evidence by [11] and [12] combine existing CNN architectures, e.g., ResNet, AlexNet, VGG16, and InceptionV3, with the Gabor filter to get high accuracy. Because of their complexity, performing those existing CNN architectures is tedious and time-consuming. Therefore, the Siamese network has a strategic role here. This network is not only able to reduce training time but also can be trained from small data [13]. Because of that, the Siamese network is more popular nowadays. The architecture has been successfully applied to recognizing handwritten signatures by [14]. With the same analogy, this architecture can be used for other handwritten data, such as the handwritten digits on the MNIST dataset. Inspired by those particular ideas, our research aims to fill the gap. We concentrate our research on their fusion of the Siamese network with the Gabor filter as a kernel on the network's first convolution layer. After the embedding process, it is forwarded to a classifier using kNN.

We also organize the rest of the chapter as follows: After this introduction, we describe the related work in Sect. 2 and the proposed network architecture in Sect. 3, then specify empirical settings consisting of three aspects: data set descriptions, a baseline model, and hyperparameters in Sect. 4. Meanwhile, Sect. 5 describes the results and discussion, and finally, we outline some conclusions in Sect. 6.

## 2   The Related Work

Multiple algorithms have been developed for handwritten recognitions on the comprehensive investigation of several research papers regarding the dataset used, accuracy performance, and limitations. In [6], the authors proposed a technique for classifying MNIST handwritten digits using a combination of NN and ELM. The findings indicated that ELM achieved superior classification accuracy and required less processing time compared to NN. It achieved an accuracy of 98.40%. Additionally, in [7], the authors introduced a CRNN that merged the strengths of CNN and RNN. This approach in [7] was also employed for classifying MNIST handwritten digits and achieved an accuracy of 98.70%. However, it should be noted that this approach entails computational complexity.

A different approach to recognizing handwritten digits was presented in [5]. The author suggested an ensemble classification technique that utilizes bagging to enhance accuracy. A hybrid system consisting of bagged-RBF, bagged-SVM, and RBF-SVM was developed and assessed using various real-world and benchmark datasets. The performance evaluations illustrated that the proposed hybrid RBF-SVM classifier delivers favorable classification outcomes. It achieved an accuracy of 98.00%. However, it should be mentioned that it is time-consuming to implement this approach because of its complexity.

Numerous classification algorithms were introduced in [8], such as naive Bayes, MLP, Bayes-nct, J48, SVM, random trees, and RF. The results showed that MLP outperforms other classifiers in recognition performance. A novel technique for computing features was introduced in [9], utilizing structural and statistical approaches. The initial stage involved preprocessing the input data to binarize, crop, and normalize it. Subsequently, four distinct feature sets were generated using cavity, zoning, FFC, and profile projection methods. The classification of key points was then carried out using the kNN algorithm. Notably, this approach [9] achieved an impressive recognition accuracy of 95.00% on the MNIST database when using FFC. However, its performance on more challenging databases may be limited.

In addition, still in cases of MNIST handwritten digits, [2] proposed a hybrid approach, which utilized a CNN for feature extraction and a hybrid classifier for classification. The resulting system achieved an accuracy of 94.40%. [15] used the sparse group lasso (SG-L1) for feature selection and a deep NN for classification, achieving a classification accuracy of 97.00%. [16] applied spiking neural networks (SNN) with normalized approximate descent (NormAD) as the learning algorithm and achieved 98.40% classification accuracy. Similarly, [17] used the spike timing dependent plasticity (STDP) based deep SNN training and achieved a classification accuracy of 98.40%. Finally, [18] utilized fractional order backpropagation (FOBP) neural networks and population extremal optimization (PEO) for network optimization, resulting in an overall classification accuracy of 96.54%. Nevertheless, from all references presented earlier, their accuracy and computing complexity could still be improved.

## 3 The Siamese Network with Gabor Filter System

Our approach was intended to integrate the Siamese network and Gabor filter. The Gabor filter theory will be introduced in Subsect. 3.1, followed by the Siamese network in Subsect. 3.2. Then, their combination will be discussed in Subsect. 3.3 at the end of this section.

### 3.1 Gabor Filters

A Gabor function is defined as the product of a sinusoid with a Gaussian distribution in mathematical form as follows,

$$g_{\Theta}(x, y) = \exp\left(-\frac{x'^2 + \gamma^2 y'^2}{2\sigma^2}\right) \exp\left(i\left(2\pi\frac{x'}{\lambda} + \phi\right)\right) \tag{1}$$

and

$$\begin{aligned} x' &= x\cos(\theta) + y\sin(\theta) \\ y' &= -x\sin(\theta) + y\cos(\theta) \end{aligned} \tag{2}$$

while $\Theta = \{\theta, \lambda, \phi, \gamma, \sigma\}$ serves as the parameter and $i$ represents the imaginary integer. Notice thus the equation (1) could be written in two forms, namely the real form (3)

$$g_{\Theta}^{\text{real}}(x, y) = \exp\left(-\frac{x'^2 + \gamma^2 y'^2}{2\sigma^2}\right) \cos\left(2\pi\frac{x'}{\lambda} + \phi\right) \tag{3}$$

and imaginary form (4)

$$g_{\Theta}^{\text{img}}(x, y) = \exp\left(-\frac{x'^2 + \gamma^2 y'^2}{2\sigma^2}\right) \sin\left(2\pi\frac{x'}{\lambda} + \phi\right). \tag{4}$$

Both components can be utilized as a filter in a convolution layer, but we restrict our experiment by using the real form only. The real form (3) contains five parameters, and every parameter has a different purpose and can take numerical values within a given interval. Additionally, we summarize the example of interval values for every parameter below,

**Orientation $\theta$.** The direction of the Gabor filter is specified by the parameter $\theta$. The acceptable values are ranging from 0 and $2\pi$. Gabor filters with several values of $\theta$ which are 0, $\pi/8$, $\pi/4$, $3\pi/8$, $\pi/2$, $5\pi/8$, $3\pi/8$ and $7\pi/8$ are displayed in Fig. 1(a). It showed the bands of Gabor filters spin in response to a change in orientation parameter.

**Wavelength $\lambda$.** In general, acceptable values of $\lambda$ should larger than or equal to 2. Considering that the Gabor function should be zero at $\lambda = 2$ and $\phi = \pi/2$, we will ensure in this experiment that $\lambda$ is greater than 2. In addition, to decrease the possibility of undesirable effects at the picture boundaries, it is necessary to set the wavelength $\lambda$ will be not greater than the pixels of the image. Therefore, to determine the maximum value of $\lambda$, we simply define $C_\lambda = \min(I_{\text{width}}, I_{\text{height}})$, where $I_{\text{width}}$ and $I_{\text{height}}$ are the width and height of the input picture. Different values of $\lambda$ which are $2, 4, 6, 8, 10, 12, 14$, and $16$ showed in Fig. 1(b). The bandwidth increases as the increasing $\lambda$.

**Phase offset $\phi$.** The Gabor function has a parameter of $\phi$ in which it represents the argument for the sine or cosine factor. It has to be real numbers between $-\pi$ and $\pi$. If the value of $\phi$ is 0, it is in accordance with center-symmetric 'center-on' and if the value is $\pi$, it is in accordance with non-center-symmetric 'center-off' functions. In addition, the Gabor function will be in accordance with anti-symmetric functions while the parameters of $\phi$ are $-\pi/2$ and $\pi/2$; otherwise, it is similar to asymmetric functions. Different values of $\phi$, from 0 to $\frac{7\pi}{8}$, are illustrated in Fig. 1(c).

**Aspect ratio $\gamma$.** This parameter defines the ellipticity of the Gabor function's support. This support will be round when the value of $\gamma$ equals 1, but this support is stretched in the position of the perpendicular lines of the function when the value of $\gamma$ is less than 1. Acceptable values of $\gamma$ are real values within interval $0 < \gamma \leq 1$. As an illustration, we use several values of $\lambda$, which are $0.1, 0.2, 0.3, 0.4, 0.5, 0.7, 0.8$, and $1.0$ to visualize Gabor filters shown in Fig. 1(d) We may observe that when the aspect ratio increases, the band length decreases.

**Generate $\sigma$.** The parameter $\sigma$ is well known as a deviation in a Gaussian distribution. In the Gabor filters, the value of $\sigma$ determines the number of bands. As we can see from Fig. 1(e), it depicts the Gabor filters when the values of $\sigma$ are set to be $0.1, 0.5, 1.0, 1.5, 2.0, 2.5, 3.0$, and $3.5$.

Further details about parametrization can be found in [19]. Traditionally, we must create a collection of Gabor filters with various combinations of their parameters in order to use them. In applying Gabor filters, the values of the parameters of the Gabor function need to be properly decided. We explained those in Subsect. 4.3 about the hyperparameters of the Gabor filters. Because this type of pipeline utilizes only hand-designed unique parameters, it may be suboptimal for particular inputs. The Gabor filter banks are derived from a comprehensible Gabor function. In contrast to classical convolution, its filters are created at random, and they are independent of one another. This is what makes a significant difference between them. In addition, all parameters in the Gabor filters have distinct meanings, whereas those in a classical convolution do not.

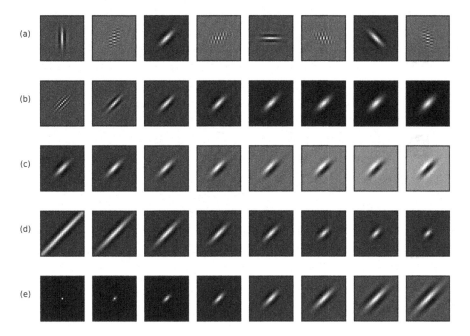

**Fig. 1.** Images with varying Gabor filter settings: (a) orientation $\theta$, (b) wavelength $\lambda$, (c) phase offset $\phi$, (d) aspect ratio $\gamma$, and (e) various values of $\sigma$.

## 3.2 Siamese Networks with Triplet Loss

The Siamese neural network is a category of network designs that typically consists of two or more identical subnetworks. The configuration, parameters, and weights of each subnetwork are identical because the parameter update is replicated on all subnetworks. [20] has reported applications of the Siamese networks not only in speech signal processing and text mining but also in dimensionality reduction [21] and face verification [22] in which the framework has shown promising results. Generally, Triplet loss is the loss function operated in Siamese networks [23]. As first introduced in [22], it was used for recognizing faces by integrating triplet loss into the deep convolutional network. To date, the triplet loss has been extensively used in a variety of image processing, such as image retrieval [24–26] as well as person re-identification [27,28].

Figure 2 shows the framework of the Siamese networks with Triplet loss. By defining three embeddings (subnetworks), there must be three input sample images, namely an anchor $(x_a)$, a positive $(x_p)$, and a negative $(x_n)$ sample image. The idea behind the Triplet loss is to ensure that an anchor image has a closer distance to a positive image in the embedding space (the positive has the same label as the anchor) than a negative image with a different label. According

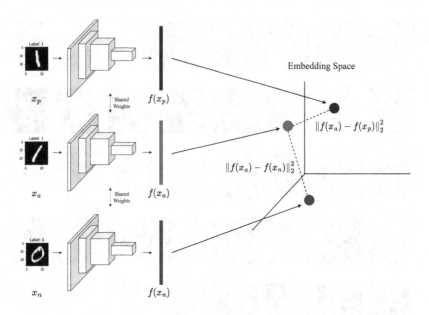

**Fig. 2.** Siamese network architecture with Triplet loss.

to [22], we can write a formula for triplet $(a, p, n)$ loss as follow,

$$L_{triplet} = max\,(d_p - d_n + \alpha, 0) \tag{5}$$

where $d_p = \|f(x_a) - f(x_p)\|_2^2$, $d_n = \|f(x_a) - f(x_n)\|_2^2$, and $\alpha$ represents a required margin to maintain a large distance between the positive and negative image. Based on the definition of the loss, there are three categories of triplets: first, easy triplets, which have a loss of 0 since $d_p + \alpha < d_n$. Second, hard triplets where the positive is further from the anchor than the negative, $d_n < d_p$, and third, semi-hard triplets where the positive is closer to the anchor than the negative but still hard because the distance is still inside the margin, $d_p < d_n < d_p + \alpha$. Selecting the right triplets is essential to achieving fast convergence. Therefore, we will use semi-hard triplets, known as the best results in [22]. In order to efficiently identify these triplets within each batch, we apply an online strategy and train from the semi-hard samples only.

We employed the architecture influenced by [29] to solve this challenge. In order to facilitate the understanding of the network, Table 1 contains a comprehensive listing of the parameters used to create the CNN layers. Mainly, we will have 2 convolution layers and 2 pooling layers with dropout regularization in the networks. Every layer creates an output with the size of N × H × W, where N, H, and W are the number of filters, the height, and the width of the output, respectively. The stride parameter is the number of movements over an image, and the size parameter refers to the pooling operation.

We use the Rectified Linear Units (ReLU) activation function for all convolutional layers throughout the network but not on the last dense layer. The first

**Table 1.** Overview of the Siamese network architecture.

| Layers | An output size | Parameters |
|---|---|---|
| Convolution 1 | $64 \times 28 \times 28$ | Size = 2, stride = 1, padding = 'same' |
| MaxPooling + Dropout | $64 \times 14 \times 14$ | Size = 2, p = 0.3 |
| Convolution 2 | $32 \times 14 \times 14$ | Size = 2, stride = 1, padding = 'same' |
| MaxPooling + Dropout | $32 \times 7 \times 7$ | size = 2, p = 0.3 |
| Flattening | 1568 | - |
| Fully Connected | 256 | - |

convolutional layer creates the $28 \times 28$ output size with 64 filters, adding a stride of 1 pixel and pooling layer along with a Dropout rate equal to 0.3. Next, the second convolutional layer is performed from the output of the first convolutional layer. It creates $14 \times 14$ output with 32 filters, adds a stride of 1 pixel and pooling layer along with the Dropout rate equal to 0.3 again. In conclusion, there are 1568 connected units (nodes) in the flattened layer, while there are 256 nodes in the fully connected layer. This suggests that the latest learned feature vector from either side of the Siamese Network has a size of 256. This indicates that the latest embeddings on each subnetwork of Siamese networks are 256 in size.

## 3.3   The Architecture of the Proposed Model

Hereinafter in this topic, we will illustrate how Siamese networks may benefit from the Gabor filter when used for handwritten recognition. Our suggested architecture is constructed by inserting the first convolutional layer of the Siamese networks with the Gabor filter. We will also perform the Siamese networks without employing the Gabor filter as a basis for comparison. Therefore, there will be two variants of architecture, with and without the Gabor filter, based on the Siamese networks. Figure 3 gives a clear idea of two variant structures. As mentioned in the previous subsection, our Siamese network consists of two convolutional layers and two pooling layers with dropout regularization in the networks.

Firstly, we will use the original architecture of Siamese networks, let it be known as "network 1". Secondly, we insert the Gabor filter into the first convolution layer in the Siamese network; let it be known as "network 2". Lastly, Both network 1 and network 2 are similar, whereas the only difference is in the first convolution layer, where network 1 will use default filters from the 2D convolution layer, while network 2 will use Gabor filters. Again, for a detailed understanding of the network, read Table 1. According to the previous section, we mentioned triplet loss in order to train those networks. We should notice that there are several types of triplets in accordance with its definition. However, we will only use the semi-hard triplet loss function. In conclusion, the embedding output, after completing the training process, can be taken as a new feature vector for training a baseline classifier such as a k-NN. Finally, the baseline classifier performs the recognition task to predict the labels on the testing images.

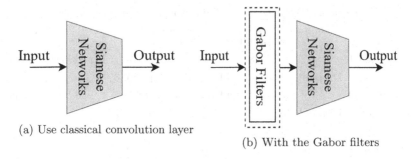

(a) Use classical convolution layer

(b) With the Gabor filters

**Fig. 3.** Proposed Siamese network.

## 4    Empirical Settings

The presented experiment evaluates the Siamese networks with the Gabor filter for MNIST handwritten digits. The experimental framework is presented in three aspects: dataset description, a baseline classifier, and hyperparameters.

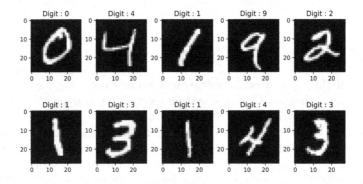

**Fig. 4.** Example of MNIST Dataset.

### 4.1    Data Set Description

In the current study, the suggested classification system has been trained and tested using MNIST, a well-known benchmark dataset of handwritten digits. The 10 digits are depicted in handwritten form in the dataset (0–9). The MNIST dataset is a portion of a larger dataset made available by the National Institute of Standards and Technology (NIST). The dataset has a total of 70000 instances, which includes 60000 instances for training and 10000 instances for testing. Initially, a $20 \times 20$ pixel matrix was used to represent the images that were contained in the NSIT database. However, these handwritten images were normalized into $28 \times 28$ pixel images [30]. We have presented a few examples of handwritten digits from the MNIST dataset in Fig. 4. Furthermore, it should be highlighted that we used the MNIST dataset because it is a complex and challenging one due to its inherent variations in digit size, scale, and angle. The images in the dataset are also affected by issues such as blurring and variations in intensity, making it still interesting for classification study.

## 4.2   A Baseline Classifier

We use the kNN for a baseline classification model. This algorithm can categorize the data based on training features. Regardless of the learning methodologies, the kNN algorithm uses basic computations, which makes it the easiest categorization method. Objects are categorized depending on the votes of their neighbors, who are symbolized by the letter $k$. In kNN, a sample is categorized into the class with the most votes. K-NN calculates the distance, specifically using Euclidian distance, between the feature vector values of each training set and the feature vector values of the testing set. The training vector is an array with several dimensions. The training pictures' class labels and feature values are each included in a row of an array, but the test vector only includes feature values. Each row in the test set receives a classification label according to Euclidian distance measurements and the number of neighbors ($k$) taken into account. The elbow method, one of the most popular methods, can help us select the optimal number of $k$.

## 4.3   Hyperparameters

In this subsection, we will specify how the hyperparameters will be ranged in our model. It consists of hyperparameters for Gabor filters and hyperparameters for learning setup.

**Gabor Filters.** We used real form (3) in order to create the number of Gabor filter banks. There are five parameters in the Gabor function such as $\theta$, $\lambda$, $\phi$, $\gamma$, and $\sigma$. In experiments, we take the value of $\theta$ be $0, \pi/4, \pi/2, 3\pi/4, \pi, 5\pi/4, 3\pi/2$, and $2\pi$. Parameter $\lambda$ is set to be 7, 11, 16, and 22. Thus, the parameter of phase offset $\phi$ is specified as 0 and $\pi/2$. Finally, we also set the aspect ratio $\gamma = 0.25$ and the values of $\sigma = 1.75$ in the whole setting. Through all possible combinations of elements in $\theta$, $\lambda$, $\phi$, $\gamma$, and $\sigma$, we will obtain 64 filters. These filters are then operated to the first convolutional layer of the Siamise networks.

**Learning and Experimental Setup.** Here is the common setup we followed to conduct experiments: The entire experiment was coded with Python 3.8.5. We also used fundamental libraries such as pandas, numpy, scikit-learn, keras and tensorflow. The training was done using standard PCs with a specification of 8 Core CPUs, 16 GB RAM, and GeForce GTX 1660 Ti and Windows 11. Next, because the datasets are already split into train and test sets, the train set was used to fit the model. We trained the networks using adaptive moment estimation (Adam) to optimize parameters to get the smallest loss and back-propagation, the method to calculate the gradient for each layer. These are widely used optimization algorithms for deep neural networks. By applying the Adam optimizer and the back-propagation algorithm together, we can update the weights of a neural network to minimize the loss function 5 by alternatively doing forward and back-propagation processes. We initiate the learning rate (LR) equal to 0.001 and the hyperparameter of $\varepsilon = 10^{-7}$. We also set the number of epochs equal to 15. Other setups are set, such as the first exponential decay rate ($1^{st}$) equal to 0.9, the second exponential decay rate ($2^{nd}$) equal to 0.999, and the batch size equal to 32. Next, the test set was then used to evaluate our proposed method's performance. Therefore, the achieved results concern test sets only. After that, comparisons with other existing methods were prepared with the use of resources from Sect. 2, and finally, we would like to emphasize that there is no training validation test split process again or any other augmentation techniques used.

## 5    Result and Discussion

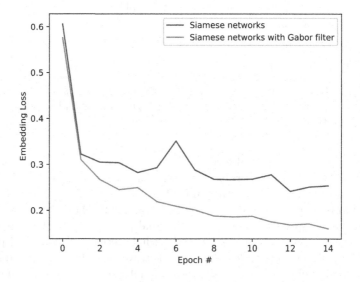

**Fig. 5.** Embedding loss.

A minimum loss of training result means that the classification was well performed. The loss of the embedding process on the training data is shown in the following Fig. 5. The training data contains 60000 images used to build the model. The network optimized the error at every iteration until 15 epochs. This comparison between those two networks shows that network 2, the Siamese network with Gabor filters, generated a better learning curve and was able to obtain better performance with a lower loss of 0.1601 rather than network 1, the original Siamese network, with a loss of 0.2536.

According to Fig. 5, the following are our conclusions: Firstly, we noticed that the Gabor filter is effective in the Siamese networks with the given parameters. As we can see from the figure during the training process, the Siamese network combined with the Gabor filter works well for the MNIST dataset. Secondly, the Gabor filters produced by the real part of the Gabor function are suitable for this network. Finally, we contended that this property is advantageous for the Siamese network. The explanation behind this is that typically, a Gabor layer relates to textural features that are effective in the lower network layers. Therefore, this suggests that we can utilize Gabor filters for replacing a classical one in the lower layers of a network to really get excellent results.

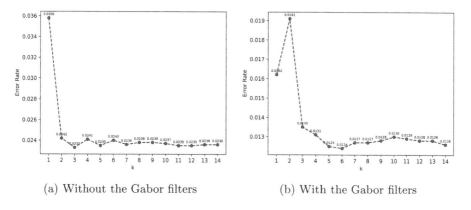

(a) Without the Gabor filters          (b) With the Gabor filters

**Fig. 6.** The optimal value of $k$ using elbow method.

After the embedding process steps were over, we employed the kNN classifier in order to classify handwritten digit images. The elbow method was executed with successive values of $k$ from 1 to 15. Figure 6 depicts a visualization of the classification error for various $k$ values. Evidently, the ideal number of $k$ equals 3 for classifying MNIST numerical digits using Siamese networks without Gabor filters (network 1). Next, the ideal number of $k$ for classifying MNIST numerical digits using Siamese networks with Gabor filters (network 1) equals 6. We get the error rates on the testing dataset on network 1 and network 2 are 0.0233 and 0.124, respectively. We also provided the differences between network 1 and network 2 in terms of the confusion matrix and the accuracy of each class shown in Fig. 7. In accuracy, our network 2 outperformed network 1 in almost all classes. Especially in class "eight", the accuracy obtained by network 2 clearly higher than network 1. Regarding the difference in accuracy, network 2 is 1.09% more accurate than network 1.

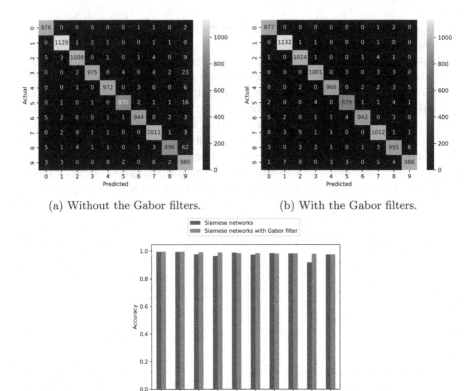

(a) Without the Gabor filters.          (b) With the Gabor filters.

(c) Class-wise accuracy values.

**Fig. 7.** Confusion matrix and the accuracy of each class.

The accuracies of our proposed network and other existing methods on the same dataset are shown in Table 2. Noteworthy is the fact that our suggested network outperforms existing approaches on MNIST datasets. A possible reason for the better results is based on the feature extraction method and the classifier used for classification. Our approach used Siamese networks with Gabor filters to classify MNIST digits and achieved an overall classification accuracy of 98.76%. On the other hand, [2] introduced a hybrid method for recognizing the MNIST dataset. They used CNN for feature extraction and fed the results to a hybrid classifier for classification. Their CNN and SVM-based hybrid classifier achieved 94.40% classification accuracy. [15] carried out the handwritten digit recognition using SG-L1 for feature selection. They obtained 97.00% classification accuracy with a deep NN as the classifier. [16] also investigated this classification task, which used SNN with NormAD as its learning algorithm and achieved 98.40% classification accuracy. [17] performed handwritten digit recognition using deep SNN training with STDP algorithm and obtained a classification accuracy of 98.40%. [18] used FOBP neural networks and PEO optimization to optimize the network and achieved an overall classification accuracy of 96.54%. Another method introduced by [31] proposed a combination of LeNet-5 for feature extraction and multi-level fusion of kNN and RF, which achieved an accuracy of 98.10%. Additionally, [32] introduced a CNN approach for classifying MNIST digits, achieving a 98.00% accuracy rate. However, we would like to emphasize that this work contained several limitations. First, cross-validation experiments were not conducted to assess the model's generalization capabilities, and second, cross-dataset evaluation for robust handwritten digit classification method also was not addressed. Consequently, this approach could be incapable of recognizing the handwritten digits from unseen samples.

**Table 2.** Evaluate the performance between proposed and other existing methods.

| References | Models | Accuracy |
|---|---|---|
| [2] | CNN + SVM | 94.40% |
| [15] | SG-L1-DNN | 97.00% |
| [16] | SNN + NormAD | 98.17% |
| [17] | Deep SNN + STDP | 98.40% |
| [18] | PEO-FOBP | 96.54% |
| [31] | LeNet-5 + fusion of kNN and RF | 98.10% |
| [32] | CNN + kNN + SVM | 98.00% |
| Network 1 | Siamese networks + kNN | 97.67% |
| Network 2 | Siamese networks + Gabor filter + kNN | 98.76% |

# 6   Conclusion and Future Work

In this paper, we have shown a good fusion of the Siamese network with the Gabor filter for handwritten digit recognition. The model combines the advantages of the Siamese network, the Gabor filter, and the kNN classifier in recognizing handwritten digits. The experimental study revealed that our suggested strategy has a classification accuracy 98.76% on the MNIST dataset. It is important to note the research on the Siamese networks with the Gabor filter is in its early stages and can be further improved. In upcoming projects, we will enhance the network's performance in the following areas. Firstly, we will improve the performance using different Gabor filter banks with learnable parameters and utilize the Gabor filters to deeper layers of the networks, as well as adapt this algorithm as a preprocessing tool. Next, we will also focus on improving some limitations of the proposed method, such as cross-validation experiments for generalization and cross-dataset evaluation for the robustness of classifying unseen samples. Finally, will try to design new configurations of Siamese networks based on the best real and imaginary forms of Gabor filters.

# References

1. Babu, U.R., Venkateswarlu, Y., Chintha, A.K.: Handwritten digit recognition using k-nearest neighbour classifier. In: Proceedings - 2014 World Congress on Computing and Communication Technologies, WCCCT 2014, pp. 60–65. IEEE Computer Society (2014)
2. Niu, X.X., Suen, C.Y.: A novel hybrid CNN-SVM classifier for recognizing handwritten digits. Pattern Recogn. **45**, 1318–1325 (2012)
3. Goltsev, A., Gritsenko, V.: Investigation of efficient features for image recognition by neural networks. Neural Netw. **28**, 15–23 (2012)
4. Hossain, A., Ali, M.: Recognition of handwritten digit using convolutional neural network (CNN). In: Proceedings of 2020 International Conference on Computing and Data Science CDS 2020, vol. 19, pp. 183–190 (2020)
5. Govindarajan, M.: Evaluation of ensemble classifiers for handwriting recognition. Int. J. Mod. Educ. Comput. Sci. **5**, 11–20 (2013). https://doi.org/10.5815/ijmecs.2013.11.02
6. Malik, H., Roy, N.: Extreme learning machine-based image classification model using handwritten digit database. In: Advances in Intelligent Systems and Computing, pp. 607–618 (2018). https://doi.org/10.1007/978-981-13-1822-1_57
7. Shi, B., Bai, X., Yao, C.: An end-to-end trainable neural network for image-based sequence recognition and its application to scene text recognition. IEEE Trans. Pattern Anal. Mach. Intell. **39**, 2298–2304 (2017). https://doi.org/10.1109/tpami.2016.2646371
8. Shamim, S.M., Miah, M.B.A., Sarker, A., Rana, M., Jobair, A.A.: handwritten digit recognition using machine learning algorithms. Indonesian J. Sci. Technol. **3**, 29 (2018). https://doi.org/10.17509/ijost.v3i1.10795
9. Dine, K.Z., Nasri, M., Moussaoui, M., Benchaou, S., Aouinti, F.: Digit recognition using different features extraction methods. In: Advances in Intelligent Systems and Computing, pp. 167–175 (2016). https://doi.org/10.1007/978-3-319-46568-5_17
10. Ji, P., Jin, L., Li, X.: Vision-based vehicle type classification using partial Gabor filter bank. In: Proceedings of the IEEE International Conference on Automation and Logistics, ICAL 2007, pp. 1037–1040 (2007)
11. Sarwar, S.S., Panda, P., Roy, K.: Gabor filter assisted energy efficient fast learning convolutional neural networks. In: Proceedings of International Symposium on Low Power Electronics and Designs, pp. 1–6 (2017)
12. Alekseev, A., Bobe, A.: GaborNet: Gabor filters with learnable parameters in deep convolutional neural networks. arXiv. (2019)
13. Koch, G., Zemel, R., workshop, R.S.-I. deep learning, 2015, undefined: Siamese neural networks for one-shot image recognition. cs.toronto.edu. http://www.cs.toronto.edu/~gkoch/files/msc-thesis.pdf. Accessed 09 Apr 2021
14. Bromley, J., et al.: Signature verification using a "Siamese" time delay neural network. Int. J. Pattern Recognit. Artif. Intell. **07**, 669–688 (1993)
15. Scardapane, S., Comminiello, D., Hussain, A., Uncini, A.: Group sparse regularization for deep neural networks. Neurocomputing. **241**, 81–89 (2017)
16. 23 Kulkarni, S.R., Rajendran, B.: Spiking neural networks for handwritten digit recognition–Supervised learning and network optimization. Neural Netw. **103**, 118–127 (2018)
17. Kheradpisheh, S.R., Ganjtabesh, M., Thorpe, S.J., Masquelier, T.: STDP-based spiking deep convolutional neural networks for object recognition. Neural Netw. **99**, 56–67 (2018)

18. Chen, M.R., Chen, B.P., Zeng, G.Q., Lu, K.D., Chu, P.: An adaptive fractional-order BP neural network based on extremal optimization for handwritten digits recognition. Neurocomputing **391**, 260–272 (2020)
19. Yuan, Y., Zhang, J., Wang, Q.: Deep Gabor convolution network for person re-identification. Neurocomputing **378**, 387–398 (2020)
20. Chicco, D.: Siamese neural networks: an overview. Methods Mol. Biol. **2190**, 73–94 (2021)
21. Chopra, S., Hadsell, R., LeCun, Y.: Learning a similarity metric discriminatively, with application to face verification. In: Proceedings of 2005 IEEE Computer and Social Conference on Computer Vision and Pattern Recognition, CVPR 2005, I, pp. 539–546 (2005)
22. Schroff, F., Kalenichenko, D., Philbin, J.: FaceNet: A unified embedding for face recognition and clustering. In: Proceedings of IEEE Computer and Social Conference on Computer Vision and Pattern Recognition 07–12-June-2015, pp. 815–823 (2015)
23. Dong, X., Shen, J.: Triplet loss in Siamese network for object tracking. In: Ferrari, V., Hebert, M., Sminchisescu, C., Weiss, Y. (eds.) ECCV 2018. LNCS, vol. 11217, pp. 472–488. Springer, Cham (2018). https://doi.org/10.1007/978-3-030-01261-8_28
24. Hoffer, E., Ailon, N.: Deep metric learning using triplet network. In: Feragen, A., Pelillo, M., Loog, M. (eds.) SIMBAD 2015. LNCS, vol. 9370, pp. 84–92. Springer, Cham (2015). https://doi.org/10.1007/978-3-319-24261-3_7
25. Zhuang, B., Lin, G., Shen, C., Reid, I.: Fast training of triplet-based deep binary embedding networks. In: Proceedings of IEEE Computer and Social Conference on Computer Vision and Pattern Recognition, 2016-December, pp. 5955–5964 (2016)
26. Song, H.O., Xiang, Y., Jegelka, S., Savarese, S.: Deep metric learning via lifted structured feature embedding. In: Proceedings of IEEE Computer and Social Conference on Computer Vision and Pattern Recognition 2016-December, pp. 4004–4012 (2015)
27. Cheng, D., Gong, Y., Zhou, S., Wang, J., Zheng, N.: Person re-identification by multi-channel parts-based CNN with improved triplet loss function. In: Proceedings of IEEE Computer and Social Conference on Computer Vision and Pattern Recognition, 2016-December, pp. 1335–1344 (2016)
28. Hermans, A., Beyer, L., Leibe, B.: In Defense of the Triplet Loss for Person Re-Identification (2017)
29. TensorFlow Addons Losses: TripletSemiHardLoss. https://www.tensorflow.org/addons/tutorials/losses_triplet. Accessed 07 July 2022
30. LeCun, Y., Cortes, C.: MNIST handwritten digit database (2010). http://yann.lecun.com/exdb/mnist/
31. Zhao, H., Liu, H.: Multiple classifiers fusion and CNN feature extraction for handwritten digits recognition. Granular Comput. **5**, 411–418 (2019). https://doi.org/10.1007/s41066-019-00158-6
32. Enriquez, E.A., Gordillo, N., Bergasa, L.M., Romera, E., Huélamo, C.G.: Convolutional neural network vs traditional methods for offline recognition of handwritten digits. In: Advances in Intelligent Systems and Computing, pp. 87–99 (2018). https://doi.org/10.1007/978-3-319-99885-5_7

# Semi-supervised Time Series Classification Through Image Representations

Bionda Rozin$^{(\boxtimes)}$ [iD], Emílio Bergamim [iD],
Daniel Carlos Guimarães Pedronette [iD], and Fabricio Aparecido Breve [iD]

Department of Statistics, Applied Mathematics and Computing (DEMAC). Sao Paulo State University (UNESP), Rio Claro, Brazil
bionda.rozin@unesp.br

**Abstract.** Time series data is of crucial importance in different domains, such as financial and medical applications. However, obtaining a large amount of labeled time series data is an expensive and time-consuming task, which becomes the process of building an effective machine learning model a challenge. In these scenarios, algorithms that can deal with reduced amounts of labeled data emerge. One example is Semi-Supervised Learning (SSL), which has the capability of exploring both labeled and unlabeled data for tasks such as classification. In this work, a kNN graph-based transductive SSL approach is used for time series classification. A feature extraction step, based on imaging time series and obtaining features using deep neural networks is performed before the classification step. An extensive evaluation is conducted over four datasets, and a parametric analysis of the nearest neighbors is performed. Also, a statistical analysis over the obtained distances is conducted. Results suggest that our methods are suitable for classification and competitive with supervised baselines in some datasets.

**Keywords:** Transductive Semi Supervised Learning · Graph · Time Series · Feature Extraction · Images · Neural Networks · Classification

## 1 Introduction

One of the greatest challenges, nowadays, is dealing with great amounts of available data. While there are huge quantities of data available, labeling it, on the other hand, is a laborious, expensive, and time-consuming task. In particular, for time series, finding annotations for data can be difficult due to the necessity of a professional or the excessive amount of instances in a dataset [47].

Time series are important in lots of different fields, such as finances [33], healthcare and medicine [42], energy [2], agriculture [34], and sensor data [12], among others. Given the importance of time series and the scarcity of labeled data, it is important to find methods to process these data without losing effectiveness.

O. Gervasi et al. (Eds.): ICCSA 2023, LNCS 13957, pp. 48–65, 2023.
https://doi.org/10.1007/978-3-031-36808-0_4

For traditional machine learning methods, a large amount of labeled data is necessary for training [47], so, in this scope, Semi-Supervised Learning (SSL) algorithms emerged as an interesting research area, using both labeled and unlabeled information to perform tasks such as classification [41]. Tasks such as disease monitoring [17], human activity recognition [35], indexing of hand-written documents [47], among others, benefit from applying semi-supervised approaches.

In this work, we use a classic transductive SSL algorithm in the task of time series classification. Known as Label Propagation, this method represents the whole dataset as a graph and then labels are propagated from labeled samples to unlabeled ones. Under this scenario, the construction of the similarity graph among pairs of samples is crucial for correct inference.

Under these circumstances, we propose transforming a time series to an image using different methods and subsequently extracting features from the images using neural networks. This step aims to improve the quality of the similarity graph and, consequently, the effectiveness of the classification task.

Our main contributions are:

– Studying different approaches for imaging of time series, extracting features from generated images using neural networks originally trained on a large image dataset, and then using the obtained features to construct a similarity graph for SSL.
– Our classification results show that the proposed methods are suitable for time series classification. We also observe that the imaging method impact results in a more meaningful way than the feature extraction methods.
– A statistical analysis of distances and similarities generated via the proposed method in order to understand classification results.

The rest of the paper is organized as follows: Sect. 2, is given a theoretical foundation about SSL and the related work; Sect. 3 gives a detailing of the proposed method; Sect. 4 outlines the experimental protocol and the used datasets; Sect. 5 presents the obtained results and a discussion; finally, Sect. 6 presents a conclusion about the work.

## 2   Theoretical Foundation and Related Work

Let $D = \{\mathbf{x}\}_{i=1}^{N}$ be a set of features such that $\mathbf{x_i} \in \mathbb{R}^n$ and $\mathcal{Y} = \{y_i\}_{i=1}^{L}$ a set of labels for the corresponding elements of $D$, with $L \leq N$. A semi-supervised classification problem appears when one has $L << N$ and wishes to determine labels for the whole dataset (in a transductive setting) or to learn a classification function $y(\mathbf{x})$ (which is called an inductive setting) [41].

Transductive Semi-Supervised Learning (SSL) algorithms are essentially graph-based and can be described as having two steps [41]:

– **Graph construction**: in this step, elements of $D$ are mapped to nodes in a graph $G = (V, E)$, where $V$ is the node set and $E$ the edge set. Weighted edges between similar nodes are drawn in order to describe class relations.

– **Inference**: a dynamic is then applied to $G$ in order to label the unlabelled elements through the previous knowledge present in $\mathcal{Y}$.

The construction of $G$ is crucial to the success of the inference step. Edges in $G$ should connect mainly nodes belonging to the same class, in order to enhance the contrast between different classes. This is related to the clustering hypothesis, which establishes that classes should be associated to clusters in order for SSL to take place [6]. Therefore, we proceed to a deeper discussion of this step.

## 2.1  Similarity Construction

Letting $d(\cdot, \cdot)$ be a distance function, a common approach to weight edges of $G$ is the Gaussian similarity:

$$w_{i,j} = \exp \left\{ \frac{-d^2(\mathbf{x}_i, \mathbf{x}_j)}{2\sigma^2} \right\} \tag{1}$$

and $d$ is usually set to be the Euclidean distance [39, 41]

After weighting, a sparsification procedure is applied [41]. Starting from the fully connected weighted graph edges between less similar nodes are deleted (which is equivalent to setting $w_{i,j} = 0$). In this work, we will use a $k-$nearest neighbors approach, where each node is connected to its $k$ nearest neighbors according to the distance $d$. This is a common approach in the field and setting $k = \log_2 N$ is known to be an effective choice [3, 39].

Tunning of $\sigma$ is also a difficult problem [41]. However, a comparison of different approaches found that the method proposed in [22] yields better results. In this case, the parameter is set to

$$\sigma = \frac{1}{3N} \sum_{i=1}^{N} d(\mathbf{x}_i, \mathbf{x}_{i_k}), \tag{2}$$

where $i_k$ is the $k-$nearest neighbor of the $i-$th element.

## 2.2  Label Propagation

The dynamics for classification on $G$ usually involve the propagation of labels from labeled nodes to unlabeled ones. In this direction, *Gaussian Random Fields* (GRF) [41, 49] is a well-established method in the SSL community, together with *Local And Global Consistency* [48]. It is also noteworthy that methods that do not rely on the said dynamics exist, such as neural network based [4, 24] and biologically inspired methods [5].

We will focus on GRF, due to its widespread use. This approach amounts to the minimization of the cost function

$$H = -\sum_{i<j} w_{i,j} \sum_{s} \psi_{i,s} \psi_{j,s}, \tag{3}$$

where $\psi_{i,s}$ denotes the probability of the $i-$th node belonging to the $s-$th class and $w_{i,j}$ is the pairwise similarity among nodes.

Minimization of $H$ is conducted under constraints on the probabilities of labeled nodes. If $i \leq L$, probabilities are frozen to known labels:

$$\psi_{i,s} = \begin{cases} 1, & \text{if } s = y_i \\ 0, & \text{otherwise.} \end{cases} \qquad (4)$$

The optimization process is then a propagation process on $G$, for which each probability at an iteration $t$ is updated as the weighted average of its neighbors in the previous iteration:

$$\psi_{i,s}^{(t+1)} \propto \sum_{j \neq i} w_{i,j} \psi_{j,s}^{(t)} \qquad (5)$$

and then normalized in order for individual probabilities to sum to 1.

The above-described method can be iterated until a maximum number of iterations $t_{max}$ or an upper bound $\epsilon$ for the difference between iterations is reached. After convergence, an unknown label $\hat{y}_i$ (with $i > L$) is determined by

$$\hat{y}_i = arg \max_s \psi_{i,s}. \qquad (6)$$

## 2.3 Time Series Classification

Regarding semi-supervised approaches for time series classification, these have been studied for quite a while [16,21,31,47], since the limitations on acquiring sufficient amounts of labeled data are present across many research areas. In this scenario, our main contribution is the study of a distance-based method for time series classification [1] using different methods for feature extraction, which will be discussed in the next section.

Under limited access to labeled data, graph-based approaches are widely employed. An earlier work employs a modified version of label propagation where at each step $t$ the unlabeled instance with higher probability in step $t - 1$ is considered as labeled [47] A more recent work uses a cluster-then-label approach [31] that aims at finding a minimum spanning tree for the similarity graph.

Approaches based on ensembles of classifiers are also popular in the field. HIVE-COTE [28] is an ensemble of classifiers for which the probability of a label is predicted in a hierarchical voting structure. Other methods in a similar direction are BOSS [37] and HESCA [19]. Despite HIVE-COTE being closer to being considered a state-of-the-art (SOTA) approach, the other two are still able to achieve better results on some datasets [28].

More recently, supervised deep learning methods have shown competitive results with more classical methods. The construction of a baseline [45] allowed for further improvements, like the use of long short-term memory layers [23] and ensembles of neural networks [15]. Semi-supervised approaches were also studied [17], finding that MixMatch is the most reliable method. This model, however, relies on augmenting unlabeled data during training.

As ensemble and deep learning methods demand a significant amount of computational resources, we focus our study on a simple classification method (Label Propagation) that can be efficiently implemented as a message-passing algorithm with time complexity $O(Nk)$, where $k$ is the number of nearest neighbors for each node in the similarity graph.

In this context of more limited computational resources, the use of networks trained in a dataset that is not related to the task at hand, called transfer learning [40], is a recurrent approach. The removal of classification layers in order to use previous layers to extract features that could be more suitable to the problem and further application of a classical machine learning method (like Label Propagation) can overcome limitations such as the time required to train a deep neural network and also show that such models learn meaningful representations of data.

## 3   Proposed Approach

In this work, we propose a graph-based semi-supervised time series classification approach. First, we convert a series to an image by using three different methods, described in Sect. 3.1. For each generated image, we perform a feature extraction using two different neural networks, which are described in Sect. 3.2. In the next step, a graph with the entire dataset is built, and a Label Propagation is performed for the semi-supervised classification task, as described in Sect. 2.

### 3.1   Image-Based Time Series Description

Different approaches were proposed for time series feature extraction over the years. Shape-based [27], Symbol-based [26,38], and Kernel-based [9] are a few examples of time series feature extractors. Each feature can give a new perspective for a machine learning algorithm about a dataset. In this way, finding a good representation of data that can generalize information in a dataset and generate improved results in machine learning problems is a challenging task. An approach for time series representation is using images to extract features [11,43]. Different methods can generate an image using specific characteristics, such as a time series trajectory. These methods can be powerful tools for time series feature extraction if used along with an image feature extractor which is able to consider color, patterns, and texture information in the image. This step can be done using deep learning networks pre-trained through transfer learning, as it was done in this work. Below we describe three methods for imaging a time series.

**Gramian Angular Fields (GAF)** [43]: This method generates an image based on the polar coordinates of a time series. Given an time series $X = \{x_1, x_2, ...x_N\}$, a new series $\tilde{X}$ is obtained from the polar coordinates of the normalized series $X$, in range $[-1, 1]$. Considering the angular perspective, $\tilde{X}$

generates a Gramian Angular Field Matrix, with $N \times N$ dimension, described in Eq. 7.

$$GAF = \tilde{X}'\tilde{X} - \sqrt{I - \tilde{X}^2}'\sqrt{I - \tilde{X}^2} \tag{7}$$

where $I$ is a unit line vector. Each point $GAF_{i,j}$ is the trigonometric sum of the intervals between these points. In this way, a Gramian Angular Field represents a temporal correlation between different time intervals in a time series.

**Markov Transition Fields (MTF)** [43]:   This method images time series based on Markov Matrixes. Given a time series $X = \{x_1, x_2, ...x_N\}$, its $Q$ quantile bins are identified, where $q_j(j\epsilon[1, Q])$ are points that divide a sorted time series into subsets with the same dimension. Given the quantile bins, the Markov Matrix $M$, with $Q \times Q$ dimension, is defined, as in the Eq. 8:

$$M = \begin{bmatrix} P(x_t\epsilon q_1|x_{t-1}\epsilon q_1) & ... & P(x_t\epsilon q_1|x_{t-1}\epsilon q_Q) \\ P(x_t\epsilon q_2|x_{t-1}\epsilon q_1) & ... & P(x_t\epsilon q_2|x_{t-1}\epsilon q_Q) \\ ... & ... & ... \\ P(x_t\epsilon q_Q|x_{t-1}\epsilon q_1) & ... & P(x_t\epsilon q_Q|x_{t-1}\epsilon q_Q) \end{bmatrix} \tag{8}$$

where $M_{i,j}$ describes the probability of $x_t$ being in the quantile bin $q_i$ given that $x_{t-1}$ is in the quantile bin $q_j$. It removes the temporal correlation in the matrix [44]. In this way, a Markov Transition Field, with $N \times N$ dimension, is constructed according to the Eq. 9:

$$MTF = \begin{bmatrix} x_1\epsilon q_i, x_1\epsilon q_j & ... & x_1\epsilon q_i, x_n\epsilon q_j \\ x_2\epsilon q_i, x_1\epsilon q_j & ... & x_2\epsilon q_i, x_n\epsilon q_j \\ ... & ... & ... \\ x_n\epsilon q_i, x_1\epsilon q_j & ... & x_n\epsilon q_i, x_n\epsilon q_j \end{bmatrix} \tag{9}$$

where $MTF_{i,j}$ is the probability of transition from a quantile bin $q_i$ to a quantile bin $q_j$. Formally, $MTF_{i,j||i-j|=k}$ denotes the probability of transition between points with a time interval $k$.

**Recurrence Plots (RP)** [11]:   A Recurrence Plot is a binary representation from a time series that gives information about the temporal correlation of a series. Given a time series $X = \{x_1, x_2, ...x_N\}$, it is obtained its trajectory $\vec{X} = \{\vec{x_i}, \vec{x_{i+\tau}}, ..., \vec{x_{i+(m-1)\tau}}\}$, $\forall i\epsilon\{1, 2, ..., N - (m - 1)\tau\}$, where $\tau$ is the temporal delay and $m$ is the trajectory dimension. A point $RP_{i,j}$ is set if the Euclidean distance between $\vec{x}(i)$ and $\vec{x}(j)$ is less or equal than a threshold. Formally, let $K = N - (m-1)\tau$, a Recurrence Plot matrix, with $K \times K$ dimension, is described in Eq. 10:

$$R_{i,j} = \begin{cases} 1, & \text{if } ||\vec{x}(i) - \vec{x}(j)|| \leq \epsilon \\ 0, & \text{else,} \end{cases} \tag{10}$$

$$\forall i, j\epsilon\{1, 2, ..., K\}$$

## 3.2 Deep Learning Methods as Image Feature Extractors

Images have lots of encoded information such as patterns, colors, textures, and shapes, among others. The use of previously trained neural networks via transfer learning, for image feature extraction, has shown great potential in this field due to its great generalization ability and strong feature learning [29]. In this work, we used a CNN ResNet-152 and a huge-sized Vision Transformers for feature extraction, both pre-trained with the ImageNet dataset [10] by using transfer learning techniques. ResNet architectures are widely used for image feature extraction [13, 30, 32] and have demonstrated excellent results in different scopes. On the other hand, although Vision Transformers have not been extensively tested for feature extraction, it has achieved competitive results in different tasks, such as image classification, making it a promising approach for this task. A brief explanation of these models is described below.

**CNN ResNet-152** [18]. A Residual Network (ResNet) is a family of Convolutional Neural Networks (CNN) that was proposed for image recognition. This network can have up to 152 layers and overcomes the "vanishing gradient" problem by using skip connections on plain networks. A skip connection, also called identity shortcut, allows a more effective training process by enabling the flow of information between layers and avoiding the loss of gradient information during backpropagation. This facilitates the training of deeper neural networks. A skip connection involves taking multiple convolutional layers and skipping them, using activation functions of the previous layer. When the network is retrained, all of these layers, known as residual parts, are used for exploring more of the feature space, improving the accuracy of the model. For feature extraction, the last fully connected layer is used as output.

**Vision Transformers (ViT)** [25]. Vision Transformers is a model proposed for image recognition that achieved state-of-the-art in tasks such as object detection and image classification. The model uses a self-attention mechanism to enable the model to focus on the most important parts of the input by weighting and processing these parts simultaneously. The input image is represented as a sequence of patches that are flattened and fed into a transformers architecture. The transformers architecture consists of an encoder, that processes the input tokens and generates a sequence of hidden states, which feed a decoder, that produces a sequence of output tokens. Both the encoder and decoder are composed of multiple layers of multi-head self-attention mechanisms and feedforward neural networks, but decoders use masked self-attention, so the model attends only to the previously generated tokens during decoding. For feature extraction, we used the pooler output.

## 4    Evaluation

This section outlines the experimental protocol for semi-supervised time series classification and the datasets used for this task. Our strategy can be summarized in four steps: first, we extract features from time series data; then, we split the data and perform semi-supervised learning (SSL); finally, we evaluate the results of our approach.

## 4.1  Datasets

Below are described the four univariate time series datasets, from the UCR Archive [8], used in the experiments. The datasets were chosen based on size, the number of classes, and domain variability. This assures that our model is versatile, robust, and can be applied to a wide range of real-world problems. All datasets were z-normalized.

- **CBF** [36][1] This is a simulated dataset, where the data from each class consists of a standard normal noise plus an offset term that varies for each class. This dataset has 930 elements of size 128, divided into 3 classes.
- **ECG5000** [7][1] This dataset is derived from a 20-hour-long ECG called BIDMC Congestive Heart Failure Database (chfdb), available on Physionet. The used record is "chf07" and the patient has congestive heart failure. Data underwent pre-processing, extracting each heartbeat, and interpolating for uniform length. After pre-processing, 5000 heartbeats of length 140 were randomly selected, composing this dataset, and the heartbeats were automatically annotated and divided into five classes.
- **Yoga** [47][1] This dataset is composed of 3300 time series, of size 426, generated from videos of actors transitioning between yoga poses. Each image of the video was converted to a time series considering the distances between the actor's contour and the image center. The problem is distinguishing the male and the female actors.
- **Electric Devices** [2][1] This dataset has 16637 time series of length 96, divided into 7 classes. Data were obtained by measuring daily the power consumption of different devices, which are washing machines, ovens, dishwashers, kettles, immersion heaters, cold groups (fridge, freezer), and screen groups (computer, television), from 187 households. The problem consists in distinguishing each device by its daily measurements.

## 4.2  Experimental Protocol

The process of time series feature extraction was conducted using Python 3.10 and all the datasets were imaged using the methods described in Sect. 3.1, while we maintained all the proposed parameters on pyts library [14]. Images were plotted and saved using the matplotlib library [20]. For the GAF and MTF methods, we set the colormap parameter to 'rainbow' and for the RP method, we used a 'binary' colormap. The neural network architectures outlined in Sect. 3.2 were, then, applied to all generated images. Subsequently, we compute the Euclidean distance among pairs of instances in order to construct the similarity matrix for

---

[1] Downloaded from https://timeseriesclassification.com/dataset.php.

label propagation. For the inference step we set $t_{max} = 10^3$ and $\epsilon = 10^{-3}$.

To evaluate our methods, we split each dataset $D$ in a labeled set $D_l$ and an unlabeled one $D_u$, ensuring that the second always contains a representative of each class. This procedure is conducted for different sizes of $D_u$. All our experiments on classification are averaged over equally sized splits of $D$, which were ten in our setup.

The effect of the number of neighbors on classification results is also evaluated by varying $k$ under a fixed size for $D_u$ and then averaging over splits.

As classification metrics we employ the accuracy and adjusted mutual information, the second being a clustering metric, that, together with the first, helps in visualizing the relationship between clustering and classification in a SSL setup [3].

Comparison with previous works is done using supervised classification methods as baselines, particularly the ones in [23,28], which aggregate the accuracy for several methods and datasets. We then compare our accuracy results with the two best methods on each dataset.

For the extracted features, we conduct a statistical analysis in terms of the distribution of pairwise distances and similarities, and their coefficient of variation, defined as the standard deviation divided by the mean. This is done in order to have a better understanding of how different methods for feature extraction compare with each other.

## 5 Results and Discussion

We first discuss our empirical evaluation of different methods for feature extraction in semi-supervised classification and then proceed to our statistical analysis of pairwise distances to elucidate some of the differences among said methods.

### 5.1 Classification Results

Our results show the proposed methods for feature extraction are suitable for the task of semi-supervised classification using label propagation (Figs. 1, 2, 3 and 4). It is also noteworthy that accuracy and AMI carry a very intimate relationship in all of the studied datasets, showing clustering and classification are indeed connected.

The Electric Devices (Fig. 1) dataset presents some of our most interesting results. In this case, supervised baselines are trained with a high rate of labeled data ($r_l \approx 0.54$) and one can clearly see that with $r_l = 0.2$ some of the proposed methods are not far away of their accuracy. It is also noteworthy that using GAF and RP achieves higher accuracies with $r_l > 0.06$ than methods using the combination LSTM+FCN [23] in the standard splits.

Another interesting feature of this dataset is that, different from the others, using raw data provides the worst results. To our knowledge, this dataset does not have a Gaussian distribution. However, the discrepancy from the other

Electric Devices, $k = \log_2 N$

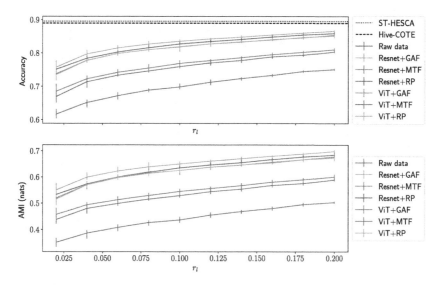

**Fig. 1.** Results for the ElectricDevices dataset as a function of $r_l$. Supervised baselines were obtained from 8926 labeled points, corresponding to $r_l \approx 0.54$.

CBF, $k = \log_2 N$

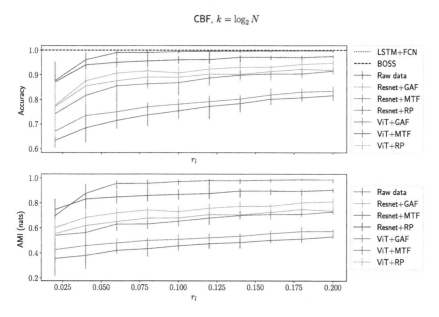

**Fig. 2.** Results for the CBF dataset as functions of the number of nearest neighbors $k$ (up) and the rate of labeled data $r_l$ (down). Supervised baselines were obtained with initially 30 labeled points, corresponding to $r_l \approx 0.03$.

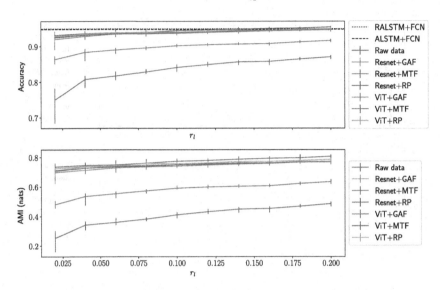

**Fig. 3.** Results for the ECG5000 dataset as a function of $r_l$. Supervised baselines were obtained with initially 500 labeled points, corresponding to $r_l = 0.1$.

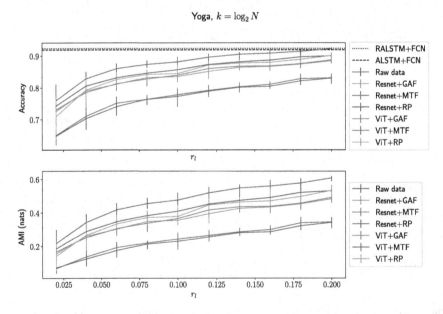

**Fig. 4.** Results for the Yoga dataset as a function of $r_l$. Supervised baselines were obtained with initially 300 labeled points, corresponding to $r_l \approx 0.09$.

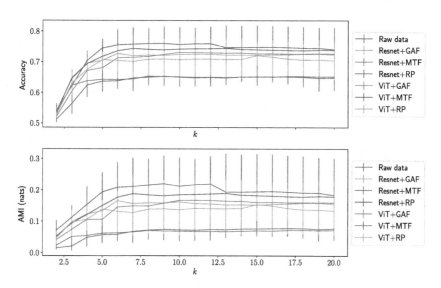

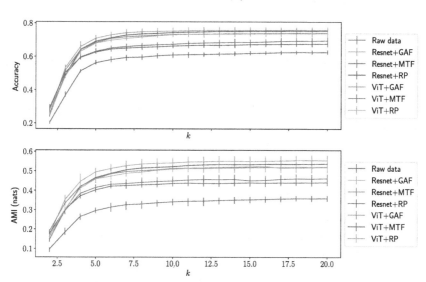

**Fig. 5.** Classification results as a function of $k$ for the Yoga (up) and Electric Devices (down) datasets.

studied sets may indicate a line of work for which our methods may provide a significant improvement.

One also sees that, with the exception of Electric Devices, the usage of raw data dominates our benchmarks in comparison with methods that use features extracted via neural networks. This could be related to CBF, ECG5000, and Yoga having some form of Gaussian property, either explicitly, as is the case of CBF, or intrinsically. This second hypothesis, however, demands a deeper evaluation to be better understood.

Drawing our attention to comparisons with previous works, on CBF (Fig. 2), previous works using neural networks [23] and also BOSS [38] trained with $r_l \approx 0.03$ achieve correctness over the whole dataset, while our methods fall shortly of that milestone. On ECG5000 we observe our methods are only marginally less accurate than LSTM+FCN ones [23]. Yoga is the hardest dataset, with our methods demanding $r_l > 0.2$ in order to compete with SOTA accuracy.

We also observe that methods that rely on MTF for imaging of time series tend to be less accurate than their counterparts using GAF and RP. This is also a strange behavior that we are not yet able to understand.

Regarding the role of graph construction on classification results, we show results for Yoga and Electric Devices (Fig. 5) under $r_l = 0.02$ and variable $k$. As noted in earlier works [3,39], there is evidence of a *plateau* in studied metrics once a sufficient amount of nearest neighbors is reached.

Fig. 5 also shows us that is the proposed feature extraction approach that renders Electric Devices its performance and not an anomaly due to graph construction. As different values of $k$ do not alter the relative classification performance among evaluated methods, we are able to confirm that our imaging of time series can indeed provide a representation of data that is more discriminative among classes.

The choice for $k$ in this method, however, defines also the computational complexity. Therefore, one should choose $k$ in a way that the method is fast and accurate. From our experiments, the initial choice of $k = \log_2 N$ seems a good one to attain these conditions.

## 5.2   Statistical Analysis of Pairwise Distances and Similarities

We now turn to analyzing the distribution of pairwise distances and similarities. This is done only on CBF, ECG5000, and Yoga due to the large size of the Electric Devices dataset.

Fig. 6 shows the kernel density estimation of the distribution of distances, obtained using the Seaborn library [46]. One then can easily see that features extracted using ViT networks produce pairwise distances that are smaller than other evaluated methods.

Another distributional aspect that draws our attention is that the distribution of pairwise distances of the most accurate methods tends to not resemble a Gaussian. In fact, some of those distributions even show a double-peaked distribution, being indicative of a separation between intraclass and outer class distances. This is the case for using raw data in ECG5000 and Resnet+RP in CBF.

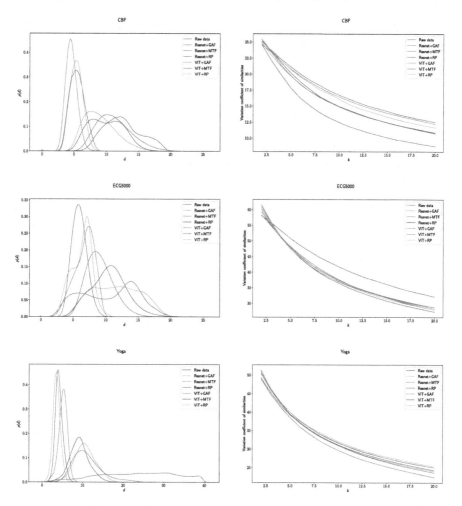

**Fig. 6.** Kernel density estimation of pairwise distances (left) and coefficient of variation of pairwise similarities as a function of $k$ (right) for CBF, ECG5000, and Yoga.

Results in Fig. 6 also outline that the combination of imaging with feature extraction from neural networks tends to smooth the distribution of distances. ResNet and ViT, however, do such in a different manner, with the second producing smaller distances.

When we turn to the analysis of the coefficient of variation of similarities (Fig. 6) we see that, on CBF, the distribution for raw data has the lowest variation. Together with our previous analysis of Fig. 6, we then conclude that similarities may reflect intraclass proximity in this case.

However, especially on the Yoga dataset, similarities calculated from MTF imaging have a lower variation. This dataset and ECG5000 are also the ones where MTF is clearly the worst imaging method. As their kernel densities (Fig. 6) show a single-peaked distribution, we presume pairwise distances of these methods suffer from an indistinguishability phenomenon.

## 6   Conclusion

We have studied imaging of time series followed by feature extraction from previously trained deep neural networks applied to semi-supervised classification.

Our results indicate that the proposed approach is useful in the problem of time series classification, showing competitive results on most datasets.

The conducted empirical evaluation, however, leaves lots of questions to be answered. Classification results on CBF, ECG5000, and Yoga are somewhat similar, where the usage of raw data instead of imaging is the most effective approach. On ElectricDevices this picture changes drastically and imaging with GAF and RP, followed by MTF, provides the best results. Understanding the causes of this phenomenon is our main research direction moving forward.

It is also noteworthy that imaging methods seem to be way more impactful on classification results than neural network architectures. In this regard, MTF is clearly the worst approach when compared to GAF and RP.

The statistical analysis of pairwise distances and similarities also helped us with some of our classification results and revealed interesting properties of features extracted from neural networks, like the fact that Vision Transformers produce more homogeneous and smaller distances. Studying such aspects also seems a fruitful research direction we aim to purchase in future work.

**Acknowledgements.** The authors are grateful to São Paulo Research Foundation - FAPESP (grants #2016/05669-4, #2022/01359-1 and #2018/15597-6), Brazilian National Council for Scientific and Technological Development - CNPq (grants #309439/2020-5 and #422667/2021-8) for financial support. This study was also financed in part by the Coordenação de Aperfeiçoamento de Pessoal de Nível Superior - Brasil (CAPES) - Finance Code 001.

We thank Prof. Dr. Denis Salvadeo, from DEMAC, for some insightful discussions and help with computational infrastructure.

## References

1. Abanda, A., Mori, U., Lozano, J.A.: A review on distance based time series classification. Data Min. Knowl. Disc. **33**(2), 378–412 (2019)
2. Bagnall, A., Davis, L., Hills, J., Lines, J.: Transformation based ensembles for time series classification. In: Proceedings of 12th SDM, April 2012. https://doi.org/10.1137/1.9781611972825.27
3. Bergamim, E., Breve, F.: On tuning a mean-field model for semi-supervised classification. J. Stat. Mech: Theory Exp. **2022**(5), 053402 (2022)
4. Berthelot, D., Carlini, N., Goodfellow, I., Papernot, N., Oliver, A., Raffel, C.A.: Mixmatch: a holistic approach to semi-supervised learning. In: Advances in Neural Information Processing Systems, vol. 32 (2019)

5. Breve, F., Zhao, L., Quiles, M., Pedrycz, W., Liu, J.: Particle competition and cooperation in networks for semi-supervised learning. IEEE Trans. Knowl. Data Eng. **24**(9), 1686–1698 (2011)
6. Chapelle, O., Schölkopf, B., Zien, A.: Semi-supervised learning. Adaptive computation and machine learning series (2006)
7. Chen, Y., Hao, Y., Rakthanmanon, T., Zakaria, J., Hu, B., Keogh, E.: A general framework for never-ending learning from time series streams. Data Min. Knowl. Disc. **29**(6), 1622–1664 (2014). https://doi.org/10.1007/s10618-014-0388-4
8. Dau, H.A., et al.: The UCR time series classification archive, October 2018. https://www.cs.ucr.edu/~eamonn/time_series_data_2018/
9. Dempster, A., Petitjean, F., Webb, G.I.: ROCKET: exceptionally fast and accurate time series classification using random convolutional kernels. Data Min. Knowl. Disc. **34**(5), 1454–1495 (2020). https://doi.org/10.1007/s10618-020-00701-z
10. Deng, J., Dong, W., Socher, R., Li, L.J., Li, K., Fei-Fei, L.: Imagenet: a large-scale hierarchical image database. In: 2009 IEEE Conference on Computer Vision and Pattern Recognition, pp. 248–255 (2009). https://doi.org/10.1109/CVPR.2009.5206848
11. Eckmann, J.P., Kamphorst, S., Ruelle, D.: Recurrence plots of dynamical systems. Europhys. Lett. (EPL). **4**, 973–977 (1987). https://doi.org/10.1209/0295-5075/4/9/004
12. Falcon, A., D'Agostino, G., Lanz, O., Brajnik, G., Tasso, C., Serra, G.: Neural turing machines for the remaining useful life estimation problem. Comput. Indus. **143**, 103762 (2022). https://doi.org/10.1016/j.compind.2022.103762
13. Fan, L., Zhang, T., Du, W.: Optical-flow-based framework to boost video object detection performance with object enhancement. Expert Syst. Appl. **170**, 114544 (2021). https://doi.org/10.1016/j.eswa.2020.114544
14. Faouzi, J., Janati, H.: PYTS: a python package for time series classification. J. Mach. Learn. Res. **21**(46), 1–6 (2020). http://jmlr.org/papers/v21/19-763.html
15. Fawaz, H.I., Forestier, G., Weber, J., Idoumghar, L., Muller, P.A.: Deep neural network ensembles for time series classification. In: 2019 International Joint Conference on Neural Networks (IJCNN), pp. 1–6. IEEE (2019)
16. González, M., Bergmeir, C., Triguero, I., Rodríguez, Y., Benítez, J.M.: Self-labeling techniques for semi-supervised time series classification: an empirical study. Knowl. Inf. Syst. **55**, 493–528 (2018)
17. Goschenhofer, J.: Deep semi-supervised learning for time-series classification. In: Wani, M.A., Palade , V. (eds.) Deep Learning Applications, Volume 4. Advances in Intelligent Systems and Computing, vol. 1434, pp. 361–384. Springer, Singapore (2022). https://doi.org/10.1007/978-981-19-6153-3_15
18. He, K., Zhang, X., Ren, S., Sun, J.: Deep residual learning for image recognition. In: 2016 IEEE Conference on Computer Vision and Pattern Recognition (CVPR), pp. 770–778 (2016). https://doi.org/10.1109/CVPR.2016.90
19. Hills, J., Lines, J., Baranauskas, E., Mapp, J., Bagnall, A.: Classification of time series by Shapelet transformation. Data Min. Knowl. Disc. **28**, 851–881 (2014)
20. Hunter, J.D.: Matplotlib: a 2d graphics environment. Comput. Sci. Eng. **9**(3), 90–95 (2007). https://doi.org/10.1109/MCSE.2007.55
21. Jawed, S., Grabocka, J., Schmidt-Thieme, L.: Self-supervised learning for semi-supervised time series classification. In: Lauw, H.W., Wong, R.C.-W., Ntoulas, A., Lim, E.-P., Ng, S.-K., Pan, S.J. (eds.) PAKDD 2020. LNCS (LNAI), vol. 12084, pp. 499–511. Springer, Cham (2020). https://doi.org/10.1007/978-3-030-47426-3_39

22. Jebara, T., Wang, J., Chang, S.F.: Graph construction and b-matching for semi-supervised learning. In: Proceedings of the 26th Annual International Conference on Machine Learning, pp. 441–448 (2009)
23. Karim, F., Majumdar, S., Darabi, H., Chen, S.: LSTM fully convolutional networks for time series classification. IEEE Access **6**, 1662–1669 (2017)
24. Kipf, T.N., Welling, M.: Semi-supervised classification with graph convolutional networks. arXiv preprint arXiv:1609.02907 (2016)
25. Kolesnikov, A., et al.: An image is worth 16 × 16 words: Transformers for image recognition at scale (2021)
26. Lin, J., Keogh, E., Wei, L., Lonardi, S.: Experiencing sax: a novel symbolic representation of time series. Data Min. Knowl. Discov. **15**, 107–144 (2007). https://doi.org/10.1007/s10618-007-0064-z
27. Lines, J., Davis, L.M., Hills, J., Bagnall, A.: A shapelet transform for time series classification. In: Proceedings of the 18th ACM SIGKDD International Conference on Knowledge Discovery and Data Mining, pp. 289–297. KDD 2012, Association for Computing Machinery, New York, NY, USA (2012). https://doi.org/10.1145/2339530.2339579
28. Lines, J., Taylor, S., Bagnall, A.: Time series classification with hive-cote: the hierarchical vote collective of transformation-based ensembles. ACM Trans. Knowl. Disc. Data **12**(5) (2018)
29. Liu, Y., Pu, H., Sun, D.W.: Efficient extraction of deep image features using convolutional neural network (CNN) for applications in detecting and analysing complex food matrices. Trends Food Sci. Technol. **113**, 193–204 (2021). https://doi.org/10.1016/j.tifs.2021.04.042
30. Mahajan, A., Chaudhary, S.: Categorical image classification based on representational deep network (ResNet). In: 2019 3rd International conference on Electronics, Communication and Aerospace Technology (ICECA), pp. 327–330 (2019). https://doi.org/10.1109/ICECA.2019.8822133
31. Marussy, K., Buza, K.: SUCCESS: a new approach for semi-supervised classification of time-series. In: Rutkowski, L., Korytkowski, M., Scherer, R., Tadeusiewicz, R., Zadeh, L.A., Zurada, J.M. (eds.) ICAISC 2013. LNCS (LNAI), vol. 7894, pp. 437–447. Springer, Heidelberg (2013). https://doi.org/10.1007/978-3-642-38658-9_39
32. Nidhyananthan, S.S., Shebiah, R.N., Kumari, B.V., Gopalakrishnan, K.: Chapter 15 - deep learning for accident avoidance in a hostile driving environment. In: Zhang, Y.D., Sangaiah, A.K. (eds.) Cognitive Systems and Signal Processing in Image Processing, pp. 337–357. Cognitive Data Science in Sustainable Computing, Academic Press (2022). https://doi.org/10.1016/B978-0-12-824410-4.00002-7
33. Pincus, S., Kalman, R.: Irregularity, volatility, risk, and financial market time series. In: Proceedings of the National Academy of Sciences of the USA, vol. 101, pp. 13709–13714 (2004)
34. Pino, F.A.: Sazonalidade na agricultura. Revista De Economia Agrícola (Printed) **61**, 63–93 (2014)
35. Saeed, A., Ozcelebi, T., Lukkien, J.: Multi-task self-supervised learning for human activity detection. CoRR abs/1907.11879 (2019)
36. Saito, N.: Local feature extraction and its applications using a library of bases. Yale University (1994)
37. Schäfer, P.: The boss is concerned with time series classification in the presence of noise. Data Min. Knowl. Disc. **29**, 1505–1530 (2015)

38. Schäfer, P.: The BOSS is concerned with time series classification in the presence of noise. Data Min. Knowl. Disc. **29**(6), 1505–1530 (2014). https://doi.org/10.1007/s10618-014-0377-7

39. de Sousa, C.A.R., Rezende, S.O., Batista, G.E.A.P.A.: Influence of graph construction on semi-supervised learning. In: Blockeel, H., Kersting, K., Nijssen, S., Železný, F. (eds.) ECML PKDD 2013. LNCS (LNAI), vol. 8190, pp. 160–175. Springer, Heidelberg (2013). https://doi.org/10.1007/978-3-642-40994-3_11

40. Tan, C., Sun, F., Kong, T., Zhang, W., Yang, C., Liu, C.: A survey on deep transfer learning. In: Kůrková, V., Manolopoulos, Y., Hammer, B., Iliadis, L., Maglogiannis, I. (eds.) ICANN 2018. LNCS, vol. 11141, pp. 270–279. Springer, Cham (2018). https://doi.org/10.1007/978-3-030-01424-7_27

41. Van Engelen, J.E., Hoos, H.H.: A survey on semi-supervised learning. Mach. Learn. **109**(2), 373–440 (2020)

42. Volna, E., Kotyrba, M., Habiballa, H.: ECG prediction based on classification via neural networks and linguistic fuzzy logic forecaster. Sci. World J. **2015**, 205749 (2015). https://doi.org/10.1155/2015/205749

43. Wang, Z., Oates, T.: Encoding time series as images for visual inspection and classification using tiled convolutional neural networks. In: Workshops at the Twenty-ninth AAAI Conference on Artificial Intelligence (2015)

44. Wang, Z., Oates, T.: Imaging time-series to improve classification and imputation. In: Proceedings of the 24th International Conference on Artificial Intelligence, pp. 3939–3945. AAAI Press (2015)

45. Wang, Z., Yan, W., Oates, T.: Time series classification from scratch with deep neural networks: a strong baseline. In: 2017 International Joint Conference on Neural Networks (IJCNN), pp. 1578–1585. IEEE (2017)

46. Waskom, M.L.: Seaborn: statistical data visualization. J. Open Sourc. Softw. **6**(60), 3021 (2021)

47. Wei, L., Keogh, E.: Semi-supervised time series classification. In: Proceedings of the 12th ACM SIGKDD International Conference on Knowledge Discovery and Data Mining, pp. 748–753 (2006)

48. Zhou, D., Bousquet, O., Lal, T., Weston, J., Schölkopf, B.: Learning with local and global consistency. In: Advances in Neural Information Processing Systems, vol. 16 (2003)

49. Zhu, X., Ghahramani, Z.: Learning from labeled and unlabeled data with label propagation (2002)

# Construction of Torus of Revolution Generated from Epicycloids

Daniel A. Flores-Cordova🆔, Carlos E. Arellano- Ramírez🆔,
Robert Ipanaqué-Chero🆔, Felícita M. Velásquez-Fernández$^{(\boxtimes)}$🆔,
and Ricardo Velezmoro-León🆔

Universidad Nacional de Piura, Urb. Miraflores s/n Castilla, Piura, Peru
{dflores,carellanor,ripanaquec,fvelasquezf,rvelezmorol}@unp.edu.pe

**Abstract.** Among the geometric bodies of revolution, the torus of revolution stands out, which can be generated from a circumference, lemniscate curves and the figure-of-eight curve. Given the classical definition used in Mathematics, interest arises in finding other curves that generate the torus of revolution when rotating around an axis. In this article, carrying out the respective analyzes and the necessary programming using the Mathematica software, allowed us to carry out the necessary calculations and geometric visualizations of the mathematical object: This is how a torus of revolution was built from epicycloid curves in their parametric form. The study was extended by determining curves that were on the torus generated by epicycloid curves, which when properly projected to planes, curves that present beautiful symmetries were obtained. When the points of these curves are taken correctly, special irregular polygons are obtained.

With the obtaining of these results, a satisfactory answer to the research question was obtained, as well as a way of defining it. In addition, it has shown us a wide path of research on the different curves that a torus of revolution can generate.

**Keywords:** Torus · revolution · epicycloides

## 1 Introduction

The word torus comes from the latin word torus which means curved elevation, it has a specific geometric shape. Topologically, it is a closed orientable surface of genus 1. Within the tori of revolution we already have three types of basic curves that generate tori of revolution, the first one based on a circumference that is well known, you can torus of revolution with Bernoulli lemniscates [1] and then it is possible to define spatial curves with curvatures and non-zero torsion that generate tori of revolution that in some cases coincide with the tori generated by circumferences. And thirdly, it is possible to generate torus of revolution by the curve of eight, in this case the equations are simpler than the lemniscatic torus [2]. Given what has been described, the research question

ⓒ The Author(s), under exclusive license to Springer Nature Switzerland AG 2023
O. Gervasi et al. (Eds.): ICCSA 2023, LNCS 13957, pp. 66–83, 2023.
https://doi.org/10.1007/978-3-031-36808-0_5

arises: can toruses of revolution be generated from epicycloidal curves? Through an exhaustive analysis and the use of Mathematica software [3–5] as a graphic visualization tool, we were able to verify that new torus of revolution can be generated. The torus of revolution have multiple applications in different fields from making geometric designs of polygons, polyhedrons [6,7] and even antennas [8], particle accelerators with their quasi-toroidal shape, in optics with toric surfaces and in the world of the video games.

## 2   The Epicycloid

The present research work is based on the definition of an epicycloid. For this we will see the formal definition of the epitrochoid [9], taking into account Fig. 1.

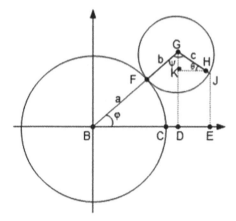

**Fig. 1.** Circle of radius b moving through another circle of radius a to generate an epitrochoid

They obtained the equation of the ep itrochoid.

$$epitro(t) = \left((a + b)cos(\varphi) - c\ cos\left(\tfrac{a+b}{b}\right)\varphi, (a + b)sin(\varphi) - c\ sin\left(\tfrac{a+b}{b}\right)\varphi\right)$$

If in the previous equation we make b=c we will have the Epicycloid equation.

$$epici(t) = \left((a + b)cos(\varphi) - b\ cos\left(\tfrac{a+b}{b}\right)\varphi, (a + b)sin(\varphi) - b\ sin\left(\tfrac{a+b}{b}\right)\varphi\right)$$

For research purposes we are interested in the case when $b > c$.
Let's look at a specific example. Previously we defined with Mathematica.

$$\text{Epitro}[t_-, \{a_-, b_-, c_-\}] := \left\{(a+b)\text{Cos}[t] - c\ Cos\left(\frac{(a+b)}{b}t\right), (a+b)\text{Sin}[t] - c\ \text{Sin}\left(\frac{(a+b)}{b}t\right)\right\}$$

$$\text{Epitro}[\ t, \{4, 4, 1.5\}]$$
$$\{10\ Cos[t] - Cos[5t], 10\ Sin[t] - Sin[5t]\}$$

$$\text{Epitro}[t, \{8, 1, 2\}]$$
$$\{9\ Cos[t] - 2\ Cos[9t], 9\ Sin[t] - 2\ Sin[9t]\}$$

$$\text{ParametricPlot}[\text{Epitro}[t, \{4, 4, 1.5\}], \{t, 0, 2\pi\}, \text{PlotStyle} \rightarrow \text{Hue}[\text{Random}[]]]$$
$$\text{ParametricPlot}[\text{Epitro}[t, \{8, 1, 2\}], \{t, 0, 2\pi\}, \text{PlotStyle} \rightarrow \text{Hue}[\text{Random}[]]]$$

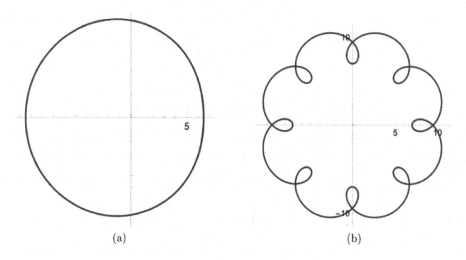

(a)                                          (b)

**Fig. 2.** (a) Epitro[t,4,4,1.5] and (b) Epitro[t,8,1,2]

## 3   Generation of the Torus of Revolution from an Epicycloid

If we have an epicycloid given in parametric form (Figs. 2, 3, 4, 5, 6, 7, 8, 9, 10, 11, 12, 13, 14, 15, 16, 17, 18, 19, 20, 21, 22):

$$\text{Epici3D}(u_-, (a_-, b_-), B) = (B, 0, 0) + \left((a+b)Cos[u] - b\ Cos\left[\frac{(a+b)}{b}u\right], 0,\right.$$
$$\left.(a+b)Sin[u] - b\ Sin\left[\frac{(a+b)}{b}u\right]\right)$$

Which obviously rests in the plane $x = B$, if it rotates around the "Z" axis then we would have the following equation:

$$\textbf{ToroEpici}(u,v,a) = \begin{pmatrix} \textbf{Cos}(v) & \textbf{Sin}(v) & 0 \\ -\textbf{Sin}(v) & \textbf{Cos}(v) & 0 \\ 0 & 0 & 1 \end{pmatrix} \begin{pmatrix} B + (a+b)\textbf{Cos}[u] - b \ \textbf{Cos}\left[\frac{a+b}{b}u\right] \\ 0 \\ (a+b)\textbf{Sin}[u] - b \ \textbf{Sin}\left[\frac{a+b}{b}u\right] \end{pmatrix}$$

Performing the matrix calculations is as follows:

$$\textbf{ToroEpici}(u,v,a) = \left(\left(B + (a+b)\textbf{Cos}[u] - b \ \textbf{Cos}\left[\frac{(a+b)}{b}u\right]\right)\textbf{Cos}[v],\right.$$

$$\left.\left(B + (a+b)\textbf{Cos}[u] - b \ \textbf{Cos}\left[\frac{(a+b)}{b}u\right]\right)\textbf{Sin}[v], (a+b)\textbf{Sin}[u] - b \ \textbf{Sin}\left[\frac{(a+b)}{b}u\right]\right) \quad (1)$$

The domain of said parameterization is defined by:
$D: -\frac{\pi}{2} < u < \frac{\pi}{2}$ y $0 < v < 2\pi$
We graph with Mathematica.
Now, we define the **ToroEpici** with the Mathematica software taking into account the definition of rotation and Eq. (1)

$$\textbf{Rotz}[\theta\_] := \{\{\textbf{Cos}[\theta], -\textbf{Sin}[\theta], \theta\}, \{\textbf{Sin}[\theta], \textbf{Cos}[\theta], \theta\}, \{0, 0, 1\}\}$$
$$\textbf{ToroEpici}[\{u\_, v\_\}, \{a\_, b\_\}, B] := \textbf{Rotz}[v] \cdot \textbf{Epici3D}[u, \{a, b\}, B]$$

Then explicitly with Mathematica we get it:

$$TorEpici[\{u, v\}, \{a, b\}, B]$$

$$\left\{\left(B + (a+b)\textbf{Cos}[u] - b \ \left[\frac{(a+b)}{b}u\right]\right)\textbf{Cos}[v],\right.$$

$$\left(B + (a+b)\textbf{Cos}[u] - b \ \textbf{Cos}\left[\frac{(a+b)}{b}u\right]\right)\textbf{Sin}[v], \quad (2)$$

$$\left.(a+b)\textbf{Sin}[u] - b \ \textbf{Sin}\left[\frac{(a+b)}{b}u\right]\right\}$$

### 3.1    Examples of Epicycloidal Torus

We will show three concrete examples:
**Example 01**
If from Eq. 2 we give the values $a = 1$, b$= \frac{1}{4}$ and $B = 2$ we obtain with the Mathematica software.

$$TorEpici[\{u,v\},\{1,\tfrac{1}{4}\},2]$$

$$\left\{\left(2+\frac{5\cos[u]}{4}-\frac{1}{4}\mathrm{Cos}[5u]\right)\mathrm{Cos}[v],\right.$$

$$\left.\left(2+\frac{5\cos[u]}{4}-\frac{1}{4}\mathrm{Cos}[5u]\right)\mathrm{Sin}[v],\frac{5\sin[u]}{4}-\frac{1}{4}\mathrm{Sin}[5u]\right\}$$

By graphing this surface we have a geometric object that looks like a yo-yo.

**g0 = ParametricPlot3D[TorEpici[$\{u,v\}$, $\{1,1/4\}$, 2], $\{u,0,2\pi\}$,**
**$\{v,0,2\pi\}$, PlotStyle → Opacity[0.6], Mesh → False, PlotPoints → 75]**

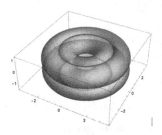

**Fig. 3.** Yo-yo surface.

We have the graphs of the u-parametric curves and the v-parametric curves.

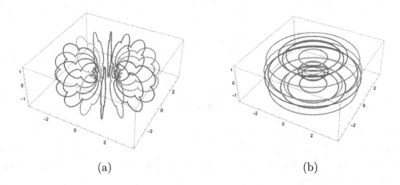

(a)                                (b)

**Fig. 4.** (a) The parametric u-curves on the yoyo surface. (b) The parametric v-curves on the yoyo surface.

**Example 02**

If from Eq. 2 we give the values $a = 1$, $b = \frac{1}{6}$ and $B = 2$ we obtain with the Mathematica software.

$$\textbf{TorEpici}[\{u, v\}, \{1, \frac{1}{6}\}, 2]$$

$$\left\{\left(2 + \frac{7\textbf{Cos}[u]}{6} - \frac{1}{6}\textbf{Cos}[7u]\right)\textbf{Cos}[v],\right.$$

$$\left.\left(2 + \frac{7\textbf{Cos}[u]}{6} - \frac{1}{6}\textbf{Cos}[7u]\right)\textbf{Sin}[v], \frac{7\textbf{Sin}[u]}{6} - \frac{1}{6}\textbf{Sin}[7u]\right\}$$

$$\textbf{g1} = \textbf{ParametricPlot3D}[\{u, v\}, \{1, \frac{1}{6}\}, 2], \{u, 0, 2\pi\}, \{v, 0, 2\pi\},$$

$$\textbf{PlotStyle} \rightarrow \textbf{Opacity}[0, 6], \textbf{Mesh} \rightarrow \textbf{False}, \textbf{PlotPoints} \rightarrow 75]$$

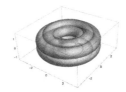

**Fig. 5.** $ToroEpici[\{u, v\}, \{1, \frac{1}{6}\}, 2]$ .

We have the graphs of the u-parametric curves and the v-parametric curves.

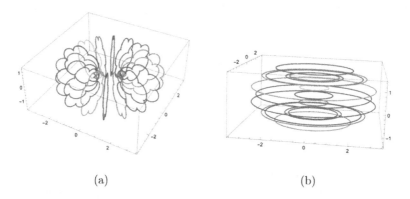

(a)                                              (b)

**Fig. 6.** (a) The parametric u curves of $ToroEpici[\{u, v\}, \{1, \frac{1}{6}\}, 2]$ and (b) The parametric v curves of $ToroEpici[\{u, v\}, \{1, \frac{1}{6}\}, 2]$

**Example 03**

If from Eq. 2 we give the values $a = 1$, $b = \frac{1}{16}$ and $B = 2$ we obtain with the Mathematica software

$$\mathbf{TorEpici}[\{u, v\}, \{1, \frac{1}{16}\}, 2]$$

$$\left\{ \left(2 + \frac{17\mathbf{Cos}[u]}{16} - \frac{1}{16}\mathbf{Cos}[17u]\right) \mathbf{Cos}[v], \right.$$

$$\left. \left(2 + \frac{17\mathbf{Cos}[u]}{16} - \frac{1}{16}\mathbf{Cos}[17u]\right) \mathbf{Sin}[v], \frac{17\mathbf{Sin}[u]}{16} - \frac{1}{16}\mathbf{Sin}[17u]\right\}$$

$$\mathbf{g2} = \mathbf{ParametricPlot3D}[\{u, v\}, \{1, \frac{1}{16}\}, 2], \{u, 0, 2\pi\}, \{v, 0, 2\pi\},$$

$$\mathbf{PlotStyle} \rightarrow \mathbf{Opacity}[0, 6], \mathbf{Mesh} \rightarrow \mathbf{False}, \mathbf{PlotPoints} \rightarrow 75]$$

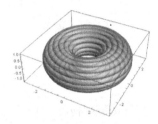

**Fig. 7.** $ToroEpici[\{u, v\}, \{1, \frac{1}{16}\}, 2]$ .

We have the graphs of the u-parametric curves and the v-parametric curves.

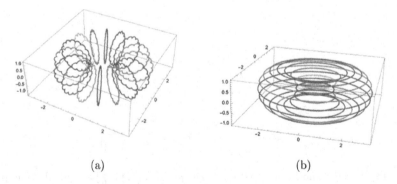

(a)                                    (b)

**Fig. 8.** (a) The parametric u curves of $ToroEpici[\{u, v\}, \{1, \frac{1}{16}\}, 2]$ and (b) The parametric v curves of $ToroEpici[\{u, v\}, \{1, \frac{1}{16}\}, 2]$

## 4    Parametric Curves in Epicycloidal Torus

Taking Eq. 2 into account, an infinite number of curves are defined in the epicyclic torus in the following way, we assume that we have a parametric function $\alpha(t) = (\alpha_1(t), \alpha_2(t))$ and we substitute in Eq. 2 $u = \alpha_1(t)$ $y$ $v = \alpha_2(t)$, with the Mathematica software it is defined in the following way.

$$\textbf{Curva1}[\textbf{t\_}, \{\textbf{a\_}, \textbf{b\_}, \textbf{B\_}\}, \alpha : \{\_, \_\}] :=$$
$$\textbf{TorEpici}[\{\textbf{u}, \textbf{v}\}, \{ \textbf{a}, \textbf{b}\}, \textbf{B}]] / .\{\textbf{u} \rightarrow \alpha[[1]], \textbf{v} \rightarrow \alpha[[2]]\}$$

(3)

### 4.1    The Curve $Curve1[t, \{1, 1/4, 2\}, \{6t, 5t\}]$

If from Eq. 3 we give the values $/a = 1$, $b = 1/4$ $and$ $B = 2, \alpha_1(t) = 6t$, $\alpha_2(t) = 5t$, we obtain with the Mathematica software.

$\textbf{Curva1}[\textbf{t}, \{1, 1/4, 2, \{6t, 5t\}]$

$$\left\{ Cos[5t] \left( 2 + \frac{5}{4}Cos[6t] - \frac{1}{4}Cos[30t] \right), \right.$$
$$\left. \left( 2 + \frac{5}{4}Cos[6t] - \frac{1}{4}Cos[30t] \right) Sin[5t], \frac{5}{4}Sin[6t] - \frac{1}{4}Sin[30t] \right\}$$

The graph is obtained with The graph of the curve alone is shown and the other the curve resting on the epicyclic torus.

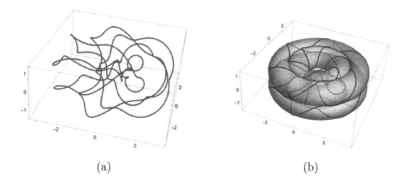

(a)                                        (b)

**Fig. 9.** (a) Curve1[t,1,1/4,2,6t,5t] (b) Curva1 resting on the epicilloidal torus that contains it.

We project this curve onto the z=0 plane and call it $\beta_1(t)$.

$\beta1[t\_] := \textbf{Delete}[\textbf{Curva1}[t, \{1, 1/4, 2\}, 6t, 5t], 3]$
$\beta1[t]$

$$\left\{ Cos[5t] \left( 2 + \frac{5}{4}Cos[6t] - \frac{1}{4}Cos[30t] \right), \left( 2 + \frac{5}{4}Cos[6t] - \frac{1}{4}Cos[30t] \right) Sin[5t] \right\}$$

The graph is obtained by

$$pc\alpha 1 = ParametricPlot[\beta 1[t], \{t, 0, 2\pi\}, PlotStyle \rightarrow Hue[0.75], Axes \rightarrow False]$$

**Fig. 10.** $Curva1 = \beta_1(t)$

The curve is symmetric about the ordinate axes and the origin.

**Some Polygons on Curva1[t].** In this curve are immersed equilateral triangles, regular hexagons, regular dodecahedrons, dodecaangulos etc.

### Dodecaangle

This polyhedron is generated from the points:

$$P_1 = \left(-sin\left[\frac{\pi}{16}\right]\left(2 + \frac{5}{4}cos\left[\frac{\pi}{8}\right] + \frac{1}{4}sin\left[\frac{\pi}{8}\right]\right), -cos\left[\frac{\pi}{16}\right]\left(2 + \frac{5}{4}cos\left[\frac{\pi}{8}\right] + \frac{1}{4}sin\left[\frac{\pi}{8}\right]\right)\right)$$

$$P_2 = \left(sin\left[\frac{\pi}{16}\right]\left(2 + \frac{5}{4}cos\left[\frac{\pi}{8}\right] + \frac{1}{4}sin\left[\frac{\pi}{8}\right]\right), -cos\left[\frac{\pi}{16}\right]\left(2 + \frac{5}{4}cos\left[\frac{\pi}{8}\right] + \frac{1}{4}sin\left[\frac{\pi}{8}\right]\right)\right)$$

These points are generated with Mathematica as follows:

$pol0 = \beta 1 /@\{11\pi/16, 5\pi/16\}$

$$\left\{\left\{-Sin\left[\frac{\pi}{16}\right]\left(2 + \frac{5}{4}Cos\left[\frac{\pi}{8}\right] + \frac{1}{4}Sin\left[\frac{\pi}{8}\right]\right), -Cos\left[\frac{\pi}{16}\right]\left(2 + \frac{5}{4}Cos\left[\frac{\pi}{8}\right] + \frac{1}{4}Sin\left[\frac{\pi}{8}\right]\right)\right\},\right.$$

$$\left.\left\{Sin\left[\frac{\pi}{16}\right]\left(2 + \frac{5}{4}Cos\left[\frac{\pi}{8}\right] + \frac{1}{4}Sin\left[\frac{\pi}{8}\right]\right), -Cos\left[\frac{\pi}{16}\right]\left(2 + \frac{5}{4}Cos\left[\frac{\pi}{8}\right] + \frac{1}{4}Sin\left[\frac{\pi}{8}\right]\right)\right\}\right\}$$

The distance of these points from the origin is

$$Norm/@polo0//Simplify$$

To generate the other points:

**rpol0 = Partition[Flatten[Table[Table[RotationMatrix[$\theta$] $\cdot$ pol0[[i]], $\{i, 2\}$]**

$\{\theta, 0, 2\pi - \frac{\pi}{3}, \frac{\pi}{3}\}]], 2];$

The length of the sides in alternating form is
{1.26829, 208969, 1.26829, 208969, 1.26829, 208969, 1.26829, 208969,
1.26829, 208969, 1.26829, 208969, }
The graph of the first polygon with the curve $\beta_1[t]$ is shown below.

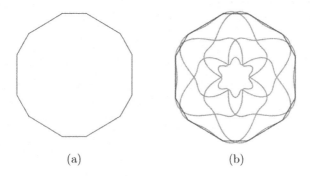

(a)                                (b)

**Fig. 11.** (a) Dodecangle (b) Dodecangle on the curve $\beta_1(t)$

## 24 sided polygon
This polyhedron is generated from the points:

$$P_1 = \left(-sin\left[\frac{\pi}{16}\right]\left(2+\frac{5}{4}cos\left[\frac{\pi}{8}\right]+\frac{1}{4}sin\left[\frac{\pi}{8}\right]\right), -cos\left[\frac{\pi}{16}\right]\left(2+\frac{5}{4}cos\left[\frac{\pi}{8}\right]+\frac{1}{4}sin\left[\frac{\pi}{8}\right]\right)\right)$$

$$P_2 = \left(sin\left[\frac{\pi}{16}\right]\left(2+\frac{5}{4}cos\left[\frac{\pi}{8}\right]+\frac{1}{4}sin\left[\frac{\pi}{8}\right]\right), -cos\left[\frac{\pi}{16}\right]\left(2+\frac{5}{4}cos\left[\frac{\pi}{8}\right]+\frac{1}{4}sin\left[\frac{\pi}{8}\right]\right)\right)$$

These points are generated with Mathematica as follows

**pol1** $= \beta1/@\{7\pi/24, 17\pi/24\}$

$$\left\{\left\{-\left(\left(2+\frac{3}{2\sqrt{2}}\right)Sin\left[\frac{\pi}{24}\right]\right), -\left(\left(2+\frac{3}{2\sqrt{2}}\right)Cos\left[\frac{\pi}{24}\right]\right)\right\},\right.$$
$$\left.\left\{\left(2+\frac{3}{2\sqrt{2}}\right)Sin\left[\frac{\pi}{24}\right], -\left(\left(2+\frac{3}{2\sqrt{2}}\right)Cos\left[\frac{\pi}{24}\right]\right)\right\}\right\}$$

The distance of these two points from the origin is:

**Norm/@pol1//Simplify**

$$\left\{\frac{1}{2}\sqrt{\frac{41}{2}+12\sqrt{2}}, \frac{1}{2}\sqrt{\frac{41}{2}+12\sqrt{2}}\right\}$$

We generate the other points as follows

**rpol1 = Partition[Flatten[Table[Table[RotationMatrix[$\theta$] · pol1[[$i$]], {$i$, 2}**
**{$\theta$, 0, 2$\pi$ − $\pi$/6, $\pi$/6}]], 2];**

The length of the sides is 0.798993.
The graph of the second polyhedron with the curve is shown below.

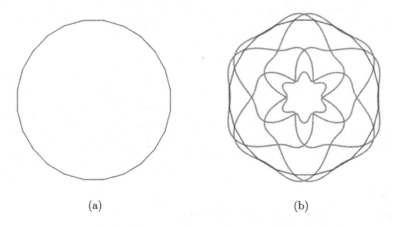

(a)                                      (b)

**Fig. 12.** (a) Dodecangle (b) Dodecangle on the curve $Curva1 = \beta_1(t)$

Obviously this 24-sided polygon has dodecagons, regular hexagons, and equilateral triangles. **_12-sided polygon._** We generate this polygon with the following pair of points FALTA

$$pol2 = \beta1/@\{17\ \pi/16, 13\ \pi/48\ \}//\text{Simplify}$$

$$\left\{\left\{\frac{1}{4}\left(-8+Cos\left[\frac{\pi}{8}\right]-5Sin\left[\frac{\pi}{8}\right]\right)Sin\left[\frac{3\pi}{16}\right], \frac{1}{4}Cos\left[\frac{3\pi}{16}\right]\left(-8+Cos\left[\frac{\pi}{8}\right]-5sin\left[\frac{\pi}{8}\right]\right)\right\}\right.$$
$$\left.\left\{\frac{1}{4}\left(-8+Cos\left[\frac{\pi}{8}\right]-5Sin\left[\frac{\pi}{8}\right]\right)Sin\left[\frac{7\pi}{48}\right], \frac{1}{4}Cos\left[\frac{7\pi}{48}\right]\left(-8+Cos\left[\frac{\pi}{8}\right]-5sin\left[\frac{\pi}{8}\right]\right)\right\}\right\}$$

We generate the other points as follows:

$$rpol2 = Partition[flatten[Table[Table[RotationMatriz[\theta] \cdot pol2[[i]], \{i, 2\}]$$
$$\{\theta, 0, 2\pi - \pi/3, \pi/3\}]], 2];$$

The length of the sides in alternating form is 0.293972 and 1.98799
The graph of the third polyhedron with the curve is shown below.

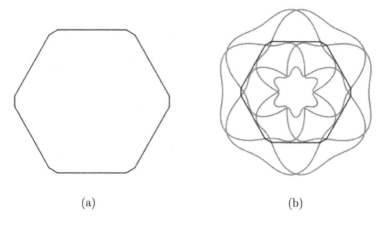

(a)                                          (b)

**Fig. 13.** (a) Dodecangle (b) Dodecangle on the curve Curve $\beta_1(t)$

## 4.2   The Curve $Curva1[t, 1, 1/6, 2, 6t, 5t]$

We define the curve as follows

$\mathbf{Curva1}[t, \{1, 1/6, 2\}, \{6t, 5t\}]//\mathbf{Simplify}$

$$\Big\{ -\frac{1}{6}Cos[5t](-12 - 7Cos[6t] + Cos[42t]),$$

$$-\frac{1}{6}(-12 - 7Cos[6t] + Cos[42t])Sin[5t], \frac{1}{6}(7Sin[6t] - Sin[42t]) \Big\}$$

The graph of the curve and the torus that contains it is shown in the following figure.

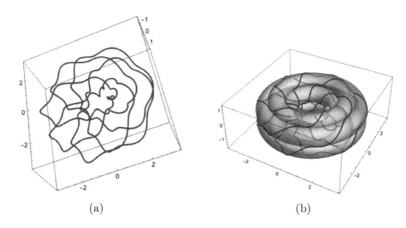

(a)                                          (b)

**Fig. 14.** (a) $Curve1[t, 1, 1/6, 2, 6t, 5t]$ (b) Curve1 resting on the epicyclic torus that contains it

We project it to the plane z=0 with.

$\beta 2[t\_] := \textbf{Delete}[\textbf{Curva1}[t, \{1, 1/6, 2\}, \{6t, 5t\}], 3]$

$$\left\{ Cos[5t]\left(2 + \frac{7}{6}Cos[6t] - \frac{1}{6}Cos[42t]\right), \left(2 + \frac{7}{6}Cos[6t] - \frac{1}{6}Cos[42t]\right)Sin[5t]\right\}$$

And we get its graph.

**Fig. 15.** Curve $\beta_2(t)$

The graph is obviously symmetric to the ordered axes and the origin.

### First Polygon in the curve $\beta_2[t]$
We generated this first polygon with:

$\textbf{Pol00} = \beta 2/@\{95\pi/64, 97\pi/64\}//Simplify$

$$\left\{\left\{-\frac{2}{3}\left(3 + 2Cos\left[\frac{\pi}{8}\right]\right)Sin\left[\frac{5\pi}{64}\right], -\frac{2}{3}Cos\left[\frac{5\pi}{64}\right]\left(3 + 2Cos\left[\frac{\pi}{8}\right]\right)\right\},\right.$$
$$\left.\left\{\left(2 + \frac{4}{3}Cos\left[\frac{\pi}{8}\right]\right)Sin\left[\frac{5\pi}{64}\right], -\frac{2}{3}Cos\left[\frac{5\pi}{64}\right]\left(3 + 2Cos\left[\frac{\pi}{8}\right]\right)\right\}\right\}$$

Then we generate 16 points in total

$\textbf{N[rPol00} =$
$\textbf{Partition}[\textbf{Flatten}[\textbf{Table}[\textbf{Table}[\textbf{RotationMatrix}[\theta] \cdot \textbf{Pol00}[[i]], \{i, 2\}] ,$
$\{\theta, 0, 2\pi - \pi/4, \pi/4\}]], 2], 3]$

$\{\{-0.785, -3.13\}, \{0.785, 3.13\}, \{1.66, -2.77\}, \{2.77, -1.66\}, \{3.13, -0.785\},$
$\{3.13, 0785\}, \{2.77, 1.66\}, \{1.66, 2.77\}, \{0.785, 3.13\}, \{-0.785, 3.13\},$
$\{-1.66, 2.77\}, \{-2.77, 1.66\}, \{-3.13, 0.785\}, \{-3.13, -0.785\}, \{-2.77, -1.66\}$
$\{-1.66, -2.77\}\}$

The internal angles have a measure of $\theta_1 = 2.74889$ radians, and the alternating side lengths are 1.57055 and 0.948419.

The graph of this polygon is:

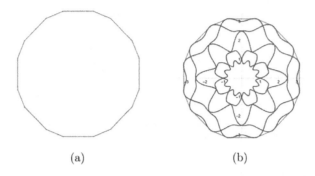

(a)                              (b)

**Fig. 16.** (a) curve $\beta 2[t]$ (b) Curve $\beta 2$ and the first 16-sided polygon

The first polygon in the curve $\beta_2[t]$ has embedded two regular octagons whose angles in radians measure 2.35619 and the length of the side is 2.47354.
The two regular octagons are shown, and also the 16-sided polygon next to the two regular octagons.

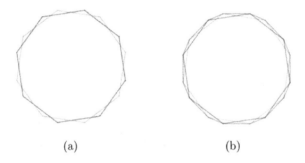

(a)                              (b)

**Fig. 17.** (a) The octagons (b) Octagons and the 16-sided polygon

**Second polygon on the $\beta 2[t]$ curve.**
We generate this polynomial with the points

**Pol2 $\beta$ 2 /@ {191Pi/128,193Pi/128} // Simplify**

$$\left\{\left\{-\frac{1}{6}Sin\left[\frac{5\pi}{128}\right]\left(12+7Cos\left[\frac{\pi}{16}\right]-Sin\left[\frac{\pi}{16}\right]\right),\right.\right.$$
$$\left.-\frac{1}{6}Cos\left[\frac{5\pi}{128}\right]\left(12+7Cos\left[\frac{\pi}{16}\right]-Sin\left[\frac{\pi}{16}\right]\right)\right\},$$
$$\left\{\frac{1}{6}Sin\left[\frac{5\pi}{128}\right]\left(12+7Cos\left[\frac{\pi}{16}\right]-Sin\left[\frac{\pi}{16}\right]\right),\right.$$
$$\left.\left.-\frac{1}{6}Cos\left[\frac{5\pi}{128}\right]\left(12+7Cos\left[\frac{\pi}{16}\right]-Sin\left[\frac{\pi}{16}\right]\right)\right\}\right\}$$

The rest of the points are generated with

**N[rPol2 =**
**Partition[Flatten[Table[Table[RotationMatrix[$\theta$] · Pol2[[i]], {i, 2}] ,**
**{$\theta$, 0, 2$\pi$ − $\pi$/4, $\pi$/4}]], 2], 2]**

nternal angles have a measure of $\theta_1 = 2.74889$ radians. And the alternating side lengths are 0.7619 and 1.65988. Next, we show the graph.

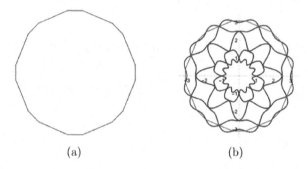

(a)                          (b)

**Fig. 18.** (a) curve $\beta2[t]$ and $\beta2[t]$ and the second 16-sided polygon

The second polygon on the curve $\beta_2[t]$ has embedded two regular octagons whose angles in radians measure 2.35619 and the length of the side is 2.38162. The two regular octagons are shown, and also the second 16-sided polygon next to the two regular octagons.

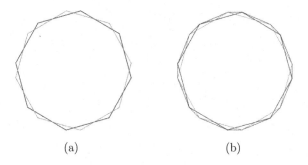

**Fig. 19.** (a) Octagons. (b) Octagons and the second 16-sided polygon.

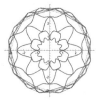

**Fig. 20.** The curve $\beta_2$ , the octagons and the two 16-sided polygons.

### 4.3  La Curva Curva1[t,1,1/16,2,6t,5t].

We take a third curve.

$$\textbf{Curva1}[\text{t},\{1,1/16,2\},\{6t,5t\}]//\text{Simplify}$$

$$\left\{ \frac{1}{16}Cos[5t]\left(32 + 17Cos[6t] - Cos[102t]\right), \right.$$
$$\left. \frac{1}{16}\left(32 + 17Cos[6t] - Cos[102t]\right)Sin[5t], \frac{1}{16}\left(17Sin[6t] - Sin[102t]\right) \right\}$$

The graph of the curve and the torus that contains it is shown in the following figure.

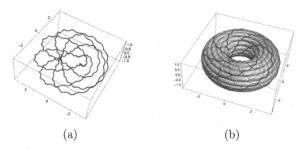

**Fig. 21.** (a) $Curve1[t, \{1, 1/16, 2\}, \{6t, 5t\}]$ (b) Curve 1 alone resting on the epicilloidal torus that contains it.

We project it to the plane z=0 with.

$$\beta 3[t] := \textbf{Delete}[\textbf{Curva1}[t, \{1, 1/16, 2\}, \{6t, 5t\}], 3]$$

$$\beta 3[t]$$

$$\left\{ Cos[5t] \left( 2 + \frac{17}{16} Cos[6t] - \frac{1}{16} Cos[102t] \right), \left( 2 + \frac{17}{16} Cos[6t] - \frac{1}{16} Cos[102t] \right) Sin[5t] \right\}$$

$$gbeta3 = ParametricPlot[\beta 3[t], \{t, 0, 2\pi\} PlotStyle \rightarrow Hue[0.75], PlotPints \rightarrow 75]$$

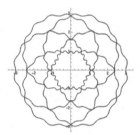

**Fig. 22.** The curve $\beta_2[t]$.

As can be seen, the graph is symmetric with respect to the axes and the origin.

## 5   Conclusions

According to the results found, it is concluded that a torus of revolution can be built in its generic form from the epicyclic curve:

$$\textbf{ToroEpici}(u, v, a) = \left( \left( B + (a + b)\textbf{Cos}[u] - b \ \textbf{Cos} \left[ \frac{(a + b)}{b} u \right] \right) \textbf{Cos}[v], \right.$$

$$\left. \left( B + (a + b)\textbf{Cos}[u] - b \ \textbf{Cos} \left[ \frac{(a + b)}{b} u \right] \right) \textbf{Sin}[v], (a + b)\textbf{Sin}[u] - b \ \textbf{Sin} \left[ \frac{(a + b)}{b} u \right] \right)$$

$$D : -\frac{\pi}{2} < u < \frac{\pi}{2} \ y \ 0 < v < 2\pi$$

Taking into account the equation: **Curva1**$[t\_, \{a\_, b\_, B\_\}, \alpha : \{\_, \_\}] :=$ **TorEpici**$[\{u, v\}, \{ a, b\}, B\}]/.\{u \rightarrow \alpha[[1]], v \rightarrow \alpha[[2]]\}$

An infinite number of curves are defined in the epicyclic torus. Some existing spatial curves on the torus generated by epicycloidal curves were analyzed, taking into account the projections to the XY plane, observing the existing symmetries. Points were taken from the curves that would be the vertices of special polygons such as: 24-sided polygons, 16-sided polygons, 12-sided polygons, octagons.

It is recommended to deepen the study of the polygons that are generated with the projection of special curves that are on the torus generated by an epicyclic curve.

# References

1. Vegas Ordinola, S.; Silupu Suarez, C. Construcción de toros de revolución, a partir de curvas planas y espaciales, con curvatura no constante o torsión no nula, utilizando el Mathematica https://alicia.concytec.gob.pe/vufind/Record/RUMP_6d7ad06b0ec78269746beb32a749f9c0/Details. Accessed 20 Aarch 2023
2. Velásquez-Fernández, F.M., Vega-Ordinola, S.P., Silupu-Suarez, C.E., Ipanaqué-Chero, R., Velezmoro-León, R.: Torus of revolution generated by curves of eight. In: Gervasi, O., Murgante, B., Hendrix, E.M.T., Taniar, D., Apduhan, B.O. (eds.) Computational Science and Its Applications - ICCSA 2022. ICCSA 2022. LNCS, vol 13375. Springer, Cham (2022). https://doi.org/10.1007/978-3-031-10522-7_27
3. Wolfram, S.: The Mathematica Book, 4th edn. Cambridge University Press, Champaign, Cambridge, Wolfram Media (1999)
4. Maeder, R.: Programming in Mathematica, 2nd edn. Addison-Wesley, Redwood City (1991)
5. Volkert, K.: On models for visualizing four-dimensional figures. Math. Intell. **39**, 27–35 (2017). https://doi.org/10.1007/s00283-016-9699-1
6. Velezmoro-León, R., Ipanaqué-Chero, R., Velásquez-Fernández, F.M., Gomez, J.J.: Construction of a convex polyhedron from a Lemniscatic Torus. In: Saraswat, M., Sharma, H., Balachandran, K., Kim, J.H., Bansal, J.C. (eds.) Congress on Intelligent Systems. LNDECT, vol. 114. Springer, Singapore (2022). https://doi.org/10.1007/978-981-16-9416-5_65
7. Velezmoro-León, R., Ipanaqué-Chero, R., Fernández, M.V., Gomez, J.J.: Construction of polyhedra whose vertices are points on curve which lying on lemniscatic torus with mathematica. In: Gervasi, O., et al. (eds.) ICCSA 2021. LNCS, vol. 12950, pp. 3–17. Springer, Cham (2021). https://doi.org/10.1007/978-3-030-86960-1_1
8. Velezmoro-León, R., Arellano-Ramírez, C.E., Flores-Córdova, D.A., Ipanaqué-Chero, R.: Using Mathematica and 4Nec2 to design and simulation of an antenna in 2100 and 3500 MHz bands. In: et al. Computational Science and Its Applications - ICCSA 2021. ICCSA 2021. LNCS, vol. 12951. Springer, Cham (2021). https://doi.org/10.1007/978-3-030-86970-0_12
9. Heredia Ordinola, A., Gonzáles Lafosse, J.: Simulación del movimiento de la luna teniendo como sistema de referencia al sol con asistencia del sotfware Mathematica https://renati.sunedu.gob.pe/handle/sunedu/3204484. Accessed 20 Aarch 2023

# Advanced and Emerging Applications

# AutoML Framework for Labor Potential Modeling

Vladislav Kovalevsky[1](✉) ⓘ, Elena Stankova[2] ⓘ, Nataly Zhukova[1] ⓘ,
Oksana Ogiy[3] ⓘ, and Alexander Tristanov[3] ⓘ

[1] St. Petersburg Federal Research Center of the Russian Academy of Sciences, St. Petersburg,
Russia
darkeol@gmail.com
[2] St. Petersburg State University, St. Petersburg, Russia
[3] Kaliningrad State Technical University, Kaliningrad, Russia

**Abstract.** Labor potential estimation is a complex analysis task of a large data sets of digital profiles of workers. Digital profile is a structure that contains heterogeneous data and has high complexity. The attribute space of digital profiles datasets has a large dimension. Individual features are distinguished by a large variability of types and include qualitative and quantitative characteristics that can be both continuous or discrete. This fact significantly complicates the use of traditional statistical methods and hinder manual selection of machine learning algorithms for labor potential estimation. Automated machine learning (AutoML) can help to deal with this problem. The results of AutoML can significantly depend on the used AutoML library. AutoML libraries differ in the set of algorithms among which they select the best one, in the constrains that are used to stop the search of the optimal solution, in the techniques used for hyperparameters optimization and in metrics that are calculated for the obtained results. In this work we develop an AutoML framework that unites several commonly used AutoML libraries and enables use of common constrains and metrics. Processing dataset about employees' performance using the developed framework we show the applicability of the AutoML for the task of labor potential estimation.

**Keywords:** AutoML · Machine learning · Hyperparameters optimization · Labor potential assessment

## 1 Introduction

### 1.1 Human Capital

One of the important sections of modern economic science is the theory of human capital, which explores the dependence of the income of an individual, enterprise and society as a whole on the abilities of people, their knowledge and skills [1]. The labor potential and its estimation is vital for enterprises to be competitive [2]. However, it should be noted that nowadays there is no single methodological approach to the definition and, especially, the measurement of labor potential.

O. Gervasi et al. (Eds.): ICCSA 2023, LNCS 13957, pp. 87–98, 2023.
https://doi.org/10.1007/978-3-031-36808-0_6

## 1.2   Labor Potential Estimation

Labor potential estimation is a complex analysis task [3] of a large data sets of digital profiles of workers. Digital profile is a structure that contains heterogeneous data type and has high complexity. The attribute space of the digital profile datasets has a large dimension and covers the attributes of four groups of parameters: socio-demographic, spiritual and moral, professional competence and socio-psychological.

The main characteristics of an individual that determine his labor potential are:

- abilities determined by such psychophysiological characteristics as gender, age, functional state of the body, operator working capacity, adaptive potential of health, current mental state, personality traits, character accentuations;
- competence - knowledge, skills, level of education/qualification, total length of service, competency proactivity;
- labor behavior determined by motivation and value orientations.

Individual features are distinguished by a large variability of types and include qualitative and quantitative characteristics that can be both continuous or discrete. This fact significantly complicates the use of traditional methods of statistical analysis.

A prominent approach to labor potential estimation assumes usage of artificial neural networks [4, 5]. However, these methods are complex and require significant efforts to define the architecture and the parameters of the networks. Another approach to labor potential estimation is based on using machine learning (ML) methods. To solve the problem of labor potential estimation various ML methods can be used that capture the dependency between input characteristics and output value based on the analyses of large amount of existing data, but the high complexity of the problem and the characteristics of the processed data, hinder manual selection of machine learning algorithm and tuning its hyperparameters. This leads to the need to automate the process of finding the best algorithm.

An approach that is not limited by only one method but instead searches through many different methods in order to find the one that process the given data in the best way is automated machine learning (AutoML). In the paper the problem of using AutoML for labor potential estimation is considered.

Contribution of this research is the following: 1) An AutoML framework was developed that enables search for appropriate model through several AutoML libraries instead of a single one with support of common metrics and constrains, 2) The efficiency of AutoML approach in solving a problem of labor potential estimation, that is a poorly formalized problem, is shown through the use of the developed framework.

The rest of the paper is organized as follows: In Sect. 2 we describe the problem of labor potential estimation, how AutoML can be used to deal with this problem, and which difficulties can arise while using AutoML. Section 3 gives general overview of the existing AutoML libraries and their comparison. In Sect. 4 we describe the architecture of the proposed AutoML framework that unites several AutoML libraries, considerations by which the libraries were chosen and common metrics that are used by all libraries in evaluation of classification results. In Sect. 5 we show the applicability of the developed framework for the task of labor potential estimation by performing experiment on a dataset that contains information about workers, their characteristics and performance. The paper concludes with a brief summary and discussion about the future work.

## 2 Problem Statement

The task of labor potential estimation can be seen from different points of view. In one cases it can be seen as a classification problem where an individual should be related to the right category of labor potential based on the various attributes that the individual possesses. In another cases labor potential can be expressed not as category, but in numeric form, then the task will be to predict the value of the labor potential given the input attributes. Another approach can be in dividing individuals into clusters based on their potential rather than finding information about specific individual.

The field of machine learning (ML) include many algorithms that build models using data. The algorithms that can be used for labor potential estimations fall in the following categories depending on the specific task that needs to be solved:

- classification - determine class of the object from predefined set of classes;
- regression - predict value of continuous parameters;
- clustering - separate objects into several classes.

Every ML algorithm has its own set of hyperparameters – values that define the work of the algorithm, and these hyperparameters also need to be tuned. Thus the task is - given some dataset find the best possible combination of learning algorithms and their hyperparameters. This task is often referred as "CASH problem" - Combined Algorithm Selection and Hyperparameter Optimization [6, 7].

AutoML methods are suitable to solve the tasks of choosing the best algorithm for the labor potential estimation. By now several AutoML libraries have been developed and thus a problem of choosing the most appropriate one arises. One way to tackle this problem is to unite several AutoML solutions in a common framework. To that end the solutions (AutoML libraries) should be examined in order to find limitations that can prevent to unite the libraries, and also common constrains and metrics that can be used across all solutions included in the framework. Thus the framework should enable following capabilities:

- unite several AutoML libraries and enable their parallel run;
- supply data preprocessing that is needed for each library;
- enable usage of common search constrains for all libraries;
- use common metrics for comparing the results of different libraries.

## 3 Existing AutoML Solutions

Currently there are several AutoML libraries that use different approaches in order to find best combination of machine learning algorithm and its hyperparameters. These solutions share common approach of using underlying machine learning library to select algorithm from. Among the known ones are Auto-WEKA [8], Hyperopt-sklearn [9], Auto-Sklearn [10], TPOT [11], H2O [12] and Auto-Keras [13]. Hyperopt-sklearn, Auto-Sklearn and TPOT search for the suitable algorithm in the Python library Scikit-Learn [14] whereas others use their own implementation of machine learning algorithms. The comparison of the characteristics of the systems is shown in Table 1.

**Table 1.** Comparison of AutoML solutions.

| Solution | Library | Language | OS | GUI |
|---|---|---|---|---|
| Auto-WEKA | WEKA | Java | Cross-platform | Yes |
| Hyperopt-sklearn | Scikit-Learn | Python | Cross-platform | No |
| Auto-sklearn | Scikit-Learn | Python | Linux | No |
| TPOT | Scikit-Learn | Python | Cross-platform | No |
| H2O | H2O | Java/Python | Cross-platform | No |
| Auto-Keras | TensorFlow | Python | Linux | No |

### 3.1 Auto-WEKA

The Auto-WEKA is one of the first AutoML solutions and is built as a plugin to the WEKA program [15] that is written in Java language. Auto-WEKA searches through machine learning algorithms that are presented in WEKA in order to find the most appropriate combination of machine learning algorithm and values of its hyperparameters that can most efficiently process a given dataset.

The search for the best solution is done by use of the Bayesian optimization, a sequential design strategy for global optimization of black-box expensive-to-evaluate functions. The SMAC (Sequential Model-Based Algorithm Configuration) algorithm based on Bayesian optimization that Auto-WEKA uses for the search is a sophisticated instantiation of the general SMBO (Sequential Model-Based Optimization) framework and works in following steps:

1. A probabilistic model of the objective function is built.
2. Hyperparameters are selected that suite best the probabilistic model.
3. Fitted hyperparameters are applied to the objective function.
4. The probabilistic model is recalculated.

### 3.2 Hyperopt-Sklearn

The popularity of Python language for the tasks of data mining gave rise to the machine learning libraries and AutoML solutions written in this language. One of the first AutoML solutions written in Python is Hyperopt-sklearn. It was also designed to solve the problem of automatic selection of the best combination of machine learning algorithm and its hyperparameters that is most efficient for processing any given dataset.

Hyperopt-sklearn searches through machine learning algorithms that present in Scikit-learn (sklearn) library but doesn't implement its own method for hyperparameters optimization and uses for this task Hyperopt library [16]. Hyperopt searches through the hyperparameter space in order to find the best values of hyperparameters. This search can be done using one of the following search and optimization algorithms which must be specified at startup:

- Random search (rand)
- Simulated annealing (anneal)
- Tree of Parzen Estimators (tpe)
- Adaptive TPE (atpe).

### 3.3  Auto-Sklearn

The Auto-sklearn is another more sophisticated AutoML solution that is also based on Bayesian optimization and searches through algorithms of Scikit-learn library. Auto-sklearn introduces two improvements to the search that previous solutions didn't have: meta-learning and ensemble. Meta-learning assumes searching for similar, previously encountered datasets to use the same search initialization as they had. The similarity of datasets is determined by comparing their meta-properties. Auto-sklearn uses 140 datasets from the OpenML [17], an open source repository, as source for meta-learning. Ensemble means usage of several algorithms that have shown good results in the final training, instead of a single algorithm, albeit the most effective one. The solution based on algorithms combination is more reliable and less prone to overfitting. Auto-sklearn considers configuration space consisting from base classifiers and excluded meta-models and ensembles that are themselves parameterized by one or more base classifiers. Such ensembles that are used by Auto-WEKA give it space of 786 hyperparameters whereas Auto-Sklearn features 110 hyperparameters. Auto-sklearn uses ensemble at the last step and not within search process that is more efficient.

### 3.4  TPOT

The TPOT (Tree-Based Pipeline Optimization Tool) software package is a Python library for automatically building a suitable machine learning data processing pipeline that is most efficient for processing a given data set and for automatically tuning the hyperparameters of the selected machine learning algorithm. This package is based on the ideas of genetic programming where many different solutions are generated and then checked in order to retain the best, modify them, check again and so on.

The result of TPOT work is a data processing pipeline - a combination of algorithms for working with a selected data set. The parts of the pipeline are:

1. Feature Preprocessing Operators
2. Feature Selection Operators
3. Algorithms for classification and regression (Supervised Classification/Regression Operators).

The algorithms from which the data processing pipeline is compiled are taken from the Scikit-learn library (sklearn).

### 3.5  H2O

H2O is an open source, in-memory, distributed, fast, and scalable machine learning and predictive analytics platform that allows build machine learning models on big data and provides easy productionalization of those models in an enterprise environment. H2O's core code is written in Java. Inside H2O, a Distributed Key/Value storage is used to access and reference data, models, objects, etc., across all nodes and machines. The algorithms are implemented on top of H2O's distributed Map/Reduce framework. This platform implements a number of supervised and unsupervised algorithms like Deep Learning, Tree Ensembles, and GLRM, and also has AutoML functionality that allows automatic search through the algorithms contained in the platform. API to Python allows use H2O from code written on Python.

### 3.6 Auto-Keras

Auto-Keras is a system that searches deep learning algorithms. This system works with algorithms from the Keras library, but since this library itself is an add-on and interface to the TensorFlow [18] library, in fact AutoKeras searches in this particular library.

Auto-Keras architecture consists of four parts: 1) search engine, 2) graph, 3) model trainer, 4) model repository. A search engine is a neural architecture search algorithm module containing Bayesian optimizers and Gaussian processes. The model trainer trains the resulting neural network using the training data. A graph is a module that processes computational graphs of neural networks managed by a search engine to perform network morphism operations. Model storage is a pool of trained models.

## 4   AutoML Framework

In order to process the data on various AutoML libraries with same constrains and then to compare their results it is worth to unite them in a common framework. To reach this goal the libraries have to be compatible. For this reason, we exclude Auto-WEKA from the further consideration, because it is written in Java which makes it hard to unite with other solutions written in Python.

Another important feature that should be considered are the constrains that each solution can use to limit the search of the algorithm and ability to divide the search into several parallel processes. Among common constraints are: time limits, memory limits. Comparison of the constrains that AutoML libraries support is shown in Table 2. It could be seen from the comparison that AutoKeras library doesn't support time constraints that other systems do, so it will be also excluded from the united framework.

Different AutoML libraries that use Scikit-Learn as a source of algorithms also cannot run together because of their dependency on different versions of libraries, in particular, Auto-sklearn cannot run together neither with TPOT nor with Hyperopt-sklearn. Therefore, two separate parts were developed, one unites Auto-sklearn and H2O and another works with TPOT, Hyperopt-sklearn and H2O.

Based on the above mentioned considerations a common framework for AutoML libraries was developed [19] in Python language. The framework takes as input information about dataset, ratio in which the data has to be splitted into train and test sets and time limit for each possible solution to run and then starts each AutoML solution with given data and limits in separate thread. The general architecture of the framework is shown in Fig. 1.

When all solutions finish their work the results are accumulated in a table. The results of each run contain various metrics which can be used to compare different solutions. These metrics include accuracy, precision, recall, f-measure and AUC.

Accuracy is a metric for assessing the quality of the classification, which shows how many objects were classified correctly relative to the total number of objects. This is the

**Table 2.** AutoML search constrains.

| AutoML library | Time limit | Memory limit | Parallel runs |
| --- | --- | --- | --- |
| AutoWEKA | Yes | Yes | Yes |
| Hyperopt-sklearn | Yes | No | No |
| Auto-sklearn | Yes | Yes | Yes |
| TPOT | Yes | No | Yes |
| H2O | Yes | No | No |
| AutoKeras | No | No | Yes |

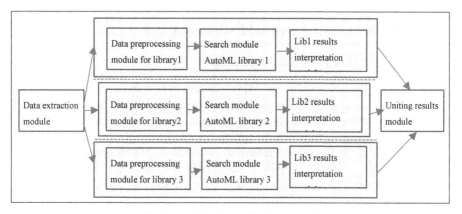

**Fig. 1.** Architecture of the framework

ratio of correctly classified objects to the total number of objects in the sample and it is calculated as follow:

$$Accuracy = \frac{tp + tn}{tp + fp + tn + fn} \quad (1)$$

where tp - true positive, tn - true negative, fp - false positive, - fn - false negative.

Precision is a metric that indicates how many of the objects classified as positive by the model are actually positive. This is the ratio of true positive objects (TP) to the total number of objects classified as positive (TP + FP).

$$precision = \frac{tp}{tp + fp} \quad (2)$$

Recall is a metric that shows how many positive objects were correctly detected by the model relative to the total number of true positive objects in the sample. This is the ratio of true positive objects (TP) to the total number of objects that are actually positive (TP + FN).

$$recall = \frac{tp}{tp + fn} \quad (3)$$

F-measure is a metric that combines precision and recall into one metric. It is calculated as a harmonic mean of precision and recall and shows how well the model classifies positive objects while minimizing false positives and false negatives.

$$F(\beta) = \left(1 + \beta^2\right) \frac{precision \cdot recall}{\beta^2 \cdot precision + recall} \qquad (4)$$

AUC (area under the curve) is a metric that shows how well the model distinguishes between positive and negative classes. The ROC curve is a graph showing the relationship between the recall and false positive rate of a model as the threshold changes. AUC indicates how well the model distinguishes between positive and negative classes, and the higher the AUC, the better is the model.

## 5   AutoML for Labor Potential Estimation

### 5.1   Datasets of Labor Potential Information

As every other statistical method AutoML needs data to be trained on. In our case data about workers, their characteristics and performance is needed. The collection of such data is beyond the scope of this work. Open source repositories include a number of already prepared datasets on which the approach could be tested. For example, Kaggle [20] repository contains Employee Performance Prediction [21], Human Resources Data Set [22], IBM HR Analytics Employee Attrition & Performance [23] and Employee Performance Analysis INX Future Inc [24]. For our purposes we decided to use the last one because it contains various information about workers and their performance. The selected dataset has records about 1200 workers, each described by 26 features.

The dataset contains following information: Age, Gender, EducationBackground, MaritalStatus, EmpDepartment, EmpJobRole, BusinessTravelFrequency, DistanceFromHome, EmpEducationLevel, EmpEnvironmentSatisfaction, EmpHourlyRate, EmpJobInvolvement, EmpJobLevel, EmpJobSatisfaction, NumCompaniesWorked, OverTime, EmpLastSalaryHikePercent, EmpRelationshipSatisfaction, TotalWorkExperienceInYears, TrainingTimesLastYear, EmpWorkLifeBalance, ExperienceYearsAtThisCompany, ExperienceYearsInCurrentRole, YearsSinceLastPromotion, YearsWithCurrManager.

The target attribute PerformanceRating has numeric value that has three possible values: 2 – poor (16%), 3 – good (73%), 4 – excellent (11%).

### 5.2   Experiments

The developed framework enables use of common data and constraints by several libraries. The records from the dataset were divided into training and test set, the latter being 1/4 from the total data and all libraries used the same ratio of train and test data. Then the search was performed using different time limits, again common for different libraries: 5 min, 10 min, 15 min, 30 min and 60 min. The visualization of the dependency between accuracy and running time of the libraries included in the framework is shown in Fig. 2.

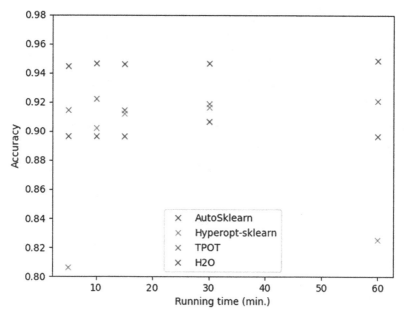

**Fig. 2.** Dependency of the accuracy from the running time

The more detailed results of the runs are given in Table 3.

GBM is standing for Gradient Boosting Machine and RF for Random Forest algorithms.

The performed experiments have shown high accuracy across all used libraries. The use of AutoML framework instead of a single library enabled to identify not only the best algorithm but also the most appropriate library from which the algorithm should be taken for the task of labor potential estimation. It was shown that in different time constrains different libraries can give better results. For example, for running time of 5 and 60 min Hyperopt-sklearn gives the worst results whereas for the time limit of 10, 15 and 30 min it outperforms Auto-sklearn and for limits of 15 and 30 min even almost reaches the accuracy of TPOT that always occupies the second place.

The experiments show that H2O provides better accuracy among other libraries, Hyperopt-sklearn more than other libraries depends on the time limits, and that increase in running time can also worsen the results, at least when the running time constraints are in the span of 1 h.

**Table 3.** Comparison of AutoML systems' suggestions and performance.

| AutoML library | Time | Selected alg | Accuracy | Precision | Recall | F-score | AUC |
|---|---|---|---|---|---|---|---|
| AutoSklearn | 5 min | adaboost | 0,896 | 0,878 | 0,812 | 0,841 | 0,967 |
| Hyperopt-sklearn | 5 min | RF | 0,806 | 0,878 | 0,605 | 0,623 | 0,660 |
| TPOT | 5 min | RF | 0,914 | 0,894 | 0,850 | 0,869 | 0,950 |
| H2O | 5 min | GBM | 0,944 | 0,970 | 0,866 | 0,910 | – |
| AutoSklearn | 10 min | adaboost | 0,896 | 0,878 | 0,812 | 0,841 | 0,967 |
| Hyperopt-sklearn | 10 min | RF | 0,902 | 0,847 | 0,874 | 0,859 | 0,951 |
| TPOT | 10 min | RF | 0,922 | 0,911 | 0,852 | 0,878 | 0,960 |
| H2O | 10 min | GBM | 0,946 | 0,927 | 0,928 | 0,927 | – |
| AutoSklearn | 15 min | adaboost | 0,896 | 0,878 | 0,812 | 0,841 | 0,967 |
| Hyperopt-sklearn | 15 min | GBM | 0,912 | 0,883 | 0,850 | 0,865 | 0,655 |
| TPOT | 15 min | RF | 0,914 | 0,894 | 0,850 | 0,869 | 0,953 |
| H2O | 15 min | GBM | 0,946 | 0,942 | 0,908 | 0,920 | – |
| AutoSklearn | 30 min | GBM | 0,906 | 0,858 | 0,883 | 0,870 | 0,962 |
| Hyperopt-sklearn | 30 min | GBM | 0,916 | 0,873 | 0,880 | 0,877 | 0,589 |
| TPOT | 30 min | RF | 0,918 | 0,895 | 0,856 | 0,874 | 0,959 |
| H2O | 30 min | xgboost | 0,946 | 0,936 | 0,914 | 0,924 | – |
| AutoSklearn | 60 min | adaboost | 0,896 | 0,878 | 0,812 | 0,841 | 0,967 |
| Hyperopt-sklearn | 60 min | RF | 0,825 | 0,772 | 0,653 | 0,697 | 0,701 |
| TPOT | 60 min | RF | 0,921 | 0,907 | 0,851 | 0,876 | 0,926 |
| H2O | 60 min | GBM | 0,948 | 0,940 | 0,911 | 0,925 | – |

## 6 Conclusion

In this work we develop an AutoML Framework that unite several commonly used AutoML libraries. To that end review and comparison of libraries were made that enabled selection of libraries that share common properties in means of metrics and constrains. The Framework is developed in Python language and consists of 4 AutoML libraries, it provides following capabilities:

- load data from local files or from openml.org website;
- input data preprocessing that is unique for each library and depends on data characteristics;
- common values of data split ratio and search time limits are shared across the used libraries;
- use of common metrics for results evaluation;
- parallel run of the libraries included in the framework.

The Framework was used to show the applicability of AutoML methods for solving the poorly formalized problem of labor potential estimation by performing search of the best model with 5 different time limits: 5, 10, 15, 30, 60 min. The experiments have shown that H2O library outperforms other AutoML libraries in all runs, giving maximum accuracy of 0,948 when maximum amount of time was allocated. AutoSklearn gave in most cases the worst results with the best result being 0,906. Hyperopt-sklearn have shown heavy dependency on running time giving accuracy of 0,806 when minimum amount of time was allocated and outperforming AutoSklearn with accuracy of 0,916 when given more time. The use of the AutoML framework allowed identify the most suitable library for the given task and in different time constrains. The performed experiments on dataset about labor potential have shown that the developed framework successfully solves the task of labor potential estimation.

The limitation of the suggested approach is that only AutoML libraries that share common properties can be united under the umbrella of the common framework. The more different metrics and constrains the framework will support the less libraries will be possible to use. Another limitation is that only libraries that written in Python or supporting it can be used.

The future work includes overcoming some of the mentioned above limitations, taking in account not only time constraint but also other constrains such as memory limits and number of runs; use of early stopping methods to stop search early in case when threshold value is reached; and enabling choose of libraries to make search in, this could be particularly useful in case when only part of libraries share some common properties.

**Acknowledgments.** This work was supported by a state grant (project No. FFZF-2022-0006) and as part of the agreement on the provision of subsidies from the federal budget for financial support for the implementation of the state task for 2023 (registration number of the EGISU NIOKTR card 1122110800010-7 28/11/2022).

# References

1. Patutina, E.S.: Main approaches to the interpretation of the concepts of "labor potential" and "human potential" as the basis for the quality of the labor force in the works of domestic and foreign scientists. In: Science Research Practice. Collection of Selected Articles Based on the Materials of the International Scientific Conference, pp. 215–220 (2020)
2. Human Resources Management: Concepts, Methodologies, Tools, and Applications, p. 1513. IGI Global, Pennsylvania (2012)
3. Page, S.E.: What sociologists should know about complexity. Ann. Rev. Sociol. **41**(1), 21–41 (2015). https://doi.org/10.1146/annurev-soc-073014-112230
4. Heravi, G., Eslamdoost, E.: Applying artificial neural networks for measuring and predicting construction-labor productivity. J. Constr. Eng. Manag. **141**(10) (2016)
5. Ogiy, O.G., Osipov, V.Yu., Tristanov, A.B., Zhukova, N.A.: The process of managing labor potential of the fishery complex as an object of modeling using artificial neural networks. In: AIP Conference Proceedings, vol. 2661, p. 030001 (2022)
6. Thornton, C., Hutter, F., Hoos, H.H., Leyton-Brown, K.: Auto-WEKA: combined selection and hyperparameter optimization of classification algorithms. In: 19th ACM SIGKDD International Conference on Knowledge Discovery and Data Mining, KDD 2013. ACM, New York (2013). https://doi.org/10.1145/2487575.2487629

7. Guo, X., van Stein, B., Bäck, T.: A new approach towards the combined algorithm selection and hyper-parameter optimization problem. In: 2019 IEEE Symposium Series on Computational Intelligence (SSCI), pp. 2042–2049. IEEE, Xiamen (2019). https://doi.org/10.1109/ssci44817.2019.9003174

8. Auto-WEKA. https://www.cs.ubc.ca/labs/algorithms/Projects/autoweka/. Accessed 07 Apr 2023

9. Hyperopt-sklearn. https://hyperopt.github.io/hyperopt-sklearn/. Accessed 10 Apr 2023

10. Feurer, et al.: Auto-Sklearn 2.0: Hands-Free AutoML via Meta-Learning. arXiv (2020)

11. Olson, R.S., Bartley, N., Urbanowicz, R.J., Moore, J.H.: Evaluation of a tree-based pipeline optimization tool for automating data science. In: Proceedings of GECCO 2016, pp. 485–492 (2016)

12. H2O.AI - The fastest, most accurate AI Cloud Platform. https://h2o.ai. Accessed 10 Apr 2023

13. Jin, H., Chollet, F., Song, Q., Hu, X.: AutoKeras: an AutoML library for deep learning. J. Mach. Learn. Res. **6**, 1–6 (2023)

14. Scikit-Learn. Machine Learning in Python. https://scikit-learn.org/stable/. Accessed 07 Apr 2023

15. Weka 3: Machine Learning Software in Java. https://www.cs.waikato.ac.nz/ml/weka/. Accessed 07 Apr 2023

16. Hyperopt: Distributed Asynchronous Hyper-parameter Optimization. http://hyperopt.github.io/hyperopt/. Accessed 07 Apr 2023

17. OpenML. A worldwide machine learning lab. https://www.openml.org. Accessed 07 Apr 2023

18. TensorFlow. An end-to-end open source machine learning platform for everyone. https://www.tensorflow.org. Accessed 07 Apr 2023

19. AutoML Framework for AutoML libraries comparison. https://github.com/DarkEol/AutoML-Framework. Accessed 07 Apr 2023

20. Kaggle. https://www.kaggle.com. Accessed 07 Apr 2023

21. Employee Performance Prediction. https://www.kaggle.com/datasets/gauravduttakiit/employee-performance-prediction. Accessed 07 Apr 2023

22. Human Resources Data Set. https://www.kaggle.com/datasets/rhuebner/human-resources-data-set. Accessed 07 Apr 2023

23. IBM HR Analytics Employee Attrition & Performance. https://www.kaggle.com/datasets/pavansubhasht/ibm-hr-analytics-attrition-dataset. Accessed 07 Apr 2023

24. Employee Performance Analysis INX Future Inc. https://www.kaggle.com/datasets/eshwarganta/employee-performance-analysis-inx-future-inc/. Accessed 07 Apr 2023

# Seismic Inversion for Fracture Model Reconstruction: From 1D Inversion to Machine Learning

Maxim Protasov[1]([✉]) [iD], Roman Kenzhin[1,2] [iD], Danil Dmitrachkov[1] [iD], and Evgeniy Pavlovskiy[2] [iD]

[1] Institute of Petroleum Geology and Geophysics, Koptyug St. 3, Novosibirsk 630090, Russia
protasovmi@ipgg.sbras.ru
[2] Novosibirsk State University, Pirogova St. 2, Novosibirsk 630090, Russia

**Abstract.** The presented paper is devoted to the numerical study of the applicability of 1D seismic inversion and 2D machine learning based inversion for fracture model reconstruction. Seismic inversion is used to predict reservoir properties. Standard version is based on a one-dimensional convolutional model, but real geological media are more complex, and therefore it is necessary to determine conditions where seismic inversion gives acceptable results. For this purpose, the work carries out a comparative analysis of one-dimensional and two-dimensional convolutional modeling. Also, machine learning methods have been adopted for 2D fracture model reconstruction. We use UNet architecture and 2D convolutional model to create a training dataset. We perform numerical experiments for a realistic synthetic model from Eastern Siberia and Sigsbee model.

**Keywords:** seismic inversion · convolution model · fractures · machine learning

## 1 Introduction

To date, seismic inversion has become a standard procedure, which is used to make a detailed model of the elastic parameters of the geological environment, which enables to predict reservoir properties [1, 2]. Researchers have defined seismic inversion as an algorithm that converts a time or migrated time seismic section into an acoustic impedance section [1, 3]. In this sense, the input data for the inversion are the seismic data time processing results, both before and after stacking [4, 5]. However, in areas with complex geology, seismic depth processing is required to build an accurate representation of the reservoir structure. In this case, the image after depth migration is transformed into the time domain, and standard inversion algorithms are applied.

But seismic inversion is based on the use of a one-dimensional convolutional model assuming horizontal layering of the medium [1, 3]. In practice, it may not satisfy this condition due to the presence of various kinds of lateral inhomogeneities, for example fractures provide them. In this case, it is necessary to switch to two-dimensional or three-dimensional convolutional models and implement the corresponding inversion

O. Gervasi et al. (Eds.): ICCSA 2023, LNCS 13957, pp. 99–109, 2023.
https://doi.org/10.1007/978-3-031-36808-0_7

algorithms. However, this does not happen in practice, and for laterally inhomogeneous media, seismic inversion is used, which is implemented within the framework of a one-dimensional convolutional model. Therefore, in the presented work, we determine the conditions where a one-dimensional seismic inversion gives acceptable results, and where it does not, through a numerical study on model examples. To do this, we compare the numerical results of one-dimensional and two-dimensional convolutional modeling, and we also compare the numerical results of seismic inversion. We carry the study out using the synthetic model Sigsbee.

At present, the problem of identifying complex carbonate reservoirs and predicting their porosity and permeability properties according to seismic data does not have an unambiguous solution [6, 7]. The irregular distribution of fractures complicates the structure of such reservoirs, which, in turn, are the main ways of fluid filtration and form the basis of the capacitive space of fractured reservoirs. 1D seismic inversion does not help in this case, therefore, as we mentioned above, there is a necessity to provide 2D and 3D inversion algorithms. On the other hand, machine learning methods shows a great potential in a solution to such kind of problems including 1D seismic inversion [8, 9]. Therefore, in this we adopt the machine learning methods for 2D fracture model reconstruction. For that, we use UNet neural network [10] and 2D convolutional modeling. We perform numerical experiments for a realistic synthetic model from Eastern Siberia.

## 2 Convolutional Modeling and Seismic Inversion

### 2.1 1D and 2D Convolutional Models

Acoustic seismic inversion is based on a one-dimensional convolutional model [1, 3]. This formulation suggests that for a horizontally layered model with a normal incidence of a plane longitudinal wave, we can represent a reflected wave field in the time domain as a convolution of the reflection coefficient trace with a seismic impulse:

$$S(t) = w(t) * R(t). \tag{1}$$

Here $S(t)$ – seismic trace, $R(t)$ – reflection coefficients, $w(t)$ – seismic impulse. In the frequency domain, expression (1) is rewritten as follows:

$$S(t) = \int \hat{W}(\omega)\hat{R}(\omega)e^{i\omega t}d\omega, \tag{2}$$

where $\omega$ is the frequency, $\hat{W}$ and $\hat{R}$ are the Fourier transforms of the seismic wavelet and reflection coefficients, respectively. Seismic inversion is performed to recover acoustic impedances directly related to reflection coefficients, where the results of time processing are input seismic traces [1, 3]. Also, in practice, an approach is often used when the image after depth migration is transformed into the time domain and standard inversion algorithms based on one-dimensional convolutional modeling are applied.

However, in the case where the medium is not horizontally layered, the results of both time and depth processing in the 2D/3D environment formally satisfy the 2D/3D convolutional model. Considering the two-dimensional case, let us turn to the result of pre-stack depth migration in true amplitudes. We know that the depth image has an expression that is very similar to a two-dimensional convolution in the frequency domain [11, 12]:

$$S(x_i, z_i) = \iint \hat{W}(\omega(p_x, p_z)) \cdot \hat{R}(p_x, p_z) \cdot e^{i(p_x x_i + p_z z_i)} dp_x dp_z, \qquad (3)$$

where $p_x, p_z$ are spatial frequencies, $\hat{W}$ is the Fourier transform of the seismic wavelet, $\hat{R}$ is the Fourier transform of the linearized reflection coefficient $R(x, z)$ in the two-dimensional medium. Similarly to the one-dimensional case, considering the normal incidence of the wave, the time frequency $\omega$ depends on the spatial frequencies as follows [11, 12]:

$$\omega(p_x, p_z) = \frac{\sqrt{p_x^2 + p_z^2}}{2} c_0(x_i, z_i), \qquad (4)$$

where $c_0$ is the migration velocity model of the medium. The image, which is got by using the direct calculation of the integral (3), we call the ideal image. Also, it is called as the result of two-dimensional convolutional modeling.

Further, in order to understand where the results of one-dimensional and two-dimensional convolutional modeling are similar and where they differ, we will compare them using specific examples. Since two-dimensional images are defined on a depth scale, and one-dimensional convolution is defined on a time scale, for their comparison, we convert depth images to a time scale using the depth-to-time transform [13].

First, we consider a horizontally layered model, and we calculate seismic traces for it by both one-dimensional and two-dimensional convolutional modeling (see Fig. 1a, 1b). In the first case, we convert the model to the time scale, and we implement one-dimensional convolution according to formula (1). In the second case, we construct images according to formula (3), and then we transform to the time scale by applying the same transform. We calculate the difference between the results as the error of the 1D simulation relative to the 2D simulation (see Fig. 1c). For the horizontally layered medium, the difference between the results of 1D and 2D modeling is mostly about 2–3%. This is partly due to the numerical errors in the approximation of the corresponding integrals. Therefore, we can say that for the model with horizontal interfaces, 1D and 2D modeling give approximately the same results.

Further, we consider a more complex media, i.e. a fragment of the Sigsbee model containing lateral inhomogeneities associated with the presence of non-horizontal layers, faults, and scattering objects. We carry out similar 1D and 2D convolutional modeling computations, and we obtain the corresponding difference in the modeling results (see Fig. 2). Here, we pay attention to the features associated with lateral heterogeneities. One can observe that the results of 1D and 2D convolutional modeling are quite close for part of the model containing interfaces, including those with a non-zero slope angle (the difference is about 2–3%). But in the presence of non-reflecting elements of the geological media such as faults, diffracting or scattering objects, the difference between the modeling results becomes significant, and can reach 40% (see Fig. 2c).

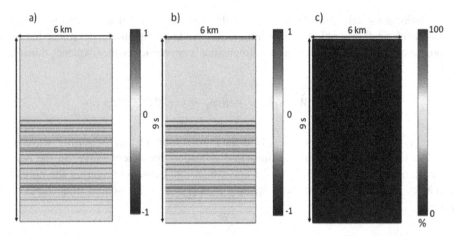

**Fig. 1.** Results of convolution modeling in the case of a horizontally layered medium: a) 1D modeling; b) 2D modeling; c) their difference.

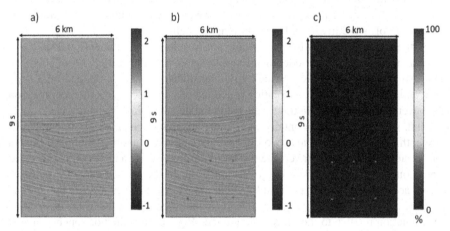

**Fig. 2.** Results of convolutional modeling in the laterally inhomogeneous Sigsbee model: a) 1D modeling; b) 2D modeling; c) their difference.

## 2.2 1D Seismic Inversion

One of the most widely used algorithms in practice is model-based inversion. Further, using it, we process the synthetic data for the Sigsbee model got by one-dimensional and two-dimensional convolutional modeling. As shown above, they slightly differ from each other at the interfaces, but significant differences appear in the area where the scattering/diffracting objects are located. The same effect appears when comparing the seismic inversion results (Fig. 3).

For a more detailed comparison, we calculate the error of the inversion results relatively to the true acoustic impedance model (Fig. 4). 1D inversion of 1D modeling data provides the inversion result within the minor error (Fig. 4a). We get such results because 1D inversion and 1D modeling are inverse operations with respect to each other. However, the results of seismic data processing in a 2D media correspond to 2D convolutional modeling, so it is necessary to track the corresponding error, which arises during 2D seismic data processing.

One can see that the inversion of 2D modeling data provides the error 3–8% in most of the media, and the error can reach 60% in the areas where scatters are located. The incorrect description of essentially two-dimensional effects by the one-dimensional modeling is the reason for such large errors. Experiments show that the application of one-dimensional model-based inversion gives a quite satisfactory result with acceptable accuracy for reflective elements of the medium (Fig. 4b, Fig. 5a). However, the use of seismic inversion in the areas with scattering objects generates significant errors (Fig. 4b, Fig. 5b). This means that 1D seismic inversion must not be applied for reconstruction of scattering objects, particularly for fracture model reconstruction.

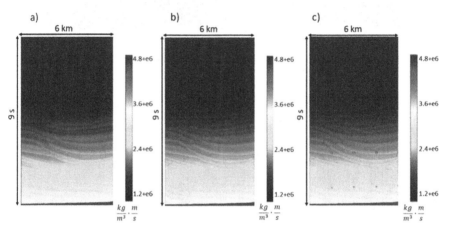

**Fig. 3.** a) True acoustic impedances. b), c) The result of the 1D inversion according to: b) 1D modeling; c) 2D modeling.

## 3   Machine Learning for Fracture Model Reconstruction

Based on the described above research results, we suggest investigating the inversion that uses the 2D depth convolutional model. The inversion in this case is not so simple as for 1D time convolutional model. But the 2D convolutional modeling is computationally a cheap procedure. Therefore, we suggest investigating machine leaning methods for 2D fracture model reconstruction.

As one can conclude from the previous section, the 1D seismic inversion provides appropriate results when the model contains reflected interfaces only, i.e. it provides reasonable inversion results of the reflective part of the model. Therefore, 1D seismic inversion can be applied for reconstruction of the reflective part of the model. It means that it is necessary to define the scattering/diffractive part of the model when the model contains the scatters/diffractors.

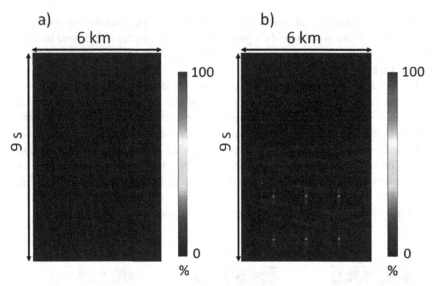

**Fig. 4.** Relative error of 1D inversion in the Sigsbee model according to: a) 1D simulation; b) 2D modeling.

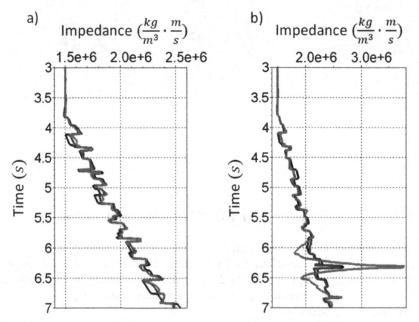

**Fig. 5.** True acoustic impedances (black), inversion result from 1D modeling data (blue) and 2D modeling data (red): a) trace does not contain scatterers; b) trace contains a scatterer. (Color figure online)

From practical datasets, we know that fractures provide localized heterogeneities of the elastic properties. Therefore, the fractures on the seismic model scale can be considered as scatters/diffractors that are scattering/diffractive part of the model. And this part of the model is the reconstruction goal. On the other hand, we have the result of the seismic depth data processing, which is the depth seismic image. As we said above, this image in the 2D case satisfies 2D convolutional model. Therefore, we create a rather big number of different 2D localized fracture models, then put this fracture model inside reflector model and finally provide the corresponding seismic image. We provide models and images easily using rather small computational resources and minimum a priori information about fractures. Thus, we construct training data set for the machine learning algorithm.

For the described problem, we apply the Unet neural network architecture [10] with changed input and output sizes. We present the architecture at the Table 1.

# 4  Numerical Experiments

## 4.1  2D Synthetic Fracture Models and Images

To test the technology, a two-dimensional seismogeological model was created based on a prototype section of one of the East Siberian fields (see Fig. 6a). The elastic model parameters are constructed based on well data. Small-scale heterogeneities typical for this field were included in the model: fractures, located in the upper part of the Riphean carbonate complex (see Fig. 6b). The petrophysical characteristics of heterogeneities were set based on the results of the analysis of the core material. The fractures belong to the class of fluid-saturated ones. We can create a variety of different fracture models with the information from the well data. In this particular case, we construct 1000 models (see one of them on the Fig. 6b). For all of them, we construct corresponding full models (see the corresponding model on the Fig. 7a) including reflective part of the model that is the same for all 1000 fracture models. And finally, we provide 2D convolution modeling in order to get the ideal image (see the corresponding image on the Fig. 6c). Thus, we construct a data set for testing the proposed machine learning approach.

## 4.2  ML Results of 2D Fracture Model Reconstruction

Then we come to the application of the proposed machine learning approach to the created data. From that dataset, we use 800 realizations for training and 200 realizations for testing of size $2000 \times 400$ pixels. We interpret the task in terms of machine learning as a semantic segmentation, i.e. to classify each pixel to belong to a background - 0, or fracture - 1. The splitting is carried out once without shuffling. The neural network is fed by samples without preprocessing. We apply a post-processing min-max image normalization at the output of the neural network. We modify the UNet architecture to work with $2000 \times 400$ input-output size (Table 1).

We define the loss function as an equal combination of Dice loss (5), binary cross-entropy (6) and mean squared error losses, which averages on all pixels of an image; $y$

a)

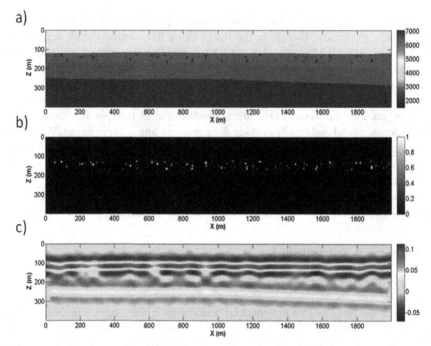

b)

c)

**Fig. 6.** a) Seismic velocity model (pressure velocity) containing main reflected horizons of Riphean carbonate complex, and one of the fracture model realization. b) The corresponding fracture model realization – indicator function showing the fractures density. c) The corresponding ideal seismic image – the result of 2D convolution modeling.

stands for the true image, and $\hat{y}$ is the predicted by UNet.

$$Dice(y, \hat{y}) = 2\frac{y \cap \hat{y}}{y + \hat{y}}, \ DiceLoss = 1 - Dice, \tag{5}$$

$$BCE(y, \hat{y}) = -\left[\hat{y} \log y + (1 - \hat{y}) \log(1 - y)\right] \tag{6}$$

Also, we use the Dice metric to measure the quality of the classifier. Neural network training parameters are the following: optimizer - AdamW, learning rate - 0.1, batch size - 2, maximum number of epochs – 25. We carry out validation on the test dataset at the end of training after the 25th epoch. The total error in the training was 0.62, on the test – 0.74.

After we finish the training, we apply the trained neural network to the images that were used in the training dataset first. One of the images and the corresponding recovered model results one can see on the Fig. 7. Recovered fractures locations have red color, the true fractures locations have blue color (Fig. 7b). There is rather good correspondence between the biggest true fracture locations and the recovered ones. Dice metric in this case is rather high, and it equals 37.0%.

Then we apply the trained neural network to the images from the testing dataset. One of the images and the corresponding recovered model results we can see on the Fig. 8.

**Table 1.** Network architecture. MP is MaxPooling2D (kernel = 2 × 2, stride = 2, padding = 0, dilation = 1), DC(x,y) is Conv2D(in = x, out = y, kernel = 7 × 7,stride = 1, padding = 3) – BatchNorm – ReLU - Conv2D(in = y, out = y, kernel = 3 × 3, stride = 1, padding = 1) – BatchNorm – ReLU.

| Layer structure | Channels | Size |
|---|---|---|
| Input | 1 | 2000 × 400 |
| DC(1,64) | 64 | 2000 × 400 |
| MP-DC(64,128) | 128 | 1000 × 200 |
| MP-DC(128,256) | 256 | 500 × 100 |
| MP-DC(256,512) | 512 | 250 × 50 |
| MP-DC(512,1024) | 1024 | 125 × 25 |
| ConvTranspose2d(1024,512,2 × 2, s = 2 × 2)-DC(1024,512) | 512 | 250 × 50 |
| ConvTranspose2d(512,256,2 × 2, s = 2 × 2)-DC(512,256) | 256 | 500 × 100 |
| ConvTranspose2d(256,128,2 × 2, s = 2 × 2)-DC(256,128) | 128 | 1000 × 200 |
| ConvTranspose2d(128,64,2 × 2, s = 2 × 2)-DC(128,64) | 64 | 2000 × 400 |
| Conv2D(64,1,1 × 1,1) | 1 | 2000 × 400 |
| Output – MinMax[0,1] | 1 | 2000 × 400 |

There is also good correspondence between the biggest true fracture locations and the recovered ones. Dice metric in this case is rather high, and it equals 28.8%.

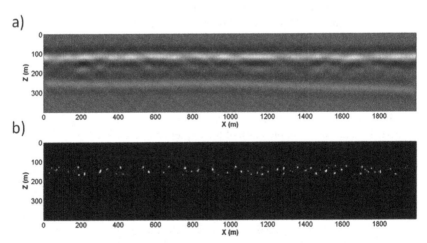

**Fig. 7.** a) The seismic image from the training dataset. b) The corresponding fracture models: blue – true fractures locations; red – recovered fractures locations. Dice metric equals to 37.0%. (Color figure online)

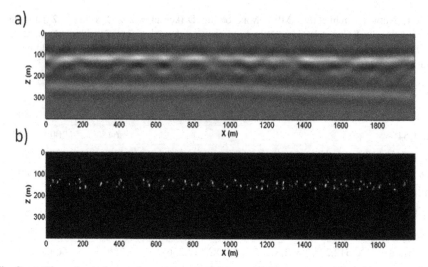

**Fig. 8.** a) The seismic image from the testing dataset. b) The corresponding fracture models: blue – true fractures locations; red – recovered fractures locations. Dice metric equals to 28.8%. (Color figure online)

## 5   Conclusions

In the paper we describe 1D and 2D convolution modeling algorithms and the implementation of seismic inversion algorithm for fracture model recovery based on 2D convolution modeling and machine learning.

We provide a numerical study of the applicability of seismic inversion for laterally inhomogeneous media. On 2D synthetic models, we show that the results of 1D convolutional modeling with acceptable accuracy (within 2–3%, including depth-time transformation errors) coincide with the results of 2D convolutional modeling both for models with horizontal reflecting boundaries and for models with boundaries with non-zero dip angle. But when the non-reflecting elements such as scattering objects (caverns, faults, fractures) are present in the media, the difference between the results of one-dimensional and two-dimensional convolutional modeling becomes significant, and can reach 40%. The numerical results of the application of the implemented seismic inversion to the 2D convolutional modeling data show that the error for the main part of the Sigsbee model is acceptable (about 3–8%). In areas of this model where faults and scatters are present, the inversion error becomes significant and reach 60%. This means that 1D seismic inversion must not be applied for reconstruction of scattering objects, particularly for fracture model reconstruction. But the 1D seismic inversion can be used as an effective tool for the recovery of the reflected component of the model.

For the fracture model reconstruction, we provide a machine learning approach. It contains two key components: 2D depth convolution modeling for creating training dataset, and UNet neural network architecture for the fracture model reconstruction. We provide the machine learning results for 2D models and images. The numerical results for realistic synthetic model from the Eastern Siberia show appropriate reconstruction of the fracture model. These results look promising for the generalization of the approach to 3D real physical models.

**Acknowledgements.** The work is supported by RSF grant 21-71-20002. The numerical results were obtained using the computational resources of Peter the Great Saint-Petersburg Polytechnic University Supercomputing Center (scc.spbstu.ru).

# References

1. Ampilov, Yu.P., Barkov, A.Yu., Yakovlev, I.V., Filippova, K.E., Priezzhev, I.I.: Almost everything is about seismic inversion. Part 1. Seismic Technol. **4**, 3–16 (2009)
2. Yakovlev, I.V., Ampilov, Yu.P., Filippova, K.E.: Almost everything is about seismic inversion. Part 2. Seismic Technol. **1**, 5–15 (2011)
3. Russell, B.H.: Introduction to Seismic Inversion Methods. Course Notes Series, Society of Exploration Geophysicists, pp. 80–101 (1988)
4. Russell, B.H., Hampson, D.P.: Comparison of poststack seismic inversion methods. In: SEG Technical Program Expanded Abstracts, pp. 876–878 (1991)
5. Hampson, D.P., Russell, B.H., Bankhead, B.: Simultaneous inversion of pre-stack seismic data. In: SEG Technical Program Expanded Abstracts, pp. 1633–1637 (2005)
6. Liu, E., et al.: Fracture characterization by integrating seismic-derived attributes including anisotropy and diffraction imaging with borehole fracture data in an offshore carbonate field. In: International Petroleum Technology Conference, IPTC-18533 (2015)
7. De Ribet, B., Yelin, G., Serfaty, Y., Chase, D., Kelvin, R., Koren, Z.: High resolution diffraction imaging for reliable interpretation of fracture systems. First Break **35**(2), 43–47 (2017)
8. Chen, Y., Schuster, G.: Seismic inversion by Newtonian machine learning. Geophysics **85**, W185–W200 (2020)
9. Pintea, S.L., Sharma, S., Vossepoel, F.C., van Gemert, J.C., Loog, M., Verschuur, D.J.: Seismic inversion with deep learning. Comput. Geosci. **26**(2), 351–364 (2021). https://doi.org/10.1007/s10596-021-10118-2
10. Ronneberger, O., Fischer, P., Brox, T.: U-Net: convolutional networks for biomedical image segmentation. In: Navab, N., Hornegger, J., Wells, W.M., Frangi, A.F. (eds.) MICCAI 2015. LNCS, vol. 9351, pp. 234–241. Springer, Cham (2015). https://doi.org/10.1007/978-3-319-24574-4_28
11. Protasov, M.I., Tcheverda, V.A.: True amplitude imaging. Dokl. Earth Sci. **407**, 441–445 (2006)
12. Protasov, M., Tcheverda, V.: True amplitude imaging by inverse generalized Radon transform based on Gaussian beam decomposition of the acoustic Green's function. Geophys. Prospect. **59**, 197–209 (2011)
13. Robein, E.: Seismic Imaging. EAGE Publications (2010)

# "Fat" Rays in Three Dimensional Media to Approximate a Broadband Signal Propagation

Dmitry Neklyudov[✉] [iD] and Maxim Protasov [iD]

Institute of Petroleum Geology and Geophysics SB RAS, prosp. acad. Koptuga 3,
Novosibirsk 630090, Russia
neklyudovda@ipgg.sbras.ru

**Abstract.** The paper presents a simple and robust approach for calculating frequency-dependent rays in three-dimensional media. The proposed ray tracing procedure simulates propagation of locally plane fragment of a wave front. Ray properties depend on velocity distribution in some sub-volume around the ray and on wavelength at each point. We provide a numerical comparison of "fat" rays approach with the "exact" Helmholtz solver using complex 3D SEG salt model. This comparison show promise of using the concept of "fat" rays in 3D seismic data processing, i.e. comparison show that "fat" rays approach needs up to several orders less resources than Helmholtz solver, while the error between "fat" rays wave filed and "exact" solution does not exceed several percent.

**Keywords:** Fat rays · Ray method · Broadband signal · Green function

## 1 Introduction

The ray method [1, 2] play an important role in seismic data processing. Its main application is to calculate the ray paths and corresponding travel times of seismic waves. It is also used for the computation of wave fields in models of moderate complexity. The classical ray theory is formulated using a high-frequency approximation of signal propagation processes. This fact produces the main limitation of all ray-based methods. Classical ray method does not take into account the fact that actual seismic signals are broadband and their spectrum are limited. A high-frequency approximation often leads to a non-physical behavior of the rays if there are significant velocity variations in a model [3, 4]. On nonplanar surfaces, the standard rays disperse abruptly and as a result, shadow zones appear in the model (i.e. the regions where the rays do not pass at all). Propagation of the signals with limited spectrum depends on velocity distribution within certain volume around the ray. These volumes are called as "Fresnel volumes". Dominant frequency of the signal determines the width of the Fresnel volume. The real signals are affected by velocity variations within the Fresnel volume [5, 6]. A number of methods are developed to go beyond the standard ray method based on high frequency approximation. The main idea behind these approaches is to consider the impact of the

O. Gervasi et al. (Eds.): ICCSA 2023, LNCS 13957, pp. 110–124, 2023.
https://doi.org/10.1007/978-3-031-36808-0_8

Fresnel zone on travel times and ray paths [7–14]. It allows to weaken the impact of the high-frequency approximation. As a result, it is possible to calculate the reliable rays in fairly complex velocity models. The principal disadvantage of the proposed approaches is the complexity of the calculations, especially in the three-dimensional case. Original approach for approximating the propagation of broadband seismic signals in complex environments was proposed in [8] where it was called "the wavelength-smoothing technique". The key point there is the fact that velocity used for ray tracing is determined by smoothing actual velocity along the normal to the ray at the current point over an aperture proportional to the wavelength. In the limiting case when the wavelength becomes infinite small, the method reduces to the standard rays described by classical ray theory. In [15], we considered this method in 2D case and proved that it might be quite promising in some seismic exploration applications. Specifically, we found that these rays can be very effective in calculating travel times in the presence of salt intrusion in a model. This work is an extension of [15] to three dimensions. We propose quite simple and robust algorithm to construct frequency dependent rays in complex 3D media. It consists of two main ingredients: 1) the velocity wavelength-smoothing technique along a 2D wave front; 2) movement of a number of points located on a plane wave front' fragment in some vicinity of a ray to determine the wave front orientation at a next point on the ray. During ray tracing process a local plane fragment of the wave front moves. Thus, ray's orientation depends on velocity distribution in some sub-volume around the ray. This is why we called such rays as "fat" rays. The term "fat" rays is already widely used in seismic [16]. Usually it means a standard ray attributed with corresponding first Fresnel zone. In our case the sense of the term is a little bit different.

The paper is organized in the following way. First, we describe simple algorithm how to construct a frequency-dependent ray in three dimensions. We then describe an approach for interpolating travel times from the irregular points on the rays to the regular 3D grid. Next, we briefly describe an approach we use to calculate ray based amplitudes. Finally, we give two numerical examples and demonstrate that "fat" rays are more stable than standard rays in complex 3D models. We conclude that the "fat" rays can provide reliable travel times and amplitudes when the standard ray method fails.

## 2 Method

### 2.1 "Fat" Ray Construction

"Fat" ray tracing is based on two main concepts. First is the wavelength-smoothing technique proposed in [8]. This technique allows to calculate locally smoothed velocity in vicinity of a ray. Smoothing is performed in particular direction, namely along a wave front, i.e. in a plane which is orthogonal to the current ray's propagation direction. The second concept is the local control points movement which is used to determine a ray propagation vector at a next point on the ray. As an input of the procedure, we define auxiliary parameter $\upsilon$ (measured in Hz), which is called "frequency" of the ray. This parameter defines the sensitivity of the ray to velocity variations. Two take-off angles $\varphi_{AZ}$, $\varphi_{Dip}$ are also given. $\varphi_{AZ}$ is the azimuthal angle (i.e. an angle between initial ray direction and X-axis in XY plane), $\varphi_{Dip}$ is dip angle (i.e. an angle between initial ray direction and Z-coordinate axis). Let $\vec{x}_p = (x_p, y_p, z_p)$ is a current point on the ray (central point). At this point, a unit tangent vector $\vec{s} = (s_X, s_Y, s_Z)$ is given which define a ray propagation direction at the current point. We construct a plane passes through the point $\vec{x}_p$ and orthogonal to the vector $\vec{s}$. In this plane, we cut a rectangular area ("patch"). The size of the rectangular is a function of local wavelength in the central point, $\lambda = \frac{v(\vec{x}_p)}{v}$ (see Fig. 1a). Local velocity value $v(\vec{x}_j)$ is defined in the regular grid of points in the patch (these points are shown as the blue stars in Fig. 1a). Smoothed velocity in the central point is calculated as

$$v_{sm}(\vec{x}_p, v) = \frac{\sum_{j=-N}^{N} w_j \cdot v(\vec{x}_j)}{\sum_{j=-N}^{N} w_j} \tag{1}$$

where $w_j$ are the smoothing weights. As a smoother we choose 2D Gaussian function. The weights are given as:

$$w_j = \exp\left\{-\left(\frac{r_j}{\lambda \cdot \theta_{max} \cdot \alpha}\right)^2\right\}, \tag{2}$$

where $r_j$ is a distance between the central point and the point $\vec{x}_j$ in the wavefront patch, predefined parameter $\theta_{max}$ (local wavelength percentage) determines the spatial size of the rectangular, parameter $\alpha$ is responsible for the shape of the Gaussian smoother. In the Fig. 2, we show how the Gaussian smoothing function (2) behaves in relation to the parameter $\alpha$. When the parameter $\alpha$ is reduced, the smoothing function becomes narrower, concentrating near the center point. When increasing the parameter $\alpha$, the Gaussian smoothing is reduced to simple averaging in the rectangular area.

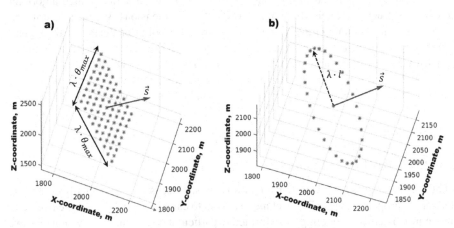

**Fig. 1.** a) Rectangular area ("patch") cut along a local wave front. Blue stars mark the points where velocity values are taken to calculate smoothed velocity at the central point (shown as a red star). Vector $\vec{s}$ denote current normal to the front (ray propagation direction). b) Control points taken around the central point. They are used calculating new normal to the front $\vec{s} + d\vec{s}$. (Color figure online)

To explain a meaning of the control points, we consider a circle lying in the same plane orthogonal to the current ray propagation direction vector $\vec{s}$. Radius of the circle is also function of the local wavelength, $R = \lambda \cdot l$ (predefined parameter $l$ controls the percentage of the local wavelength which one want to use). We choose a number of points lying on the circle with constant angular increments (see Fig. 1b). We shall refer to these points as "control" points. They are used for calculating vector $\vec{s} + d\vec{s}$ in the next point on the ray.

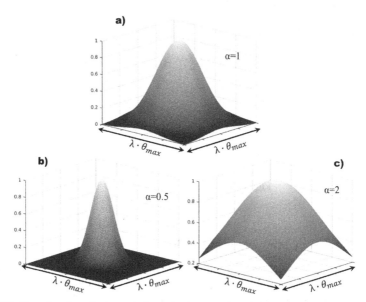

**Fig. 2.** 2D Gaussian functions used for velocity wavelength-smoothing along the front for different value of parameter $\alpha$.

Let us define the time step along the ray as $dt$. To move along the "fat" ray we apply the following scheme (see Fig. 3).

1) We calculate the wavelength-smoothed velocity at the central point, $\bar{v}_p = v_{sm}(\vec{x}_p, v)$ using the formulas (1), (2). During the time interval $dt$, the central point $\vec{x}_p$ moves to the point $\vec{x}_p + d\vec{x}_p$, $d\vec{x}_p = (dx_p, dy_p, dz_p)$ along the vector $\vec{s}$:

$$dx_p = \bar{v}_p dt \cdot s_x, \quad dy_p = \bar{v}_p dt \cdot s_y, \quad dz_p = \bar{v}_p dt \cdot s_z, \tag{3}$$

It gives us a position of a next point on the ray. Now we need to determine new ray propagation direction vector $\vec{s}_{new}$ (or in other words, new local wavefront orientation).

2) For each control point, we calculate corresponding smoothed velocities using the same orthogonal plane as for the central point: $\bar{v}_j = v_{sm}(\vec{x}_j, v)$. For the same time interval $dt$ each control point will travel different distances, $dx_j = \bar{v}_j dt \cdot s_x$, $dy_j = \bar{v}_j dt \cdot s_y$, $dz_j = \bar{v}_j dt \cdot s_z$. Control points in updated positions, $\vec{x}_j + d\vec{x}_j$ might not lie in the same plane. We define numerically a plane which is closest to all points $\vec{x}_j + d\vec{x}_j$ in the least-squares sense. Thus, we solve the classical three-dimensional linear regression problem. As a result, new ray direction vector $\vec{s}_{new}$ is defined. We attach $\vec{s}_{new}$ to the new central point position $\vec{x}_p + d\vec{x}_p$ and repeat the process. There is

a step-by-step movement along the ray. Note that the "fat" ray tracing is performed in a certain volume of the medium. Simultaneous movement of all control points determines the next orientation of the front.

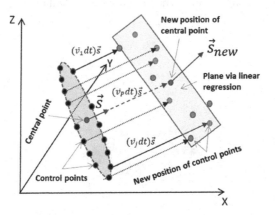

**Fig. 3.** Scheme of "fat" ray tracing.

## 2.2 Ray Travel Time Interpolation in 3D Regular Grid

When constructing rays, we determine the travel times at the points of the medium through which each ray passes. These points are quite irregular. For seismic applications, ray-based travel times must often be evaluated within a standard 3D grid. Such an array, consisting of the first arrival travel times given in the regular grid points, is called a travel time table.

Let we have constructed the number of rays for a large set of take-off angles. We presume that the rays cover the whole model. For each ray, we have a set of travel times at each point of the ray: $T_i^j(x_i^j, y_i^j, z_i^j)$, where $j = 1, \ldots, N_{rays}$ is an index of the ray, $i$ is an index of a point on the ray, $i = 1, \ldots, N_{segm}^j$, $N_{segm}^j$ is a total number of ray segment for $j$th ray. We need to make a map $T_i^j\left(x_i^j, y_i^j, z_i^j\right) \rightarrow T_{table}(x_k, y_l, z_m)$ for all $j$, where $T_{table}$ are traveltimes given in the regular grid points $x_k, y_l, z_m$ ($k = 1, \ldots, N_X$; $l = 1, \ldots, N_Y$; $m = 1, \ldots, N_Z$).

Consider successively the ray tubes, which are formed by three adjacent rays, first with the take-off angles ($\varphi_{AZ}, \varphi_{Dip}$), second ($\varphi_{AZ}, \varphi_{Dip} + d\varphi_{Dip}$), third ($\varphi_{AZ} + +d\varphi_{AZ}, \varphi_{Dip}$), where $\varphi_{AZ}$ is azimuthal take-off angle, $\varphi_{Dip}$ is dip take off angle, $d\varphi_{AZ}$, $d\varphi_{Dip}$ are corresponding angles increments. A ray tube may be decomposed into elementary prismatic cells which bottom corresponds to travel time $T_j$ and top corresponds to $T_{j+1} = T_j + dt$ (see Fig. 4). Next, a parallelepiped which cover the prismatic cell with the regular grid points is determined. Every regular grid point of the parallelepiped domain is verified to be inside the prism cell. If so, the travel times at the prism cell vertices (marked as 11, 21, 31, 12, 22, 32 in the Fig. 4) are interpolated at the grid point using the method proposed in [17]. Overwise, the grid point gets ignored from consideration at the current stage. It is repeated for each ray cell and each ray tube. As a result, a regular travel time table is constructed if the model has been illuminated by the rays adequately.

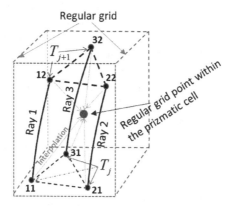

**Fig. 4.** Scheme of ray travel times interpolation to a regular grid.

## 2.3  Green's Function Calculation

In seismic imaging, it is often necessary to calculate Green's functions for scalar wave equation or its frequency domain counterpart, Helmholtz equation:

$$\Delta G(\vec{x}, \vec{x}_S; \omega) + \frac{\omega^2}{v^2(\vec{x})} G(\vec{x}, \vec{x}_S; \omega) = \delta(\vec{x} - \vec{x}_S) \tag{4}$$

where $\vec{x}_S = (x_S, y_S, z_S)$ is the source position, $\omega$ is a fixed frequency. Below we describe briefly an approach which we choose to calculate the frequency domain Green's functions by the ray method.

In the tree-dimensional case, the expression for the ray-based asymptotic Green's function calculated at point R with the source in the point S is defined as [2, 18]:

$$G(R; S) = A(S, R) \exp\{i\omega\tau(S, R)\}, \tag{5}$$

where $\tau(S, R)$ is traveltime along a ray between the points S (source) and R (receiver), $A(S, R)$ is an amplitude factor provided by the ray method:

$$A(S, R) = \frac{1}{4\pi} \sqrt{\frac{v(R)}{v(S) \cdot J(S, R)}}, \tag{6}$$

$v(x)$ is a value of velocity in corresponding point of velocity model, $J(S, R)$ is geometrical spreading along a ray. The geometrical spreading is defined here by the expression

$$J = \frac{dS}{d\Omega} \tag{7}$$

where $dS$ is the elementary oriented surface of an orthogonal ray tube section at R and $d\Omega$ is the elementary solid angle associated with the ray tube at the source. We compute finite-difference approximation of geometrical spreading factor using the theory provided in [2] (expression 3.10.33). To use this approximation of geometrical spreading we need to consider three adjacent rays with a small increment in the take-off angles as we described in the previous section. In this case, ray coverage (or ray density) within the target area should be sufficient. Amplitudes calculated along the ray tubes are interpolated on the regular grid in the same manner as the travel times. As a result, an amplitude table is obtained. Note, if ray-based travel time and amplitude tables are calculated, it is possible to calculate the Green function very quickly for any frequency because no additional raytracing is required. As an alternative to the approach outlined above, it is possible to use much more computationally expensive dynamic ray tracing [2].

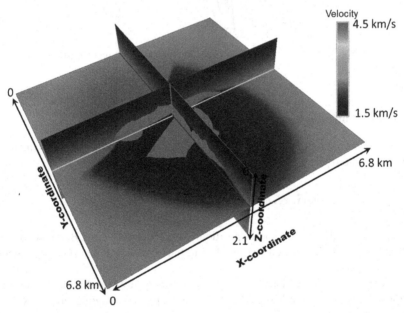

**Fig. 5.** Original 3D SEG Salt velocity model (scaled to the grid size 10 m). (Color figure online)

## 3  Numerical Examples

### 3.1  Travel Time Calculation in 3D SEG Salt Velocity Model

Significant problems arise when the ray method is applied in models with rapid seismic wave's velocity variations. In these cases, standard ray's behavior becomes unphysical. At sharp, non-planar boundaries the standard rays scatter and as a result "shadow" zones occur in travel times distribution. It is expected, because "by the origin" the ray method is valid if the range of velocity variations is much greater than the wavelength. In seismic exploration applications, one of the most challenging conditions for the ray method occurs when the salt intrusions are presented in a model. Salt bodies might have a very complex shape. Seismic wave's velocity in salt is much higher than in sedimentary rocks surrounding an intrusion. Usually, it is very problematic to construct reliable rays passing through a salt body and to calculate the corresponding travel times. Below we show that "fat" rays can resolve these issues.

Figure 5 presents a well-known 3D SEG Salt velocity model [19] with a salt body of complex shape (shown in red). The model has the following parameters. Top of the model is water layer with pressure wave velocity 1500 m/s. Seismic wave velocity in salt is 4500 m/s meanwhile in surrounding area (which model sedimentary rocks) it doesn't exceed 3200 m/s. Number of grid points in each direction is $N_X = 676$, $N_Y = 676$, $N_Z = 211$ with grid steps $dx = dy = dz = 10$ m. Total spatial size of the model is $6750 \times 6750 \times 2100$ m. A point source is located in the center of the model in a point with coordinate $X_S = 3200$ m, $Y_S = 3200$ m, $Z_S = 100$ m. We want to calculate the corresponding ray based first arrival travel times in each point of the regular velocity grid (travel time table). For standard raytracing we used a code taken from well-known Madagascar freeware package. "Fat" rays are calculated using the code we developed.

Below, for "fat" ray construction we used the following parameters: "ray frequency" parameter $\upsilon = 5$ Hz, $l = 0.5$, $\theta_{max} = 0.5$, $\alpha = 1$. Number of control points was equal to 30. Figure 6a, 6b show a 3D view of 50 rays calculated for a fixed azimuth angle ($\varphi_{AZ} = 0$) and uniform dip angle increment. In Fig. 7a, 7b projections of the rays at XY plane are demonstrated (top view). One can immediately note that the standard and "fat" rays are substantially different. Behavior of "fat" rays looks much more regular. They cover much wider area of the model. Note that the rays are substantially three-dimensional. They go far beyond the plane $Y = Y_S = 3200$ m where the source is located. To calculate travel times in the whole model we must shoot the rays quite densely with small dip and azimuth angular increments. Take off angles should cover the whole intervals $\varphi_{AZ} = [0, 360°]$, $\varphi_{Dip} = [0, 360°]$. We used a bunch of $500 \times 500$ rays, i.e. the take off angles increment is $0.72°$. In Fig. 8 we show travel time tables corresponding to each method. Standard rays produce "holes" in the travel time table, i.e. there are areas where the rays do not arrive at all due to complexity of the model and limitation of the ray method (at these areas travel times are zero). It is an obvious contradiction with the real physical process of wave propagation. Numerical tests proved that even the standard rays will be traced densely, this does not help to achieve adequate ray coverage everywhere. Figure 8b shows the "fat" rays travel times. "Fat" rays pass through the salt body and produce quite regularly distributed travel times. The residuals between the "fat" rays' travel times and exact first arrival travel times provided by the 3D finite difference method does not exceed 0.006 s which can be considered quite satisfactory.

If the "ray frequency" parameter increases, the "fat" rays tends to be closer to the standard rays. At a certain point ($\upsilon$ 30 Hz), they become indistinguishable. It is very expected behavior. Note that, for a given rays' density, "fat" ray calculation requires much more computational time than the standard ray. One of the reason is the fact that at each time step along the "fat" ray multiple accesses to the velocity model (i.e. memory access) are required to calculate the averaged velocity along the current position of the front. The number of control points chosen for ray tracing increase the computation time almost linearly. The number of control points should be sufficient to account for the 3D velocity variation around a ray. If the number of control points is insufficient, the ray calculation can be unstable. An overabundance results in a significant increase in computational time without any visible improvement of the final result.

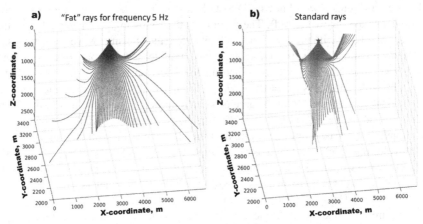

**Fig. 6.** 3D view of rays calculated in the original 3D SEG Salt velocity model for one source (marked as a star) and one fixed azimuth angle, $\varphi_{AZ} = 0$: a) "fat" rays calculated for the "frequency" parameter $\upsilon = 5$ Hz; b) standard rays.

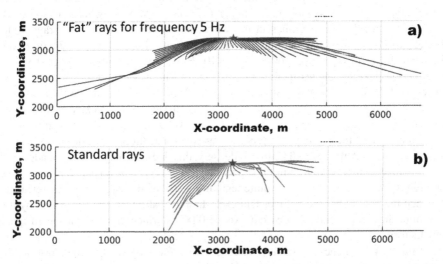

**Fig. 7.** Projection at XY plane of rays calculated in the original 3D SEG Salt velocity model for one fixed azimuth angle, $\varphi_{AZ} = 0$: a) "fat" rays constructed for the frequency parameter $\upsilon = 5$ Hz; b) standard rays.

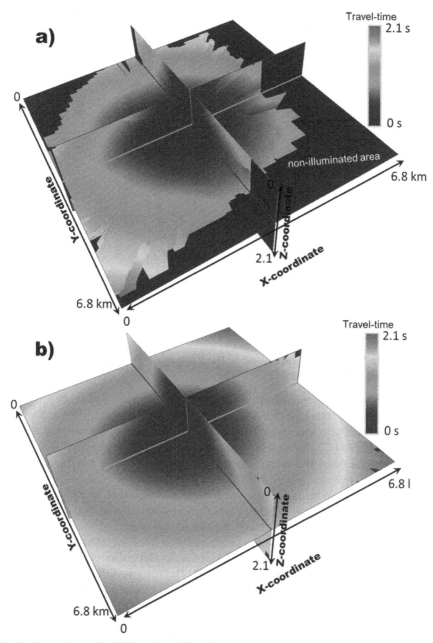

**Fig. 8.** Travel time table (TT) in original 3D SEG Salt velocity model: a) TT calculated using the standard rays ("shadow" zones have zero travel time); (b) TT calculated using the "fat" rays with the "frequency" parameter $\upsilon = 5$ Hz.

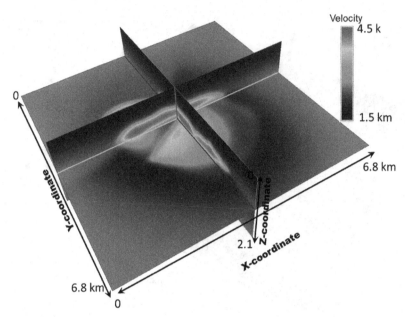

**Fig. 9.** Smoothed 3D SEG Salt velocity model used for acoustic wave field simulation.

## 3.2 Acoustic Wave Field Simulation in the Frequency Domain in Smoothed 3D SEG Salt Velocity Model

Now, we present an example of 3D acoustic wave field simulation in the frequency domain. We compare the asymptotic wave field provided by the ray method based on the "fat" rays with the "exact" wave field which is calculated by the numerical solution of Helmholtz Eq. (4). The exact wave field will contain reflected waves if the velocity model used for the simulation is non-smooth. But we apply the ray method to model first arrivals only. No reflected waves will occur in the ray-based simulation. To make the comparison of the wave fields more fair, we will use a smoothed version of the SEG Salt 3D velocity model (see Fig. 9) in order to avoid reflected waves in the "exact" wave field. The smoothed model was obtained with the spatial convolution of the original model with the 3D Gaussian function having a length of 200 m in each direction. "Exact" wave field calculation in the frequency was performed using Helmholtz iterative solver with semi-analytical preconditioner proposed in [20]. The iterative solver is applied using the same grid where the velocity model is given. The velocity model grid parameters are the same as in the previous numerical example, $N_X = 676$, $N_Y = 676$, $N_Z = 211$, $dx = dy = dz = 10$ m. Point source has coordinates $X_S = 3200$ m, $Y_S = 3200$ m, $Z_S = 100$ m. In Fig. 10a a real part of "exact" wave field at frequency 5 Hz is presented. For ray based wave field simulation we used a bunch of $500 \times 500$ rays. Even though the model is smoothed, the standard rays do not provide the required illumination for the calculation of the amplitudes. Standard rays leave holes in travel times and amplitude tables. "Fat" rays resolve the issue successfully. For "fat" ray calculation we use the same parameters as in previous example: $\upsilon = 5Hz$, $l = 0.5$, $\theta_{max} = 0.5$, $\alpha = 1$. In Fig. 10b we present "fat" rays - based wave field for frequency 5 Hz in comparison with "exact" wave field (Fig. 10a). One can observe good fit between them. In Fig. 11, we compare the vertical and horizontal sections of the wave fields from Fig. 10 for the finite difference solution (shown in blue) and for the "fat" rays (red). The traces were taken at the plane Y = 2000 m. Quite satisfactory match is obvious. The solution error provided by "fat" rays in comparison with "exact" solution does not exceed 8% even for such a complex model as 3D SEG salt model.

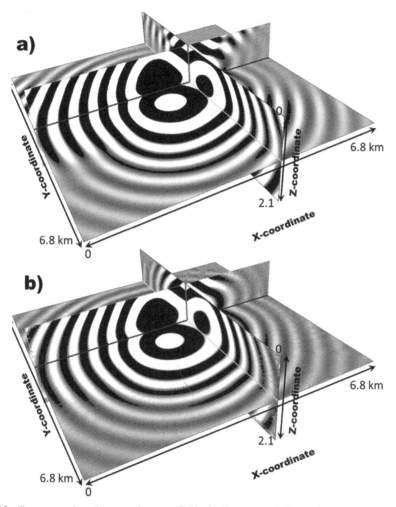

**Fig. 10.** Frequency domain acoustic wave fields for frequency 5 Hz (real part): a) obtained by solution of Helmholtz equation ("exact" wave field); (b) simulated using the "fat" rays. (Color figure online)

All computations presented above are performed on a personal desktop computer with Intel Core i7-3770K 3.50 GHz CPU (4 core) and 32 Gb RAM. The total cycle of "fat ray"-based Green function calculation for one source takes ~6 min of total computation time (all 4 CPU core was used). The most time consuming part is raytracing. It takes almost 85% of total time. "Exact" wave field simulation using highly optimized iterative solver [20] requires ~7 min in the same setup (the same grid, number of CPU cores, etc.). The computation time for the "exact" solver will increase considerably with the frequency of the simulation increase. For example, for frequency of 10 Hz and 20 Hz "fat ray"-based Green function calculation for one source take ~6 min for both also, while "exact" wave field simulation using highly optimized iterative solver requires minimum 20 min for 10 Hz. We note also, if ray-based travel time and amplitude tables are ready, Green function for high frequencies can be computed very fast (seconds). There is no need to repeat ray tracing procedure.

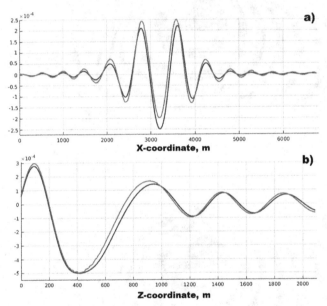

**Fig. 11.** 1D sections of 3D wave fields form Fig. 10.: a) horizontal (Z = 1000 m) sections; (b) vertical (X = 2000 m) sections. Exact (finite difference) wave field is shown in blue, "fat" ray based wave field is shown in red.

## 4   Conclusions

We consider a concept of "fat" rays for approximation frequency-dependent signal propagation in three dimensional media. "Fat" ray computation consists of two main ingredients: 1) local velocity smoothing along a 2D plane wave front; 2) control points movement to determine a wave front orientation at a next point on the ray. The procedure approximates propagation of a local plane fragment of the wave front. Ray properties depends on velocity distribution in some sub-volume around the ray and on wavelength in each point. We perform a comparative analysis of the "fat" rays versus the standard rays for calculating travel times in complex media. It shows that "fat" rays are more stable than the standard rays and can provide reliable travel times when the standard ray method fails. Using the "fat" rays we simulate frequency domain acoustic wav field and compare it with the "exact" wave field provided by the solution of Helmholtz equation. This comparison showed a satisfactory agreement between the quality of the results. "Fat" rays wave filed in comparison with "exact" solution does not exceed 8% even for such a complex model as 3D SEG salt model. Comparison of the computational times show that "fat" rays approach needs much less (up to several orders for high frequencies) resources than Helmholtz solver. Such numerical results provide the promise of using the concept of "fat" rays in seismic exploration in a complex three-dimensional environment.

**Acknowledgments.** The reported study was funded by RFBR and GACR, project number 20-55-26003.

# References

1. Babich, V.M., Buldyrev, V.S.: Asymptotic Methods in Short-Wavelength Diffraction Theory. Alpha Science (2009)
2. Cerveny, V.: Seismic Ray Theory. Cambridge University Press, Cambridge (2001)
3. Kravtsov, Y.A., Orlov, Y.I.: Geometrical Optics of Inhomogeneous Media. Springer, Heidelberg (1990)
4. Ben-Menahem, A., Beydoun, W.B.: Range of validity of seismic ray and beam methods in general inhomogeneous media –I. General theory. Geophys. J. Int. **82**, 207–234 (1985)
5. Marquering, H., Dahlen, F.A., Nolet, G.: Three-dimensional sensitivity kernels for finite-frequency traveltimes: the banana-doughnut paradox. Geophys. J. Int. **137**, 805–815 (1999)
6. Dahlen, F.A., Hung, S.-H., Nolet, G.: Fréchet kernels for finite-frequency traveltimes—I. Theory. Geophys. J. Int. **141**, 157–174 (2000)
7. Cerveny, V., Soares, J.E.P.: Fresnel volume ray tracing. Geophysics **57**, 902–915 (1992)
8. Lomax, A.: The wavelength-smoothing method for approximating broad-band wave propagation through complicated velocity structures. Geophys. J. Int. **117**, 313–334 (1994)
9. Vasco, D.W., Peterson, J.E., Majer, E.L.: Beyond ray tomography: wavepaths and Fresnel volumes. Geophysics **60**, 1790–1804 (1995)
10. Bube, K.P., Washbourne, J.K.: Wave tracing: ray tracing for the propagation of band-limited signals: part 1 – theory. Geophysics **73**, VE377–VE384 (2008)
11. Yarman, C.E., Cheng, X., Osypov, K., Nichols, D., Protasov, M.: Band-limited ray tracing. Geophys. Prospect. **61**, 1194–1205 (2013)
12. Vasco, D.W., Nihei, K.: Broad-band trajectory mechanics. Geophys. J. Int. **216**, 745–759 (2019)
13. Foreman, T.L.: An exact ray theoretical formulation of the Helmholtz equation. J. Acoust. Soc. Am. **86**, 234–246 (1989)
14. Protasov, M., Gadylshin, K.: Computational method for exact frequency-dependent rays on the basis of the solution of the Helmholtz equation. Geophys. J. Int. **210**, 525–533 (2017)
15. Neklyudov, D., Protasov, M.: Acoustic wavefields simulation by the ray method with approximation of a broadband signal propagation. In: Gervasi, O., Murgante, B., Hendrix, E.M.T., Taniar, D., Apduhan, B.O. (eds.) ICCSA 2022. LNCS, vol. 13376, pp. 84–96. Springer, Cham (2022). https://doi.org/10.1007/978-3-031-10450-3_7

16. Jordi, C., Schmelzbach, C., Greenhalgh, S.: Frequency-dependent traveltime tomography using fat rays: application to near-surface seismic imaging. J. Appl. Geophys. **131**, 202–213 (2016)
17. Bulant, P., Klimeš, L.: Interpolation of ray theory traveltimes within ray cells. Geophys. J. Int. **139**(2), 273–282 (1999)
18. Lucio, P.S., Lambaré, G., Hanyga, A.: 3D multivalued travel time and amplitude maps. PAGEOPH **148**, 449–479 (1996)
19. Aminzadeh, F., Burkhard, N., Long, J., Kunz, T., Duclos, P.: Three dimensional SEG/EAGE models - an update. Lead. Edge **15**(2), 131–134 (1996)
20. Belonosov, M., Dmitriev, M., Kostin, V., Neklyudov, D., Tcheverda, V.: An iterative solver for the 3D Helmholtz equation. J. Comput. Phys. **345**, 330–344 (2017)

# Visualization, Analysis and Collaborative Discussion of Severe Weather Events

Robson Siscoutto[1], Luan Silva[1], Lucas Santos[1],
Marcelo de Paiva Guimarães[2]([⊠]), Diego R. C. Dias[3], Reinaldo Silveira[4],
and José Remo Brega[5]

[1] Universidade do Oeste Paulista - Unoeste, Presidente Prudente, Brazil
robson@unoeste.br, luanpp@live.nl
[2] Universidade Federal de São Paulo (UNIFESP- EPPEN), Osasco, Brazil
marcelo.paiva@unifesp.br
[3] Universidade Federal de São João del-Rei (UFSJ), João del-Rei, Brazil
diegodias@ufsj.edu.br
[4] Sistema Metereológico do Paraná (SIMEPAR), Curitiba, Brazil
reinaldo.silveira@simepar.br
[5] Universidade Estadual Paulista (Unesp), Bauru, Brazil
remo@unesp.br

**Abstract.** Designing effective collaboration, visualization, and analysis of severe weather events (e.g., excessive rainfall accumulation, floods, severe thunderstorms, tornadoes, and droughts) for meteorologists on the web is challenging because it requires processing huge amounts of data from different sources, diverse technologies, as well as using appropriate visualization techniques. This paper presents an innovative web toolset for visualization, collaborative discussion, and analysis of severe weather events. It is composed of the tool Viewing events on Maps (VIMAPS), which allows users to visualize and analyze severe weather events using maps enriched with multivariate data glyphs to observe spatial relations from any desired angle; and the tool called Collaborative system for Meteorological Data Analysis (COMETA) that allows the collaborative analysis of severe weather events between remote users synchronously or asynchronously. These tools were tested using real data and showed that they fulfill the usability requirements of this class of application.

**Keywords:** severe weather · visualization · analysis · collaboration · maps

## 1 Introduction

The World Meteorological Organization (WMO) provides many guidelines on information systems that provide early warning to severe weather conditions [6]. Weather events (e.g., tornados, wind, rain, temperature inversions, and lightning) bring several consequences to the city population, either on economic or health aspects. The primary purpose of such guidelines is to help the construction of tools and rules for preparing the National Weather Services worldwide to

O. Gervasi et al. (Eds.): ICCSA 2023, LNCS 13957, pp. 125–143, 2023.
https://doi.org/10.1007/978-3-031-36808-0_9

deal with severe weather events. That is the case of storms followed by floods, especially in urban areas, causing mortality due to drowning, landslides, and buildings' collapse. Most of the time, such situations are followed by death and without an appropriate weather warning.

Severe weather is either becoming more frequent or reported more often. The latter has been possible mainly due to better information technology and the increasing number of observations. Nonetheless, it is necessary to have appropriate computational tools to help specialists visualize and analyze such events to prevent death and loss of property. Computational tools are necessary to define resources for prevention, and the anticipation of weather events, minimizing damage caused by the severe events [7, 10]. Although technological advances have made it possible to tackle complex problems in diverse areas, such as those related to weather [2, 8, 12, 14, 20, 23–25], it is still a challenging task to design and develops systems to assist in the visualization, analysis, and collaborative discussion of severe weather events. This paper presents a web toolset for the visualization, collaborative understanding, and analysis of severe weather events. The Visualizing Events compose it on Maps tool called VIMAPS (VIewing events on MAPS), which provides a user-friendly environment, allowing users to interact with weather data and analyze severe weather information. The toolset also includes the Collaborative System for Meteorological data Analysis Tool (COMETA) that allows collaborative analysis and discussion between remote users in a synchronous way [4], where everyone interacts in real-time, or an asynchronous way, where the interaction can be distributed over time. Usability tests were applied to the developed tools through an evaluation guided by five experts.

This paper's remainder is organized as follows: Sect. 2 presents related works on this subject; Sect. 3 presents the VIMAPS tool, including its architecture, details about the maps enriched with glyph icons, and the 3D charts. It also describes the usability tests that were performed; Sect. 4 shows the COMETA tool. It also shows the usability test performed and the obtained results; and finally, the implications of this work are discussed in Sect. 5.

## 2    Related Work

Related work has been found in data analysis and mitigation of natural hazards due to excessive rainfall accumulations, for instance, and all sorts of extreme weather events. These studies describe the intrinsic characteristics of the associated weather phenomena concerning the evidence of natural disasters. Thus, we investigated studies that bring alternative or innovative ways of using technology for weather data analysis or the prediction of severe weather events. The technology described in such studies included all types of sensors, such as radar, satellites and meteorological stations, lightning sensors, or numerical weather prediction model data.

Ohneiser et al. [19] present a prototype that highlights the meteorological conditions and routes of affected aircraft. Their approach gives concrete advice based on the 4D trajectory for redirection, taking into account the complete arrival flow. The authors assume that this ongoing support can help flight controllers optimize highly dynamic air traffic flow, even if they do not fully follow the automatically generated plan. However, all approach operations to severe weather conditions remain supported by controller assistance systems.

Li et al. [11] developed a weather data visualization system capable of performing preprocessing, transformation, and rendering. The study's primary purpose was to optimize the use of a graphics processing unit (GPU) and a central processing unit (CPU) to speed up a general geo-visualization process. They used sandstorms as case studies. To compare the two approaches (GPU and CPU), visualization components based on each architecture were developed and analyzed. According to the experiments, both multi and many-core architectures can improve mathematical calculations and rendering using multi-threaded techniques.

The mentioned studies have common characteristics when historical data on maps, images, or geometric shapes enhance a given region. The proposed visualizations are based on a 2D plan; the drawback of such an approach is the lack of detailed insight of the selected area, hampering analysis and an understanding of valuable information for accurate decision making. Those approaches do not use graphical and interactive techniques for manipulating 3D charts, which can be applied in different areas and situations, such as natural disasters.

Kern et al. [9] proposed a visualization approach to analyze three-dimensional atmospheric fronts' structures and their physical and dynamic processes. Their approach aimed to build three-dimensional models from traditional 2D models. This transformation is possible by using the temperature change's magnitude along the gradient of a potential wet temperature field as the primary identification factor.

Theuss et al. [22] presented a 3D environment to visualize the cyclonic storm Chapala. Their research aimed to predict the cyclone's movement and characteristics, which was the second most robust tropical cyclone on record in the Arabian Sea. Therefore, they customized the solution for a specific problem. Feng and Fan [3] simulated snow, rain, and fog conditions in ZuiYi city, GuiZhou province, China. However, the solution is not integrated with a natural resource.

Many studies use virtual reality to visualize weather-related content, such as [22], which presents a 3D immersive environment in which users can better visualize the thick ice layer of a cyclone to better understand the relationship between distinct aspects of the data. Murata et al. [15] presented a real-time 3D visualization system for observing data of an X-band phased array weather radar (PAWR) in conjunction with ecosystems provided by a cloud service. Although this research works with real data and creates 2D and 3D visualization, it does not promote collaboration between users.

Stäli, Rudi, and Raubal [21] presented a 3D user-centered approach (the usual method is 2D). They focused on the visualization of weather-related graphics used during flight preparation. The authors conducted a study with 64 pilots. In their results, it was evident that using a 3D approach, there was a decrease in cognitive load, but an increase in spatial awareness and usability.

Afzal et al. [1] present a review on the state of the art of ocean and atmospheric data set visual analysis approaches. They interviewed researchers, experts, and professionals working with datasets related to the study objects. The authors discuss techniques, systems, and tools, categorizing them using the following taxonomy: task requirements, interaction methods, visualization techniques, machine learning and statistical methods, evaluation methods, data types, data dimensions and size, spatial scale, and application areas. Based on the professionals' answers, the authors present trends, challenges, and opportunities for future research in the area, making clear that there are several questions to be addressed regarding the taxonomy defined by them.

A common gap in the reviewed works is the lack of collaboration between remote users. The value of the collaborative analysis of severe weather events proposed here lies in the exchange of information to improve the understanding of underlying features in the multi-source data. The research is focused on building a collaborative solution to be used in practice. So far, in the literature, very few attempts have been made in this direction.

## 3   VIMAPS

VIMAPS aims to allow users to visualize and analyze severe weather events through easy interaction with meteorological data, helping them in their decision-making. It processes and adds weather events (e.g., wind, rain, temperature inversions, and lightning) represented by glyph icons on maps in which the users navigate and interact, and analyze the events. These functionalities allow, for example, visualization when lightnings occur in the air or when it strikes the ground, and also its incidence (low, medium, or high) and the position on the map; and weather data (e.g., temperature, wind direction, wind speed, and pressure). Details are presented when the mouse pointer is over the glyph icons. The more the view is closer to the ground, the more details are presented.

### 3.1   Essential Features of VIMAPS

The essential features of VIMAPS are:

a) Process and position data from Atmospheric Electrical Discharge (AED) and Weather Events under maps, allowing the user to visualize, navigate, interact and analyze data represented by two-dimensional and three-dimensional interactive objects (3D symbols on the map). Through this functionality, the visualization of the information of atmospheric electrical discharges (AED) from the cloud to the ground or vice versa, latitude, longitude and current, date and time) Furthermore, meteorological data (station code, date, time, instantaneous temperature, maximum temperature, minimum temperature, instantaneous humidity, maximum humidity, minimum humidity, dew point, maximum dew point, minimum dew point, pressure, maximum pressure, minimum pressure, wind direction, wind speed, wind gust, radiation, and precipitation) run through layers or levels (zoom), where the user can view the groupings of this data represented by 3D objects (symbols) on online maps. By positioning the mouse on these objects, detailed information (represented by two-dimensional data) regarding the meteorological events in question is displayed, and the closer to the ground, the greater the number of objects the user will visualize. For processing and positioning, VIMAPS uses the concept of GIS (Geographic Information Systems) to convert geographic coordinates into geometries, making it easier to manipulate spatial data and calculate a region's area, the distance between points, data exports for use in GISs, among others. This functionality is detailed in Sect. 2.

b) From a depth on the map and selected data sets, allow navigation, exploration, and interaction with a 3D representation, resulting from a combination of visualization techniques, which relate electrical discharge data, data from surface weather stations and their locations.

Through this functionality, the process of understanding a vast amount of data is simplified since the interactive 3D representations are organized in a tree structure that represents the data grouped by geographical regions and indexed by the types of electrical discharge data: cloud and soil. The division of a geographic region represents each graph into four parts (quadtree). Each part groups the sum of the sets of electrical discharges in that area. The data captured by the meteorological stations, referring to the area in question, are integrated into the graphic, creating the relationship between them in the visualization. This functionality is detailed in Sect. 2.

## 3.2   Vimaps Architecture

– Visualization module, which provides two types of interaction: global and specific. "Global" refers to manipulating the angles of the map, facilitating the visualization of the terrestrial globe and its objects. Specific interaction occurs when the user hovers over a particular map area. Users can visualize and analyze the data using maps enriched with multimedia elements (e.g., glyph icons, text, and images). Users can view and analyze data using 2D maps or an environment composed of 3D representations;
– Engine module, which consists of algorithms used to manipulate the data:
  • Mapping of multimedia elements that are superimposed on the environment; and
  • Data mining allows users to manipulate the database (by applying filters - e.g., levels of rain accumulation, humidity, and lightning).
– Database module, VIMAPS uses PostGIS [30] stores the severe events data from different sources; and
– Web technologies, which are the back-end solution implemented. It follows the web technologies described by [30–32], developed using HTML5 and Javascript as they can be used to develop complex web applications compatible with all major browsers, whether on PCs or mobile devices. These

browsers can also render 3D charts, as they support the Web-based Graphics Library (WebGL) [33], which brings hardware-accelerated 3D graphics to the browser without the use of plug-ins:

- Three.js Javascript library was used to abstract WebGL through virtual objects and environments;
- Cesium.js Javascript library was used to create 3D globes and 2D maps in web browsers without using plugins; and
- Node.js, a runtime system used for creating server-side applications, is built on Google Chrome's JavaScript Engine (V8 Engine).

### 3.3  Visualization Using 2D Maps

VIMAPS can use maps from any provider, such as Microsoft, Google, and the OpenStreet community. Usually, these maps also offer an application programming interface (API) with a set of functions, classes, methods, and standards to be used in an application without understanding the details of their implementation. Using the APIs, one can have access, in real-time and constant updating, to satellite images and their coordinates, computational methods for requesting data (for example, latitude and longitude of a given place), and different types of satellite images, among others. Client applications can use these providers via HTTP requests or by using their Software Development Kit (SDK); in both cases, service access keys are required. When communication between the application and the library is performed, an environment for manipulating the map is loaded, making requests through the Internet for images and/or information. The providers distribute the resources, which use data structures, hardware, and software mechanisms to organize and disseminate this information.

The hierarchical navigation was based on quadtree [34], and it allows the user to select pieces of data (subsets) according to specific interests. This feature was implemented using the CesiumJS framework. This framework, which was developed using JavaScript, allows 3D globes and 2D maps to be created in web browsers without using plug-ins. It uses WebGL for hardware-accelerated graphics. The implementation of hierarchical navigation in VIMAPS was based on the camera distance concept in the globe. Therefore, the smaller the distance, the greater the level of detail, and when there is an inclination of the camera on the map, different tiles levels are presented. The slope is a user interactivity function, with the map allowing the user to view the glyphs in depth, facilitating the analysis process.

The operation of VIMAPS can be demonstrated using real data on lightning flashes. On January 1st, 2014, a mesoscale convective system quickly developed over South of Brazil, being associated with a cold front active in the region. This weather system propagated from Paraguay to the Brazilian east coast in Santa Catarina in about two hours. It brought many severe weather activities, including strong thunderstorms and lightning, as depicted in Fig. 1. The civil defense authorities had to warn the population about floods and landslides in 13 cities in the eastern portion of Santa Catarina state, as reported by local newspapers.

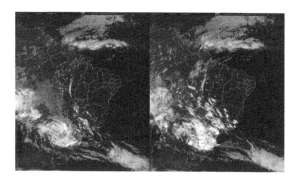

**Fig. 1.** Eumetsat satellite images on January 1st, 2014, at 16:00 local time (right) and 18:30 local time (left). The red arrow indicates the city of Florianopolis, Santa Catarina, Brazil (Color figure online)

Glyph icons are associated with lightning data (electrical discharge weather events) in a cloud format, inserted over the map in its corresponding position. Glyphic discharge icons can be recognized by the number of events in a region of the quadtree. An example is when an event is registered over a region presented by two types: cloud or cloud-ground. The cloud type is only when an electrical discharge is in the sky (there is no contact with the ground), while the cloud-ground is when there is contact with the ground (presented as a green region below the cloud).

The lightning and meteorological data related to Fig. 1 were introduced in VIMAPS and 1706 flashes were counted in the period of thunderstorm activity. This hierarchical visualization figure depicts the bounding boxes (cross-cross yellow lines painted) covering the map on VIMAPS. Each box represents some part of the map that is being indexed, with the root node covering the entire area. Each box is divided such that it contains a maximum of four children (quadtree). Each child is either a point or a smaller box. The map on the left highlights a box with a blue cloud in the center; it received 1706 electric discharges during the thunderstorm activity. The map on the right shows details of this area, divided into four smaller areas, which still sum 1706 flashes. This area corresponds to the beginning of lightning activity, and successive updates of the maps (not shown) suggested that the activity would follow the east, i.e., in the Great Florianopolis metropolitan region. The COMETA tool (Sect. 3), a collaborative environment, allows users to interact with the system and draw conclusions regarding the weather system's real-time development.

VIMAPS uses PostGIS [34], a spatial database extension, for the PostgreSQL database. It allows location queries to be run in Structured Query Language (SQL) for geographic objects. This tool was used mainly to convert geographic coordinates into geometries. Hence, it is easier to manipulate spatial data (such as data conversions using only a single SQL line) and to perform functions, such as calculations of the area of a region or a distance between points, and exports of data for use in a geographic information system (GIS). PostGIS supports geometries such as points, line sequences, polygons, multiple points, multiple polygons, a collection of geometries, and multiple line sequences. We received text files from the meteorological institutes that had to be preprocessed before uploading them into our database.

In the VIMAPS graphical user interface (Fig. 2), the user can view the globe using different maps. Icons are available to allow searches by address or specific references. It is also possible to return to the starting point of the visualization, change the map image provider or the visualization parameters (weather events/electrical discharges and date ranges for viewing the events), and view the map's quadtree divisions as well as information. Figure 2 depicts data related to meteorological events captured by automatic ground weather stations in Brazil's southern part. By clicking on a weather station (antenna icons), users are presented with a window (left side) showing data captured by the station (e.g., wind direction, atmospheric pressure, rainfall accumulation, air humidity, and air temperature). In the option box (right), the user can select the details in which he/she is interested.

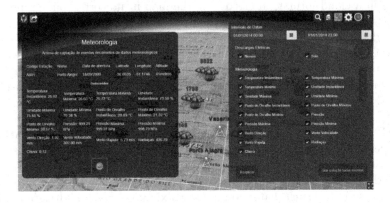

**Fig. 2.** VIMAPS graphical user interface

## 3.4   Interactive Three-Dimensional Environment

VIMAPS collects large amounts of different and isolated data, making it difficult to understand and relate to them. As presented in Sect. 2, data on electrical discharges and weather events are presented under maps with no relationship between them to allow faster and more punctual navigation, exploration, and analysis.

We created different epistemic actions to increase the user's attention to the different views. We also intended to facilitate the interaction between the views of details and context, seeking to decrease the cognitive load and increase the rate of capture of information. To achieve this goal, we created an interactive three-dimensional juxtaposed context environment to present the relationship between various data related to meteorological events. We used information regarding latitude, longitude, date, time, the radius of coverage, and position/distance of weather event capture stations. This information can help create three-dimensional representations that can support analyzing complex sets of information for quick, accurate, and safe decision-making.

Also, we organized the 3D representations in a tree structure, following the quadtree groupings, where the leaf nodes have no other subdivisions. This form of organization allows different depth levels and contents so that the lower the depth level, the more detailed the region observed will be. It is worth noting that the representations show the viewer's direction and angle, connected by lines that visually link each secondary representation to its source, creating an easy hierarchical structure.

Another critical point is related to the user's distinction from multiple windows to view and manipulate data in both VIMAPS and COMETA. This way, it is possible to use each system separately without confusing the user. Each window presents details and allows data manipulation uniquely and autonomously, with defined policies, functionalities, and hierarchies. Using VIMAPS, large data spaces can coexist in one or more windows, aiming to demonstrate a more extensive and detailed part of the data space, improving the presentation and readability of text and information. It proves an alternative visual representation (3D context) for the data, locations, and directions, allowing navigation, manipulation, and work on these representations.

After uploading the events in VIMAPS, the user can navigate/interact with the map and can also perform these activities in the 3D context environment, being able to switch between the environment and the map at any time. A representation is formed by five rows and six columns, with row one consisting of the groupings by divisions; row two by the groupings by types of discharge; and rows three, four, and five by weather events. In addition, the current geographic position and the range of the data presented in the representation are indicated. All the data displayed are related to each other by means of latitude, longitude, date, time, the radius of coverage, and position/distance of the weather event capture stations.

In Fig. 3, we present a Level 3 grouping on the VIMAPS. In the line of the grouping by divisions, we can see the green color bar that represents the grouped amount of electric discharges of current Level 3 in the quadtree hierarchy. Level 3 is indicated by the icon at the top and represents the current level of the scene on the map, based on the camera's position relative to the Z-axis. On the line, the white color bar represents the Level 2 grouping, referring to the number of electrical discharges of its parent in the quadtree hierarchy. The orange bars show the Atmospheric Electrical Discharge groupings of the quadtree subregions (Level 4) of the current one (Level 3) represented in the form of clusters (Cluster A, Cluster B, Cluster C, and Cluster D). The sum of the quantities of the Level 4 clusters (sum of the divided regions) total the value of Level 3. In Depth 2, we have the grouping by discharge types: cloud or cloud-ground and their corresponding quantities. Lines 3, 4, and 5 present weather events captured by automatic surface weather stations, such as temperature, humidity, dew point, pressure, wind direction, wind gust, radiation, wind speed, and rain.

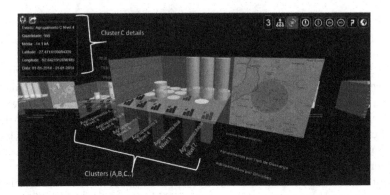

**Fig. 3.** Accurate view of the region selected (electrical discharges)

In this visualization environment, a set of icons is available for navigation, for example, icons to allow navigating and manipulating individual elements of a chart. Some bars in the chart have navigation functions. For example, it allows the user to navigate directly to another chart in the hierarchical order. The user can navigate freely using the mouse by clicking on a particular chart or navigating between the charts by moving the mouse left/right or forward/backward by clicking the corresponding left and right mouse buttons.

### 3.5   Usability Tests of VIMAPS

The usability evaluation verifies the relation established between users, tasks, hardware, applications, and other aspects in which users use the software. Problems can occur whenever users find it challenging to perform a task or access the documentation. Several methods can be attempted to evaluate applications, such as usability inspection, involving just expert users, while end-users can perform usability tests. One way to verify the users' opinion is by using questionnaires.

As part of this research, we prepared a questionnaire for usability inspecting of our application, based on heuristic evaluation [18]. This evaluation method is one of the most well-known ways to inspect usability, and it is a low-cost inspection method since it does not involve the final users. A few expert users can carry it out, and it can be applied when the software is already implemented. According to Nielsen [17], the best results from usability tests come from small tests with no more than five users. Nielsen [16] proposed heuristics, and some of them had to be adapted. The questionnaire evaluated aspects such as the objective, design, level of difficulty, documentation, help, and user satisfaction. All these aspects are important because they influence the system's acceptance.

A group of five experts that are specialist in visualization, and analysis of severe weather events performed the following steps in the usability test:

1. The experts were accommodated in the computer laboratory (each user was visually isolated from each other);

2. The experts filled out a pre-test questionnaire, which aimed to identify their profile (age, sex, education attainment and technological literacy). Each one had 5 min to fill the questionnaire;
3. VIMAPS was explained by an instructor for 30 min;
4. Each expert had 30 min to use VIMAPS; and
5. The experts filled out the usability questionnaire - each one had 15 min to complete the questionnaire.

We determined the users' profiles by analyzing the pre-test questionnaire results: five expert users between 30 and 45. A Likert scale [13] has been adopted (1 - Strongly disagree, 2 - Disagree, 3 - Neither agree nor disagree, 4 - Agree, 5 - Strongly agree) in the questionnaire. The heuristics adapted by the authors were assigned to a template to organize the information. Our questionnaire is an informal inspection tool, which is intended to be practical and answered by specialists. We aimed to identify usability problems and to classify and quantify the problems encountered. We also selected and prioritized the problems that needed to be corrected. We chose some Nielsen heuristics, whose initial focus was on desktop applications in the 1990 s and extended it, and we included satisfaction, according to ISO 9241-11:

– Ease of use: it refers to how comfortable and secure a user feels in using the application, both on the 2D map and the 3D objects: Question 1 It is easy to understand how to use the application and what purpose it serves.
– Accuracy: it deals with how precisely the symbols (rays) are positioned on the maps: Question 6 The objects (electrical discharges, clouds) are merged correctly with the maps (position, texture, scale).
– Satisfaction: this is how well the user's expectations are met: Question 13 The application is pleasant to use. Question 14 I would like to use the application again.

Table 1 depicts the consolidated report with evaluation results from the experts. VIMAPS was very well accepted by experts, indicating a perceived benefit in mixing 2D maps and 3D charts as part of one visualization solution. It is necessary to consider improvements in some functionality for novice users who have a low learning curve (question 12 had the lower grade). Even though VIMAPS is a complex application, involving a large amount of data, as well as unconventional interface and interaction, the answers to the usability questionnaire showed a high acceptance rate of the system, obtaining an average of 4.3 between all the questions.

## 4   COMETA

COMETA is a collaborative web application that allows multiple users to discuss weather information. During a collaboration session, users can add multimedia elements (video, images, and text) and also drawn objects (arrows, lines, circles) over 2D images captured from VIMAPS canvas (screenshot). In this way,

**Table 1.** VIMAPS usability results

| Questions | Heuristics | Average | Standard deviation |
|---|---|---|---|
| 1) It is easy to understand how to use the application and what purpose it serves. | Flexibility and efficiency of use | 4.8 | 0.4 |
| 2) Error messages are clear and easy to understand (i.e., video, text, audio). | Error prevention | 4.4 | 0.8 |
| 3) The interaction and navigation follow real-world conventions, thereby making the actions appear in a natural and logical order. | Match between system and the real world | 4.2 | 0.4 |
| 4) I never get lost when using the application, not knowing what to do. | Visibility of system status | 4.0 | 1.2 |
| 5)The application has a 2D interface for visualizing maps and 3D charts. I was not confused by the use of both. | Flexibility and efficiency of use | 4.0 | 1.0 |
| 6) The glyph icons (i.e., electrical discharges, clouds) are merged correctly with the maps (i.e., position, texture, scale). | Match between system and the real world | 4.6 | 0.5 |
| 7) The actions/feedback are standardized (i.e., same actions to trigger the same functionality). | Consistency and standards | 4.0 | 1.2 |
| 8) The interface has an appropriate design (i.e., icons, messages). | Aesthetic and minimalist design | 4.8 | 0.4 |
| 9) The system provides help and documentation (i.e., video, audio, text). | Help and documentation | 4.2 | 1.0 |
| 10) The help and documentation are easy to understand. | Help and documentation | 4.4 | 0.8 |
| 11) I felt I had freedom to interact and navigate with the visual elements (i.e., users can have different perspectives). | Flexibility and efficiency of use | 4.2 | 0.8 |
| 12) I believe novice users can easily use the application. | Flexibility and efficiency of use | 3.8 | 1.6 |
| 13) The application is pleasant to use. | Satisfaction | 3.8 | 0.4 |
| 14) I would like to use the application again. | Satisfaction | 4.6 | 0.5 |
| 15) It is easy to understand how to use the application and what purpose it serves. | Satisfaction | 4.6 | 0.5 |
| | **Overall average** | 4.3 | |

COMETA creates a shared workspace where participants can annotate, draw, brainstorm, and convey ideas during a synchronous or asynchronous discussion between participants in the collaborative session.

The rest of this Section is organized as follows: Sect. 3.1 presents the key motivating features of COMETA, Sect. 3.2 details COMETA architecture, as well as the usability tests performed.

## 4.1   Essential Features of COMETA

The essential features of COMETA are:

– It provides a set of tools that allows the creation of collaborative sessions for meteorological data analysis between remote users in a way that all interact in real-time, synchronously or asynchronously, and the interaction can be distributed over time. Through this feature, the user can capture an image (screenshot of the canvas) of the current VIMAPS scene view and its parameterized URL, and send it to COMETA to be added to a collaborative session. A collaborative session is formed by one or more images (called session object(s)) and between two or more participants. Collaborative discussions can occur synchronously or asynchronously. In synchronous form, two or more participants are collaborating in a session and on a session object and talking through an audio conference and using the interactive multimedia elements (any modification is updated, in real-time, for all participants, in its web interface). Asynchronously, the user enters a collaborative session, individually, opens a session object, and adds interactive multimedia elements, which will be available to the other participants at the time of opening the session. Therefore, a collaborative session can be viewed and analyzed later, allowing for its continuity, as well as being built synchronously among its participants.

– A collaborative session consists of session objects made up of an image (screenshot of the canvas) created with VIMAPS referring to the desired meteorological data, and interactive multimedia elements made available by COMETA. Through these elements, participants can add audio, video, images, texts, markers, graphics, geometric shapes positioned and organized chronologically, when the same element has more than one input. It is worth mentioning that the multimedia element will have a name and a color that indicates the user who owns the element. Moreover, the use of screenshots (2D images) simplifies and minimizes the computational cost in collaboration, if compared with the real-time processing and positioning of meteorological data (VIMAPS).

## 4.2   COMETA Architecture and Usability Test

– The Visualization Module, which allows users to create collaborative sessions. Images exported from VIMAPS, including multimedia elements and drawn objects, are shared during a collaboration session. It follows the paradigm What You See Is What I See (WYSIWIS) [5]:
  • Map Canvas is an area where VIMAPS 2D images are rendered;
  • Multimedia elements, through which users make a voice or video call with any participant. It also allows video, sound, and texts to be added; and
  • Drawn objects, which allows users to drawn over an image from VIMAPS. A tool palette allows the user to pick various drawing tools, such as a paintbrush or an eraser.

– The Engine Module, which manages and manipulates data from VIMAPS: it captures and exports images from VIMAPS to COMETA. VIMAPS allows capturing a 2D image and its URL parameterized to be visualized in COMETA. It is possible to visualize the meteorological data presented in VIMAPS. Through the URL, it is possible to load the data into VIMAPS precisely where the image was captured. The URL has the actual positions (coordinate systems, level, weather data used, slope, depth, and filters) obtained when the session object was created. While the user is visualizing the image in a collaborative session, when questions arise, they can click on the image and request its opening on VIMAPS. Through the URL, VIMAPS is loaded with the information (weather data) that generated this image, so the user can interact and analyze it in real-time. The user can restart the process if they want to capture a new image for the session;

- Real-time session sharing allows users to keep track of changes as they occur, without refreshing the browser. All elements added over the images are updated automatically. They can be recovered from the database;
- Drawn on canvas, which draws objects over the images. The objects can be recovered from the database;
- Voice chat allows communications between users via a voice channel;
- Audio/Video sharing, which manages voice and video calls;
- The Relational Database module manages and stores the session data (e.g., maps, drawings, texts, videos) that are retrieved during asynchronous sessions. It was implemented using the NHibernate framework and the SQL Server database; and
- Web technologies, which are the back-end solution implemented. ASP.NET is a framework designed for web development that allowed dynamic web pages and services to be produced. SignalR is a library for ASP.NET developers that facilitated the addition of real-time web functionality to the applications. WebRTC is a web framework that enabled real-time communication over peer-to-peer connections in the browser.

Computers and modern networks enable users to work together toward a common goal in real-time. COMETA users can overlap elements over a map; thus, it is necessary to preserve consistency across instances of the tool opened in different browser windows/tabs, which means that the state of objects and the history of operations must be the same for all users. In order to prevent inconsistencies and conflicts, objects were locked. Each object has a color that identifiers the user responsible for it. The architecture adopted was centralized that the server controls the distributed work of all users. The server collects and decides what to do with all users' events and where to display the output. This architecture's advantage is that the synchronization is easy, as state information always remains consistent since it is all located on the same computer [42].

COMETA works in an integrated way with VIMAPS, so it was necessary to consider using both tools to evaluate the collaboration. The questionnaire and the help of the usability experts described in Sect. 2 were used to evaluate the collaborative environment provided by COMETA and VIMAPS. The five experts who had already completed the pre-test questionnaire during the VIMAP test and performed the following tasks:

a) Use VIMAPS to visualize weather events about the city of Florianopolis, Brazil, and export the resulting map to COMETA. This task required users to navigate the map hierarchy in VIMAPS to the eighth level of depth (Fig. 4). Glyph icons represent weather events, and the user can click on them to see the details about them. The user is directed to the three-dimensional context environment when a user clicks on the glyph.

b) Use the 3D chart environment of VIMAPS to find the same meteorological events found in item a); navigate it, and export an image to COMETA.

c) Each expert must discuss the meteorological events of Florianópolis found on the item a) and b) with two other participants. Users were free to use collaborative tools (i.e., voice chat, video, lines, circles).

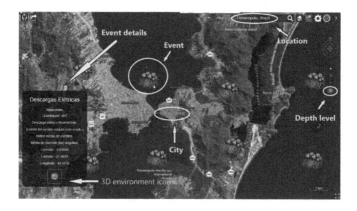

**Fig. 4.** 2D map of the city of Florianópolis on VIMAPS with overlapping 3D and 2D elements

The following steps were performed for the COMETA usability test:

1. The experts were accommodated in the computer laboratory (each user was visually isolated from the others);
2. COMETA integration with VIMAPS was explained by an instructor for 15 min;
3. Each expert had 30 min to use the tools however they wanted;
4. The tasks were explained;
5. Each expert had 10 min to solve each task; and
6. Each expert had 30 min to answer the questionnaire.

Table 2 depicts the results of the collaborative usability test. We chose some Nielsen heuristics, whose initial focus was on desktop applications in the 1990 s and extended it, and we included satisfaction, according to ISO 9241-11. Satisfaction aims to evaluate how much COMETA surpasses user expectations. We consider that reviews were consistent across experts and questions since the variations were not significant. Even though the results are preliminary, they proved useful in the validation of the applications. However, during the COMETA usability test, the collaborative test had the lowest score for question 12. This was expected since this class of application involves a large amount of data and requires diverse functionalities. This feedback review is important for improving applications.

The experiment successfully demonstrated the usability and usefulness of both VIMAPS and COMETA as tools for synchronous and asynchronous discussion. It appears that the users' engagement, motivation, participation, and awareness during the task led them to become unaware of the distance between them and cooperated naturally.

**Table 2.** Collaborative session using VIMAPS and COMETA - usability results

| Questions | Heuristics | Average | Standard deviation |
|---|---|---|---|
| 1) It is easy to understand how to use the application and what purpose it serves. | Flexibility and efficiency of use | 4.8 | 0.4 |
| 2) Error messages presented are clear and easy to understand (i.e., video, text, audio). | Error prevention | 4.4 | 0.5 |
| 3) The interaction and navigation follow real-world conventions, thereby making the actions appear in a natural and logical order. | Match between system and the real world | 4.6 | 0.5 |
| 4) I never get lost when using the application, not knowing what to do. | Visibility of system status | 4.4 | 0.5 |
| 5) The application has a 2D interface to map visualization and a 3D interface to chart visualization. This mixture does not cause confusion. | Flexibility and efficiency of use | 4.2 | 0.8 |
| 6) The interactive multimedia elements (text, video, audio, for example) are positioned correctly in the environment. | Match between system and the real world | 4.8 | 0.4 |
| 7) The actions/feedback are standardized (i.e., same actions to trigger the same functionality). | Consistency and standards | 4.6 | 0.5 |
| 8) The interface has an appropriate design (i.e., icons, messages). | Aesthetic and minimalist design | 4.6 | 0.5 |
| 9) The system provides help and documentation (i.e., video, audio, text). | Help and documentation | 4.4 | 0.8 |
| 10) The help and documentation are easy to understand. | Help and documentation | 4.4 | 0.8 |
| 11) User have freedom to interact and navigate (i.e., users can rotate the 3D charts easily). | Flexibility and efficiency of use | 4.8 | 0.4 |
| 12) Novice users can use the application easily. | Flexibility and efficiency of use | 4.6 | 0.5 |
| 13) The application is pleasant. | Satisfaction | 4.0 | 0.7 |
| 14) I would like to use the application again. | Satisfaction | 4.8 | 0.4 |
| 15) It is easy to understand how to use the application and what purpose it serves. | Satisfaction | 5.0 | 0.0 |
| | **Overall average** | 4.3 | |

# 5   Conclusions

This paper presented a web toolset to easily and flexibly facilitate the visualization, analysis, and discussion of severe weather events. It is composed of VIMAPS, which allows users to visualize and analyze severe weather events using 2D maps and a 3D chart environment to visualize spatial relations from any desired angle. Moreover, COMETA allows the collaborative analysis of severe weather events between remote users synchronously or asynchronously. The collaborative approach presented here lies in the broad exchange of information to better understand the underlined features hidden in the multi-source data. This tool set's main scientific benefits include understanding weather systems' characteristics and studies related to trajectories of thunderstorms.

VIMAPS and COMETA were tested using real data and showed that they fulfill their class of application's performance and usability requirements. VIMAPS, naturally a complex application, was very well accepted by experts, indicating that it is possible to perform detailed observations of a region over time, using 2D maps and a 3D chart environment. This approach allows users to visualize objects of interest in detail and, at the same time, get an overview. However, the VIMAPS usability test indicates that some of its aspects must be improved;

for example, novice users should be enabled to learn how to use the application as fast as possible.

Tools such as VIMAPS are necessary to study and discuss severe weather events and define resources for prevention and the anticipation of services, minimizing the damage caused by extreme climatic events. Images have always been used to improve how people visualize information, primarily using charts and figures. However, 3D environments can amplify the user's ability to process data in more dimensions. It also supports multimodal interactions, allowing for more intuitive use of the applications.

Decision-makers need appropriate tools to prepare for future severe weather events and engage in appropriate actions. A collaborative tool such as COMETA is necessary to facilitate information exchange among experts to assist decision-makers in taking action efficiently. COMETA works in an integrated way with VIMAPS, and then both tools were considered to evaluate collaboration. The experiment was very successful, although some improvements are also necessary, for example, a mechanism to ensure the user never gets lost when using the application.

From the observed results, we can conclude that our tool has achieved its purpose. For future work, we intend to adapt VIMAPS and COMETA to support the visualization, analysis, and discussion of other data, such as epidemic information (for such things as the Zika virus, dengue fever, chikungunya, and H1N1), electoral data, information on deforestation, fire data, the latest global data on drug production, trafficking and consumption, and crime data, among others.

We believe that future advances will be made by better promoting collaborative work between scientists interested in climate forecasts. Decision-makers will thus be able to take proactive actions to avoid or minimize damages. Also, the use of immersive visualization of interactive three-dimensional representations can allow easy attention between detail and context views to improve the process of data analysis.

# References

1. Afzal, S., et al.: The state of the art in visual analysis approaches for ocean and atmospheric datasets. In: Computer Graphics Forum, vol. 38, pp. 881–907. Wiley Online Library (2019)
2. Alder, J.R., Hostetler, S.W.: Web based visualization of large climate data sets. Environ. Model. Softw. **68**, 175–180 (2015)
3. Feng, H., Fan, H.: 3d weather simulation on 3d virtual earth. In: 2012 IEEE International Geoscience and Remote Sensing Symposium, pp. 543–545. IEEE (2012)
4. Ghate, P.V., Pati, H.K.: Collaborative distributed communication in heterogeneous environments: a comprehensive survey. J. Netw. Comput. Appl. **61**, 1–20 (2016). https://doi.org/10.1016/j.jnca.2015.10.006, https://www.sciencedirect.com/science/article/pii/S1084804515002271
5. Greenberg, S., Hayne, S., Rada, R.: Designing groupware for real-time drawing (1995)

6. Jacks, E., Davidson, J., Wai, H.: Guidelines on early warning systems and application of nowcasting and warning operations. World Meteorological Organization (2010)
7. Jakob, D., Walland, D.: Variability and long-term change in Australian temperature and precipitation extremes. Weather Climate Extremes **14**, 36–55 (2016)
8. Kelley, O.A.: Adapting an existing visualization application for browser-based deployment: a case study from the tropical rainfall measuring mission. Comput. Geosci. **51**, 228–237 (2013)
9. Kern, M., Hewson, T., Schätler, A., Westermann, R., Rautenhaus, M.: Interactive 3d visual analysis of atmospheric fronts. IEEE Trans. Visual. Comput. Graph. **25**(1), 1080–1090 (2018)
10. Lewis, S.C., King, A.D.: Evolution of mean, variance and extremes in 21st century temperatures. Weather Climate Extremes **15**, 1–10 (2017)
11. Li, J., Jiang, Y., Yang, C., Huang, Q., Rice, M.: Visualizing 3d/4d environmental data using many-core graphics processing units (GPUS) and multi-core central processing units (cpus). Comput. Geosci. **59**, 78–89 (2013)
12. Li, Z., et al.: A high performance web-based system for analyzing and visualizing spatiotemporal data for climate studies. In: Liang, S.H.L., Wang, X., Claramunt, C. (eds.) W2GIS 2013. LNCS, vol. 7820, pp. 190–198. Springer, Heidelberg (2013). https://doi.org/10.1007/978-3-642-37087-8_14
13. Likert, R.: A technique for the measurement of attitudes. Archives of psychology (1932)
14. Liu, P., Gong, J., Yu, M.: Visualizing and analyzing dynamic meteorological data with virtual globes: a case study of tropical cyclones. Environ. Model. Softw. **64**, 80–93 (2015)
15. Murata, K.T., et al.: Real-time 3d visualization of phased array weather radar data via concurrent processing in science cloud. In: 2016 IEEE 7th Annual Information Technology, Electronics and Mobile Communication Conference (IEMCON), pp. 1–7. IEEE (2016)
16. Nielsen, J.: Usability Engineering. Morgan Kaufmann, Burlington (1994)
17. Nielsen, J.: Why you only need to test with 5 users (2000)
18. Nielsen, J., Molich, R.: Heuristic evaluation of user interfaces. In: Proceedings of the SIGCHI Conference on Human Factors in Computing Systems, pp. 249–256 (1990)
19. Ohneiser, O., Kleinert, M., Muth, K., Gluchshenko, O., Ehr, H., Groß, N., Temme, M.M.: Bad weather highlighting: advanced visualization of severe weather and support in air traffic control displays. In: 2019 IEEE/AIAA 38th Digital Avionics Systems Conference (DASC), pp. 1–10. IEEE (2019)
20. Papathomas, T.V., Schiavone, J.A., Julesz, B.: Applications of computer graphics to the visualization of meteorological data. In: Proceedings of the 15th Annual Conference on Computer Graphics and Interactive Techniques, pp. 327–334 (1988)
21. Stähli, L., Rudi, D., Raubal, M.: Turbulence ahead-a 3d web-based aviation weather visualizer. In: Proceedings of the 31st Annual ACM Symposium on User Interface Software and Technology, pp. 299–311 (2018)
22. Theußl, T., Dasari, H.P., Hoteit, I., Srinivasan, M.: Simulation and visualization of the cyclonic storm chapala over the Arabian sea: a case study. In: 2016 4th Saudi International Conference on Information Technology (Big Data Analysis)(KACSTIT), pp. 1–6. IEEE (2016)

23. Yang, C., Raskin, R., Goodchild, M., Gahegan, M.: Geospatial cyberinfrastructure: past, present and future. Comput. Environ. Urban Syst. **34**(4), 264–277 (2010)
24. Zhang, T., Li, J., Liu, Q., Huang, Q.: A cloud-enabled remote visualization tool for time-varying climate data analytics. Environ. Model. Softw. **75**, 513–518 (2016)
25. Ziegeler, S., Moorhead, R.J., Croft, P.J., Lu, D.: The metvr case study: meteorological visualization in an immersive virtual environment. In: Proceedings Visualization, 2001. VIS 2001, pp. 489–596. IEEE (2001)

# Urban and Regional Planning

# Investigating Alternative Clustering Algorithms for a Cluster-First, Route-Second Truck and Drone Scheduling Algorithm

Sarah Dillon, Rudolf Ernst, and Jacomine Grobler$^{(\boxtimes)}$ (ID)

Department of Industrial Engineering, Stellenbosch University,
Stellenbosch, South Africa
`jacomine.grobler@gmail.com`

**Abstract.** This paper investigates alternative clustering algorithms as part of a cluster-first, route-second method for solving a vehicle routing problem with drones. The problem consists of multiple purpose-built trucks, each having a single drone that can be launched to make deliveries, which set out to deliver products to customers. The drones are able to intercept and land on a moving truck after making a delivery, which speeds up the synchronisation and delivery time. Various different clustering algorithms are evaluated as part of a self-adaptive neighbourhood search differential evolution algorithm and applied to fifteen publicly available datasets, containing three types of customer distributions: double-centred, single-centred, and uniform. The customer nodes are segmented into clusters and each cluster is serviced by one truck and drone pair. Each cluster is solved as a travelling salesman problem with drone with interceptions using the nearest neighbour heuristic for initial solutions self-adaptive neighbourhood search differential evolution algorithm. A k-means clustering algorithm, the Gaussian mixture model, and agglomerative nesting are evaluated. From the study, it is conclusive that the Gaussian mixture model is the best clustering algorithm for double-centred datasets. The k-means algorithm is the best clustering algorithm for single-centred and uniform datasets. The contributions of this paper include the only cluster first-route second approach to solving the vehicle routing problem with drone with interceptions. This paper contributes to the computational sciences by using advanced computing capabilities for decision support to improve the performance of an intelligent transport system.

**Keywords:** Clustering · Drone delivery · Vehicle routing problem with drones

## 1 Introduction

Drone technology has been on the rise in recent years, and it continues to improve, which broadens the application of drones for personal and commercial use. Due to their unique capabilities, drones can play an essential role in a

O. Gervasi et al. (Eds.): ICCSA 2023, LNCS 13957, pp. 147–162, 2023.
https://doi.org/10.1007/978-3-031-36808-0_10

variety of industries, including agriculture, security, distribution, and commercial delivery [1]. Last-mile delivery refers to the transportation of goods from the warehouse or depot to the final destination [2]. Despite the shorter delivery time expected by customers, the e-commerce industry has remained chiefly dependent on trucks for last-mile delivery operations [1]. Generally, products are housed in warehouses and transported to local depots. From the depots, the products are delivered to the customer's door. Trucks complete the movement of goods from the warehouses and the movement of goods from the depots to the customers, also known as the "last mile." However, due to increased customer expectations and the growth of the e-commerce industry, the traditional method of truck-only deliveries might not necessarily be the most optimal. In addition, an increase in traffic congestion and fuel prices affects the price that the customer pays for the delivery, which needs to be factored in along with the desired delivery speed [3].

One method to improve a last-mile delivery system is to include drones in the delivery process. Drones have the advantage of travelling faster than trucks and do not have to follow a fixed route, such as a road [4]. However, both the capacity and flight distance of drones are limited. If drones were launched directly from the depot, deliveries could not be made to customers outside of the drone's service range. The limitations mentioned above can be overcome by using a combination of trucks and drones. A *Drone-truck combined operations* (DTCO) system refers to a drone and truck working together to perform tasks [4].

Clustering refers to the grouping of elements that are of the same type or appear close together [5]. An optimally clustered group of orders will result in an effective delivery schedule. A truck and drone would service each cluster individually; therefore, each cluster is assigned a truck with a drone onboard. The truck would drive through the cluster and service specific customers, while the drone would assist with the other customers. Therefore, the overall delivery route distance that the truck travels is impacted by the effectiveness of the clustering algorithm applied. The DTCO system can significantly improve the last-mile delivery process by harnessing the advantages of both vehicles involved. The new system will optimise the delivery process by decreasing the delivery price and time, as efficient routes cannot be obtained without effective clustering.

In this paper, a *VRP with drones with interceptions* (VRPDi) is solved using a cluster-first, route-second approach. The results indicate that the k-means algorithm is best for clustering double-centred and larger uniform datasets, while the Gaussian mixture model is preferred for single-centred and smaller uniformly distributed datasets.

The paper is significant, since the clustering algorithm utilised in a cluster-first, route-second algorithm, has a marked impact on routing performance. Investigating the impact of alternative clustering algorithms has, however, not yet received priority in drone scheduling research.

The paper organisation is as follows: A literature review is presented in Sect. 2. The problem is described in Sect. 3. The empirical evaluation of the alternative clustering algorithms is documented in Sect. 4. A conclusion of the paper is presented in Sect. 5.

## 2    Literature Review

The clustering algorithms evaluated in this study are introduced in Sect. 2.2, along with information about where they have been applied to DTCO problems. Literature on DTCO problems is covered in Sect. 2.1. Next in Sect. 2.3, the nearest neighbour heuristic for initial solutions self-adaptive neighbourhood search differential evolution (NNHis SaNSDE) algorithm is introduced, which is used to schedule the truck and drone deliveries of each cluster.

### 2.1    DTCO Research

DTCO problems have been addressed in multiple survey papers. Otto et al. (2018) [6], Khoufi et al. (2019) [7], Chung et al. (2020) [4], Poikonen and Campbell (2020) [8]; Moshref-Javadi and Winkenbach (2021) [9], and Liang and Luo (2022) [10] all published survey papers where they addressed the most prominent and important research with regard to DTCO problems.

Research on where drones and trucks can intercept each other between customer nodes is sparse, as it is a new addition to current DTCO problem variants. Notable examples include Li et al. [11], Salama and Srinivas [12], and Thomas et al. [13], where drones can be dispatched and retrieved on the arc between two customers.

### 2.2    Clustering Literature

The k-means clustering algorithm is a centroid-based method for clustering a dataset with the objective of minimising the variance of the data points within each cluster [14]. The k-means clustering algorithm is commonly applied in a cluster-first, route-second approach when solving drone and truck scheduling problems. Ferrandez (2016) [15], investigated an optimisation algorithm that aimed to minimise the total delivery time of the DTCO system. The truck travelled through the centres of clusters that were obtained using the k-means clustering algorithm. Chang and Lee (2018) [16], proposed a new approach for routing the DTCO system, which used shift weights to move the cluster centres closer to the depot. The clusters used in this approach were determined using k-means.

Distribution-based clustering methods group data points based on the likelihood of the points belonging to the same probability distribution within the dataset [17]. Each cluster has a centre, and as the distance from that centre increases, the probability of a data point being a member of that cluster decreases [14]. The probability distribution applied in this paper is the *Gaussian* distribution (GMM) [18]. To the best of the author's knowledge, the Gaussian mixture model has not been used to perform the clustering of a cluster-first, route-second approach for solving DTCO problems.

Hierarchical-based clustering algorithms separate the dataset into clusters based on a measure of similarity. The objective is not to find the best cluster, but to merge the closest pair of data points or split the farthest pair [19].

*agglomerative nesting* (AGNES) is applied in this paper. Hierarchical clustering has frequently been applied to solve TSPs. Changyou Wu and Xisong Fu (2020) [20] applied an *agglomerative greedy brainstorm optimization* (AG-BSO) algorithm to a TSP. The algorithm applied a greedy algorithm to the TSP and replaced the traditional k-means clustering algorithm with the AG-BSO algorithm. Marco Lama and John Mittenthal (2013) [21], proposed a hierarchical clustering-based heuristic for a multi-depot location-routing problem. Abdulah Fajar (2011) [22] applied hierarchical clustering to a Euclidean TSP. To the best of the author's knowledge, hierarchical clustering has not been used to perform the cluster-first, route-second approach for solving DTCO problems.

## 2.3    NNHis SaNSDE Algorithm

The NNHis SaNSDE algorithm is a population-based metaheuristic applied in this paper to determine the routing and allocation of nodes to drones and trucks after clustering the data. The NNHis SaNSDE was introduced by Ernst et al. (2023) [23], where it was applied with great success to a TSP with drones with interceptions. The NNHis SaNSDE built on the SaNSDE-based algorithm introduced by Yang et al. [24], combined with problem-specific nearest neighbour heuristics that introduced good solutions into the initial population to guide the search process.

By introducing several good initial solutions into the starting population, it was possible for the NNHis SaNSDE to improve these solutions and find even better routes with shorter delivery times in the neighbourhood of the solutions. The six initial solutions introduced into the first population of the NNHis SaNSDE are explained below:

- The first solution is generated using a *nearest neighbour heuristic* (NNH). The depot is considered the first node. The node with the smallest distance from the depot is chosen as the second node to visit. Thereafter, the node closest to the second node is allocated as the next stop. This process is continued until all nodes have been allocated and the final node is again assigned as the depot. All nodes are to be visited by the truck, and the drone is stationary.
- The second solution is generated using two parallel NNHs. Two different routes are generated, both starting from the depot. After allocating all nodes, the second route is reversed and connected onto the end of the first half of the route to ensure that the depot is visited first and last. Again, all nodes are visited by a truck.
- The third solution is generated using two parallel NNHs, as in solution 2. However, in the third solution, nodes are continuously added to either route depending on which endpoint is nearest to any unallocated node. The second route is again reversed after all nodes are allocated and connected to the first route to construct one full route where the depot is visited at the start and end of the route with truck-only nodes.

- The fourth solution is generated using an *alternating nearest neighbour heuristic* (ANNH). The first node, which is the depot, is allocated to the truck. Thereafter, the node with the smallest distance to the first node is allocated to the drone. The nearest node to the drone node is then chosen and allocated to the truck. This procedure is continued until all the nodes have been allocated, and the last node is then again allocated as the depot.
- The fifth solution is generated using two parallel ANNHs, combining solutions two and four, by alternating between allocating truck and drone nodes. This process is continued until all nodes have been added. The second half of the route is again reversed and added onto the end of the first half of the route to ensure that the depot is visited first and last.
- The sixth solution is generated similarly to the third solution, except that nodes are now alternated between the truck and the drone (thus combining solutions three and four).

The SaNSDE NNHis makes use of decision variables, which are stochastic continuous values between a an upper bound, $u_b$, and lower bound, $l_b$, which are converted to determine the allocation and routing of solutions. The SaNSDE alters these decision variable values as it moves through the search space. Each solution contains $2 * n$ decision variable values, where $n$ is the number of customer nodes to be visited. The first $n$ decision variables, called priority values, are sorted in descending order, which then gives the permutation or order that nodes are visited. The second $n$ decision variables, called allocation variables, are used for allocating nodes. Any decision variable value bigger than or equal to zero is allocated to the truck, while values smaller than zero are allocated to the drone, thereby discretising the search space.

One of the restrictions of the VRPDi model is that only one drone delivery is allowed per drone flight, whereafter the drone has to return to the truck. The continuous values, which are used to determine the routing and allocation of nodes, can often lead to solutions that have multiple consecutive drone nodes. Consecutive drone nodes are not allowed, and thus repair mechanisms are used to turn these infeasible solutions into valid ones. The repair mechanism changes the second consecutive drone node into a truck node by changing the decision variable value to $u_b/2$ (from the negative number it was before). The repair process ensures that the previously infeasible nodes will now be visited by a truck node, but also that the SaNSDE's search process can still change the decision variable values to find different solutions.

## 3    Problem Description

The VRPDi is based on a set of trucks and drones that work together to complete the last-mile delivery of a predetermined number of packages. A set of trucks and drones depart from the depot simultaneously. Each of the drones can be launched from its corresponding stationary truck at any of the nodes. Once the drone has completed a delivery, it either intercepts the truck while it is in motion or flies straight to the next truck node if an interception is not possible due to the truck arriving at the next node before the drone is able to intercept it. This model seeks to optimise the drone's flying time since the drone attempts to not have to fly to the next customer node. Rather, the drone can fly to a predetermined optimal point where it intercepts the truck, resulting in less waiting time. After an interception, the drone remains on the truck until the truck reaches the next customer node. Once the truck has reached the next customer, the drone can again be launched to complete another delivery. The model explanation follows as provided in [25].

- $n$ is the number of customers to be serviced.
- $T_{ijk}$ denotes the total time for the scenario where a drone delivers to node $j$ while the truck delivers to nodes $i$ and $k$. $T_{ijk}$ is calculated based on the drone and truck intercepting each other after the drone delivery. This interception point is calculated using the standard mathematical equations for two objects interceptions explained in [25].
- $T_{ik}$ denotes the total time for the scenario where the truck delivers to nodes $i$ and $k$ when there is not a drone delivery in between.
- $w$ is the drone offload time

With the following decision variables:

- $u_i$ is used to eliminate sub-tours.

$$x_{ijk} = \begin{cases} 1 & \text{if the truck services customer } i \text{ before } k \text{ while the drone services } j \text{ in between} \\ 0 & \text{otherwise} \end{cases}$$

$$b_j = \begin{cases} 1 & \text{if the customer } j \text{ is serviced by the drone} \\ 0 & \text{if customer } j \text{ is serviced by the truck} \end{cases}$$

$$z_{ik} = \begin{cases} 1 & \text{if the truck travels between customer } i \text{ and } k \\ 0 & \text{otherwise} \end{cases}$$

$$\min \sum_{i=1}^{n} \sum_{k=1}^{n} \sum_{j=1}^{n} x_{ijk} T_{ijk} + \sum_{i=1}^{n} \sum_{k=1}^{n} z_{ik} T_{ik} \left(1 - \sum_{j=1}^{n} x_{ijk}\right) - w \tag{1}$$

Subject to:

$$z_{ii} = 0 \qquad \forall i \in \{1, ..., n\} \tag{2}$$

$$x_{iii}, x_{iij}, x_{iji}, x_{ijj} = 0 \qquad \forall i, j \in \{1, ..., n\} \tag{3}$$

$$z_{ik} = \left(\sum_{j=1}^{n} x_{ijk} = 1\right) => (z_{ik} = 1) \qquad \forall i, k \in \{1, ..., n\} \tag{4}$$

$$b_j = \sum_{i=1}^{n} \sum_{k=1}^{n} x_{ijk} \qquad \forall j \in \{1, ..., n\} \tag{5}$$

$$\sum_{i=1}^{n} z_{iq} - \sum_{k=1}^{n} z_{qk} = 0 \qquad \forall q \in \{1, ..., n\} \tag{6}$$

$$(b_i = 0) => (\sum_{k=1}^{n} z_{ik} = 1) \qquad \forall i \in \{1, ..., n\} \tag{7}$$

$$(b_k = 0) => (\sum_{i=1}^{n} z_{ik} = 1) \qquad \forall k \in \{1, ..., n\} \tag{8}$$

$$\sum_{j=1}^{n} x_{ijk} \leq 1 \qquad \forall i, k \in \{1, ..., n\} \tag{9}$$

$$u_i + z_{ij} \leq u_j + (n-1)(1 - z_{ij}) \qquad \forall i, j, j \neq 1 \in \{1, ..., n\} \tag{10}$$

$$u_1 = 0 \tag{11}$$

$$x_{ijk}, b_i, z_{ik} \in \{0, 1\} \qquad \forall \, i, j, k \in \{1, ..., n\} \tag{12}$$

- The objective function (1) minimises the total time that the drone and truck travel, which includes the travel time of all truck deliveries which do not include a drone release and intercept.
- Constraints (2) and (3) simplify the model by ensuring that the truck and drone cannot travel from the current node back to a previously visited node.
- Constraints (4) links $z_{ik}$ and $x_{ijk}$.
- Constraints (5) links $b_j$ and $x_{ijk}$.
- Constraints (6) ensure that if a delivery is conducted at a customer location, the truck or drone leaves that same customer.
- Constraints (7) and (8) ensure that each customer is arrived at from exactly one other customer (by truck), and that from each customer there is a departure to exactly one other customer (by truck). If node $j$ is serviced by a drone, then no trucks enter or exit node $j$.
- Constraints (9) ensure that only one drone delivery can occur between two truck deliveries.
- Constraints (10) and (11) eliminate any sub-tours.
- Constraints (12) restricts the decision variables to binary values.

## 4   Empirical Evaluation

The VRPDi is solved by first clustering the customer nodes and then routing each cluster using a *Nearest Neighbour Heuristic for initial solutions Self-adaptive Differential Evolution with Neighbourhood Search* (NNHis SaNSDE) algorithm. A single truck and drone are assigned to each cluster. The clustering is performed on multiple different datasets from Bouman [26], with varying distributions. Single-centred datasets contain a central location where most nodes are scattered around it; double-centred datasets contain two centres with nodes scattered around both; and uniform datasets contain uniformly scattered nodes and no centre.

Each clustering algorithm is applied once per dataset, whereafter the NNHis SaNSDE is applied to each cluster for 30 optimisation runs. The resulting delivery times are then taken as the average over the 30 optimisation runs, which are reported in this section. The boundary values of $u_b$ and $l_b$ are chosen as –100 and 100.

Tables 1, 2, 3 provide a summary of the most important results. Tables 1, 2, and 3 present the average delivery time of the cluster with the longest delivery time for each dataset-clustering algorithm pair. The longest average delivery time from the clusters represents the overall average delivery time for the truck and drone systems to service the dataset, since the longest average delivery time is the limiting time.

### 4.1  Double-Centred Datasets Results

Examples of the final clusters for the datasets of size 250 are plotted in Fig. 1, 2, Fig. 3. The cluster size distribution for the three clustering algorithms was relatively even due to the clear separation of the double-centred datasets. While this trend is not present in the smaller datasets, the larger the dataset, the more apparent the trend becomes.

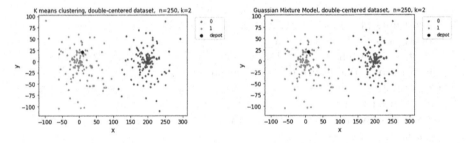

**Fig. 1.** k-means doublecenter-3-n250 clus-   **Fig. 2.** GMM doublecenter-3-n250 clusters
ters

The average delivery times for the double-centred datasets are presented in Table 1. The Gaussian mixture model resulted in the shortest average delivery time for each of the double-centred dataset sizes. The k-means clustering and AGNES algorithms resulted in longer average delivery times. The k-means clustering algorithm and AGNES obtained similar results for most datasets, but the AGNES algorithm performed the worst for the doublecenter-5-n500 by a significant margin of almost 30 time units.

### 4.2  Single-Centred Datasets Results

Examples of the final clusters for the datasets of size 250 are plotted in Fig. 4, 5, Fig. 6, showing the distributions of the different clustering algorithms. The

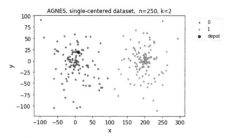

**Fig. 3.** AGNES doublecenter-3-n250 clusters

**Table 1.** Double-centred dataset results

| Name | Clustering algorithm | k | Average delivery time |
| --- | --- | --- | --- |
| doublecenter-alpha3-61-n20 | k-means | 2 | 57.32 |
| | Gaussian Mixture Model | 2 | **57.29** |
| | AGNES | 2 | 57.32 |
| doublecenter-91-n100 | k-means | 2 | 96.91 |
| | Gaussian Mixture Model | 2 | **94.52** |
| | AGNES | 2 | 99.36 |
| doublecenter-3-n250 | k-means | 2 | 173.84 |
| | Gaussian Mixture Model | 2 | **166.12** |
| | AGNES | 2 | 173.69 |
| doublecenter-3-n375 | k-means | 2 | 243.40 7 |
| | Gaussian Mixture Model | 2 | **214.52** |
| | AGNES | 2 | 243.40 |
| doublecenter-5-n500 | k-means | 2 | 240.99 |
| | Gaussian Mixture Model | 2 | **240.86** |
| | AGNES | 2 | 270.65 |

clusters are spread fairly evenly in terms of the number of customers per cluster, with a clear central cluster and three spread-out clusters around it.

The average delivery times for the single-centred datasets are presented in Table 2. For the single-centred datasets, the k-means clustering algorithm resulted in the shortest average delivery time for the datasets of sizes 100, 250, 375, and 500. For the size 20 dataset, the Gaussian mixture model resulted in the shortest average delivery time, and the AGNES algorithm resulted in the shortest total truck distance. However, despite the short truck distance, the AGNES algorithm also resulted in the longest average delivery time.

Figs. 7, 8, 9 present the average delivery time per cluster for the singlecenter-6-n500 dataset. The graphs show that the average delivery time is highly consistent across the clusters for the k-means clustering algorithm. The variance for the k-means clustering algorithm's average delivery times is 124.04. The Gaussian mixture model and AGNES algorithm have greater variances of 482.37 and

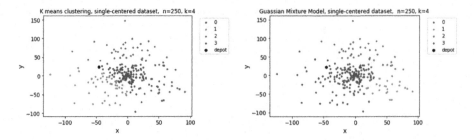

**Fig. 4.** k-means singlecenter-1-n250 clus-  **Fig. 5.** GMM singlecenter-1-n250 clusters
ters

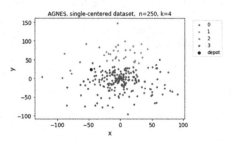

**Fig. 6.** AGNES singlecenter-1-n250 clusters

1149.40, respectively. Therefore, the k-means clustering algorithm results in the most uniform average delivery time distribution when the NNHis SaNSDE is applied to each cluster.

## 4.3   Uniform Dataset Results

Examples of the final clusters for the datasets of size 250 are plotted in Figs. 10 and 12. The clusters obtained by k-means and GMM are very similar, while the clusters obtained by AGNES have a much larger variance in size and an average number of nodes per cluster. The average delivery times for the uniform datasets are presented in Table 3.

The uniform datasets do not appear to have one clustering algorithm that tends to deliver a shorter average delivery time or total truck distance. The k-means clustering algorithm has the best performance on the larger datasets, while the AGNES algorithm greatly outperformed the other algorithms on the uniform-62-n20 dataset.

Figs. 13, 14, 15 show the cluster average delivery time distribution of the uniform-8-n500 dataset. The most uniform average delivery time distribution is observed for the k-means clustering algorithm. The variance in average delivery time over all clusters for the k-means clustering algorithm is 29.25. The variances for the Gaussian mixture model and the AGNES algorithm's average delivery

**Table 2.** Single-centred dataset results

| Name | Clustering algorithm | k | Average delivery time |
|------|---------------------|---|----------------------|
| singlecenter-61-n20 | k-means | 4 | 24.79 |
| | Gaussian mixture model | 4 | **24.61** |
| | AGNES | 4 | 29.23 |
| singlecenter-100-n100 | k-means | 4 | **36.84** |
| | Gaussian mixture model | 4 | 47.22 |
| | AGNES | 4 | 47.64 |
| singlecenter-1-n250 | k-means | 4 | **59.46** |
| | Gaussian mixture model | 4 | 64.35 |
| | AGNES | 4 | 131.24 |
| singlecenter-1-n375 | k-means | 4 | **62.17** |
| | Gaussian mixture model | 4 | 70.01 |
| | AGNES | 4 | 143.52 |
| singlecenter-6-n500 | k-means | 5 | **77.49** |
| | Gaussian mixture model | 5 | 101.35 |
| | AGNES | 5 | 109.18 |

times are 151.34 and 174.57, respectively. The trend is observed across all the dataset sizes for the k-means clustering algorithm.

Next, the results of the VRPDi study are validated in the form of Mann-Whitney U statistical tests. The statistical tests compare the delivery time results of the different clustering algorithms for a statistical difference with a significance level of 0.05. The results are measured as wins-draws-losses and presented in Table 4. A win (or loss) indicates the number of times each algorithm statistically significantly differs in average delivery time when compared.

It is clear from Table 4 that no clustering algorithm, after a NNHis SaNSDE is applied to solve each cluster, significantly outperforms the other clustering

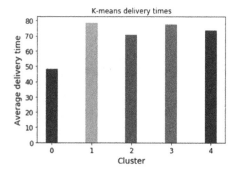
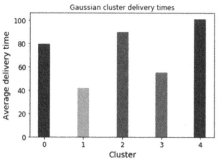

**Fig. 7.** k-means sc-6-n500 delivery time distribution

**Fig. 8.** Gaussian sc-6-n500 delivery time distribution

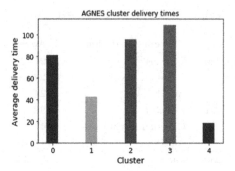

**Fig. 9.** AGNES sc-6-n500 delivery time distribution

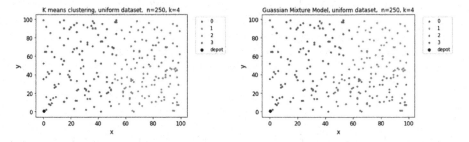

**Fig. 10.** k-means uniform-8-n250 clusters     **Fig. 11.** GMM uniform-8-n250 clusters

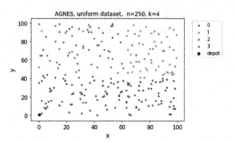

**Fig. 12.** AGNES uniform-8-n250 clusters

algorithms when the three distributions are combined. Therefore, in order to choose an algorithm that will have a higher statistical chance of performing well, it is necessary to know the distribution of the dataset.

**Table 3.** Uniform dataset results

| Name | Clustering algorithm | k | Average delivery time |
|------|---------------------|---|----------------------|
| uniform-62-n20 | k-means | 4 | 21.74 |
| | Gaussian Mixture Model | 4 | 19.50 |
| | AGNES | 4 | **15.80** |
| uniform-91-n100 | k-means | 4 | 49.91 |
| | Gaussian Mixture Model | 4 | **48.08** |
| | AGNES | 4 | 48.66 |
| uniform-8-n250 | k-means | 4 | 49.91 |
| | Gaussian Mixture Model | 4 | **48.09** |
| | AGNES | 4 | 48.67 |
| uniform-1-n375 | k-means | 4 | **57.43** |
| | Gaussian Mixture Model | 4 | 60.65 |
| | AGNES | 4 | 66.33 |
| uniform-8-n500 | k-means | 4 | **66.62** |
| | Gaussian Mixture Model | 4 | 70.51 |
| | AGNES | 4 | 81.03 |

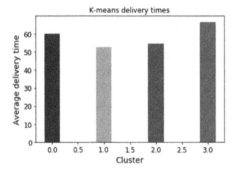

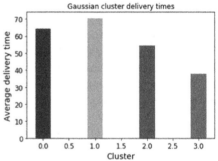

**Fig. 13.** k-means u-8-n500 delivery time distribution

**Fig. 14.** Gaussian u-8-n500 delivery time distribution

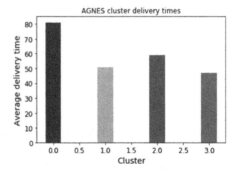

**Fig. 15.** AGNES u-8-n500 delivery time distribution

**Table 4.** Combined hypothesis test results

|  | k-means | Gaussian mixture model | AGNES |
|---|---|---|---|
| k-means | X | 7-2-6 | 6-2-7 |
| Gaussian mixture model | 6-2-7 | X | 6-3-6 |
| AGNES | 7-2-6 | 6-3-6 | X |

## 5   Conclusion

This paper considered a VRP with drones with interceptions [25], where a cluster-first, route-second approach was used to solve the last-mile delivery problem. K-means, a Gaussian mixture model, and the AGNES algorithm were applied to cluster customers from pre-determined datasets. Each dataset was then solved in the form of a TSP, where a truck with a drone that can be launched from it to make deliveries was applied to each cluster. Each cluster was routed with the NNHis SaNSDE algorithm [23]. The results indicated that the distribution of the dataset is an important factor when deciding which clustering algorithm to apply. The Gaussian mixture model performed the best for double-centred datasets. The k-means algorithm significantly outperformed the other clustering algorithms for single-centred datasets. The k-means algorithm performed the best for larger, uniformly distributed datasets but was outperformed by the Gaussian mixture model and AGNES for smaller, uniform datasets.

In this paper, only three clustering algorithms were investigated and tested. Further research can investigate clustering algorithms that were not considered. To allow for direct comparison between the clustering algorithms, the elbow method was used to solve for the $k$-value for all the clustering algorithms. However, there are other methods that can be used to solve for the optimal $k$-value. It is possible that a different method, such as the silhouette metric, could provide a better solution. Future work can thus consider applying different methods for determining the $k$-value. Different algorithms can also be applied instead of the NNHis SaNSDE algorithm when routing each of the clusters. Finally, the realism of the model can be improved to, for example, take into account weather conditions and traffic congestion.

**Acknowledgements.** This work is based on the research supported in part by the National Research Foundation of South Africa (Grant Number: 129340).

## References

1. Salama, M., Srinivas, S.: Joint optimization of customer location clustering and drone-based routing for last-mile deliveries. Transp. Res. Part C: Emerg. Technol. **114**, 620–642 (2020)
2. DoveTail. 5 strategies for effective last-mile delivery logistics. https://www.dovetail.co.za/5-strategies-for-effective-last-mile-delivery-logistics/

3. Francois Emil Knoetze. Solving a last mile truck and drone delivery schedule to optimality (2021)

4. Chung, S.H., Sah, B., Lee, J.: Optimization for drone and drone-truck combined operations: a review of the state of the art and future directions. Comput. Oper. Res. **123**, 105004 (2020)

5. Simpson, J.A., Weiner, E.S.C.: Oxford English Dictionary. Claredon Press, Oxford (1989)

6. Otto, A., Agatz, N., Campbell, J., Golden, B., Pesch, E.: Optimization approaches for civil applications of unmanned aerial vehicles (UAVs) or aerial drones: a survey. Networks **72**(4), 411–458 (2018)

7. Khoufi, I., Laouiti, A., Adjih, C.: A survey of recent extended variants of the traveling salesman and vehicle routing problems for unmanned aerial vehicles. Drones **3**(3), 66 (2019)

8. Poikonen, S., Campbell, J.F.: Future directions in drone routing research. Networks **77**(1), 116–126 (2021)

9. Moshref-Javadi, M., Winkenbach, M.: Applications and research avenues for drone-based models in logistics: a classification and review. Expert Syst. Appl. **177**, 114854 (2021)

10. Liang, Y.J., Luo, Z.X.: A survey of truck-drone routing problem: literature review and research prospects. J. Oper. Res. Soc. China **10**, 1–35 (2022)

11. Li, H., Chen, J., Wang, F., Zhao, Y.: Truck and drone routing problem with synchronization on arcs. Naval Res. Logist. (NRL) **69**(6), 884–901 (2022)

12. Salama, M.R., Srinivas, S.: Collaborative truck multi-drone routing and scheduling problem: package delivery with flexible launch and recovery sites. Transp. Res. Part E: Logist. Transp. Rev. **164**, 102788 (2022)

13. Thomas, T., Srinivas, S., Rajendran, C.: Collaborative truck multi-drone delivery system considering drone scheduling and EN-route operations. Available at SSRN 4080821

14. McGregor, M.: 8 clustering algorithms in machine learning that all data scientists should know. https://www.freecodecamp.org/news/8-clustering-algorithms-in-machine-learning-that-all-data-scientists-should-know/

15. Ferrandez, S.M., Harbison, T., Weber, T., Sturges, R., Rich, R.: Optimization of a truck-drone in tandem delivery network using k-means and genetic algorithm. J. Ind. Eng. Manag. (JIEM) **9**(2), 374–388 (2016)

16. Chang, Y.S., Lee, H.J.: Optimal delivery routing with wider drone-delivery areas along a shorter truck-route. Expert Syst. Appl. **104**, 307–317 (2018)

17. Prasad, S.: Different types of clustering methods and applications. https://www.analytixlabs.co.in/blog/types-of-clustering-algorithms

18. Delua, J.: Unsupervised learning: what's the difference? https://www.ibm.com/cloud/blog/supervised-vs-unsupervised-learning

19. Zhang, T., Ramakrishnan, R., Livny, M.: Birch: a new data clustering algorithm and its applications. Data Min. Knowl. Disc. **1**(2), 141–182 (1997)

20. Changyou, W., Xisong, F.: An agglomerative greedy brain storm optimization algorithm for solving the tsp. IEEE Access **8**, 201606–201621 (2020)

21. Lam, M., Mittenthal, J.: Capacitated hierarchical clustering heuristic for multi depot location-routing problems. Int. J. Logist. Res. Appl. **16**(5), 433–444 (2013)

22. Fajar, A., Herman, N.S., Abu, N.A., Shahib, S.: Hierarchical approach in clustering to Euclidean traveling salesman problem. In: Shen, G., Huang, X. (eds.) ECWAC 2011. CCIS, vol. 143, pp. 192–198. Springer, Heidelberg (2011). https://doi.org/10.1007/978-3-642-20367-1_30

23. Ernst, R., Grobler, J., Moremi, T., Knoetze, F., Knoetze, F.: Differential evolution algorithms for the travelling salesman problem with drones with interceptions. Submitted Comput. Ind. Eng. (2023)
24. Yang, Z., Tang, K., Yao, X.: Self-adaptive differential evolution with neighborhood search. In: 2008 IEEE Congress on Evolutionary Computation (IEEE World Congress on Computational Intelligence), pp. 1110–1116. IEEE (2008)
25. John, M.T., et al.: An Ant Colony Optimisation Approach to Scheduling Truck and Drone Delivery Systems. PhD thesis, Stellenbosch University (2022)
26. Bouman, A.N.P., Schmidt, M.: Instances for the tsp with drone, April 2015. https://dx.doi.org/10.5281/zenodo.22245

# Strategic Directions of Ensuring the Financial Stability of the Transport Enterprise

George Abuselidze[1]([✉]) [iD], Yuliia Nehoda[2] [iD], and Yuliia Bilyak[2] [iD]

[1] Batumi Shota Rustaveli State University, Batumi, Georgia
george.abuselidze@gmail.com, george.abuselidze@bsu.edu.ge
[2] National University of Life and Environmental Sciences of Ukraine, Kyiv, Ukraine

**Abstract.** The article is devoted to the study of methodological features and justification of practical measures in the organization of strategic directions to ensure the financial stability of the transport enterprise. It is proved that financial analysis is a set of measures that are used in the process of studying the financial condition of a transport enterprise. The main indicators of the results of its business activities to identify summarize the weaknesses and strengths of the enterprise. Financial stability is a very important indicator of the real state of affairs of both the financial condition of the transport enterprise and the effectiveness of the cash flow management policy. Attention is focused on the fact that the level of financial stability of the enterprise directly depends on the chosen policy and strategy of financial stability management. Based on this, it should be said that the directions of minimizing the risks of reducing the financial stability of the enterprise are included in the system of financial controlling and management policy of the transport enterprise itself. It is established that to maintain the necessary level of financial stability of the insurance company in the transport industry and minimize the risk of reducing financial stability, it is important to have a quality management policy and the selected type and model of management of the main items that affect it, which include the level of current assets, reserves and sources of their formation. It is also necessary to research and allocate items in time to increase their own sources and provide them with material working capital. It is revealed that the optimal ratio of financial resources is also important. With the help of which it is possible to ensure an effective uninterrupted process of production and sale of products, goods and services due to their effective disposal. This, in turn, will contribute to the expansion and updating of the results of the company's activities.

**Keywords:** Financial stability · Balance · Sustainability · Financial planning · Strategy · Transport Enterprise

## 1 Introduction

Today, enterprises are in a complex market economy, in which there are certain requirements that must be met to achieve a stable financial state of the development of its economy as a whole. That is why for the development of the enterprise and ensuring its financial stability and autonomy, the management should be able to analyze both the current financial condition of the enterprise and its past indicators, which characterize how successful, profitable and it is financially stable. It is necessary to pay attention in time to the dynamics and trends of individual financial indicators of the enterprise, such as the indicator of financial stability, which reflects its financial independence. Ensuring the sustainable development of an enterprise is its main and difficult task, and to achieve this, it is necessary to be able to analyze certain factors and financial indicators that affect the financial condition of the enterprise and the financial stability as a whole.

With the help of the analysis of the financial condition of the enterprise, the management of the enterprise has the opportunity to evaluate the effectiveness of a particular policy, apply it in the activities of the enterprise, determine the feasibility of managing and using resources in the enterprise for the period under study and whether they meet the requirements of the market. It is the analysis of financial stability indicators that gives an idea of the level of solvency, and therefore the level of success of the enterprise. Therefore, when searching for an answer to the question of effective management of the activities of any enterprise, the study of the indicators of the financial stability of the enterprise is one of the key and most important characteristics, describes the financial stability of the enterprise, that is, its stability in the given conditions of the market economy and environment, is a very relevant and significant task.

The objectives of the study in accordance with these problems and the relevance of the study is: highlighting the importance of the financial stability of the enterprise and identifying new facts of the impact of risks on it by performing the necessary calculations; Studies of the main indicators of this analysis, their specific weight in the formation of the financial independence of the enterprise and the financial and economic condition; As well as the search for new recommendations to minimize the risk of reducing the financial stability of the enterprise.

The purpose of the study is to analyze the financial condition of the economic entity under study, to analyze the main indicators of the financial stability of the economic entity under study and the directions of minimizing the risk of reducing the financial stability of the enterprise, as well as the influence of external and internal factors on the financial stability of the economic entity under study and its main directions of increasing financial stability.

## 2   Methodological Foundations

The need to ensure the financial stability of enterprises is reflected in the scientific literature. The works of domestic and foreign authors, such as Karanina et al., (2018); Delas et al., (2015); Novikov and Novikova, (2014); Natocheeva et al., (2019); Zhovnovach et al., (2021); Semin et al., (2016); Shmygol and Kasianok (2020); Cherep et al., (2020); Kosova et al., (2020); Dudin et al., (2014) are devoted to this problem [1–10].

Some aspects of the theoretical and methodological substantiation of the essence of the activities of insurance companies and ensuring their financial stability are considered in the works of such Western experts as Mamatkulova (2020); D'yakonova et al., (2018); Kuz'minov et al., (2017); Letkiewicz and Mandera (2018); Gregova et al., (2020); Neri et al., (2021) [11–17].

However, the components of financial stability and the reserves for ensuring it at enterprises remain insufficiently considered.

The achievement of the research goal was based on a systematic approach and comparative economic analysis. In the course of the study, the following methods were used: theoretical methods (synthesis, comparison and systematization of indicators and generalization); empirical methods (observation, comparison, analysis and generalization of indicators of financial stability of the enterprise); methods of mathematical processing of research results (processing of data and graphical objects of indicators and results).

## 3  Results and Discussion

In the modern conditions of the market economy, the process of formation and development of the activities of various enterprises and business entities is an integral part of the mechanism of development of the world economy and the key to the growth of financial stability and independence of both a certain sector of human activity and the economy of a certain country or the world as a whole. Therefore, the theoretical and practical importance of the professional conditions of business activities and clearly (confidently) assessing the real situation of affairs of a particular enterprise is increasing. Based on its strengths and weaknesses identify shortcomings in management and discover priority areas of economic activity of a particular enterprise. In other words, financial analysis is important for conducting business, and it is with the help of this analysis that the effective management of any enterprise becomes possible.

Financial analysis is a set of measures that are used in the process of studying the financial condition of the enterprise and the main indicators of the results of its business activities to identify and summarize the weaknesses and strengths of the enterprise. Thanks to the ability to analyze the current financial condition of any enterprise, the management has the ability to effectively manage the income and expenses of the enterprise, improve and ensure the effective development of its enterprise. One of the most important characteristics of the performance and financial condition of any enterprise is financial stability, the analysis of the main indicators of which is the main integral component in the process of all financial analysis.

Financial stability is a state of financial resources of the enterprise, in which the rational use of them is a guarantee of the availability of own funds, stable profitability and ensuring the process of expanded reproduction. Financial stability is one of the main factors that affect the achievement of a company's financial balance and financial stability [18–22].

In the enterprise, when studying the financial stability of an enterprise, the practical significance is expressed in determining the limits of its financial stability, since with an insufficient level of financial stability, the enterprise becomes simply insolvent and unable to fulfill its current financial and investment obligations, in the worst case, it can lead to the bankruptcy of the enterprise [23–32].

If the indicators of the financial stability analysis are excessive, then this can lead to certain obstacles in the development of this enterprise, since at the same time the costs of creating excess stock and reserves will be constantly increased. Therefore, only with an optimal ratio and knowledge of the acceptable limits of the level of financial stability of certain indicators, the company will be able to improve its own financial condition and increase financial stability [33, 34].

In the economic literatures [3, 4, 21, 22, 31–35] and in practice, depending on the level of coverage of various types of sources, the amount of reserves and costs of financial stability is distinguished by its following degrees (Fig. 1).

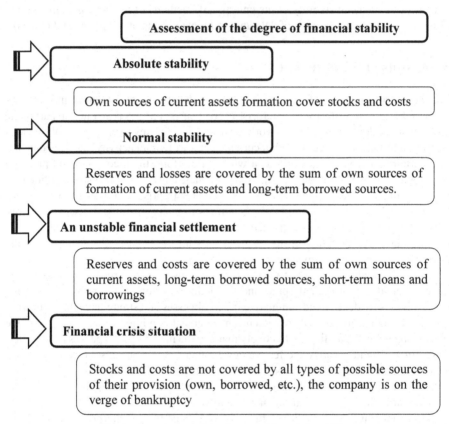

**Fig. 1.** Assessment of the degree of financial stability.

From this scheme, it can be understood that there are only four levels of financial stability that an enterprise can have, based on the main economic indicators of its activities, five levels can be distinguished. But based on the research and analysis of financial stability, after studying all the necessary indicators, the company is made a conclusion about its overall financial stability and assigned the so-called "status" of assessing the level of its financial stability, and if the conclusion of the company is the level of absolute stability, then this should mean that it is financially reliable and secured, if the opposite is true - this indicates negative consequences and requires immediate intervention in the policy of managing financial affairs and choosing the necessary course to minimize losses. Financial stability is a very important indicator of the real state of affairs of both the financial condition of the enterprise and the effectiveness of the cash flow management policy.

Therefore, there are many ways and methods of analyzing the financial stability of an enterprise. Despite the different approaches to the analysis of financial stability, in the economic literature, it is customary to distinguish two main stages of the analysis of financial stability in enterprises, during which various methods and techniques are used for the necessary indicators [3, 4, 21, 22, 31–37]. These steps are shown in Fig. 2.

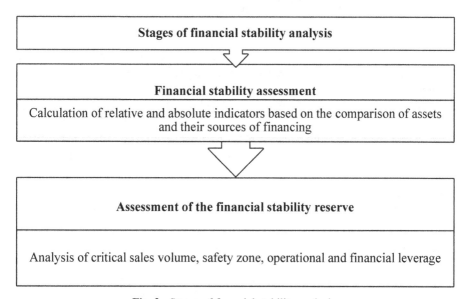

**Fig. 2.** Stages of financial stability analysis.

Based on various studies of this topic and the stages of conducting an analysis of the financial stability of an enterprise, it is usually customary to apply two main generally accepted approaches:

– Absolute assessment of financial stability;
– Relative assessment of financial stability.

When applying the first approach to assessing the financial stability of an enterprise, the insufficiency or excess of funds used in the formation of stocks and costs is determined and analyzed, thereby determining the difference between the amount of funds to cover expenses and the amount of stocks themselves [36, 37]. In the absolute assessment of financial stability, absolute indicators are used, which show the level of availability of reserves with sources of own financing. Such a ratio of stocks and sources that provide their financing can indicate and explain the type of financial stability of the enterprise. In other words, thanks to this, it is possible to draw a conclusion about the level of financial stability of the enterprise.

To determine the type of financial stability, consider all the items on the company's Balance Sheet and determine the items related to stocks and general sources of inventory financing. Thus, inventory can include: finished products, production stocks, work in progress, goods, expenses of future periods, etc. And common sources of inventory financing may include equity and short-term loans from the bank and current liabilities.

For this analysis, it is customary to use the calculation of the following three indicators:

1. Availability of own working capital (OWC) - the difference between the company's own capital (COC) and irreversible assets (IA):

$$OWC = COC - IA \qquad (1)$$

2. The availability of own working capital and long-term borrowed funds (working capital, (WC) - is calculated by increasing the result of the first indicator by the amount of long-term liabilities (LT):

$$WC = OWC + LT \qquad (2)$$

3. Availability of total working capital (TWC) - calculated by increasing the result of the previous indicator by the amount of short-term liabilities of banks (LB):

$$TWC = WC + LB \qquad (3)$$

These three indicators correspond to three indicators of the level of supply of stocks and costs with sources that form (F):

1. Insufficiency or excess of own working capital:

$$F(OWC) = OWC - \left( C\left(\frac{Q}{2}\right) + F\left(\frac{D}{Q}\right) \right) \qquad (4)$$

where,
$\left( C\left(\frac{Q}{2}\right) + F\left(\frac{D}{Q}\right) \right)$ is the total value of inventory and costs.

2. Insufficient or excessive working capital:

$$F(WC) = WC - \left( C\left(\frac{Q}{2}\right) + F\left(\frac{D}{Q}\right) \right) \qquad (5)$$

3. Insufficiency or excess of all sources:

$$F(TWC) = TWC - \left( C\left(\frac{Q}{2}\right) + F\left(\frac{D}{Q}\right) \right) \qquad (6)$$

After calculating these indicators, a three-dimensional indicator is determined, which determines the type of financial stability of the enterprise. And so [37–39]:

– If the exponent F > 0, then S (F) = 1
– If the exponent F < 0, then S (F) = 0

So, according to this criterion, you can analyze the above indicators, which will determine the level of financial stability and refer the company to a particular type of financial situation. As already noted in the previous paragraph of the work, there are four main types of financial stability of the enterprise, namely:

– Absolute stability;

- Normal stability;
- Unstable financial situation;
- Financial crisis.

And thanks to the calculation of these indicators, you can get results that indicate exactly what type of financial stability should be attributed to the studied business entity.

Today JSC "UPSK" is included in the list of the best insurance companies in the Ukrainian insurance market and is steadily developing, strengthening its position in the transport industry market. The insurance company specializes in providing services of other types of insurance, except for life insurance, reinsurance services to both legal entities and individuals and its activities are carried out on the basis of licenses obtained in accordance with the Laws of Ukraine and provides insurance services for 20 types of voluntary and 16 types of compulsory insurance (Fig. 3).

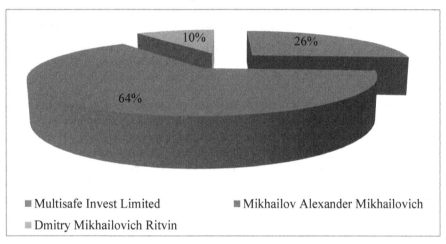

**Fig. 3.** Owners of significant participation in the Management Board of UPSK JSC. Source: author's development based on data [38–40]

Insurance premiums are an equally important indicator of the effectiveness and profitability of insurance activities. Net insurance premiums and payments are gross insurance premiums (or payments) less funds from domestic reinsurance, that is, less other components of the premium, relate to domestic service. Net insurance premiums and payments are gross insurance premiums (or and based on the final data on the amount of gross and net insurance premiums in the statement of financial results for 2016–2020, Adjusted for their dynamics (Fig. 4).

As can be seen from the diagram, the dynamics of insurance premiums, both gross and net, tends to increase in recent years, and the fact that the amount of net earned insurance premiums is not too less than gross can indicate the profitable activity of the insurance company under study. Insurance reserves are also a very important indicator in the study of the liquidity of an insurance company.

Insurance reserves - funds formed by insurers in order to ensure future payments of insurance amounts and insurance compensation, depending on the types of insurance

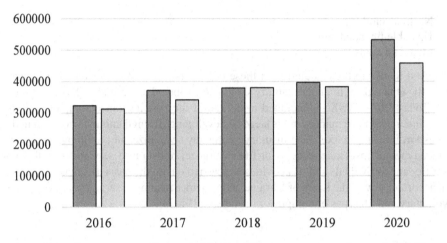

◪ Gross insurance premiums, th. UAH    ▫ Net insurance premiums, th. UAH

**Fig. 4.** Dynamics of gross and net insurance premiums of UPSK JSC for 2016–2020. Source: Compiled by the authors on the basis of the company's financial statements.

(reinsurance). The moments of receipt of insurance premiums and payment of insurance compensation, as a rule, do not coincide; this allows the insurer to accumulate significant funds in the form of insurance reserves. The amount of these reserves at any time must be sufficient for the insurer to comply with the terms of the insurance contract [33, 34].

Therefore, the insurance reserves of UPSK JSC were examined and based on the data of the official audit report on the company, it can be said that the insurance reserves represent the most significant liabilities of the Company (91.3% of all the Company's liabilities) and consist of the reserve of unearned premiums and the reserve of losses (the reserve of losses incurred but not declared, as well as the reserve of declared but not paid losses) and also based on these notes to the financial statements for 2016–2020. It is possible to distinguish the indicators of the amount of insurance reserves and their components (Table 1).

As can be seen from this table, the amount of insurance reserves has increased in recent years, and at the same time, the reliability and solvency of the insurance company JSC "UPSK" has increased, which has a positive effect on its financial condition. It should be noted that the financial stability of the enterprise largely depends on the policy of effective management of financial resources. The values of indicators that calculate financial stability depend directly on the optimal structure of assets, as well as on the ratio of own and borrowed funds, assets and sources of their financing.

The purpose and main objective of the analysis of the financial stability of the insurance company is to determine the level of solvency in the event of certain adverse conditions and the impact of negative factors and factors that may occur when conducting insurance activities in the insurance market of Ukraine. The dynamics of the results of the financial autonomy indicator can be depicted in Fig. 5.

The dynamics of the results of the financial dependence indicator is shown in Fig. 6.

**Table 1.** Insurance reserves of UPSK JSC for 2016–2020 (Thousand)

| Title of the article | 2016 | 2017 | 2018 | 2019 | 2020 |
|---|---|---|---|---|---|
| Insurance reserves | 151293,5 | 174381,9 | 169852,6 | 182797,6 | 263645,9 |
| Reserve of unearned premiums | 112532,3 | 135203,8 | 130054,8 | 139664,0 | 208362,5 |
| Provision for claimed but unpaid losses | 27360,7 | 24722,5 | 21472,0 | 24738,90 | 20736,9 |
| Provision for losses incurred but not claimed | 11400,5 | 14455,6 | 18325,8 | 18394,70 | 34546,5 |
| Reinsurer's share in insurance reserves | 3847,5 | 888,5 | 1599,3 | 734,3 | 3948,7 |

Source: compiled by the authors on the basis of the company's financial statements

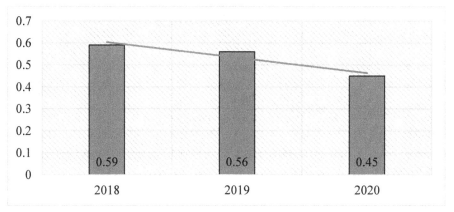

**Fig. 5.** Dynamics of the indicator of financial autonomy of JSC "UPSK" for 2018–2020. Source: compiled by the authors on the basis of the company's financial statements.

After performing calculations on the financial stability indicators of the insurance company, we group and enter the data in the table, determine the absolute deviation of these coefficients for the last year from the base one (in this case, 2018), shown in Table 2.

As can be seen from the table, almost all indicators of the financial stability of the insurance company are in the normative value, and their absolute deviation over the past year in almost all indicators has a positive value, which indicates the dynamics of the growth of the financial stability of the insurance company JSC "UPSK" and its rapid development in the insurance market of Ukraine. Therefore, it can be argued that the company has the appropriate level of financial stability for the smooth conduct of insurance activities. Despite the results of the analysis of financial stability, we can say with full confidence that the solvency of the insurance company in the event of certain adverse conditions and the influence of negative factors and factors that may occur in

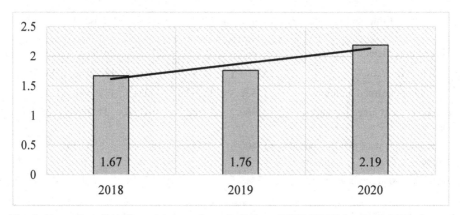

**Fig. 6.** Dynamics of the financial dependence indicator of JSC UPSK for 2018–2020. Source: compiled by the authors on the basis of the company's financial statements.

**Table 2.** Results of calculation of financial stability coefficients of JSC "UPSK" for 2018–2020, %

| Indicator | Indicator value | | | Normative value | Absolute ratio (2018–2020) |
|---|---|---|---|---|---|
| | 2018 | 2019 | 2020 | | |
| Financial autonomy | 0,59 | 0,56 | 0,45 | From 0,5 | −0,14 |
| Financial dependence | 1,67 | 1,76 | 2,19 | 1,67–2,5 | 0,52 |
| Concentration coefficient | 0,4 | 0,43 | 0,52 | 0,4–0,6 | 0,12 |
| Maneuverability coefficient | 0,76 | 0,82 | 0,86 | Within the limits of 1 | 0,1 |
| Financial strength ratio | 0,96 | 0,96 | 0,95 | 0,7–0,9 | −0,01 |

Source: compiled by the authors on the basis of the company's financial statements

the conduct of its activities in the insurance market of Ukraine, the company will be able to withstand them and continue its activities.

Therefore, the level of financial stability of the enterprise directly depends on the chosen policy and strategy of financial stability management. Based on this, it should be said that the directions of minimizing the risks of reducing the financial stability of the enterprise are included in the system of financial controlling and management policy of the enterprise itself. Therefore, the solution to the problems associated with the risks of reducing the financial stability of the enterprise depends on the chosen type of financial policy and the strategic financial management tools that the enterprise chooses.

Since the acceptable value of the level of profitability and risks depends on the type of financial stability management policy chosen by the enterprise, it is necessary to familiarize yourself with the main possible types of enterprise policies and their characteristics (Fig. 7).

| Conservative type | Moderate type | Aggressive type |
|---|---|---|
| • minimum level of borrowed resources;<br>• average level of return on sales;<br>• no financial leverage effect;<br>• high level of capital price;<br>• low sales and business growth rates. | • optimal level of debt-equity ratio;<br>• average level of return on sales;<br>• positive effect of financial leverage;<br>• average capital price level;<br>• average sales and business growth rates. | • excess of borrowed resources;<br>• high level of return on sales;<br>• negative effect of financial leverage;<br>• low equity price level;<br>• high sales and business growth rates. |

**Fig. 7.** Types of financial policy of the enterprise. Source: systematized by the author on the basis of data [38–40].

And in any case, one or another model of the current assets financing policy reflects the indicator of net current assets, that is, net working capital. And the level of the ratio of return on equity and the risk of reducing the financial stability and solvency of the enterprise are interrelated from each other. Therefore, since the availability of sources of inventory formation is a positive factor for achieving the financial stability of the transport enterprises, and the negative factors are the volume of inventory itself, the main tips for minimizing the risks of reducing financial stability are [41–47]:

• Increased sources and flows of inventory generation;
• Improvement and restructuring of inventory sources;
• A reasonable and deliberate gradual reduction in the level of the stocks themselves.

To achieve these actions, there are a dozen ways, shown in Fig. 8.

In addition, we should not forget that there are many methods to improve the efficiency of the management of current assets and reserves, among which we can distinguish the usual collection of receivables, because even with the strengthening of its collection, there may be an acceleration in the turnover of funds in the enterprise and an increase in the security of its own working capital, which leads to an increase in the solvency indicators of the sole proprietor.

So, we can conclude that the main indicators when using the management policy in the direction of minimizing the risks of reducing the financial stability of the enterprise is the choice of the correct type and model of financial management and approaches to financing and managing current assets, reserves and sources of their formation. At the same time, it is necessary to promptly investigate and allocate items to increase their own sources and provide them with material working capital. The optimal balance of financial resources is also of great importance, with the help of which it is possible to ensure an effective uninterrupted process of production and sale of products, goods and

> **Ways to get out of an unstable and crisis financial state:**

> –an increase in real equity due to an increase in the size of the authorized capital, as well as due to the accumulation of retained earnings (used if the company does not incur uncovered losses for the analyzed period, otherwise it can not give special results).

> –development of a competent financial strategy of the company, which would allow the company to attract both short-term and long-term borrowed funds, while maintaining the optimal proportions between its own and borrowed capital;

> –view the weighted average values of product stocks in warehouses for a day, week, or month. The decrease in the inventory level occurs as a result of the planning of inventory balances, as well as the sale of unused inventory items. An overstated inventory size affects the accounts payable, which is therefore unfavorable for the company.

**Fig. 8.** Ways to get out of an unstable and crisis financial state.

services due to their effective disposal and maneuvering, which in turn will contribute to the expansion and updating of the results of the enterprise's activities.

## 4   Conclusions

On the basis of the above-mentioned material, it can be concluded that in the modern conditions of the market economy, the process of formation and development of the activities of business entities is an integral part of the mechanism for the development of the world economy and the key to the growth of financial stability and independence of society. To maintain the proper level of operation of enterprises in such conditions, there is a need for professional business management and the ability to clearly and confidently assess the true state of affairs of the enterprise, identify shortcomings in management and identify priority areas of their management. It is the analysis of the financial stability of the enterprise that is designed to ensure the fulfillment of these tasks for the management of the business entity.

One of the most important characteristics of the performance and financial condition of any enterprise is financial stability, the analysis of the main indicators of which is the main integral component in the process of all financial analysis.

In the course of the research and analysis of the financial condition of JSC UPSK, the analysis of the main indicators of insurance activity was carried out, namely: insurance premiums and insurance payments, insurance reserves. In addition, a horizontal and vertical analysis of the insurer's balance sheet was carried out. According to the conclusion of the analysis, it can be argued that the main performance indicators of the company are at a sufficiently high and sufficient level for the quality of the enterprise, and their amount is increasing. Therefore, even minor fluctuations in the specific weight of the balance sheet indicators, as well as the uniformity of their decrease, indicate that these phenomena are most likely caused by external factors, such as inflation and a decrease in the exchange rate, in turn, devalued money and accordingly reduced it in the Balance Sheet, but this did not significantly affect the financial and economic activities of the enterprise. Therefore, the financial condition of JSC UPSK is satisfactory, and the level of its financial security is sufficient for further activities.

In addition, when analyzing the financial stability, it was found that almost all indicators of the financial stability of the insurance company are in the normative value, and their absolute deviation over the past year in almost all indicators has a positive value, which indicates the dynamics of the growth of the financial stability of the insurance company JSC "UPSK" and its rapid development in the insurance market of Ukraine. It can be argued that the company has the appropriate level of financial stability for the smooth conduct of insurance activities.

Therefore, despite the results of the analysis of financial stability, we can say with full confidence that the solvency of the insurance company in the event of certain adverse conditions and the influence of negative factors and factors that may occur in the conduct of its activities in the insurance market of Ukraine, the company will be able to withstand them and continue its activities.

To maintain the necessary level of financial stability of the insurance company and minimize the risk of reducing financial stability, it is important to have a quality management policy and the selected type and model of management of the main items that affect it, which include the level of current assets, reserves and sources of their formation. It is also necessary to research and allocate items in time to increase their own sources and provide them with material working capital. The optimal balance of financial resources is also of great importance, with the help of which it is possible to ensure an effective uninterrupted process of production and sale of products, goods and services due to their effective disposal and maneuvering, which in turn will contribute to the expansion and updating of the results of the enterprise's activities.

## References

1. Karanina, E., Ryazanova, O., Gritsuk, N.: Conceptual approach to the assessment of economic security of economic entities on the example of transport enterprises. MATEC Web Conf. **193**, 01031 (2018). https://doi.org/10.1051/matecconf/201819301031
2. Delas, V., Nosova, E., Yafinovych, O.: Financial security of enterprises. Proc. Econ. Finance **27**, 248–266 (2015). https://doi.org/10.1016/S2212-5671(15)00998-3
3. Novikov, A.O., Novikova, M.M.: Modeling of financial and economic security of transport enterprises based on factor analysis. Sci. Transp. Progr. Bull. Dnipropetrovsk Natl. Univ. Railw. Transp. **6**(54), 42–49 (2014). https://doi.org/10.15802/stp2014/32769
4. Natocheeva, N., Borodin, A., Rud, N., Kutsuri, G., Zholamanova, M., Namitulina, A.: Development of tools for realizing the potential of financial stability of enterprises. Entrep. Sustain. Issues **7**(2), 1654–1665 (2019). https://doi.org/10.9770/jesi.2019.7.2(60)

5. Zhovnovach, R., Levchenko, O., Muzychenko, A., Koval, L., Vyshnevska, V.: Ensuring safety of the use of transport enterprises' resources participating of air carriers' international alliances. E3S Web Conf. **255**, 01050 (2021). https://doi.org/10.1051/e3sconf/202125 501050
6. Semin, V.G., Grigoreva, S.V., Dmitrieva, T.V., Ilyina, E.A.: A process model of risk management in the system of management of strategic sustainability of cargo motor transport enterprises. In: 2016 IEEE Conference on Quality Management, Transport and Information Security, Information Technologies (IT&MQ&IS), pp. 172–175. IEEE (2016). https://doi.org/10.1109/ITMQIS.2016.7751951
7. Shmygol, N., Kasianok, M.: Analysis of financial and economic sustainability of enterprises based on the use of accounting and analytical instruments. Sci. J. Cahul State Univ. "Bogdan Petriceicu Hasdeu" Econ. Eng. Stud. **7**(1), 29–35 (2020)
8. Cherep, A., Babmindra, D., Khudoliei, L., Kusakova, Y.: Assessment of the level of financial and economic security at machine-building enterprises: evidence from Ukraine. Probl. Perspect. Manag. **18**(1), 33–47 (2020). https://doi.org/10.21511/ppm.18(1).2020.04
9. Kosova, T., Yaroshevska, O., Solomina, G.: Financial diagnostics and regulation of the potential of strategic cost-oriented development of corporate enterprises. Efektyvna Ekonomika **4** (2020). https://doi.org/10.32702/2307-2105-2020.4.2
10. Dudin, M., Lyasnikov, N., Yahyaev, M., Kuznecov, A.: The organization approaches peculiarities of an industrial enterprises financial management. Life Sci. J. **11**(9), 333–336 (2014)
11. Mamatkulova, N.: Theoretical and practical aspects and indicators of financial security of enterprises. Int. J. Psychosoc. Rehabil. **24**(4), 4819–4823 (2020). https://doi.org/10.37200/ijpr/v24i4/pr201580
12. D'yakonova, I., Nikitina, A., Sukhonos, V., Zhuravka, F.: Methodological bases of estimating the efficiency of economic security management of the enterprises in the global environment. Invest. Manag. Financ. Innov. **15**(2), 145–153 (2018). https://doi.org/10.21511/imfi.15(2).2018.13
13. Kuz'minov, A.N., Dzhukha, V.M., Ternovsky, O.A.: Methodology of structural stability management for industrial enterprises. Eur. Res. Stud. **20**(3B), 260 (2017)
14. Letkiewicz, A., Mandera, E.: The determinants of the internal audit in road cargo transport enterprises. In: Suchanek, M. (ed.) TranSopot 2018. SPBE, pp. 161–169. Springer, Cham (2019). https://doi.org/10.1007/978-3-030-17743-0_14
15. Gregova, E., Valaskova, K., Adamko, P., Tumpach, M., Jaros, J.: Predicting financial distress of Slovak enterprises: comparison of selected traditional and learning algorithms methods. Sustainability **12**(10), 3954 (2020). https://doi.org/10.3390/su12103954
16. Abuselidze, G., Bilyak, Y., Mračkovskaya, N.K.: Methodological and practical issues of the organization of the personnel of the enterprise and the implementation of changes to its structure. Stud. Appl. Econ. **39**(8) (2021). https://doi.org/10.25115/eea.v39i8.4449
17. Neri, A., Cagno, E., Lepri, M., Trianni, A.: A triple bottom line balanced set of key performance indicators to measure the sustainability performance of industrial supply chains. Sustain. Prod. Consum. **26**, 648–691 (2021). https://doi.org/10.1016/j.spc.2020.12.018
18. Tropina, V., Rybakova, T.: Financial mechanisms of foreign economic activity regulation in top trading countries. In: 6th International Conference on Strategies, Models and Technologies of Economic Systems Management (SMTESM 2019), pp. 257–261. Atlantis Press (2019). https://doi.org/10.2991/smtesm-19.2019.50
19. Klapkiv, Y.M., Niemczyk, L., Vakun, O.V.: Financial mechanism of the insurance business. Sci. Bull. Polissia **12** (2017)
20. Wall, L.D., Eisenbeis, R.A., Frame, W.S.: Resolving large financial intermediaries: banks versus housing enterprises. J. Financ. Stab. **1**(3), 386–425 (2005). https://doi.org/10.1016/j.jfs.2005.02.009

21. Adrian, T., Shin, H.S.: Financial intermediaries, financial stability, and monetary policy. FRB of New York Staff Report 346 (2008). https://doi.org/10.2139/ssrn.1266714

22. Abuselidze, G.: The impact of banking competition on economic growth and financial stability: an empirical investigation. Eur. J. Sustain. Dev. **10**(1), 203–220 (2021). https://doi.org/10.14207/ejsd.2021.v10n1p203

23. Abuselidze, G., Beridze, L.: The role of alternative investments in the development of capital markets in terms of the transformation of Georgia with the EU. In: Proceedings of the 4th International Conference on European Integration 2018, pp. 29–40 (2018)

24. Abuselidze, G., Slobodianyk, A.: Analysis and control of bankruptcy and reorganization processes: case studies using accounting data. E3S Web Conf. **164**, 09036 (2020). https://doi.org/10.1051/e3sconf/202016409036

25. Akhmetshin, E.M., Artemova, E.I., Vermennikova, L.V., Shichiyakh, R.A., Prodanova, N.A., Kuchukova, N.M.: Management of investment attractiveness of enterprises: principles, methods, organization. Int. J. Appl. Bus. Econ. Res. **15**(23), 71–82 (2017)

26. Karlibaeva, R.: Structure of the capital and financial stability of the enterprises in condition of modernization of economics. Sci. Res. Arch. **35**(1), 22–26 (2020)

27. Vasylieva, D., Kudyk, T., Lisovska, V., Abuselidze, G., Hryvkivska, O.: Ensuring the issuance of investment-attractive corporate bonds. E3S Web Conf. **295**, 01008 (2021)

28. Fedorova, E.A., Gilenko, E.V., Dovzhenko, S.E.: Models for bankruptcy forecasting: case study of Russian enterprises. Stud. Russ. Econ. Dev. **24**(2), 159–164 (2013). https://doi.org/10.1134/S1075700713020044

29. Datsii, O., Levchenko, N., Shyshkanova, G., Platonov, O., Abuselidze, G.: Creating a regulatory framework for the ESG-investment in the multimodal transportation development. Rural Sustain. Res. **46**(341), 39–52 (2021). https://doi.org/10.2478/plua-2021-0016

30. Knyshek, O.O., Tarasenko, I.O.: Financial analysis of enterprise activity in conditions of economic instability. Econ. Scope (139), 171–181 (2018). https://doi.org/10.30838/p.es.2224.271018.171.282

31. Xianglan, W., Xingfeng, F.: Research on financial analysis of modern enterprise based on economic added value and DuPont financial analysis. In: Proceedings of the 5th International Conference on Social Sciences and Economic Development (ICSSED 2020) (2020). https://doi.org/10.2991/assehr.k.200331.013

32. Iurieva, L.V., Dolzhenkova, E.V.: Financial stability management of an industrial enterprise based on the formation of signal indicators. IOP Conf. Ser.: Earth Environ. Sci. **666**(6), 062104 (2021). https://doi.org/10.1088/1755-1315/666/6/062104

33. Sylkin, O., Kryshtanovych, M., Zachepa, A., Bilous, S., Krasko, A.: Modeling the process of applying anti-crisis management in the system of ensuring financial security of the enterprise. Bus.: Theory Pract. **20**, 446–455 (2019). https://doi.org/10.3846/btp.2019.41

34. Sosnovska, O., Zhytar, M.: Financial architecture as the base of the financial safety of the enterprise. Balt. J. Econ. Stud. **4**(4), 334–340 (2018). https://doi.org/10.30525/2256-0742/2018-4-4-334-340

35. Mavlutova, I., Babenko, V., Dykan, V., Prokopenko, N., Kalinichenko, S., Tokmakova, I.: Business restructuring as a method of strengthening company's financial position. J. Optimiz. Ind. Eng. **14**(1), 129–139 (2021). https://doi.org/10.22094/JOIE.2020.677839

36. Betaneli, F.T., Nikitina, N.V., Zhelev, P.: Managing the financial stability of an enterprise in a digital economy. In: Ashmarina, S.I., Mantulenko, V.V. (eds.) Current Achievements, Challenges and Digital Chances of Knowledge Based Economy. LNNS, vol. 133, pp. 267–272. Springer, Cham (2021). https://doi.org/10.1007/978-3-030-47458-4_31

37. Kim, S., Mehrotra, A.: Managing price and financial stability objectives in inflation targeting economies in Asia and the Pacific. J. Financ. Stab. **29**, 106–116 (2017). https://doi.org/10.1016/j.jfs.2017.01.003

38. Mishra, A.K., El-Osta, H.S., Sandretto, C.L.: Factors affecting farm enterprise diversification. Agric. Financ Rev. **64**(2), 151–166 (2004). https://doi.org/10.1108/00214660480001160

39. Shah, S.F.H., Nazir, T., Zaman, K., Shabir, M.: Factors affecting the growth of enterprises: a survey of the literature from the perspective of small-and medium-sized enterprises. J. Enterp. Transform. **3**(2), 53–75 (2013). https://doi.org/10.1080/19488289.2011.650282

40. Hasan, N., Miah, S.J., Bao, Y., Hoque, M.R.: Factors affecting post-implementation success of enterprise resource planning systems: a perspective of business process performance. Enterp. Inf. Syst. **13**(9), 1217–1244 (2019). https://doi.org/10.1080/17517575.2019.1612099

41. Abuselidze, G.: Competitiveness analysis of the Georgian transport and logistics system in the black sea region: challenges and perspectives. In: Gervasi, O., et al. (eds.) ICCSA 2021. LNCS, vol. 12952, pp. 133–148. Springer, Cham (2021). https://doi.org/10.1007/978-3-030-86973-1_10

42. Abuselidze, G., Gogitidze, I.: Tax policy for business entities under the conditions of association with the European Union: features and optimization directions. E3S Web Conf. **166**, 13013 (2020). https://doi.org/10.1051/e3sconf/202016613013

43. Abuselidze, G.: Analysis and forecasts of the impact of non-performing loans on the economy in pandemic conditions. In: Alareeni, B., Hamdan, A., Khamis, R., Khoury, R.E. (eds.) ICBT 2022. LNNS, vol. 620, pp. 129–143. Springer, Cham (2023). https://doi.org/10.1007/978-3-031-26953-0_14

44. Jauch, L.R., Osborn, R.N., Glueck, W.F.: Short term financial success in large business organizations: the environment-strategy connection. Strateg. Manag. J. **1**(1), 49–63 (1980). https://doi.org/10.1002/smj.4250010106

45. Levchenko, N., Shyshkanova, G., Abuselidze, G., Zelenin, Y., Prykhodko, V., Kovalskyi, M.: Global trends of decarbonisation as a determining factor for the development of external economic activity of metallurgical enterprises. Rural Sustain. Res. **47**(342), 61–75 (2022)

46. Henager, R., Cude, B.J.: Financial literacy and long-and short-term financial behavior in different age groups. J. Financ. Couns. Plan. **27**(1), 3–19 (2016)

47. Larkin, Y.: Brand perception, cash flow stability, and financial policy. J. Financ. Econ. **110**(1), 232–253 (2013). https://doi.org/10.1016/j.jfineco.2013.05.002

# New Geographies of Fuel Purchase During the COVID-19 Pandemic: Evidence from the Italian Northeastern Border Zone

Giorgia Bressan[1](✉) (ID) and Gian Pietro Zaccomer[2] (ID)

[1] Tor Vergata University of Rome, Via Columbia 1, 00133 Rome, Italy
giorgia.bressan@uniroma2.it
[2] University of Udine, Via Petracco 8, 33100 Udine, Italy
gianpietro.zaccomer@uniud.it

**Abstract.** Under normal conditions, favorable connections with Slovenia and Austria allow residents of the Italian region of Friuli Venezia Giulia to take advantage of the different market conditions abroad. However, due to pandemic-issued border closures, the privilege of unbounded mobility was compromised. This contribution aims to understand the implications of a temporary border closure on the fuel retailing market by exploring quantitative data on fuel purchases made available by diverse public entities. In the first year of the pandemic, despite a national situation in which a strong contraction in sales of fuels was recorded, the Friuli Venezia Giulia region behaved significantly differently from Italy, especially in its border provinces of Gorizia and Trieste. The return to an open border has triggered strong international competition. As such, the results advance our knowledge of the impact of customer (im)mobility on the economy of a borderland.

**Keywords:** COVID-19 · Border closure · Fuel retail market · Geography of consumption · Friuli Venezia Giulia (Italy)

## 1 Introduction

The first autochthonous case of COVID-19 in Italy was confirmed in the Lombardy region on February 21, 2020. After a few days, the rapid increase in reported COVID-19 infections in some regions of northern Italy led the competent authorities to make tough decisions to contain the spread of the virus, such as the closure of the schools. The worsening of the situation meant that the population of the whole national territory was subject to a national-wide lockdown from 10 March 2020. In northern Italy, the routine of inhabitants living in proximity to international terrestrial crossings were further compromised in the first stages of the pandemic. Both measures adopted by Italy to contain the spread of the coronavirus and those taken by neighboring states to regulate access to their countries created a temporary impermeability of the international border[1].

---

[1] For a chronology of rules to cross-border displacements from 04 February 2021 to 21 February 2022, refer to the internet resources made available by the Italian Trade & Investment Agency, https://www.ice.it/it/mercati/slovenia/lubiana/disposizioni-su-covid-19. For the previous period, the reconstruction of the history of the notices relating to the mobility to/from

© The Author(s), under exclusive license to Springer Nature Switzerland AG 2023
O. Gervasi et al. (Eds.): ICCSA 2023, LNCS 13957, pp. 179–196, 2023.
https://doi.org/10.1007/978-3-031-36808-0_12

The measures in place only made it possible for Italian citizens or foreigners residing in Italy to enter. For outbound fluxes from Italy to abroad, travel for the sole purpose of tourism was prohibited, as were those related to shopping. Very few exceptions were granted to special categories of people.

A permeable border and a good network of road infrastructure between the Italian region of Friuli Venezia Giulia (onward, FVG) and the nearby Austria and Slovenia usually allow borderland residents to travel easily abroad to take advantage of the different market conditions in terms of price and/or product range. Among them, the conditions of the foreign fuel market are a strong stimulus to the cross-border mobility of Italians. Motorists of FVG have a consolidated habit of taking advantage of the proximity to Slovenian filling stations to refuel [1]. In addition to offering a generally cheaper product, the foreign facility can, in some cases, also be the closest store in spatial terms to their home. As illustrated later, national and regional lawmakers are well aware of this problem, which creates a loss of fiscal revenues without remediation actions. Italians living in the surroundings of the eastern border zone do not go abroad often just for this purpose. It is quite common to combine refueling with other activities, such as the purchase of cigarettes and meat [25]. However, people do not just frequently cross the border for shopping, but because they work abroad, own agricultural lands or visit family members. In addition, recreational activities, such as casinos, attract Italians (not only those residing in the borderland) to Slovenia.

This article aims to understand the implications of the COVID-19 pandemic on the fuel retailing market in the northeastern Italian region of the FVG. Contrary to other types of shopping, the physical movement of customers to shop is needed to purchase goods. Specifically, the article analyzes the trends in the sale of gasoline and diesel in regional filling stations in an unprecedented situation of border closure and forced stay of people in their homes. In this Italian border region, two relevant phenomena overlapped during spring 2020. At the national level, the Italian measures to contain the pandemic severely limited internal mobility, basically allowing movement within the municipality of residence only in the presence of specific reasons. Second, in the border area, regional consumers were unable to consider the usual attractivity of the foreign market in their spending decisions due to travel restrictions, so that the demand for fuel was met only by Italian stores. In the case of border closure, price differentials are irrelevant to final consumers given that the crossing of the border for shopping is simply not allowed.

The research relies on the analysis of different datasets on quantities of fuel sold. These datasets were originally assembled on the basis of data published by regional and national authorities. In Italy, at the national level, the Ministry of Economic Development (MISE) is responsible for publication through its Oil Bulletin of monthly data concerning the quantities of fuel sold at the province and regional levels. In the case of FVG, additional data are available. The existence of a monitoring system of fuel quantity sold that considers different geographical extents, compared to the "traditional" provincial level, allows analysis of other aspects of the regional fuel market. This wealth of data is possible because in this region, various economic policies have been in place since 1997 with the aim of prompting local residents to attend regional filling stations. Due to

Slovenia was possible thanks to the material purposely provided for the research by the Italian Ministry of Foreign Affairs and International Cooperation.

transparency reasons and the need to verify the efficiency of the policy, regional bodies produce these additional statistics. It is expected that during the border closure, a context of exceptionality was created, with the "forced" attendance of regional filling stations. The loss of sales is expected to be smaller at regional filling stations than that recorded at the national level.

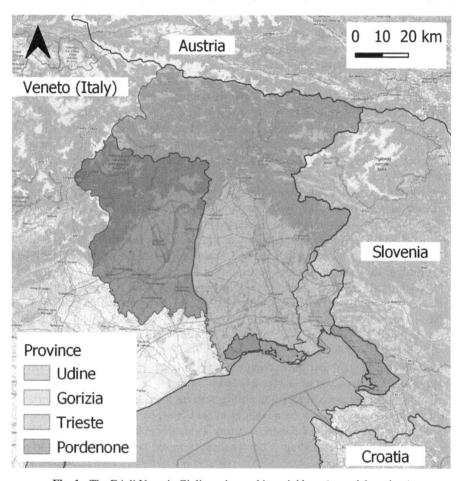

**Fig. 1.** The Friuli Venezia Giulia region and its neighbors (own elaborations)

Many reasons justify the interest in the case study (Fig. 1). The first is demograph-ics. Own elaborations 2022 resident population statistics show that the sole population living in the municipalities sharing an international border to Austria and/or Slovenia amounts to almost 300,000 inhabitants (a quarter of the total population of the region). These borderland municipalities have a limited population, under 15,000 inhabitants, with the exceptions of Trieste (c. 200,000) and Gorizia (c. 33,000). Another interesting feature comes from the strong interconnection of the region with other countries, mainly determined by a thick road transport network intersecting a favorable geography. On the

Italian-Slovenian border, the plain and hilly nature of the terrain facilitate movements across the border [19]. The mountainous nature of the upper part of the region does not permit the creation of an analogous pattern of international crossings. However, the presence of the motorway A23, by connecting the city of Udine with Tarvisio – the most northeastern municipality in Italy – and then Villach (Austria), via the Austrian Süd Autobahn, makes this tool road one of the most important links between Northeast Italy and Central Europe. Third, the history of the current Italian and Slovenian borderlands is strongly intertwined, and the exceptional limitations to what formally should be called international mobility damaged in several dimensions the livelihood of who consider living in a unique, borderless, context [14, 22]. It is about a "real" interconnected European border region, where the imposition of impermeable borders has the potential to cause major disruptions to social, economic, institutional international ties [16].

This study contributes to the wave of studies aimed at analyzing the rebordering practices triggered by the coronavirus pandemic [12]. While focusing specifically on the fuel market, the insights emerging from this article could be particularly useful to enrich our knowledge on the exceptionality of the health emergency, answering the stimulus offered by Brunet-Jailly and Carpenter [4] to observe how COVID-19 border closure looks like from inside a borderland. Retailers located in the country with higher prices are normally penalized by the proximity to the terrestrial border, especially if competition is only based on prices. The decision to attempt to curb the diffusion of the virus with forms of strong impermeability of the international borders has determined an unprecedented situation. From here, there exists the need to reflect on whether it had temporarily advantaged such retailers operating in border areas. The analysis was carried out from the outbreak of the pandemic to mid-March 2023. This note is relevant, as the topic is in progress from a normative point of view, and the interpretation of some trend in the market might vary with the release of new data that were not available at the time of this writing.

The remainder of this paper is organized as follows: Sect. 2 discusses the interplay between border closure and the economy. Section 3 concerns the case study. It first illustrates the various schemes that have been introduced in the borderland region of the FVG to favor the purchase of fuel at the filling stations located in the regional territory. Then, it analyzes the trend in the quantities of sold fuels, by focusing in particular on the pandemic times. Section 4 illustrates actors' dynamics at the time of the pandemic, allowing a deeper understanding of the challenges raised with the pandemic in this market. Section 5 concludes.

## 2   Border Closure: A Friend or Foe for the Local Economy?

Since the first autochthonous cases of novel coronavirus have appeared in diverse geographical contexts, various measures consisting of imposing isolation on infected individuals and limiting the displacement of people potentially at risk of infection have been introduced. A process labeled bordering of the world was also at work, which consisted of the majority of the nation-state introducing restrictions to international travel by altering the usual permeability of borders [6]. Interventions based on territorial control were thus used to contain the COVID-19, with the effect – in the academic domain – to give rise to interesting reflections on the consequences of such territorial thinking [20, 28].

The spread of the new coronavirus has constituted an unprecedented occasion to think about how a health emergency, having an incredible worldwide propagation pattern, had the power to resurface the notion of state sovereignty. The territorial borders were revived because they marked the spatial extent to which a certain emergency measure – for instance, one that foresaw the partial lockdown of some economic activities or the exclusion of the entrance in the national borders to some categories of people – was in force. Such observed large-scale border closures induced by the pandemic instituted a rethinking of how economic relations are spatially organized.

In economic geography, pandemic-induced measures have been the backdrop of peer reviewed articles aimed at studying reconfiguration production networks following the forced slowdown of certain economic sectors and the vivacity of others called to cope urgently with increasing demands [8, 9, 17]. It should be acknowledged that it was not the primary objective of such articles to contribute to border theory but rather to understand whether the risk related to the global health crisis led to a contraction of the production network [2, 24], a trend that, by the way, was already in place before the outbreak of COVID-19 [23]. While the changes in worldwide flows of goods have attracted quite strong attention, not the same interest has sprung up in terms of the changes in cross-border contacts.

Among the reviewed literature, Malkowski and Mazur [15] explores the impact of international travel restrictions during the outbreak of the pandemic for some selected counties in the northern part of the Polish-German border. During this period, border marketplaces, shopping centers and numerous service points in Poland, which are regarded as drivers of local development, became inaccessible to tourists coming from the West. The article offers various cues for reflection, being based on secondary data and authors' own research data, but here it worth highlighting that the interviews conducted over the phone to a random group of entrepreneurs during the period of border indicate that the closure of the borders had a substantial impact on their economic situation. Most respondents (over 70%) express that their turnover fell by up to 80%. Interviews also reveal that respondents identified the uncertainty of how much longer the borders would remain closed as one of the most important problems in such a context.

Paül et al. [18] considers the border between Galicia (Spain) and Northern Portugal, which is a highly integrated cross-border economy. The research makes use of fieldwork and interviews with representatives of the local political, institutional and economic sphere to collect perceptions on the impacts of border closure on the various business sectors and on daily life. The other part of the work is quantitative in nature and aims to explore the contraction of the regional economy by considering the diverse economic sectors that made up the economy in the selected municipalities, utilizing a novel methodology. The quantitative analysis shows that the lockdown effect explains approximately 94 percent of GDP contraction in the region, and the remaining is attributable to border closures. A different boundary effect in the two countries emerges, with Portugal being more penalized than Spain by travel restrictions.

Outside the European continent, Richardson and Cappellano [21] assesses how the mobility restrictions affected a border region of the U.S.-Canada border and another of the U.S.-Mexico border, which are both characterized for hosting innovative business ecosystems. The work, based mainly on interviews with a wide range of local stake-holders but also on participant observation and textual analysis of relevant material, suggests that the border closures had generated limited impacts on business activity. Despite the difficulty of generalizing the insights coming from a diverse number of companies from this contribution, it seems unanimous that with regard to business relations, the use of remote working and virtual meetings have contributed to alleviating the disruption of partial border closures. Interviews reveal the existence of disruptions in terms of supply chain and hiring practices and a strategy based on "spot, think, and act", which contributed to coping with the different contexts emerging during the height of the pandemic.

The few available studies having mainly an economic focus differ in themes, research methods, and geographical contexts. Clearly, due to the timing given by the peer review process, the existing contributions concern 2020. The lack of such studies is somewhat disappointing, especially in geographical contexts where remarkable differences between the two sides of the border exist. In these settings, the analysis of this unprecedented condition is even more relevant because with the pandemic, in addition to a drop in cross-border contacts, there might have been a willingness of the institutional structures on the most disadvantaged side to take this context of crisis to rethink their policy actions, with the aim of improving the jurisdiction's economic position. This contribution has this ambition, looking at a market that is chronically in difficulty in a European border region.

## 3   The Impact of the Closure of the Borders

First, in compliance with international agreements and the laws of the European Union, at the end of 1995, the Italian State granted the regional administrations the possibility of reducing the sale prices of motor fuels, including both gasoline and diesel. This price reduction concerned only citizens residing in a specific region – thus excluding local businesses – and was obtained through the sole reduction of excise duties on fuels.

After introducing the main features of the scheme in force in the region under analysis, this section intends to investigate the effects of the closure of the borders on the quantities of fuels sold at the regional level, both for the fuel sold at a reduced price (resulting from the application of the regional law, as will be explained later) and at full price.

### 3.1   The Evolution of the Scheme in Force in Friuli Venezia Giulia

The Italian Region of FVG immediately took advantage of the possibility of reducing the sale price of fuels. With Regional Law (RL) 47 of December 1996, the Region put in place the first economic measure to reduce gasoline prices starting from April 1997, while diesel was included in the scheme only from 2002. This measure was launched with the explicit aim of containing fuel tourism, which, for market issues directly linked to the various national tax systems, at that time mainly concerned nearby Slovenia.

It is essential to remember that this first scheme was linked to the concept of a "discount" on the price charged at the filling station and the geographical concept of "inverse proportionality" between the road distance (calculated between the municipality of residence of the citizen, that is, the motorist, and the border from Slovenia) and the discount applied. Since the municipalities involved were more than 200, the regional administration decided to group these municipalities into five zones. The greater discount was attributed to the area closer to the Slovenian border, which included all municipalities in the provinces of Gorizia and Trieste[2]. The smaller discount was assigned to the furthest area of the international border. From an operational point of view, each motorist resident in the region was equipped with an identification card equipped with a microchip, and each regional filling station was endowed with a POS system. This electronic system allowed not only the identification of the owner of the vehicle to whom the discount could be applied, but also the application of the discount regardless of the location of the filling station[3] [25].

At the end of the first decade of the 2000s, mainly due to the international economic situation and the suppression of the Free Zone of Gorizia and Trieste, the loss of efficiency of this scheme became evident since not only fuel tourism toward Slovenia restarted again, but it also began to be convenient to refuel in Austria and in the nearby Italian region of Veneto. In the latter case, the reason was not linked to a different taxation system but to the presence in the fuel market of new unbranded economic operators. Alongside these economic issues, there was also a legal problem, as the European Commission deemed that the concept of "discount" constituted a violation of its Directive 2003/96/EC on the taxation of energy products.

For all these reasons, the regional lawmaker preferred to introduce a new law, known as RL 14 of August 2010. This latter modified the key principles of the previous one, not referring to the concept of receiving a discount at the filling station, but of a direct "contribution" paid by the regional administration to resident motorists for the purchase of fuel. Additionally, previous geographical zones were abolished, and the principle of inverse proportionality was completely eliminated. Two new "areas" were identified, namely, one where residents were eligible for an ordinary contribution (A2) and one for an increased contribution (A1). This latter area was made up of not only municipalities sharing an international border, but also the most economically disadvantaged ones – located above all in the mountain area – in line with European directives. All these changes were made in the hope of resolving any dispute with the European Commission [26]. The new economic scheme began to produce its effects only from the end of 2011 and at the time of the outbreak of the pandemic it was the one in force.

## 3.2 Analysis of the Time Series of the Quantities Sold

Before starting the quantitative analysis, it is necessary first to illustrate the characteristics of the official data published by the regional bodies of the FVG region. RL 14 of 2010 contains an evaluation clause that requires the Regional Government to submit a Report

---

[2] The maximum discount range also included 25 border municipalities in the province of Udine.

[3] The system applied the same price reduction in every filling station of the regional territory since the discount was fixed in relation to the municipality of residence and not to that of the refueling site. In this way, a borderland resident, who was entitled to receive the maximum discount, was subject to the same price reduction at any regional filling station.

on the state of implementation of the law (referred to as the "implementation report", for brevity) to the Regional Council in June of each year. The evaluation clause contains specific requirements, and two of these are exclusively quantitative. They concern the trend in sales of automotive fuels, that is, the liters sold of gasoline and diesel, while the second concerns the amount of contributions handed out and the number of active cards, which allow refueling at reduced prices. In addition, the evaluation clause also requires presenting in the implementation report the criticalities that emerge during the years of application of the law.

To carry out the following analysis, it was therefore necessary to search and assemble the data available on all the reports that were published in the Official Bulletin of the Autonomous Region of FVG into a single database. Alongside these sources, the preliminary notes and opinions published online by the Committee of Legislation, Monitoring and Evaluation Committee (which is a body of the Regional Council) were also employed. Their importance stands in the fact they analyze the implementation reports, integrate certain aspects with the aim of assessing the ability of the scheme to produce the envisioned impact, in this case to curb fuel tourism, and produce knowledge to support future political choices.

The examination of all these official documents highlighted several issues. For this study, the most important of these are the temporal ones. At the time of the analysis, all the years starting from the introduction of the law were not yet available (including 2021). With the documentation prepared by the Committee, however, it was possible to fill some gaps by identifying, specifically, the annual historical series of liters sold from 2012 to 2020 (here in Table 1), while for the monthly series, it was not possible to identify the complete time series, as data for the years 2012, 2014 and 2021 was completely missing. Finally, it should be emphasized that, regarding the critical issues identified in the implementation reports, due to the requirements linked to the evaluation clause, most of the attention has gone exclusively on the evolution of appeals against the same law, both at the national and European levels (dimension explored later); therefore, the reports have never investigated economic problems, such as fluctuations in market prices. Additionally, the effects of the pandemic on the consumption of automotive fuels were also never analyzed by regional bodies, thus legitimizing the study carried out here.

Table 1 shows how the trends are different, above all by type of fuel: in general, there is a progressive decrease in the quantities of gasoline sold in favor of diesel. This phenomenon was already observed at the time of the previous law since 2002 [25]. As far as gasoline is concerned, the reduction concerns, exclusively, the fuel sold at a reduced price for both contribution areas, while that sold at full price is increasing. In the increased contribution area A1, sales between 2012 and 2020 decreased by 36.6%. In the A2 ordinary area, on the other hand, sales decreased by 39.5%. Conversely, sales at full price increased by 21.9%. In summary, as regards the gasoline sold in FVG, if in 2012 approximately 270 ML were sold, in 2020 just 212.6 ML were sold with an overall reduction of 20.9%. Considering diesel, as anticipated, this presents a very different trend from that of gasoline: there is a continuous growth in the liters sold of all its annual time series, at both reduced and full prices, except for the setback caused by the 2020 pandemic: total sales increased by 9.7% between 2012 and 2020. This increase

**Table 1.** Time series from 2012 to 2020 for fuel sales (in millions of liters sold)

| GASOLINE | 2012 | 2013 | 2014 | 2015 | 2016 | 2017 | 2018 | 2019 | 2020 |
|---|---|---|---|---|---|---|---|---|---|
| Reduced price A1 | 101.7 | 105.3 | 100.6 | 98.6 | 93.5 | 88.9 | 84.4 | 79.4 | 64.5 |
| Reduced price A2 | 90.2 | 87.6 | 83.5 | 81.5 | 77.8 | 74.9 | 73.1 | 71.3 | 54.6 |
| Full price | 76.7 | 73.6 | 72.8 | 75.5 | 76.4 | 77.2 | 76.9 | 85.9 | 93.5 |
| *Total* | 268.7 | 266.6 | 256.9 | 255.6 | 247.7 | 241.1 | 234.4 | 236.6 | 212.6 |
| DIESEL | 2012 | 2013 | 2014 | 2015 | 2016 | 2017 | 2018 | 2019 | 2020 |
| Reduced price A1 | 36.6 | 42.2 | 44.6 | 48.6 | 50.5 | 52.5 | 54.3 | 53.6 | 46.8 |
| Reduced price A2 | 41.0 | 48.9 | 52.3 | 56.6 | 58.5 | 60.8 | 62.6 | 62.7 | 49.6 |
| Full price | 217.5 | 208.5 | 206.2 | 212.9 | 214.9 | 222.9 | 227.0 | 244.4 | 227.3 |
| *Total* | 295.1 | 299.5 | 303.2 | 318.1 | 323.8 | 336.1 | 343.9 | 360.6 | 323.8 |

Source: our elaborations on official data of the Autonomous Region of FVG

was strongly driven by the sale at a reduced price since the change was 27.9% in the increased contribution area and 21.1% in that with ordinary contribution.

### 3.3 The Impact of the Pandemic on the Quantities Sold

To assess the impact of the pandemic, the annual variations in the quantities sold between 2019 and 2020 are considered. The year 2020 was affected not only by the international border closure but also by the measures taken by the national government in terms of internal mobility, which in this context had an impact on trips to the neighboring Veneto region. The absolute and relative variations are shown in Table 2.

Analyzing the overall annual reductions between 2019 and 2020 in gasoline and diesel, it emerges that these were very similar, 10.1% and 10.2%, respectively, but these variations hide different dynamics. If these are compared to the positive annual changes recorded between 2018 and 2019 of 0.9% and 4.9%, respectively, one can immediately understand how the impact of the pandemic on sales has hit diesel the most. In fact, the latter observed a contraction of 36.8 ML compared to the 24 ML of gasoline. Considering the contribution areas, on the other hand, it can be observed that, in general, the reduction in liters sold is much stronger for fuel at a reduced price, in particular in the area with ordinary contribution, compared to those at full price: the sale of full price gasoline even increased by 8.8%.

These data seem to contradict what one might suppose: if the borders remained closed and mobility was severely limited for long periods in 2020, how is it possible that fuel decreased in FVG since motorists are no longer able to refuel abroad? To answer this question, several considerations are necessary. The first relates to the fact that, in 2020, traffic restrictions led to a general collapse of fuel sales nationwide, as will be highlighted shortly. The second consideration concerns the fact that, as explained above, the current law no longer considers the requirement of inverse proportionality, as the first law on reduced pricing did. To understand the dynamics at the borderland, it is necessary to use other data that refer to administrative partitions at the NUTS 3 level

**Table 2.** Absolute and relative change (in millions of liters sold) in fuel sales

| GASOLINE | Variation 2020/2012 | | Variation 2019/2018 | | Variation 2020/2019 | |
|---|---|---|---|---|---|---|
| | absolute | relative | absolute | relative | absolute | relative |
| Reduced price A1 | −37.2 | −36.6% | −5.0 | −5.9% | −14.8 | −18.7% |
| Reduced price A2 | −35.7 | −39.5% | −1.8 | −2.5% | −16.7 | −23.5% |
| Full price | 16.8 | 21.9% | 9.0 | 11.8% | 7.6 | 8.8% |
| *Total* | −56.1 | −20.9% | 2.2 | 0.9% | −24.0 | −10.1% |
| DIESEL | Variation 2020/2012 | | Variation 2019/2018 | | Variation 2020/2019 | |
| | absolute | relative | absolute | absolute | relative | absolute |
| Reduced price A1 | 10.2 | 27.9% | −0.6 | −1.2% | −6.8 | −12.7% |
| Reduced price A2 | 8.6 | 21.1% | 0.1 | 0.1% | −13.0 | −20.8% |
| Full price | 9.9 | 4.5% | 17.3 | 7.6% | −17.0 | −7.0% |
| *TOTAL* | 28.7 | 9.7% | 16.8 | 4.9% | −36.8 | −10.2% |

Source: our elaborations on official published data of the FVG Autonomous Region

(Province, in the Italian context), which allows for better identification of sales trends near the borders.

On the basis of these considerations, in Zaccomer and Bressan [27], the data of the Ministry of Economic Development on fuel sales in Italy were used. These data are published monthly in the Oil Bulletin[4] broken down by NUTS 2 (regions) and NUTS 3 (provinces) levels. Through these data, it is possible to know the market outcomes for the provinces of Gorizia and Trieste, both of which border the Slovenian Republic. Data referring to the province of Udine, which shares the border with Austria and Slovenia but is very wide in terms of surface, do not make it possible to study in detail the effect of closure on its border zone (Fig. 1). However, it should be remembered that the ministerial data do not distinguish residents entitled to buy regional fuel at lower prices, and consequently, the data include the fuel sales of businesses and those of nonresidents. Despite these differences, the data made available by the Ministry, in Table 3, clearly highlight what happened during the first year of the pandemic[5].

In FVG, the sales of automotive fuels in 2020, compared to the previous year, underwent a reduction that is lower than the one recorded in Italy, both for gasoline (by 13.9% against 21.2% nationally) and for diesel (by 9.1% against 16.2% nationally). Going into the regional detail, it is enlightening to observe that the provinces of Gorizia and Trieste, unlike those of Udine and Pordenone, which are decreasing, have registered increases in sales equal to 10.1% and 30.4% for gasoline and 19.9% and 33.7% for diesel, respectively. It is confirmed that the predominantly border provinces behaved in a very different way from those farther away from Slovenia.

---

[4] See https://dgsaie.mise.gov.it/bollettino-petrolifero.

[5] In Zaccomer and Bressan [27], provisional data from the first half of 2020 were used for an initial assessment of the effects of the pandemic on fuel sales.

**Table 3.** Sales of gasoline and diesel for transport (in millions of tons sold)

| GASOLINE | Annual sales | | | Relative variation | | |
|---|---|---|---|---|---|---|
| | 2019 | 2020 | 2021 | 2020/19 | 2021/20 | 2021/19 |
| Gorizia | 15.8 | 17.4 | 21.5 | 10.1% | 23.8% | 36.3% |
| Pordenone | 40.0 | 34.1 | 37.8 | −14.7% | 10.9% | −5.4% |
| Trieste | 15.7 | 20.5 | 26.6 | 30.4% | 29.9% | 69.4% |
| Udine | 101.9 | 77.4 | 89.4 | −24.1% | 15.5% | −12.3% |
| FVG | 173.4 | 149.3 | 175.3 | −13.9% | 17.4% | 1.1% |
| Italia | 7,334.8 | 5,780.6 | 7,051.5 | −21.2% | 22.0% | −3.9% |
| DIESEL | Annual sales | | | Relative variation | | |
| | 2019 | 2020 | 2021 | 2020/19 | 2021/20 | 2021/19 |
| Gorizia | 24.7 | 29.6 | 36.0 | 19.9% | 21.7% | 45.9% |
| Pordenone | 90.4 | 83.6 | 93.3 | −7.5% | 11.6% | 3.3% |
| Trieste | 21.7 | 29.0 | 37.4 | 33.7% | 29.2% | 72.7% |
| Udine | 260.2 | 218.6 | 239.7 | −16.0% | 9.7% | −7.9% |
| FVG | 396.8 | 360.7 | 406.4 | −9.1% | 12.7% | 2.4% |
| Italia | 23,796.4 | 19,930.3 | 23,121.3 | −16.2% | 16.0% | −2.8% |

Source: our elaborations on data from the MISE Oil Bulletin, updated to September 2022

This last observation allows us to indirectly justify how, with respect to the variations reported in Table 2, A1, the area entitled to a greatest contribution, has more limited contractions than that of ordinary contribution: for gasoline 18.7% versus 23.5%, while for diesel 12.7% versus 20.8%. However, the apparent contradiction is still unresolved: why were full-price sales better than those at reduced prices?

With open borders, the purchase of fuel at full price in regional filling stations is done, for the most part, from businesses, nonresidents and residents who rarely use the car. During the closure of the borders, the sales at full price include not only those categories, but also those who traditionally prefer to refuel abroad and who have never refueled at reduced prices because they never asked the electronic card managed by the Chamber of Commerce or who have let the electronic card expire.

To understand what happened, it is necessary to consider data provided by the regional administration on the number of identification cards. Some of the regional motorists, who were forced to refuel in Italy during the periods of border closure, immediately applied in 2020 to reactivate the expired cards or request new ones. The data show that if the overall regional increase between 2019 and 2020 was 4.3%, that relating to the provinces of Trieste and Gorizia alone reaches 10% (more precisely 7.1% for gasoline and 21% for diesel).

As anticipated, ministerial data allow for an understanding of what happened in 2021. From Table 3, it is possible to observe how the increases in sales during the second year of the pandemic, again for the provinces of Gorizia and Trieste, are truly remarkable when compared to the regional and national ones. When 2019 is taken as the baseline, these increases are 36.3% and 69.4% compared to the regional 1.1% for gasoline and 45.9% and 72.7% compared to the 2.4% regional for diesel, respectively. Furthermore, it should be noted that the regional variation - driven by the sales of the two border provinces - despite being limited, is positive in value, in contrast with the national contraction of 3.9% for gasoline and 2.8% for diesel.

Even if the periods of total or partial closure of the borders did not exactly follow the monthly calendar, it is interesting to note that the regional data published in the implementation reports show a collapse, especially in the period March-May 2020, particularly in April. This fall is entirely consistent with the official chronology of traffic restrictions [10]: the first Italian national lockdown began on 10 March 2020, while the reopening with international borders took place on 13 June 2020 in the case of Slovenia and two days later with Austria.

In the period March-April 2020, compared to the same period of the previous year, the drop in total sales amounted to 42.6% for gasoline and 39.1% for diesel. By focusing attention on the month of greatest contraction, namely, April 2020, compared to the same month in 2019, according to the implementation report, total sales fell by 67.6% for gasoline and 60.8% for diesel. It is not surprising that the greatest collapse was recorded for sales at a reduced price, especially in the ordinary contribution area with 76.8% and 77.2%, respectively. More limited, albeit still dramatic, was the full-price decline of 54% for both types of fuel. The extent of these monthly reductions stresses how strong the effect of the pandemic has been on the sale of fuels of both types, both at a reduced price and at full price.

Monthly ministerial data can also be explored. The collapse of the overall sales of automotive fuels recorded in the month of April 2020, compared to the sales of the corresponding month of the previous year, is confirmed with a reduction for gasoline of 63.9% at the regional level and 74% at the national level and of 48.7% and 58.5% for diesel. Provincial data instead present smaller contractions compared to the regional and national ones both for the province of Gorizia and Trieste, but the latter still manages to record an increase of 23% when diesel is concerned.

## 4   Actor Dynamics at the Time of the Pandemic

As seen before, in the case of the Italian borderland region of FVG, it is evident that alongside the various market players, there is a strong influence on the market outcomes of both the regional public administration, which must always act within the limits imposed by national and European Union regulations, and of neighboring states. The focus is now on some aspects of the behavior of some of these actors during the first year of the pandemic, as the trends in fuel sales were directly affected.

The analysis of the data presented here highlights how the outbreak of the pandemic and the introduction of restrictions on national and international circulation have produced a contraction in annual sales of motor fuels at a national level, while at a regional level, such a reduction was more contained. This result was directly influenced by the fact that with the limitation in mobility for some periods of the year, it was no longer possible to refuel as usual in the nearby Veneto region and, to a greater degree, abroad.

The regional contraction derives from the fact that, despite the boom in sales in the border provinces of Gorizia and Trieste, these two matter less in terms of absolute fuel sales than those of Pordenone and Udine. The period from March to May 2020 was the most affected by traffic restrictions due to a lockdown never experienced before in Italian history. It was therefore not surprising to verify that the monthly data identify the month of April of the same year as the one of greatest criticality in terms of sales.

In the first part of 2020, economic actors suffered a great blow due to the pandemic, which took everyone by surprise. However, the intense work of the regional Chambers of Commerce, especially that of Venezia Giulia (for the provinces of Gorizia e Trieste), should be remembered, which, despite the limitations on access to public offices, had to cope with the intensified requests made by local motorists in relation to the issue of new cards or the reactivation of expired ones.

With the reopening of the Slovenian border on 13 June 2020, the situation changed drastically. From the early morning, the first queues of Italian motorists at the crossings, especially the minor ones of Gorizia, were registered[6]. This was only the first sign of what would have happened in the following days. In fact, given the enormous economic damage caused by border closure to the many filling stations present on Slovenian territory close to the Italian border (since a significant portion of their clientele lives in FVG), the Government of Ljubljana modified its excise duties on fuels to allow filling stations to charge a price just below the psychological threshold of 1 Euro per liter, while Austria, without any official announcement, regulated itself in such a way as to charge a price slightly higher than the unit price. This then triggered what the Italian press of the FVG region called the "gasoline war".

From the Italian side, the reaction of the regional government was immediate by opening crisis talks with all the actors involved to decide how to react to the actions of foreign states. In particular, an agreement was sought above all with the oil companies, which have been long accused – even by consumers themselves – of keeping prices high (compared to those charged in neighboring Veneto) with the excuse of transport costs. It was proposed to bring, for the A1 area alone, the regional contribution to 29 cents per liter for gasoline and 20 cents per liter for diesel in the face of a reduction of 5 cents per liter of the price list charged by oil companies. The agreement was reached, and the increase in the contributions was operationalized from the end of August 2020, especially with the aim of limiting the strongly rooted habit of fuel tourism close to the Slovenian border.

It is far more complex to comment on the dynamics of the regional fuel market during the second part of 2020. In fact, fuel sales may reflect other effects, such as the tendency to avoid long-distance trips and the contraction in mobility caused by the closure of various economic activities, which generate purchases of fuel at a reduced price when workers go to the workplace with their own car. Finally, there is a further problem: following the resumption of the pandemic after the summer break, Slovenia declared a state of health emergency and closed, albeit with various exceptions, its borders starting from 26 October 2020 (and gradually reopened them only in the year following), while Austria did not close the borders but, to enter its territory, a negative test was required

---

[6] See    https://www.ansa.it/friuliveneziagiulia/notizie/2020/06/13/fase-3-fila-al-confine-di-gor izia-in-slovenia-per-benzina_20813f43-6d34-41c8-85ea-2da1dfca6c3c.html.

whose cost offset any possible savings in fuel purchase. From a quantitative point of view, the regional data of the implementation reports show an increase in the period November-December 2020 compared to the same months of the previous year, only for gasoline, equal to 9.1%. This figure is also in line with a new wave of requests for activating cards from the Chambers of Commerce.

At the time of the reopening of the borders in June 2020, a further change in legislation was asked at both the political and economic levels. The request was to locally introduce the so-called "Bolzano model", which is in force in the Italian autonomous province of Bolzano (bordering Austria and Switzerland) and, similar to what happens in FVG, is aimed at curbing fuel tourism. According to this scheme, the recipients of the contributions are classified into two groups, according to the residency in two "zones", up to 10 km and from 10.1 to 20 km from the international border[7].

In reality, in the FVG region, the possibility of modifying the second regional fuel law was, in fact, precluded until the beginning of 2021 when the European proceedings against the 2010 regional law were finally concluded. As previously explained, the first change of law was derived not only by the loss of efficiency of the first scheme but also by the remarks of the European Commission, which considered the regional law not in compliance with its own directives on the taxation of energy products. The reason for the dispute was also assumed to exist for the 2010 law, to the point that the Commission appealed to the European Court of Justice. In January 2021, the Court issued the final judgment in favor of the FVG, in this way closing the dispute. Only at this point did the regional lawmaker begin to think about an improvement in the law – keeping the principles of the second law that the Court had judged correct – since the increase in the contribution was not successful in halting fuel tourism after the borders reopened.

The first talks to revise the law between the regional administration and the actors involved began in the first months of 2021. In May 2021, the admission criterion for municipalities in the increased contribution area was redefined, specifying that all municipalities within the 10 km band from the border should be included within this area. This change followed, not surprisingly, the provisions of the Bolzano model.

With the outbreak of the war in Ukraine, this improvement in legislation seemed, at least until September 2022, to lose importance since the energy problems concerning above all the prices of gas, electricity and transport costs incurred by local companies were becoming more urgent.

The state cut of 30 cents per liter for gasoline introduced during 2022 by the government led by Mario Draghi[8] was not able to offset completely in the borderland the incentive to cross the border. In fact, in September 2022, due to the entry into force of the new Slovenian price lists on fuel prices charged off the highways, there was still a fair amount of convenience to refuel across the border. This is why the regional government promulgated the new RL 20 at the end of 2022, which introduced again the geographical concept of "distance from the border", a key aspect of the first law but not of the second.

---

[7] For more details, see the website of the Autonomous Province of Bolzano https://www.provin cia.bz.it/it/servizi-a-z.asp?bnsv_svid=1004463.

[8] The fuel price reduction was introduced by the Italian government in March 2022 as a result of the economic effects of the Ukrainian crisis. After the general election of September 2023, the new government did not renew such initiative.

That is made by enabling the inhabitants of the "Zero Area", which consists of a set of Municipalities with a distance of 10 km from the state borders, to receive a further contribution when refueling at regional pumps[9]. The new LR 20 took effect in 2023, but there is no data yet to understand its effects.

## 5   Conclusion

The temporary higher attendance of regional petrol pumps in comparison to the average situation recorded in Italy highlights the disadvantaged contexts that business operators usually face in this border area. From the perspective of car drivers, the temporary closure of the border meant a restricted range of shopping options. For retailers, it basically meant the possibility of relying on a share of customers who normally opt for the foreign market.

The business activity is, for definition, imbued with risk, and the coronavirus-issued lockdown has shown how external shocks can pose additional challenges, especially to businesses where online shopping or home delivery cannot be applied. In the case of Italy, a lower demand for fuel was registered, with consequences not only for business but also for the state, in terms of lower fiscal revenues. In border zones, the risk seems to be higher, and this is visible by the fact that during the period of border closure, larger volumes of fuel were sold in the border zone of high-taxation countries, despite limited mobility.

Studies concerning the economic impacts of pandemic-issued border closure are limited. This paucity could probably be explained by the fact that online retailing has attracted the most scholarly interest [5, 13]. E-commerce is not a novelty, as its emergence can be traced back to the 1990s, but the rest-at-home policy has consolidated its role [3]. Another reason for this scarceness could be found in the methodological challenges characterizing borderland research and, in the case where the focus is on the economy, the fact that quantitative data referring to small areas are limited or absent. It highlights the need to develop ad hoc surveys or rely, as was the case of this contribution, on data produced by other bodies for other purposes, which strengthens the importance of the study. With the available data, it is possible to know how many liters were sold and how many contributions were granted, but still it is not possible to affirm whether there has been a reduction in fuel tourism. Only with data relating to the flows at border crossings would it be possible to affirm with greater certainty that there has been a reduction in full tourism beyond what the accounting data say. Our ability to comment on the possible achievement of a "business new normal" status is also limited by the fact that the 2021 data on the quantities sold by contribution area are not yet published.

The issue of border closures can be analyzed from many perspectives. This paper does not investigate what happened in the other side of the border in terms of quantity sold, for example. An examination of the data concerning the neighboring countries would have enabled an assessment whether an advantage of some Italian petrol pumps corresponds to the loss for others who normally benefit from an open border. As acknowledged earlier, the strong reduction in fuel prices with the reopening of the border registered in Slovenia hints that a significant drop in fuel purchases occurred. If such data are

---

[9] See https://www.consiglio.regione.fvg.it/pagineinterne/Portale/IterLeggi/IterLeggiDettaglio.aspx?Leg=5&ID=1935.

undoubtedly interesting, it should be said that international comparisons are always difficult to make, as the measures adopted to fight the pandemic were different in the various European Union member states [11], with the consequence that the demand for mobility cannot be fully compared.

The focus on the article was one of the quantities sold, but this is not the only impact concerning the fuel retailing market. It is expected that the decision over the price charged was different during the lockdown period compared to a business-as-usual situation. In the context of the almost absence of international fluxes of car drivers, petrol stations can consider that the regional demand for fuel is satisfied locally. A hypothesis is that there are no differences in the prices charged in the same regional territory. Some hints were provided on the fierce international competition on prices by revisiting what happened after the border reopening, especially in terms of the willingness of the regional lawmaker to change the current scheme. The state, through the lowering of the value of excise duties or ad hoc legislation to lower fuel prices, has a strong power in determining the direction of motorists' trips and the fate of the local fuel market. This creates uncertainty of international oil companies or local operators, who need to ponder the possible decision of locating one of their stores in such a variable environment.

Here an economic aspect of border closure was investigated, but there are other dimensions that deserve to be analyzed. Given that cross-border trips are not only made to take advantage of price differentials, it is expected that border closure severely affects the wellbeing of those who normally rely on goods, services and – especially – people located on the other side of the border. Interestingly, Docherty et al. [7] question how the rhythms of towns and cities will be in the future due to the impact of pandemic-induced restrictions on people's livelihoods. This stimulus promotes further reflections on the medium- and long-term impacts of the pandemic on border connectivity. Everyday mobility and car ownership among borderland inhabitants can also be affected if working from home continues to be a significant trend in the post-COVID period. The compression of one's space of life might cause long-term transformation to borderland livelihood and the way in which borderland residents take advantage of opportunities at the other side of the border. On the other hand, there are reasons to believe that daily flows will return to pre-pandemic times or even increase. The pandemic might have moved to the background shared modes of transport due to the perception of the private vehicle as a safer mode of transport. To conclude, it should be observed that the pandemic has impacted people's routines and because of the general willingness to restore the pre-COVID situation and the surge of new global challenges, a new equilibrium in the economy has yet to be found.

# References

1. Bressan, G.: Power, mobility and the economic vulnerability of borderlands. J. Borderl. Stud. **32**(3), 361–377 (2017)
2. Bryson, J.R., Vanchan, V: Covid-19 and alternative conceptualisations of value and risk in GPN research. Tijdschrift voor economische en sociale geografie **111**(3), 530–542 (2020)

3. Bryson, J.R.: COVID-19 and the immediate and longer-term impacts on the retail and hospitality industries: dark stores and turnover-based rental models. In: Bryson, J.R., Andres, L., Ersoy, A., Reardon, L. (eds.) Living with Pandemics: Places, People and Policy, pp. 202–216. Edward Elgar, Cheltenham (2021)
4. Brunet-Jailly, E., Carpenter, M.J.: Introduction: borderlands in the era of covid-19. Bord. Glob. Rev. **2**(1), 7–11 (2020)
5. Dannenberg, P., Fuchs, M., Riedler, T., Wiedemann, C.: Digital transition by Covid-19 pandemic? The German food online retail. Tijdschr. Econ. Soc. Geogr. **111**(3), 543–560 (2020)
6. Delmas, A., Goeury, D.: Bordering the world in response to emerging infectious diseases: the case of SARS-CoV-2. Bord. Glob. Rev. **2**(1), 12–22 (2020)
7. Docherty, I., Marsden, G., Anable, J., Forth, T.: Mobility during and after the pandemic. In: Bryson, J.R., Andres, L., Ersoy, A., Reardon, L. (eds.) Living with Pandemics: Places, People and Policy, pp. 184–193. Edward Elgar, Cheltenham (2021)
8. Free, C., Hecimovic, A.: Global supply chains after COVID-19: the end of the road for neoliberal globalization? Account. Audit. Account. J. **34**(1), 58–84 (2021)
9. Gibson, C., Carr, C., Lyons, C., Taksa, L., Warren, A.: COVID-19 and the shifting industrial landscape. Geogr. Res. **59**(2), 196–205 (2021)
10. Giovanetti, M., et al.: SARS-CoV-2 shifting transmission dynamics and hidden reservoirs potentially limit efficacy of public health interventions in Italy. Commun. Biol. **4**, 489 (2021)
11. Guild, E.: Covid-19 using border controls to fight a pandemic? Reflections from the European union. Front. Hum. Dyn. **2**, 606299 (2020)
12. Lara-Valencia, F., Laine, J.P.: The Covid-19 pandemic: territorial, political and governance dimensions of bordering. J. Borderl. Stud. **37**(4), 665–677 (2022)
13. Li, J., Hallsworth, A.G., Coca-Stefaniak, J.A.: Changing grocery shopping behaviours among Chinese consumers at the outset of the COVID-19 outbreak. Tijdschr. Econ. Soc. Geogr. **111**(3), 574–583 (2020)
14. Jurić Pahor, M.: Border as method: impact of the Covid-19 pandemic on the border area between Italy and Slovenia and on the Slovene minority in Italy. Treaties Doc. J. Ethn. Stud. **85**, 57–81 (2020)
15. Malkowski, A., Mazur, R.: The impact of border closure on the economy of a border region – as exemplified by the Polish-German borderland. Prace Naukowe Uniwersytetu ekonomicznego we wroclawiu, Res. Pap. Wroclaw Univ. Econ. Bus. **64**(8), 72–82 (2020)
16. Opiłowska, E.: The Covid-19 crisis: the end of a borderless Europe? Eur. Soc. **23**(S1), S589–SS600 (2021)
17. Panwar, R., Pinkse, J., De Marchi, V.: The future of global supply chains in a post-COVID-19 world. Calif. Manag. Rev. **64**(2), 5–23 (2022)
18. Paül, V., Trillo-Santamaría, J.-M., Martínez-Cobas, X., Fernández-Jardón, C.: The economic impact of closing the boundaries: the lower Minho Valley cross-border region in times of Covid-19. J. Borderl. Stud. **37**(4), 761–779 (2022)
19. Pelc, S.: Peripherality and marginality of Slovenian border areas along the Italian border. In: Geographical Marginality as a Global Issue. General, Theoretical and Methodological Aspects, vol. 1, pp. 96–113 (2010)
20. Radil, S.M., Castan, P.J., Ptak, T.: Borders resurgent: towards a post-Covid-19 global border regime? Space Polity **25**(1), 132–140 (2021)
21. Richardson, K.E., Cappellano, F.: Sieve or shield? High tech firms and entrepreneurs and the impacts of COVID-19 on North American border region. J. Borderl. Stud. **37**(4), 805–824 (2022)
22. Sorgo, L., Lukanovič, S.N.: The Italian national community in Slovenia during the Covid-19 epidemic. Treaties Doc. J. Ethn. Stud. **85**, 101–117 (2020)

23. Vanchan, V., Mulhall, R., Bryson, J.: Repatriation or reshoring of manufacturing to the U.S. and UK: dynamics and global production networks or from here to there and back again. Growth Change **49**(1), 97−121 (2018)
24. Vanchan, V.: Global pandemic disruptions, reconfiguration and glocalization of production Networks. In: Bryson, J.R., Andres, L., Ersoy, A., Reardon, L. (eds.) Living with Pandemics: Places, People and Policy, pp. 195−201. Edward Elgar, Cheltenham (2021)
25. Zaccomer, G. P.: Carburanti, statistiche e prezzi. Esperienze di ricerca legate alla manovra di riduzione dei prezzi delle benzine e del diesel per autotrazione in Friuli Venezia Giulia. Forum, Udine (2011)
26. Zaccomer, G.P.: La manovra di riduzione dei prezzi dei carburanti in Friuli Venezia Giulia: un quadro di sintesi dal 1997 al 2012. Rivista di Economia e Statistica del Territorio **2**, 34–59 (2012)
27. Zaccomer, G.P., Bressan, G.: Le manovre di riduzione dei prezzi dei carburanti in Friuli Venezia Giulia tra feedback passati e futuri. Considerazioni all'epoca della pandemia di Covid-19. In: Dini, F., Martellozzo, F., Randelli, F., Romei, P. (eds.) Memorie Geografiche, pp. 83–89. Società di Studi Geografici, Florence (2021)
28. Wang, F., Zou, S., Liu, Y.: Territorial traps in controlling the COVID-19 pandemic. Dialogues Hum. Geogr. **10**(2), 154–157 (2020)

# Local Budget Revenue Formation Reality, Obstacles and Prospects in Georgia: An Empirical Examination and Creative Approach

George Abuselidze(✉) ⓘ

Batumi Shota Rustaveli State University, Ninoshvili, 35, 6010 Batumi, Georgia
george.abuselidze@gmail.com

**Abstract.** The purpose of this research is to investigate the creation of financial resources in municipal budgets and to highlight significant concerns. Local self-government is crucial for the development of a robust economy in a nation, but without a balanced budget, a municipality cannot be independent or powerful. As a result, it's crucial to identify the mechanisms for optimization and assess the difficulties associated with creating local budgets. In the study, the sources of Georgian municipal budget creation are examined and discussed. The difficulties that now exist are highlighted based on the analysis of the study findings, and modifications that should be made are suggested based on the aforesaid facts. These changes will be crucial for the efficient operation of the local budgets.

**Keywords:** Budget policy · Budget system · Local budget · Local taxation · subsidies and revenue

## 1 Introduction

In modern conditions, the experience of many countries reveals that the process of decentralization makes a great contribution to the economic development of the country. It is essential for any state to distribute power in such a way that it is not monopolized. Decentralization and financial independence in the state guarantee that the municipality will be able to exercise its powers. If the municipality does not have enough sources of its own income, then it will not be able to carry out expenses at its own discretion. Accordingly, the independence of municipalities and the effectiveness of the functioning of the program budget will be called into question.

Recently, the role of self-government in the country's financial, economic, and social development is a particularly relevant issue in Georgia. In this direction, reforms have been carried out many times for its productivity. However, today there are still gaps that need to be studied, analyzed, and the development of elimination mechanisms.

The aim of the work is to present the problems of the formation of financial resources of local self-government budgets and to determine recommendations and ways of overcoming them based on their analysis. In addition, the presentation of the main hindering factors preventing the decentralization process.

O. Gervasi et al. (Eds.): ICCSA 2023, LNCS 13957, pp. 197–209, 2023.
https://doi.org/10.1007/978-3-031-36808-0_13

The paper objectives are:

1. To determine the degree of dependence of the municipality's budgets on the central budget, as well as to study the relationship between the dependence of the municipality's revenues and expenses.
2. To determine the level of decentralization, study of individual components in the municipality's income.

## 2 Methodology for Studying Formation Local Budgets

The theoretical-methodological foundation of the research is the articles of many scientists on the research subject, where local budgeting, financial mechanisms for territorial unit growth and the peculiarities of state fiscal arrangement models are explored. Works by Melkers and Willoughby (2005), LaFrance and Balogun (2012), Mullins and Pagano (2005), Lysiak et al. (2020), Pokrovskaia and Belov (2020), Karianga (2016), Morgan et al. (2017), Seal (2003), Rossikhina et al. (2018), Patytska et al. (2021), Oprea and Bilan (2015), Glushchenko and Kozhalina (2019), Petrushenko (2014), Pelinescu et al. (2010), Ismoilova (2022), Dvoryadkina and belousova (2018), Storonyanska et al. (2021), Panday and Chowdhury (2020), Godwin (2018), Mussari et al. (2016), Sintomer et al. (2008), Abuselidze (2020, 2021), Ivanyuta et al. (2022), and others are included [1–26]. They researched and published extensively on the subjects of state governance system construction and improvement, budget regulation, financial equalization, and budget relations organization. The articles [1–3, 6–8, 15–21, 24–26] focuses particularly on budgeting for capital investments, alternative service delivery, financial management, budgeting and budget reform, and intergovernmental finance. According to Duncan and Sabirianova [27], progressivity decreases inequality in observed income but has a far lesser influence on real inequality as estimated by consumption-based Gini indices. Tax, as a key component of the system of economic interactions, is so intricate in the absence of fiscal alternatives that it always becomes an actual problem in public debates [22]. The majority of OECD nations use various sorts of progressive income tax arrangements, in which tax rates rise as income rises [28]. In the present day, the study of the optimization of taxable income taxes is not just science but also a major issue for practitioners. First and foremost, the severity of this tax is based on income tax analysis and has an influence on societal welfare. Second, it is one of the key tax collections for the budget, which is more or less predictable and is dependent on the state's functioning to cover the essential expenditures. It is well acknowledged that the tax burden impacts not only budget revenues but also investments, production factors, pricing standards, and so on. Lastly, all of the above has an impact on the country's socioeconomic standing [5, 9, 12, 22–26]. According to Denek and Dylewski [29], financial sustainability indicates not just the ability to create enough income, but also how income and spending responsibilities are satisfied. The consequences of decentralization between 2015 and 2020, according to the conducted empirical study [24–26, 30, 31], include a slowing in the pace of current rural population decline, the rate of new rural population decline, and the level of rural employment. Decentralization has increased rural development levels, which helps to ensure that there is less regional disparity in rural development. According to the findings of the paper [6], the Good Financial Governance concept has been the focus of extensive research in its understanding as a new paradigm for local financial management. Yet, in practice, it has certain flaws, notably with regard to the accountability and legitimacy of its foundation. That is, financial sustainability indicates the budget's balance and the probability of its breach. These researchers have highlighted issues in this subject, but the fiscal arrangement and fiscal system require ongoing development and investigation. The Local Self-Government Code of Georgia, the Budget Code of Georgia, the Tax Code of Georgia, the Law of Georgia on Grants, and the Law of Georgia on Local Fees control the economic and financial foundations of self-governing entities. Moreover, Georgia has accepted the European Charter of Self-Government, on which self-government law is founded. Organic laws primarily govern fiscal relations: the Local Self-Government Law, the Tax Code of Georgia, and the Budget Code. Local self-government is Georgian people' right and chance to control and manage matters of local relevance in line with the population's interests through local self-government authorities. The Code of Self-Government outlines self-government powers, which are classified as delegated, self-governing, and voluntary (Local Self-Government Code). To reduce socioeconomic disparity across various territorial entities, it is required to examine regional welfare circumstances and implement legislative rules.

## 3    Results and Discussion

When discussing the independence of municipalities and the decentralization process, we mean first of all the existence of financial resources necessary for independence. Based on the fact that in the process of formation of the budget revenues of the municipalities of Georgia, certain peculiarities were revealed, in the paper, A systematic, empirical research has been used, which distinguishes the peculiarities of the revenues of 69 municipalities of Georgia.

To assess how important tax revenues are in total revenues at the municipal level, we have identified several indicators:

- Indicator 1: ratio of municipal tax revenues to total revenues;
- Indicator 2: ratio of tax revenues of the municipality to expenses;
- Indicator 3: Ratio of municipal grants to total revenues.

The mentioned indicators best reflect how financially independent the municipality is because only its sources of income ensure the determination of expenses at the discretion of the municipality.

As a result of the study of 69 municipalities according to indicator 1, it was revealed that the situation is quite complicated in this regard, as several municipalities were identified, whose tax revenues are meager and in fact they depend on other types of revenues. As a result of empirical research, the table presents the 5 municipalities whose ratio of tax revenues to total revenues was the least among 69 municipalities:

According to data, in 2016–2018 there were municipalities whose own incomes in the form of taxes were only up to 10%. This point to the fact that the municipalities were actually managed by the central government and decentralization is not possible for municipalities with such a budget.

As a result of the 2019 change in the mechanism of distribution of tax revenues to municipalities, the situation of the mentioned municipalities' changes:

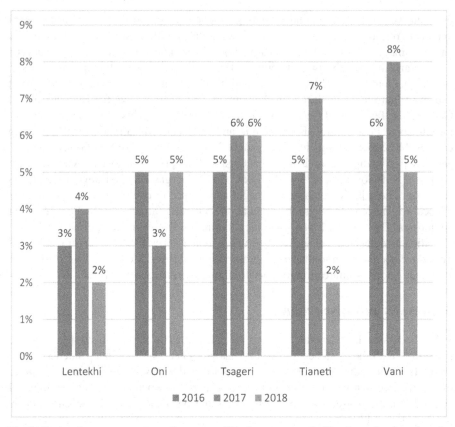

**Fig. 1.** Ratio of tax revenues to total revenues (%). Source: compiled by the author based on the data of the Ministry of Finance of Georgia [32–34]

As we can see, the situation changes after 2019, when the reform was carried out and 19% of VAT was assigned to local governments. However, it is interesting how the value- added tax (VAT) was distributed among the municipalities shown in the Fig. 4:

The difference in the increase of the tax revenues of the municipalities in the mentioned years is quite noticeable. From a financial point of view, of course, the distribution of 19% of VAT is beneficial for municipalities, but how fairly the said financial funds are distributed and how it affects the development of municipalities in the long term is already a controversial issue.

Since 2019 the least tax revenues have been received by the municipalities in Fig. 2 and Fig. 3. Until 2018, completely different municipalities received the lowest tax revenues. Until 2018, they received income from both property tax and certain categories of income tax. Therefore, the municipalities shown in Fig. 1 are the least economically active.

As we can see, 4 municipalities have received the smallest amount of VAT: Bolnisi, Borjomi, Kazbegi, and Shuakhevi. As a result, they are at the top of the list with the least amount of tax revenue in total revenue. While the municipalities in Fig. 2 had the least

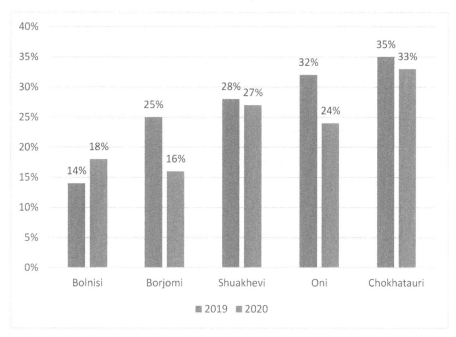

**Fig. 2.** Ratio of taxes to total revenues in 2019–2020 (%). Source: compiled by the author based on the data of the Ministry of Finance of Georgia [32–34]

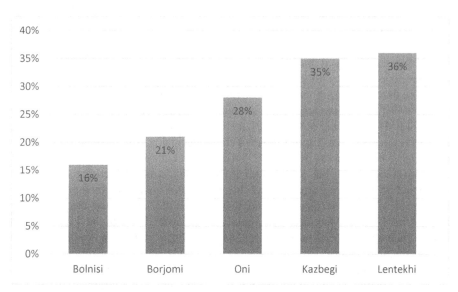

**Fig. 3.** Ratio of taxes to total revenues in 2021 (%). Source: compiled by the author based on the data of the Ministry of Finance of Georgia [32–34]

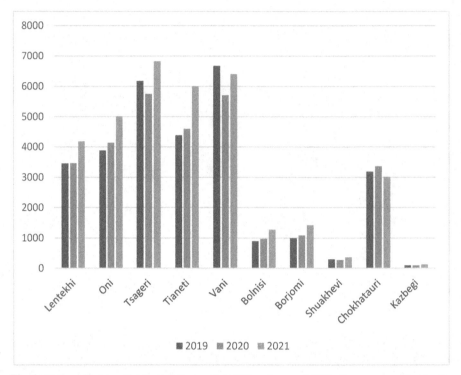

**Fig. 4.** Value added tax distribution by municipalities, thousand GEL. Source: compiled by the author based on the data of the Ministry of Finance of Georgia [32–34]

tax revenue, they received much more revenue from the distribution of VAT than other more developed municipalities.

To see the difference more clearly, consider the following Fig. 5:

According to the diagram, the tax revenues of the municipalities whose economic activity was the lowest in 2018, by 2019, their tax revenues are increasing several times. Moreover, their revenues exceed those of the municipality, whose tax revenues were much higher before the distribution of VAT. The amount distributed from the value-added tax is included in the tax revenues of the municipalities, therefore their distribution should be done in accordance with the added value created by the municipalities. Based on all of the above, questions arise that question the fairness and adequacy of the distribution of VAT. VAT replaces the equalization transfer, but with the difference that the distribution of financial resources in this form imposes certain frameworks on more developed municipalities.

The research has identified the factors indicating the presence of certain gaps in the existing system of financing of the municipality. Accordingly, it is necessary to consider separately the distribution of VAT and its objectivity.

The Fig. 6 shows the 5 municipalities that received the largest share of VAT according to the 2021 budget law:

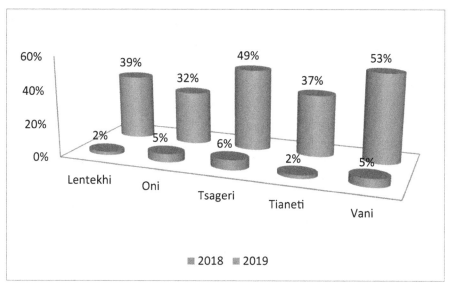

**Fig. 5.** Change in tax revenues in 2018–2019. Source: compiled by the author based on the data of the Ministry of Finance of Georgia [32–34]

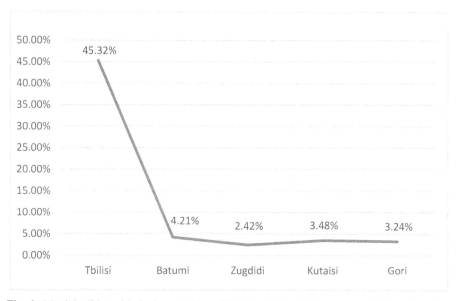

**Fig. 6.** Municipalities with the largest share of VAT by 2021, %. Source: compiled by the author based on the data of the Ministry of Finance of Georgia [32–34]

Municipalities that were more active compared to other municipalities receive the least revenue from value-added tax (Fig. 7). For instance, consider Kazbegi, which receives the lowest value-added tax by 2021. Until 2019, the ratio of Kazbegi tax revenues

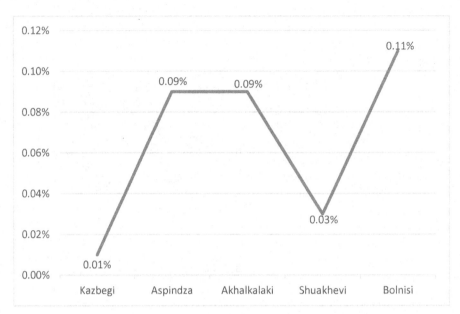

**Fig. 7.** Municipalities with the lowest share of VAT by 2021, %. Source: compiled by the author based on the data of the Ministry of Finance of Georgia [32–34]

to total revenues was: 50% in 2016, 45% in 2017, and 45% in 2018. Accordingly, Kazbegi is among the municipalities of Georgia that create significant added value on the territory of the country, although it receives the least revenue from the state when distributing VAT.

It is much easier for municipalities to administer other types of tax than value-added tax. As we have seen, it is common in European countries to assign a share of income tax to local governments. Georgia also has a similar experience, although the incomes received in this way were not enough for the activities of the local self-government. Hence the government can also consider assigning profit tax to municipalities.

As an indicator of the municipality's independence, we can also apply how it can manage to cover expenses with its sources of income. Therefore, we defined the next indicator as the ratio of taxes and expenses (Table 1 and Table 2).

As we can see, since the municipalities in Fig. 7 received the least tax revenues, their ability to cover the expenses is the least. Therefore, the obtained results clearly show and emphasize that the tax revenues received by the municipalities are not enough to cover their expenses. The situation is changing again in 2019 when the tax revenues increase, and the ability of the municipalities to cover the expenses they incur increases accordingly.

In addition, it should be noted that until 2018 only 6 municipalities (Akhalkalaki, Aspindza, Kazbegi, Gardabani, Shuakhevi) were allocated on average, whose tax revenues covered 100% or more of the municipality's expenses Since 2019, when local governments retain 19% of VAT, the number of such municipalities has increased to 30.

**Table 1.** Ratio of taxes and expenses in 2016–2018 (%)

| Municipality | 2016 year | 2017 year | 2018 year |
|---|---|---|---|
| Lentekhi | 5% | 7% | 3% |
| Tianeti | 7% | 8% | 7% |
| Khoni | 10% | 10% | 10% |
| Tsageri | 10% | 11% | 11% |
| Oni | 12% | 9% | 11% |

Source: compiled by the author based on the data of the Ministry of Finance of Georgia [32–34]

**Table 2.** Ratio of taxes and expenses in 2019–2021 (%)

| Municipality | 2019 year | 2020 year | 2021 year |
|---|---|---|---|
| Bolnisi | 19% | 29% | 22% |
| Borjomi | 45% | 29% | 36% |
| Tkibuli | 53% | 70% | 78% |
| Chokhatauri | 57% | 63% | 72% |
| Dedoplistskaro | 65% | 68% | 68% |

Source: compiled by the author based on the data of the Ministry of Finance of Georgia [32–34]

Accordingly, almost half of the 69 municipalities have the opportunity to cover their expenses with their tax revenues and without depending on the state budget.

Another important indicator, by which we can judge how dependent the budget of municipalities is on the state budget, is the share of grants in total revenues. Most grants are received by those municipalities with small tax revenues. However, it is worth emphasizing the fact that there are quite a lot of municipalities whose incomes are half or more from grants.

The data obtained from the research result are presented in the Fig. 8:

As we can see, the dependence of municipalities on grants is quite high until 2020, however, after 2020, there is a tendency to decrease. At first glance, it seems that the dependence of municipalities on the state budget is decreasing, however, we must take into account the fact that the revenues of municipalities have increased significantly with the allocation of 19% of VAT, therefore the percentage share of grants in total revenues has decreased.

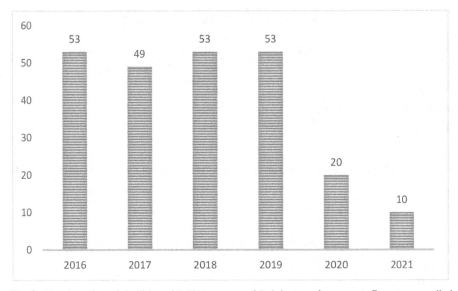

**Fig. 8.** Number of municipalities with 50% or more of their income from grants **Source:** compiled by the author based on the data of the Ministry of Finance of Georgia [32–34]

## 4 Conclusions

The financial dependence of the center and municipalities is determined via the budgets. Perfection of the formation of municipal budgets provides a guarantee of economic development of local self-government. The municipalities have been granted independence in the process of forming the program budget; however, its revenues do not allow the power to be effectively exercised. Improving revenue generation ensures that municipalities can manage their finances independently, which is a prerequisite for decentralization.

During the study of the formation of municipal budgets, certain problems were revealed. Based on the statistical analysis of the mentioned problems, we can draw the following conclusions:

- The only tax that belongs 100% to the municipalities is the property tax. It is necessary to review (evaluate) its fiscal effectiveness and by introducing progressive taxation, formulate the optimal tax burden;
- In Georgia today, economic inequality between municipalities remains an actual topic, therefore, canceling the equalization transfer contradicts the role of the state to ensure the economic equalization of the country's territorial units. It would be better to leave the equalization transfer, however, with the implementation of an effective mechanism for its redistribution;
- The 2019 change related to the distribution of 19% of VAT to municipalities increases the dependence on the central budget. The research identified the increased incomes of the municipalities, although it is confirmed that the amounts received from the mentioned distribution are not objective, it is impossible to determine which municipality belongs to the value-added tax depending on the level of its economic activity;

- To increase the municipality's income and at the same time stimulate its economic activity, it would be better to develop a legal framework that would leave the income and/or profit tax in the budget of the municipalities. This would help to encourage the municipality in terms of attracting additional jobs or investments in the territorial unit. However, leaving the income tax in an unequal position will put those municipalities where the share of employees is relatively less. Therefore, the state should implement an effective equalization policy.

Thus, the implementation of changes only in one direction will not be enough to overcome the problems of the formation of municipal budgets. A complex approach and analysis of the strengths and weaknesses of each municipality is needed. To complete the process of decentralization of Georgia, it is necessary to carry out specific reforms that ensure the raising of the financial independence of municipalities and the fair distribution of financial funds.

**Acknowledgement.** This research was carried out by a scientific grant from the Batumi Shota Rustaveli State University (Georgia) under the title "Prospects for the Development of an Innovative Economy in the Region in the context of Global Economic and Business Challenges".

# References

1. Melkers, J., Willoughby, K.: Models of performance-measurement use in local governments: understanding budgeting, communication, and lasting effects. Public Adm. Rev. **65**(2), 180–190 (2005). https://doi.org/10.1111/j.1540-6210.2005.00443.x
2. LaFrance, T.C., Balogun, E.A.: Public participation in the local budgeting process: definitions, impediments, and remaining questions. Am. J. Econ. **2**(1), 1–7 (2012). https://doi.org/10.5923/j.economics.20120201.01
3. Mullins, D.R., Pagano, M.A.: Local budgeting and finance: 25 years of developments. Public Budg. Financ. **25**(4s), 3–45 (2005). https://doi.org/10.1111/j.1540-5850.2005.00002.x
4. Lysiak, L., Kachula, S., Hrabchuk, O., Filipova, M., Kushnir, A.: Assessment of financial sustainability of the local budgets: case of Ukraine. Public Munic. Financ. **9**(1), 48–59 (2020). https://doi.org/10.21511/pmf.09(1).2020.05
5. Pokrovskaia, N.V., Belov, A.V.: Tax revenues of local budgets in unitary states: a case study of Japan. J. Tax Reform **6**(1), 73–89 (2020). https://doi.org/10.15826/jtr.2020.6.1.076
6. Karianga, H.: New Paradigm for local financial management: a review of local budgeting system. Hasanuddin Law Rev. **2**(3), 398–408 (2016). https://doi.org/10.20956/halrev.v2i3.700
7. Morgan, D., Robinson, K.S., Strachota, D., Hough, J. A.: Budgeting for Local Governments and Communities. Routledge (2017). https://doi.org/10.4324/9781315716534
8. Seal, W.: Modernity, modernization and the deinstitutionalization of incremental budgeting in local government. Financ. Account. Manage. **19**(2), 93–116 (2003). https://doi.org/10.1111/1468-0408.00165
9. Rossikhina, H., Svitlychna, Y., Brusakova, O.: Local taxes and charges in local budgets'income generation. Baltic J. Econ. Stud. **4**(4), 291–294 (2018). https://doi.org/10.30525/2256-0742/2018-4-4-291-294
10. Patytska, K., Panukhnyk, O., Popadynets, N., Kramarenko, I.: Forming the territorial communities' local budgets in Ukraine under decentralization: current condition and management tasks. J. Optim. Indust. Eng. **2021**, 201–208 (2021)

11. Oprea, F., Bilan, I.: An evaluation of the economic and financial crisis's impact on local budgetary aggregates: the Romanian case. Procedia Econ. Financ. **20**, 467–477 (2015). https://doi.org/10.1016/s2212-5671(15)00098-2

12. Glushchenko, J., Kozhalina, N.: Development trends of local taxes in the system of local budgets in Ukraine. Public Munic. Financ. **8**(1), 104–111 (2019). https://doi.org/10.21511/pmf.08(1).2019.09

13. Petrushenko, Y.M.: Analysis of the stability of local budgets in the context of financial policy of the territorial communities development. Eur. J. Econ. Stud. **9**(3), 170–176 (2014). https://doi.org/10.13187/es.2014.3.170

14. Pelinescu, E., Anton, L.V., Ionescu, R., Tasca, R.: The analysis of local budgets and their importance in the fight against the economic crisis effects. Roman. J. Econ. Forecast. **13**, 17–32 (2010)

15. Ismoilova, S.Y.: Theoretical issues of implementing effective use of local budgets funds. Am. J. Econ. Bus. Manag. **5**(11), 56–61 (2022)

16. Dvoryadkina, E.B., Belousova, E.A.: Factors and trends in the development of local budgets of rural territories. Revista ESPACIOS **39**(39) (2018)

17. Storonyanska, I., Melnyk, M., Benovska, L., Sytnyk, N., Zakhidna, O.: Economic activity vs generation of local budgets' revenues: regional disparities in COVID-19 instability. Public Munic. Financ. **10**, 94–105 (2021). https://doi.org/10.21511/pmf.10(1).2021.08

18. Panday, P.K., Chowdhury, S.: Responsiveness of local government officials: insights and lessons from participatory planning and budgeting. Asia Pac. J. Public Admin. **42**(2), 132–151 (2020). https://doi.org/10.1080/23276665.2020.1742753

19. Godwin, M.L.: Studying participatory budgeting: democratic innovation or budgeting tool? State Local Govt. Rev. **50**(2), 132–144 (2018). https://doi.org/10.1177/0160323x18784333

20. Mussari, R., Tranfaglia, A.E., Reichard, C., Bjørnå, H., Nakrošis, V., Bankauskaitė-Grigaliūnienė, S.: Design, trajectories of reform, and implementation of performance budgeting in local governments: a comparative study of Germany, Italy, Lithuania, and Norway. In: Kuhlmann, S., Bouckaert, G. (eds.) Local Public Sector Reforms in Times of Crisis. GPM, pp. 101–119. Palgrave Macmillan UK, London (2016). https://doi.org/10.1057/978-1-137-52548-2_6

21. Sintomer, Y., Herzberg, C., Röcke, A.: Participatory budgeting in Europe: potentials and challenges. Int. J. Urban Reg. Res. **32**(1), 164–178 (2008). https://doi.org/10.1111/j.1468-2427.2008.00777.x

22. Abuselidze, G.: Optimality of tax policy on the basis of comparative analysis of income taxation. Eur. J. Sustain. Dev. **9**(1), 272–293 (2020). https://doi.org/10.14207/ejsd.2020.v9n1p272

23. Abuselidze, G., Mamuladze, L.: The peculiarities of the budgetary policy of Georgia and the directions of improvement in association with EU. SHS Web Conf. **73**, 01001 (2020). https://doi.org/10.1051/shsconf/20207301001

24. Abuselidze, G.: The intergovernmental relations and their regulation in the context of decentralization of fiscal policy. In: E3S Web of Conferences, vol. **280**, 02010 (2021). https://doi.org/10.1051/e3sconf/202128002010

25. Ivanyuta, P., Kartashov, E., Datsii, N., Kovalskyi, M., Abuselidze, G., Aleinikova, O.: Right ownership as the particularization of territorial formations in the conditions of decentralization reform of Ukraine. In: Gervasi, O., Murgante, B., Hendrix, E.M.T., Taniar, D., Apduhan, B.O. (eds.) Computational Science and Its Applications – ICCSA 2022. ICCSA 2022. LNCS, vol. 13376, pp. 126–143. Springer, Cham (2022). https://doi.org/10.1007/978-3-031-10450-3_10

26. Abuselidze, G., Sudak, I., Bilyak, Y., Nehoda, Y.: Political features of federalization of the most powerful countries in the world: experience for Ukraine. Int. Multidiscipl. Sci. GeoConf. SGEM, **21**(5.1), 445–452 (2021). https://doi.org/10.5593/sgem2021/5.1/s21.096

27. Duncan, D., Sabirianova Peter, K.: Unequal inequalities: do progressive taxes reduce income inequality? Int. Tax Public Financ. **23**(4), 762–783 (2016). https://doi.org/10.1007/s10797-016-9412-5
28. Olsen, J., Kogler, C., Stark, J., Kirchler, E.: Income tax versus value added tax: a mixed-methods comparison of social representations. J. Tax Adm. **3**(2), 87–107 (2017)
29. Denek, E., Dylewski, M.: Szacowanie poziomu zadłużenia jednostek samorządu terytorialnego w warunkach zwiększonego ryzyka utraty płynności finansowej, p. 332. (Difin, Warszawa, 2013). https://ksiegarnia.difin.pl/szacowaniepoziomu-zadluzenia-jednosteksam orzadu-terytorialnego-wwarunkach-zwiekszonego-ryzykautraty-plynnosci-finansowej1
30. Davydenko, N., Wasilewska, N., Boiko, S., Wasilewski, M.: Development of rural areas in Ukraine in the context of decentralization: an empirical study. Sustainability **14**, 6730 (2022). https://doi.org/10.3390/su14116730
31. Davydenko, N., Dibrova, A., Onyshko, S., Fedoryshyna, L.: The Influence of the gross regional product on the formation of the financial potential of the region. J. Optim. Indust. Eng. **14**(1), 153–157 (2021)
32. Ministry of Finance of Georgia, Selected economic and financial indicators (2023)
33. Ministry of Finance of Georgia, Central Government Operations (2023)
34. Ministry of Finance of Georgia, Budget of autonomous republics and municipalities (2023)

# Design Principles for Platform-Based Innovation in Smart Cities

Rui José$^{(\boxtimes)}$ and Helena Rodrigues

Centro Algoritmi/LASI, University of Minho, Guimarães, Portugal
{rui,helena}@dsi.uminho.pt

**Abstract.** Smart Cities represent the next big frontier for computational science. However, the real-world impacts of this transformation have been considerably slower than other domains of digital innovation. In this work, we study the interplay between the core properties of digital platforms and the urban innovation contexts that aim to promote digital transition as a means to generate value for cities and its citizens. The research methodology is based on a literature review, which aimed to characterise the key limitations preventing smart city initiatives from attaining the same level of fast paced innovation as other areas of computational science, and seek for alternative innovation practices. The results suggest that innovation practices in the context of smart city initiatives seem to be framed by a key trade-off between the idea that only global solutions may be able to capture the full benefits of digital innovation and the idea that each city is unique and must pave its own way towards digital transition. From the analysis of those results, we derive five design principles for new service-based platforms. These principles represent a new direction to address the specificities of smart cities and unleash the real-world impact of digital innovation in smart and sustainable cities.

**Keywords:** Smart Cities · Digital Platforms · Digital Innovation

## 1 Introduction

Becoming a smart city is now a common aspiration for any city aiming to provide their citizens with better services and more socioeconomic development. In recent years, many cities and urban regions have established strategies to promote the digital transformation of their territories, embracing a broad range of dimensions, such as mobility, energy, digital governance, sustainability or the entrepreneurial context. Digital technologies, in general, can have a very profound impact in addressing long-term problems of city life, and thus, there is a legitimate expectation that we may start to witness a progressive and positive impact emerging from their increasing presence in urban contexts.

However, there is also a general sense of disappointment about the real-world impacts of this transformation. While there are numerous smart cities initiatives

This research has been supported by FCT - Fundação para a Ciência e Tecnologia within the R&D Units Project Scope: UIDB/00319/2020.

aiming to leverage the disruptive potential of digital innovation to address urban problems, the results are still somewhat limited in regard to the initial expectations and the investments involved. The innovation pace seems much slower than in other areas of Computational Science and there are even growing signs of backlash against what is seen as an excessive presence of computing technology in urban settings. There is thus an increasing pressure to deliver real value and show evidences of relevant progress. In this context, it is timely and relevant for the whole field of smart cities to study the fundamental causes behind this limited progress and seek for alternative innovation directions that may offer a better fit between the unique properties of digital innovation and the concrete needs of cities.

## 1.1 Objectives

In this work, we seek to uncover the key limitations faced by innovation initiatives aiming to explore the application of digital technology in urban contexts. We also seek to identify novel innovation patterns that may unlock the innovation potential of computational science in smart and sustainable cities. Digital platforms and local innovation ecosystems have been at the centre of these processes of digital transformation for cities. Our study is thus focused on the interplay between the core properties of digital platforms and the urban innovation contexts that aim to promote digital transition as a medium to generate value for cities and its citizens. These broader goals can be represented by the following two research questions:

– RQ1: What are key limitations that may be preventing current smart city initiatives from attaining the same level of fast paced innovation as other areas of computational science?
– RQ2: What type of alternative innovation practices may help to unleash the real-world impact of digital platforms in smart cities?

With the first research question, we aim to contribute to the understanding of the limitations that are shaping the concrete results produced by smart city initiatives and offer a framework for the subsequent analysis of alternative paths for smart city innovation. With the second research question, we aim to inform the exploration of novel platform design approaches that are more effective at capturing the potential of digital innovation for the benefit of urban life.

In the remainder of the paper, in Sect. 2, we review prior work on platforms for smart cities, an then in Sect. 3, we describe the execution of a Systematic Literature Review on urban innovation ecosystems, from which we gathered evidences about the fundamental challenges faced by smart city innovation. In Sect. 4, we present the result of the review, which highlight the existence of a key trade-off between two quite distinct approaches to urban digital innovation. In Sect. 5, we discuss those results and their implications for platform design, resulting in the proposal of five fundamental design principles for new service-based architectures for smart cities.

## 2    Related Work

Platform development has been a major topic in smart cities literature, as researchers seem determined to define an explicit smart city architecture to facilitate the actual deployment of smart city applications [26]. The core motivation is strongly associated with the goals of interoperability and development optimization. As described by Santana et al. [23], most solutions focus on a specific domain, target a specific problem, and were developed from scratch, with little software reuse. Since they do not interoperate, they lead to duplication of work, incompatible solutions, and non-optimized resource use. The conclusion is the need for a Unified Reference Architecture that can offer a novel and comprehensive software platform to support application development, integration, deployment, and management.

Saborido and Alba [26], analyse several platforms and claim that most existing smart city deployments are based on closed systems that use private software systems sold by a particular vendor, who does not provide many details about its software design and architecture. As a consequence, although there is a variety of smart city software systems, their benefits and limitations are still unknown. Tsampoulatidis et al. [29] report on the inherent heterogeneity of Internet-of-Things (IoT) devices and how it leads to many different architectures and communication protocols for exchanging data streams. They conclude that this diversity disrupts the creation of smart city ecosystems and prohibits the establishment of holistic and universal access models.

Lim et al. [15] address Big Data for smart cities and propose a set of reference models, challenges, and considerations to offer a framework for data usage in smart cities. This focus on data management has led to many data-driven platforms. A common pattern is the organization of functionality across a set of layers, such as sensing, transmission, data management, and application. However, this data-centric perspective faces the lack of open data initiatives and depends on the willingness of vendors and integrators to support interoperability [25]. Singh et al. [26], claim that, while theoretically feasible, the viability of a common smart city architecture for deployment in the real world is far away from reality and general architectural guesses are limited by major changes in required functionality.

There is thus extensive work on architectures and development paradigms for Smart Cities, and there are many elements related to the design, development, deployment, and management of smart city platforms that still challenge the research community. Our work moves away from specific architectural designs and data interoperability issues, and focus instead on the fundamental properties of digital innovation as the core principles for the design of digital platforms for smart cities. To the best of our knowledge, this is a relevant and novel contribution to this field, with the capability to open fundamentally new innovation practices for smart cities.

# 3   Methodology

The methodology for this study is based on a Systematic Literature Review (SLR) on the topic of smart city innovation. The main advantage of a SLR is the ability to uncover common issues across a wide range of smart city initiatives. There is a considerable body of research literature reporting on the results of various types of innovation strategies. This is thus a meaningful and timely review that reflects on the limitations of the prevalent innovation paradigms. Its results should help to inform new urban innovation strategies that might be more efficient at capturing the specific sources of value offered by digital innovation.

The review protocol follows the general guidelines proposed by Kitchenham and Charters [12], and the PRISMA reporting guidance [18]. The formulation of the review protocol is centred on the two research questions defined for this study, which drive the selection of primary studies included in the review and the analytical approaches used to uncover evidences from those publications.

The eligibility criteria considers research studies, in English, published in the last 5 years and reporting findings about the creation, operation, challenges and outcomes of urban innovation ecosystems created as part of smart city initiatives. To search for the relevant bibliography, we used Scopus, a major bibliographic database, recognized as suitable for a variety of tasks, from journal and literature selection or personal career tracking to large-scale bibliometric analyses and research evaluation practices [20]. It also largely overlaps with the other major bibliography indexing databases, including Web of Science (WoS) [33].

Our search strategy comprises two separate queries. Both queries included the same five years time frame and used *smart cities* as a selection keyword. The first query used the term *innovation ecosystem* and the second used the term *helix*, which is often used in the literature to describe different stakeholder combinations in local innovation ecosystems. This led to the formulation of the two complementary search strings presented in Table 1.

**Table 1.** Search string for the two scopus queries.

Query 1 "Innovation ecosystem": TITLE-ABS-KEY ( innovation AND ecosystem ) AND LANGUAGE ( english ) AND ( LIMIT-TO ( PUBYEAR , 2023 ) OR LIMIT-TO ( PUBYEAR , 2022 ) OR LIMIT-TO ( PUBYEAR , 2021 ) OR LIMIT-TO ( PUBYEAR , 2020 ) OR LIMIT-TO ( PUBYEAR , 2019 ) ) AND ( LIMIT-TO ( EXACTKEYWORD , "Smart City" ) )

Query 2 "helix": ( TITLE-ABS-KEY ( helix ) AND ( TITLE-ABS-KEY ( city ) OR TITLE-ABS-KEY ( urban ) ) ) AND LANGUAGE ( english ) AND ( LIMIT-TO ( PUBYEAR , 2023 ) OR LIMIT-TO ( PUBYEAR , 2022 ) OR LIMIT-TO ( PUBYEAR , 2021 ) OR LIMIT-TO ( PUBYEAR , 2020 ) OR LIMIT-TO ( PUBYEAR , 2019 ) ) AND ( LIMIT-TO ( EXACTKEYWORD , "Smart City" ) )

The search was performed in February 2023. The list of results was screened for a quick eligibility assessment, based only on the analysis of the title and abstract of each of the publications. All papers that seemed to match the eligibility criteria were selected. To reduce bias and clarify the selection decisions, we also used an exclusion criteria to eliminate any studies where the contribution was strongly associated with a specific technology. The results of the complete data selection process are summarized in Fig. 1.

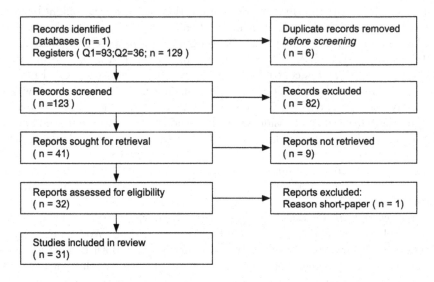

**Fig. 1.** Data selection process

The selected publications were then analyzed according to a semi-structure coding process, supported by a software tool for Qualitative Data Analysis. The coding was framed by the two research questions, which became the two top-level code categories, one for core challenges for smart city initiatives; and the other for novel opportunities for smart city innovation. Under these top-level codes, coding was based on an open coding process. At the end, the resulting codes were aggregated to combine similar codes and organized them under representative second-level categories. The information extracted within each category was then used to synthesize a qualitative overview of the respective topic.

## 4   Results

The results of this review have shown the diversity and breadth of the challenges that may be preventing current smart city platforms from attaining the same level of fast paced innovation as other areas of computational science.

The most fundamental challenges can be described as intrinsic to the depth and magnitude of the transformation process itself. The concept of smart city is a major paradigm transition, which necessarily challenges established practices and perceptions, causing imbalances of power, frustrations, organizational stress, communication difficulties. More than annoyances, these elements can become major obstacles to the transition itself, either through the inability to devise appropriate strategies, to deal with decision in a context of major uncertainty or to assume the risks associated with a profound change.

These challenges seem to be exacerbated by the strongly ambiguous nature of the concept of 'smart city' and the many unique ways in which it can be interpreted. The literature reports the existence of numerous definitions of 'smart city', but, more importantly, it clearly emphasises how despite those definition attempts, the concept remains largely ambiguous [6,14,28]. Appio et al. [2] highlight how the ambiguity generated by these many perspectives can significantly challenge policy makers in setting a proper smart cities development agenda. Other authors emphasise the inherently evolutionary nature of the process of urban transformation [4], and its need to constantly re-invent itself as it unfolds through a set of contingent and relational processes shaped by local governance practices, political priorities, political economic context and institutional settings [6]. Sarv et al. [24] suggest moving the focus to the situated interpretation of the concept within the specific context of a given territory, which means each smart city project would be made unique because of its own geographical, cultural, and economic context. This need for a local interpretation of the concept represents in itself a major challenge because it requires a strong alignment with the local reality and, ideally, a strongly participatory process. A strong strategic vision is thus essential, but is normally absent. It is extremely complex for any city to congregate the drive, the knowledge, and the collective support needed to define, plan and execute a long-term vision and corresponding strategy for its digital transition.

Even when city managers are genuinely motivated to move forward and know what they want to accomplish, they still need to face all sorts of barriers. According to Borghys [3], cities identify the lack of (sustainable) resources, experience, and capacity as the main bottleneck in addressing smart city challenges. Common examples include outmoded procurement processes and regulations [6], provision models that are optimized for predictable and well-known solutions, not for innovative solutions [8], or slow decision-making, which breaks expectations and trust from private partners [8]. Most city governments are not well equipped to explore digital technologies as a solution to urban challenges due to rigid management structures and limited resources, both financial and Human [16]. These obstacles are often underestimated, but the reality of smart city initiatives is always made of these organizational misalignments and multiple forms of resistance.

Finance is another critical issue for these local innovation ecosystems. The technological infrastructures and services promoted by smart city initiatives cannot be created or exist without adequate capital expenditures [11]. Since municipal budgets are very short, they are only able, at most, to fund ongoing tasks, not the type of strategic investment, over a period of at least several years, that is required by most smart city initiatives. Also, classical models of financing, with traditional annual budget cycles, can limit the flexible management of projects, especially in the case of unexpected business and technological opportunity that can arise [8]. According to Sarv et al. [24] many cities assess their chances of smart development as low or very low.

Digital transition is thus a major paradigm chance for cities. They miss the expertise, the tools and the forms of governance that are needed to deal with the breadth and complexity of these changes. To embrace this highly dynamic context and benefit from its many opportunities, they need to find partnerships that allow them to mitigate their limitations and accelerate their digital transition process. In our review, we have identified two major directions for the promotion of these collaborations. While not necessarily exclusive, they seem to represent two very distinct perspectives about the role of digital platforms in smart cities. The first direction is based on partnerships with technology companies, in some cases large global platforms, which can offer them the technical expertise or the services they need to develop parts of their digital agenda. The second direction involves the promotion of local innovation ecosystems to address the digital transformation of the respective territory. This section, will now describe in more detail each of these directions and their implications for urban innovation.

## 4.1   The Challenges of Digital Platforms

As they feel pressured to be seen as smart cities, a technology-centred partnership may seem like an easy way forward. It allows the city to draw on the competencies held within industry, which possesses sufficient expertise to guide city administrators in delivering better city services. These partnerships are often associated with a double-helix structured collaboration between a local government and an ICT company. They may emerge in the form of public-private partnerships (PPP), leasing, deregulation and market competition, or outright privatisation [6]. Considering the complex challenges associated with developing a strategic vision and the necessary capabilities, this type of collaboration may seem very attractive for cities. The collaborations are simpler than those associated with a larger ecosystem and they do not normally involve major upfront investment, which helps to address the lack of resources of local governments. It is also something that may seem less risky, as it may deliver visible results in a much shorter period of time and allow experimentation to be done within relatively controlled contexts. On top of that, cool technology can be exciting and generate positive press coverage, as most people can relate very easily with techno-utopias [10] and technology determinism [21].

However, attempting to transfer to the private sector a large share of the responsibility for developing, managing and promoting a smart city initiative, does not provide the necessary intellectual capital to drive smart city development [16]. The city benefits from the expertise, guidance and solutions of the partner companies, but in that process it may fail to address the real challenges of the city [6]. According to Mora et al. [16], this is essentially a partnership between information technology corporations offering their technological solutions and local governments, which are persuaded to underpin smart city development by adopting such proprietary technologies. Therefore, this technology-led model may fail to cope with the complexity of smart city development, and is most likely to promote a utopian and technological deterministic interpretation of smart cities that serves nothing but the interests of companies working in the technology industry. Many cities have also expressed a specific concern about the risk of vendor lock-in [17], which they fear may hamper the necessary flexibility to deal with the natural evolution of the projects. Data interoperability seems to be the most common concern, with cities fearing the consequences of endless data formats and complementary solutions that cannot communicate between each other.

This techno-centric perspective is also at the centre of the "platformization" trend, in which services that significantly shape cities, e.g. ride-hailing, property rental, or electric scooter sharing, are delivered by major private players and are rarely co-designed with cities [3]. These smart city technologies are developed and marketed by multinational high-tech corporations as universal solutions to urban issues [6]. They address the city as a tabula rasa for innovation, layering their technology onto the city and replacing existing city systems, infrastructures, organisational structures or established modes of practice. The disruptive nature of these platforms and the ways in which they are able to generate user involvement, has propelled a very quick growth, often beyond the control of local governments, which are thus compelled to consider their role in this ecosystem. The concept of "platform urbanism" [9] has emerged to describe these dynamics and reveal a complex platform-based ecosystem encompassing organizations and citizens and challenging the smart city framework as a planning and development paradigm.

These platforms are valuable to citizens and often convenient for cities, but they can be hard to align with any local strategy for the smart city. They often operate in an uncertain regulatory state, with questions related to privacy, ethical working conditions, use of and access to data or the commodification of the public space [3]. Cities can lose control of their own strategy and platforms may reach a monopoly situation in which they will have acquired the power to shape urban policies. Among other risks, this approach may lead to a smart city, dominated by expensive technologies and capital-intensive infrastructure, and only accessible to young, healthy, and rich residents [11].

A smart city initiative is thus a very broad challenge that goes far beyond its enabling technologies. The smart city should also provide human capital development opportunities, as a way to foster knowledge and creativity; should deal with sustainability solutions, to cope with the changing urban environment; and, at the end of the day, should offer quality of life to its citizens [4]. Therefore, an approach only focusing on the technical aspects and economic possibilities is not sufficient. Truly smart cities need to employ a holistic approach and engage in a co-creative open innovation process [27].

## 4.2    The Challenges of Local Innovation Ecosystems

The promotion of a local innovation ecosystem has become a common practice to drive the development of smart city initiatives beyond mere technological fixes. These 'smart ecosystems' can involve a wide spectrum of stakeholders engaged in a continuous collaboration on a human-oriented knowledge and learning process toward 'intelligent' solutions to urban challenges [28]. They can combine the contributions of governments, universities and industry (triple-helix structure), along with those expressed by citizens and civil society organizations (quadruple-helix structure) [16]. The overall goal is to create an environment that is conducive to innovation, by fostering collaboration and partnerships between these different groups and providing easier access to resources, such as funding and specialized knowledge. They may help to overcome the lack of financial resources and technological capabilities of public organizations, and also to expand access to innovators, skilled human resources, and other loci of knowledge, where tacit know-how is shared and exploited [8]. Despite the widespread recognition of the role that local innovation ecosystem may play in the promotion of smart city initiatives, the review results highlight that no ecosystem can fully address all the core challenges of smart city development and that the creation and promotion of an effective ecosystem is also a challenge on its own.

The first major challenge is to bring together a set of stakeholders with the right combination of contributions to create a valuable innovation ecosystem. Key activities at this formation stage involve partner search, partner identification and value creation [17]. This is always a challenging task, but it can be particularly difficult for smaller cities or villages, either because of the lack of resources of the local government or the lack of relevant partners in the respective territory [7]. Even when those partners are available, it can be very challenging to progress from the formation stage to the coordination stage of these initiatives [17], and transform a group of partners into a thriving and effective urban innovation ecosystem. Weak interactions between partners can hamper the growth of smart city projects and lead to a misalignment between key actors [17]. A large number of heterogeneous stakeholders is also a challenge for knowledge sharing. According to Robaeyst et al. [22], an heterogeneous multi-stakeholder ecosystem corresponds to a variety of knowledge 'assets' distributed within the regional space, which can be the main driver of regional innovation, as long as there is the ability to transfer innovations and knowledge among entities. Without the ability to access and share that knowledge, innovative insights from external partners are more difficult to emerge [1].

Panori et al. [19] recognise that many smart city initiatives fail to grow beyond their initial pilot phase and suggest that internal adjustment between stakeholders to coordinate value creation and value capture activities can be the key to foster growth in smart city initiatives. In particular, to continuously generate, capture and protect value, it is necessary to carefully manage the trade-off between public and private value [17]. While private stakeholders may favour approaches that aim to protect their business cases, public stakeholders may seek the value emerging from scalability, openness and interoperability. According to Ferraris [8], public actors represent one of the main drivers of "cooperation failure" because they have: weak absorptive capacities and innovation capabilities; low pressure to innovate; poor technological knowledge; short-term pressures associated with politics and re-election cycles; insufficient funding; and risk-aversion. These elements create a significant distance between public and private partners and may significantly impact the ability to successfully manage a cooperative behaviour.

Ecosystem governance is recognised as essential, but it often seems to be missing or to be largely misunderstood. Typical roles attributed to governance entities may include: promoting, executing, financing, warrantying and certifying projects; coordinating stakeholders (including citizens) and manage the respective information flows [2]. However, many cities seem to prefer other actors to take up this coordinating role and are still experimenting with different ways to organize, foster, and sustain these initiatives [3]. Clement et al. [5] claim that this central role of local government in managing the ecosystem is essential, but only up to a certain point, after which, diseconomies are likely to arise because the local government is unable to standardize the dynamics in the collaborative ecosystem. This suggests that collaboration with more stakeholders increases coordination costs, which ultimately leads to an optimal size that offers the best combination between the value that can be brought by the presence of more stakeholders and the added costs associated with those collaborations. This may be seen as a negative reinforcement loop that prevents urban innovation ecosystems from growing beyond an optimal number of stakeholders. This barrier often emerges when smart city initiatives attempt to expand to the regional or national level [17]. Indirectly, this natural limitation in the number of stakeholders can also limit the range of domains in which any ecosystem is able to produce significant innovation as each problem domain requires different types of knowledge assets, which necessitates many theme-specific stakeholders. [22]

## 5  Discussion

The insights from the review suggest that innovation practices in smart city initiatives seem to be framed by a key trade-off between the idea that only global solutions may be able to capture the full benefits of digital innovation and the idea that each city is unique and must pave its own way to digital transition.

On the one hand, it is widely recognized that the local context should play a key role when transforming broader smart city concepts into specific policy actions [13], and that the promotion of a local innovation ecosystem with multiple stakeholders can significantly increase the ability of a city to pursue its own smart city initiatives. However, this policy of many city-specific ecosystems, leads to many local solutions, all of which face many challenges in regard to their dissemination and replication, leading to an inefficient innovation context.

On the other hand, a global solution has a unique capability to congregate the multidisciplinary knowledge, the capital and the domain expertise that are required to address the growing complexity of urban information systems and produce solutions of excellence. They may also provide a context for the emergence of large scale and distributed innovation, where multiple entities can benefit from and learn with innovation anywhere in the system. However, platforms are often conceived as universal solutions that rely on the assumption that cities can be shaped to align with the design principles embedded in the platform operation [6], when the exact opposite would be expected. This may compromise the autonomy and uniqueness of each smart city initiative.

These results suggests that the answer to our second research question, regarding alternative innovation practices for digital platforms in smart cities, may be associated with the ability to untangle this trade-off, addressing the issue of how to enable cities to leverage the transformative force of platforms while also preserving their many specificities and their own digital transformation paths.

Based on the analysis of the challenges described in Sect. 4, we elaborated five design principles for digital platforms in smart cities, which aim to align smart city development with the capabilities of digital innovation. These principles are independent of any particular platform technology, and should be applicable across a wide range of platform models.

**Principle 1: A Platform of Many Independent Services.** The first principle is to explore a platform design inspired by micro-service architectures. Under this principle, the digital infrastructure of the smart city, would be composed of a multitude of smaller and autonomous services. Each service is conceived as a self-contained unit of logic, with its own unique functionality, data storage, business model and interoperability mechanisms. These services should follow a service-dominant logic [31], with a profound understanding of the concrete nature of the target problem and strong insights about value co-creation [32]. They should also offer a strong solution to a specific, bounded and relevant problem that is common across many cities. The assumption is that these services would be developed independently by multiple providers to address multiple, very diverse and possibly overlapping needs, creating a heterogeneous offer that cuts across the many dimensions of urban digital transition.

By breaking down the vision of large global platform systems and focusing instead on compositions of smaller services, this principle should significantly facilitate the continuous and mutual alignment between a strategic vision for the smart city and the information infrastructures needed to pursue that vision. A strategy based on the composition of smaller services can offer a smoother development path based on the progressive, but steady integration of technology. Smart city initiatives in the early stage, would no longer be constrained by the lack of a strong strategic vision and they would no longer be pushed into large and risky investments under conditions of major uncertainty. Instead, they could start with simpler and less risky steps and, then, learn with the process to continuously realign their strategic vision and their technology infrastructure. Small services can thus offer a much-needed flexibility to allow the strategic vision and the technological infrastructure to evolve independently, and still be able to mutually adjust as needed.

A development strategy based on smaller services targeting concrete problems is also more likely to align investments with concrete value creation and, thus, reduce the risks associated with technology-centred views of smart city development. A focus on smaller, but more concrete problems, makes it easier to create offers that are much closer to concrete city needs and can thus be much more efficient at delivering real value, rather than just technological infrastructures. Technology development could follow a lean paradigm, based on smaller viable solutions that promote diversity, reduce risks, support experimentation and allow innovation to emerge from simpler and more concrete steps. Services that fail to deliver real value should be easy to identify and be discarded before becoming a waste of resources or an obstacle to better solutions.

A steady and incremental development of the technological ecosystem can also be very beneficial from the perspective of funding. Instead of complex upfront investments, funding can be transformed into a predictable budget. This may help to safeguard economic sustainability and is more aligned with the funding restrictions of many local governments. Finally, smaller service units offered by multiple independent providers can help to reduce dependencies from any single provider and thus avoid vendor lock-in. The fact that services address a smaller scope, also means they should be easier to replace by similar ones.

**Principle 2: Global Solutions.** The second principle is the assumption that these services will be offering globally available solutions to be used across many cities. Most urban problems are largely shared by many cities. For most cases, only a global solution will have the capability to congregate the capital, the multidisciplinary knowledge, the domain expertise and the multi-deployment insights that are required to address the growing complexity of urban information systems. These services would be much smaller than large global platforms, but within the scope of their target value proposition, they should offer the type of top-quality solution that today can only be found in larger platforms.

The vision of global services should still be compatible with the specificities of each city. Different strategic visions and development priorities should be matched by specific selections of global services. Unlike platforms that promote homogenization, this platform model would be composed of many smaller heterogeneous value propositions, allowing cities to pursue their specific strategy, without necessarily recurring to city-specific technology. This would provide a direct path to address the trade-off between the quality of technical solutions and the specificities of each smart city initiative.

These global solutions will offer an obvious channel to scale the distribution of expert knowledge across multiple cities. By being embedded with top expertise, these services can significantly reduce the expertise demand on each city and help to mitigate the lack of advanced knowledge that permeates local innovation ecosystems. This congregation of knowledge becomes seamlessly available to all the cities using the service. Services will thus become a context for the provision and scalable distribution of expertise that can help local governments to mitigate their own limitations.

As global solutions, these services should also become the enablers for specific value chains involving diverse collaboration patterns between multiple types of stakeholders. This would be very different from local innovation ecosystems where these collaborations need to be explicitly promoted and are normally limited to a small number of stakeholders. Instead, in these services, collaborations between multiple stakeholders are directly embedded into the service design, which defines its own value chain, and the roles of the various types of stakeholders involved. This should allow interactions between stakeholders to be orchestrated to optimise the value generation process and the concrete value proposition offered by the service. As a consequence, collaborations can be much more scalable, because they are based on low-cost interactions, and much more effective, because they are already part of value co-creation processes embedded in the service design. This reduces collaboration barriers and enables collaborations between large numbers of potentially very diverse stakeholders.

**Principle 3: Multi-city Communities.** A fundamental challenge emerging from the review is the fragmentation of urban innovation ecosystems. Each city tends to develop its own ecosystem, and collaborations between cities are far from being the rule, even when they are dealing with the exact same issues. Despite their many specificities in terms of strategy, stakeholder composition and territories, urban innovation systems will always share many similar problems, challenges and even solutions. It is highly inefficient that each of them may operate as an isolated reality and be unable to share the innovation process with other territories.

Platform services should thus be conceived as more than global applications ready to address the similar needs of many different cities with a common solution. They should also provide a context that promotes their collaboration, either explicitly or not, as part of the solution itself. While, global solutions may offer the benefits of scale and access to advanced expertise, the shared collaborative environment of a multi-city operation should bring the benefits of connected intelligence. Services should thus be able to explore the collective wisdom and the co-creation possibilities that can emerge from the availability of data and activities that cut across all those territories.

According to Panori et al., [19] there are two ways in which digital technologies and digital platforms can become the enabler for connected intelligence: on the one hand, by bringing many people together they allow collective intelligence to appear, and on the other, by using machine competences, such as online collaboration, data analytics, object classification or forecasting, they allow analytics and AI to further enhance human skills. A multi-city operation provides the context for these two sources of innovation, by producing crowdsourced knowledge, advanced analytics, AI, and large scale distributed learning. This is essential to unleash some of the most powerful capabilities of digital innovation that rely on the ability to connect human, collective, and machine intelligences

Despite serving as a generic solution, a service designed for many cities should be policy agnostic, avoiding any major assumptions about local urban policies.

Instead, there should be an explicit separation between service features and any parameterization that may define how those features are affected by different urban policies. This should allow cities to define their own operational settings to match their specific strategies. This is essential to preserve the uniqueness of each territory, but is also a driver for shared innovation. The diversity of strategies explored by different territories within the scope of the same service should become an important source of value, experimentation and shared innovation, allowing city-specific strategies to be combined with larger knowledge flows that can significantly expand the breath, depth and sustainability of the innovations involved.

This layer of collaboration between multiple cities is not meant to replace the role of urban innovation ecosystems, but it complements those ecosystems with the ability to trigger the explosion and multiplication of innovation actors (nodes); multiple forms of crowdsourcing and user engagement; glocalisation of knowledge and specialisation by mixing local and global competence and know-how; informed intelligence and discovery based on data [19]. These services can become the enablers for many new types of boundary-spanning collaborations that cut across multiple local ecosystems [27,30,34]. As they have the ability to frame low-cost and very scalable collaborations between many stakeholders, these services should not be bound by the constraints that normally define the maximum number of partners in an effective collaboration.

**Principle 4: Service Recombinations.** The downside of the division into many smaller and autonomous service units is the risk of fragmentation, with each service becoming its own data and functionality island. Despite their autonomy, these services should maintain their ability to share resources and promote collaborative innovation. These are the same motivations that are commonly used to justify the need for data-centric architectures that aim to abstract core data needs and allow services to be built on top of those common data layers. However, such data-layers are often based on strong assumptions about the nature of the data and the types of applications that will use it. Unlike data-centric architectures, we propose a mainly vertical organization of those services, where each service is focused on a specific value proposition for cities. Any data interoperability should be shaped by the needs and opportunities associated with the delivery of that value proposition. This is the opposite of common data-centric approaches where data is expected to come first, and then applications will naturally emerge.

The goal is to enable arbitrary and unexpected connections between multiple services to become a tool for open innovation. These should be loosely coupled associations, most likely based on indirect communication models in which any service can potentially be recombined with others through the exchange of specific data resources that can act as convergence points between multiple services. The use of well-know or standard data formats or APIs should offer many opportunities to promote the emergence of such convergence points. Still, these connections should never be seen as essential for the service operation, and should only emerge as additional value generation opportunities resulting from the shared used of data produced by those services.

**Principle 5: Platform Governance.** Another dimension of fragmentation involves the many functional elements that may be offered with significant advantages at the platform level rather than at the service level. The first group involves features that are common across most of the services, and do not benefit from many unique implementations across the various services. These features should be identified, characterised and developed as common platforms services. Common examples may include generic horizontal services, such as identity management, service discovery and service subscriptions. Like any middleware strategy, this should reduce development effort and significantly increase the quality of those implementations. This would be more convenient for service developers and would allow turn-key solutions with reduced barriers for new ideas [2].

The other group involves coordination features that can only be addressed from a collective perspective, rather than from the perspective of a single service. For example, a service platform should offer marketplace services to create awareness about existing services. The existence of a coordination layer above the multitude of endless and diverse services offered by multiple providers, can significantly enhance the efficiency of the whole system, in a number of ways. A system-wide perspective enables new valuable perspectives that would never be possible from a single service perspective, e.g. matching problems to possible services, matching services to territories with compatible resources or matching services to convergence resources.

## 6   Conclusions

Digital Innovation represents a major transformation force for cities. However, cities are highly complex ecosystems where innovation relies on contextual elements that can be hard to align with the properties that can make digital innovation a source of powerful and fast paced innovation. This results in a much slower progress or even frustration with the smart city concept.

The first contribution of this work is the identification of key limitations associated with current innovation processes in smart city initiatives. Based on the results of a Systematic Literature Review, we analysed those limitations and nailed down the problem to a trade-off between the idea that only global solutions may be able to capture the full benefits of digital innovation in smart cities and the idea that each city is unique and must pave its own way towards digital transition. The second contribution is a set of five design principles that aims to address those limitations and provide new directions for the design of digital platforms for smart cities

These new directions should support the ability to pursue large scale shared innovation, without imposing any homogeneous view about smart city priorities, policies or collaboration patterns. Platforms designed under these principles should embrace the diversity of urban ecosystems as the essence of what cities are, and never as a problem. They should also embrace this diversity as the essence of innovation itself, by offering broader innovation ecosystems where the independent experimentation of many alternative directions may become a major source of innovation. This implies that the knowledge generated by those experiments can be shared, leading to a thriving multi-city innovation ecosystem, with the capability to learn much faster and much more efficiently than what is possible today.

# References

1. Acuto, M., Steenmans, K., Iwaszuk, E., Ortega-Garza, L.: Informing urban governance? Boundary-spanning organisations and the ecosystem of urban data. Area **51**(1), 94–103 (2019). https://doi.org/10.1111/area.12430
2. Appio, F.P., Lima, M., Paroutis, S.: Understanding smart cities: innovation ecosystems, technological advancements, and societal challenges. Technol. Forecast. Soc. Change **142**, 1–14 (2019). https://doi.org/10.1016/j.techfore.2018.12.018
3. Borghys, K., van der Graaf, S., Walravens, N., Van Compernolle, M.: Multi-stakeholder innovation in smart city discourse: quadruple helix thinking in the age of "platforms". Front. Sustain. Cities **2**(March), 1–6 (2020). https://doi.org/10.3389/frsc.2020.00005
4. Camboim, G.F., Zawislak, P.A., Pufal, N.A.: Driving elements to make cities smarter: evidences from European projects. Technol. Forecast. Soc. Change **142**, 154–167 (2019). https://doi.org/10.1016/j.techfore.2018.09.014
5. Clement, J., Manjon, M., Crutzen, N.: Factors for collaboration amongst smart city stakeholders: a local government perspective. Government Inf. Q. **39**(4), 101746 (2022). https://doi.org/10.1016/j.giq.2022.101746
6. Coletta, C., Heaphy, L., Kitchin, R.: From the accidental to articulated smart city: the creation and work of 'Smart Dublin'. Eur. Urban Regional Studies **26**(4), 349–364 (2019). https://doi.org/10.1177/0969776418785214
7. Doering, C., Schmidtner, M., Timinger, H.: Collaboration for innovation between universities and smart cities. In: 2021 IEEE European Technology and Engineering Management Summit, E-TEMS 2021 - Conference Proceedings, pp. 82–86 (2021). https://doi.org/10.1109/E-TEMS51171.2021.9524896
8. Ferraris, A., Santoro, G., Pellicelli, A.C.: Openness of public governments in smart cities: removing the barriers for innovation and entrepreneurship. Int. Entrepreneurship Manag. J. **16**(4), 1259–1280 (2020). https://doi.org/10.1007/s11365-020-00651-4
9. van der Graaf, S., Ballon, P.: Navigating platform urbanism. Technol. Forecast. Soc. Change **142**, 364–372 (2019). https://doi.org/10.1016/j.techfore.2018.07.027
10. Grossi, G., Pianezzi, D.: Smart cities: Utopia or neoliberal ideology? Cities **69**, 79–85 (2017). https://doi.org/10.1016/j.cities.2017.07.012
11. Jonek-Kowalska, I., Wolniak, R.: Economic opportunities for creating smart cities in Poland. Does wealth matter? Cities **114** (2021). https://doi.org/10.1016/j.cities.2021.103222
12. Kitchenham, B., Charters, S.: Guidelines for performing systematic literature reviews in software engineering. EBSE Technical Report EBSE-2007-01. School of Computer Science and Mathematics, Keele University. Technical Report. January, Technical report, EBSE Technical Report EBSE-2007-01 (2007)

13. Komninos, N., Kakderi, C., Collado, A., Papadaki, I., Panori, A.: Digital transformation of city ecosystems: platforms shaping engagement and externalities across vertical markets. J. Urban Technol. **28**(1–2), 93–114 (2021). https://doi.org/10.1080/10630732.2020.1805712
14. Kummitha, R.K.R., Crutzen, N.: How do we understand smart cities? An evolutionary perspective. Cities **67**, 43–52 (2017). https://doi.org/10.1016/j.cities.2017.04.010
15. Lim, C., Kim, K.J., Maglio, P.P.: Smart cities with big data: reference models, challenges, and considerations. Cities **82** (2018). https://doi.org/10.1016/j.cities.2018.04.011
16. Mora, L., Deakin, M., Reid, A.: Strategic principles for smart city development: a multiple case study analysis of European best practices. Technol. Forecast. Soc. Change **142**, 70–97 (2018). https://doi.org/10.1016/j.techfore.2018.07.035
17. Oomens, I.M., Sadowski, B.M.: The importance of internal alignment in smart city initiatives: an ecosystem approach. Telecommun. Policy **43**(6), 485–500 (2019). https://doi.org/10.1016/j.telpol.2018.12.004
18. Page, M.J., et al.: The PRISMA 2020 statement: an updated guideline for reporting systematic reviews. BMJ **372** (2021). https://doi.org/10.1136/bmj.n71
19. Panori, A., Kakderi, C., Komninos, N., Fellnhofer, K., Reid, A., Mora, L.: Smart systems of innovation for smart places: challenges in deploying digital platforms for co-creation and data-intelligence. Land Use Policy **111**, 104631 (2021). https://doi.org/10.1016/j.landusepol.2020.104631
20. Pranckutė, R.: Web of science (Wos) and scopus: the titans of bibliographic information in today's academic world. Publications **9**(1) (2021). https://doi.org/10.3390/publications9010012
21. Reeves, S.: Envisioning ubiquitous computing. In: Proceedings of the 2012 ACM Annual Conference on Human Factors in Computing Systems - CHI 2012, p. 1573 (2012). https://doi.org/10.1145/2207676.2208278
22. Robaeyst, B., Baccarne, B., Duthoo, W., Schuurman, D.: The city as an experimental environment: the identification, selection, and activation of distributed knowledge in regional open innovation ecosystems. Sustainability (Switzerland) **13**(12) (2021). https://doi.org/10.3390/su13126954
23. Santana, E.F.Z., Chaves, A.P., Gerosa, M.A., Kon, F., Milojicic, D.S.: Software platforms for smart cities: concepts, requirements, challenges, and a unified reference architecture. ACM Comput. Surv. **50**(6) (2017). https://doi.org/10.1145/3124391
24. Sarv, L., Kibus, K., Soe, R.M.: Smart city collaboration model: a case study of university-city collaboration. In: ACM International Conference Proceeding Series, pp. 674–677 (2020). https://doi.org/10.1145/3428502.3428601
25. Silva, B.N., Khan, M., Han, K.: Towards sustainable smart cities: a review of trends, architectures, components, and open challenges in smart cities (2018). https://doi.org/10.1016/j.scs.2018.01.053
26. Singh, T., Solanki, A., Sharma, S.K., Nayyar, A., Paul, A.: A decade review on smart cities: paradigms. Challenges Opportunities (2022). https://doi.org/10.1109/ACCESS.2022.3184710
27. Suzic, B., Ulmer, A., Schumacher, J.: Complementarities and synergies of quadruple helix innovation design in smart city development. In: 2020 Smart Cities Symposium Prague, SCSP 2020 (2020). https://doi.org/10.1109/SCSP49987.2020.9133961

28. Taratori, R., Rodriguez-Fiscal, P., Pacho, M.A., Koutra, S., Pareja-Eastaway, M., Thomas, D.: Unveiling the evolution of innovation ecosystems: an analysis of triple, quadruple, and quintuple helix model innovation systems in European case studies. Sustainability (Switzerland) **13**(14) (2021). https://doi.org/10.3390/su13147582

29. Tsampoulatidis, I., Komninos, N., Syrmos, E., Bechtsis, D.: Universality and Interoperability Across Smart City Ecosystems. In: Lecture Notes in Computer Science (including subseries Lecture Notes in Artificial Intelligence and Lecture Notes in Bioinformatics), vol. 13325, LNCS (2022). https://doi.org/10.1007/978-3-031-05463-1_16

30. Vallance, P., Tewdwr-Jones, M., Kempton, L.: Building collaborative platforms for urban innovation: newcastle city futures as a quadruple helix intermediary. Eur. Urban Regional Stud. **27**(4), 325–341 (2020). https://doi.org/10.1177/0969776420905630

31. Vargo, S.L., Lusch, R.F.: Evolving to a new dominant logic. J. Mark. **68**(January), 1–17 (2004). https://doi.org/10.1509/jmkg.68.1.1.24036

32. Vargo, S.L., Maglio, P.P., Akaka, M.A.: On value and value co-creation: a service systems and service logic perspective. Eur. Manag. J. **26**(3), 145–152 (2008). https://doi.org/10.1016/j.emj.2008.04.003

33. Visser, M., van Eck, N.J., Waltman, L.: Large-scale comparison of bibliographic data sources: scopus, web of science, dimensions, crossref, and microsoft academic. Quant. Sci. Stud. **2**(1), 20–41 (2021). https://doi.org/10.1162/qss_a_00112

34. Wang, P.: Theorizing digital innovation ecosystems: a multilevel ecological framework. In: Proceedings of the 27th European Conference on Information Systems (ECIS). Stockholm and Uppsala, Sweden (2019)

# Analysis of an Enterprise's Compliance with the Authorized Economic Operator Status in the Context of the Customs Policy of Ukraine

Olena Vakulchyk[1] , Valeriia Fesenko[1] , Oksana Knyshek[1] ,
Lyudmyla Babenko[1] , Liudmyla Horbach[2] , George Abuselidze[3](✉) ,
and Oleksandr Datsii[2]

[1] University of Customs and Finance, Vladimir Vernadsky, 2/4, Dnipro 49000, Ukraine
[2] Interregional Academy of Personnel Management, Frometivska, 2, Kyiv 03039, Ukraine
[3] Batumi Shota Rustaveli State University, Ninoshvili, 35, 6010 Batumi, Georgia
george.abuselidze@gmail.com, george.abuselidze@bsu.edu.ge

**Abstract.** In view of international trade transactions increase worldwide along with the Customs policy of Ukraine aimed at reducing government control and pressure over business, the issue of assigning the Authorized Economic Operator (AEO) status is becoming more and more important. Therefore, there is a strong need to develop a methodology for objective quantitative assessment of the qualitative characteristics of enterprises involved in international trade operations during Customs diagnostics in order to determine whether they comply with Customs laws to obtain the AEO status or not. A methodical approach to Customs diagnostics based on an integral indicator of compliance of an enterprise's quality characteristics with Customs rules divided into five thematic blocks has been worked out, which allows determining an enterprise's rating and avoid subjectivity in assigning a company the AEO status. To make a decision whether to assign a company the AEO status or not, it has been proposed to use a scale of compliance of an enterprise's rating with one of the committee's conclusions such as unconditionally positive, positive, conditionally positive, negative, refusal to assign the status.

**Keywords:** Customs policy · Foreign economic activity · Customs diagnostics · Integral indicator · Rating assessment · Authorized Economic Operator

## 1 Introduction

The current situation of international economic relations development is characterized by a dramatic global division of labor and growing pace of Country's integration into the world trade [1–3]. The expansion of companies' foreign economic activity and accelerated globalization processes require adaptation and improvement of the organizational and economic mechanism of Customs control of international transactions.

Carrying out foreign economic transactions is inherently accompanied by Customs control, which makes it important to seek for effective ways of interaction between

© The Author(s), under exclusive license to Springer Nature Switzerland AG 2023
O. Gervasi et al. (Eds.): ICCSA 2023, LNCS 13957, pp. 228–241, 2023.
https://doi.org/10.1007/978-3-031-36808-0_15

business and Customs authorities. The current Ukrainian Customs policy implies that one of possible forms of such cooperation is simplified Customs procedures through the mechanism of assigning an enterprise the AEO status.

Along with the adoption of the Customs Code of Ukraine [4], which introduced the possibility for domestic exporters and importers to obtain the AEO status, there occurred a requirement to draw out and implement a range of criteria for assessing whether a company is worthy of the AEO status or not. This status provides Ukrainian companies with obvious benefits in European markets and a number of preferences, which significantly saves time and simplifies Customs procedures. The benefits include: preferences and special simplifications; enhanced trust from Customs authorities; good reputation in the market; Customs post-audit once every 30 months; increased speed of supplies; greater compliance of management system with European standards. All these are bound to considerably improve trade conditions and facilitate export of domestic goods into European markets. However, the procedure of assigning the AEO status still has not been implemented due to the lack of criteria and rules developed by the government.

In 2013 the Ministry of Revenue and Duties of Ukraine proposed a draft order "On assigning a company the AEO status" [5], which provided that a subject of foreign economic activity should make self-assessment according to the questionnaire of a standard form, while the auditors from the Ministry of Revenues and Duties were to verify this information by conducting factual and documentary checks. Despite the ultimate need for settling up the relationships in the field of assigning the AEO status, public discussion of this project did not lead to a decision on its final adoption. Therefore, the question of objective assessment of the qualitative characteristics of an enterprise remains open and still challenging.

In early 2016 the Ministry of Finance of Ukraine worked out and the Cabinet of Ministers of Ukraine approved a draft amendment to the Customs Code of Ukraine in terms of assigning the AEO status [5]. The law entails five thematic units to assess a company's compliance with Customs requirements, which are described in detail and contain characteristics against which a company is to make self-assessment of compliance with certain criteria ("yes" – complies with the criteria, "no" - does not comply). Then a special committee of the Customs authority at its discretion may decide to assign the AEO status or refuse it. Yet this law has not been adopted so far because of the change of the Ukrainian government in the spring of 2016 and sequential withdrawal of all government bills.

In October 2019 the Verkhovna Rada adopted the Law of Ukraine "On amendments to the Customs Code of Ukraine related to certain issues of Authorized Economic Operator functioning", which clarifies the procedure for assigning the AEO status as well as special simplifications and benefits for certified enterprises.

This situation leaves the issue of objective assessment of the qualitative characteristics of subjects of foreign economic activity open and even more challenging in the light of the Customs policy of Ukraine aimed at reducing government control over domestic business participating in global trade. Still a lack of a universal method of integral quantitative assessment of the qualitative characteristics of subjects of foreign economic activity is obvious and, to our mind, the system of Customs diagnostics of an enterprise developed by the authors of this paper can help resolve this problem.

The issues of diagnostics, evaluation and analysis of enterprises have been studied by a number of Ukrainian scientists including Mitsenko (2012), Kostyrko (2008), Kovalchuk (2005), Dovbnya (2015), Datsii et al. (2021) and others [6–18]. Methods of integral assessment have been researched and developed by Bassova (2012), Ignatenko (2014), Larikova (2014), Rushchyshyn (2007), Khrushchev (2011) etc. [19–21]. The procedure of obtaining the AEO status as a new option in the field of Customs services, the questions of computerization of this process, defining the impact of AEO on supply chain security are covered in the works of such foreign researchers as B.K. Bachtiar (2021), Fletcher (2007), Grottel (2013), Huang (2016), Chang (2015), Erceg (2014), Knysh (2013), Laszuk (2016), Manuj (2008), Torello (2020) [22–31].

However, the methodology of quantitative measurement of qualitative characteristics of an enterprise and the integration of assessments of its compliance with Customs rules still require further development and improvement.

The purpose of the paper is to work out a methodological approach to Customs diagnostics of a subject of external economic activity based on an integral and rating assessment of its qualitative characteristics in order to make a decision whether a company deserves the AEO status or not.

## 2 The Model of Assessment of a Company's Compliance with the Requirements Put Forward for Authorized Economic Operators

While assessing a large number of different parameters of a company's activity, it is feasible to group them thematically by areas of Customs control and in accordance with the objects of management within the company. The basis for choosing the parameters of diagnostics within each thematic group should be the qualitative characteristics of a company stated in the questionnaire of its self-assessment [5] as well as grounded on European best practices Authorized Economic Operators (AEO) [32].

As following from the analysis of laws and regulations developed to legally establish the procedure of assigning the AEO status and the methodology for assessing company's reports [33, 34], the authors of the paper propose to identify the main thematic blocks ($j1, j2, j3, j4, j5$), according to which an assessment procedure can be carried out (Fig. 1).

Each block has its own set of parameters (mj) used to analyze and assess the compliance of a company's business with Customs rules for assigning the AEO status. To make an objective evaluation of the given parameters, we have presented several types of characteristics of the degree of compliance according to each parameter, while the result of the assessment is selected from the options provided, which are measured in a certain number of points.

Evaluation points for each parameter are summed up within a separate thematic block ($j$), while the evaluation result for this block ($Bj$) is determined in accordance

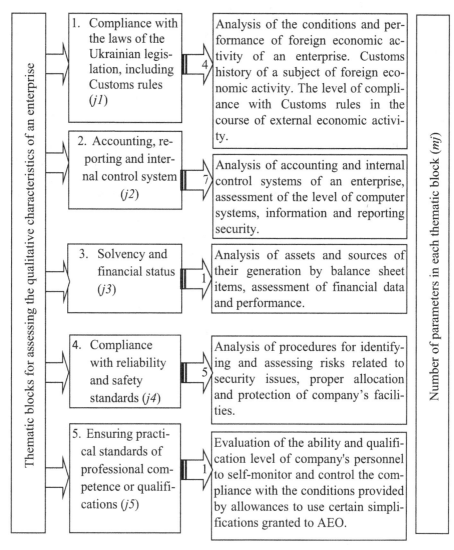

**Fig. 1.** Thematic blocks and their parameters for assessment and analysis of compliance of qualitative characteristics of an enterprise with Customs laws

with the number of parameters in it:

$$B_j = \frac{\sum\limits_{i=1}^{m_j} \beta_c^{(j)}}{m_j}, \tag{1}$$

where $\beta$ is the number of points, which assess the compliance of the parameter with Customs laws; $j$ is a block of indicators; $c$ is a parameter of block $j$; $m_j$ is the number of parameters in block $j$, $i$ is a parameter number.

The integral indicator of compliance of a company's qualitative characteristics with Customs laws (hereinafter - INT), which takes into account the result of the assessment of all 5 blocks, is equal to:

$$INT = \frac{\sum\limits_{j=1}^{d} B_j}{d} \qquad (2)$$

where d is the number of blocks (d = 5).

The quantitative assessment of the quality of each parameter is proposed to be made by using evaluation indicators ranging from 1 to 3, where indicator "1" corresponds to the lowest quality of the studied parameter within a company, and indicator "3" shows the highest quality (Table 1).

**Table 1.** The scale of assessment of a company's qualitative characteristics during Customs diagnostics

| Number of points | Quality level of the parameter | Characteristic features of the parameter |
|---|---|---|
| 1 | Low | Presence of certain elements of compliance of the block parameters with Customs laws, which in general do not ensure the absence of risks |
| 2 | Middle | Partial compliance of the block parameters with Customs laws, but a risk of loss of trust remains |
| 3 | High | Full compliance of the block parameters with Customs rules |

Further we will present the procedure for assessing the quality characteristics of machine building producers of Ukraine against each parameter of this thematic block. It will be done on the example of block 2 "Accounting, reporting and internal control system", which contains 7 separate parameters (Table 2, *compiled using data*: Official site Public Joint-Stock Company Dnipropetrovsk Turning Plant, Official site Public Joint-Stock Company Poltava turbomechanical plant, Official site Public Joint Stock Company Glukhovsky Plant "Electropanel", Official site Public Joint Stock Company "Scientific-Production Joint-Stock Company" VNIICompressormash") [35–41].

Below the assessment of a company's qualitative characteristics according to parameter 2.1 "Compliance of a company's accounting systems with the purpose of Customs control" of thematic block 2 "Accounting, reporting and internal control system" will be presented (Table 3).

**Table 2.** Quantitative assessment of compliance of a company's qualitative characteristics with Customs laws according to the parameters of block 2 "Accounting, reporting and internal control system"

| Block parameter (j) | The number of points by means of which the degree of compliance of an enterprise's parameter with Customs laws is assessed | | | | | | | | | | | |
| --- | --- | --- | --- | --- | --- | --- | --- | --- | --- | --- | --- | --- |
| | Public joint-stock company "Dnipropetrovsk Railway Switch Plant" | | | Private joint-stock scientific-production company "VNDICOMPRESSORMACH" | | | Private joint-stock company "Poltava Turbomechanical Plant" | | | Private joint-stock company Glukhiv Plant "Electropanel" | | |
| | 2018 | 2019 | 2020 | 2018 | 2019 | 2020 | 2018 | 2019 | 2020 | 2018 | 2019 | 2020 |
| 2.1. Compliance of accounting systems with the purpose of Customs control | 2 | 2 | 2 | 2 | 2 | 2 | 2 | 2 | 3 | 2 | 3 | 3 |
| 2.2. Introduction of automated systems of accounting and reporting of foreign economic transactions | 3 | 2 | 3 | 2 | 2 | 2 | 2 | 2 | 3 | 2 | 2 | 3 |
| 2.3. Implementation of an efficient logistics system | 2 | 2 | 2 | 2 | 3 | 3 | 2 | 2 | 2 | 2 | 2 | 2 |
| 2.4. Incorporation of internal control (audit) procedures | 1 | 2 | 2 | 1 | 1 | 2 | 1 | 2 | 2 | 2 | 2 | 2 |
| 2.5. Compliance of goods tracking management systems with the purposes of Customs control | 2 | 2 | 2 | 2 | 2 | 2 | 2 | 2 | 2 | 2 | 2 | 2 |
| 2.6. Ensuring the protection and storage of documents, data and information (including those created electronically) | 2 | 2 | 2 | 1 | 2 | 2 | 2 | 2 | 2 | 2 | 2 | 2 |
| 2.7. Protection of computer (information and telecommunication) systems from unauthorized access | 3 | 3 | 3 | 1 | 2 | 2 | 1 | 2 | 2 | 2 | 2 | 2 |
| Assessment result within the block (j2) | 2.14 | 2.14 | 2.29 | 1.57 | 2 | 2.14 | 1.71 | 2 | 2.29 | 2 | 2.14 | 2.29 |

**Table 3.** Estimates according to parameter 2.1 "Compliance of a company's accounting systems with the purpose of Customs control" of thematic block 2 "Accounting, reporting and internal control system"

| The number of points to assess the degree of compliance of a company's parameter with Customs laws | | |
|---|---|---|
| **3** (high level of quality) | **2** (middle level of quality) | **1** (low level of quality) |
| **Compliance:**<br>The performance of the accounting system corresponds to a company's size and scale of its transactions<br>There are no inconsistencies in the functional allocation of staff responsibilities for accounting of goods and vehicles<br>The company meets the following conditions:<br>- documented control procedures to detect suspicious transactions have been introduced;<br>- computer programs used for accounting ensure a mutual correspondence of all types of accounting data;<br>- the company plans operations with goods;<br>- the company provides trainings for its staff on the use of accounting systems and related software | **Compliance:**<br>The accounting system corresponds to a company's size and scale of its transactions<br>There are no inconsistencies in the functional allocation of staff responsibilities for accounting of goods and vehicles<br>**Noncompliance:**<br>However, monitoring the use of the accounting system, staff work arrangement, quality of accounting management etc. pave the way for concealing illegal transactions | **Noncompliance:**<br>The accounting system is incompatible with the generally accepted accounting rules adopted in Ukraine, or there is such evidence as:<br>- incorrect and/or incomplete record of transactions in the accounting system;<br>- insufficient consistency between the records of the accounting system;<br>- the accounting system does not fully perform the functions and tasks of accounting in terms of ensuring integrity and continuity of the accounting process;<br>- the accounting system does not allow Customs authorities to have access to the records to be checked;<br>- Customs authorities can not audit the accounting system;<br>- monitoring the use of the accounting system, staff work arrangement, quality of accounting management etc. pave the way for concealing illegal transactions |

# 3  Defining a COMPAny's Rating While Assigning the AEO Status

For each block a quantitative assessment of qualitative parameters is carried out and on the basis of this estimate an integral indicator is determined, which defines a company's rating. An integral assessment complements and expands the scope of traditional analysis, since it allows comparing indicators with different dimensions and characteristics between each other (Table 4).

**Table 4.** Quantitative assessment of compliance of a company's qualitative characteristics with Customs laws within each thematic block (*compiled using data*: Official site Public Joint-Stock Company Dnipropetrovsk Turning Plant, Official site Public Joint-Stock Company Poltava turbomechanical plant, Official site Public Joint Stock Company Glukhovsky Plant "Electropanel", Official site Public Joint Stock Company "Scientific-Production Joint-Stock Company" VNIICompressormash")

| Thematic block | Year | The number of points to assess the degree of compliance of a company's parameters within each thematic block with Customs laws | | | |
| | | Public joint-stock company "Dniproptrovsk Railway Switch Plant" | Private joint-stock scientific-production company "VNDICOMPRESSORMACH" | Private joint-stock company "Poltava Turbomechanical Plant" | Private joint-stock company Glukhiv Plant "Electropanel" |
|---|---|---|---|---|---|
| 1. Compliance with the provisions of the Ukrainian legislation, including Customs laws | 2018 | 2,25 | 2,00 | 1,75 | 2,25 |
| | 2019 | 2,25 | 2,50 | 2,00 | 2,25 |
| | 2020 | 2,50 | 2,25 | 2,25 | 2,50 |
| 2. Accounting, reporting and internal control system | 2018 | 2,14 | 1,57 | 1,71 | 2,00 |
| | 2019 | 2,14 | 2,00 | 2,00 | 2,14 |
| | 2020 | 2,29 | 2,14 | 2,29 | 2,29 |
| 3. Solvency and financial status | 2018 | 2,80 | 1,20 | 1,90 | 1,80 |
| | 2019 | 2,40 | 1,20 | 2,70 | 1,70 |
| | 2020 | 2,90 | 1,40 | 2,30 | 2,00 |
| 4. Compliance with reliability and safety standards | 2018 | 3,00 | 2,40 | 2,60 | 2,60 |
| | 2019 | 3,00 | 2,40 | 3,00 | 2,60 |
| | 2020 | 3,00 | 2,00 | 2,00 | 2,20 |
| 5. Ensuring practical standards of competence or professional qualifications | 2018 | 2,00 | 2,00 | 3,00 | 2,00 |
| | 2019 | 3,00 | 3,00 | 2,00 | 2,00 |
| | 2020 | 3,00 | 3,00 | 3,00 | 3,00 |
| **INT** | 2018 | 2,44 | 1,83 | 2,19 | 2,13 |
| | 2019 | 2,56 | 2,22 | 2,34 | 2,14 |
| | 2020 | 2,74 | 2,16 | 2,37 | 2,40 |

The public joint-stock company "Dnipropetrovsk Railway Switch Plant" shows the greatest value of the integral indicator of Customs diagnostics. Moreover, this value is noticed to increase each and every year, which is explained by the enterprise's development in the analyzed period. The calculated indicators and tendency of their growth indicate that the company can qualify for AEO status. The integral indicators of Customs diagnostics of the private joint-stock company "Poltava Turbomechanical Plant" and the private joint-stock company Glukhiv Plant "Electropanel" vary almost to the same extent, as they belong to the same concern "Ukrrosmetal", while the private joint-stock scientific-production company "VNDICOMPRESSORMACH" shows the lowest level and pace of growth of INT indicator.

To make a decision whether to assign a company the AEO status or not, we propose to define its rating by means of the following gradation of INT indicator (Table 5).

**Table 5.** The scale of compliance of a company's rating with the conclusion on assigning the AEO status

| Gradation of INT indicator | Company's rating | Conclusion on assigning the AEO status | Comments |
|---|---|---|---|
| 3,00 – 2,60 | R1 | Unconditionally positive | Assign the AEO status with a subsequent audit in 3 years. Include in the Unified Register of AEOs |
| 2,59 – 2,20 | R2 | Positive | Assign the AEO status. Include in the Unified Register of AEOs. Carry out a follow-up audit in a year in the areas where inconsistencies were found during Customs diagnostics |
| 2,19 – 1,80 | R3 | Roughly positive | Assign the AEO status in case of the correction of identified inconsistencies within 3 months. Then include in the Unified Register of AEOs. Carry out a follow-up audit in a year, on the result of which to make a conclusion as to retaining the AEO status or depriving of it |
| 1,79 – 1,40 | R4 | Negative | Refuse to assign the AEO status. Reconsider assigning the AEO status after another Customs diagnostics not earlier than in a year |
| 1,39 – 1,00 | R5 | Refusal to assign the AEO status | Refuse to assign the AEO status. Reconsider assigning the AEO status after another Customs diagnostics not earlier than in 3 years |

Based on the calculated value of the INT indicator and the proposed gradation scale, we have specified an integral-rating assessment of enterprises during Customs diagnostics for the assignment of the AEO status (Table 6).

**Table 6.** Integral-rating assessment of an enterprise when assigning the AEO status

| Enterprise | 2018 | | 2019 | | 2020 | |
|---|---|---|---|---|---|---|
| | INT | Rating | INT | Rating | INT | Rating |
| Public joint-stock company "Dnipropetrovsk Railway Switch Plant" | 2,438 | R2 | 2,558 | R2 | 2,737 | R1 |
| Private joint-stock company "Poltava Turbomechanical Plant" | 2,192 | R3 | 2,340 | R2 | 2,367 | R2 |
| Private joint-stock company Glukhiv Plant "Electropanel" | 2,130 | R3 | 2,138 | R2 | 2,397 | R2 |
| Private joint-stock scientific-production company "VNDICOMPRESSORMACH" | 1,834 | R3 | 2,220 | R2 | 2,159 | R3 |

The findings presented in Table 6 show that the public joint-stock company "Dnipropetrovsk Railway Switch Plant" is prepared best to obtain the AEO status. Every year the rating of this company rose and in 2019 reached the highest level R1. This enterprise, estimated by the scale of compliance invented by us (see Table 5), deserves to be given an "unconditionally positive" conclusion on assigning the AEO status. The private joint-stock company "Poltava Turbomechanical Plant" and the private joint-stock company Glukhiv Plant "Electropanel" can be provided with a "positive" conclusion on granting the AEO status. These companies succeeded in their rating increase. In particular, in 2018 they could only get a "conditionally positive" conclusion, while in 2019–2020 their quality characteristics improved to the level of "positive" conclusion on assigning the AEO status. The private joint-stock scientific-production company "VNDICOMPRESSORMACH" is also entitled to receive an AEO certificate based on a "conditionally positive" conclusion, but subject to elimination of inconsistencies within three months.

# 4 Conclusion

The presented methodological approach to the quantitative assessment of compliance of a company's qualitative characteristics with Customs laws through certain thematic blocks allows taking unbiased decision whether to assign the AEO status or not. In addition, the detailed information used to calculate the integral indicator facilitates identifying management and internal control weaknesses as well as other risk areas to create appropriate risk profiles that can be useful for effective Customs control further on.

The Customs policy of Ukraine stipulates that since the date of receipt of the AEO certificate it is a company's responsibility to self-monitor its own level of compliance of quality characteristics with Customs laws by means of the internal control system adapted to the concept of Committee of Sponsoring Organizations of the Tread way Commission (COSO) [42, 43]. The internal audit of an enterprise's compliance with Customs laws should be carried out through the analysis of deviations from the integral indicator INT.

A separate stage is to develop and put forward a number of measures to ensure the effectiveness of an internal control system, which include making managerial solutions aimed at achieving such a level of a company's quality characteristics as compliant with Customs laws.

A prospective further direction of the research into Customs policy of Ukraine in the field of AEO implementation can be creating an algorithm for collecting, accumulating, arranging, summarizing and analyzing detailed information of a required type as to the transactions of enterprises participating in foreign economic activity in order to provide information for identifying the factors that affect the integral rating indicator of Customs diagnostics.

# References

1. Babenko, V., Pasmor, M., Pankova, J., Sidorov, M.: The place and perspectives of Ukraine in international integration space. Probl. Perspect. Manag. **15**(1), 93–98 (2017)
2. Abuselidze, G.: European integration of Georgia and financial-economic condition: achievements and Challenges. Eur. J. Sustain. Dev. **8**(1), 53–68 (2019). https://doi.org/10.14207/ejsd.2019.v8n1p53
3. Shpachuk, V., Hornyk, V., Kravchenko, S., Vizirov, B., Aleinikova, O., Abuselidze, G.: State policy of cooperation between countries and global institutions: condition and prospects. E3S Web Conf. **371**, 05004 (2023)
4. The Law of Ukraine. Customs Code of Ukraine. The Verkhovna Rada of Ukraine (2012). https://zakon4.rada.gov.ua/laws/show/4495-17
5. The Draft Order of Ukraine. About granting an enterprise the status of authorized economic operator. (The Ministry of Income and Collections of Ukraine (2013). http://www.mdoffice.com.ua/pls/MDOffice/aSNewsDic.getNews?dat=18102013&num_c=372761
6. Mitsenko, N., Duliaba, N.: Diahnostyka diievosti ekonomichnoho mekhanizmu torhovel'noho pidpryiemstva [Diagnostics of the efficiency of the economic mechanism of a trading enterprise]. L'viv: L'vivs'ka komertsijna akademiia, p. 223 (2012). (in Ukr.)
7. Kostyrko, L.: Diahnostyka potentsialu finansovo-ekonomichnoi stijkosti pidpryiemstva. Diagnostics of the potential of financial and economic stability of the enterprise. Kharkiv: Faktor, p. 336 (2008). (in Ukr.)
8. Kovalchuk, T.: Diahnostychnyy analiz v systemi upravlinnia pidpryiemstvom: metodolohiia ta metodyka. Diagnostic analysis in enterprise management system: methodology and methodology]. Ekonomika ahropromyslovoho kompleksu. **2**, 59–63 (2005). (in Ukr.)
9. Dovbnia, S.: Metodolohiia formuvannia dvorivnevoi systemy upravlins'koi diahnostyky pidpryiemstva [Methodology of forming a two-level system of managerial diagnostics of the enterprise]. Ekonomichnyj visnyk Natsional'noho hirnychoho universytetu. **1**(49), 118–124 (2015). (in Ukr.)
10. Datsii, O., Datsii, N., Zborovska, O., Ivashova, L., Cherkashyna, M., Ingram, K.: Financing of environmental programs for industrial waste management in times of crisis. Naukovyi Visnyk Natsionalnoho Hirnychoho Universytetu. **2021**(1), 130–136 (2021). https://doi.org/10.33271/nvngu/2021-1/130

11. Abuselidze, G., Bilyak, Y., Mračkovskaya, N. K.: Methodological and practical issues of the organization of the personnel of the enterprise and the implementation of changes to its structure. Stud. Appl. Econ. **39**(8), (2021). https://doi.org/10.25115/eea.v39i8.4449

12. Sakhno, A., Salkova, I., Abuselidze, G., Yanchuk, T., Buha, N.: Evaluation of efficiency of small agricultural enterprises economic activity under sustainable development conditions. Lect Notes Netw. Syst. **575**, 2262–2271 (2023). https://doi.org/10.1007/978-3-031-21219-2_254

13. Ohanisian, A., Levchenko, N., Shyshkanova, G., Abuselidze, G., Prykhodko, V., Banchuk-Petrosova, O.: Organic farms are the fundamental basis for the sustainable foreign economic activities of agrarians in Ukraine. Environ. Socio-econ. Stud. **10**(2), 49–61 (2022). https://doi.org/10.2478/environ-2022-0011

14. Mohylevska, O., Abuselidze, G., Dragan, O., Gorovij, V., Opanasiuk, V.: Theoretical and practical aspects of the formation of an integrated quality management system in milk processing enterprises. E3S Web Conf. **295**, 01036 (2021). https://doi.org/10.1051/e3sconf/202129501036

15. Stehnei, M., Irtysheva, I., Khaustova, K., Boiko, Y.: Modeling of strategic control system in the context of sustainable development of enterprise. Probl. Perspect. Manag. **15**(3), 212–223 (2017)

16. Abuselidze, G., et al.: The economic mechanism of marketing activity management of food enterprises. E3S Web Conf. **371**, 05002 (2023). https://doi.org/10.1051/e3sconf/202337105002

17. Levchenko, N., Shyshkanova, G., Abuselidze, G., Zelenin, Y., Prykhodko, V., Kovalskyi, M.: Global trends of decarbonisation as a determining factor for the development of external economic activity of metallurgical enterprises. Rural Sustain. Res. **47**(342), 61–75 (2022). https://doi.org/10.2478/plua-2022-0008

18. Yakobchuk, V., Zborovska, O., Dombrovska, S., Dragan, I., Blyznyuk, A., Abuselidze, G.: Model of the state policy for the development of enterprises in the hospitality industry. E3S Web Conf. **371**, 05012 (2023). https://doi.org/10.1051/e3sconf/202337105012

19. Bassova O., Doksova, K.: Intehralna otsinka finansovogo stanu pidpryiemstva [Integral assessment of the financial condition of the enterprise (2012). http://www.rusnauka.com/4_SND_2012/Economics/3_99525.doc.htm

20. Ihnatenko, T.: Rejtynhova otsinka iak zasib vyznachennia efektyvnosti rezul'tativ finansovo hospodars'koi diial'nosti sehmentiv. [Rating estimation as a means of determining the effectiveness of the results of financial and economic activities of the segments]. Visnyk sotsial'no-ekonomichnykh doslidzhen **1**(52), 197–200 (2014). (in Ukr.)

21. Larikova, T.: Osoblyvosti rozrakhunku intehral'noi otsinky finansovoho stanu sub'iektiv hospodariuvannia. Features of the calculation of the integrated assessment of the financial condition of economic entities. Naukovyj visnyk Khersons'koho derzhavnoho universytetu ("Ekonomichni nauky") **6**, 228–233 (2014). (in Ukr.)

22. Ruschyshnyn, N.: Intehral'na otsinka efektyvnosti funktsionuvannia torhovel'nykh pidpryiemstv ta metody rozrakhunku intehral'nykh pokaznykiv [Integral assessment of the efficiency of trading enterprises and methods of calculating integral indicators]. Naukovyj visnyk Natsional'noho lisotekhnichnoho universytetu Ukrainy **17**, 176–180 (2007). (in Ukr.)

23. Khrusch, N.: Intehralna otsinka rivnia finansovoho potentsialu pidpryiemstv u sferi telekomunikatsij. Integral assessment of the level of financial potential of enterprises in the field of telecommunications. Visnyk Khmel'nyts'koho natsional'noho universytetu **6**(2), 304–307 (2011). (in Ukr.)

24. Bachtiar, B., et al.: Analysis of Authorized Economic Operator Policy in the Tanjung Priok Customs and Excise Service Office: Strengths and Weaknesses. In: Asia-Pacific Research in Social Sciences and Humanities Universitas Indonesia Conference APRISH 2019. Atlantis Press. pp. 310–317 (2021)

25. Fletcher, T.: Authorized Economic Operator (AEO) programs: IBM'S perspective. World Customs J. **1**(2), 61–65 (2017)
26. Grottel, M.: The status of authorized economic operator – a new quality of customs services. Int. Bus. Global Econ. **32**, 109–110 (2013)
27. Huang, H-H: Authorized economic operator: joint international conference on economics and management engineering. In: (ICEME 2016) and International Conference on Economics and Business Management (EBM 2016) (USA, Lancaster, December 2, 2016), Lancaster: Economics and Management Engineering
28. Chang, H-L., Wu, J.: Exploring company ability to meet supply chain security validation criteria. Int. J. Phys. Distrib. Logist. Manag. **45**(7), 691–710 (2015)
29. Erceg, A.: Influence of authorized economic operator on supply chain security. In: Proceedings of the Business logistic in modern Management: 14th International Scientific Conference (Croatia, October 16, 2014), Osijek: Business logistic in modern Management, pp. 93–101 (2014)
30. Knysh, Y.: Development of evaluation principles of regional economy operation efficiency. Probl. Perspect. Manag. **11**(1), 106–109 (2013)
31. Laszuk, M., Ryciuk, U.: The importance of authorized economic operator institution for the security of supply chain in the international goods turnover of Polish enterprises. Eur. J Bus. Manag. **4**(1), 32–41 (2016)
32. Manuj, I., Mentzer, J.T.: Global supply chain risk management strategies. Int. J. Phys. Distrib. Logist. Manag. **38**(3), 192–223 (2008)
33. Torello, A.: The Simplification of Customs Formalities: The Role of the Authorized Economic Operator (AEO) in Vietnam and in the EU. Emerging Markets. (IntechOpen, 2020)
34. Authorised Economic Operators. Guidelines. The European Commission (2012). Doc. TAXUD/B2/047/2011 – Rev.3. http://ec.europa.eu/taxation_customs/resources/documents/customs/policy_issues/customs_security/aeo_guidelines2012_en.pdf
35. Pratama, D.H., Everett, S.: Supply chain security initiatives: the authorized economic operator and Indonesia's experience. J. Int. Logist. Trade **15**(1), 10–18 (2017)
36. The Law of Ukraine. On amendments to the Customs Code of Ukraine (regarding the authorized economic operator and simplifications of customs formalities).(The Verkhovna Rada of Ukraine, 2016). https://www.minfin.gov.ua/uploads/
37. The Law of Ukraine. On Amendments to the Customs Code of Ukraine on Some Issues of Functioning of Authorized Economic Operators. (The Verkhovna Rada of Ukraine, 2019). https://zakon.rada.gov.ua/laws/show/141-20
38. Ofitsijnyj Sajt Publichne Aktsionerne Tovarystvo Dnipropetrovs'kyj Strilochnyj Zavod [Official site Public Joint-Stock Company Dnipropetrovsk Turning Plant]. http://dsz.dp.ua/ua/inf ormatciya_dlya_obnarodovaniya/rchna_fnansova_zvtnst (in Ukr.)
39. Ofitsijnyj Sajt Publichne Aktsionerne Tovarystvo Dnipropetrovs'kyj Strilochnyj Zavod (2021). [Official site Public Joint-Stock Company Poltava turbomechanical plant]. http://old.ptmz.com.ua/content/dokumenty-0 (in Ukr.)
40. Ofitsijnyj Sajt Publichne Aktsionerne Tovarystvo Dnipropetrovs'kyj Strilochnyj Zavod "ELEKTROPANEL'" [Official site Public Joint Stock Company Glukhovsky Plant "Electropanel"]. http://elpa.com.ua/documents.html (in Ukr.)
41. Ofitsijnyj Sajt Publichne Aktsionerne Tovarystvo Dnipropetrovs'kyj Strilochnyj Zavod "VNDIKOMPRESORMASH" [Official site Public Joint Stock Company "Scientific-Production Joint-Stock Company" VNIICompressormash"]. http://old.vnii.com.ua/content/dokumenty (in Ukr.)

42. The Committee of Sponsoring Organizations of the Treadway Commission (2017). https://www.coso.org/documents/COSO%202013%20ICFR%20Executive Summary.Pdf
43. Vakulchyk, O., Fesenko, V., Knyshek, O.: Internal control and audit of enterprises' compliance with Customs requirements while conducting foreign economic activity. Baltic J. Econ. Stud. **3**(4), 38–46 (2017)

# A Usage and Analysis of Measured $CO_2$ Levels in Japanese Community Buses with IoT Sensors

Toshihiro Uchibayashi[1]([✉]) [iD], Chinasa Sueyoshi[2], Hideya Takagi[2], Yoshihiro Yasutake[2], and Kentaro Inenaga[2]

[1] Kyushu University, Fukuoka, Japan
uchibayashi.toshihiro.143@m.kyushu-u.ac.jp
[2] Kyushu Sangyo University, Fukuoka, Japan
{sueyoshi,remilab,yasutake,inenaga}@is.kyusan-u.ac.jp

**Abstract.** Since 2020, COVID-19 has raged throughout the world, and with recommendations to open windows and ventilate enclosed spaces, such as buses and trains, attention has been drawn to the issue of indoor environmental pollution. Therefore, it was hypothesized that measuring and reporting the air quality inside buses would allow passengers peace of mind. In this research, Internet of Things (IoT) sensors were installed inside buses, and the measured data were analyzed. With the cooperation of Sue Town in Japan, IoT sensors were installed in regional public transportation systems (i.e., Japanese Community Buses) and data that temperature, humidity, $CO_2$, noise, and pressure were collected. The measured data were displayed in real-time on signage inside the bus. As a preliminary step to predict the ability of the buses to maintain normal air quality inside the vehicles at all times, data accumulated on three buses over a six-month period were analyzed.

**Keywords:** Community Bus · Regional Public Transportation · $CO_2$ · IoT Sensor · Analysis · Usage

## 1 Introduction

Buses play a central role in public transportation systems in the regional cities of Japan, particularly those that primarily consist of buses operating within specific regions. However, the number of regional public transportation service users is on the decline due to competition with private cars. This is particularly true for buses that primarily operate within a given region, as opposed to buses that link cities. Even given this competition, there are expectations that buses will continue to play a central role in regional public transportation, as a means to address environmental issues and cater to an aging society. In particular, community buses and demand-driven transportation, which are operated mainly by local governments, play a vital role in Japan [1], where over 40% of the population is expected to consist of elderly citizens, over 65 years old, by 2050. Thus, buses operated primarily by local governments are highly important for social welfare.

ⓒ The Author(s), under exclusive license to Springer Nature Switzerland AG 2023
O. Gervasi et al. (Eds.): ICCSA 2023, LNCS 13957, pp. 242–255, 2023.
https://doi.org/10.1007/978-3-031-36808-0_16

Since 2020, when the COVID-19 pandemic first started, the spread of a new approach was seen, which differs from conventional wisdom. There have been recommendations [2] to open windows and ventilate the confined spaces in buses and railways, and this has drawn attention to indoor environmental pollution. In particular, the concentration of $CO_2$ emitted by humans has been used as a barometer for measuring indoor environmental pollution. Many recommendations and studies have used this metric, due to the widespread use of sensors and the ease of measurement.

This research team collaborated with more than 10 local authorities within Fukuoka Prefecture in Japan and carried out activities to support regional public transportation on buses and ferries. The support activities included posting route information on Google Maps, through the maintenance of General Transit Feed Specification (GTFS), a system for collecting and displaying location information on buses in real-time, as well as the summary and analysis of a passenger survey application [3–6]. Community buses operated by local governments often have a capacity of 30 or fewer people, and there are concerns about the risk of pollution to the indoor environment. It was considered necessary, therefore, to collect environmental information within the bus in real-time, and communicate this both to passengers who have already boarded and those who are about to board.

In this paper, as a preliminary step to determining how to maintain normal air conditions inside the vehicle at all times, the measured data from inside the bus were analyzed. With the cooperation of the Sue Town, in Kasuya-gun, Fukuoka Prefecture, Internet of Things (IoT) sensors were installed for periods of up to six months, collecting data on the environment inside community buses, and said data were analyzed. In Sect. 2, related research is introduced. In Sect. 3, in addition to providing an overview of the Sue Town and the community buses, an explanation is given regarding the installation of the IoT sensors. In Sect. 4, the data collected by the IoT sensors are analyzed, and a summary is provided in Sect. 5.

## 2   Related Works

Chun-Fu Chiu et al. [7] investigated whether the accident ratio increased as the concentration of $CO_2$ within the bus increased. Verification was performed by measuring the $CO_2$ concentrations and temperature within three tour buses with a passenger capacity of 43 people during a three-day/two-night school excursion. The results of the verification indicated that the $CO_2$ concentration greatly exceeded the standard values. As the air in the air conditioners within the tour buses circulated, there was a significant lack of air being exchanged with the outside air, and the researchers warned that this may have a negative effect on transportation safety. This suggests that increasing the opportunities for ventilation within tour buses would maintain safety during travel, and would be extremely beneficial for increasing the quality of the trip.

Kevin Weekly et al. [8] developed data-driven partial differential equations and ordinary differential equation models to predict the respective $CO_2$ concentrations in conference rooms resulting from a human presence or user-controlled ambient $CO_2$. Three cases were considered, and an actual conference room was used for the simulation. For the estimation of exogenous inputs, $CO_2$ concentrations were measured at two indoor locations, and these were used for the design and validation of a model-based observer.

Andrzej Gajewski [9] discussed the quality of air inside a bus. An experiment was performed in which 24 passengers and one driver boarded a bus, and the $CO_2$ concentration was measured on the outbound and inbound routes. On the outbound route, the concentration of $CO_2$ exceeded the allowable limit of 1,000 ppm, whereas, on the inbound route, a maximum of 2,400 ppm was measured. Based on the result of the experiment, an analysis was performed, calculating the ratio of fresh air required to satisfy the standard allowable limit.

## 3   Measurement Environment

The measurements of environmental data within a regional public transportation service were taken on Sue Town community buses. Therefore, Sue Town, the community bus, and the IoT sensors used for measurement will be introduced in this section.

### 3.1   Sue Town

Sue Town [10] is located slightly northwest of the central region of Fukuoka Prefecture, approximately 10 km east of Fukuoka City. It is bordered by towns on all four sides. It has a total area of 16.31 $km^2$ comprised of 7.1 km east to west, and 4 km north to south. The Sue River flows from east to west through the center of town, and the central region is in the southwest part of town. In the western region of the town is Mt. Bota, which straddles the towns of Kasuya and Shime. The northwestern and southwestern parts of Sue Town have been increasingly developed in recent years as a bedroom community for Fukuoka City. The population, as of April 2022, was 28,840, and three prefectural roads pass through the town, functioning as arterial roads. The Kyushu Expressway was established to run through the town, and the Sue parking area was established on both the inbound and outbound roads. In the parking area, a national social experiment called the Sue Smart Interchange (limited to mini and standard-sized vehicles equipped with ETC on board equipment) was conducted and is now in full operation following the experiment's completion in October 2006. This Sue Smart Interchange has become entrenched in the community and is viewed as an important facility essential for life in the region. In addition, three JR railway lines pass through the town, and there are three stations in town: JR Sue-Chuo Station, JR Shimbaru Station, and JR Sue Station. Three bus routes are operated by the main transportation company in the prefecture, Nishi-Nippon Railroad Bus, and these connect Fukuoka Airport and Fukuoka City. Furthermore, the community bus operation started in February 2010, which aimed to supplement regional transportation in areas through which the railway or bus routes did not pass.

## 3.2    Community Bus

Community buses in Japan are planned for and operated by local governments in order to eliminate transportation gaps and inconvenience. Unlike bus routes operated by corporations, which are the mainstay of public transportation in metropolitan areas and core regional cities, community buses are not intended to make profits. The main objectives are to fill the blank areas or areas where buses are not convenient, to provide an alternative to commuting by car, to support the elderly and disabled in areas lacking welfare bus services, and to connect and revitalize commercial facilities in the city center.

In Sue Town, five buses, including one held in reserve, operate from the base point of Sue Town Hall (Fig. 1). The passenger capacity ranges from nine to 28 people depending on the bus (Table 1). The number of bus runs is a maximum of 10 per day, and the buses run every day except for weekends and public holidays, as well as the period at the end/start of the year. Rather than being operated by Sue Town directly, all operations are outsourced by Sue Town to taxi operators within the town. There are seven routes in total, including routes running from the central region of the town to the outskirts, and routes confined to the central region (Table 2). In terms of the number of bus stops, route 1 has 20, route 2 has 13, route 3 has 15, route 4 has 14, route 5 has 20, route 6 has 10, and route 7 also has 10. All buses start from the welfare center in the center of the town, and after visiting the designated bus stops, return to the welfare center (Fig. 2). The Sue Town community buses are operated such that one bus straddles multiple routes. For example, the PINK bus follows a fixed route order every day: $3 \rightarrow 3 \rightarrow 7 \rightarrow 3 \rightarrow 3 \rightarrow 3 \rightarrow 7 \rightarrow 3 \rightarrow 7 \rightarrow 3 \rightarrow 3$.

The Toyota HIACE buses are allocated to route 6, where there are many narrow streets, because of the ability to turn in a small radius. The fare is fixed at 100 yen per person, and the charge is reduced for children of elementary school age and below, those 65 years old and above, and users with disabilities. Furthermore, the driver records on paper the number of people boarding and alighting from the bus at each bus stop.

Table 1. Summary of Sue Town community buses.

| Bus name | Bus type | Passenger capacity |
| --- | --- | --- |
| PINK | Pon'cho | 24 |
| BLUE | Pon'cho | 26 |
| GREEN | Pon'cho | 26 |
| SILVER | HIACE | 9 |
| (Reserve bus) | (Reserve bus) | 28 |

## 3.3    IoT Sensors

IoT sensors were installed in three of the Hino Pon'cho community buses (PINK, BLUE, and GREEN), which had a comparatively high degree of spare capacity

Fig. 1. Sue Town community bus vehicles.

**Table 2.** Operating routes.

| Route No. | Route name | No. of bus stops |
|---|---|---|
| 1 | Ichibanda-Kami-Sue route | 20 |
| 2 | Otsuueki-Sue-Shiroyama route | 13 |
| 3 | Tabiishi-Yamanokami-Shimbaru route | 15 |
| 4 | Satani-Kawago route | 14 |
| 5 | Satani-Kenshoji route | 20 |
| 6 | Hirabaru-Oma route | 10 |
| 7 | Central circulation route | 10 |

in terms of space and electricity. The sensors were installed on top of the front and rear handrails within the vehicles so that the passengers would not touch them by accident. Netatmo [11] IoT sensors were used, which come in a pair con-

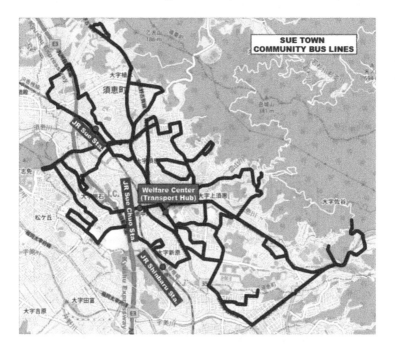

**Fig. 2.** Route map that includes seven lines.

sisting of a main unit supplied with electricity via USB, and a battery-powered handset. The main unit is able to measure temperature, humidity, $CO_2$, noise, and pressure, whereas the handset can only measure temperature, humidity, and $CO_2$. The measured data were uploaded and stored on the Netatmo Cloud every 10 minutes. In addition to being able to confirm the accumulated data through graphs and figures using a dedicated application or website, it is also possible to download the accumulated data through the prepared API. The main unit was installed at the front of the bus and the handset was installed at the back. The bus installation locations and images of the installed sensors are shown in Fig. 3. In addition, an in-vehicle Wi-Fi router [12] was installed inside the bus to facilitate automatically sending the data to the Netatmo Cloud via the Internet. The installation periods for the IoT sensors were March 2021, November 2020, and September 2021 for the PINK, BLUE, and GREEN buses, respectively. As all buses undergo repairs several times a year, data could not be acquired during those periods.

## 4   Usage and Analysis of IoT Sensor Data

### 4.1   Data Usage

A prototype of the digital signage was installed on the GREEN bus. An image of the actual digital signage is shown in Fig. 4. Within the digital signage, the

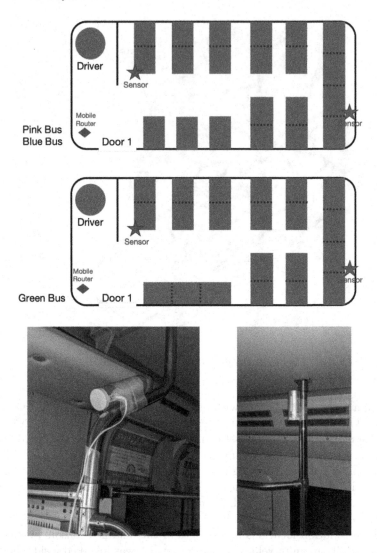

**Fig. 3.** IoT sensor installation locations and images.

current location is derived from location information obtained separately from the bus location system, and the bus stop guidance and delay information are updated and displayed in real-time. As part of this, the temperature within the bus and the $CO_2$ value from the Netatmo sensor are displayed in real-time to communicate the state of the environment inside the bus to the passengers. The passengers, by looking at this value and opening or closing the windows, can regulate the $CO_2$ concentration within the bus. Moving forward, by predicting $CO_2$ concentration based on the analyzed results, the researchers believe that advance warning can be provided.

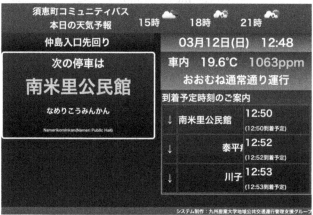

**Fig. 4.** Digital signage monitor within the GREEN bus.

## 4.2   Data Analysis

An analysis was performed on the data measured using the IoT sensors installed on the Sue Town community buses. Among the measured data, the analysis mainly focused on the CO$_2$ concentration values.

In Japan, the recommendation of the Ministry of Health, Labor, and Welfare for indoor CO$_2$ concentration is that it be kept below 1,000 ppm [13]. The European Federation of Air Conditioning Associations [14] has stated the importance of confirming that indoor CO$_2$ concentration does not exceed the standard value of 1,000 ppm (with a recommended value of 800 ppm). The air environment guidelines for the Hong Kong Environmental Protection Agency [15] recommend an indoor CO$_2$ concentration of 2500 ppm or below.

Figure 5 shows the measured $CO_2$ concentration values. The values from the IoT sensors at the front of each bus from the date of installation to March 2022 were rounded and plotted on a line graph in five-minute intervals. The areas where the data is blank are the intervals during which data could not be acquired due to difficulties connecting to the IoT sensors or the Internet, or periods during which the bus was being repaired. In addition, as the values were not stable during the initial phase after installation, the valid periods used were July 1, 2021 to March 30, 2022 for the PINK bus, April 2021 to March 30, 2022 for the BLUE bus, and September 2021 to March 30, 2022 for the GREEN bus. The number of valid data items for the PINK bus was 9,316, with the mean in-vehicle temperature being 24.3% and the mean humidity being 50.7% (maximum 43.7% and 90%, minimum 17.5% and 33%) across all processes. The mean and median values for $CO_2$ concentration were 967.3 ppm and 335 ppm, respectively, with a maximum value of 2,112 ppm and a minimum value of 555 ppm. The number of valid data items for the BLUE bus was 17,355, with the mean in-vehicle temperature being 24.2% and the mean humidity being 47.4% (maximum 36.6% and 89%, minimum 19.4% and 23%) across all processes. The mean and median values for $CO_2$ concentration were 923.1 ppm and 335.8 ppm, respectively, with a maximum value of 3,409 ppm and a minimum value of 264.2 ppm. The number of valid data items for the GREEN bus was 16,346, with the mean in-vehicle temperature being 23.1% and the mean humidity being 38.6% (maximum 35.7% and 81%, minimum 1.3% and 19%) across all processes. The mean and median values for $CO_2$ concentration were 582.7 ppm and 256.3 ppm, respectively, with a maximum value of 1,700 ppm and a minimum value of 0 ppm. Although the $CO_2$ reference value of 1,000 ppm recommended by the Japanese guidelines and the European Federation of Air Conditioning Associations are exceeded, some of the buses are within the air conditioning environment guidelines of 2500 ppm set by the Hong Kong Environmental Protection Agency. The fact that the periods and number of data items are not proportionate is due to the periods during which the buses were being repaired. As the data volume for the GREEN bus is insufficient, and the blank areas are conspicuous, for this paper, only the data measured from the PINK and BLUE buses were analyzed.

Next, to investigate the transition in $CO_2$ concentration over time, the $CO_2$ concentrations for the valid period were wrapped in five-minute intervals and plotted on a heat map (Fig. 6). The reason that there are blank periods during the PINK lunch breaks is that, as the power to the bus was cut, the power to the sensors was also cut, meaning that the data could not be measured. It appears that the $CO_2$ concentration increases linearly as the number of passengers increases but decreases linearly in a smooth manner when the doors are opened or when the number of passengers decreases. Furthermore, in areas where the values are exceptionally low, this is likely when the doors were left open during the gaps when changing routes. During the period as a whole, the PINK bus had a $CO_2$ concentration of 2,500 ppm in specific timeframes three or four times in the mornings and four times in the afternoons, and these are seen as the peak values. The BLUE bus had a $CO_2$ concentration of around 3,000 ppm once each in the morning and afternoon (09:00-11:00, 13:00-16:00), which was the peak value. Thus, routine multiple increases in $CO_2$ concentration followed by decreases during a single day of operation is the cycle repeated throughout the seasons, though there may be some seasonal variation. The route each bus takes throughout the day is fixed, and so this is thought to be related to whether there are boarding or alighting passengers at specific bus stops.

Therefore, to consider the relationship between the season, $CO_2$ concentration, and temperature within the vehicle, a scatter diagram plotting the relationship between $CO_2$ concentration and vehicle temperature for the summer (July) and winter (January) is shown (Fig. 7). The mean and median temperatures within the PINK bus in the summer were 24.6 °C and 24.8 °C, respectively. In contrast, in the winter the respective mean and median temperatures were 23.2 °C and 23.7 °C. Furthermore, the mean $CO_2$ concentration in the summer was 971.3 ppm and the median was 940 ppm, whereas in the winter the mean was 746 ppm and the median was 664 ppm. The mean and median temperatures within the BLUE bus in the summer were 24.6 °C and 23.9 °C, respectively, whereas in the winter the respective mean and median temperatures were 24.4 °C and 24.8 °C. The mean $CO_2$ concentration in the summer was 1,026.6 ppm and the median was 1037 ppm, whereas in the winter the mean was 860 ppm and the median was 793 ppm. Although the distribution trends were the same regardless of the season, both temperature and $CO_2$ concentration tended to be higher in the winter than in the summer. These characteristics were similar for both the PINK and BLUE buses.

Thus, although the values varied according to the season, the distribution trends between in-vehicle temperature and $CO_2$ concentration were extremely similar. The variation in the $CO_2$ concentration measured during one day of operation was verified. When confirming the variation, by comparing this with the number of passengers, for which there is considered to be an extremely close relationship with $CO_2$ concentration variation, it was possible to analyze the relationship. When performing the analysis, Sue Town Hall provided the summary data for the number of passengers boarding and alighting the PINK and BLUE buses from March 2020 to September 2021. This summary data contains the number of boarding and alighting passengers recorded by the bus driver at each bus stop. The number of passengers on board the bus was calculated for each bus stop based on the number of boarding and alighting passengers. It was assumed that if the bus arrived at the bus stop at a fixed time and there were no passengers there, the doors were not opened. The $CO_2$ passenger data for August 29, 2021 is shown in Fig. 8. The mean $CO_2$ concentration and passenger numbers for every five-minute interval were output and plotted. Service started t 08:20, and the $CO_2$ concentration gradually increased from that time. The $CO_2$ concentration was near zero around 12:30 because this was the lunch break period in which the bus was not in operation. The graph shows that the $CO_2$ concentration and passenger numbers are linked, with a delay of approximately 1020 minutes. The reason for the error in the transition of $CO_2$ concentration and passenger numbers is thought to be because, contrary to the number of passengers, which is in non-linear form, the linear $CO_2$ concentration values are gradually increasing and decreasing. Thus, the increase and decrease in values when boarding or alighting means that the doors were opened and closed and that the $CO_2$ concentration fell at that time, regardless of the number of passengers. However, if a bus departs with one or more passengers on board, the $CO_2$ concentration will increase again. The speed of increase in the $CO_2$ concentration toward the upper limit is faster the more passengers are aboard. Furthermore, the fact that the $CO_2$ concentration never went below 500 ppm is due to the fact that the driver was always present.

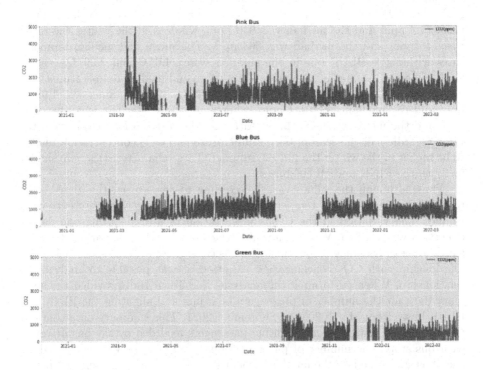

**Fig. 5.** Measured $CO_2$ concentration data.

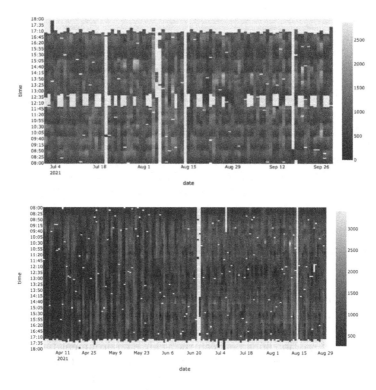

**Fig. 6.** Five-minute interval heat map.

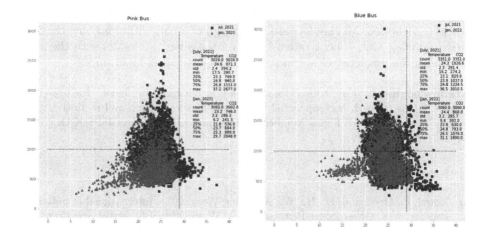

**Fig. 7.** Relationship between CO₂ concentration and temperature.

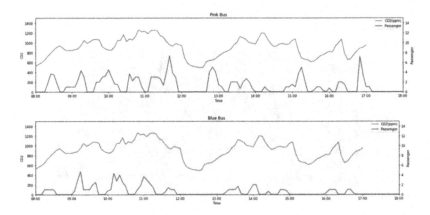

**Fig. 8.** $CO_2$ concentration and number of passengers (August 29, 2021).

## 5    Conclusion

In this study, IoT sensors were installed on three Sue Town community buses to measure environmental data. The $CO_2$ concentration data are displayed in real-time on a digital signage monitor inside the bus to encourage passengers to ventilate. By analyzing the environmental data measured within the bus, the nature of variations and relationships between the vehicle environment parameters and the number of passengers were derived. In addition, the installed monitor can aid in the avoidance of congestion within the vehicle environment. As a result of analyzing the measured $CO_2$ concentration data, it was found that the $CO_2$ concentration increased and decreased based on the season, but in the fixed cycle within one day of operation, variation in the $CO_2$ concentration clearly occurred. As factors in the variation, the opening and closing of doors with the boarding and alighting of passengers, and the number of passengers who had boarded the bus were identified. Moving forward, the design of an algorithm is being considered to predict $CO_2$ concentration based on the analyzed results with the aim to publish the predicted $CO_2$ concentration to passengers in advance.

**Acknowledgment.** The authors would like to thank Sue Town, Kasuya-gun, Fukuoka. This research was supported by Kyushu Sangyo University Practical Application Support Research Funds Number K060243 and K060064, and JSPS KAKENHI Grant Number JP 21K18021.

## References

1. Kowal, P., Goodkind, D., He, W.: An Aging World 2015. International Population Reports, U.S. Government Printing Office, Washington DC. http://www.census.gov/library/publications/2016/demo/P95-16-1.html. Accessed 27 Jan 2023
2. "Onboard ventilation capacity for sightseeing buses and local buses". https://www.mlit.go.jp/jidosha/anzen/top/data/covid19_info_shyanaikanki.pdf (in Japanese). Accessed 27 Jan 2023

3. Chinasa, S., Takagi, H., Uchibayashi, T., Inenaga, K.: An analysis of the number of passengers in consecutive national vacation collected with a practical management support system. Int. J. Intell. Transp. Syst. Res., pp. 279–287 (2022)
4. Sueyoshi, C., Takagi, H., Inenaga, K.: Analysis of the number of passengers in consecutive national holiday collected with a practical management support system in the case of community bus of Shingu Town in Japan. In: 11th International Green and Sustainable Computing Workshops (IGSC), pp. 1–8 (2020)
5. Sueyoshi, C., Takagi, H., Inenaga, K.: Development of route shape measurement application to create transit data for regional public transportation. In: Proceedings of the International Symposium on Innovation in Information Technology and Applications (ISIITA 2020), pp. 57–58 (2020)
6. Sueyoshi, C., Takagi, H., Yasutake, Y., Inenaga, K.: Building and publishing fundamental transit data for regional public transportation provided by municipalities. In: 8th International Conference on Transportation and Traffic Engineering (ICTTE 2019), vol. 308, no. 01005, pp. 23–28 (2019)
7. Chiu, C.-F., Chen, M.-H., Chang, F.-H.: Carbon dioxide concentrations and temperatures within tour buses under real-time traffic conditions. PLoS ONE, vol. 10, no.4 (2015)
8. Weekly, K., Bekiaris-Liberis, N., Jin, M., Bayen, A.M.: Modeling and estimation of the humans' effect on the $CO_2$ dynamics inside a conference room. In: 53rd IEEE Conference on Decision and Control, pp. 1301–1306 (2014)
9. Gajewski, A.: Indoor air quality in a bus. WIT Trans. Built Environ. **134**, 749–757 (2014)
10. "Sue Town". https://www.town.sue.fukuoka.jp/. Accessed 27 Jan 2023
11. "Netatmo : same home, just smarter". https://www.netatmo.com/. Accessed 27 Jan 2023
12. "DCT-WR100D — PIONEER". https://jpn.pioneer/ja/carrozzeria/wifi_router/wifi_router/dct-wr100d. Accessed 27 Jan 2023
13. "Ventilation to improve "poorly ventilated enclosed spaces" in winter". https://www.mhlw.go.jp/content/000698866.pdf (in Japanese). Accessed 27 Jan 2023
14. "Guidance for Schools". https://www.rehva.eu/fileadmin/user_upload/REHVA_COVID19_Guidance_School_Buildings.pdf. Accessed 27 Jan 2023
15. "Practice Note for Managing Air Quality in Air-conditioned Public Transport Facilities". https://www.epd.gov.hk/epd/sites/default/files/epd/english/resources_pub/publications/files/pn03_2.pdf. Accessed 27 Jan 2023

# Assessment of Spatial Inequality in Agglomeration Planning

Georgii Kontsevik$^{(\boxtimes)}$ ⓘ, Igor Lavrov ⓘ, Aleksandr Morozov ⓘ, Leonid Kharlov ⓘ, and Sergey Mityagin ⓘ

ITMO University, Birzhevaya Line, 14, Saint-Petersburg, Russia
kontsevik@niuitmo.ru, mityagin.spb@gmail.com

**Abstract.** The paper considers the problem of spatial inequality of agglomerations. The paper proposes an approach to the estimation of spatial inequality based on the intermodal transport graph and data on the placement of urban services in the agglomeration cities. This approach has been experimentally tested on the agglomeration of St. Petersburg. The result is an assessment of the influence of cities in relation to each other, as well as the evaluation of each city by the availability of a particular type of service.

**Keywords:** Network modeling · City graph · Agglomeration · Settlement system · Urban planning · Urban Environment Model · Informational Model · Algorithms on Graphs · Urban Neighborhood Model · Urban Environment Model · Urban Neighborhood Centrality · Urban Neighborhood Profile

## 1 Introduction

The article is about spatial inequality of urban agglomerations. The spatial inequality is defined as the socio-economic inequality of the population caused by differences in the development of territories. Such distinctions, in turn, can be caused not only by geographical, but also historical, cultural and other reasons [1].

The concept of spatial inequality is closely connected with the assessment of the quality of life for the population of the studied territory. There are many studies on the implementation of such an assessment in terms of one or more factors – for example, the level of income or level of education [2], but there is no consensus among researchers on the rules for building a comprehensive assessment of the quality of life for the population of a particular territory. This is partly due to the fact that there is no unified definition of what "quality of life" is and what parameters it includes. In particular, the following groups of parameters can be identified [3]: physical, mental, psychological, social, cultural, economic, political and environmental, but there is no clear understanding of how they can be formalized to build an integral assessment for the purpose of comparing different territories with each other.

The heterogeneity of the quality of life is clearly manifested when considering such urban systems as agglomerations. The concept of "agglomeration" itself is quite vague: it is not part of a formal administrative-territorial division and has no clear boundaries.

O. Gervasi et al. (Eds.): ICCSA 2023, LNCS 13957, pp. 256–269, 2023.
https://doi.org/10.1007/978-3-031-36808-0_17

In this regard, the same agglomeration, depending on the chosen approach to defining its boundaries, may include different towns and villages [4]. An urban agglomeration is a group of cities that are territorially close and have stable economic, labor, recreational and cultural relations [5]. The region where an urban agglomeration is located should have a highly developed transport infrastructure, be spatially compact and economically closely integrated [6]. Urban agglomeration is a natural stage of urban development and urbanization, when cities in specific regions begin to "cooperate", not just compete with each other [7]. Urban agglomerations have some characteristics, such as the integrity of economic markets, functional connectivity of territories, which are achieved due to the developed transport infrastructure [8].

This paper studies the concept of spatial inequality of territories and proposes an approach to its assessment for agglomerations based on the construction of the transport graph and data on the availability of services in the cities of agglomerations. Experimental testing of the method was carried out on the example of the agglomeration of St. Petersburg (Russia), which includes a number of territories of the city itself and the surrounding cities of the Leningrad Oblast. This agglomeration is the second largest in the Russian Federation (after Moscow agglomeration) and is of interest for the study partly because of the known heterogeneity of population on its territory.

## 2   Territorial Dissimilarities in Settlement Systems

The settlement system in this paper is defined as a set of settlements that are territorially close and functionally interconnected [9]. One of the actual problems both within one and between several settlement systems is the differences in the quality of settlement life caused not only by geographical differences of territories, but also by the historically established socio-economic disparities in their development.

On one scale of consideration, agglomerations can be chosen as a settlement system. In general, agglomerations can be defined as sets of cities and surrounding territories, united by stable links of various types (labor, cultural, infrastructural) between their populations. However, the delimitation of the boundaries of agglomerations, as well as the boundaries of other settlement systems, is subject for a discussion due to the lack of a unified approach among researchers.

### 2.1   Approaches for Delimitation of Agglomeration Borders

The question of delimiting the boundaries of agglomeration depends on which processes are chosen as fundamental for the formation of such a system of human settlement. The two main categories of approaches to defining the concept of agglomeration can be distinguished as economic and functional [10].

The economic approach is based on statistical data on the socio-economic processes in which the territory in question is involved. Such data for agglomerations can be the following [11]:

- number of cities with population over a certain threshold;
- per capita GDP;
- non-agricultural industries' impact on the GDP;

- clear distinction of economic belts of certain transportation radii.

The functional approach is based on actual data on the human settlement and inter-connections between settlements. The advantage of the approach is a broader set of data that is publicly available: the number of population of territories and their parts, the characteristics of transport infrastructure, the location and parameters of services – locations of interest to the population satisfying certain needs. In this regard, this approach was chosen for the construction of the agglomeration assessment model in the framework of this work.

### 2.2 Spatial Inequality Problem: Case Study and Countermeasures

One of the reasons of spatial inequality is different opportunities for earning money between more advantaged areas with more amenities and services and peripheries and rural areas that become poorer in comparison. Mastronardi and Cavallo's study demonstrates that income inequality appears to be greater in "densely populated urban centers with a high incidence of tertiary activities and young population" [12].

However, it would be unreasonable to avoid creating urban centers since while rural areas exhibit lower inequality, they also often lack basic healthcare, education, and mobility services. In fact, setting up infrastructure in sparsely populated areas would be too costly. So, rather than abolishing metropolises, Mastronardi and Cavallo suggest redistributive policies that are supported by policies that affect market functioning, corporate governance, intergenerational transmission of advantages and disadvantages, and the link between structural and sectorial policies [12].

Other studies also demonstrate that "high mobility areas have (i) less residential segregation, (ii) less income inequality, (iii) better primary schools, (iv) greater social capital, and (v) greater family stability" [13] while "policies that exogenously improve amenities in low-public good communities may increase segregation" [14]. Besides, as the model of Sun et al. suggests, market-driven residential redevelopment tends to exacerbate spatial inequality through facilitating income sorting (concentration of people with high income in the advantaged areas) [15].

Reducing the spatial inequality of agglomerations can be carried out in different ways:

(1) local actions – adding new opportunities for the population by creating new services in needy settlements;
(2) connecting actions – improving the transport connectivity of the agglomeration through measures to improve its transport system;
(3) administrative actions – by means of dispositive correction of the composition of agglomerations through stimulating measures for the settlement of people.

## 3 Spatial Inequality Modeling

Cities located outside the agglomeration core cannot always provide the full range of services and opportunities to residents that are available in the "center" [16, 17]. There are several common reasons why residents of peripheral cities travel to neighboring or central cities [18]: work, education, retail, recreation.

In this paper, spatial inequality is assessed through the accessibility/sufficiency of large shopping and entertainment centers. Travelling from one city to another within an agglomeration for the purpose of shopping is one of the most common after work and study [18]. Data on labor migration is not openly available, so it is not expected to be used.

Retail trade is an important component of the urban economy. Large objects of trade can have a wide service area and a large temporary transport accessibility (from 30 min) [19]. Cities and towns where such shopping centers are located can be points of attraction, serving the needs of neighboring territories.

## 3.1 Selected Agglomeration Description

St. Petersburg agglomeration (the second largest in Russia) was chosen for the analysis due to the known heterogeneity of population on its territory. The selected agglomeration is shown on Fig. 1.

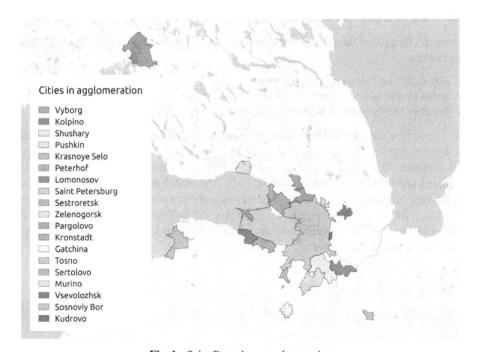

**Fig. 1.** Saint Petersburg agglomeration

For the analysis and assessment of spatial inequality, the cities and settlements that are part of St. Petersburg and the Leningrad Oblast were selected according to the studies dedicated to the identification of the boundaries of the St. Petersburg agglomeration [16, 18]:

- St. Petersburg (Central, Admiralteisky, Petrogradsky, Vasi-leostrovsky, Kalininsky, Krasnogvardeisky, Nevsky, Frunzensky, and Kirovsky administrative districts as a whole; Primorsky district without the municipal entity Lakhta-Olgino and the settlement of Lisy Nos; Vyborgsky district without the settlement of Levashovo and Pargolovo; Moscow district without the territories of Aviagorodok and Pulkovo; Krasnoselsky district without Krasny Selo and Gorelovo);
- cities within the administrative boundary of St. Petersburg (Kol-pino; Pushkin; Peterhof; Shushary; Krasnoye Selo; Kronstadt; Pargolovo; Lomonosov; Sestroretsk; Zelenogorsk);
- cities within the Leningrad Oblast (Gatchina; Vyborg; Vsevolozhsk; Sosnovy Bor; Sertolovo; Murino; Tosno; Kudrovo).

### 3.2 Data Selection and Preprocessing

To model the spatial inequality of the St. Petersburg agglomeration the following data are needed:

- population and cities in the agglomeration;
- about shopping and entertainment centers and their areas;
- intracity and external public transport routes.

Population data are taken from the Federal State Statistics Service of the Russian Federation Rosstat according to the results of the census for 2020 [20]. Geometries of the agglomeration cities and data on shopping centers were obtained using the open mapping service OpenStreetMap (OSM) [21]. The routes and stops of intracity (bus, trolleybus, streetcar, metro) and external (trains and electric trains) public transport are also taken from OSM by appropriate tags. The CityGeoTools library for modeling the intermodal graph [22] is used to calculate the time of accessibility of shopping centers and travel time between cities.

### 3.3 Accessibility Graph: Algorithm and Construction

A public transport graph was used to model service availability. The general scheme of the algorithm is shown in Fig. 2:

**Fig. 2.** General outline of the algorithm

The first step is to select the types of transport used for modeling, as well as the cities included in the agglomeration. Types of public transport selected for modeling the intermodal transport graph: tram, trolleybus, bus, train, subway. It is necessary to consider intra-city modes of public transport, as accessibility is modeled between the centers of cities. In this paper, we have not considered accessibility by private car, as this was not the purpose of the work.

At the second stage, an intermodal graph was constructed for each city. The general scheme of graph construction for one city is shown in Fig. 3 below:

**Fig. 3.** Graph modeling algorithm for one city

The graph modeling algorithm is taken from the work [23]. At the first stage, routes and stops for the selected type of transport are loaded from OSM. Then they are combined into a single network for each type of transport. At the end, all types of transport are combined into one network, forming a single graph. The weights of the edges is the time between the nodes (PT stops) of the graph. The difference from the work [23] in this case is that to build a graph for agglomeration it is necessary not to cut the transport routes by the geometry of the city, as it is done in the mentioned work (but it is possible to limit them by the geometry of the selected area to discard unnecessary information). Thus, a route from the OSM data relating to a city can go beyond the city, for example,

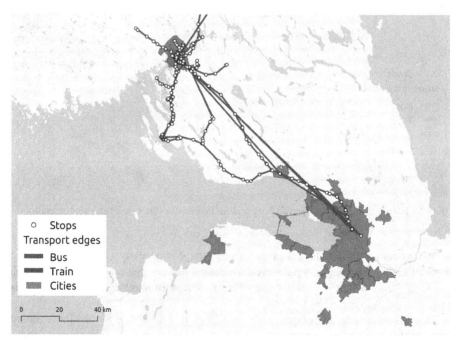

**Fig. 4.** Transportation routes outside the city

when a bus or train travels from one city to another. This change made it possible to obtain data on connections between cities.

The transport graph for one city, without cutting the routes by the city boundaries is shown in Fig. 4.

It is important to note that Vyborg and St. Petersburg are connected by a high-speed train line. The most distant from the other cities of the agglomeration, still connected to the analyzed city centers, is Vyborg. Since in the current method the train speed is the same everywhere in the graph, the weight of the edge was manually changed in order to highlight the line. The high-speed train line on the transport subgraph is highlighted for clarity in Fig. 5. Such a line exists only between these two cities in the agglomeration and this reflects the inequality of the spatial component of the equity in high-speed railways (HSR) [24]. Thus, this train allows Vyborg to be a full-fledged part of the St. Petersburg agglomeration and maintain a good level of influence in the cotext of social services, such as aforementioned "malls".

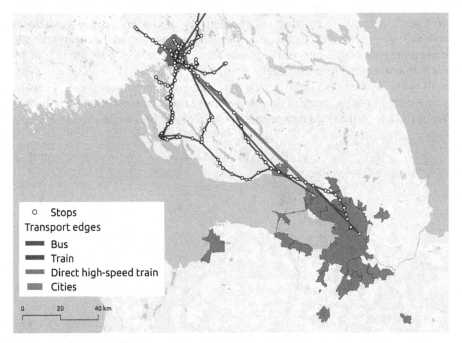

**Fig. 5.** High-speed train between Vyborg and St. Petersburg (the core of the agglomeration)

After obtaining the transport graph of one city, it is necessary to connect it to the graph of the neighboring city. However, we cannot be sure that one route in the graph of one city ends where the next route of another type in another graph begins. This mismatch can be seen in the following Fig. 6:

In order to connect the graphs of the two cities it is necessary to take into account the possible transfers between one or more modes of transport. Thus, the nearest nodes of the graphs (stops) within a radius of 100 m were connected by a line. This connection

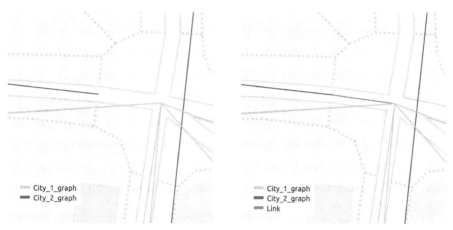

**Fig. 6.** Non-intersecting transport graphs of cities; and united non-intersecting transport graphs of cities

reflects the possibility of walking between stops. Accordingly, the weight of such an additional edge will be the Euclidean distance between the points (the length of the edge) divided by the speed of a pedestrian. It should be noted that in this case it was not possible to construct a path between two selected points on the pedestrian graph, because sometimes transport routes end at the stations, where there is no pedestrian graph.

As a result, a transport graph covering the entire St. Petersburg agglomeration was obtained, which is shown in Fig. 7:

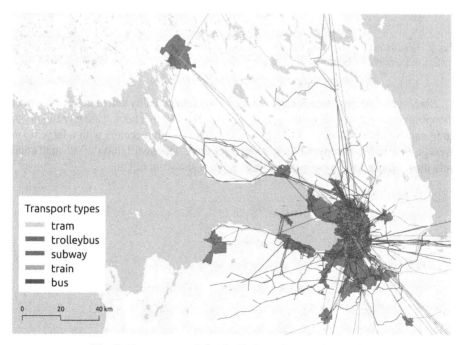

**Fig. 7.** Transport graph for the St. Petersburg agglomeration

In order to calculate the distances between cities on the transport graph it is necessary to use the following algorithm, as is shown in Fig. 8:

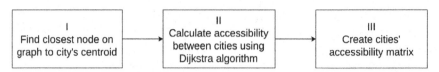

**Fig. 8.** The algorithm for calculating accessibility between cities

This algorithm calculates accessibility between cities by different types of transport using transfers between them.

The distribution of shopping centers in St. Petersburg and Leningrad Oblast by area is shown in Fig. 9:

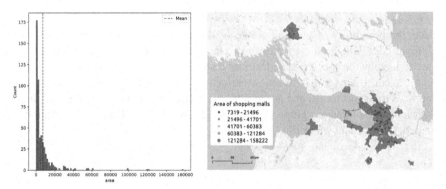

**Fig. 9.** Distribution of Shopping Centers in Leningrad Oblast by area and distribution of shopping centers in Leningrad Oblast with area larger than average

Since the OSM data does not always accurately reflect reality and there may be small shopping centers under the mall tag, and to reflect the fact that people are more likely to go to another city for a large shopping center, only shopping centers with a larger than average area in the Leningrad Oblast were selected. The distribution of all malls and only those whose area is larger than the average is shown in Fig. 9.

In order to estimate the spatial inequality in the agglomeration, it is necessary to calculate the inequality coefficient:

Let $K$ - be the number of cities in the agglomeration:

• $link_{ij}$ - normalized connectivity between cities $i$ and $j$. Constraint: $link_{ij} < 120min$.;
*Services* - the number of services in the city;
• $I_i$ - the inequality indicator for the selected city;
*Population* - the population in the selected city.

$$I_i = \frac{Services_i}{Population_i} + \sum_{j=1}^{K} link_{ij} \cdot \frac{Services_j}{Population_j} \tag{1}$$

In this paper, we use normalized weighting coefficients, because we compare cities only within the agglomeration and not with the target value. As a result of calculating the coefficient of spatial inequality between the cities of the St. Petersburg agglomeration, we obtained an estimate for each city based on its distance from the other cities and the number of services in the considered and the nearest cities. The right side of the equation is shown in Figs. 10 and 11. Figure 10 shows directly the weighting coefficient of the connection between the cities ($link_{ij}$). Figure 11 shows the impact of cities on each other, taking into account transport connectivity and the presence or absence of the services in question. The results are presented as a map in Fig. 12 below. The values of the obtained indicators are presented in Table 1.

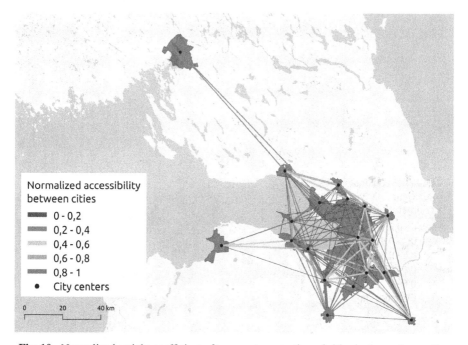

**Fig. 10.** Normalized weight coefficient of transport connection of cities in the agglomeration

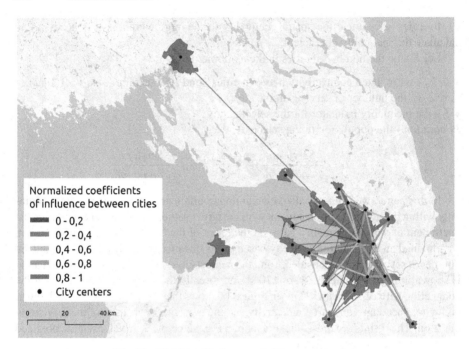

**Fig. 11.** Weights of influence of cities on each other

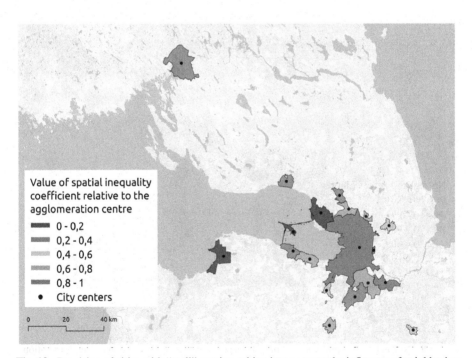

**Fig. 12.** Provision of cities with "mall" service, taking into account the influence of neighboring cities

**Table 1.** Indicator threshold values

| Minimum value | Maximum value | Description |
| --- | --- | --- |
| 0 | 0.2 | The territory practically lacks the necessary number of places providing the service; the transport connection with the neighboring territories provided with the service is very poor |
| 0.2 | 0.4 | There are few or almost no service points in the area, but the transport connection to the neighboring service areas is good |
| 0.4 | 0.6 | The area is well provided with the service and has stable transportation links with neighboring areas, compensating the lack of its own needs |
| 0.6 | 0.8 | Territory is well provided with the service, covering its own needs, but cannot cover the needs of neighboring areas |
| 0.8 | 1 | Territory is provided with the service to the extent that fully covers its and neighboring territories' needs |

## 4 Discussion

The calculation of the indicator in this paper is based on the transport graph of the region and data on the location of individual services. The indicator allows to compare the spatial inequality of individual cities of the agglomeration and thereby identify the most problematic places. Solutions to reduce the spatial inequality can be either adding new service points to the cities with the lowest index value, or improving their transport connections with neighboring cities with the best index values through the development of intercity transport infrastructure.

At the same time, real passenger flows and the capacity of service points are not taken into account due to the lack of detailed data. In addition, transport interconnections are considered as potentially possible for the existing infrastructure - in reality, without a survey it is difficult to predict the purpose of trips of specific passengers, i.e. the demand for specific services and the need to move between the cities of the agglomeration for a specific service. This aspect should be considered in further studies of intra-regional spatial inequality.

## 5 Conclusion

The paper considers the concept of urban agglomeration, spatial inequality. The assessment of spatial inequality was carried out by constructing an intermodal transport graph with the selected type of service on the example of "mall" and its application on the example of St. Petersburg agglomeration.

As a result of modeling, it was possible to see the influence of cities on each other in the agglomeration, taking into account their transport connectivity. It can be seen that the cities that are closer to the center of the agglomeration are not equal to the more distant cities. This happened due to their poor connectivity and the lack of points of attraction (selected services) within these cities.

**Acknowledgements.** This research is financially supported by the Russian Science Foundation, Agreement 17-71-30029 (https://rscf.ru/en/project/17-71-30029/), with co-financing of Bank Saint Petersburg.

# References

1. D.i., U.: Theoretical and methodological foundations of economic inequality of regions. Vestnik (Herald) of Belgorod State Technological University named after V. G. Shukhov, pp. 120–126 (2018)
2. Galster, G., Sharkey, P.: Spatial foundations of inequality: a conceptual model and empirical overview. RSF: The Russell Sage Foundation. J. Soc. Sci. **3**, 1–33 (2017)
3. Sinha, B.R.K.: Introduction: an overview of the concept of quality of life. In: Sinha, B.R.K. (ed.) Multidimensional Approach to Quality of Life Issues, pp. 3–23. Springer, Singapore (2019). https://doi.org/10.1007/978-981-13-6958-2_1
4. Liang, J., Li, F., Mao, L.: Review of the methods of delimitation for the spatial scope of urban agglomeration. In: 18th International Conference on Geoinformatics, pp. 1–10 (2010)
5. Fang, C., Yu, D.: China's Urban Agglomerations. Springer Geography (2020). https://doi.org/10.1007/978-981-15-1551-4
6. Fang C., Yu D.: Overview of the fundamental connotation and strategic position of China's urban agglomerations. Springer Geography, 1–63 (2020)
7. Georgievich, A.E.: Outlines of the theory of urban agglomerations' self-development. Reg. Econ. **1**, 231–235 (2012)
8. Tokunova, G.: Transport Infrastructure as a factor of spatial development of agglomerations (Case Study of Saint Petersburg Agglomeration). Transp. Res. Procedia **20**, 649–652 (2017)
9. Tkachenko, A.A.: Key concepts of the theory of resettlement: an attempt to rethink. Vestnik (Herald) of Moscow University. Series 5. Geography, pp. 10–15 (2018)
10. Antonov, E.V., Makhrova, A.G.: Largest urban agglomerations and super-agglomerations in Russia. Izvestiya Rossiiskoi akademii nauk. Seriya geograficheskaya **4**, 31–45 (2019)
11. Fang, C., Yu, D.: Urban agglomeration: an evolving concept of an emerging phenomenon. Landsc. Urban Plan. **162**, 126–136 (2017)
12. Mastronardi, L., Cavallo, A.: The spatial dimension of income inequality: an analysis at municipal level. Sustainability. **12**, 1622 (2020)
13. Chetty, R., Hendren, N., Kline, P., Saez, E.: Where is the land of opportunity? The geography of intergenerational mobility in the United States. Q. J. Econ. **129**, 1553–1623 (2014)
14. Banzhaf, H.S., Walsh, R.P.: Segregation and Tiebout sorting: the link between place-based investments and neighborhood tipping. J. Urban Econ. **74**, 83–98 (2013)
15. Sun, W., Fu, Y., Zheng, S.: Local public service provision and spatial inequality in Chinese cities: the role of residential income sorting and land-use conditions. J. Reg. Sci. **57**, 547–567 (2017)
16. Reznikov, I.L.: Vyyavlenie granic Sankt-Peterburgskoj gorodskoj aglomeracii. Vestnik Sankt-Peterburgskogo universiteta Nauki o Zemle. **64**, 89–103 (2017)
17. Joel, G.: Edge City: Life on the New Frontier, 548p. (1992)
18. Lachininsky, S.S., Sorokin, I.S.: Spatial structure and the development of settlements in the Saint Petersburg agglomeration. Baltic Region. **13**, 48–69 (2021)

19. Yigitcanlar, T., Sipe, N., Evans, R., Pitot, M.: A GIS-based land use and public transport accessibility indexing model. Aust. Plan. **44**, 30–37 (2010)
20. Rosstat — Vserossijskaya perepis' naseleniya 2020 goda. https://rosstat.gov.ru/vpn_popul. Accessed 4 July 2023
21. OpenStreetMap. https://www.openstreetmap.org/#map=10/59.9512/30.2303. Accessed 15 Apr 2023
22. CityGeoTools - python package of methods developed for analysis of the urban environment. https://github.com/iduprojects/CityGeoTools. Accessed 15 Mar 2023
23. Mishina, M., Khrulkov, A., Solovieva, V., Tupikina, L., Mityagin, S.: Method of intermodal accessibility graph construction. Procedia Comput. Sci. **212**, 42–50 (2022)
24. Cavallaro, F., Bruzzone, F., Nocera, S.: Spatial and social equity implications for high-speed railway lines in Northern Italy. Transp. Res. Part A Policy Pract. **135**, 327–340 (2020)

# Assessment of Spatial Inequality Through the Accessibility of Urban Services

Aleksandr Morozov[1]([✉])⬡, Irina A. Shmeleva[1]⬡, Nikita Zakharenko[2]⬡,
Semen Budenny[2,3]⬡, and Sergey Mityagin[1]⬡

[1] ITMO University, Birzhevaya Line, 14, Saint Petersburg, Russia
asmorozov@itmo.ru
[2] Sber AI Lab, Moscow, Russia
[3] Artificial Intelligence Research Institute, Moscow, Russia

**Abstract.** This paper examines a method for assessing spatial inequality through access to opportunities and urban services based on modeling an intermodal graph of accessibility of urban areas. The goal is to obtain ratings on the difference in physical access to services and opportunities on public transport by social groups. This is done by collecting data on the city's residential areas and urban amenities that serve the functions of education, health, sports, and leisure. Calculation of travel time by public transport to the nearest service of each type is carried out using an intermodal graph. The result of the work is an assessment of the accessibility of services in terms of travel time, compared with urban planning standards.

**Keywords:** Spatial Inequality · Transport Accessibility · Sustainability · Sustainable Mobility

## 1 Introduction

Until the 1980s, city transport planning focused solely on increasing demand for car travel. As a result, great emphasis was placed on building infrastructure for road transport, prioritizing cars on the roads over public transport. One of the clearest examples of a car-centric urban transport policy is found in the cities of the United States - the sprawl of suburbs and cities in width forces residents to buy a personal car and use it daily as a primary type of transport. As a result of such a policy, many cities in the world have felt all the negative effects of motorization: deteriorating air quality, noise pollution, climate change, traffic congestion, increased deaths due to traffic accidents, inefficient use of urban space, inequality in access to services and opportunities [1]. However, it remains obvious that mobility, safety, and time travel affect the sustainability of cities. An efficient public transportation network is not only the main characteristic of a well-functioning and sustainable city [2], but also the most essential condition for improving the quality of life [3] and spatial equity [4].

The urban environment is becoming an increasingly important factor for economic and social development. One of the key aspects is the accessibility of urban services, such as schools, medical facilities, recreational facilities, and others. However, the accessibility of these services is not the same for all citizens, and this leads to spatial inequality in the city. Studies show that regions with high mobility exhibit several positive outcomes, including lower levels of residential segregation, income inequality, and greater social capital, as well as better primary schools and family stability [5]. Conversely, efforts to improve amenities in low-public good communities through external policies may exacerbate segregation [6]. Existing studies have looked at access to urban services by car, while accessibility by public transport has not been studied as often [7,8]. Much attention is given to the study of pedestrian and bicycle accessibility, which is an important element of a sustainable and smart city, to vital urban services [9].

In large cities and metropolitan areas, public transportation plays an important role in residents' daily movements. Residents who do not own cars usually need more time and effort to get to their destinations because of the time it takes to walk to and from stops, the frequent stops on routes, and waiting times [10]. Urban policies that encourage and promote the principles of sustainable mobility in cities increase the focus not only on the use of public transport as the mainstay but also on the incorporation of equal access to services and opportunities through planning and monitoring [11].

This article focuses on assessing spatial inequality in the city through the public transport accessibility of urban services. We use data on the public transport network of the city and the location of urban services to evaluate how easy or difficult it is for residents of different city areas to access these services. Our approach not only assesses the accessibility of individual services but also evaluates the overall accessibility of urban services in different city areas.

## 2  Related Works

At the turn of the 20th-21st century, the problem of urban mobility was considered in terms of criticism of the car-oriented transport policies of world cities. Many works can be considered in two directions:

- A significant study of the problems of international transport (mobility). Such works reveal the problem of urban transport systems.
- The study of sustainable urban mobility in various aspects of the city and its description in such areas as the environment, health, urban planning, and design. In other words, sustainable mobility is perceived as an integral part of other urban systems.

Many cities are dependent on the constant use of private vehicles, with courses the lose their functionality and efficiency and become inconvenient for people [1]. The discrepancy between transport demand and the capacity of urban transport networks creates congestion in the road infrastructure [1]. These problems negatively affect the health and mobility of citizens.

The issue of sustainable mobility in terms of transport systems is considered in detail in the work of P. Newman and D. Kenworthy "Sustainability and Cities" [12]. The authors provide the concept of sustainable development and how it applies to cities with heavy car dependency, consider the changing urban economy in the information age, and describe the extent of car dependency worldwide. Great emphasis is placed on the study of the effect of reverse demand in transport planning. City administrations that pursued a car-oriented transport policy (an increase in street and road networks) actually created in the future an even greater burden on the road network, which it could not cope with [12]. From this, we can conclude that the problem of traffic congestion cannot be solved by developing and expanding road networks - owners of private cars who refused to travel because of traffic jams were motivated to use a personal vehicle, thereby increasing the load on highways and roads, resulting in more congestion.

Studies of transport systems in the US and the UK by Robert Noland and Lewison Lehn contain calculations and measurements of the reverse demand effect: a 10% increase in road capacity increases car traffic on the road by 2.9% in the short term [13], and even more in the long term - up to 10% [14].

Summarizing the above, we can recall the Downes paradox, which was identified by the American economist Anthony Downes back in 1962 - the expansion of the road network provokes an increase in traffic jams and congestion instead of reducing them, especially if public transport is not a priority in urban planning [15]. The cheaper and more attractive a private car becomes to use, the more people will use personal transport, thereby increasing the load on the road network. Due to the provoked demand effect in the US, traffic congestion increased by 144% from 1993 to 2017 [16].

The Downes-Thomson paradox essence is that the weighted average speed of personal vehicles on the road network directly depends on the speed at which users of off-street public transport get from the starting point to the endpoint (meaning the railway, metro, buses, and trams moving along the dedicated lane). There is a Downes-Thomson paradox due to the transition of passengers from public to personal transport under the influence of pent-up demand. The outflow of passengers from public transport reduces the profits of its operators and forces them to increase intervals, which forces other passengers to switch to private vehicles. However, at the same time, the traffic situation is also deteriorating - believing in the improvement of the traffic capacity of the road during rush hours, drivers who previously tried to use the road outside peak hours begin to use it. Both of these factors upset the transport balance, resulting in an explosive increase in the flow of vehicles on the widened road, causing even more congestion and deteriorating public transport services [15] [17].

A separate Pigou-Knight-Downs paradox is a consequence of the Downs-Thomson paradox that, in the presence of public transport, an increase in the capacity of public roads leads not to an improvement, but to a deterioration in the traffic situation [18]. A similar effect was shown by Dietrich Braes in the so-called Braes Paradox: according to it, adding alternative paths to a transport network with independent ("selfish") load distribution on its elements can reduce its efficiency [19].

Mobility is one of the key indicators of urban areas, determining the speed and movement comfort of all people in the city. Sustainable mobility is an important part of UN SDG 11 (United Nations Sustainable Development Goals). This goal assumes by 2030 the introduction of the practice of using universal public inclusive transport, improving road safety, and reducing the negative environmental impact of transport systems on the environment [20]. All the ideas of the SDGs imply a close relationship between all areas: the measures and actions of any goal have a positive effect on the implementation of other goals. Sustainable mobility involves the development of:

– pedestrian infrastructure, promoting the priority of pedestrians in cities;
– public transport;
– alternative modes of transport.

The city is a space for every resident of the city, and public transport uses it more efficiently than private vehicles. Public transport frees up road space for use by all residents of the city and reduces the level of street congestion, which makes cities unattractive places to live and work. The distribution of street space between modes of transport is determined by carrying capacity - the number of passengers that one or another system is able to provide for one available lane. The carrying capacity of a 3.5 m wide lane for a bus and bicycles is approximately the same - about 4 thousand consumers per hour, which is about 4 times higher than the carrying capacity of road transport (about 1000–1200 passengers per hour) [21].

Studies show that when transported by bus, pollutant emissions can be reduced by 1.3-5 times compared to transportation by individual cars, and when transported by rail (taking into account energy production) - by 4-1000 times [22]. Electric public transport, taking into account the generation of electricity at power plants, emits ten times less pollution than personal automobile transport [23].

The impact of sustainable mobility on the ecological situation in cities is considered within the framework of the theory of "urban metabolism" in the book "Understanding Urban Metabolism". The ideas of urban metabolism see the city as a system that exchanges and transforms energy, water, carbon, and pollutants in cities. The authors argue that the understanding of all urban processes is directly related to urban planning [24]. The key characteristics in the concept of developing a sustainable city should be safety, the level of pedestrianization and transport accessibility of territories, and livability. The authors point to a clear relationship between an ecological approach to mobility and reducing the negative impact of transport systems on the environment, reducing the consumption of urban resources and energy, as well as emissions of harmful substances [24].

It is also necessary to note the importance of the efficiency of public transport as one of the key aspects of sustainable mobility within the framework of a transit-oriented concept [25]. The importance of the transport "framework" is indicated, which includes high-speed isolated public transport routes in the planning structure of the city [25]. The paper emphasizes the idea of the importance of transit points, around which it is most profitable to place trade facilities, business centers, and compact housing. Such a planning structure is multifunctional and allows minimizing the load on the transport network due to the presence of everything necessary in one area [26].

The concept of a compact city is closely related to the idea of transit-oriented development: the compact location of residential, social, and economic facilities in the city contributes to the development of achieving a balance between the negative and positive effects of high population concentration [27].

Transport planners have developed a strong tradition of using the scientific method to solve urban transport problems using the classical deductive approach (gathering data, defining goals and objectives, forecasting future needs) [28]. This approach takes land use as a given and does not suggest that transport planners should advocate land use change to create a more efficient transport system. However, from a sustainability perspective, urban transport planning cannot be considered in isolation from land use and the environment without compromising the goal of sustainability [29].

Urban areas have an important criterion in terms of mobility - transport accessibility [30]. Traditionally, transport accessibility has been defined as "the potential for interaction" [31] and can be thought of as the extent to which land use and transportation systems allow people to get to their destinations, to 'connect with each other' through a combination of transport modes [32]. This indicator can be considered as an important social score that reflects the quality of life of people in cities for sustainable smart development [33,34]. The vitality of urban areas depends largely on the quality of the environment, the availability of urban amenities, and their accessibility in particular [30].

Modern urban planning must pay great attention to the development of places with high accessibility and to improving the efficiency of public systems [35]. Quick access to city services is one of the main targets of the 11th UN Sustainable Development Goal (Sustainable Cities) [36]. There are differences in urban planning between mobility and accessibility. The first is associated with increased efficiency of transportation systems, and the second with improved access to opportunities and services that meet the needs of city residents [37]. But mobility is inseparable from accessibility since access depends largely on the "quality" of the network. The goal is not just "movement," but "access" to goods and services. Research shows that accessibility "planning" should be based on high levels of connectivity between urban functions (services) and improved quality of life, rather than on predictions of future traffic volumes and congestion [38,39].

There are several types of accessibility [39,40]:

- Accessibility of the transport system (physical access) depends on the time, distance, and effort required to reach the network.
- System-facilitated accessibility, which evaluates the user's ability to get to a destination and includes the cost of travel time.

– Integral accessibility, which considers access to the number of possible destinations.

## 3   Method

This section presents a method for assessing spatial inequality in access to urban services. Inequality is assessed through the transport accessibility of a residential neighborhood (block) to the nearest service of each type. The intermodal graph developed at the Urban Data Analysis Lab at ITMO University is used to calculate the transport accessibility of services [41]. Intermodal routes consider providing greater flexibility in the movement of citizens when modeling the transport accessibility of the urban environment. Travel time calculations do not include the use of personal or shared transportation, including micro-mobility. For each type of service, the accessibility time is scaled in accordance with city planning standards [42]. Based on the time value to the nearest service, each living block is assigned a score. The proposed method is considered in Saint Petersburg, Russia's second most populous city. It's located in the northwest of the country on the Gulf of Finland and the Neva River estuary. Population: 5,598,486 (2023) people.

### 3.1   Data

To model spatial inequality through transport accessibility, the following data are needed: a geo-layer with urban blocks, services, residential buildings, data on public transport stops, pedestrian and public transport routes. The spatial unit for which the accessibility of services will be assessed is a block. To get the city blocks, it is necessary to have geolayers with administrative and district boundaries of the city, geometry of water bodies (rivers, canals, bays, etc.), graph of the street and road network. The data sets of city boundaries and its blocks, street and road network, residential buildings, urban services, and appropriate tags from the open map service OpenStreetMap (OSM) [43] are uploaded. To build an intermodal transport accessibility graph, we require data on transit routes, stops and walking routes [41].

### 3.2   Construction of Living Blocks

The spatial unit for which the accessibility of services will be assessed is a block - a section of an urbanized area, bounded on all sides by the street and road network. To obtain the geometry of blocks, geo-layers of the administrative boundaries of the city, water bodies (rivers, lakes, etc.), as well as the city's road network, are needed. Figure 1a shows the boundaries of the municipalities of Saint Petersburg in the form of a map obtained from OSM. Figure 1b shows the geometries of all water bodies. Using the OSMnx [44] package to work with spatial data, a graph of the Saint Petersburg street and road network is unloaded (Fig. 1c).

The geometries of roads and water bodies are cut from the geometry of the city. Objects of the MultiPolygon type may appear - several polygons combined into one object. They need to be divided into separate polygons.

The result is shown in Fig. 1d. These blocks may not coincide with the division into land plots, as in the cadastral register. Data on living buildings and city services are added to the received blocks on the map. Blocks in which there are residential buildings are shown in Fig. 2a.

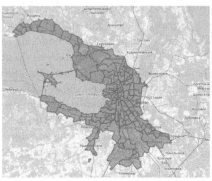

(a) Geolayer with the boundaries of Saint Petersburg municipalities

(b) Geolayer with boundaries of water bodies in Saint Petersburg

(c) Geolayer with the Saint Petersburg street and road network

(d) Geolayer with Saint Petersburg blocks

**Fig. 1.** Obtaining city blocks

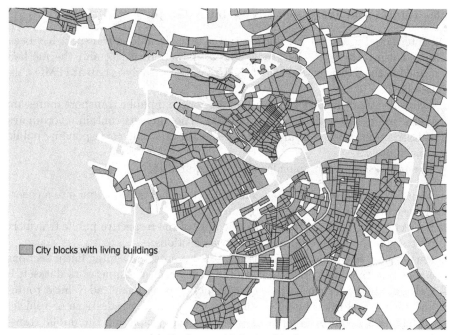

(a) Geolayer with living blocks

(b) Geolayer with city services

**Fig. 2.** Data on living blocks and city services

### 3.3    Intermodal Transport Accessibility Graph

The intermodal graph for calculating travel times by public transport has been compiled using the City Geo Tools spatial data library [45] and the method described in the paper by the staff of the Urban Data Analysis Lab at ITMO University [41].

Datasets about the pedestrian urban network and public transport routes are uploaded using appropriate tags from OSM. The datasets contain: coordinates of pedestrian sections, coordinates of transport routes, and corresponding public transport stops.

Pre-processing of the uploaded data is required [41]:

1. Transform linear objects into a coherent pedestrian network and into a coherent network of public transport routes;
2. Projecting the points of stops onto the lines of the respective public transport routes and the nearest lines of pedestrian sections;
3. Partitioning linear features at the projected points and adding linear sections connecting the point projections to the pedestrian urban network dataset;
4. Calculating the lengths of linear segments of pedestrian and vehicle routes and their travel times based on the average speed of a pedestrian or vehicle;
5. Obtaining a graph by combining the pedestrian graph and the public transport graph at the vertices corresponding to stops.

The edges of this graph are the pedestrian ways, and public transport routes are the nodes are the points of connection between the pedestrian sections and public transport stops (Fig. 3).

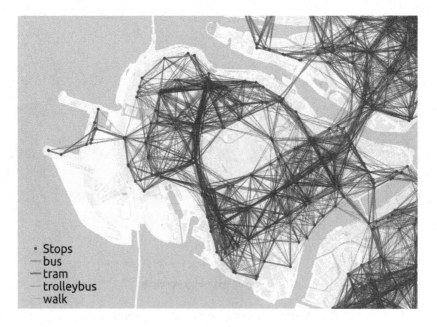

**Fig. 3.** Intermodal transport graph

## 3.4 Calculating Accessibility Times

To calculate the travel time between all the city blocks, the city blocks and the intermodal transport accessibility graph must be mapped. For each city block, a centroid is constructed, and the nearest node on the graph (the beginning of a pedestrian route or a public transport stop) is searched from it. From this node the distance and time on the intermodal graph to all other nodes that represent other city blocks is calculated using the Dijkstra algorithm [46]. Unlike similar methods, Dijkstra's algorithm searches for the optimal route from one given node to all other nodes. Along the way, it calculates the path length - the total weight of the edges it passes along this route. The result is a similarity matrix of distances among all blocks.

## 3.5 Calculating the Travel Time to the Nearest Service of Each Type for Each Living Block

A list of services with accessibility times is shown in Table 1. To calculate the travel time to the nearest service for each living block, the following steps must be performed:

1. From all the blocks in the horizontal similarity matrix, select only residential blocks (i.e., those with residential houses);
2. For each type of service, a different similarity matrix of times between blocks is produced;
3. Then, in the matrix, the blocks with no services are deleted vertically;
4. For each residential block, the closest service of each type by the lowest time value is found, and the time attribute is added to each living block.

It is worth noting that if the nearest service is located in a living block, the value of the in-transit time is 0.

**Table 1.** City Services

| City infrastructure | City function | Type of service | Accessibility time |
|---|---|---|---|
| Leisure infrastructure | Culture, entertainment, creativity | Library | up to 30 min |
| | | Zoo | up to 60 min |
| | | Cinema | up to 60 min |
| | | Museum | up to 60 min |
| | | Theatre/Concert Hall | up to 60 min |
| Leisure infrastructure | Sport | Swimming pool | up to 30 min |
| | | Sports ground | up to 30 min |
| Social infrastructure | Healthcare | Hospital | up to 60 min |
| | | Children Hospital | up to 60 min |
| | | Children's Clinic | up to 15 min |
| | | Clinic | up to 15 min |
| Social infrastructure | Education | Kindergarten | up to 10 min |
| | | University | up to 60 min |
| | | College | up to 60 min |
| | | School | 15–30 min |

## 3.6    Scoring Accessibility

For each block, an accessibility score is given according to the travel time to the nearest service of each type (Table 2). For the basic accessibility time values are taken from the urban planning standards of Saint Petersburg [42]. If the block is provided with service within the time accessibility according to the standard, then the accessibility score is considered to be normal. If less time is spent than according to the standard, then the accessibility score is considered high, and if more time is spent than according to the standard, then low.

**Table 2.** Time accessibility of city services

| Accessibility time of city services | | | | | |
|---|---|---|---|---|---|
| Accessibility time | Up to 10 min | Up to 15 min | Up to 30 min | Up to 60 min | |
| Services | Kindergarten | Children's Clinic, Clinic | School, Library, Swimming pool, Sports ground | Zoo, Cinema, Museum, Theatre/Concert Hall, Hospital, Children hospital, University, College | |
| Score | 0-4 min | 0-5 min | 0-10 min | 0-20 min | 5 (High) |
| | 4-7 min | 5-10 min | 10-20 min | 20-40 min | 4 (Good) |
| | 7-10 min | 10-15 min | 20-30 min | 40-60 min | 3 (Allowable) |
| | 10-14 min | 15-20 min | 30-40 min | 60-70 min | 2 (Low) |
| | More 14 min | More 20 min | More 40 min | More 70 min | 1 (Poor) |

If the value of the time to the nearest service is equal to the boundary value, then the accessibility score is set to a large value. The overall assessment of the transport accessibility of the block is calculated according to the arithmetic mean. The assessed results of accessibility of each type of service are put on the map and highlighted with colors according to the score.

## 4    Results

The method presented above is applied to selected types of services in Saint Petersburg (Table 1). Figure 5 shows, as an example, the assessments of kindergarten accessibility for living blocks.

The blocks are colored according to the accessibility of the nearest service. The results show that there are more living blocks in the central part of the city (Fig. 5a) with the accessibility of 3 and above points. However, the distant blocks from the center (Fig. 5b) have poor accessibility to kindergartens, which may be due to the small number of services themselves. Consequently, residents of remote areas have unequal access to kindergartens in terms of travel time.

The accessibility of each service individually indicates that, in a block of determination, a group of people will spend more/less time getting to the service.

In neighborhoods where services have better accessibility, residents are potentially less stressed to get to the needed service. As accessibility times increase, so does the inequality between residents in different parts of the city. If the travel time to a destination by public transportation is too long, it is likely that residents will use private motorized transportation more often. This eventually encourages the irrational use of cars, and the functionality and efficiency of the city are lost.

All the selected services are divided into 4 groups according to the accessibility time according to city planning standards - up to 10, 15, 30 and 60 minutes (Table 2). For the obtained results the distribution of the accessibility time was made (Fig. 4). Group 1 service accessibility time satisfies the requirements of urban norms [42] for residential neighborhoods to the extent of 43.43%, Group 2–33.87%, Group 3–75.5% and Group 4–77.25%.

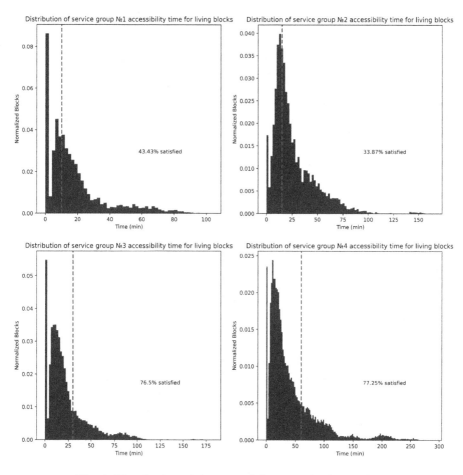

**Fig. 4.** Distribution of the accessibility time for living blocks

**(a)**

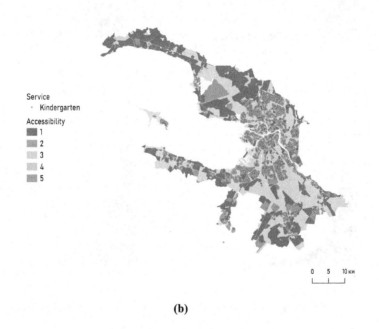

**(b)**

**Fig. 5.** Accessibility of Kindergartens

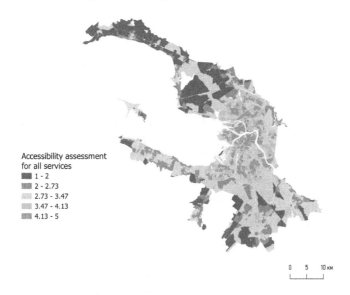

**Fig. 6.** The overall assessment of the service accessibility

# 5 Discussion

The approach to the assessment of spatial inequality through the accessibility of urban services allows one to assess in which parts of the urban area under study social groups can potentially be stressed with access to urban benefits. The proximity of a service is not the main criterion of choice for city residents. Complex and costly demand models are used to account for such complex aspects as a choice, behavior, and people's preferences. However, it is not always possible to predict what urban services people will use. That is why the closest service is worth considering as the minimum base or basis that can be provided by the territory.

# 6 Conclusion

In the course of this work, it is possible to propose a method for assessing spatial inequality through access to urban services, using open data sources. This approach allows to see the weak spots, where there is unequal access to urban amenities, in combination with settlement models and methods for estimating transportation in a city, such as the average travel time, and transport connectivity. It is possible to obtain an estimate of transport accessibility using an intermodal transport graph, which considers not only public transport routes but also pedestrian routes. This allows a more accurate estimation of travel time to a service that is within walking distance and to a remote service on PT. On the basis of this method, plans can be proposed not only for the development of the public transport system but also for land use, and the placement of new service points.

**Acknowledgements.** This research is financially supported by the Russian Science Foundation, Agreement 17-71-30029 (https://rscf.ru/en/project/17-71-30029/), with co-financing of Bank Saint Petersburg.

# References

1. Vuchic, V.R.: Transportation for Livable Cities. Routledge, Milton Park (2017)
2. Kujala, R., Weckström, C., Mladenović, M.N., Saramäki, J.: Travel times and transfers in public transport: comprehensive accessibility analysis based on pareto-optimal journeys. Comput. Environ. Urban Syst. **67**, 41–54 (2018)
3. Zolnik, E.J.: Strategies for sustainable mobilities: opportunities and challenges. J. Reg. Sci. **55**, 681–682 (2015)
4. Bhusal, S., Blumenberg, E., Brozen, M.: UCLA reports title access to opportunities primer permalink. https://escholarship.org/uc/item/98g9d5p4. publication date, January 2021
5. Chetty, R., Hendren, N., Kline, P., Saez, E.: Where is the land of opportunity? The geography of intergenerational mobility in the united states. Q. J. Econ. **129**(4), 1553–1623 (2014)
6. Banzhaf, H.S., Walsh, R.P.: Segregation and Tiebout sorting: the link between place-based investments and neighborhood tipping. J. Urban Econ. **74**, 83–98 (2013)
7. Mao, L., Nekorchuk, D.: Measuring spatial accessibility to healthcare for populations with multiple transportation modes. Health & Place **24**, 115–122 (2013)
8. Kelobonye, K., McCarney, G., Xia, J.C., Swapan, M.S.H., Mao, F., Zhou, H.: Relative accessibility analysis for key land uses: a spatial equity perspective. J. Transp. Geogr. **75**, 82–93 (2019)
9. Pellicelli, G., Caselli, B., Garau, C., Torrisi, V., Rossetti, S.: Sustainable mobility and accessibility to essential services. an assessment of the San Benedetto Neighbourhood in Cagliari (Italy). In: Gervasi, O., Murgante, B., Misra, S., Rocha, A.M.A.C., Garau, C. (eds.) Computational Science and Its Applications— ICCSA 2022 Workshops. ICCSA 2022. Lecture Notes in Computer Science, vol. 13382, pp. 423–438 (2022). https://link.springer.com/chapter/10.1007/978-3-031-10592-0_31
10. Blumenberg, E., Pierce, G.: Multimodal travel and the poor: evidence from the 2009 national household travel survey. Transp. Lett. **6**(1), 36–45 (2014)
11. Zeng, X., Yu, Y., Yang, S., Lv, Y., Sarker, M.N.I.: Urban resilience for urban sustainability: concepts, dimensions, and perspectives. Sustainability **14**(5), 2481 (2022)
12. Newman, P., Kenworthy, J.: Sustainability and Cities: Overcoming Automobile Dependence. Island press, Washington (1999)
13. Noland, R.B., Lem, L.L.: A review of the evidence for induced travel and changes in transportation and environmental policy in the us and the UK. Transp. Res. Part D: Transp. Environ. **7**(1), 1–26 (2002)
14. Litman, T., Colman, S.B.: Generated traffic: implications for transport planning. ITE J. **71**(4), 38–46 (2001)
15. Downs, A.: The law of peak-hour expressway congestion. Traffic Q. **16**(3) (1962)
16. Bellis, R.: The congestion con: How more lanes and more money equals more congestion, Washington, DC, T4America **3**(6) (2020). Accessed 2020
17. Thomson, J.M.: The value of traffic management. J. Transp. Econ. Policy, 3–32 (1968)

18. Ding, C., Song, S.: Traffic paradoxes and economic solutions. J. Urban Manag. **1**(1), 63–76 (2012)
19. Braess, D.: Über ein paradoxon aus der verkehrsplanung. Unternehmensforschung **12**(1), 258–268 (1968)
20. UN-Habitat OECD. Global state of national urban policy. OECD, Programme, March 2018
21. Filippova, R., Buchoud, N.: A Handbook on Sustainable Urban Mobility and Spatial Planning: Promoting Active Mobility. No. ECE/TRANS/298, UNECE, Geneva (2020)
22. Kalenoja, H.: Energy consumtion and enviromental effects of passenger transport modes-a life cycle study on passenger transport modes. In: Proceedings from the Annual Transport Conference at Aalborg University, vol. 3 (1996)
23. Public transport and the environment | Transport for greater Manchester. https://tfgm.com/environment/public-transport
24. Chrysoulakis, N., de Castro, E.A., Moors, E.J. (eds.): Understanding Urban Metabolism. Routledge, Milton Park (2014)
25. Deatrick, J.F.: Transit oriented development and sustainable cities: economics, community and methods. Edited by Richard D. Knowles and fFona Ferbrache. J. Urban Aff. **43**, 225–227 (2021)
26. Knowles, R.D., Ferbrache, F.: Introduction to transit oriented development and sustainable cities: economics, community and methods. In: Transit Oriented Development and Sustainable Cities, pp. 1–10. Edward Elgar Publishing (2019)
27. Crane, R.: Suburban nation: the rise of sprawl and the decline of the American dream. Am. Plan. Assoc. bf 68(1), 104 (2002)
28. Banister, D.: Transport planning. In: Handbook of Transport Systems and Traffic Control. Emerald Group Publishing Limited (2001)
29. Geerlings, H., Stead, D.: The integration of land use planning, transport and environment in European policy and research. Transp. Policy **10**(3), 187–196 (2003)
30. Garau, C., Annunziata, A.: A method for assessing the vitality potential of urban areas. the case study of the Metropolitan city of Cagliari, Italy. City, Territory Archit. **9**, 1–23 (2022). https://link.springer.com/articles/10.1186/s40410-022-00153-6
31. Hansen, W.G.: How accessibility shapes land use. J. Am. Inst. Plann. **25**(2), 73–76 (1959)
32. Geurs, K.T., van Wee, B.: Accessibility evaluation of land-use and transport strategies: review and research directions. J. Transp. Geogr. **12**, 127–140 (2004)
33. Bocarejo S, J.P., Oviedo H, D.R.: Transport accessibility and social inequities: a tool for identification of mobility needs and evaluation of transport investments. J. Transp. Geogr. **24**, 142–154 (2012)
34. Garau, C., Pavan, V.M.: Evaluating urban quality: indicators and assessment tools for smart sustainable cities. Sustainability **10**, 575 (2018). https://www.mdpi.com/2071-1050/10/3/575/htm
35. Coppola, P., Papa, E.: Accessibility planning tools for sustainable and integrated land use/transport (LUT) development: an application to Rome. Procedia - Soc. Behav. Sci. **87**, 133–146 (2013)
36. Vaidya, H., Chatterji, T.: SDG 11 sustainable cities and communities. In: Actioning the Global Goals for Local Impact, pp. 173–185. Springer, Cham (2020)
37. Inturri, G., Ignaccolo, M., Pira, M.L., Caprì, S., Giuffrida, N.: Influence of accessibility, land use and transport policies on the transport energy dependence of a city. Transp. Res. Procedia **25**, 3273–3285 (2017)

38. Solá, A.G., Vilhelmson, B., Larsson, A.: Understanding sustainable accessibility in urban planning: themes of consensus, themes of tension. J. Transp. Geogr. **70**, 1–10 (2018)
39. Inturri, G., Giuffrida, N., Le Pira, M., Fazio, M., Ignaccolo, M.: Linking public transport user satisfaction with service accessibility for sustainable mobility planning. ISPRS Int. J. Geo Inf. **10**(4), 235 (2021)
40. Lei, T.L., Church, R.L.: Mapping transit-based access: integrating GIS, routes and schedules **24**, 283-304 (2010). http://dx.doi.org/10.1080/13658810902835404, https://www.tandfonline.com/doi/abs/10.1080/13658810902835404
41. Mishina, M., Khrulkov, A., Solovieva, V., Tupikina, L., Mityagin, S.: Method of intermodal accessibility graph construction. Procedia Comput. Sci. **212**, 42–50 (2022)
42. Approval of the standards for urban planning of Saint Petersburg on April 11 2017 (in russian). https://docs.cntd.ru/document/456056520
43. Openstreetmap. https://www.openstreetmap.org/#map=10/59.9512/30.2303
44. Boeing, G.: OSMnx: new methods for acquiring, constructing, analyzing, and visualizing complex street networks. Comput. Environ. Urban Syst. **65**, 126–139 (2017)
45. Github - citygeotools. https://github.com/iduprojects/CityGeoTools
46. Dijkstra, E.W.: A note on two problems in connexion with graphs. Edsger Wybe Dijkstra, pp. 287–290, July 2022. https://dl.acm.org/doi/10.1145/3544585.3544600

# PHD Showcase Papers

# Topic Modelling for Characterizing COVID-19 Misinformation on Twitter: A South African Case Study

Irene Francesca Strydom[(✉)] and Jacomine Grobler

Department of Industrial Engineering, Stellenbosch University,
Stellenbosch, Western Cape, South Africa
strydomfrancesca@gmail.com, jacomine.grobler@gmail.com
https://ie.sun.ac.za/

**Abstract.** The COVID-19 pandemic has recently shed light on the potential for social media as a means of spreading mis-, dis-, and mal-information. This paper investigates embedding and cluster-based topic modelling to characterise the COVID-19 infodemic on South African Twitter, which has largely remained unstudied during the COVID-19 pandemic. The best performing model is able to identify specific misinformation narratives, but these narratives are mostly found within more general topics. A more fine-grained model is trained, and is able to much better isolate rumour/misinformation topics from more general topics. Finally, the paper makes several suggestions for dealing with the multilingual and code-switched nature of South African Twitter, as well as for the exploration and development of new dynamic topic modeling approaches that could be especially valuable for tracing the development of specific misinformation or rumour narratives over time. The paper presents novel insights and results on the application of a combination of data mining, machine learning and optimisation for addressing the pressing issue of misleading information on social media.

**Keywords:** Misinformation · Transformers · Social media · Twitter · Topic modelling · Natural language processing

## 1 Introduction

The COVID-19 pandemic has brought to light the potential of social media as a platform for the widespread and rapid dissemination of misinformation. In South Africa, misinformation has also made an appearance. Examples from early 2020 include rumours that 5G radio signals cause COVID-19 and rumours about COVID-19 relief funds provided to citizens by the South African government. Nearly 3 years later, in January 2023, some of these rumours are still circulated in one form or another.

Unlike many social media narratives in countries such as the United States and the United Kingdom, the South African social media narratives about

© The Author(s), under exclusive license to Springer Nature Switzerland AG 2023
O. Gervasi et al. (Eds.): ICCSA 2023, LNCS 13957, pp. 289–304, 2023.
https://doi.org/10.1007/978-3-031-36808-0_19

COVID-19 have remained largely unstudied, especially regarding their development over time. In January 2020, internet penetration in South Africa was at 62% and the number of social media users was approximately 37% of the total population. By the start of 2022, South Africa's internet penetration rate had increased to 68.2% of the total population, and the number of social media users to 46.4% of the total population [11]. The number of social media users in South Africa is likely to continually increase as more South Africans gain access to the internet, making it all the more important to understand the dynamics of information dissemination on these platforms, since they are likely to play important roles in information dissemination and public sensemaking during future crises and emergencies. Without knowing what role these platforms played at the height of the COVID-19 pandemic, it is impossible to plan effectively or mitigate potential risks related to social media misinformation in future health crises, or any large scale crisis for that matter.

Machine learning (ML) and natural language processing (NLP) are useful tools to study the large amounts of social media being generated at a rapid pace. Research efforts devoted to analysing social media narratives about COVID-19, including misinformation narratives, have successfully utilized supervised ML techniques for classifying misinformation, while others have opted for unsupervised learning and data mining techniques to study the characteristics related to misinformation. Since supervised methods require labelled training data, and such training data are not yet available for the South African context, supervised methods are not yet applicable. Unsupervised learning techniques, such as topic modelling, are therefore considered instead.

This paper uses the BERTopic topic modelling algorithm [7] to extract salient themes from South African Twitter data. The study evaluates the use of this unsupervised topic modelling approach specifically for characterising mis- /disinformation on South African Twitter. This study is the first in-depth assessment of the performance of topic modelling on South African COVID-19 Twitter data. Consequently, the analysis provides new insight to the relevant misinformation topics discussed on South African Twitter during COVID-19. Additionally, topics unrelated to misinformation provide insight to the perceptions and experiences of South Africans during the pandemic. The paper also highlights specific challenges faced when working with multilingual code-switched data for which there are limited NLP resources available.

The rest of the paper is structured as follows: Sect. 2 discusses past research in the relevant fields of study, Sect. 3 describes the methodology applied in the study, and the results are discussed in Sect. 4. The study is concluded and recommendations for future work are made in Sect. 5.

## 2   Related Work

Following the outbreak of COVID-19 in 2020 and the multiple resulting global crises, there has been an explosion of research on methods for addressing misinformation on social media. ML and NLP have proven to be especially popular techniques to apply to social media data at scale. Many studies follow a supervised learning approach to address the problem, in which the aim is to train a supervised classification model to detect misinformation among general information. Supervised methods naturally require labelled data for training, and social media misinformation datasets (specifically related to COVID-19) have been curated over the past three years precisely for this purpose [4,9,14,16]. Studies by [1] and Kaliyar *et al.* [10], for example, used labelled Twitter datasets to train models, and achieve F1-scores of more than 95% on their test data.

In the South African context, however, there are no labelled COVID-19 misinformation datasets, and so researchers must rely on publicly available misinformation datasets from other countries for training data. Strydom and Grobler [19] collected labelled data from four publicly available Twitter datasets and trained a neural network misinformation classifier. Although their best performing model attained good results on their test data (an F1-score of 89.9%), when applied to South African Tweets, their classifier did not perform as well. The reasons cited for this are that the differences in datasets relating to events, entities involved, and use of language are too substantial.

In addition to the aforementioned difficulties in finding appropriate, suitable training datasets, the often complex and nuanced nature of misinformation makes using static, labelled datasets problematic in any real-life setting. In many datasets what is labelled as misinformation is not necessarily false, it is simply 'unverifiable' or not backed by any evidence at that particular moment in time. Consequently, situations could arise where information that is questionable at one moment in time (and thus labelled as misinformation) may be verified at the next moment in time, immediately making certain labels outdated. The recently reported events related to claims about COVID-19 vaccines and their efficacy are one example of such a situation. Another issue with labelled datasets is that they do not necessarily reflect the official policy of local governments for what constitutes instances of mis-/dis-/malinformation. In South Africa, Real411, is an online platform for reporting digital misinformation. Developed by Media Monitoring Africa, the platform relies on technical and legal experts, alongside journalists to judge whether reported content constitutes disinformation, hate speech, incitement, or harassment. In this manner Real411 ensures that its assessments are in line with the South African constitution.

An unsupervised approach that identifies topics that are potentially *controversial/contentious* or *risk topics*, and that leaves the final evaluation of veracity to human experts in the field, is therefore a much more attractive option for dealing with misinformation in a holistic and sustainable manner. Topic modelling is an unsupervised text mining technique that extracts salient themes or topics from large corpora of text and has been applied in a variety of COVID-19 social media studies. In their South African study, [15] apply the latent Dirichlet allocation (LDA) topic modelling algorithm to a corpus of COVID-19 Tweets and identify 9 broad topics, two of which are related to misinformation narratives. These studies are not focused on misinformation, however, and so the opportunity to study misinformation on South African social media in more depth remains. Furthermore, LDA was proposed nearly 20 years ago, in 2003; the state of the art for NLP has advanced drastically since then and many alternative, advanced topic modelling techniques have been developed accordingly.

Word embedding models have played an especially important role in advancing NLP. These models are pre-trained on large corpora of text and convert words into numerical representations (embeddings) that capture the semantic meaning of the words. Earlier models simply return the same embedding for a word regardless of its context, but more recent contextualised embedding models (such as the famous BERT model [5]) are now able to adjust a word's embeddings based on the context it is used in, thus more accurately capturing its semantic meaning.

BERTopic [7], a novel topic modelling technique, makes use of a combination of pre-trained embeddings, dimensionality reduction, clustering and term importance scores for words to generate useful and accurate topic representations. The technique is modular and therefore extremely flexible and simple to implement. Fig. 1 shows the standard configuration of the BERTopic algorithm, which utilizes sentence transformers [18] (for creating embeddings), uniform manifold approximation and projection [13] (UMAP, for dimensionality reduction), hierarchical density-based spatial clustering of applications with noise [2,3] (HDBSCAN, for clustering), CountVectorizer [17] (for creating bag-of-words representations) and class-based term frequency inverse document frequency [7] (c-TF-IDF, for creating topic representations). BERTopic's modular nature allows for easy experimentation and supports a number of variations of topic modelling.

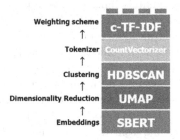

**Fig. 1.** The default configuration of the BERTopic topic modelling algorithm, as illustrated by [8]

## 3   Method

This section describes the method followed to apply the BERTopic topic modelling technique to a corpus of South African Tweets about COVID-19. Section 3.1 describes the data collection and pre-processing steps followed to collect the relevant Tweets. Section 3.2 describes the modelling process in terms of each component of the topic model, including hyperparameter optimization. Section 3.4 presents additional experiments with regards to fine-grained topic models conducted based on observations made from the results in Sect. 3.2.

## 3.1 Data Collection and Pre-processing

The Twitter dataset contains 143 228 Tweets about COVID-19 that were posted in South Africa from 1 March 2020 to 30 April 2020. The Tweets were collected from the Twitter API using a combination of search parameters. The collected Tweets (1) contain either one of the keywords "covid", "coronavirus", "covid-19", "pandemic", or the Tweet context annotation "COVID-19", and (2) are geo-tagged with the "ZA" place country tag. The "ZA" tag ensures that only Tweets posted from locations within South Africa, and presumably Tweets by South Africans, are returned. Not all Tweets necessarily have location data, but the "ZA" place country tag is the only way to filter Tweets by location, since sensitive user profile information (such as country of residence) is kept private. The corpus of Tweets was pre-processed before being passed to the BERTopic model. Duplicate Tweets, user mentions, hyperlinks, emojis, and Tweets with two or less words were all removed. Tweets referencing videos or images were also removed, since they either contain no text at all, or contain text that references the videos or images. The cleaned text is then passed to the "all-MiniLML6-v2" pre-trained sentence transformer, which converts each Tweet's text to a 384-dimensional embedding.

## 3.2 Modeling

The embedded Tweets are then passed to the BERTopic model. First UMAP reduces the dimensionality of each embedding from 384 to five, and these reduced embeddings are then passed to the clustering algorithm, HDBSCAN. The topic representations are then calculated from the clusters of documents output by HDBSCAN.

The BERTopic algorithm, as described in Sect. 2, has a number of parameters that influence its performance and the manner in which topics are formed and represented. A brief description of each parameter and the value selected for it follows. $top\_n\_words$ refers to the number of terms that are extracted to represent each topic. This value was set to ten, as is best practice in topic modelling. The higher this number, the less coherent topic representations tend to become. $n\_components$ refers to the number of dimensions that UMAP must reduce the text embeddings to. This value is set to five. $n\_gram\_range$ is the range that the number of words which can count as a single term can fall within. Extending the range beyond one allows for phrases like "Cape Town" or "President Ramaphosa" to be represented as a single term in the corpus, while also preserving the individual words that make up the phrases. The wider the range, the more computationally expensive modelling becomes. This value is set to a minimum of one and a maximum of two. $umap\_metric$ refers to the distance metric used to calculate the similarity between embeddings. The cosine distance metric was selected, since it is known to perform well with high dimensional data, such as the 384-dimensional embeddings output by the sentence transformer model. *hdbscan_metric* refers to the distance metric used to calculate similarity between the reduced embeddings output by UMAP, i.e. the distance metric to be used for clustering. The Euclidean distance metric was selected, since it is computationally efficient when working with lower dimensional data.

In addition to the fixed parameter values, the values of two additional parameters, *nn* and *mts*, were determined by evaluating the performance of the models for different combinations of values for these two parameters. The first of these, *nn*, refers to the number of neighbouring points that UMAP takes into account when approximating the manifold. The smaller this number, the more local structure is preserved; the larger the number, the more global structure is preserved. The second parameter, *mts*, simply refers to the minimum number of data points that may constitute a cluster.

Coherence is most often the metric of choice when evaluating and comparing the performance of topic models. The BERTopic modelling process is stochastic, and, therefore, produces a slightly different output every time it is run, even if all parameters are fixed. Therefore, a set of 30 models was trained for each combination of *nn* and *mts* values, and the average performance score for each set calculated. The metric used to assess the performance and topic representation of trained topic models is the UMass coherence score. Table 1 shows the different combinations of the two parameters tested, while Fig. 2 shows the average UMass coherence score obtained for each combination of values.

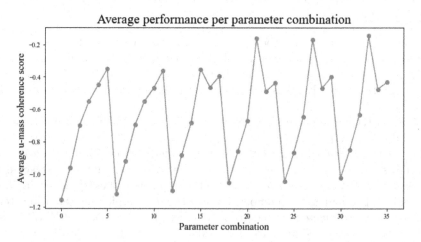

**Fig. 2.** The average UMass coherence score obtained for different combinations of *n_neigbours* and *mts*

To determine which combinations of values produced *statistically significant* increases in performance over other values, the Mann Whitney U-test, a non-parametric test for independent samples, was used. Each set of models was compared to every other set (with the Mann Whitney U-test) and the number of *wins, losses* and *draws* were recorded for each sample. A win is recorded if a sample distribution is statistically different from and has a higher mean coherence than another sample, a loss is recorded if a sample is statistically different from and has a lower mean coherence than another sample, and a draw is recorded if there is no statistically significant difference between the samples. The results of each set of Mann Whitney U-tests are shown in Table 1. The results for combinations 22, 28, and 34 are ignored, since these values produce models with only three topics that do not present any meaningful insights. Combination 6, with 31 wins, 3 losses, and 1 draw, thus provides the best performance. Consequently, the final model was trained with the values of 50 for $nn$ and 500 for $mts$, as described in Sect. 3.3.

**Table 1.** The number of wins, draws and losses obtained for each combination of $nn$ and $mts$

| Combination (nn, mts) | Wins | Draws | Losses | Combination (nn, mts) | Wins | Draws | Losses |
|---|---|---|---|---|---|---|---|
| 1 (50, 50) | 0 | 0 | 35 | 19 (300, 50) | 3 | 1 | 31 |
| 2 (50, 100) | 6 | 0 | 29 | 20 (300, 100) | 9 | 2 | 24 |
| 3 (50, 200) | 12 | 1 | 22 | 21 (300, 200) | 15 | 2 | 18 |
| 4 (50, 300) | 18 | 1 | 16 | 22 (300, 300) | 33 | 2 | 0 |
| 5 (50, 400) | 23 | 4 | 8 | 23 (300, 400) | 20 | 5 | 10 |
| 6 (50, 500) | 31 | 1 | 3 | 24 (300, 500) | 26 | 2 | 7 |
| 7 (100, 50) | 1 | 0 | 34 | 25 (400, 50) | 3 | 1 | 31 |
| 8 (100, 100) | 7 | 0 | 28 | 26 (400, 100) | 9 | 2 | 24 |
| 9 (100, 200) | 12 | 2 | 21 | 27 (400, 200) | 14 | 3 | 18 |
| 10 (100, 300) | 18 | 1 | 16 | 28 (400, 300) | 33 | 1 | 1 |
| 11 (100, 400) | 21 | 5 | 9 | 29 (400, 400) | 20 | 5 | 10 |
| 12 (100, 500) | 30 | 1 | 4 | 30 (400, 500) | 28 | 2 | 5 |
| 13 (200, 50) | 2 | 0 | 33 | 31 (500, 50) | 5 | 0 | 30 |
| 14 (200, 100) | 8 | 0 | 27 | 32 (500, 100) | 9 | 2 | 24 |
| 15 (200, 200) | 13 | 3 | 19 | 33 (500, 200) | 14 | 3 | 18 |
| 16 (200, 300) | 20 | 12 | 3 | 34 (500, 300) | 34 | 1 | 0 |
| 17 (200, 400) | 21 | 5 | 9 | 35 (500, 400) | 20 | 3 | 12 |
| 18 (200, 500) | 28 | 2 | 5 | 36 (500, 500) | 25 | 3 | 7 |

## 3.3   Final Model Training

The final model was trained with the best performing parameters identified previously, and produced 34 topics and attained a UMass coherence score of -0.39. In addition to the 34 topics generated, an additional group of outlier documents (labelled as -1) was produced. These outliers are not assigned to any topic and correspond to 'junk topics' often generated by other kinds of topic models. There are two approaches for addressing the outliers generated by the model, which are: (1) to ignore the outliers in the analysis of results (this approach is recommended by the authors of BERTopic and HDBSCAN); (2) to pass outliers to the model and assign them to the most similar clusters based on a set threshold. In this study, the first approach was followed and the outliers were not considered in the analysis of the model's output.

### 3.4 Additional Experiments

An additional experiment was performed in addition to the one described in Sect. 3.2. A fine-grained model with a larger number of topics (and thus smaller topics) was trained to test if it would better separate and isolate potential misinformation topics from general topics. The model was trained with a *mts* of 100 and *nn* of 50 and produced 157 topics, attaining a UMass coherence score of $-1.04$.

## 4  Discussion

The topics produced by the final model (described in Sect. 3.3) were inspected and labeled, as shown in Tables 2 and 3. Topics were labeled according to their top ten representative terms, as well as sample Tweets belonging to each topic. Out of the 34 identified topics, three could be directly linked to COVID-19 misinformation. These are topics 15, 20, and 23, whose word clouds are shown in Fig. 3. A number of COVID-19 rumours were identified by inspecting each of these topics' Tweets, hashtags, mentions, entities, and other related metadata.

The three identified misinformation topics are 15 (China), 20 (News and leadership), and 23 (Ethnicity).

The first official cases of COVID-19 were identified in China and a number of theories regarding the origin of the virus are also associated with China. As seen in Table 4, one theory is that the virus was manufactured and is a form of biological warfare. Donald Trump famously called COVID-19 the 'Chinese virus', and this is a term that evidently has spread to South African social media as well, evidenced by the hashtags found in the topic. Interestingly, a link between 5G mobile technology, China, and COVID-19 is also found in this topic, as illustrated by Tweets 1 and 2 in Table 4. A sense of mistrust towards China and the World Health Organization's (WHO) reported number of COVID-19 infections and deaths is also reflected in the Tweets. Additionally, calls for boycotting Chinese products and businesses are also present.

Although topic 20 does address fake news, it is (in most cases) difficult to tell what the fake news is about from only the Tweet text, since many Tweets are comments on URL links contained within the Tweets, which were removed when training the model. Inspecting the URL links contained in these texts does, however, trace the comments to other Tweets or websites that contain the alleged fake news. Examples of these original Tweets are shown in Table 5.

One rumour identified in topic 23 is that Africans are immune to COVID-19, as shown by example Tweets in Table 6.

**Table 2.** The number of Tweets and top ten terms for topics 0–17

| Topic | Label | Count | Top ten terms |
|---|---|---|---|
| 0 | Working from home | 11201 | home, working home, working, work, work home, data, stay, stay home, know, time |
| 1 | Lockdown 1 | 8819 | lockdown, lockdown, ke, le, day, end, extended, ka, day lockdown, going |
| 2 | Business responses | 6280 | cases, coronavirus, confirmed, covid_19sa, deaths, covid19southafrica, covid19insa, fund, world, relief |
| 3 | Quarantine | 4898 | quarantine, quarantined, self, self quarantine, quarantine quarantine, day, day quarantine, chill, quarantine chill, stream |
| 4 | South Africa | 3950 | south, africa, south africa, cape, africans, south africans, western, african, cases, lockdown |
| 5 | Corona | 3780 | corona, corona corona, time, le, know, time corona, going, ke, want, le corona |
| 6 | Coronavirus | 2635 | virus, corona virus, corona, coronavirus, coronavirussa, coronavirusinsa, infected, coronavirusoutbreak, immune, cure |
| 7 | Entertainment | 2491 | lockdown, music, party, lockdownhouseparty, togetherathome, dj, house party, house, lockdown house |
| 8 | Sanitary measures | 2198 | hands, wash, masks, wash hands, mask, sanitizer, water, hand, hand sanitizer, gloves |
| 9 | Food & groceries | 2161 | food, lockdown, chicken, cook, bread, eat, eating, buy, cooking, weight |
| 10 | Addresses | 2012 | lockdownsa, cyrilramaphosa, lockdownsouthafrica, covid19southafrica, coronavirusinsa, covid_19sa, lockdown, covid19sa, covid19insa, shutdownsouthafrica |
| 11 | Alcohol ban | 1657 | alcohol, liquor, wine, lockdown, drink, drinking, alcohol lockdown, bottle, ban, stores |
| 12 | Religion | 1656 | god, church, pray, jesus, lord, prayer, churches, amen, prayers, pastors |
| 13 | Global situation | 1550 | pandemic, global pandemic, pandemic pandemic, global, world, time, country, going, need, middle |
| 14 | Education | 1492 | school, schools, students, teachers, education, kids, grade, learners, learning, parents |
| 15 | China | 1446 | china, chinese, chinese virus, virus, wuhan, coronavirus, world, trump, corona, korea |
| 16 | Social distancing | 1275 | distancing, social distancing, social, distancing social, practice, practice social, practicing social, practicing, isolation, socialdistancing |
| 17 | COVID-19 testing | 1207 | tested, test, testing, positive, tested positive, tests, kits, results, symptoms, screening |

The analysis of topics and related Tweets reveals both the strengths and weaknesses of the unsupervised topic modelling approach. It is evident from the analysis that information disorder is present on South African Twitter. The topics output by the model make sense within the context of the pandemic and correspond with key issues faced by South Africans as identified by other studies, such as the cigarette and alcohol bans [6,12]. In particular, topics identified

**Table 3.** The number of Tweets and top ten terms for topics 18–33

| Topic | Label | Count | Top ten terms |
|---|---|---|---|
| 18 | Sports | 962 | league, football, liverpool, sports, cancelled, players, coronavirus, psl, cancel, season |
| 19 | Economic repercussions | 953 | lockdown, pay, money, paid, economy, work, salaries, rent, leave, income |
| 20 | News and leadership | 879 | news, fake news, fake, leadership, president, mr president, spreading fake, leader, mr, good news |
| 21 | Italy | 877 | italy, spain, italian, italians, deaths, coronavirus, france, usa, 10, friends |
| 22 | President Ramaphosa | 861 | ramaphosa, cyril ramaphosa, president, cyril, president cyril, president ramaphosa, address, nation, coronavirussa, address nation |
| 23 | Ethnicity | 830 | black, white, blacks, race, whites, racist, virus, black person, corona, racism |
| 24 | Exercise | 816 | gym, dogs, dog, workout, exercise, walk, lockdown, jogging, day, walking |
| 25 | Lockdown 2 | 780 | 21, days, 21 days, lockdown, days lockdown, extended, lockdown 21, weeks, lockdown extended, months |
| 26 | Law enforcement & crime | 742 | police, arrested, arrest, lockdown, crime, criminals, law, jail, soldiers, regulations |
| 27 | Twitter | 655 | tweet, twitter, tweets, social media, lockdown, media, tweeting, tl, retweet, social |
| 28 | Cigarette ban | 621 | cigarettes, smoking, cigarette, smoke, smokers, ban, tobacco, lungs, sale, alcohol |
| 29 | Birthdays | 586 | birthday, happy birthday, happy, lockdown birthday, lockdown, birthday lockdown, lockdown happy, hope, day, enjoy |
| 30 | Personal care | 512 | hair, lockdown, nails, barber, haircut, beard, makeup, hair lockdown, skin |
| 31 | Relationships | 509 | lockdown, relationships, relationship, sex, married, partner, love, dating, lockdown lockdown |
| 32 | Lockdown 3 | 506 | cyrilramaphosa, cyril, lockdown, bayithemovie, cyrilramaphosa lockdown, extended, bayithemovie bayithemovie, lockdown cyrilramaphosa |
| 33 | COVID-19 statistics | 505 | numbers, 100, number, stats, million, brand, 1000, increasing, gathering, scary |

also correspond with specific topics identified by topic models applied in other studies [15]. The BERTopic model also identified topics that contain examples of information disorder, that were not identified in the studies mentioned earlier, namely topics 15 (China), 20 (News and leadership), and 23 (Ethnicity).

The nature of topic modelling, however, makes it difficult to distinguish within a topic between information disorder and general information, opinions, and questions on the level of individual Tweets. That is, the granularity of the model in Sect. 3.4 means that Tweets in a topic, if it indeed includes information disorder, will likely be a mixture of both information disorder Tweets and general

(a) Word cloud for topic 15          (b) Word cloud for topic 20

(c) Word cloud for topic 23

**Fig. 3.** Word clouds for misinformation topics

**Table 4.** Examples of Tweets in topic 15

| | Tweet |
|---|---|
| 1 | Remember those trade bans USA had on China last year? The war for 5G could be linked to Covid19 |
| 2 | @eugenegu @realDonaldTrump This coronavirus is a hoax just to give China a boost!!-Just look at their stock market, the last 7 https://t.co/6zOtUmP8l9 not forget 5G... |
| 3 | You may hate on @realDonaldTrump... and say He is racist, But the truth of the matter is This #COVID-19 is being called wrong it should Be called The #ChineseVirus. |
| 4 | I wonder if the UN is going to take action against China fir their creation of the COVID-19. The WHO must also institute charges on China. #UnitedNations #StopCovid19 #ChinaMustPay |

Tweets. These results are conceivably still more useful than a classifier that only distinguishes between information disorder Tweets and general Tweets, such as those trained in [19], since information disorder is better described and positioned in relation to other topics and types of information. In this respect, the model proves useful in analysis and determining the overall consensus towards a topic and an appropriate response (or non-response) to the dialogue/information present on Twitter.

To a certain extent, the complexity of information disorder is reflected in this occurrence. A more fine-grained approach, i.e. a topic model with more

**Table 5.** Examples of Tweets in topic 20

| | Tweet |
|---|---|
| 1 | Isn't this #FakeNews in violation of the regulations? Hello @SAPoliceService https://t.co/2fDNwF8LBN |
| 2 | How come some people want to feed us with #FakeNews ? https://t.co/qdDNvONTrB |
| 3 | FAKE NEWS ALERT \| WhatsApp voicenote 'was not from me' - Groote Schuur virologist How do we know anything on News24 is not fake news? Who do you believe? https://t.co/1Y4taH5HA2? Shared via @Health24com |
| 4 | News24 always with the sensational journalism https://t.co/MuJcUuaCuj |

**Table 6.** Examples of Tweets in topic 23

| | Tweet |
|---|---|
| 1 | And know that they will not show themselves when they are on the receiving end of things, CoronaVirus is a neumonia like virus attacking the lungs, But it can't do so kuBlack Man! #MelaninOurProtectorAgainstCovid19 That's why they say we have 65 cases, and not say what race is it |
| 2 | News is our black skin is resistant to Corona Virus, meaning we as black people are immune to this disease. I have never heard of black person having corona. I hope it's true |
| 3 | Is there any black person infected with Corona Virus yet ? Because I'm starting to think this virus is for white people only like they said back then HIV is for black people. |
| 4 | Idrise Elba is lying. White people begged him to say this nonsense so that it seem that blacks suffer as much as whites from corona. Blacks don't suffer much from corona. |

(and smaller) topics that better subdivides the larger topics identified in Sect. 4, could perform better. These smaller topics would be more representative of the specific narratives and language patterns that are often hallmarks/characteristic of information disorder and could possibly allow for identifying more uniform and 'pure' information topics. The coherence score utilised earlier may not be optimal in such an instance, but what is optimal depends on the context of the problem. Here the results suggest that the context requires another way of measuring performance. The coherence measure may be useful for more traditional uses of topic modelling (i.e. summarising and categorising texts) but may not be ideal for fine-grained analysis if misinformation is anomalous (some niche rumours may be different than mainstream widely spread rumours).

To explore this assumption, the results obtained from the fine-grained topic model with a *mts* of 100 (as described in Sect. 3.4) were inspected. The fine-grained model produced 157 topics, the largest comprising 4 507 Tweets, and the smallest comprising 100 Tweets. Potential mis-/disinformation topics identified from the fine-grained model output are shown in Table 7. It is important to note that the parameters of this model were not optimised and only serve to illustrate the potential benefit of utilising a more fine-grained topic model specifically for characterising information disorder. The model does particularly well in splitting the larger topics from the model in Sect. 3.3 into smaller coherent themes, and evidently also identifies smaller niche rumours, as expected. Topic 97, for example, contains Tweets that discuss the similarities between films about pandemics and the coronavirus pandemic, and many view the 2011 thriller film, *Contagion*, as a prediction of the COVID-19 pandemic. Topic 114 is specifically focused on rumours about 5G causing COVID-19, and topic 121 is specifically focused on the discussion about the virus's effects on different population groups. Conspiracies related to Bill Gates and his alleged involvement in vaccine development are represented in topic 122. Other conspiracies related to vaccines are found in topic 117.

**Table 7.** The number of Tweets and top ten terms for each topic

| Topic | Count | Top ten terms |
|---|---|---|
| 9 | 1463 | china, chinese, chinese virus, virus, wuhan, coronavirus, world, trump, korea, virus china |
| 12 | 1351 | corona virus, virus, corona, coronavirus, virus corona, coronavirus corona, virus coronavirus, cure, symptoms, like |
| 26 | 606 | virus, infected, immune, infect, people, virus virus, spreading, spread, infection, spread virus |
| 62 | 297 | fake news, fake, news, spreading fake, spreading, media, news24, arrested, news fake, stop spreading |
| 81 | 246 | whatsapp, whatsapp group, group, whatsapp groups, messages, groups, whatsapp number, 060, 3456, 012 3456 |
| 84 | 235 | cuba, cuban, doctors, cuban doctors, cubans, cubandoctors, vaccine, fidel, medical, castro |
| 86 | 220 | flu, covid, covid 19, 19, symptoms, cure, immune, cure covid, disease, flu covid |
| 88 | 212 | vaccine, vaccines, lupus, 19 vaccine, trials, vaccine vaccine, covid, covid 19, 19, patients |
| 89 | 209 | led, ignorance, shame, stupidity, stupid, idiot, ignorance bliss, bliss, dumb, ignorant |
| 97 | 194 | movie, contagion, movie contagion, contagion movie, 2011, watch, sabc, watching, watch movie, watched |
| 114 | 158 | 5g, 5g towers, radiation, towers, conspiracy, 5g corona, technology, 5g coronavirus, 5g technology, causes |
| 117 | 152 | ebola, vaccine, vaccines, french, africa, french doctors, tested, africans, test, tested africa |
| 121 | 147 | black, black people, white, white people, blacks, black person, virus, people, corona virus, corona |
| 122 | 146 | gates, vaccine, potential coronavirus, coronavirus vaccine, confident potential, gates confident, vaccines, work africa, africa, vaccine work |
| 134 | 127 | lies, lie, lying, facts, lies lies, lies detected, lied, detected, liar, spreading lies |

# 5   Conclusion

In this study, a topic model, BERTopic, was applied to a corpus of unlabelled South African Tweets about COVID-19. The topics produced by the final model were able to reveal information disorder on South African Tweets. Three topics could be directly linked to information disorder related to origin theories linking China to the creation of the virus (topic 15), the effect of the virus on specific population groups (topic 23), and general discussions about COVID-19 fake news (topic 20). An additional fine-grained model was also trained (without hyperparameter optimization) to test if it would better isolate misinformation topics.

There is still much potential for expanding and refining the topic modelling approach to characterizing misinformation on South African social media. As discussed in Sect. 4, coherence may not be the optimal metric to evaluate the performance of a topic model for characterizing misinformation. Other metrics, such as topic diversity and topic significance, will be utilized in future work.

The Tweets identified as belonging to potential misinformation topics may be used as a starting point for curating labelled COVID-19 misinformation datasets specifically for South African Twitter, and could aid in future research studies that wish to use these datasets for supervised learning. As noted in Sect. 2, the changing and complex nature of health related information must be kept in mind when curating these kinds of datasets.

Additionally, a classification model trained to classify Tweets according to the topics identified by the topic modelling approach may be trained, as well as a stance classifier which can classify whether a Tweet supports, denies, or is neutral towards a specific issue or topic.

An important area for future research is that of dynamic topic modelling (DTM), which models the evolution of topics over time. Some rumours and misinformation seem to spread rapidly, others build up more slowly, and some only surface at specific intervals in time. The temporal aspect of misinformation dissemination has largely been ignored in NLP approaches and therefore needs further attention.

The pre-trained sentence transformer model used to create embeddings was trained on English data only. While the topic model is able to identify salient topics related to misinformation, multilingual Tweets containing primarily non-English words may likely have been labelled as outliers. A more in-depth analysis of the outliers is thus necessary to confirm this supposition. Future work therefore aims to address the multilingual nature of the data by investigating methods for working with low-resource languages, such as isiXhosa, in the South African data.

**Acknowledgements.** This work is based on the research supported in part by the National Research Foundation of South Africa (Grant number: 129340).

# References

1. Abdelminaam, D.S., Ismail, F.H., Taha, M., Taha, A., Houssein, E.H., Nabil, A.: CoAID-DEEP: an optimized intelligent framework for automated detecting COVID-19 misleading information on twitter. IEEE ACCESS **9** (2021). https://doi.org/10.1109/ACCESS.2021.3058066
2. Campello, R.J.G.B., Moulavi, D., Sander, J.: Density-based clustering based on hierarchical density estimates. In: Pei, J., Tseng, V.S., Cao, L., Motoda, H., Xu, G. (eds.) PAKDD 2013. LNCS (LNAI), vol. 7819, pp. 160–172. Springer, Heidelberg (2013). https://doi.org/10.1007/978-3-642-37456-2_14
3. Campello, R.J., Moulavi, D., Zimek, A., Sander, J.: Hierarchical density estimates for data clustering, visualization, and outlier detection. ACM Trans. Knowl. Discovery Data (TKDD) **10**(1), 1–51 (2015)
4. Cui, L., Lee, D.: CoAID: COVID-19 healthcare misinformation dataset. Comput. Res. Repository (2020)
5. Devlin, J., Chang, M.W., Lee, K., Toutanova, K.: BERT: pre-training of deep bidirectional transformers for language understanding. In: Proceedings of the 2019 Conference of the North American Chapter of the Association for Computational Linguistics: Human Language Technologies, vol. 1, pp. 4171–4186 (2019)
6. Filby, S., van der Zee, K., van Walbeek, C.: The temporary ban on tobacco sales in south Africa: lessons for endgame strategies. Tob. Control (2021)
7. Grootendorst, M.: BERTopic: neural topic modeling with a class-based TF-IDF procedure. arXiv preprint: arXiv:2203.05794 (2022)
8. Grootendorst, M.: BERTopic algorithm (2023). https://maartengr.github.io/BERTopic/algorithm/algorithm.html. Accessed 20 Oct 2021
9. Hayawi, K., Shahriar, S., Serhani, M., Taleb, I., Mathew, S.: ANTi-Vax: a novel twitter dataset for COVID-19 vaccine misinformation detection. Publ. Health **203**, 23–30 (2022)
10. Kaliyar, R.K., Goswami, A., Narang, P.: A hybrid model for effective fake news detection with a novel COVID-19 dataset. In: ICAART (2), pp. 1066–1072 (2021)
11. Kemp, S.: Digital 2022: South Africa (2022). https://datareportal.com/reports/digital-2022-south-africa. Accessed 30 Aug 2022
12. Matzopoulos, R., Walls, H., Cook, S., London, L.: South Africa's COVID-19 alcohol sales ban: the potential for better policy-making. Int. J. Health Policy Manag. **9**(11), 486 (2020)
13. McInnes, L., Healy, J., Melville, J.: UMAP: uniform manifold approximation and projection for dimension reduction. arXiv preprint: arXiv:1802.03426 (2018)
14. Memon, S.A., Carley, K.M.: Characterizing COVID-19 misinformation communities using a novel twitter dataset. Comput. Res. Repository (2020)
15. Mutanga, M.B., Abayomi, A.: Tweeting on COVID-19 pandemic in south Africa: LDA-based topic modelling approach. Afr. J. Sci. Technol. Innov. Dev. **12**, 1–10 (2020)
16. Patwa, P., et al.: Fighting an infodemic: COVID-19 fake news dataset. In: Chakraborty, T., Shu, K., Bernard, H.R., Liu, H., Akhtar, M.S. (eds.) CONSTRAINT 2021. CCIS, vol. 1402, pp. 21–29. Springer, Cham (2021). https://doi.org/10.1007/978-3-030-73696-5_3
17. Pedregosa, F., et al.: Scikit-learn: machine learning in Python. J. Mach. Learn. Res. **12**, 2825–2830 (2011)

18. Reimers, N., Gurevych, I.: Sentence-BERT: sentence embeddings using Siamese BERT-networks. In: Proceedings of the 2019 Conference on Empirical Methods in Natural Language Processing and the 9th International Joint Conference on Natural Language Processing (EMNLP-IJCNLP), pp. 3982–3992. Association for Computational Linguistics, Hong Kong, November 2019. https://doi.org/10.18653/v1/D19-1410, https://aclanthology.org/D19-1410
19. Strydom, I.F., Grobler, J.: Transformers for COVID-19 misinformation detection on twitter: a south African case study. In: Giuseppe, N., et al. (eds.) Machine Learning, Optimization, and Data Science: 7th International Conference (LOD 2022), pp. 197–210. Springer, Cham (2022). https://doi.org/10.1007/978-3-031-25599-1_15

# Investigating the Use of Topic Modeling for Social Media Market Research: A South African Case Study

Irene Francesca Strydom[✉][iD], Jacomine Grobler[iD], and Euodia Vermeulen[iD]

Department of Industrial Engineering, Stellenbosch University, Stellenbosch,
Western Cape, South Africa
`strydomfrancesca@gmail.com, jacomine.grobler@gmail.com, euodia@sun.ac.za`
`https://ie.sun.ac.za/`

**Abstract.** Businesses are increasingly investigating the use of data science and machine learning techniques for market research. This paper investigates the use of topic modeling as a tool for social media market research, specifically the influence and impact of this technology within market research practice. As an example of the use of topic modeling, three different topic modeling algorithms are applied to a single dataset extracted from Reddit, and their performance compared. The latent Dirichlet allocation (LDA) algorithm was trained as a baseline and compared to the Correlated topic model (CTM) and the Gibbs sampling for Dirichlet multinomial mixtures (GSDMM) model. The CTM outperformed the LDA model, while the GSDMM was unable to improve on the baseline. The 25 topics produced by the final CTM were investigated in greater detail and interpreted within the context of market research. Although five of these topics did not prove useful, the remaining topics were easily interpreted and divided into six categories related to (1) features, (2) software, (3) acquisition, (4) workouts, (5) physical design, and (6) physiological monitoring. Each category's topics were able to provide valuable insight regarding consumers' opinions about and experiences of the related product.

**Keywords:** Machine learning · Text mining · Topic modeling · Latent Dirichlet allocation · Correlated topic model · Dirichlet multinomial mixture · Market research · Social media

## 1 Introduction

Market research is one of the core competencies of most successful businesses today, and the advent of the internet and social media has provided businesses with near limitless sources of data about consumers' habits, opinions and needs. As such, the modern business must leverage this data effectively to differentiate itself and maintain a competitive advantage. Literature reveals that businesses are increasingly investigating the use of data science and

© The Author(s), under exclusive license to Springer Nature Switzerland AG 2023
O. Gervasi et al. (Eds.): ICCSA 2023, LNCS 13957, pp. 305–320, 2023.
https://doi.org/10.1007/978-3-031-36808-0_20

machine learning techniques for market research [9], since traditional market research methods are becoming less effective. These traditional methods suffer from dwindling response rates, are costly and do not necessarily gather input from large audiences [13]. Traditional methods also commonly follow an 'asking' approach, where all initiative is taken by the market researcher. In contrast, social media provides an excellent opportunity for businesses to follow a 'listening' approach. The competitive nature of the booming fitness wearables industry makes a compelling case for businesses in this industry to also listen closely to what their customers are saying about their products on social media. A human movement analysis laboratory has therefore commissioned the research in this paper to determine whether the opinions and experiences of fitness wearable users could reveal potential business opportunities.

An abundance of machine learning techniques are used to analyse the data generated on social media, and these include text mining techniques like topic modeling [1,3]. Topic modeling has mainly been used for information retrieval and organising large corpora of unstructured text. The ease of access to public social media data, however, has led to an increased use of topic modeling to extract themes from social media datasets. The aims of this paper is to assess whether topic modeling is a feasible social media market research tool, what the influence and impact of this technique can be within market research practice, and to conduct a case study comparing the performance of three different topic models as applied to social media data extracted from Reddit.

This paper is significant, since to the best of the authors' knowledge, it is the first to compare the performance of the topic models latent Dirichlet allocation (LDA), the correlated topic model (CTM), and Gibbs sampling for Dirichlet multinomial mixtures (GSDMM) within the context of market research.

The rest of this paper is organised as follows: First an overview of market research and topic modeling is provided, after which data collection and data preparation, are described. Next, the experimental setup and how the algorithms compare are described. The results of the best performing topic modeling algorithm are then interpreted. The paper concludes with findings and recommendations for future work.

## 2    Relevant Literature

This section presents the literature relevant to the paper. A brief overview of the field of market research and the increased use of data science within this field is presented. The premise of topic modeling, the three topic modeling algorithms relevant to this paper, as well as the chosen method for evaluating the models in this paper are described thereafter.

### 2.1    Data Science and Market Research

The intersection of data science and market research provide unique opportunities for businesses to innovate and better understand their customers.

The ultimate goal of market research is to enable a business to gain and maintain a competitive advantage through understanding the customers' needs and then catering for those needs. The field of market research is relatively new compared to ancient business fields like transport or logistics, yet it has quickly become indispensable to many corporate businesses around the world. Market research has also changed drastically since its early days, largely owing to the huge amounts of data that researchers now have access to [12]. For the most part, market research relies heavily on quantitative studies, since the data is usually structured and therefore more easily processed and analysed in large volumes [10]. [4], however, explained that customers often have more intricate and nuanced views that cannot be captured by structured data. They use the example of a numerical service rating scale for a hotel's services. If a customer finds room service excellent, but cleaning services terrible, how would they rate their experience? Different customers would give different ratings, but none of these ratings would accurately describe their experience. Bendle and Wang further noted: "By summarizing complex thoughts in a single number, the reasons that informed the choice are lost". A solution might be to add a comment box, in which a customer might express exactly what they feel about each element of their experience. This simple example illustrates the more nuanced nature of qualitative data and how it can provide more insightful and actionable information to a business. The added benefit of conducting research with qualitative *social media* data is that the data is produced without any encouragement from some corporate entity and so provides a unique opportunity to access consumers' genuine and unfiltered opinions. Data mining from social media, therefore, mimics observational studies, which makes it possible to draw out potential associations between the attributes of products and the behaviour of customers. Traditional qualitative studies, however, demand large amounts of time and resources, since nearly every response requires a human to interpret the content [10]. As such, these studies are costly and according to [10], mostly drive quantitative studies or are only used in specific cases. Topic modeling, however, is a method to analyse unstructured, qualitative data on the same scale as structured, quantitative data.

## 2.2 Topic Modeling

Topic modeling is a text mining technique that is used to identify the latent semantic structure of a corpus, in the form of coherent themes or topics [6]. The assumption is generally that a topic consists of a probability distribution over words or terms, and that each document consists of a probability distribution over topics. Topic models can be classified as unsupervised, supervised, or semi-supervised. This paper focuses solely on three unsupervised topic models. These models are all probabilistic generative models, since they assume that the documents in the training corpus were generated by some probabilistic procedure defined by specific parameters. A topic model aims to infer the set of parameters that best explains the observed terms in documents. Any additional information or assumptions that the analyst has about the corpus is incorporated into the model through priors, which influence the characteristics of the generative process. Software implementations of topic modeling train the models with a variety of learning algorithms, including collapsed Gibbs samplers and variational inference [2]. These learning algorithms estimate the parameters of the model, since calculating them precisely is intractable.

The topic models considered here are referred to as *bag-of-words* (BOW) models, since only the frequency, and not order, of words in documents are taken into account. In the context of social media, a document could refer to a post, comment or thread. Each document consists of a number of *tokens*, and each token could be assigned a single word, part of a word or multiple words, each referred to as a *term*. The number of unique terms (after pre-processing) is called the vocabulary.

**Latent Dirichlet Allocation.** LDA, proposed by [6] in 2003, is widely used and considered in literature to be a reliable industry standard for topic modeling. LDA is a probabilistic generative model of a corpus of documents. The assumption is that a document is a multinomial distribution over topics and a topic is a multinomial distribution over terms. In LDA each of these distributions is drawn from a separate Dirichlet distribution $\mathcal{D}$, parameterized by $\boldsymbol{\alpha}$, for drawing the document-topic distributions $\boldsymbol{\theta}$, and $\boldsymbol{\beta}$, for drawing the topic-term distributions $\boldsymbol{\Phi}$. Both $\alpha$ and $\beta$ are concentration parameters that influence how many topics are present in a document or how many terms make up a topic. The LDA model assumes that the terms in each of the $M$ documents in the corpus are generated by the following process:

1. Sample the term probabilities $\boldsymbol{\Phi}_i \sim \mathcal{D}(\boldsymbol{\beta})$ for each topic $i$,
2. Sample the topic mixtures of the document $\boldsymbol{\theta}_d \sim \mathcal{D}(\alpha)$ for each document $d$,
3. Sample the topic assignment $z_{dn} \sim \mathcal{M}(\boldsymbol{\theta}_d)$ for each token $n$ in the document,
4. Sample a term $w_{dn} \sim \mathcal{M}(\boldsymbol{\Phi}_{z_{dn}})$ for each topic assignment $z_{dn}$.

**Correlated Topic Model.** CTM is, after LDA, the most widely used topic model and was also proposed by [5] in 2005. Oftentimes the presence of one topic is correlated with the presence of another topic. The underlying Dirichlet distribution used to model the topic mixtures in LDA, however, assumes that the components of these distribution vectors are independent, and therefore fails to directly model the correlations between different topics. To address this problem, CTM utilizes the more flexible logistic normal distribution to model topic proportions for each document. The logistic normal distribution assumes that each document topic distribution $\boldsymbol{\Phi}_i$ is normally distributed with a mean $\mu_i$. Correlations between the different topics are modeled through the covariance matrix $\boldsymbol{\Sigma}$ of the normal distribution. The CTM model assumes a generative process similar to that of LDA, except that the topic proportions for each document are drawn from a logistic normal distribution, rather than a Dirichlet distribution.

**Gibbs Sampling for Dirichlet Multinomial Mixtures.** Topic models were originally developed for and tested on longer documents such as journal and newspaper articles or Wikipedia pages. The increased interest in analysing social media data has led to the development of new topic models specifically catering to shorter documents, such as those found in social media. [14] conducted a comprehensive survey of short text topic modeling and clustering techniques, each belonging to one of three broad categories, namely: (1) Dirichlet multinomial mixture (DMM) based methods, (2) global term co-occurrence based methods, and (3) self-aggregation based methods. In this paper, the GSDMM algorithm [16] is considered. This algorithm first randomly assigns each document to one of $k$ clusters (hereon referred to as a topic) and then iteratively re-assigns each document in turn with two conditions: (1) the document must be assigned to a topic with more documents than its current topic, and (2) the document must be assigned to a topic where the documents contain similar words to the re-assigned document. If $k$ is large enough, some topics may disappear, while others grow larger. GSDMM can thus infer the optimal number of topics if $k$ is large enough. If $k$ is not large enough, no topics will be discarded. The GSDMM assumes a similar generative process to that of LDA, except that a document is assumed to be generated by a single topic, and not a mixture of topics as assumed by LDA and CTM.

**Evaluating Topic Models.** Probabilistic models are often evaluated by measuring the log-likelihood of a held-out test [1,7]. The model is trained with the largest part of the data forming the training set, and the rest of the data being held out to test how well the trained model fits this data. For an LDA model the test set is a selection of unseen documents $D$ and the log-likelihood $\mathcal{L}$ represents the probability of the unseen documents being generated given the learned topic and term distributions. A higher log-likelihood therefore implies a better fit. For topic models the perplexity $\mathcal{P}$ of $D$ is more often used as the indicator and is evaluated as:

$$\mathcal{P}(D) = exp(-\frac{\mathcal{L}(D)}{f}), \tag{1}$$

where $f$ is the number of tokens in the corpus, and a lower perplexity implies a better model.

The perplexity of a model may be a good indicator of how well a model fits unseen data, but it is often not correlated with how well a human can interpret the topics and their top terms [7,8], since it only measures the probability of observations and not the association of top terms with each other. If human interpretability of topics is important (as would be the case with market research), it is often more useful to determine the *coherence* of topics. The coherence of a topic refers to the semantic similarity of the top terms of the topic and provides a good way to distinguish between topics that are useful for humans and those that are only statistically the best fit for the data.

[8] devised the so called *word intrusion task* to assess the coherence of topics produced by a model through human evaluation. In this task, human subjects are

presented with a list of randomly ordered words, and the subject must identify the word that does not belong with the rest of the words, i.e. the intruder. When the list of words without the intruder fit together, the subjects should easily be able to identify the intruder, implying a topic of good coherence. If none of the words fit together, subjects will most likely choose an intruder randomly, implying a topic of poor coherence. Manually inspecting topics with the word intrusion task can easily become time-consuming, since some large corpora may produce more than 100 topics. Since the main advantage of topic modeling is the automated analysis of large corpora of text, it would not make much sense to again revert back to manual methods to evaluate the topics of a model for market research.

The need to automatically evaluate the coherence of topic models in a way that corresponds with the human interpretability of topics led to the development of so-called *coherence scores* [11]. These scores are calculated by measuring the association of different subsets of the top $n$ words of each topic. Each topic obtains a score, and the overall score is the averaged score of the topic scores. [15] investigated several existing topic coherence measures, and also proposed new measures by combining elements of existing measures. Some of these newly proposed measures - most notably the $C_v$ coherence measure - performed better than existing measures, and are now included in popular topic modeling packages such as *gensim* and *tomotopy*. As such, the $C_v$ coherence score is used to measure the performance of the models in this study.

## 3    Data Collection

For this paper, data were collected from a forum or community of Reddit users (called a *subreddit*) dedicated to the discussion of a popular brand of wearable fitness devices, hereon referred to as Brand Y. Brand Y's subreddit has more than 49 000 members, and a range of discussions take place daily on this subreddit. Consequently, this subreddit is a treasure trove of information about customers' opinions, experiences and expectations regarding Brand Y's products. A discussion, or thread, typically consist of a single post, which dictates the theme of the discussion, and a number of comments and subcomments made in reply to this post. A single thread could contain anything from a handful to hundreds of comments from any number of users. Posts and comments may contain text, images, videos, and web links. All threads on public subreddits can be accessed via the Reddit application programming interface (API), for which the only requirement is a Reddit account. Several packages in Python, R, and Java have also been developed to interface with the Reddit API, allowing greater ease of access to the data. A combination of *Pushift.io* (an API that interfaces with the Reddit API) and the *praw* package was used to extract the data. The final dataset contains 13 523 posts and 88 927 comments made on Brand Y's subreddit between 1 January 2017 and 1 January 2020.

# 4    Data Preparation

Before the topic models can be applied to the dataset, the data must first be pre-processed. The objectives of pre-processing are fourfold: (1) to ensure that the model receives input in the correct format, (2) to ensure that the model produces useful and high quality output, (3) to remove irrelevant information in order to speed up the training process, and (4), to address any data quality issues. The effect of each pre-processing step on the corpus and vocabulary size is shown in Table 1. First, each post was combined with all of its corresponding comments to form a thread, and all the threads represent the documents in the corpus. Next, tokenisation was performed, where each document was split into a list of single terms, called tokens. A single list of standard stopwords was then compiled by combining each of the *nltk*, *spacy*, and *gensim* packages' stopword lists. All the terms on this list were removed from the corpus. Even though the standard stopword list contained only 412 terms, it more than halved the size of the corpus (see Table 1). Next, during lemmatisation, each term was reduced to its most basic morphological unit, or lemma. The software used to perform this step uses a parts of speech (POS) tagger to determine what the lemma of a word should be. The word 'connected' for example, is tagged as an adjective and changed to the lemma 'connect', while the word 'connection' is tagged as a noun and the lemma remains 'connection'. Ideally, both words should be changed to the lemma 'connect'. To solve this problem, the POS tagger was disabled. It is noted, however, that a few terms were still not completely reduced to the correct lemma. Thereafter, a list of custom stopwords was compiled and these also removed from the corpus. Custom stopwords include terms that only appear once, terms unique to Reddit (such as 'subreddit' or 'upvote') and terms that carry little semantic meaning in the context, such as 'really' or 'hello'. Bigrams and trigrams were then identified with the *gensim* package and included as single terms in the documents. Examples of identified bigrams and trigrams are: 'battery_life', 'customer_support', and 'health_insurance_discount'. The last step is to convert the corpus into a format that can be fed into the topic model. An id is assigned to each term in the vocabulary and term frequencies in each document are indicated by id-frequency pairs for each document, e.g. the pair (1, 5) indicates that term one appears five times in the document.

# 5    Modeling

This section describes how the three topic modeling algorithms were applied to the data, and how their performance was evaluated. The LDA algorithm is the most widely used topic modeling algorithm in literature, and as such, was used to establish a baseline against which the CTM and GSDMM algorithms were compared.

**Table 1.** Pre-processing steps and their effect on the number of terms in the corpus and vocabulary.

| Pre-processing Step | Terms in Corpus | Terms in Vocabulary |
|---|---|---|
| Combining posts and comments | 3 976 985 | 31 766 |
| Tokenisation | 3 976 985 | 31 766 |
| Standard stopword removal | 1 804 221 | 31422 |
| Lemmatisation | 1 804 221 | 23 962 |
| Custom stopword removal | 1 414 956 | 7 334 |
| Collocation discovery | 1 356 137 | 8 785 |

The *gensim* package was used to train and optimise the LDA models. *Gensim* includes a feature that allows the LDA training algorithm to learn the optimal values of $\alpha$ and $\beta$ during training, and this feature was enabled to ensure the best results. Therefore, the only remaining hyperparameter that had to be optimized was $k$, which was done by conducting a structured statistical test. In the test, a number of models with values of $k$ set to different values between five and 65 were trained. Thirty models were trained for each value of $k$, and the average of the coherence scores for each set of 30 models was calculated. Each of these models were trained over 100 iterations. Figure 1 shows a plot of the average coherence scores. The average scores confirm that the value of $k$ has a significant effect on the performance measures: $k = 25$ and $k = 30$ have relatively high scores, while there is a decrease in scores for values of $k$ on both sides of the $k = 25$ to 30 interval.

To determine which values for $k$ produce *statistically significant* increases in performance over other values for $k$, the Mann Whitney U-test, a non-parametric test for independent samples, was used at the 5% significance level. Each sample (set of models with a set value for $k$) was compared to every other sample and the number of *wins, losses* and *draws* for each sample were recorded. A win is recorded if a sample distribution is statistically different from and has a higher mean coherence than another sample, a loss is recorded if a sample is statistically different from and has a lower mean coherence than another sample, and a draw is recorded if there is no statistically significant difference between the samples. The results of each set of Mann Whitney U-tests are shown in Tables 2 and 3, with $k = 30$ yielding the most wins (22), and $k = 25$ in second place with 21 wins.

**Table 2.** Results of the statistical procedure for $k = 5$ to $k = 20$

| k | 5 | 6 | 7 | 8 | 9 | 10 | 11 | 12 | 13 | 14 | 15 | 16 | 17 | 18 | 19 | 20 |
|---|---|---|---|---|---|---|---|---|---|---|---|---|---|---|---|---|
| Wins | 0 | 1 | 1 | 3 | 3 | 3 | 3 | 7 | 7 | 7 | 7 | 10 | 8 | 10 | 10 | 11 |
| Draws | 0 | 1 | 1 | 3 | 3 | 3 | 3 | 5 | 4 | 12 | 15 | 20 | 13 | 20 | 20 | 21 |
| Losses | 32 | 30 | 30 | 26 | 26 | 26 | 26 | 20 | 21 | 13 | 10 | 2 | 11 | 2 | 2 | 0 |

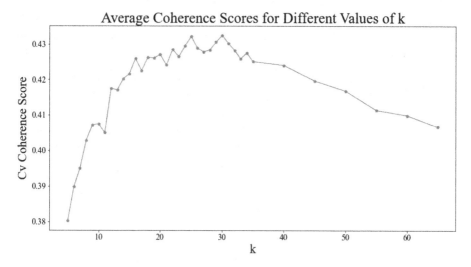

**Fig. 1.** The average $C_v$ coherence scores for each value of $k$. There is a steady increase in performance from $k = 5$ to $k = 25$. Two peaks at $k = 25$ and $k = 30$ are observed. After $k = 30$, the performance gradually decreases.

**Table 3.** Results of the statistical procedure for $k = 21$ to $k = 40$

| k | 21 | 22 | 23 | 24 | 25 | 26 | 27 | 28 | 29 | 30 | 31 | 32 | 33 | 34 | 35 | 40 |
|---|---|---|---|---|---|---|---|---|---|---|---|---|---|---|---|---|
| Wins | 9 | 13 | 11 | 15 | 21 | 15 | 14 | 14 | 15 | 22 | 15 | 15 | 10 | 12 | 9 | 9 |
| Draws | 16 | 19 | 19 | 17 | 11 | 17 | 18 | 18 | 17 | 10 | 17 | 17 | 20 | 19 | 21 | 14 |
| Losses | 7 | 0 | 2 | 0 | 0 | 0 | 0 | 0 | 0 | 0 | 0 | 0 | 2 | 1 | 2 | 9 |

The results of the statistical testing procedure performed indicated that a model with $k = 30$ yields the best coherence score. It is however noted that $k = 25$ has 21 wins (only one less than $k = 30$), while the four closest runners up ($k = 24, 29, 31$, and $32$) have only 15 wins. The sample with $k = 25$ also did not differ from the sample with $k = 30$ in a statistically significant way. Final models for each of the two best performing values of $k$ were therefore trained, and their coherence scores and human topic interpretability compared. The training algorithms for the final models were allowed to run for 1 500 iterations. The final model with $k = 30$ achieved a coherence score of 0.482, while the model with $k = 25$ achieved a score of 0.5. It is interesting to note that even though the statistical procedure indicated $k = 30$ as the optimal choice, a 3.7% higher coherence score is obtained for the final model with $k = 25$. Next, the topics for the two final LDA models were labeled by inspecting the top 20 terms for each topic (i.e. the terms with the highest probabilities of occurring, given a topic) and assigning a label based on the interpreted meaning of the terms. The technical nature of the texts in the corpus and the context in which it was created (social media) mean that domain knowledge is of critical importance. The domain includes not only wearable fitness devices in general, but also knowledge of the chosen brand's products and services, as well as their features. If the top 20 terms of a topic did not provide any clear, coherent meaning, the topic was marked as a *junk topic*, while if the top 20 terms indicated that more than one concept or meaning is represented by the topic, it is marked as a *mixed topic*. The outcomes of this process are shown in Table 4. The model with $k = 30$ produced worse results than expected. A total of four topics for this model are marked as junk topics, and two are marked as mixed topics. The model with $k = 25$ performed better than expected, with only two topics marked as mixed. The coherence score for the final LDA model with $k = 25$ was the highest, and also produced no junk topics, as opposed to the LDA model with $k = 30$, that produced four junk topics.

**Table 4.** Outcomes of the topic labeling process.

| k | 25 | 30 |
|---|---|---|
| Labeled | 22 | 24 |
| Mixed | 3 | 2 |
| Junk | 0 | 4 |

Due to the better interpretability and coherence score of the final LDA model with $k = 25$, the CTM and GSDMM algorithms are also trained with the same value for $k$. The CTM algorithm is applied to the dataset using the *tomotopy* package. The inputs for the CTM algorithm are $k$ and $\eta$. The value for $k$ was set to 25, and the value for $\eta$ was set to 0.1. A sample of 30 CTM models was trained over 600 iterations each, and an average coherence score of 0.516 was obtained. The final model was trained over 1600 iterations, and achieved a coherence score of 0.527. Finally, a similar procedure is followed to train the GSDMM models using the *gpym_tm* package. The inputs for the GSDMM algorithm are $k$, $\alpha$, and $\beta$. The value for $k$ was set to 25, while $\alpha$ and $\beta$ were both set to 0.1. A sample of 30 GSDMM models with $k = 25$ were trained over 25 iterations each, and an average coherence score of 0.404 was achieved. The final model was trained over 50 iterations, and achieved a coherence score of 0.392. The average and final coherence scores for each algorithm are shown in Table 5.

**Table 5.** Average and final coherence scores for models trained with each algorithm.

| Coherence | LDA | CTM | GSDMM |
|---|---|---|---|
| Average over 30 models | 0.432 | 0.516 | 0.404 |
| Final Model | 0.500 | 0.527 | 0.392 |

The Mann-Whitney U-test was then used to compare the results of each of the algorithms and determine which performed best. The results of the procedure are shown in Table 6. From Tables 5 and 6, it is clear that based on $C_v$ coherence scores, the CTM algorithm performed better than the LDA algorithm, while the GSDMM performed worse than the LDA algorithm.

**Table 6.** Results of the statistical test.

| Algorithm | LDA | CTM | GSDMM |
|-----------|-----|-----|-------|
| Wins | 1 | 2 | 0 |
| Draws | 0 | 0 | 0 |
| Losses | 1 | 0 | 2 |

# 6    Interpretation of Topics

The CTM model performed the best, with an average coherence score of 0.516 for the 30 trained models, and a score of 0.527 for the final trained model. The topics produced by this model were then labeled by applying the same procedure as described in the Modeling section for labeling the LDA topics. The label and the top 10 terms for each topic are shown in Table 7, as well as the number of tokens assigned to each topic.

The number of tokens assigned to each topic gives an indication of the size and importance of each topic. Each of the topics were organised into one of seven categories. These categories are: (1) features, (2) connectivity, (3) acquisition, (4) workouts, (5) physical design, (6) physiological monitoring, and (7) miscellaneous. Figure 2 shows the seven categories and the relative size of each category.

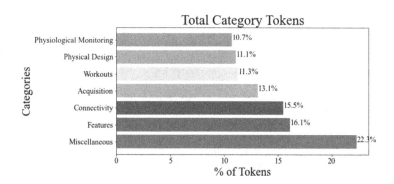

**Fig. 2.** Categories of topics and the number of tokens assigned to each category.

**Table 7.** Top terms and number of tokens assigned to each topic.

| Label | Top 10 Terms | % of Tokens |
|---|---|---|
| Junk1 | long, end, hope, case, post, wonder, couple, okay, similar, let | 4.76% |
| Information | start, delete, check, fine, idea, late, link, numb, user, website | 4.70% |
| Customisation Features | datum, way, add, option, miss, edit, amp, save, possible, available | 4.66% |
| Junk2 | pretty, bite, little, reason, actually, definitely, hard, easy, feel, expect | 4.56% |
| Purchasing | wearable3, new, year, buy, month, old, wait, release, return, replace | 4.56% |
| Junk3 | day, week, change, hour, minute, today, notice, normal, lose, yesterday | 4.48% |
| Accuracy | time, read, different, tell, guess, experience, correct, close, assume, example | 4.46% |
| Junk4 | wearable2, come, right, far, switch, leave, sound, live, reply, comment | 4.29% |
| Settings | phone, set, turn, button, bluetooth, setting, stop, pair, mode, connection | 4.24% |
| Junk5 | point, mean, base, stuff, understand, basically, useful, information, real, kind | 4.19% |
| Size/Weight | wear, wrist, big, small, compare, feel, vs, light, size, fit | 4.15% |
| Syncing | app, connect, sync, track_app, os, download, competitor1_phone, create, upload, file | 4.13% |
| Updates | update, notification, support, send, remove, software, version, firmware, contact, install | 4.02% |
| Statistics | run, cycle, metric, test, load, drop, fast, long, min, short | 3.94% |
| Upgrades | wearable1, plus, price, wearable8, model, upgrade, series, worth, deal, pro | 3.79% |
| Logging | activity, step, record, walk, count, exercise, calory, goal, log, active | 3.70% |
| $VO_2$-max | accurate, high, low, weight, vo_max, rest, accuracy, measure, average, level | 3.68% |
| Water Features | feature, swim, fitness, sport, wearable10, prefer, runner, decide, water, touchscreen | 3.67% |
| Heart Rate | hr, heart_rate, strap, sensor, hrm, monitor, chest_strap, wearable4, optical, ant | 3.63% |
| Planning | workout, train, pace, plan, distance, mile, zone, lap, treadmill, race | 3.62% |
| Watch Band | band, online_store, buy, sapphire, scratch, black, sell, mm, sale, discount | 3.47% |
| Watchface | screen, battery, charge, face, battery_life, display, widget, field, power, wearable11 | 3.45% |
| General Health | track, sleep, competitor2, bike, ride, night, wearable7, stress, tracker, body_battery | 3.39% |
| Geolocation | gps, map, hike, course, route, elevation, trail, weather, location, altimeter | 3.31% |
| Audio | music, competitor1, pay, smart, play, spotify, competitor1_wearable, control, wifi, smartwatch | 3.14% |

The features category is, except for the miscellaneous category, the largest, and constitutes 16.1% of all the tokens in the corpus. It consists of the customisation, accuracy, water features, and geolocation topics. These topics are an indication of what kind of features consumers are interested in. The customisation topic suggests that consumers expect a large degree of control over how their wearable device functions and how they interact with it. Words like 'possible', 'available', 'miss', and 'option' could point to users' increased interest in finding out if such options do exist. The accuracy topic suggests that consumers sometimes find that readings do not match expectations or are not logical and thus not accurate. Closer inspection of representative documents also seem to suggest a keen interest in how certain measurements are obtained or how certain metrics are calculated. The water features topic is mainly concerned with how the wearable device behaves in water with regards to touchscreen sensitivity. The geolocation topic suggests that consumers often use their devices in the outdoors and use a wide variety of sensors, such as altimeters, barometers, and temperature sensors to monitor their environment.

The software category constitutes 15.5% of all the tokens in the corpus, and consists of the audio, device connection, syncing, and updates topics. These topics are all related to software and connectivity, and inspection of these topics' representative documents suggest that issues in this regard are numerous. The audio topic is mainly related to controlling audio feedback (mainly music) on other devices through the user's wearable. The top words also contain other brand names, indicating which other devices or music apps the wearables are most often used alongside. The settings topic is related to how users can access and change different features and modes on their devices. Similar to the customisation topic, the top terms suggest that having control over how the wearable functions is very important to consumers. The syncing topic is related to the data that is shared between different apps, devices, and platforms, and how users interact with this data. The top terms and representative documents signal the use of multiple apps and devices for daily activities, and that it is expected that these must be able to communicate and transfer data seamlessly. The updates topic concerns the continued software support and enhancements that Brand Y's devices receive.

The acquisition category consists of the information seeking, upgrades, and purchasing topics, and 13.1% of all tokens are assigned to this category. The information seeking topic is about where users find information and the different resources that they consult when seeking help or making a decision. The upgrades topic revolves around product offers and new versions of devices, and whether these compare well with what users already own. It also seems that these users actively look for discounts and deals when considering an upgrade. The purchasing topic is closely related to the upgrade topic, with users comparing different models and deciding whether to buy now or wait, but this topic also concerns issues such as shipping and availability of different models in different countries.

The workouts category constitutes 11.3% of all tokens in the corpus, and contains the statistics, logging, and planning topics. The planning topic's top terms indicate that being able to plan multiple aspects of a workout (such as distance, sequence, and pace) and comparing them with actual performance is important to users. The logging topic suggests that setting goals and logging activities that contribute towards those goals is also important to users. These goals also include special rewards or badges for completing challenges designed by Brand Y. The statistics topic indicates that users increasingly analyse their own fitness data and are interested in trends in their health and fitness.

The physical design category constitutes the watch band, watch face, and size/weight topics. The watch face topic seems to mainly focus on the screen and displays of watches, and their effect on the battery life of the watch. The watch band topic seems mainly concerned with the buying and selling of watch bands of different colours and materials. The size/weight topic reflects the importance of comfort and fit and how the size and weight of the watch affects this.

The physiological monitoring category consists of 10.7% of the tokens and, it includes the general health, heart rate, and $VO_2$-max topics. The general health topic is focused on the daily habits and lifestyle patterns that the wearables are able to track, such as sleeping, heart rate variability, and stress. The heart rate topic signals the importance of this single measurement to users, and the representative documents suggest a keen interest in its accuracy. The $VO_2$-max is also indicative of this specific metric's importance to users.

All junk topics were assigned to the miscellaneous category, since it is difficult to discern any single concept related to wearables from these topics' top terms. The top terms include 'wonder' and 'hope' in junk 1, 'actually' and 'expect' in junk 2, 'today' and 'notice' in junk 3, 'far' and 'come' in junk 4 and 'understand' and 'useful' in junk 5. These are all terms typically found in discussion forums where users share their experiences and opinions with others, and so it is not surprising that these words often occur together and appear as top terms for this specific dataset. The more emotive and descriptive nature of these words, however, mean that they do not add much value in terms of identifying specific aspects of products that are important to consumers. Additional cleaning and more extensive inspection of the corpus and vocabulary could prevent the formation of such junk topics.

## 7   Conclusion

This paper explored the influence and impact of topic modeling on market research practice and tested the performance of three topic modeling techniques as applied to a social media dataset extracted from Reddit, within the context of market research in the fitness wearable industry. An optimised LDA model with $k = 25$ was used as the baseline against which to measure the CTM and GSDMM algorithms. GSDMM provided worse results than the LDA, while CTM provided better results. The 25 topics produced by the CTM were then labeled by inspecting each topic's top 20 terms and its most representative documents.

Twenty of these topics were easily interpreted and received appropriate labels, while no appropriate labels could be found for the remaining five topics, and they were consequently labeled as 'junk'. The labeled topics were found to fall within larger categories, and each category was interpreted. The top terms for each topic gives an indication of *what* is important to customers, while the number of tokens belonging to each category provide information on the *degree* of importance of each category. There also exists the opportunity to use the topic categories to perform customer or product segmentation. The appearance of competitor brand names or their products in the top terms of topics may also provide an indication of the company's largest competitors from the consumers point of view. Perhaps the greatest advantage of using topic modeling for market research is the automatic and time-efficient extraction of topics from large corpora of social media text, which would otherwise require an exorbitant amount of time or manpower. The observational nature of the research may lead to the formulation of further research questions and provide direction for more focused and in-depth market research. The human analyst plays an important role in interpreting, labeling and categorising the topics, and in making the final decision about the number of topics that provides the best insight.

Future research may include the optimisation of hyperparameters for both CTM models and the GSDMM models, which includes finding the optimal number of topics and concentration parameters. In addition, added cleaning steps to remove semantically meaningless words could prevent the formation of a large number of junk topics.

**Acknowledgements.** This work is based on the research supported in part by the National Research Foundation of South Africa (Grant number: 129340), and the school for Data Science and Computational Thinking at Stellenbosch University.

# References

1. Aggarwal, C.C., Zhai, C.: Mining Text Data. Springer, New York (2012). https://doi.org/10.1007/978-1-4614-3223-4
2. Asuncion, A., Welling, M., Smyth, P., Teh, Y.W.: On smoothing and inference for topic models. In: Proceedings of the 25th Conference on Uncertainty in Artificial Intelligence, UAI 2009, pp. 27–34 (2009)
3. Batrinca, B., Treleaven, P.C.: Social media analytics: a survey of techniques, tools and platforms. AI Soc. **30**(1), 89–116 (2015). https://doi.org/10.1007/s00146-014-0549-4
4. Bendle, N.T., Wang, X.S.: Uncovering the message from the mess of big data. Bus. Horiz. **59**(1), 115–124 (2016)
5. Blei, D., Lafferty, J.: Correlated topic models. In: Advances in Neural Information Processing Systems, vol. 18, p. 147 (2006)
6. Blei, D.M., Ng, A.Y., Jordan, M.I.: Latent dirichlet allocation. J. Mach. Learn. Res. **3**, 993–1022 (2003)
7. Boyd-Graber, J., Mimno, D., Newman, D.: Care and Feeding of Topic Models: Problems, Diagnostics, and Improvements. CRC Press, Boca Raton (2014)

8. Chang, J., Boyd-Graber, J., Wang, C., Gerrish, S., Blei, D.M.: Reading tea leaves: how humans interpret topic models. In: Neural Information Processing Systems, vol. 22, pp. 288–296. Citeseer (2009)
9. Chernova, V., Starostin, V.: Leading trends in marketing research: a case of big data. In: 5th International Conference on Social, Economic, and Academic Leadership (ICSEALV 2019), pp. 210–215. Atlantis Press (2020)
10. Cluley, R., Green, W., Owen, R.: The changing role of the marketing researcher in the age of digital technology: practitioner perspectives on the digitization of marketing research. Int. J. Mark. Res. 62(1), 27–42 (2020)
11. Newman, D., Lau, J.H., Grieser, K., Baldwin, T.: Automatic evaluation of topic coherence. In: Human Language Technologies: The 2010 Annual Conference of the North American Chapter of the Association for Computational Linguistics, pp. 100–108 (2010)
12. Nunan, D., Di Domenico, M.: Market research and the ethics of big data. Int. J. Mark. Res. 55(4), 505–520 (2013)
13. Patino, A., Pitta, D.A., Quinones, R.: Social media's emerging importance in market research. J. Consum. Mark. 29(3), 233–237 (2012)
14. Qiang, J., Qian, Z., Li, Y., Yuan, Y., Wu, X.: Short text topic modeling techniques, applications, and performance: a survey. IEEE Trans. Knowl. Data Eng. 34(3), 1427–1445 (2020)
15. Röder, M., Both, A., Hinneburg, A.: Exploring the space of topic coherence measures. In: Proceedings of the Eighth ACM International Conference on Web Search and Data Mining, pp. 399–408 (2015)
16. Yin, J., Wang, J.: A dirichlet multinomial mixture model-based approach for short text clustering. In: Proceedings of the 20th ACM SIGKDD International Conference on Knowledge Discovery and Data Mining, pp. 233–242 (2014)

# Mitigating Traffic Congestion in Smart and Sustainable Cities Using Machine Learning: A Review

Mikkay Wong Ei Leen[1]([✉]) [iD], Nurul Hanis Aminuddin Jafry[2] [iD],
Narishah Mohamed Salleh[1] [iD], HaJin Hwang[1] [iD], and Nasir Abdul Jalil[2] [iD]

[1] Sunway Business School, Sunway University, Petaling Jaya, Malaysia
mikkayw@sunway.edu.my
[2] School of Liberal Studies, Universiti Kebangsaan Malaysia, Bandar Baru Bang, Malaysia

**Abstract.** Machine Learning (ML) algorithms can analyze large amounts of traffic data, learn from patterns and past behaviors, and provide insights into the current and future traffic flow. ML can also optimize traffic management, including traffic signal control, route optimization, and demand forecasting. Traffic prediction is a key application of ML in traffic management, with studies showing that ML outperforms traditional methods in predicting traffic congestion. ML is an effective tool for managing traffic, particularly for projecting traffic demand, predicting traffic congestion, and optimising routes. Studies have revealed that ML is more efficient than conventional techniques in these areas, leading to decreased journey times, improved traffic flow, and better traffic management in general. As the demand for efficient and sustainable transportation systems rises, ML integration in traffic management is expected to be vital in addressing these requirements. Nevertheless, there are obstacles and restrictions that must be overcome, such as shortcomings in the reliability of data and model interpretability. Despite these challenges, ML has the potential to mitigate traffic congestion and enhance urban mobility in smart and sustainable cities. Further research is needed to address these challenges and fully realize the potential of ML in traffic management.

**Keywords:** Traffic congestion · Machine learning · Smart cities · Sustainable cities · Traffic management

## 1 Introduction

Irrespective of nation, traffic congestion is a major issue that affects all urban areas around the globe. Traffic congestion is fast becoming a critical problem that influences not only transportation but also the economy, environment, and quality of life in urban regions as cities continue to expand and their populations rise. The idea of smart and sustainable cities has emerged as a possible remedy to this problem. The creation of more effective, livable, and ecologically friendly urban environments is a goal of smart and sustainable cities. In order to improve traffic movement and lessen congestion, smart and sustainable cities use cutting-edge transportation technologies and data analytics.

O. Gervasi et al. (Eds.): ICCSA 2023, LNCS 13957, pp. 321–331, 2023.
https://doi.org/10.1007/978-3-031-36808-0_21

Machine learning techniques have recently demonstrated great promise for reducing traffic congestion in smart, sustainable communities [1]. By analyzing large datasets and predicting traffic patterns, machine learning algorithms can help to improve traffic flow and reduce travel time, making urban transportation more efficient and sustainable.

Traffic congestion can frustrate and stress commuters by extending journey times, slowing down traffic, and decreasing travel speeds [2]. Apart from contributing to increased fuel consumption and air pollution, congestion also has a detrimental impact on the environment and public health [3]. Furthermore, traffic congestion could result in a damaging effect on the economy in terms of higher transportation expenses, lower productivity, and a decline in competitiveness [4].

Addressing traffic congestion in urban areas is therefore essential to create more efficient, sustainable, and livable cities [5]. Reducing congestion can lead to shorter travel times, increased productivity, and lower transportation costs. It can also improve the environment and public health by reducing air pollution and greenhouse gas emissions [6] [7]. Moreover, mitigating traffic congestion can lead to a more sustainable urban transportation system, reducing the need for single-occupancy vehicles and promoting alternative modes of transportation such as public transit, biking, and walking. As such, addressing traffic congestion is a critical component of building smart and sustainable cities for the future.

The purpose of this paper is to review the current state of research on the use of machine learning techniques for mitigating traffic congestion in smart and sustainable cities. The scope of the paper includes an overview of the concept of smart cities and their role in addressing traffic congestion, an examination of various machine learning techniques used for traffic congestion prediction and mitigation, a review of case studies and examples of machine learning applications in traffic congestion mitigation, and a discussion of the challenges and future directions of machine learning in the context of urban transportation systems. The paper aims to provide insights into the potential of machine learning techniques for reducing traffic congestion in smart and sustainable cities and to identify key areas for future research and development in this field.

## 2 Smart Cities and Traffic Congestion

A smart city is a city that uses digital technologies and data-driven approaches to improve the quality of life for its citizens, enhance sustainability, and streamline urban services [8]. One of the key areas in which smart cities can have a significant impact is in the mitigation of traffic congestion, which is a major challenge faced by urban areas around the world. Smart cities use a range of technologies, such as sensors, GPS, and data analytics, to monitor traffic patterns and optimize transportation systems. By analyzing traffic data in real time, smart cities can identify congestion hotspots and deploy resources to alleviate traffic flow, such as adjusting traffic signal timing, rerouting traffic, or providing real-time traffic information to drivers. Smart cities can also use machine learning algorithms to predict traffic patterns and proactively address potential congestion issues before they occur. Overall, the use of smart city technologies can help to reduce traffic congestion, improve traffic flow, and enhance the overall quality of life for citizens [9].

Traffic congestion in urban areas is a complex issue that poses a range of challenges for cities and their residents. One of the key challenges is the negative impact on quality of life, as traffic congestion can lead to increased travel times, air pollution, noise pollution, and stress for commuters [10]. Additionally, traffic congestion can have significant economic costs, including lost productivity due to delays, increased fuel consumption and emissions, and increased transportation costs. Moreover, congestion can create safety risks for drivers, cyclists, and pedestrians, leading to accidents and injuries.

Another challenge associated with traffic congestion is the difficulty in predicting and mitigating congestion effectively. Traffic patterns can be highly variable and influenced by a range of factors, such as weather, special events, and road construction. Traditional traffic management approaches, such as adding more lanes or increasing public transportation options, can be costly and take a long time to implement. Therefore, there is a need for more effective and efficient approaches to mitigating traffic congestion in urban areas [11]. Finally, addressing traffic congestion requires collaboration and coordination among a range of stakeholders, including transportation agencies, city planners, businesses, and residents. This can be challenging, as different stakeholders may have competing priorities and interests. As such, effective solutions to traffic congestion require a comprehensive, multi-faceted approach that considers the needs and perspectives of all stakeholders.

Machine learning techniques have the potential to significantly improve the ability of cities to address traffic congestion [1]. One key advantage of machine learning is its ability to analyze large volumes of data quickly and accurately, which can provide insights into traffic patterns and congestion hotspots [12]. Machine learning algorithms can use historical traffic data to predict future traffic patterns and identify potential congestion issues, allowing transportation agencies to proactively deploy resources to alleviate traffic flow.

Furthermore, machine learning algorithms can be used to integrate data from multiple sources, such as traffic sensors, weather forecasts, and social media, to provide a more comprehensive and accurate picture of traffic patterns and congestion. This can allow transportation agencies to make more informed decisions about traffic management and allocate resources more effectively.

Overall, the potential of machine learning techniques in addressing traffic congestion is significant, and these techniques are likely to play an increasingly important role in the development of smart and sustainable cities. However, there are also challenges and limitations associated with the use of machine learning in this context, such as the need for high-quality data, the potential for biases and errors in the algorithms, and the need for collaboration and coordination among a range of stakeholders.

## 3  Machine Learning Techniques for Traffic Congestion Mitigation

Traffic congestion is a growing problem in urban areas, with significant negative impacts on the economy, environment, and quality of life. Machine learning techniques have emerged as a powerful tool for predicting and mitigating traffic congestion. This paper provides an overview of various machine learning techniques that can be used for traffic congestion mitigation, including Artificial Neural Networks (ANNs), Support Vector Machines (SVMs), Decision Trees, Random Forests, Deep Learning, and Reinforcement Learning [13].

There are several machine learning techniques that can be used for traffic congestion prediction and mitigation. Some of the most commonly used techniques include:

a) **Artificial Neural Networks (ANNs)** [14, 15]:

ANNs are a type of deep learning algorithm that are modeled after the human brain. They consist of layers of interconnected nodes that can learn to identify complex relationships between different variables. ANNs are often used for traffic prediction and congestion mitigation by analyzing historical traffic data to identify patterns and make predictions about future traffic flow. ANNs can handle both linear and nonlinear relationships and are flexible in adapting to different types of data. However, they require large amounts of training data and can be computationally expensive.

b) **Support Vector Machines (SVMs)** [16, 17]:

SVMs are a type of machine learning algorithm used for both classification and regression tasks. They work by mapping data into a high-dimensional feature space and identifying a hyperplane that separates the data into different classes. In traffic prediction and congestion mitigation, SVMs can be used to analyze historical traffic data and make predictions about future traffic flow. They are particularly useful in optimizing traffic signal timings. However, SVMs can be sensitive to the choice of kernel function and can struggle with large datasets.

c) **Decision Trees** [18, 19]:

Decision trees are a simple and intuitive machine learning technique that can be used for both classification and regression tasks. They work by breaking down a dataset into smaller and smaller subsets based on specific rules or conditions until the subsets are as small as possible and can be classified or predicted. Decision trees are often used for traffic prediction and congestion mitigation by analyzing a range of factors such as weather, time of day, and road conditions. However, decision trees are prone to overfitting and can be unstable when used on small datasets.

d) **Random Forests** [20, 21]:

Random forests are an extension of decision trees that improve their accuracy and robustness by combining multiple trees. Random forests work by building a multitude of decision trees at training time and outputting the class that is the mode of the classes (classification) or mean prediction (regression) of the individual trees. They are often used for traffic prediction and congestion mitigation by analyzing multiple factors and identifying the most important factors contributing to congestion. Random forests are robust to noisy data and can handle missing values, but can be computationally expensive and require more memory compared to decision trees.

e) **Deep Learning** [22, 23]:

Deep learning is a type of machine learning that uses neural networks with multiple layers to learn hierarchical representations of data. It can be used for a range of traffic prediction and optimization tasks, including traffic flow prediction, congestion detection, and traffic signal optimization. Deep learning algorithms can handle complex data and have achieved state-of-the-art results in many applications. However, they require large amounts of data and can be computationally expensive.

f) **Reinforcement Learning** [24, 25]:

Reinforcement learning is a type of machine learning used for decision-making tasks. It involves an agent that interacts with an environment and receives feedback in the form of rewards or penalties. Reinforcement learning can be used to optimize traffic signal timings and improve traffic flow by learning from feedback received from the environment. However, reinforcement learning requires significant computational resources and may not be suitable for real-time applications.

Overall, each of these machine learning techniques has its own strengths and weaknesses, and the choice of technique will depend on the specific task and data available. However, the use of machine learning techniques in traffic prediction and mitigation has shown promising results and is likely to play an increasingly important role in the development of smart and sustainable cities [26].

Machine learning techniques have shown great potential for traffic congestion prediction and mitigation in smart cities. In this section, the strengths and limitations of each of the techniques mentioned above will be discussed.

Firstly, artificial neural networks (ANNs) have been widely used for traffic congestion prediction due to their ability to handle complex nonlinear relationships between traffic flow and various factors affecting it. ANNs have been shown to perform well in predicting traffic flow in urban areas with high accuracy [27, 28]. However, ANNs require large amounts of data for training, which can be a challenge for small-scale urban areas with limited data availability [14]. Additionally, ANNs have high computational requirements, which can be a limitation for real-time traffic prediction and control [29].

Secondly, support vector machines (SVMs) have also been used for traffic flow prediction with promising results. SVMs have been shown to outperform traditional statistical methods in predicting traffic flow, especially in urban areas with complex traffic patterns [30, 31]. However, SVMs can be computationally expensive, and their performance can be sensitive to the choice of kernel function and tuning parameters.

Thirdly, decision trees have been used for traffic prediction due to their ability to handle both categorical and continuous data [18, 32]. Decision trees are relatively easy to interpret, making them a useful tool for understanding the relationship between traffic flow and various factors affecting it. However, decision trees can be prone to overfitting, especially in cases where there are many input variables [33].

Fourthly, random forest (RF) is an ensemble learning technique that uses multiple decision trees to improve the accuracy of traffic flow prediction. RF has been shown to perform well in predicting traffic flow, especially in cases where there are a large number of input variables [34]. RF is also robust to overfitting and can handle missing data [35]. However, RF can be computationally expensive, especially when dealing with a large number of decision trees.

Finally, deep learning techniques such as convolutional neural networks (CNNs) and recurrent neural networks (RNNs) have shown promising results in predicting traffic flow [36]. CNNs have been used for traffic image classification, while RNNs have been used for time series prediction of traffic flow. Deep learning techniques can handle complex patterns in traffic flow, but they require large amounts of data and computational resources for training.

In summary, each machine learning technique has its own strengths and limitations. ANNs and SVMs are powerful tools for predicting traffic flow, but they can be computationally expensive and require large amounts of data. Decision trees and RF are relatively easy to interpret and can handle missing data, but they can be prone to overfitting and computationally expensive in some cases. Finally, deep learning techniques such as CNNs and RNNs can handle complex patterns in traffic flow but require large amounts of data and computational resources. Choosing the most appropriate machine learning technique for traffic prediction and mitigation in smart cities requires careful consideration of the specific urban area and available data.

## 4  Applications of Machine Learning Techniques in Traffic Congestion Mitigation

There are several case studies and examples of machine learning techniques being applied to traffic congestion mitigation in smart cities. One such example is the implementation of a machine learning-based traffic control system in Hangzhou, China. The system uses real-time data from sensors installed on the roads to predict traffic flow and adjust traffic signals accordingly. The system has shown to be effective in reducing congestion and improving travel times.

Another example is the use of machine learning algorithms to predict traffic congestion in New York City. New York City implemented a system that uses machine learning algorithms to predict traffic congestion based on historical data. The system suggests alternate routes to drivers in real-time to avoid congestion. The city installed sensors and cameras throughout the city to collect real-time traffic data. The system has successfully reduced congestion on some of the busiest streets and improved traffic flow by distributing traffic more evenly across the city.

In Singapore, machine learning techniques have been used to optimize the city's bus network. The system uses data from GPS devices on buses to predict travel times and adjust bus schedules accordingly. This has resulted in more efficient use of the city's bus network and reduced wait times for passengers.

Smart cities around the world are implementing machine learning techniques to mitigate traffic congestion. In San Francisco, a machine learning algorithm was developed to predict traffic congestion caused by construction sites. The city of Stockholm, Sweden has implemented a system that uses machine learning algorithms to optimize traffic signal timing. Amsterdam, Netherlands has implemented a machine learning-based system that uses data from traffic cameras and other sensors to predict traffic congestion and adjust traffic signals.

Similarly, the city of Toronto, Canada implemented a machine learning-based system that uses real-time data from GPS devices on buses to predict travel times and adjust bus schedules. In Rio de Janeiro, Brazil, a machine learning algorithm was developed to predict traffic congestion caused by major events. The city of Seoul, South Korea implemented a system that uses machine learning algorithms to predict traffic congestion and adjust toll prices on highways.

Dubai, United Arab Emirates, also implemented a machine learning-based system that predicts traffic congestion caused by accidents. The city of Boston, United States, uses data from traffic cameras and other sensors to predict traffic congestion and adjust traffic signals. Delhi, India, developed a machine learning algorithm that predicts traffic congestion caused by air pollution. Finally, Copenhagen, Denmark, implemented a system that uses machine learning algorithms to predict traffic congestion and adjust traffic signals based on the number of cyclists on the roads.

These machine learning techniques have proven to be effective in mitigating traffic congestion in urban areas. They have reduced travel times, improved traffic flow, and resulted in more efficient use of transportation networks. However, they also come with limitations such as the need for accurate data, the complexity of implementation, and the potential for biases in the algorithms. Overall, the use of machine learning in traffic congestion mitigation shows promise for creating more sustainable and efficient smart cities.

The effectiveness of the machine learning applications for traffic congestion mitigation varies depending on the specific use case and implementation. In San Francisco, the algorithm for predicting traffic congestion caused by construction sites has been effective in reducing delays and improving traffic flow. The Stockholm system for optimizing traffic signal timing has also been successful, resulting in reduced travel times and improved traffic flow. Similarly, the Amsterdam system for predicting and adjusting traffic signals has shown significant reductions in congestion.

Overall, the effectiveness of machine learning applications for traffic congestion mitigation is highly dependent on the quality of the data used and the specific implementation. However, many of these applications have shown promising results and have the potential to significantly improve traffic flow and reduce delays in smart cities.

Machine learning techniques have the potential to significantly impact urban transportation systems. By improving traffic flow and reducing congestion, these techniques can lead to more efficient transportation networks, decreased commute times, and improved air quality. Additionally, the use of machine learning can lead to more accurate and timely predictions of traffic patterns and congestion, enabling better decision-making by transportation authorities and more effective use of resources [37].

Moreover, the use of machine learning can also enhance the safety of urban transportation systems [38]. By identifying potential hazards and predicting accidents, transportation authorities can take proactive measures to prevent them. For example, machine learning algorithms can be used to detect near-collisions and alert drivers, reducing the likelihood of accidents.

However, there are also potential drawbacks to the use of machine learning in urban transportation systems. One concern is the possibility of bias in algorithms, leading to unequal treatment of certain communities or individuals. Additionally, there are concerns around data privacy and security, as these systems rely on the collection and analysis of large amounts of personal data. Finally, there is the risk of over-reliance on these technologies, leading to a lack of human oversight and decision-making in transportation systems.

Despite these challenges, the potential benefits of machine learning in urban transportation systems cannot be ignored. As cities continue to grow and face increasing challenges related to transportation, the use of machine learning will become increasingly important in optimizing transportation networks and reducing congestion. With careful consideration and planning, the integration of machine learning techniques into urban transportation systems has the potential to create safer, more efficient, and more sustainable cities for future generations.

## 5  Challenges and Future Directions

As with any emerging technology, machine learning techniques for traffic congestion prediction and mitigation in smart cities face several challenges and limitations. These challenges include the availability and quality of data, the complexity of urban transportation systems, the need for interdisciplinary collaboration, and the potential for unintended consequences. However, despite these challenges, machine learning techniques have shown great promise in addressing traffic congestion and improving the efficiency and sustainability of urban transportation systems. As the field continues to evolve, it is important to consider these challenges and work towards addressing them while also exploring new opportunities for the use of machine learning in smart cities.

One major challenge is the lack of data standardization across different cities and regions, which can make it difficult to develop and train machine learning algorithms [39]. This challenge can be compounded by the fact that traffic data can be highly variable, making it difficult to develop generalized models that can be applied across different contexts.

Another challenge is the need for high-quality data inputs. Machine learning algorithms rely on accurate and timely data to make predictions, and any errors or delays in data collection can significantly impact the effectiveness of these algorithms. Additionally, there may be issues with data privacy and security, particularly when sensitive information such as real-time traffic data is being collected and analyzed.

Despite these challenges, there is a growing recognition of the potential impact of machine learning on urban transportation systems. As technology continues to advance and cities become increasingly connected, there is a tremendous opportunity to leverage machine learning algorithms to address some of the most pressing transportation challenges facing urban areas today. To realize this potential, it will be important to address the challenges associated with data standardization, data quality, integration with existing infrastructure, and ongoing monitoring and evaluation.

As machine learning techniques continue to evolve and urban transportation systems become more sophisticated, there are several areas for future research and development. One promising area is the use of reinforcement learning algorithms to optimize traffic signal timing in real-time. This would involve using data from sensors and cameras to learn how traffic patterns change throughout the day and adjusting traffic signals accordingly. This could lead to significant reductions in traffic congestion and travel times.

Furthermore, there is a need to explore the potential of machine learning techniques for predicting and mitigating traffic congestion in multi-modal transportation systems. This would involve integrating data from various sources, including public transportation, ride-sharing services, and personal vehicles, to develop a more comprehensive understanding of traffic patterns and potential solutions.

In summary, while machine learning techniques show great promise for mitigating traffic congestion in smart cities, there are still several areas for future research and development. These include the integration of reinforcement learning algorithms, autonomous vehicles, multi-modal transportation systems, extreme weather events, and data privacy and security. Addressing these challenges will be essential for the continued success and sustainability of urban transportation systems.

## 6 Conclusion

In summary, this paper discussed the challenges associated with traffic congestion in urban areas and the potential of machine learning techniques to mitigate this issue in the context of smart cities. Various machine learning techniques used for traffic congestion prediction and mitigation were presented, along with their strengths and limitations.

The paper also provided case studies and examples of machine learning techniques applied to traffic congestion mitigation in smart cities, including San Francisco, Stockholm, Amsterdam, Toronto, Rio de Janeiro, Seoul, Dubai, Boston, Delhi, and Copenhagen. These examples demonstrated the potential of machine learning to improve traffic flow, reduce travel times, and enhance the efficiency of transportation systems.

However, the paper also highlighted the challenges associated with implementing machine learning techniques for traffic congestion mitigation in smart cities, such as data privacy concerns, cost, and the need for continuous maintenance and updates. The paper also identified areas for future research and development, such as exploring the use of machine learning in combination with other technologies, addressing ethical concerns related to algorithmic bias, and developing more sophisticated predictive models.

Overall, the paper emphasized the importance of incorporating machine learning techniques into transportation planning and management in smart cities to address traffic congestion, improve the efficiency of transportation systems, and enhance the quality of life for residents.

Smart and sustainable cities can benefit greatly from the use of machine learning techniques for traffic congestion mitigation. By optimizing traffic flow, we can reduce fuel consumption and emissions, contributing to a cleaner environment and a healthier population. Additionally, machine learning can improve public transportation systems, making them more efficient and convenient for commuters, leading to a shift away from personal vehicles and towards greener modes of transportation.

## References

1. Meena, G., Sharma, D., Mahrishi, M.: Traffic prediction for intelligent transportation system using machine learning. In: 2020 3rd International Conference on Emerging Technologies in Computer Engineering: Machine Learning and Internet of Things (ICETCE), 2020, pp. 145–148. IEEE (2020)
2. Munuhwa, S., Govere, E., Mojewa, B., Lusenge, A.: Alleviating urban traffic congestion: case of Gaborone City. J. Econ. Sustain. Dev. 11 (2020)
3. Samal, S., Kumar, P.G., Santhosh, J.C., Santhakumar, M.: Analysis of traffic congestion impacts of urban road network under Indian condition. IOP Conference Series: Materials Science and Engineering, 2020, vol. 1006, no. 1, p. 012002: IOP Publishing (2020)

4. Zain, R.M., Salleh, N.H.M., Zaideen, I.M.M., Menhat, M.N.S., Jeevan, J.: Transportation Engineering.
5. Weisbrod, G., Vary, D., Treyz, G.: Measuring economic costs of urban traffic congestion to business. J. Transp. Res. **1839**(1), 98–106 (2003)
6. Fazal, S.J.E.: Addressing congestion and transport-related air pollution in Saharanpur, India. Environ. Urban. **18**(1), 141–154 (2006)
7. Rajé, F., Tight, M., Pope, F.D.J.C.: Traffic pollution: a search for solutions for a city like Nairobi. Cities **82**, 100–107 (2018)
8. Halegoua, G.: Smart Cities. MIT Press (2020)
9. Mora, L., Deakin, M.: Untangling Smart Cities: From Utopian Dreams to Innovation Systems for a Technology-Enabled Urban Sustainability. Elsevier (2019)
10. Ali, L., *et al.*: Dynamics of transit oriented development, role of greenhouse gases and urban environment: a study for management and policy. Sustainability **13**(5), 2536 (2021)
11. Cheng, Z., Pang, M.-S., Pavlou, P.A.J.I.S.R.: Mitigating traffic congestion: the role of intelligent transportation systems. Inf. Syst. Res. **31**(3), 653–674 (2020)
12. Hernandez, L., Castillo, A.: Management, "applications of cloud computing in intelligent vehicles: a survey." J. Artif. Intell. Mach. Learn, Manag. **7**(1), 10–24 (2023)
13. Zhou, H., *et al.*: Review of learning-based longitudinal motion planning for autonomous vehicles: research gaps between self-driving and traffic congestion. J. Transp. Res. **2676**(1), 324–341 (2022)
14. Akhtar, M., Moridpour, S.: A review of traffic congestion prediction using artificial intelligence. J. Adv. Transp. **2021,** 1–18 (2021)
15. ShirMohammadi, M.M., Esmaeilpour, M.J.P., Software, C.: The traffic congestion analysis using traffic congestion index and artificial neural network in main streets of electronic city (case study: Hamedan city). Program. Comput. Softw. **46**, 433–442 (2020)
16. Luo, C., *et al.*: Short-term traffic flow prediction based on least square support vector machine with hybrid optimization algorithm. Appl. Math. Model. **50**, 2305–2322 (2019)
17. Lin, H., Li, L, Wang, H.: Survey on research and application of support vector machines in intelligent transportation system. J. Front. Comput. Technol. **14**(6), 901 (2020)
18. AlKheder , S., AlOmair, A.: Urban traffic prediction using metrological data with fuzzy logic, long short-term memory (LSTM), and decision trees (DTs). Nat. Hazard. **111**, 1685–1719 (2021)
19. Mystakidis, A., Tjortjis, C., Big data mining for smart cities: predicting traffic congestion using classification. In: 2020 11th International Conference on Information, Intelligence, Systems and Applications (IISA), 2020, pp. 1–8. IEEE (2020)
20. Zafar, N., Ul Haq, I.: Traffic congestion prediction based on estimated time of arrival. PLoS ONE **15**(12), e0238200 (2020)
21. Stepanov, N., Alekseeva, D., Ometov, A., Lohan, E.S.: Applying machine learning to LTE traffic prediction: comparison of bagging, random forest, and SVM. In: 2020 12th International Congress on Ultra Modern Telecommunications and Control Systems and Workshops (ICUMT), 2020, pp. 119–123. IEEE (2020)
22. Tedjopurnomo, D.A., Bao, Z., Zheng, B., Choudhury, F.M., Qin, A.K.: A survey on modern deep neural network for traffic prediction: Trends, methods and challenges. IEEE Trans. Knowl. Data Eng. **34**(4), 1544–1561 (2020)
23. A. Ata, M. A. Khan, S. Abbas, G. Ahmad, and A. J. N. N. W. Fatima, "Modelling smart road traffic congestion control system using machine learning techniques," vol. 29, no. 2, pp. 99–110, 2019
24. C. Pholpol, T. J. I. J. o. C. N. Sanguankotchakorn, and Communications, "Traffic Congestion Prediction using Deep Reinforcement Learning in Vehicular Ad-hoc Networks (vanets)," vol. 13, no. 4, pp. 1–19, 2021

25. M. Abdoos and A. L. J. E. s. w. a. Bazzan, "Hierarchical traffic signal optimization using reinforcement learning and traffic prediction with long-short term memory," vol. 171, p. 114580, 2021

26. A. Heidari, N. J. Navimipour, M. J. S. C. Unal, and Society, "Applications of ML/DL in the management of smart cities and societies based on new trends in information technologies: A systematic literature review," p. 104089, 2022

27. Q. Hou, J. Leng, G. Ma, W. Liu, Y. J. P. A. S. M. Cheng, and i. Applications, "An adaptive hybrid model for short-term urban traffic flow prediction," vol. 527, p. 121065, 2019

28. V. Najafi Moghaddam Gilani, S. M. Hosseinian, M. Ghasedi, and M. J. M. p. i. e. Nikookar, "Data-driven urban traffic accident analysis and prediction using logit and machine learning-based pattern recognition models," vol. 2021, pp. 1–11, 2021

29. A. Javed, J. Harkin, L. McDaid, and J. Liu, "Exploring spiking neural networks for prediction of traffic congestion in networks-on-chip," in *2020 IEEE International Symposium on Circuits and Systems (ISCAS)*, 2020, pp. 1–5: IEEE

30. A. Boukerche, Y. Tao, and P. J. C. n. Sun, "Artificial intelligence-based vehicular traffic flow prediction methods for supporting intelligent transportation systems," vol. 182, p. 107484, 2020

31. A. H. Alomari, T. S. Khedaywi, A. R. O. Marian, and A. A. J. H. Jadah, "Traffic speed prediction techniques in urban environments," vol. 8, no. 12, p. e11847, 2022

32. S. Inkoom, J. Sobanjo, A. Barbu, X. J. S. Niu, and I. Engineering, "Prediction of the crack condition of highway pavements using machine learning models," vol. 15, no. 7, pp. 940–953, 2019

33. M.-J. J. I. J. o. G. I. S. Jun, "A comparison of a gradient boosting decision tree, random forests, and artificial neural networks to model urban land use changes: The case of the Seoul metropolitan area," vol. 35, no. 11, pp. 2149–2167, 2021

34. Q. Shang, D. Tan, S. Gao, and L. J. J. o. A. T. Feng, "A hybrid method for traffic incident duration prediction using BOA-optimized random forest combined with neighborhood components analysis," vol. 2019, 2019

35. X. Zhou, P. Lu, Z. Zheng, D. Tolliver, A. J. R. E. Keramati, and S. Safety, "Accident prediction accuracy assessment for highway-rail grade crossings using random forest algorithm compared with decision tree," vol. 200, p. 106931, 2020

36. K. Guo *et al.*, "Optimized graph convolution recurrent neural network for traffic prediction," vol. 22, no. 2, pp. 1138–1149, 2020

37. M. K. Nabi, "The uses of big data in smart city transportation to accelerate the business growth," in *Vehicular Communications for Smart Cars*: CRC Press, 2021, pp. 67–84

38. Bangui, H., Buhnova, B.: Recent advances in machine-learning driven intrusion detection in transportation: survey. Procedia Comput. Sci. **184**, 877–886 (2021)

39. Kong, W., Luo, Y., Feng, G., Li, K., Peng, H.J.E.: Optimal location planning method of fast charging station for electric vehicles considering operators, drivers, vehicles, traffic flow and power grid. vol. Energy **186**, 115826 (2019)

# Urban Resilience Key Metrics Thinking and Computing Using 3D Spatio-Temporal Forecasting Algorithms

Igor Agbossou(✉)

Laboratoire ThéMA, UMR 6049, Université de Franche-Comté, IUT NFC, Belfort, France
igor.agbossou@univ-fcomte.fr

**Abstract.** The vagueness of the concept of resilience makes it difficult to define unanimously, and it becomes even more problematic when it comes to measuring it, while urban resilience metrics can be considered as key indicators transmitting vital information to the decision makers on the observed characteristics about the city. The motivations and goals of such a metric are as different as the proponents who defend them. As for cities, due to growing urbanization in a global context of climate change, the concept of urban resilience is essential and requires scientific attention backed by a methodology with an operational aim. Based on 3D spatio-temporal forecasting algorithms, this paper revisits the concept and presents a novel approach to measuring and computing key metrics of resilience applied to urban systems. Some results show that spatio-temporal forecasting algorithms can significantly improve the accuracy and timeliness of urban resilience metrics compared to traditional methods. Our methodology can help urban planners and policymakers make more informed decisions and enhance the resilience of urban systems. However, the methodology also has limitations and challenges, such as data quality issues and algorithmic complexity, that require further research. This paper contributes to the literature on urban resilience and spatio-temporal forecasting by providing a comprehensive framework for measuring and forecasting key metrics of urban resilience using advanced computational methods.

**Keywords:** Urban resilience · Metrics framework · Forecasting algorithms

## 1 Introduction

It has become undeniable that as we move forward into the 21st century, the increase in world population accompanied by mass urbanization is becoming our reality which constitutes a major challenge [1]. Among other attempts to contain its excesses have led to the theorization of the concept of urban resilience [2–10]. The concept has gained increasing attention in recent years as cities around the world face a range of environmental and social challenges, including climate change, natural disasters, economic disruptions, and social unrest [4, 5, 7–11]. Urban resilience refers to the ability of urban systems to absorb and recover from shocks and stresses while maintaining their essential functions and structures. Measuring and forecasting key metrics of urban resilience is essential for identifying potential vulnerabilities and enhancing the adaptability and anticipation of urban systems [9–13]. Traditional methods of measuring urban resilience metrics are often limited by data quality, timeliness, and spatial resolution [14–20]. Census data and land use maps are typically used to measure urban characteristics such as population density and land use diversity [14, 16, 20], but they are often outdated and lack spatial detail. Infrastructure connectivity and social cohesion are more difficult to measure due to the lack of comprehensive data sources [21, 22]. In addition, traditional methods of forecasting these metrics often rely on simplistic statistical models that cannot capture the complex spatio-temporal dynamics of urban systems [17, 18]. Recent advances in spatio-temporal forecasting algorithms [15, 18, 23, 24] and 3D modeling techniques [25] offer new opportunities for more accurate and timely assessment of urban resilience metrics. These methods can combine data from multiple sources and use advanced computational techniques to capture the complex dynamics of urban systems. However, there are still significant challenges in applying these methods to real-world urban contexts, including issues of data quality, algorithmic complexity, and model validation [12, 13, 18, 23].

In this paper, we propose a methodology framework for measuring and forecasting key metrics of urban resilience using 3D spatio-temporal forecasting algorithms, which represents a novel approach to the problem of urban resilience assessment. The primary objective of this study is to develop a methodology for measuring and forecasting key metrics of urban resilience using 3D spatio-temporal forecasting algorithms. To achieve this objective, the following research questions will be addressed: 1) What are the key metrics of urban resilience that can be measured and forecasted using 3D spatio-temporal forecasting algorithms? 2) What data sources and validation techniques are needed to ensure the accuracy and reliability of the forecasting results? 3) How can 3D spatio-temporal forecasting algorithms be used to capture the complex spatio-temporal dynamics of urban systems? 4) How can the proposed methodology be applied to a real-world case study of a medium-sized city?

By addressing these research questions, this study aims to contribute to the field of urban resilience by proposing a comprehensive methodology for measuring and forecasting key metrics using advanced computational methods and real-world data sources. After providing an overview of the concept of urban resilience and its importance for modern cities, we discuss the current challenges faced by urban areas in terms of resilience assessment methodologies and highlight the gaps in the existing approaches in Sect. 2. The rest of the paper is organized as follows according to its main contributions. Section 3 presents our methodology framework for measuring and forecasting key metrics of urban resilience accompanied by the underlying principles, techniques, and key features. Section 4 describes the details about the specific 3D spatio-temporal forecasting algorithms we use, its capabilities and how they contribute to the overall methodology. We discuss the data requirements for the spatio-temporal forecasting algorithms and how one collected and pre-processed the data. Section 5 analyses the results and evaluation of our methodology concerning effectiveness in measuring and forecasting key metrics of urban resilience. We also compare the results with existing major approaches and highlight the strengths and limitations of our approach. Ultimately, Sect. 6 concludes this paper and future work.

## 2 Resilience Concept Background and Related Works

### 2.1 Theoretical Review from Disciplinary Perspectives

The word "resilience" is said to come from the Latin resilire, resilio and the concept has spawned a "long history of multiple and interconnected meanings in art, literature, law, science, and engineering [26, 27]. Semantically, some of its uses invoked a positive outcome or state of being, while others invoked a negative outcome. Before the 20th century, its main meaning was "to rebound" [27]. The notion is widely present in different academic disciplines [10] and now urban planning [3–5, 8, 9]. Another conceptual approach was introduced by Holling [6] in his influential publication "Resilience and Stability of Ecological Systems". The author rejected the idea of restricting resilience solely to the ability of ecosystems to return to their previous state following a disturbance. Instead, he proposed to distinguish resilience more clearly from stability. Indeed, he considers that resilience would be a much more appropriate concept to understand and manage the dynamics of ecosystems, since these systems are defined by multiple states of stability. Another approach to resilience based on the analysis of the interaction of social and ecological systems has been developed [28, 29] by integrating aspects of adaptability, learning and transformation. In this approach, the idea of bouncing has increasingly been replaced by the metaphor of 'bouncing forward'; a view considered more appropriate as it admits the interplay of disturbance and reorganization, as well as long-term societal adaptation processes [30]. More recently, at the level of national and international institutions, the concept has taken a prominent place in the definition and implementation of operational disaster risk management strategies and policies, infrastructure planning, as well as urban development [31]. Urban resilience has also received considerable attention due to other symptoms of crises [30–35]. For example, the financial crisis of 2007/2008 and its repercussions on city budgets, the COVID 19 crisis as well as rapid urban changes and their enormous impacts on urban infrastructure. Most definitions of urban resilience therefore offer suggestions on how to improve the "generic adaptability, flexibility or adaptability" of urban areas [21, 23, 24, 26, 30, 31]. Research continues to explore the concept more deeply and broadly.

### 2.2 Review and Challenges of Current Urban Resilience Frameworks

Urban resilience frameworks have emerged as a useful tool for assessing and enhancing the ability of urban systems and communities to withstand, adapt to, and recover from various shocks and stresses. In recent years, several major frameworks have been developed to guide resilience efforts in cities around the world. Among these frameworks, we can identify the City Resilience Framework (CRF) [36], the Urban Resilience Framework (URF) [37], the 100 Resilient Cities Framework (100RC) [38], the Disaster Risk Reduction Framework (DRR) [39] and the Four-Capital Framework (4CF) [40].

One of the main strengths of current urban resilience frameworks is their holistic approach to assessing and enhancing urban resilience. They recognize that urban systems and communities are complex and interconnected, and they emphasize the importance of addressing multiple dimensions of resilience, such as social, economic, and environmental factors. The frameworks also recognize that cities face different types of shocks and stresses, including climate change, natural disasters, and economic downturns, and they provide guidance on how to address these challenges. It was possible for us to identify these challenges after scrutinizing each framework in detail. Also, the result of this work is recorded in Table 1.

**Table 1.** Challenges related to the limitations of current urban resilience frameworks.

| Challenge | Description |
| --- | --- |
| Lack of flexibility and adaptiveness | Current resilience frameworks often rely on predefined indicators and dimensions of resilience, which may not reflect the unique characteristics and challenges of each urban area. This can lead to inflexible approaches that fail to account for the dynamic and complex nature of urban systems and communities. Resilience efforts require a flexible and adaptive approach that can account for the unique characteristics and challenges of each urban area |
| Limited stakeholder engagement | Some frameworks may not effectively engage with diverse stakeholder groups, such as community members and local organizations, in the development and implementation of resilience strategies. This can limit the effectiveness and sustainability of these strategies, as they may not reflect the needs and priorities of these stakeholders |
| Emphasis on shock events | Many frameworks prioritize the ability of urban systems and communities to withstand and recover from acute shock events, such as natural disasters or terrorist attacks. However, chronic stresses, such as poverty, inequality, and climate change, can also pose significant challenges to urban resilience, and may require different approaches and solutions |
| Inadequate consideration of equity | Resilience frameworks may not adequately address the underlying social and economic factors that contribute to vulnerability and inequality in urban areas, leading to uneven resilience outcomes |
| Lack of measurement and evaluation | Resilience frameworks may not provide clear metrics or benchmarks for measuring and evaluating resilience outcomes, making it difficult to assess progress and adjust strategies as needed |

(*continued*)

**Table 1.** (*continued*)

| Challenge | Description |
|---|---|
| Inadequate data and monitoring science | Resilience frameworks may not effectively integrate with other policy areas, such as sustainability, urban planning, or public health. This can limit the potential for synergies and collaboration across these policy areas and may result in fragmented or disjointed approaches to urban development and resilience. Indeed, although they often rely on data and monitoring systems to track progress and identify areas for improvement but do not fully incorporate data science approaches, such as data analytics and 3D spatio-temporal forecasting algorithms, which could enhance the effectiveness of resilience planning and response |

## 3 Novel Methodology Framework

### 3.1 Formalization of Urban System Dynamics Faces to Disruptive Event

Urban systems are complex [41] and dynamic [42], with a range of interdependent components and processes that can be disrupted by various events, such as natural disasters, pandemics, or terrorist attacks. To better understand the behavior of urban systems in the face of disruptive events, it is important to formalize the dynamics of these systems and develop models that can capture their behavior over time. The formalization of urban system dynamics involves the identification of key components and processes within urban systems and the development of mathematical models that can describe the behavior of these components and processes over time. One key challenge in the formalization of urban system dynamics is the incorporation of feedback loops and nonlinear relationships between different components and processes. Figure 1 describes the resilience dynamics of urban system over time.

The starting point of the system's usual state is represented by the initial horizontal line (anticipation state). When a disruptive event occurs (marked by a star icon), the system's performance quickly drops as it absorbs the shock. Once the threat has passed, the system enters the recovery phase. An event is composed of three elements: magnitude, duration, and location. The level of resilience recovered by the system depends on various factors. Limited resources may impede the system from fully regaining its original functionality, while ample resources and wise application of lessons learned may enable the system to attain a greater level of performance. Effective system management should aim to flatten out the entire curve, including vectors Ab, Re, and Ad, to eliminate the disturbance basin during the period dt. Indeed, following a disruption, the initial performance ($U_{res}$) experiences some change ($dU_{res}$) before eventually reaching a new steady state of performance. The time required for recovery after the disruption ($dt$) is a crucial element of resilience. Resilience can be improved by decreasing the magnitude of the disturbance (vector Ab), shortening the recovery period (vector Re) to change the

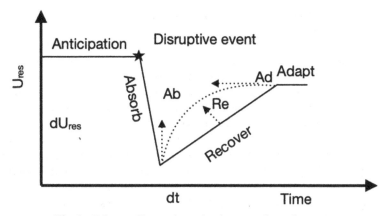

**Fig. 1.** Urban resilience dynamics face to a disruptive event.

shape of the recovery curve to gradually match the level of adaptation to that of before the crisis (vector Ad). Ab, Re, and Ad are keys metrics vectors.

Let E be a disruptive event that affects the urban system. E can be characterized by a set of attributes such as its magnitude, duration, and location (or region).

$$E = \{magnitude, duration, location\} \tag{1}$$

The master equation for the urban system dynamics faces to disruptive event be formalized as follows:

$$\frac{dU_{res}}{dt} = U_{res} - \omega\left(\vec{E}\right) + \varphi(\overrightarrow{Ab}, \overrightarrow{Re}, \overrightarrow{Ad}) \tag{2}$$

$$U_{res}^{t} = \int \left(U_{res} - \omega\left(\vec{E}\right) + \varphi\left(\overrightarrow{Ab}, \overrightarrow{Re}, \overrightarrow{Ad}\right)\right)dt \tag{3}$$

$\frac{dU_{res}}{dt}$ is the rate of change of the urban resilience $U_{res}$ variables over time.

$\omega\left(\vec{E}\right)$ is the impact of the disruptive event according to its magnitude, duration, and spatial location.

$U_{res}^{t}$ is the composite urban resilience at time t.

$\varphi(\overrightarrow{Ab}, \overrightarrow{Re}, \overrightarrow{Ad})$ is the effect of resilience strategies such as emergency response, infrastructure repair, and resource reallocation during the recovery phase depending social, economic, environmental, governance, and physical dimensions of the urban system.

By developing models that capture the complexity and dynamics of urban systems, we can better prepare for and respond to a range of disruptive events and enhance the resilience of our cities and communities. One key challenge in the formalization of urban system dynamics is the incorporation of feedback loops and nonlinear relationships between different major components of dynamics of city and its processes.

### 3.2 Construction of the Urban Resilience Metrics Matrix

The development of the urban resilience metrics matrix is a crucial step towards measuring and enhancing the resilience of urban systems. A resilient city is one that has the capacity to withstand and recover from a range of shocks and stresses, such as natural disasters, economic downturns, or social unrest. To develop an effective resilience strategy for a city, it is important to have a comprehensive set of metrics that can measure the resilience of the city across different domains.

The development of an urban resilience metrics matrix involves the identification of key resilience domains and the selection of appropriate metrics to measure the resilience of these domains. These domains include social, economic, environmental, governance, and physical aspects of the urban system. In constructing the urban resilience metrics matrix (Fig. 2), the focus is on ways to explicitly capture system capacity throughout the timeline of a disruptive event. In the Anticipate column, metrics should be selected to measure the city's ability to anticipate and prepare for potential shocks and stresses. Examples include the city's emergency preparedness plan, the number of trained emergency responders, and the availability of warning systems. In the Absorb column, metrics should be selected to measure the city's ability to absorb and manage the impacts of shocks and stresses. Examples include the capacity of critical infrastructure systems (such as water, power, and transportation) to continue functioning during and after a disruptive event, the availability of emergency shelters, and the accessibility of healthcare services. In the Recover column, metrics should be selected to measure the city's ability to recover from a disruptive event. Examples include the speed and efficiency of debris removal and restoration of critical infrastructure, the availability of financial resources for recovery efforts, and the effectiveness of post-disaster support programs. In the Adapt column, metrics should be selected to measure the city's ability to adapt to changing conditions and to build long-term resilience. Examples include the level of community engagement in resilience planning and decision-making, the adoption of sustainable development practices, and the diversity and flexibility of the local economy.

### 3.3 Urban 3D Data Collection Sources

Data collection is a critical component of any urban resilience strategy, and it involves the gathering of information on a wide range of factors that can influence the resilience of the urban system. Key metrics that are commonly collected as part of urban resilience data collection efforts include demographic data, economic indicators, environmental conditions, infrastructure performance, and social factors. OpenStreetMap 3D [43, 44], CityJSON [45], Cityscapes [45], Google Earth [46], and LIDAR [47] are some of the open databases available for 3D urban data collection. OpenStreetMap 3D provides open-source 3D maps with detailed information on urban infrastructure and buildings, and it can be used for a range of applications, including urban planning and disaster management. CityJSON is a format that allows for the easy exchange of 3D urban data, including buildings, roads, and landmarks. Cityscapes provides high-quality images and semantic annotations of urban scenes [48], which can be used for developing algorithms for urban scene understanding. Google Earth provides high-resolution satellite images and 3D models of urban environments, which can be used to extract building and

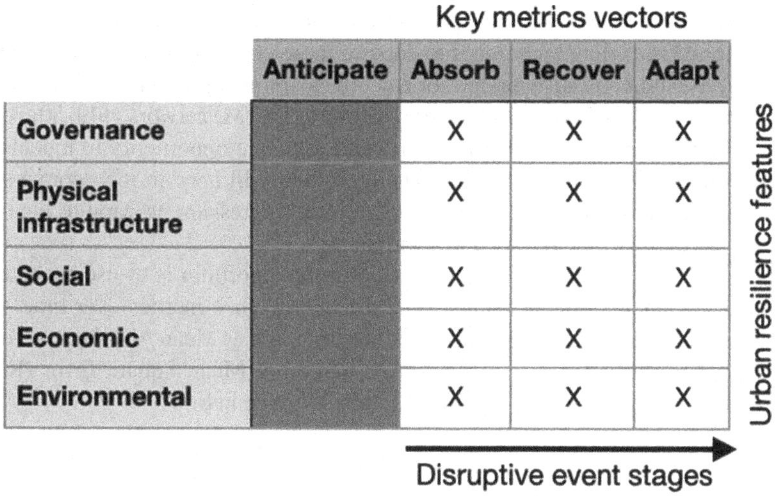

## Key metrics vectors

|  | Anticipate | Absorb | Recover | Adapt |  |
|---|---|---|---|---|---|
| **Governance** |  | X | X | X |  |
| **Physical infrastructure** |  | X | X | X |  |
| **Social** |  | X | X | X |  |
| **Economic** |  | X | X | X |  |
| **Environmental** |  | X | X | X |  |

Urban resilience features

→ **Disruptive event stages**

**Fig. 2.** An overview of urban resilience metrics matrix construction.

infrastructure information. LIDAR technology, on the other hand, uses laser scanning to provide high-precision 3D data on urban structures and infrastructure. The combination of these databases can enhance the accuracy and efficiency of 3D spatio-temporal forecasting algorithms for urban resilience analysis.

## 4 Urban Resilience Measurement Algorithm

### 4.1 3D Spatio-Temporal Forecasting Algorithm (STFA) Principles

One of the key challenges in measuring urban resilience is the ability to accurately predict and assess the impact of disruptive events. In recent years, STFA have emerged as a powerful tool for predicting urban system dynamics and identifying critical areas for resilience investments. The motivation of applying STFA is Transfer Learning (TL) from multisource data [49]. The purpose of TL is to mining the potential knowledge within the source domain. In this case, it is the data in line with the matrix of Fig. 2. Simultaneously, multitask learning paradigm [50] is integrated into the design STFA. So, when engaging in multisource transfer learning, it's essential to not only consider the connections between the target domain and multiple source domains as shown in Fig. 1, but also to consider the relationships between the various source domains themselves as depicted in Fig. 2. The general algorithm is deployed according to the following steps: 1) Data preprocessing: 3D dataset provides a large amount of geospatial data on urban areas, including images, point clouds, and semantic annotations. The first step in the algorithm is to preprocess this data and extract relevant features and metrics, such as land use patterns, building heights, and population density. 2) Dimensionality reduction: Given the large size of the 3D dataset, it may be necessary to perform dimensionality reduction techniques, such as principal component analysis, to reduce the complexity of the data and improve computational efficiency. 3) Temporal modeling: Urban resilience metrics are often dynamic and change over time, so the algorithm will need to incorporate temporal modeling techniques to capture these changes. This may include time series analysis, autoregressive models, or machine learning algorithms such as recurrent neural networks (RNNs) or long short-term memory (LSTM) networks [49, 50]. 4) Spatial modeling: The 3D nature of dataset provides a unique opportunity to model urban resilience metrics in three dimensions. The algorithm will need to incorporate spatial modeling techniques, such as geostatistics or spatial regression, to capture the spatial relationships between different features and metrics.

Forecasting and evaluation: The final step in the algorithm is to use the temporal and spatial models to generate forecasts of urban resilience metrics over time. These forecasts will be evaluated using a variety of metrics, such as Mean Absolute Percentage Error (MAPE), Mean Average Error (MAE) and Root Mean Square Error (RMSE) respectively. The equation defining the n samples is given below.

$$RMSE\left(\widehat{X}_i, X_i\right) = \sqrt{\frac{1}{n} \sum_{i=1}^{n} \left(\widehat{X}_i - X_i\right)^2} \tag{4}$$

$$MAE\left(\widehat{X}_i, X_i\right) = \frac{1}{n} \sum_{i=1}^{n} \left|\widehat{X}_i - X_i\right| \tag{5}$$

$$MAPE\left(\widehat{X}_i, X_i\right) = \frac{1}{n} \sum_{i=1}^{n} \frac{\left|\widehat{X}_i - X_i\right|}{X_i} \tag{6}$$

Our STFA relies on three fundamental principles: spatial data modeling, temporal data modeling, and data integration. Spatial data modeling is achieved by representing the urban environment as a 3D grid, where each cell represents a specific location within the city. This approach allows the algorithm to capture the nuances of the urban environment, such as building height, density, and street width, and use this information to make predictions. Temporal data modeling involves analyzing historical data to identify patterns and trends in urban development. This information is then used to make predictions about future changes in the urban environment. Finally, data integration involves combining various data sources, such as satellite imagery, sensor data, and social media data, to create a comprehensive picture of the urban environment.

Several studies have investigated the use of STFA in urban environments. For example, a study by Chen et al. [51] applied a spatio-temporal forecasting algorithm to predict the demand for shared bikes in urban areas. The authors used data from bike-sharing systems and various environmental factors, such as weather, to develop a model that accurately predicted bike usage patterns. Another study by Wu et al. [52] used an STFA to predict air quality levels in urban areas. The authors integrated data from various sources, including satellite imagery, meteorological data, and land-use data, to develop a model that accurately predicted air quality levels in different locations. These studies demonstrate the potential of STFA in urban environments and highlight the importance of integrating various data sources to achieve accurate predictions.

### 4.2 Urban Resilience Key Metrics Computation Algorithm

The STFA for urban resilience metrics vector based on the Cityscapes database will need to incorporate a range of data preprocessing, modeling, and evaluation techniques to capture the complex and dynamic nature of urban resilience metrics. The pseudocode of is presented in detail in Table 2. The algorithm consists of four main steps: preprocessing, model training, forecasting, and evaluation. During the first step, the input data is preprocessed to prepare it for training the model. This includes tasks such as data cleaning, normalization, and feature extraction. Once the data is preprocessed, the algorithm trains a machine learning model on the input data to learn the patterns and relationships in the data. This second step involves selecting an appropriate machine learning algorithm and setting its hyperparameters to optimize the performance of the model. After the model has been trained, it can be used to make predictions on new data. The forecasting step involves feeding the model with new input data and using it to generate predictions. In the final step, the performance of the model is evaluated to determine how well it performs on the task at hand. This step involves using various metrics to assess [53, 55] the accuracy and reliability of the model's predictions.

## 5 Experiments

### 5.1 Experimental City and Dataset

Located in the Auvergne-Rhône-Alpes region of France, the city of Lyon (Fig. 3), has been selected as the experimental area for the implementation of our 3D Spatio-Temporal Forecasting Algorithm. The city is known for its rich cultural heritage, gastronomy, and vibrant urban life. With a population of over 500,000 and an area of 47.87 km$^2$ Lyon is a bustling metropolis with a complex and dynamic urban system. The implementation of the STFA in Lyon will provide a valuable opportunity to test and refine the algorithm in a real-world urban environment. The Cityscapes dataset, along with other available data sources such as OpenStreetMap 3D, CityJSON, and LIDAR, were utilized to collect and process the required 3D spatio-temporal data. Disruptive events such as traffic congestion (TC), extreme weather events (EW), and infrastructure failures (IF) were considered in the development of the key metrics vectors for urban resilience. These metrics were used to train the forecasting model to predict the impact of disruptive events on the urban system in Lyon.

The evaluation of the forecasting results provided insights into the performance of the algorithm and its potential for practical applications in urban planning and management. The insights gained from this experiment aim to contribute to the advancement of the field of urban resilience and the development of effective strategies for managing urban systems in the face of disruptive events.

**Table 2.** Urban resilience key metrics forecasting algorithm.

| |
|---|
| Inputs: |
| - Cityscapes dataset (3D urban model with attributes such as building height, street-layout, and land use) |
| - Other GeoDataset (OpenStreetMap 3D data, CityJSON data, Google Earth data, LIDAR data, ...) |
| - Other data sources (e.g., social, economic, environmental, and governance of the urban system) |
| - Time series data of urban resilience metrics |
| - Spatial boundaries of the study area |
| - Disruptive event characteristics E = {magnitude, duration, location} |
| - Time frame for forecasting |
| Outputs: |
| - Forecasted key metrics vectors $\overrightarrow{Ab}, \overrightarrow{Re}, \overrightarrow{Ad}$ for the urban area affected by the disruptive event. |
| - The composite urban resilience $U_{res}^t$ from Eq. (3) |
| 1. Preprocessing: |
| - Load 3D dataset and other relevant data. |
| - Identify the affected area based on the location of the disruptive event. |
| - Extract the relevant 3D spatial and temporal features from input datasets. |
| - Normalize features and split datasets into training and testing sets. |
| 2. Model training: |
| - Train the 3D spatio-temporal forecasting model using the extracted features. |
| - Use the disruptive event characteristics E to adjust the model parameters. |
| - Tune the model hyperparameters to optimize the forecasting accuracy. |
| 3. Forecasting: |
| - Apply the trained model to forecast the key metrics vectors. |
| - Deliver the outputs. |
| 4. Evaluation: |
| - Evaluate the forecasting performance using metrics such as mean squared error or mean absolute error. |
| - Refine the model and forecasting process based on the evaluation results |

To effectively test our algorithm, the dataset includes various socio-economic indicators such as population density, employment rates, public services, and transportation systems. We cover the period from 2000 to 2023. These indicators were collected from official sources such as the National Institute of Statistics and Economic Studies (INSEE), the Urban Community of Lyon (Grand Lyon), Météo France, and the Ministry of Transport. A synoptic view of the data is presented in Table 3. The dataset also includes environmental data such as air quality index (AQI), average temperature (AT), and rainfall.

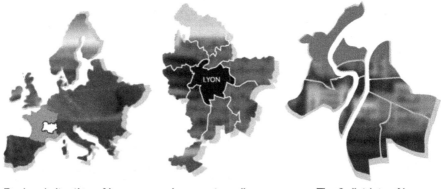

Regional situation of Lyon        Lyon metropolis        The 9 districts of Lyon

**Fig. 3.** The 9 districts of city of Lyon as study area for urban resilience forecasting computing.

**Table 3.** A synoptic view of the dataset.

| District | 3D GeoData | Population (Average) | Households (Average) | Median Households Income (€) | TC (%) | EW | IF (X) | AQI | AT (°C) |
|---|---|---|---|---|---|---|---|---|---|
| 1st | Available | 30,142 | 16,677 | 29,742 | 18–32 | Rain | 0–2 | 19–35 | 12–19 |
| 2nd | Available | 30,898 | 18,785 | 32,604 | 20–28 | Snow | 1–4 | 20–28 | 11–17 |
| 3rd | Available | 102,752 | 51,304 | 27,839 | 19–27 | Rain | 0–5 | 22–30 | 12–20 |
| 4th | Available | 36,369 | 38,203 | 29,859 | 21–40 | Snow | 2–4 | 18–26 | 9–21 |
| 5th | Available | 50,473 | 23,546 | 29,705 | 18–41 | Snow | 3–4 | 23–38 | 10–21 |
| 6th | Available | 52,568 | 24,925 | 37,768 | 20–38 | Rain | 2–5 | 19–32 | 11–18 |
| 7th | Available | 82,105 | 41,725 | 22,999 | 21–41 | Rain | 1–5 | 23–36 | 9–20 |
| 8th | Available | 86,110 | 41,574 | 24,489 | 23–40 | Snow | 1–2 | 20–29 | 12–19 |
| 9h | Available | 51,262 | 23,282 | 26,673 | 22–39 | Rain | 2–3 | 24–34 | 11–18 |

## 5.2  Experimental Settings

To achieve accurate forecasting of urban resilience, it is crucial to utilize multiple spatio-temporal datasets to their full potential. In recent years, advanced deep learning methods have been introduced for spatio-temporal modeling, but a main challenge remains: designing appropriate neural architectures to effectively fuse multi-scale spatio-temporal data and improve forecasting accuracy. Therefore, extensive experiments were conducted to evaluate a proposed model on real-world datasets from different domains and sources as depicted in Fig. 4. Based on key work in spatio-temporal forecasting [55–59], the effectiveness of STFA was evaluated by comparing it to five reference approaches. Models selected for comparison include Historical Average (HA) [49], XG-Boost [53], ConvLSTM [56], PredRNN [57] and ST-ResNet [58].

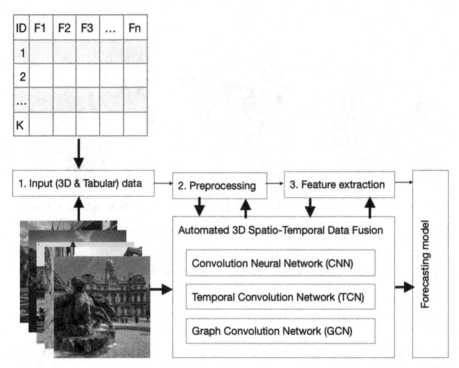

**Fig. 4.** The framework of STFA.

Automated 3D Spatio-Temporal Data Fusion (A3DSTDF) module is the crucial component in our proposed framework on which is developed our STFA (Fig. 4). CNN which has gained remarkable success in image recognition tasks in computer vision, can also be utilized for extracting spatial features in spatio-temporal forecasting. The fundamental learning mechanism of CNN is based on a sliding operation applied to image-like data followed by aggregating neighboring features through a series of filters of fixed size. These filters have learnable parameters and allow the network to automatically learn relevant features at multiple spatial resolutions. When compared to recurrent neural network, TCN is a more efficient method for modeling time series data. Like CNN, TCN's learning mechanism is based on sliding filters with learnable parameters, but the difference is that TCN's filters only slide in the 1D time dimension. GCN is a specialized extension of CNN used to handle structured data in non-Euclidean space. In contrast to a geographic grid map, where spatial semantic relations are defined in a regular Euclidean space, such relations do not exist in non-Euclidean space, and hence GCN is employed for spatial semantic learning. Adjacency matrices are used to represent the spatial semantic relations. HA is a widely used time series forecasting technique, which is simple in nature. It involves averaging the input series and using the resulting average as the forecasted value for the next time step. In this study, the input time step is set at 12. XGBoost is an ensemble learning model that employs decision regression tree models to extract and merge various features from the data in parallel. In our experiment, the input time step is set to 12, while the number of iterations and the maximum depth of trees are set to 100 and 10, respectively. ConvLSTM is a deep learning model that integrates spatial and temporal information for precipitation prediction by employing convolution operations in LSTM units. The model has 2 layers with the number of hidden dimensions set to [32]. The size of convolutional filters is set to 33, and the input time step is set to 12. The learning rate is set to 0.001. PredRNN is an extension of ConvLSTM that addresses the issue of information loss between different cells by using spatio-temporal memory units. The model also has 2 layers with the number of filters set as [32]. The size of convolutional filters is set to 33, and the input time step is 12. The learning rate is set to 0.001. ST-ResNet is a region-wise spatial-temporal forecasting model that employs the ResNet unit, an improved variant of CNN, to capture spatial-temporal features in different time granularity. In this study, the model only uses the closeness time granularity to ensure its generalizability across different domains. The ResNet unit consists of 4 CNN layers with filter sizes of 3*3. The input time step is set to 6, and the learning rate is set to 0.001.

## 5.3  Experimental Results

We evaluate the effectiveness of our proposed STFA model on three different disruptive events (traffic congestion: TC, extreme weather: EW, and infrastructure failures: IF) in the urban resilience computing of Lyon city. To compare the performance of STFA with five other region-wise spatio-temporal forecasting models, we use three evaluation metrics: Mean Absolute Percentage Error (MAPE), Mean Average Error (MAE), and Root Mean Square Error (RMSE). While MAE and RMSE measure the errors between the forecasting results and actual data, RMSE is more sensitive to outliers. On the other hand, MAPE is a relative error metric that can eliminate the influence of data scale when measuring forecasting accuracy. Lower values for these metrics indicate better performance of the models. Table 4 summarizes the performance of urban resilience forecasting for each disruptive event.

**Table 4.** Performance of our STFA for urban resilience metrics computing

| Method | Traffic Congestion (TC) | | | Extreme Weather (EW) | | | Infrastructure Failures (IF) | | |
|---|---|---|---|---|---|---|---|---|---|
| | RMSE | MAE | MAPE | RMSE | MAE | MAPE | RMSE | MAE | MAPE |
| HA | 1.4782 | 0.4213 | 0.0916 | 0.2265 | 0.0743 | 0.0689 | 0.3895 | 0.1382 | 0.0473 |
| XGBoost | 0.8135 | 0.2707 | 0.0568 | 0.1572 | 0.0514 | 0.0278 | 0.2610 | 0.0866 | 0.0286 |
| ConvLSTM | 0.7458 | 0.2336 | 0.0481 | 0.1146 | 0.0421 | 0.0196 | 0.2201 | 0.0702 | 0.0210 |
| ST-ResNet | 0.7425 | 0.2316 | 0.0471 | 0.1104 | 0.0406 | 0.0193 | 0.2189 | 0.0697 | 0.0204 |
| **PredRNN*** | **0.7378** | **0.2289** | **0.0466** | **0.1083** | **0.0401** | **0.0190** | **0.2174** | **0.0694** | **0.0199** |
| **STFA (ours)** | **0.6146** | **0.1872** | **0.0353** | **0.0864** | **0.0314** | **0.0157** | **0.1814** | **0.0573** | **0.0173** |
| Improvement | +17% | +18% | +24% | +20% | +22% | +17% | +17% | +17% | +13% |

The comparison of different spatio-temporal forecasting methods using three evaluation metrics indicates that the traditional time series model (HA) and statistical learning model (XGBoost) perform poorly compared to other methods, as they fail to capture spatial correlations and consider only temporal information. The results highlight the importance of spatial dependencies in spatio-temporal forecasting. Among the five reference models, PredRNN performs the best, but STFA outperforms all other spatio-temporal deep learning methods and PredRNN in all three evaluation metrics. The performance improvement of STFA can be attributed to three reasons. First, our model captures both Euclidean and non-Euclidean semantic correlations, allowing for better utilization of multi-scale spatial data. Second, STFA employs a TCN approach to capture both short-term and long-term temporal dependencies. This is a significant improvement over other models that focus only on short-term dependencies. Finally, STFA employs the A3DSTDF approach to effectively fuse multi-scale spatio-temporal data, which results in a better adaptation to different data scenarios and superior architectures. Future research will incorporate more refined spatio-temporal learning and fusion operators in the search space of the framework and incorporate additional exogenous information to further improve prediction accuracy.

## 6   Conclusion and Future Work

In this paper, we proposed a novel 3D Spatio-Temporal Forecasting Algorithm (STFA) based on an Automated 3D Spatio-Temporal Data Fusion (A3DSTDF) framework for computing urban resilience metrics. The proposed model was extensively evaluated on three different disruptive events and compared with state-of-the-art baselines using various evaluation metrics. The experimental results demonstrated that the STFA approach outperformed the baselines in terms of forecasting accuracy, highlighting the effectiveness of our proposed method. Furthermore, we presented case studies to illustrate the neural architectures learned by our proposed STFA model for various data attributes. One of the strengths of our framework is its scalability, as it can accommodate various spatio-temporal learning and fusion operators for different urban resilience forecasting tasks. However, we acknowledge that our proposed framework has some limitations. For instance, it currently uses relatively simple modules to fuse multi-scale spatio-temporal data.

To overcome this limitation, we plan to incorporate more refined spatio-temporal learning and fusion operators in the search space of our framework. This will enable us to effectively fuse spatio-temporal data from multiple sources and address large-scale geodata fusion. In addition, we aim to incorporate more exogenous information into the framework to further improve prediction accuracy. Overall, the proposed STFA model and A3DSTDF framework have significant potential for enhancing urban resilience metrics computation, and we believe that our future research will address the limitations and advance the state-of-the-art in this field. Our future research focus on two major directions to further advance the proposed STFA model and A3DSTDF framework for urban resilience forecasting. The proposed framework for urban resilience forecasting could benefit from the integration of more advanced and complex multi-scale spatio-temporal learning and fusion operators. This would enhance the framework's adaptability and scalability for different forecasting tasks. One such method is the exploration of graph neural networks (GNNs) and attention mechanisms, which can capture semantic and temporal dependencies across multiple scales. Moreover, to improve the accuracy of the predictions, the framework could be extended to incorporate more diverse data sources such as social data and remote sensing data. This could help to capture more comprehensive and diverse urban resilience indicators that are not directly observable, leading to a more accurate forecasting model.

# References

1. Khodadad, M., Aguilar-Barajas, I., Khan, A.Z.: Green infrastructure for urban flood resilience: a review of recent literature on bibliometrics, methodologies, and typologies. Water **15**(3), 523 (2023). https://doi.org/10.3390/w15030523
2. Ahern, J.: From fail-safe to safe-to-fail: sustainability and resilience in the new urban world. Landsc. Urban Plan. **100**(4), 341–343 (2011). https://doi.org/10.1016/j.landurbplan.2011.02.021
3. Ahern, J., Cilliers, S., Niemela, J.: The concept of ecosystem services in adaptive urban planning and design: a framework for supporting innovation. Landsc. Urban Plan. **125**, 254–259 (2014). https://doi.org/10.1016/j.landurbplan.2014.01.020
4. Meerow, S., Newell, J.P., Stults, M.: Defining urban resilience: a review. Landsc. Urban Plan. **147**, 38–49 (2016). https://doi.org/10.1016/j.landurbplan.2015.11.011
5. Leventon, J., Meerow, S.: Developing a comprehensive approach to urban resilience metrics. Sustainability **11**(16), 4363 (2019). https://doi.org/10.3390/su11164363
6. Holling, C.S.: Resilience and stability of ecological systems. Annu. Rev. Ecol. Syst. **4**(1), 1–23 (1973). https://doi.org/10.1146/annurev.es.04.110173.000245
7. Gencer, E., Akar, G.: Developing a resilience matrix for cities. Sustainability **9**(10), 1774 (2017). https://doi.org/10.3390/su9101774
8. Wang, Y., Zhang, L., Guo, C., Li, J.: Urban resilience: a review. Urban Sci. **3**(2), 45 (2019). https://doi.org/10.3390/urbansci3020045
9. Collier, M.J., Hayes, T.M.: Conceptualizing urban resilience: a framework for analysis. Sustainability **10**(10), 3609 (2018). https://doi.org/10.3390/su10103609
10. Cote, M., Nightingale, A.J.: Resilience thinking meets social theory: situating social change. In: socio-ecological systems (SES) research. Prog. Hum. Geogr. **36**(4), 475–489 (2012). https://doi.org/10.1177/0309132511425708
11. Ostadtaghizadeh, A., Ardalan, A., Paton, D., Jabbari, H., Khankeh, H.R., Khorasani-Zavareh, D.: A systematic review of the factors affecting resilience of urban areas against earthquakes and floods. J. Urban Health **94**(6), 746–759 (2017). https://doi.org/10.1007/s11524-017-0209-9
12. Chiu, C.: Theorizing public participation and local governance in urban resilience: reflections on the "provincializing urban political ecology" thesis. Sustainability **12**, 1–12 (2020). https://doi.org/10.3390/su122410307
13. Aguilar-Barajas, I., Sisto, N.P., Ramirez, A.I., Magan~a-Rueda, V.: Building urban resilience and knowledge co-production in the face of weather hazards: flash floods in the Monterrey Metropolitan Area (Mexico). Environ. Sci. Policy **99**, 37–47 (2019). https://doi.org/10.1016/j.envsci.2019.05.021
14. Albers, M., Deppisch, S.: Resilience in the light of climate change: useful approach or empty phrase for spatial planning? Eur Plan Stud **21**(10), 1598–1610 (2013). https://doi.org/10.1080/09654313.2012.722961

15. Armenakis, C., Nirupama, N.: Estimating spatial disaster risk in urban environments. Geomat. Nat. Haz. Risk **4**(4), 289–298 (2013). https://doi.org/10.1080/19475705.2013.818066

16. Cui, P., Li, D.: Measuring the disaster resilience of an urban community using ANP-FCE method from the perspective of capitals. Soc. Sci. Q. **100**, 2059–2077 (2019). https://doi.org/10.1111/ssqu.12699

17. Cutter, S.L.: The landscape of disaster resilience indicators in the USA. Nat. Hazards **80**(2), 741–758 (2015). https://doi.org/10.1007/s11069-015-1993-2

18. Cutter, S.L., Derakhshan, S.: Temporal and spatial change in disaster resilience in US counties, 2010–2015. Environ. Hazards **19**, 10–29 (2018). https://doi.org/10.1080/17477891.2018.1511405

19. Davidson, K., Nguyen, T.M.P., Beilin, R., Briggs, J.: The emerging addition of resilience as a component of sustainability in urban policy. Cities **92**, 1–9 (2019). https://doi.org/10.1016/j.cities.2019.03.012

20. Marzi, S., Mysiak, J., Essenfelder, A.H., Amadio, M., Giove, S., Fekete, A.: Constructing a comprehensive disaster resilience index: the case of Italy. PLoS ONE **14**, Article e0221585 (2019). https://doi.org/10.1371/journal.pone.0221585

21. Fratini, C.-F., Geldof, G.-D., Kluck, J., Mikkelsen, P.-S.: Three Points Approach (3PA) for urban flood risk management: a tool to support climate change adaptation through transdisciplinarity and multifunctionality. Urban Water J. **9**(5), 317–331 (2012). https://doi.org/10.1080/1573062X.2012.668913

22. Crowe, P.-R., Foley, K., Collier, M.-J.: Operationalizing urban resilience through a framework for adaptive co-management and design: five experiments in urban planning practice and policy. Environ. Sci. Policy **62**, 112–119 (2016). https://doi.org/10.1016/j.envsci.2016.04.007

23. Mahmoud, H., Chulahwat, A.: Spatial and temporal quantification of community resilience: Gotham City under attack. Comput.-Aid. Civil Infrastruct. Eng. **33**, 353–372 (2018). https://doi.org/10.1111/mice.12318

24. Wilson, G.A., Piper, J.K.: The social construction of urban resilience: reflections on the urban resilience framework in context. Urban Stud. **57**(3), 581–596 (2020). https://doi.org/10.1177/0042098018820041

25. Yonghuai, L., et al.: 3D Imaging, Analysis and Applications. 2nd edn. Springer, Cham (2022). https://doi.org/10.1007/21978-3-030-44070-1

26. Davoudi, S.: Resilience, a bridging concept or a dead end?'. Plan. Theory Pract. **13**(2), 299–307 (2012). https://doi.org/10.1080/14649357.2012.677124

27. Alexander, D.E.: Resilience and disaster risk reduction: an etymological journey. Nat. Hazards Earth Syst. Sci. **13**(2707–2716), 2013 (2013). https://doi.org/10.5194/nhess-13-2707-2013

28. Brand, F.S., Jax, K.: Focusing the Meaning(s) of resilience: resilience as a descriptive concept and a boundary object. Ecol. Soc. **12**(1), (2007). http://www.jstor.org/stable/26267855. Accessed 26 Mar 2023

29. Bruijne, M., Boin, A., Eeten, M.: Resilience: exploring the concept and its meanings. In: Comfort, L.K., Boin, A., Demchak, C.C. (eds.) Designing Resilience. Preparing for Extreme Events, pp. 13–32. University of Pittsburgh Press (2010)

30. Romero-Lankao, P., Gnatz, D.M., Wilhelmi, O., Hayden, M.: Urban sustainability and resilience: from theory to practice. Sustainability **8**(12), 1224, 1–19 (2016)

31. Weichselgartner, J., Kelman, I.: Geographies of resilience: challenges and opportunities of a descriptive concept. Prog. Hum. Geogr. **39**(3), 249–267 (2014)

32. Carpenter, A.: Resilience in the social and physical realms: lessons from the Gulf Coast. Int. J. Dis. Risk Reduct. **14**, 290–301 (2015). https://doi.org/10.1016/j.ijdrr.2014.09.003

33. Brown, A., Dayal, A., del Rio, C-R.: From practice to theory: emerging lessons from Asia for building urban climate change resilience. Environ. Urban. **24**(2), 531–556 (2012). https://doi.org/10.1177/0956247812456490

34. Boyd, E., Juhola, S.: Adaptive climate change governance for urban resilience. Urban Stud. **52**(7), 1234–1264 (2015). https://doi.org/10.1177/0042098014527483

35. Balsells, M., Barroca, B., Amdal, J.-R., Diab, Y., Becue, V., Serre, D.: Analysing urban resilience through alternative stormwater management options: application of the conceptual Spatial Decision Support System model at the neighbourhood scale. Water Sci. Technol. **68**(11), 2448–2457 (2013). https://doi.org/10.2166/wst.2013.527

36. Index, City Resilience. "City resilience framework." The Rockefeller Foundation and ARUP 928 (2014). https://www.urban-response.org/system/files/content/resource/files/main/city-resilience-framework-arup-april-2014.pdf. Accessed 26 Mar 2023

37. Ribeiro, P.J.G., Gonçalves, L.A.P.J.: Urban resilience: a conceptual framework, Sustain. Cities Soc. **50**, 101625 (2019). https://doi.org/10.1016/j.scs.2019.101625

38. Galderisi, A., Limongi, G., Salata, K.-D.: Strengths and weaknesses of the 100 resilient cities initiative in Southern Europe: Rome and Athens' experiences. City Territory Archit. **7**(1), 1–22 (2020). https://doi.org/10.1186/s40410-020-00123-w

39. Aitsi-Selmi, A., Egawa, S., Sasaki, H., Wannous, C., Murray, V.: The sendai framework for disaster risk reduction: renewing the global commitment to people's resilience, health, and well-being. Int. J. Dis. Risk Sci. **6**(2), 164–176 (2015). https://doi.org/10.1007/s13753-015-0050-9

40. Costanza, R., Kubiszewski, I.: A nexus approach to urban and regional planning using the four-capital framework of ecological economics. In: Hettiarachchi, H., Ardakanian, R. (eds.) Environmental Resource Management and the Nexus Approach, pp. 79–111. Springer, Cham (2016). https://doi.org/10.1007/978-3-319-28593-1_4

41. Batty, M.: The New Science of Cities. MIT Press, Boston (2013)

42. Agbossou, I.: Cerner le contexte spatial par les voisinages dans les modèles cellulaires en géographie, Rencontres interdisciplinaires sur le contexte dans les systèmes complexes naturels et artificiels, Jan 2010, Megève, France

43. Li, X., Zhou, Z., Liu, X., Liu, Y.: An improved approach for extracting building footprints from OpenStreetMap 3D Data. Remote Sens. **13**(7), 1315 (2021). https://doi.org/10.3390/rs13071315

44. Biljecki, F., Ledoux, H., Stoter, J.: Gaps in OpenStreetMap building data: a case study for five cities. Comput. Environ. Urban Syst. **75**, 140–153 (2019). https://doi.org/10.1016/j.compenvurbsys.2018.11.002

45. Zhang, Y., Huang, Q., Wang, S., Zhang, S.: Urban scene segmentation with CityJSON and Cityscapes datasets using multi-task learning. ISPRS Int. J. Geo Inf. **10**(2), 72 (2021). https://doi.org/10.3390/ijgi10020072

46. Zhang, W., Wang, J., Fang, H., Yang, Y.: Combining Google Earth imagery and social media data to investigate the spatial distribution of urban functions in Shenzhen China. Sustainability **11**(22), 6268 (2019). https://doi.org/10.3390/su11226268

47. Liao, M., Yuan, Y., Chen, L.: Building damage assessment model for earthquake events based on LiDAR data. ISPRS Int. J. Geo Inf. **10**(4), 257 (2021). https://doi.org/10.3390/ijgi10040257

48. Cordts, M., et al.: The cityscapes dataset for semantic urban scene understanding. In: Proceedings of the IEEE Conference on Computer Vision and Pattern Recognition, pp. 3213–3223 (2016). https://doi.org/10.1109/CVPR.2016.350

49. Song, C., Lin, Y., Guo, S., Wan, H.: Spatial-temporal synchronous graph convolutional networks: a new framework for spatial-temporal network data forecasting. Proc. AAAI Conf. Artif. Intell. **34**(01), 914–921 (2020). https://doi.org/10.1609/aaai.v34i01.5438

50. Wenjia, K., Haochen, L., Chen, Y., Jiangjiang, X., Yanyan, K., Pingwen, Z.: A deep spatio-temporal forecasting model for multi-site weather prediction post-processing. Commun. Comput. Phys. **31**(1), 131–153 (2021). https://doi.org/10.4208/cicp.OA-2020-0158

51. Chen, Y., Li, W., Liu, X., Gao, F., Li, X.: Spatio-temporal forecasting algorithm for bike-sharing demand prediction. Sustainability **12**(5), 1997 (2020). https://doi.org/10.3390/su1 2051997
52. Wu, C., Huang, Y., Wang, Y., Zeng, W.: A spatio-temporal forecasting algorithm for air quality level prediction in urban areas. Sustainability **11**(13), 3713 (2019). https://doi.org/10.3390/su11133713
53. Chen, T., Guestrin, C.: XGBoost: a scalable tree boosting system. In: Proceedings of the 22nd ACM SIGKDD International Conference on Knowledge Discovery and Data Mining, pp. 785–794 (2016)
54. Yu, F., Koltun, V.: Multi-scale context aggregation by dilated convolutions. In: ICLR (2015). https://doi.org/10.48550/arXiv.1511.07122
55. Guangyin, J., Qi, W., Cunchao, Z., Yanghe, F., Jincai, H., Xingchen, H.: Urban fire situation forecasting: deep sequence learning with spatio-temporal dynamics, Appl. Soft Comput. **97**, Part B, 106730, (2020). https://doi.org/10.1016/j.asoc.2020.106730
56. Shi, X., Chen, Z., Wang, H., Yeung, D.Y., Wong, W. K., Woo, W.C.: Convolutional LSTM network: a machine learning approach for precipitation nowcasting. Adv. Neural Inf. Process. Syst. **28** (2015)
57. Wang, Y., et al.: PredRNN: A recurrent neural network for spatiotemporal predictive learning. IEEE Trans. Pattern Anal. Mach. Intell. **45**(2), 2208–2225 (2022)
58. Zhang, J., Zheng, Y., Qi, D.: Deep spatio-temporal residual networks for citywide crowd flows prediction. In: Proceedings of the AAAI Conference on Artificial Intelligence (vol. 31, No. 1) (2017)
59. Guangyin, J., Hengyu, S., Zhexu, X., Jincai, H.: Urban hotspot forecasting via automated spatio-temporal information fusion, Appl. Soft Comput. **136**, (2023). https://doi.org/10.1016/j.asoc.2023.110087

# A Framework for the Analysis of Metaheuristics for the Travelling Salesman Problem with Drone with Interceptions

Rudolf Ernst[1]([✉]), Tsietsi Moremi[1], Jacomine Grobler[1], and Phil M. Kaminsky[2]

[1] Department of Industrial Engineering, Stellenbosch University, Stellenbosch, South Africa
rudolfernst1998@gmail.com
[2] Department of Industrial Engineering and Operations Research, University of California at Berkeley, Berkeley, USA

**Abstract.** This paper proposes a framework for utilising continuous metaheuristic algorithms for solving drone delivery scheduling problems with interceptions. The use of the framework is illustrated through the application of a particle swarm optimisation-based algorithm, a differential evolution-based algorithm, and a covariance matrix adaptation-evolution strategy for Moremi's travelling salesman problem with drone with interceptions (TSPDi) [1]. A single drone can be launched to make a delivery while a truck is delivering packages to customers. The drone then either intercepts the purpose-built truck after completing a delivery when possible or meets up with the truck at the next customer location. The optimisation algorithms are tested on benchmark datasets and compared against Moremi's ant colony optimisation-based drone scheduling algorithm. Algorithm performance is measured with regards to total delivery time and total truck travel distance. An in-depth analysis of algorithm performance is conducted in the form of an efficiency study. The efficiency study specifically considers the number of duplicate and feasible solutions as the different algorithms handle the TSPDi constraints. It is shown that the metaheuristics are especially useful when a smaller number of deliveries are required, whereas performance deteriorates significantly when the number of nodes to be visited grows.

The contributions of this paper include the only in-depth analysis of the performance of continuous-based metaheuristics in drone scheduling literature, as well as the first framework for utilising continuous-based metaheuristics for solving drone delivery scheduling problems with interceptions. This paper contributes to the computational sciences by using advanced computing capabilities for decision support to improve the performance of an intelligent transport system.

**Keywords:** Drone delivery · Metaheuristics · Routing and optimisation · TSP with drone with interceptions

© The Author(s), under exclusive license to Springer Nature Switzerland AG 2023
O. Gervasi et al. (Eds.): ICCSA 2023, LNCS 13957, pp. 351–368, 2023.
https://doi.org/10.1007/978-3-031-36808-0_23

# 1   Introduction

Last-mile freight is considered the final delivery step of goods from a fixed distribution facility to end-users [2]. The coordination of the "last mile" is a common problem in built-up environments. The closer to the aggregated demand point, the bigger the loss in efficiency and capacity is observed, due to the complexity of sequencing and allocating deliveries in an optimal manner [3]. With the growth of online shopping and accessibility to it, last-mile delivery companies are constantly seeking faster and more efficient ways to deliver products to customers in order to gain a competitive advantage [4].

In recent years, companies have investigated using "innovation vehicles" as well as collaborative or cooperative logistics, among others, to improve the efficiency of last mile deliveries [5]. One of these "innovation vehicles" being considered is a drone delivery vehicle or an unmanned aerial vehicle (UAV). Many practical applications of drones have been referenced in literature. The applications of drones range from the retailing and e-commerce sectors (Amazon, 2013 [6]; Flirtey, 2016 [7]), postal services and package delivery (United Postal Service, 2017 [8]; DHL, 2016 [9]), food and beverage delivery (Flirtey for Domino's Pizza, 2016 [10]; Alphabet for Chipotle, 2016 [11]) as well as healthcare and emergency services (Matternat for blood samples in Lesotho, 2016 [12]; Zipline for blood samples in Rwanda, 2017 [13]; Flirtey for medical supplies in Virginia, 2015 [14]).

Specifically, this paper proposes a framework that considers a problem based on the travelling salesman problem with drone (TSPD), as first presented by Agatz et al. [15], where a single truck and drone are used for pre-determined deliveries. The research involves a truck and drone waiting for one another at customer locations in the process of making deliveries. Agatz' research was expanded on by Moremi [1] to allow the drone to intercept the truck while in motion (TSPDi), on the arc between customer locations. The interceptions improve completion times and decrease waiting time, which is especially undesirable for drones due to security risks.

In this paper, a self adaptive neighbourhood search differential evolution (SaNSDE), guaranteed convergence particle swarm optimization (GCPSO), and covariance matrix adaptation evolution strategy (CMA-ES)-based algorithms are developed and evaluated as part of the framework. Two alternative repair mechanisms are implemented for the SaNSDE and GCPSO, as explained in Sect. 5. The algorithms are tested on benchmark datasets ranging from 10 to 250 nodes [16] and compared to the ant colony system (ACS) results of Moremi [1]. Furthermore, an in-depth efficiency study is conducted to understand the performance of the different metaheuristics applied to the TSPDi.

The results show that the SaNSDE performs the best on smaller datasets, whereas the CMA-ES performs the best among bigger datasets when only considering the algorithms implemented in this study. The CMA-ES is the most consistent performer, as it also finds good enough solutions for the smaller datasets. The efficiency study highlights the complications of applying metaheuristics to combinatorial optimisation problems such as the TSPDi. The metaheuristics generate large numbers of infeasible solutions but are able to navigate the solution space effectively, having minimal numbers of duplicate solutions.

The main contribution of this paper is that it is, to the best of the authors' knowledge, the first framework developed for utilising continuous-based metaheuristic algorithms, such as PSO, DE, and CMAES, for solving drone delivery scheduling problems with interceptions. The contributions of this paper include the only in-depth analysis of the performance of continuous-based metaheuristics in drone scheduling literature. The paper gives guidance as to applying metaheuristics to the truck drone scheduling problem as well as results to illustrate which metaheuristics perform better on different-sized datasets.

The rest of the paper is organised as follows: Sect. 2 introduces a literature survey of important drone and truck delivery research. Section 3 describes the mathematical model of the TSPDi, followed by the algorithm background in Sect. 4. The framework and experimental setup is presented in Sect. 5, while the empirical evaluation of the algorithms implemented on the TSPDi is done in Sect. 6. An efficiency study is presented in Sect. 7 and a conclusion is given in Sect. 8.

## 2 Literature Review

A significant amount of research has focused on optimising the last mile of deliveries, specifically with respect to the vehicle routing problem. Solomon and Desrosiers (1988) [17], Laporte et al. (1992) [18], Toth and Vigo (2012) [19], Kumar and Panneerselvam (2012) [20], and Lin et al. (2014) [21], amongst others, published surveys of vehicle routing literature. Extensive surveys, focusing on drones for deliveries, were conducted by Otto et al. (2018) [22], Khoufi et al. (2019) [23], Chung et al. (2020) [24], Poikonen and Campbell (2020) [25]; Moshref-Javadi and Winkenbach (2021) [26], and Liang and Luo (2022) [27].

Single truck and drone problems are mainly categorised and differentiated between a travelling salesman problem with drone (TSP-D) (Agatz and Bouman (2018) [15], Ha et al. (2018) [28]) or flying sidekick travelling salesman problem (FSTSP) (Murray and Chu (2015) [29], Boysen et al. (2018) [30]). TSP-D uses the concept of operations, while FSTSP uses the concept of sorties to model the problem [24]. Most of these problems considered in literature require either the drone or truck to wait for the other at customer locations when making deliveries before synchronising or meeting up again. Lastly, a truck and drone routing problem with synchronisation on arcs (TDRP-SA) (Li et al. 2022 [31]) allows for moving drone launch and retrieval locations. Drones are thus able to be launched to deliver a package and then land on a moving truck when returning. Salama and Srinivas [32] and Thomas et al. [33] also considered models where drones could be dispatched and retrieved on the arc between two customers.

A common extension of the FSTSP is allowing for multiple drones (mFSTSP) (Ferrandez et al. (2016) [34], Chang and Lee (2018) [35], Murray and Raj (2019) [36]). mFSTSP requires the truck to be stationary while the drones make deliveries, only moving to the next location when all drones have returned. On the other hand, the TSP-D is transformed into a TSP with multiple drones (TSP-mD) (Yoon (2018) [37], Tu et al. (2018) [38]), where the truck is allowed to move until the drones complete their deliveries, whereafter it is stationary until they return. Murray and Chu (2015) [29] also presented the parallel drone scheduling travelling salesman problem (PDSTSP) formulation, where a single truck and multiple identical drones service customers directly from a depot. The next natural step in literature allows multiple trucks and drones to make deliveries (VRP-D), which is not covered in this paper.

## 3   Problem Background

The problem consists of a truck and drone having to make multiple pre-determined deliveries to customers. A truck and a drone that can be launched from the truck leave the depot together when setting out to make deliveries. Whenever the drone makes a delivery, it is launched from the preceding truck node. After the drone completes a delivery, it either intercepts the truck, if possible, while it is in motion on the arc between two customer locations or meets up with the truck at the next customer location. The process is executed until all customers have been visited, whereupon the truck and drone reroute back to the depot. The mathematical formulation of the TSPDi is given below, while the full explanation of the TSPDi can be found in [1].

- $n$ is the number of customers to be serviced.
- $T_{ijk}$ denotes the total time for the scenario where a drone delivers to node $j$ while the truck delivers to nodes $i$ and $k$. $T_{ijk}$ is calculated based on the drone and truck intercepting each other after the drone delivery. This interception point is calculated using the standard mathematical equations for two objects interceptions explained in [1].
- $T_{ik}$ denotes the total time for scenario where the truck delivers to nodes $i$ and $k$ when there is not a drone delivery in between.
- $w$ is the drone offload time

With the following decision variables:

- $u_i$ is used to eliminate sub-tours.

$$x_{ijk} = \begin{cases} 1 & \text{if the truck services customer } i \text{ before } k \text{ while the drone services } j \text{ in between} \\ 0 & \text{otherwise} \end{cases}$$

$$b_j = \begin{cases} 1 & \text{if the customer } j \text{ is serviced by the drone} \\ 0 & \text{if customer } j \text{ is serviced by the truck} \end{cases}$$

$$z_{ik} = \begin{cases} 1 & \text{if the truck travels between customer } i \text{ and } k \\ 0 & \text{otherwise} \end{cases}$$

$$\min \sum_{i=1}^{n}\sum_{k=1}^{n}\sum_{j=1}^{n} x_{ijk}T_{ijk} + \sum_{i=1}^{n}\sum_{k=1}^{n} z_{ik}T_{ik}\left(1 - \sum_{j=1}^{n} x_{ijk}\right) - w \qquad (1)$$

Subject to:

$$z_{ii} = 0 \qquad \forall i \in \{1, ..., n\} \qquad (2)$$

$$x_{iii}, x_{iij}, x_{iji}, x_{ijj} = 0 \qquad \forall i, j \in \{1, ..., n\} \tag{3}$$

$$z_{ik} = (\sum_{j=1}^{n} x_{ijk} = 1) => (z_{ik} = 1) \qquad \forall i, k \in \{1, ..., n\} \tag{4}$$

$$b_j = \sum_{i=1}^{n} \sum_{k=1}^{n} x_{ijk} \qquad \forall j \in \{1, ..., n\} \tag{5}$$

$$\sum_{i=1}^{n} z_{iq} - \sum_{k=1}^{n} z_{qk} = 0 \qquad \forall q \in \{1, ..., n\} \tag{6}$$

$$(b_i = 0) => (\sum_{k=1}^{n} z_{ik} = 1) \qquad \forall i \in \{1, ..., n\} \tag{7}$$

$$(b_k = 0) => (\sum_{i=1}^{n} z_{ik} = 1) \qquad \forall k \in \{1, ..., n\} \tag{8}$$

$$\sum_{j=1}^{n} x_{ijk} \leq 1 \qquad \forall i, k \in \{1, ..., n\} \tag{9}$$

$$u_i + z_{ij} \leq u_j + (n - 1)(1 - z_{ij}) \qquad \forall i, j, j \neq 1 \in \{1, ..., n\} \tag{10}$$

$$u_1 = 0 \tag{11}$$

$$x_{ijk}, b_i, z_{ik} \in \{0, 1\} \qquad \forall \, i, j, k \in \{1, ..., n\} \tag{12}$$

- The objective function (1) minimises the total time that the drone and truck travel, which includes the travel time of all truck deliveries which do not include a drone release and intercept.
- Constraints (2) and (3) simplify the model by ensuring that the truck and drone cannot travel from the current node back to a previously visited node.
- Constraint (4) links $z_{ik}$ and $x_{ijk}$.
- Constraint (5) links $b_j$ and $x_{ijk}$.
- Constraint (6) ensures that if a delivery is conducted at a customer location, the truck or drone leaves that same customer.
- Constraints (7) and (8) ensure that each customer is arrived at from exactly one other customer (by truck), and that from each customer there is a departure to exactly one other customer (by truck). If node $j$ is serviced by a drone, then no trucks enter or exit node $j$.
- Constraint (9) ensures that only one drone delivery can occur between two truck deliveries.
- Constraints (10) and (11) eliminate any sub-tours.
- Constraint (12) restricts the decision variables to binary values.

## 4   Algorithm Background

The SaNSDE, GCPSO and CMA-ES algorithms are explained in this section along with their relevant background and implementation.

## 4.1 Differential Evolution

The *differential evolution* (DE) algorithm is a population-based, stochastic optimisation algorithm. The DE is successful due to the difference vectors that determine the step sizes applied to the individuals in the population. The difference between two solutions is the core driver of the algorithm toward better solutions [39]. A differential mutation operator allows for the step sizes of the algorithm to automatically adapt to the objective function landscape [39]. Before a population converges around a specific optimum, the randomly sampled individuals are usually far apart in different regions of the search space. Larger step sizes will then be allowed when greater exploration of the search space is desired. These larger steps also make it possible to escape local optima. In the later iterations, when convergence around a good solution is desired, smaller step sizes are automatically applied due to the close proximity of all individuals in the search space. This strategy allows the DE algorithm to exploit the region around the optimum in search of even better solutions.

The *Self-adaptive DE with Neighbourhood Search* (SaNSDE) [40] algorithm applied in this paper has been developed by combining the best features of the *Neighbourhood Search DE* (NSDE) [40] algorithm and the *Self-adaptive DE* (SaDE) [41] algorithm.

## 4.2 Guaranteed Convergence Particle Swarm Optimisation

Particle swarm optimization (PSO) is a random population-based optimisation algorithm first implemented by Kennedy and Eberhart [42]. The PSO algorithm represents each candidate solution by the position a particle resides in within a multi-dimensional hyperspace. New candidate solutions, or positions, are determined through displacement and velocity updates, which move particles to new positions, allowing for exploration of the search space [43]. The magnitude of any particle's velocity at time $t$ is the result of three vectors; the particle velocity at time $t-1$, a vector representing the best solution or position found up to time $t$ by the specific particle, and the vector representing the overall best solution or position found up to time $t$ by any particle.

The *guaranteed convergence PSO* (GCPSO) algorithm ensures that a random search around the global best particle position is executed by the *gbest* particle to avoid stagnation of the algorithm. The search space adjusts according to the number of successive successes or failures of the particle in improving the objective function. A success is recorded when there is an improvement in the objective function value.

## 4.3 Covariance Matrix Adaptation Evolution Strategy

The *Covariance Matrix Adaptation Evolution Strategy* (CMA-ES) is an algorithm operating in the continuous domain that has been successfully applied to many unconstrained or bounded constraint optimisation problems. The CMA-ES works in three phases, namely selection and recombination, covariance matrix adaptation, and step size control.

The CMA-ES algorithm is a combination of an evolutionary approach and a fitness landscape model [44]. A set of parameters describing an individual model, called sample points, are used to generate a new set or population of points, where the subset of points with the best fitness values survives to the next generation [44]. Specifically in the CMA-ES, the differences in the average fitness as well as the covariance between subsequent populations are used to move the population towards the optimum. The knowledge gathered from the interactions between parameters is iteratively saved in a covariance matrix [44] and used to allocate new sampling points, which drives the search process. Unfavourable premature convergence is avoided by the variable property of the step size.

## 5    Framework Description

Initially, a random population of $N$ real-valued vectors is created, meaning $N$ solutions are evaluated per iteration. The dimensions of the vectors are $2*(n-1)$ with decision variables between the bounds of $l_b$ and $u_b$. These decision variables change throughout the algorithm's execution and are assigned to each operation. The activity diagram in Fig. 1 shows the framework, with the implementation of the metaheuristics, which is explained next.

To evaluate the fitness of the population in each iteration, the continuous values are converted into a schedule or route to follow by making use of priority-based mapping [45]. The first $n$ values are sorted in descending order to find the permutation of nodes to be visited. The second $n$ allocation variables are used to determine whether a node is visited by a truck or a drone, where a value smaller than zero is a drone node and a value bigger than or equal to zero is a truck node, in effect discretising the search space. For example, the following ten hypothetical decision variables are to be used to determine the sequence that **five** customers will be visited, as well as by which vehicle:

$$[6\ 71\ -99\ 62\ -20\ 13\ 59\ -5\ -20\ 3]$$

The first five priority values are re-sorted in descending order by the function, leading to the following order of nodes to be visited being obtained:

$$\text{Depot} \rightarrow \text{Node 2} \rightarrow \text{Node 4} \rightarrow \text{Node 1} \rightarrow \text{Node 5} \rightarrow \text{Node 3} \rightarrow \text{Depot}$$

The priority values are altered throughout the algorithm execution to guide the process of searching the solution space and are reassigned at each operation. The second $n$ allocation variables are then used to determine which vehicle visits each of the $n$ customers. The vehicle completing each of the deliveries, indicated by a D for drone and a T for truck, are now added in round brackets, with the allocation variable value.

$$\text{Depot} \rightarrow \text{Node 2 [59](T)} \rightarrow \text{Node 4 [-20](D)} \rightarrow \text{Node 1 [13](T)} \rightarrow \text{Node 5 [3](T)} \rightarrow \text{Node 3 [-5](D)} \rightarrow \text{Depot}$$

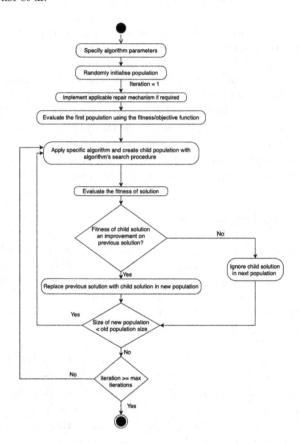

**Fig. 1.** Activity diagram showing framework

A repair process is required in cases where two consecutive drone nodes are scheduled, which does not conform to the TSPDi constraints. Two different procedures are developed for repairing the infeasible solutions, and both result sets are documented in an effort to understand the effect of applying metaheuristics to solve combinatorial optimisation problems. The first repair mechanism changes the second consecutive drone node to a truck node without altering the allocation variable. In the first instance, the algorithm is thus finding a fitness function for a "different solution" than it actually calculates. The second repair procedure changes the allocation variable of the second consecutive drone node to $u_b/2$, to ensure that there are no consecutive drone nodes. The value of $u_b/2$ is chosen, as this ensures that a truck node is scheduled, but that there is still room for the algorithm to move through solutions and change the value towards a negative number (and thus a drone node). The second repair process changes the mechanism the algorithm uses to move through the search space. Only the first repair process is implemented on the CMA-ES.

The framework and metaheuristics are evaluated on 13 datasets from Bouman and Schmidt [16] with varying sizes and coordinate spreads. It is assumed that the truck travels 10 distance units per time unit, whereas the drone travels 20 distance units per time unit. 0.1 time units are added per drone and truck delivery. $N$ is chosen as 100 individuals per population, while $u_b$ and $l_b$ values of $-100$ and 100 are initialised.

## 6    Empirical Evaluation

The means of the delivery times and truck distances with their standard deviations over 30 optimisation runs are presented in Table 1 for all algorithms, as well for an ant colony system (ACS-DT2) of Moremi [1]. The first and second executions of repair mechanisms are shown separately for the SaNSDE and GCPSO. The performance indicator shows the % deterioration or improvement in the algorithm result when compared against the ACS-DT2. Optimal results for the TSPDi model by Knoetze [46] are presented for the small datasets. The time measurement is the most important factor and objective of the problem, but the distance results are included as a secondary measurement. Throughout the rest of the paper, any mention of results is related to the total time measurement, while small datasets are those with 20 nodes or less and large datasets are those with more than 20 nodes. The framework is able to provide final, feasible solutions for the TSPDi.

The framework and most algorithms instantiations are able to improve on the ACS-DT2 result for small datasets, while only the CMA-ES improves on the ACS-DT2 for several larger datasets. The SaNSDE-1 is able to improve up to 16.4% on the smaller datasets while performing poorly with large datasets, obtaining results that are up to 65.8% worse than the ACS-DT2. The SaNSDE-2 is able to improve up to 15.6% on the small datasets, while having a 67.1% worse result on the large datasets. The GCPSO algorithm has the worst results of the candidates. The GCPSO-1 is able to obtain up to 8.2% better results than the ACS-DT2 while having up to 75.9% decline on larger datasets. The GCPSO-2 algorithm obtains a 7.9% improvement at best, having up to 103.1% worse average results on larger datasets.

Most of the algorithms averaged solutions that were equal to or close to the optimal results obtained by Knoetze. These results indicate how well the metaheuristics perform on the TSPDi for small datasets. Problems larger than 20 can currently not be solved optimally, which highlights the benefit of using metaheuristics that find "good enough" solutions in a reasonable amount of time.

The standard deviation is relatively small for the metaheuristics on smaller datasets, but the large standard deviations on larger datasets highlights erratic performance, especially for the GCPSO. The SaNSDE-1 algorithm is the best candidate for smaller datasets, as it is able to gain the best results of any of the algorithm executions. The SaNSDE is underperforming on 100-node or larger datasets. The CMA-ES improves on the results of the ACS-DT2 for the 50 node datasets and one of the 100 node datasets. The CMA-ES is thus considered the best algorithm from this study for larger datasets.

## Table 1. Algorithm Results

| Datasets | Nodes | Optimal Time | ACS-DT2 | | SaNSDE-1 | | | SaNSDE-2 | | | GCPSO-1 | | | GCPSO-2 | | | CMA-ES | | |
|---|---|---|---|---|---|---|---|---|---|---|---|---|---|---|---|---|---|---|---|
| | | | Time | Std Dev | Time | Std Dev | Perf | Time | Std Dev | Perf | Time | Std Dev | Perf | Time | Std Dev | Perf | Time | Std Dev | Perf |
| Uniform-51-n10 | 10 | 25.47 | 25.87 | 0.25 | 25.47 | 0.00 | 1.5% | 25.47 | 0.00 | 1.5% | 25.61 | 0.24 | 1% | 25.76 | 0.43 | 0.4% | 25.76 | 0.88 | 4.2% |
| Uniform-52-n10 | 10 | 20.3 | 20.71 | 0.20 | 20.35 | 0.07 | 1.7% | 20.36 | 0.08 | 1.7% | 20.63 | 0.29 | 0.4% | 20.61 | 0.01 | 0.5% | 20.94 | 0.54 | -1.1% |
| Uniform-53-n10 | 10 | 20.2 | 20.98 | 0.10 | 20.20 | 0.00 | 3.7% | 20.20 | 0.00 | 3.7% | 20.59 | 0.49 | 1.9% | 20.70 | 0.52 | 1.3% | 21.21 | 0.56 | -1.1% |
| Uniform-61-n20 | 20 | 25.49 | 32.67 | 0.63 | 27.31 | 0.94 | 16.4% | 27.57 | 1.28 | 15.6% | 29.98 | 2.43 | 8.2% | 30.08 | 2.25 | 7.9% | 30.92 | 1.51 | 5.3% |
| Uniform-62-n20 | 20 | 28.87 | 33.87 | 0.33 | 30.05 | 0.69 | 11.3% | 30.24 | 0.62 | 10.7% | 32.67 | 1.59 | 3.5% | 32.67 | 1.59 | 3.5% | 35.93 | 2.03 | -6% |
| Uniform-63-n20 | 20 | 28.62 | 33.95 | 0.94 | 28.79 | 0.32 | 15.2% | 28.83 | 0.34 | 15.1% | 33.38 | 3.28 | 1.7% | 33.66 | 2.56 | 0.9% | 35.34 | 3.62 | -4.3% |
| Uniform-71-n50 | 50 | | 83.34 | 3.17 | 85.90 | 5.55 | -3.1% | 85.54 | 4.25 | -2.6% | 89.75 | 8.34 | -7.7% | 93.64 | 10.54 | -12.4% | 81.18 | 5.30 | 2.6% |
| Uniform-72-n50 | 50 | | 85.56 | 1.49 | 95.45 | 3.77 | -11.6% | 92.79 | 4.29 | -8.5% | 94.44 | 9.13 | -10.4% | 99.46 | 9.56 | -16.3% | 83.99 | 5.55 | 1.8% |
| Uniform-73-n50 | 50 | | 83.56 | 1.22 | 89.30 | 4.04 | -6.8% | 88.51 | 3.60 | -5.9% | 90.15 | 9.56 | -7.9% | 95.41 | 10.21 | -14.2% | 88.36 | 7.13 | -5.7% |
| Uniform-91-n100 | 100 | | 161.09 | 3.08 | 202.34 | 5.41 | -25.6% | 202.62 | 6.60 | -25.8% | 209.22 | 10.35 | -29.9% | 221.02 | 14.66 | -37.2% | 157.05 | 8.61 | 2.5% |
| Uniform-92-n100 | 100 | | 149.18 | 2.30 | 200.27 | 6.32 | -34.2% | 201.59 | 5.41 | -35.1% | 211.25 | 17.00 | -41.6% | 213.97 | 12.93 | -43.4% | 159.44 | 8.71 | -6.9% |
| Uniform-1-n250 | 250 | | 382.98 | 5.30 | 634.89 | 9.30 | -65.8% | 640.00 | 9.90 | -67.1% | 673.62 | 32.00 | -75.9% | 778.14 | 65.43 | -103.2% | 422.48 | 20.99 | -10.3% |
| Uniform-2-n250 | 250 | | 385.04 | 7.62 | 626.88 | 7.27 | -62.8% | 633.17 | 11.15 | -64.4% | 659.68 | 30.99 | -71.3% | 754.33 | 53.64 | -95.9% | 409.17 | 15.55 | -6.3% |

| Datasets | Nodes | Optimal Dist | ACS-DT2 | | SaNSDE-1 | | | SaNSDE-2 | | | GCPSO-1 | | | GCPSO-2 | | | CMA-ES | | |
|---|---|---|---|---|---|---|---|---|---|---|---|---|---|---|---|---|---|---|---|
| | | | Dist | Std Dev | Dist | Std Dev | Perf | Dist | Std Dev | Perf | Dist | Std Dev | Perf | Dist | Std Dev | Perf | Dist | Std Dev | Perf |
| Uniform-51-n10 | 10 | | 250.98 | 2.18 | 248.31 | 0.00 | 1.1% | 248.31 | 0.00 | 1.1% | 248.42 | 0.68 | 1% | 250.30 | 4.24 | 0.3% | 249.47 | 4.59 | 0.6% |
| Uniform-52-n10 | 10 | | 195.22 | 3.32 | 191.79 | 1.39 | 1.8% | 191.93 | 1.39 | 1.7% | 194.88 | 4.14 | 0.2% | 194.08 | 4.31 | 0.6% | 193.24 | 5.54 | 1% |
| Uniform-53-n10 | 10 | | 182.92 | 6.85 | 190.48 | 0.00 | -4.1% | 190.48 | 0.00 | -4.1% | 192.11 | 3.19 | -5% | 193.12 | 3.88 | -5.6% | 193.01 | 7.01 | -5.5% |
| Uniform-61-n20 | 20 | | 287.03 | 14.98 | 235.63 | 10.35 | 17.9% | 235.85 | 17.78 | 17.8% | 258.85 | 27.14 | 9.8% | 262.63 | 29.40 | 8.5% | 247.33 | 23.84 | 13.8% |
| Uniform-62-n20 | 20 | | 315.17 | 7.83 | 275.98 | 6.84 | 12.4% | 277.56 | 6.42 | 11.9% | 301.20 | 15.42 | 4.4% | 301.20 | 15.42 | 4.4% | 308.84 | 36.81 | 2% |
| Uniform-63-n20 | 20 | | 311.44 | 13.09 | 274.00 | 5.93 | 12% | 274.43 | 4.10 | 11.9% | 307.23 | 31.60 | 1.4% | 311.88 | 26.82 | -0.1% | 317.18 | 27.97 | -1.8% |
| Uniform-71-n50 | 50 | | 732.46 | 59.76 | 720.41 | 55.54 | 1.6% | 701.47 | 55.72 | 4.2% | 765.80 | 80.07 | -4.6% | 813.53 | 117.95 | -11.1% | 680.45 | 65.53 | 7.1% |
| Uniform-72-n50 | 50 | | 741.82 | 47.97 | 802.25 | 54.41 | -8.1% | 782.66 | 54.01 | -5.5% | 809.91 | 82.78 | -9.2% | 878.29 | 97.49 | -18.4% | 720.96 | 55.94 | 2.8% |
| Uniform-73-n50 | 50 | | 730.77 | 25.68 | 751.33 | 54.33 | -2.8% | 747.67 | 53.90 | -2.3% | 781.56 | 89.60 | -7% | 845.42 | 96.08 | -15.7% | 754.39 | 58.85 | -3.2% |
| Uniform-91-n100 | 100 | | 1400.48 | 34.08 | 1635.97 | 97.17 | -16.8% | 1642.26 | 99.42 | -17.3% | 1751.24 | 128.38 | -25% | 1908.00 | 175.52 | -36.2% | 1263.12 | 84.34 | 9.8% |
| Uniform-92-n100 | 100 | | 1294.68 | 68.68 | 1652.34 | 82.41 | -27.6% | 1663.78 | 59.89 | -28.5% | 1774.03 | 160.17 | -37% | 1808.59 | 154.58 | -39.7% | 1301.16 | 85.21 | -0.5% |
| Uniform-1-n250 | 250 | | 3093.95 | 153.67 | 5217.9 | 198.87 | -68.6% | 5250.31 | 164.57 | -69.7% | 5610.62 | 343.99 | -81.3% | 6909.78 | 619.82 | -123.3% | 3377.06 | 186.62 | -9.2% |
| Uniform-2-n250 | 250 | | 3234.35 | 74.98 | 5145.57 | 143.81 | -59.1% | 5209.33 | 147.41 | -61.1% | 5523.64 | 336.98 | -70.8% | 6646.18 | 554.17 | -105.5% | 3297.91 | 129.58 | -2% |

The convergence graphs for all algorithm executions on the uniform-52-n10 and uniform-2-n250 are presented in Fig. 2 and Fig. 3. The convergence graphs show how the algorithm improves on its best objective function value. The convergence around optimal solutions is much faster on smaller datasets, whilst the algorithms progressively improve on the fitness function over the iterations for larger datasets.

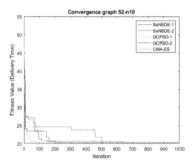
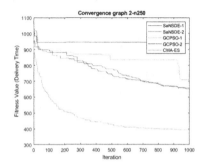

**Fig. 2.** Convergence graph for Uniform-52-n10 dataset

**Fig. 3.** Convergence graph for Uniform-2-n250 dataset

The SaNSDE-1 algorithm shows similar performance to the SaNSDE-2, indicating that the repair mechanism does not have a significant influence on the SaNSDE. The performance difference is below the 1 percentile point for most datasets, with a maximum difference of 1.3%. The results indicate that the GCPSO performs better when allowed to naturally search the solution space without feeding the repaired decision variable values to the algorithm for determining the next population of solutions. For smaller datasets, the repair mechanism does not significantly influence performance, but for the larger datasets, the performance difference is up to 15.5% in favour of the GCPSO-1.

Non-parametric Mann-Whitney U statistical tests are performed for each of the five algorithm combinations. The results are presented in Table 2. For each entry, the algorithm in row $i$ is measured against the algorithm in column $j$. The entries are in the form Wins-Draws-Losses, indicating the number of times (out of the 13 datasets) each algorithm statistically significantly differs in average delivery time, at a significance of 0.05. The SaNSDE-1 algorithm outperforms the SaNSDE-2 algorithm twice while drawing on 10 occasions and losing once. The GCPSO-1 outperforms the GCPSO-2 on three datasets, drawing on 10 occasions. The SaNSDE-1 is superior to the GCPSO-1 on 11 occasions, drawing in 2 comparisons. Lastly, the SaNSDE combinations draw six times against the CMA-ES, while drawing once and losing on six of the datasets.

**Table 2.** Hypothesis Test Results

**Table 2.** Hypothesis Test Results

|          | SaNSDE-1 | SaNSDE-2 | GCPSO-1 | GCPSO-2 | CMA-ES |
|----------|----------|----------|---------|---------|--------|
| SaNSDE-1 | X        | 2-10-1   | 11-2-0  | 12-1-0  | 6-1-6  |
| SaNSDE-2 | 1-10-2   | X        | 11-2-0  | 13-0-0  | 6-1-6  |
| GCPSO-1  | 0-2-11   | 0-2-11   | X       | 3-10-0  | 4-3-6  |
| GCPSO-2  | 0-1-12   | 0-0-13   | 0-10-3  | X       | 4-2-7  |
| CMAE-ES  | 6-1-6    | 6-1-6    | 6-3-4   | 7-2-4   | X      |

# 7   Efficiency and Feasibility Study

Further analysis in the form of an efficiency and feasibility study is executed to analyse the algorithm results on the TSPDi. Different key performance indicators (KPIs), specifically the duplicate solutions, inherent duplicates, algorithm efficiency, and infeasible solutions, are analysed for the algorithm-repair mechanism combinations and presented in graphic and tabular forms. The KPIs chosen are used to analyse how effective the algorithms are when attempting to improve on the best solution. The main KPIs consider the feasibility of solutions and their ability to search the entire solution space. The KPIs are measured over the 30 optimisation runs of the TSPDi study, as described in Sect. 6.

## 7.1   Duplicates Solutions

Firstly, the average % of duplicate solutions per optimisation run is presented in Table 3. Duplicate solutions are solutions with the same objective function value, which is the total delivery time. Solutions containing different routes that lead to the same total delivery time are considered duplicates. In more technical terms, when different genotypes have the same phenotype, they are considered to be duplicates. The nature of the optimisation processes of the different algorithms will always lead to multiple duplicate solutions, as metaheuristics can come across the same solution more than once. The theory is that due to multiple solutions in the decision space mapping to a single solution in the objective space, it is possible that continuous priority-based metaheuristics are inefficient for solving combinatorial optimisation problems.

Duplicate solutions are not clear indicators of poor algorithm performance, although research on the genetic algorithm, which is also a population-based metaheuristic, has shown that duplicates degrade quality early in an optimisation run [47]. The quality loss is attributed to diversity loss through duplicate solutions, which can be a serious weakness in population-based heuristics. Superior performance is associated with moving through a greater area of the search space and is attained through minimal duplicates, which are an indication that fewer solutions are repeatedly analysed and more of the search space is explored.

**Table 3.** Average % of duplicates per run

| Dataset | Nodes | SaNSDE-1 | SaNSDE-2 | GCPSO-1 | GCPSO-2 | CMA-ES |
|---|---|---|---|---|---|---|
| Uniform-51-n10 | 10 | **82.76%** | 83.03% | 93.07% | 92.78% | 94.64% |
| Uniform-52-n10 | 10 | **80.83%** | 81.00% | 91.92% | 90.80% | 95.37% |
| Uniform-53-n10 | 10 | 79.99% | **78.98%** | 91.14% | 90.58% | 94.28% |
| Uniform-61-n20 | 20 | 67.64% | **67.31%** | 76.12% | 76.29% | 88.03% |
| Uniform-62-n20 | 20 | 63.09% | **62.73%** | 74.17% | 74.71% | 86.77% |
| Uniform-63-n20 | 20 | 63.30% | **62.93%** | 75.56% | 75.41% | 86.64% |
| Uniform-71-n50 | 50 | 82.78% | 82.16% | 87.22% | 86.00% | **77.96%** |
| Uniform-72-n50 | 50 | 85.00% | 84.56% | 87.68% | 85.34% | **80.51%** |
| Uniform-73-n50 | 50 | 83.90% | 83.90% | 86.73% | 85.91% | **77.52%** |
| Uniform-91-n100 | 100 | 81.24% | **80.11%** | 84.67% | 82.13% | 84.69% |
| Uniform-92-n100 | 100 | 81.35% | **80.16%** | 84.50% | 81.91% | 84.85% |
| Uniform-1-n250 | 250 | 67.69% | **66.06%** | 77.56% | 85.14% | 69.36% |
| Uniform-2-n250 | 250 | 67.92% | **66.57%** | 78.13% | 83.19% | 69.62% |

Overall, the SaNSDE algorithm is the best performing algorithm when considering the average % duplicate solutions per optimisation run. The CMA-ES is performing slightly worse than the GCPSO algorithm among smaller datasets. The CMA-ES, however, generates the fewest duplicates for the 50-node datasets and performs better than the GCPSO as the dataset sizes increase beyond 50. The GCPSO, specifically the GCPSO-2, is the overall worst-performing algorithm combination, generating more than 80% duplicate solutions for all but the 20-node datasets. The overall good performance of the CMA-ES on the 50-node datasets is attributed to its much better performance during early iterations.

## 7.2  Inherent Duplicates

The next KPI, inherent duplicates, are solutions with exactly the same decision variables. In order for two solutions to be inherently duplicate, identical genotypes, that will automatically have the same phenotypes, must be present. There will thus always be a 'less than or equal' number of inherent duplicates than duplicates, as inherent duplicates also have the same objective function value and are normal duplicates of one another. Inherent duplicates are much scarcer than duplicates, as the algorithms alter the decision variables when attempting to move through the solution space. Early convergence around a perceived optimal can lead to inherent duplicates. The inherent duplicates are presented in Table 4.

Clearly, neither of the GCPSO combinations generate any inherent duplicates, whereas the CMA-ES has a few inherent duplicates in the small datasets. Interestingly, the SaNSDE algorithm is the only algorithm generating a substantial number of inherent duplicates, considering it generates the least total number of duplicates.

**Table 4.** Inherent duplicates

| Dataset | Nodes | SaNSDE-1 | SaNSDE-2 | GCPSO-1 | GCPSO-2 | CMA-ES |
|---|---|---|---|---|---|---|
| Uniform-51-n10 | 10 | 1.42% | 1.31% | 0% | 0% | 0.01% |
| Uniform-52-n10 | 10 | 1.23% | 1.16% | 0% | 0% | 0.05% |
| Uniform-53-n10 | 10 | 1.24% | 1.24% | 0% | 0% | 0% |
| Uniform-61-n20 | 20 | 3.62% | 3.34% | 0% | 0% | 0% |
| Uniform-62-n20 | 20 | 3.51% | 3.36% | 0% | 0% | 0% |
| Uniform-63-n20 | 20 | 3.01% | 3.28% | 0% | 0% | 0% |
| Uniform-71-n50 | 50 | 6.42% | 6.47% | 0% | 0% | 0% |
| Uniform-72-n50 | 50 | 6.65% | 6.66% | 0% | 0% | 0% |
| Uniform-73-n50 | 50 | 7.08% | 7.17% | 0% | 0% | 0% |
| Uniform-91-n100 | 100 | 6.09% | 6.06% | 0% | 0% | 0% |
| Uniform-92-n100 | 100 | 7.27% | 7.34% | 0% | 0% | 0% |
| Uniform-1-n250 | 250 | 6.95% | 5.88% | 0% | 0% | 0% |
| Uniform-2-n250 | 250 | 6.35% | 5% | 0% | 0% | 0% |

## 7.3   Algorithm Efficiency

To obtain the number of true duplicates, the inherent duplicates have to be deducted from the total number of duplicates. The true duplicates are then used to calculate the efficiency of the algorithms. The overall efficiency is simply determined as the percentage of unique solutions generated on average per run, as in Table 5.

The SaNSDE combinations are almost twice as efficient as the GCPSO and CMA-ES combinations on all of the datasets. The repair mechanisms do not significantly change the SaNSDE efficiency, with only a small difference in efficiency observed in favour of the GCPSO-1 for large datasets. The average efficiency over the combined SaNSDE combinations is 28.93%. The SaNSDE is 12.79% more

**Table 5.** Algorithm efficiency

| Dataset | Nodes | SaNSDE-1 | SaNSDE-2 | GCPSO-1 | GCPSO-2 | CMA-ES |
|---|---|---|---|---|---|---|
| Uniform-51-n10 | 10 | **18.66%** | 18.28% | 6.93% | 7.22% | 5.37% |
| Uniform-52-n10 | 10 | **20.4%** | 20.16% | 8.08% | 9.2% | 4.68% |
| Uniform-53-n10 | 10 | 21.25% | **22.26%** | 8.86% | 9.42% | 5.72% |
| Uniform-61-n20 | 20 | 35.98% | **36.03%** | 23.88% | 23.71% | 11.97% |
| Uniform-62-n20 | 20 | 40.42% | **40.63%** | 25.83% | 25.29% | 13.23% |
| Uniform-63-n20 | 20 | 39.71% | **40.35%** | 24.44% | 24.59% | 13.36% |
| Uniform-71-n50 | 50 | 23.64% | **24.31%** | 12.78% | 14% | 22.04% |
| Uniform-72-n50 | 50 | 21.65% | **22.1%** | 12.32% | 14.66% | 19.49% |
| Uniform-73-n50 | 50 | 23.18% | **23.27%** | **13.27%** | 14.09% | 22.48% |
| Uniform-91-n100 | 100 | 24.85% | **25.95%** | 15.33% | 17.87% | 15.31% |
| Uniform-92-n100 | 100 | 25.92% | **27.18%** | 15.5% | 18.09% | 15.15% |
| Uniform-1-n250 | 250 | 39.26% | **39.82%** | 22.44% | 14.86% | 30.64% |
| Uniform-2-n250 | 250 | **38.43%** | **38.43%** | 21.87% | 16.81% | 30.38% |

**Table 6.** Infeasible Solutions

| Dataset | Nodes | SaNSDE-1 | SaNSDE-2 | GCPSO-1 | GCPSO-2 | CMA-ES |
|---------|-------|----------|----------|---------|---------|--------|
| Uniform-51-n10 | 10 | 98.42% | 98.00% | 99.76% | 94.26% | **68.05%** |
| Uniform-52-n10 | 10 | 98.11% | 97.23% | 98.29% | 93.09% | **53.05%** |
| Uniform-53-n10 | 10 | 97.78% | 97.14% | 96.03% | 88.84% | **57.96%** |
| Uniform-61-n20 | 20 | 99.95% | 99.86% | 99.99% | 98.92% | **81.03%** |
| Uniform-62-n20 | 20 | 99.96% | 99.85% | 99.99% | 98.16% | **90.48%** |
| Uniform-63-n20 | 20 | 99.94% | 99.84% | 99.99% | 98.21% | **72.77%** |
| Uniform-71-n50 | 50 | 99.99%+ | 99.99%+ | 100% | **99.99%** | 100% |
| Uniform-72-n50 | 50 | 100% | **99.99%** | 100% | 99.99%+ | 100% |
| Uniform-73-n50 | 50 | 100% | 99.99% | 99.99% | **98.25%** | 100% |
| Uniform-91-n100 | 100 | 100% | **99.99%+** | 100% | 100% | 100% |
| Uniform-92-n100 | 100 | 100% | **99.99%+** | 100% | 99.09% | 100% |
| Uniform-1-n250 | 250 | 100% | 100% | 100% | **99.78%** | 100% |
| Uniform-2-n250 | 250 | 100% | 99.99% | 100% | **99.95%** | 100% |

efficient than the CMA-ES, which has an overall efficiency of 16.14%. The average GCPSO has an efficiency of 16.21%, which is 12.7% less than the SaNSDE.

### 7.4 Infeasible Solutions

Next, the average percentage of infeasible solutions per optimisation run is measured. A solution is considered infeasible when the decision variable values of an individual map to a route that contains consecutive drone nodes in its solution, which is invalid. The nature of the population-based metaheuristics considered for the TSPDi ultimately leads to large numbers of infeasible solutions, usually initialised already by the random decision variable values in the initial population. Only considering feasible solutions reduces the search space, and therefore, although worrying, infeasible solutions are part of the search process (Table 6).

The algorithms struggle with consistently generating feasible solutions on the benchmark datasets. Only the CMA-ES performs decently on small datasets. The high number of individuals requiring a modification to their genotypes will indefinitely lead to worse fitness values, as changing a drone node to a truck node will not only increase the truck distance and delivery time, but the modification does not consider the effect on the objective function value.

When navigating through the solution space, the metaheuristics struggle with steering the solutions in a way that would lead to mostly feasible routes. For the smaller datasets, the CMA-ES is able to create child populations more optimally by avoiding generating as many infeasible solutions as the other algorithms. Although the SaNSDE and GCPSO generate an overwhelming number of infeasible solutions for all the datasets, the second repair mechanism performs slightly better. The CMA-ES is considered the best-performing algorithm, while the other algorithms generate almost only infeasible solutions.

Ultimately, the continuous population-based algorithms are not very efficient in moving through the search space, especially when considering the large numbers of infeasible solutions being generated. A need for developing better mechanisms to move through the search space is required, which will greatly improve algorithm performance.

## 8    Conclusion

This paper proposes a framework and implements SaNSDE, GCPSO, and CMA-ES-based algorithms for the TSPDi on benchmark datasets ranging from 10 to 250 nodes. Two versions of the SaNSDE and GCPSO are implemented to test different repair mechanisms. The algorithms are then compared to an ACS algorithm of Moremi [1]. The SaNSDE-1 algorithm is the best-performing algorithm when 20 or fewer nodes are present in the system, while the CMA-ES performs best for larger datasets. Different KPIs are measured to understand the performance of the metaheuristics on the TSPDi, specifically the duplicate solutions and infeasible solutions being generated.

Future research can apply alternative algorithms within the framework, specifically the genetic algorithm, simulated annealing, or tabu search. There is also an opportunity to apply problem-specific heuristics and operators to the developed metaheuristics. Lastly, an opportunity arises to expand the problem to a VRPD, where multiple trucks and drones are used to serve customers.

**Acknowledgements.** This work is based on the research supported in part by the National Research Foundation of South Africa (Grant Numbers: 129340).

## References

1. Tsietsi John, M., et al.: An ant colony optimisation approach to scheduling truck and drone delivery systems. Ph.D. thesis, Stellenbosch University (2022)
2. Allen, J., et al.: Understanding the impact of e-commerce on last-mile light goods vehicle activity in urban areas: the case of London. Transp. Res. Part D: Transp. Environ. **61**, 325–338 (2018)
3. De Souza, R., Goh, M., Lau, H.-C., Ng, W.-S., Tan, P.-S.: Collaborative urban logistics-synchronizing the last mile a Singapore research perspective. Procedia. Soc. Behav. Sci. **125**, 422–431 (2014)
4. Lim, S.F.W., Jin, X., Srai, J.S.: Consumer-driven e-commerce: a literature review, design framework, and research agenda on last-mile logistics models. Int. J. Phys. Distrib. Logist. Manag. **48**(3), 308–332 (2018)
5. Ranieri, L., Digiesi, S., Silvestri, B., Roccotelli, M.: A review of last mile logistics innovations in an externalities cost reduction vision. Sustainability **10**, 782 (2018)
6. Wallace, G.: Amazon says drone deliveries are the future (2013). http://money.cnn.com/2013/12/01/technology/amazon-dronedelivery/index.html
7. Glaser, A.: 7-eleven beats Google and Amazon to the first regular commercial drone delivery service in the US (2016)
8. Perez, S., Kolodny, L.: UPS tests show delivery drones still need work (2017). https://techcrunch.com/2017/02/21/ups-tests-show-delivery-drones-still-need-work

9. Franco, M.: DHL uses completely autonomous system to deliver consumer goods by drone. New Atlas, 10 May 2016
10. Murphy, M.: The future is here: drones are delivering Domino's pizzas to customers (2016). https://qz.com/838254/dominos-is-delivering-pizza-with-autonomousdrones-to-customers-in-new-zealand
11. Levin, A.: Alphabet and Chipotle are bringing Burrito delivery drones to campus (2016). https://www.bloomberg.com/news/articles/2016-09-08/burrito-by-dronecoming-to-campus-in-test-of-alphabet-s-delivery
12. Wang, D.: The economics of drone delivery. IEEE Spectr. (2016)
13. Ackerman, E., Strickland, E.: Medical delivery drones take flight in East Africa. IEEE Spectr. **55**, 34–35 (2018)
14. Vanian, J.: This drone startup just achieved a milestone in doorstep delivery, 2016 (2016). http://fortune.com/2016/03/25/flirtey-drone-legal-delivery-urban
15. Agatz, N., Bouman, P., Schmidt, M.: Optimization approaches for the traveling salesman problem with drone. Transp. Sci. **52**, 965–981 (2018)
16. Bouman Paul, A., Schmidt, M.: Instances for the TSP with drone (2015). https://doi.org/10.5281/zenodo.22245
17. Solomon, M.M., Desrosiers, J.: Survey paper-time window constrained routing and scheduling problems. Transp. Sci. **22**, 1–13 (1988)
18. Laporte, G.: The vehicle routing problem: an overview of exact and approximate algorithms. Eur. J. Oper. Res. **59**, 345–358 (1992)
19. Toth, P., Vigo, D.: The Vehicle Routing Problem. SIAM (2002)
20. Kumar, S.N., Panneerselvam, R.: A survey on the vehicle routing problem and its variants (2012)
21. Lin, C., Choy, K.L., Ho, G.T., Chung, S.H., Lam, H.: Survey of green vehicle routing problem: past and future trends. Expert Syst. Appl. **41**, 1118–1138 (2014)
22. Otto, A., Agatz, N., Campbell, J., Golden, B., Pesch, E.: Optimization approaches for civil applications of unmanned aerial vehicles (UAVs) or aerial drones: a survey. Networks **72**, 411–458 (2018)
23. Khoufi, I., Laouiti, A., Adjih, C.: A survey of recent extended variants of the traveling salesman and vehicle routing problems for unmanned aerial vehicles. Drones **3**, 66 (2019)
24. Chung, S.H., Sah, B., Lee, J.: Optimization for drone and drone-truck combined operations: a review of the state of the art and future directions. Comput. Oper. Res. **123**, 105004 (2020)
25. Poikonen, S., Campbell, J.F.: Future directions in drone routing research. Networks **77**, 116–126 (2021)
26. Moshref-Javadi, M., Winkenbach, M.: Applications and Research avenues for drone-based models in logistics: a classification and review. Expert Syst. Appl. **177**, 114854 (2021)
27. Liang, Y.-J., Luo, Z.-X.: A survey of truck-drone routing problem: literature review and research prospects. J. Oper. Res. Soc. China **10**, 343–377 (2022). https://doi.org/10.1007/s40305-021-00383-4
28. Ha, Q.M., Deville, Y., Pham, Q.D., Há, M.H.: On the min-cost traveling salesman problem with drone. Transp. Res. Part C Emerg. Technol. **86**, 597–621 (2018)
29. Murray, C.C., Chu, A.G.: The flying sidekick traveling salesman problem: optimization of drone-assisted parcel delivery. Transp. Res. Part C Emerg. Technol. **54**, 86–109 (2015)
30. Boysen, N., Briskorn, D., Fedtke, S., Schwerdfeger, S.: Drone delivery from trucks: drone scheduling for given truck routes. Networks **72**, 506–527 (2018)

31. Li, H., Chen, J., Wang, F., Zhao, Y.: Truck and drone routing problem with synchronization on arcs. Nav. Res. Logist. (NRL) **69**, 884–901 (2022)
32. Salama, M.R., Srinivas, S.: Collaborative truck multi-drone routing and scheduling problem: package delivery with flexible launch and recovery sites. Transp. Res. Part E Logist. Transp. Rev. **164**, 102788 (2022)
33. Thomas, T., Srinivas, S., Rajendran, C.: Collaborative truck multi-drone delivery system considering drone scheduling and en-route operations. Available at SSRN 4080821
34. Ferrandez, S.M., Harbison, T., Weber, T., Sturges, R., Rich, R.: Optimization of a truck-drone in tandem delivery network using k-means and genetic algorithm. J. Ind. Eng. Manag. (JIEM) **9**, 374–388 (2016)
35. Chang, Y.S., Lee, H.J.: Optimal delivery routing with wider drone-delivery areas along a shorter truck-route. Expert Syst. Appl. **104**, 307–317 (2018)
36. Raj, R., Murray, C.: The multiple flying sidekicks traveling salesman problem with variable drone speeds. Transp. Res. Part C Emerg. Technol. **120**, 102813 (2020)
37. Yoon, J.J.: The traveling salesman problem with multiple drones: an optimization model for last-mile delivery. Ph.D. thesis, Massachusetts Institute of Technology (2018)
38. Tu, P.A., Dat, N.T., Dung, P.Q.: Traveling salesman problem with multiple drones. In: Proceedings of the Ninth International Symposium on Information and Communication Technology, pp. 46–53 (2018)
39. Price, K., Storn, R.M., Lampinen, J.A.: Differential Evolution: A Practical Approach to Global Optimization. Springer, Heidelberg (2006). https://doi.org/10.1007/3-540-31306-0
40. Yang, Z., Tang, K., Yao, X.: Self-adaptive differential evolution with neighborhood search. In: 2008 IEEE Congress on Evolutionary Computation (IEEE World Congress on Computational Intelligence), pp. 1110–1116 (2008)
41. Qin, A.K., Suganthan, P.N.: Self-adaptive differential evolution algorithm for numerical optimization. In: 2005 IEEE Congress on Evolutionary Computation, vol. 2, pp. 1785–1791 (2005)
42. Kennedy, J., Eberhart, R.: Particle swarm optimization. In: Proceedings of ICNN 1995 - International Conference on Neural Networks, vol. 4, pp. 1942–1948 (1995)
43. Sahab, M.G., Toropov, V.V., Gandomi, A.H.: A review on traditional and modern structural optimization: problems and techniques. In: Metaheuristic Applications in Structures and Infrastructures, pp. 25–47 (2013)
44. Jedrzejewski-Szmek, Z., Abrahao, K.P., Jedrzejewska-Szmek, J., Lovinger, D.M., Blackwell, K.T.: Parameter optimization using covariance matrix adaptation - evolutionary strategy (CMA-ES), an approach to investigate differences in channel properties between neuron subtypes. Front. Neuroinform. **12**, 47 (2018)
45. Grobler, J., Engelbrecht, A.P., Kok, S., Yadavalli, S.: Metaheuristics for the multi-objective FJSP with sequence-dependent set-up times, auxiliary resources and machine down time. Ann. Oper. Res. **180**, 165–196 (2010). https://doi.org/10.1007/s10479-008-0501-4
46. Knoetze, F.E.: Solving a last mile truck and drone delivery schedule to optimality. Bachelor's thesis, University of Stellenbosch (2021)
47. Ronald, S.: Duplicate genotypes in a genetic algorithm. In: 1998 IEEE International Conference on Evolutionary Computation Proceedings. IEEE World Congress on Computational Intelligence (Cat. No. 98TH8360), pp. 793–798 (1998)

# Value-Oriented Management of City Development Programs Based on Data from Social Networks

B. A. Nizomutdinov[1](✉), A. B. Uglova[2], and A. S. Antonov[1]

[1] Institute of Design and Urban Studies, ITMO University, Saint Petersburg, Russia
boris@itmu.ru

[2] Institute of Psychology, The Herzen State Pedagogical University of Russia, Saint Petersburg, Russia

**Abstract.** The paper presents the results of a pilot study of the possibility of using a value-based approach to managing city development programs. The value model of a person includes a static description of the values, motivations and expectations of a person, taking into account his social, demographic group and life situation. The value model of life in the city involves the description of transitions between motivated and non-motivated social groups. City development management is considered from the point of view of the composition of development projects, which requires the formation of a way of presenting the project in the "language" of a value management model, which includes an assessment of the timeliness of the city development project. The paper proposes to determine the values of residents through social media profiles and comments generated by users. Values are described using the Schwartz method. The work contains comments from sources - Google Maps, Telegram, Vkontakte. To validate the information received, a survey of residents was conducted, to compare a real person with a virtual profile, using the revealed correlations, it was concluded that with the help of information from social networks, it is possible to determine values and use them to manage city development programs.

**Keywords:** value-oriented · urban planning · parsing · data collection · mathematical modeling

## 1 Introduction

Today, urban development is one of the most important tasks of humanity. The quality of life depends on the quality of the environment that the city forms. All residents of megacities and small towns are part of their location. Their lifestyle, habits, requests, needs and values shape the environment, on an equal footing with environmental and economic factors.

The development of the cities themselves depends on the type of economy of the country and other features, however, the principle itself is often similar. A state may have one global document indicating the vector of development of mountains, for example, a development strategy up to a certain year. Based on such programs, global documents for individual cities can be formed, which also describe a development strategy that contains goals and objectives for the development of the city. But among other things, such strategies may contain separate local programs - city development programs that already affect certain industries - security, medicine, affordable housing, social policy and other areas.

But how to correctly allocate priorities between these specific individual programs? How do we know that this year we need to strengthen the development of security in the city, and not medicine? There are different approaches in classical urban studies and urban management theory. For example, based on the economic indicators of last year, macroeconomic regions, in the negative case, such decisions can be made based on the desires of individual leaders associated with political popularity. All these methods are significantly outdated, and require improvement for the sustainable development of cities.

The weak side of management is the lack of statistical methods for determining the implementation of the strategy. To date, statistics represent a limited set of indicators for municipalities, among which one can distinguish the size of territories, population, employment and wages, industrial production, construction, environmental protection and others. In addition, there is a long time interval between the presentation of statistical information and decision-making; at the same time, the information provided does not always reflect the real situation in the city. The problem in the field of management is that the social component of the object of management – the values of citizens - is not taken into account. There is no correlation between the distribution of the program budget among themselves with the significance for people in terms of values and needs.

To solve these problems, this paper considers the possibility of using a value-oriented approach to the management of city development programs, using the example of St. Petersburg.

## 2 Research Design

To ensure sustainable development and high quality of life in an urban environment, it is necessary to use intelligent urban technologies and pay special attention to the practice of taking into account eco-psychological technologies [1–3].

In the process of urban infrastructure development, it is necessary to take into account the cosmopolitanism of urban culture, the peculiarities of material and immaterial traditions, the values and needs of city residents at different levels of the urban environment in order to achieve ecological, cultural and economic sustainability of the entire city [4]. A modern city can be represented as a dynamic, semiotic structure that unites many life worlds of individuals [5], which exist in an inseparable socio-cultural unity. Currently, the interconnection of heterogeneous urban elements is supported primarily by information technologies that provide communication links between residents, the managing sector and infrastructure

One of the most effective approaches to managing the development of the city's infrastructure can be considered a value-oriented approach [6]. This approach takes into account cultural and value transformations in local communities of the city for territorial expansion of infrastructure. The values, needs and hobbies of each individual resident of the city are not independent concepts, but are intertwined, determined by con-text, culturally diverse and related to how we see ourselves and perceive the urban environment.

The relationship between the psychological state of a person and the urban environment in which he exists is widely discussed by various specialists in the framework of sociology, psychology, urban studies, anthropology, etc. In order to create an accessible environment that meets the values and needs of modern man, constant monitoring of human interaction with his spatial environment is necessary. An important part of such studies is the study of visual-semiotic elements of urban space and their impact on the psychological state and stress level of city residents [7], studies of autobiographical and historical memory of the city, the attitude of residents to architectural objects of the city, studies of semantic cognitive maps of the city [8], studies of urban identity, studies of socio-cultural capital of the city, studies devoted to the study of the influence of landscaping and noise levels on the psychological state of a citizen [9]

It is worth noting that often the theory of urban space design does not take into account the results of socio-psychological research, the complexity and variability of the emotional experience of residents, which is important when planning convenient infrastructure. Following Reinald D. and Elffers H. rethinking and expanding the concept of "protected space" O. It can be said that a successful urban space planning should be based on an analysis of the daily interaction of city residents with infrastructure facilities that ensure the satisfaction of basic needs, the realization of values and interests. In the study Karami S., Ghafary M., Fakhrayee A. It is indicated that satisfaction with the state of the surrounding urban environment is closely related to the fulfillment of the needs of residents, as well as the degree of openness and dialogicity of the space they create [10].

The daily introduction of information technology into our lives has changed our understanding of urban space, and most importantly has changed the experience of inter-action of a city resident with the environment. Virtual space is mixed with physical space and is often replaced through a large number of visual images [11]. A resident of a modern city has the opportunity to "be present" in any corner of the city, any socio-cultural location, at any event in real time through social networks and media space. Such inclusion allows you to actively change the urban environment to realize your socio-psychological needs and creates a new complex form of urban space that needs to be studied and monitored.

Value-based management is a tool for ensuring the quality of life in the city [14]. A smart city is characterized by services for the population aimed at meeting the needs, and on the other hand, a city management system to ensure sustainable development and improve the quality of life of residents. Studies indicate that the quality of living depends on and is determined by the structure of the needs and values of residents, while they can change over time due to changes in the urban environment and differ for different socio-demographic groups.

Based on these concepts, it is proposed to transform a value-oriented approach for managing city development programs.

## 3 Management Object

In this paper, the process of formation and management of city development programs is considered on the example of St. Petersburg. It is proposed to transform a conventional decision-making system, the effectiveness of which is measured on the basis of economic indicators based on an approach based on value indicators.

St. Petersburg development programs are measures to solve social and economic problems to improve the well-being of the city's residents. They are developed for a certain period of time (most often for 5–10 years), and include strategic objectives and goals, as well as ways to achieve them. City development programs may include infrastructure projects (for example, the construction of roads, school complexes and kindergartens), social and economic initiatives aimed at improving the standard of living and business development in the city. St. Petersburg development programs are usually developed with the participation of the public, the business community, city authorities and other interested parties. They cover many areas, such as ecology, transport, healthcare, small and medium-sized business development, tourism, education and culture.

The current management process has the disadvantage that there is no direct connection between residents and the state, there is a large time interval between the results of the implementation of programs and the distribution of the budget for the next year. Based on the performance indicators, a program is formed for the next year, without paying attention to the values of citizens. That is why, in this paper, we propose a management process based on a value-oriented approach that will take into account, in addition to actual metrics, also indirect ones that are related to the real needs and values of citizens (Fig. 1).

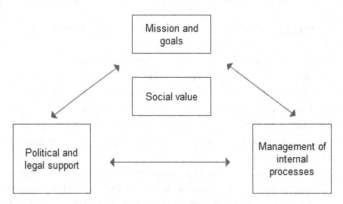

**Fig. 1.** Value-based management scheme

The development of a new method of managing city development programs with the application of a value-based approach will allow assessing the effectiveness of management through integral characteristics of the state of society and quality of life and the ability of projects to improve this quality of life.

A value-oriented approach to management is a methodology based on the iden-tification of key values that guide managers and co-workers in their professional activities.

My work describes the composition of urban problems, the current management process, and demonstrates at what stage it is possible to use a value-oriented approach. To test the method, information sources on the Internet were selected, to collect information about the values of citizens, the following sources were selected: geoinformation service - Google Maps, Vkontakte social network, Telegram messenger.

For completeness of the data, 3 types of text sources have been specially selected, the processing of which will allow determining the values and requests of citizens to the city in real time.

Figure 2 shows the general scheme of data collection and processing to determine the values of citizens.

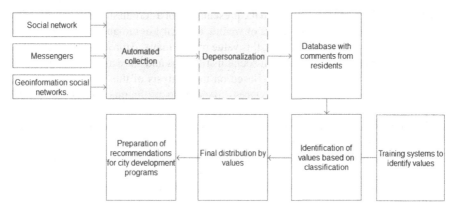

**Fig. 2.** General scheme of data collection and processing to identify values and needs

Schwartz's theory of basic individual values is used as a fundamental theory. Schwartz's theory of basic individual values is a theory that describes universal motives associated with people's value behavior. Schwartz's theory suggests that people pursue several basic values in their lives, which are key factors for explaining their behavior and preferences. These values range from personality characteristics to the socio-cultural context in which they live. Schwartz's theory is widely used in interpersonal and cross-cultural studies, where it is used to explain why people perceive and react differently to the same situations in different cultures.

The design of the study was based on the ideas of Widodo J., who points out that in order to successfully improve infrastructure, it is necessary to build a dialogue with city residents, take into account their cultural and digital experience in interaction with tangible and intangible values at different levels of the urban environment [12]. The paper presents the results of research conducted in Indonesia, which may be applicable to other emerging economies. The author examines practical and basic principles that can help cities better understand the interaction between people and the urban environment, and take the right steps to preserve the health and well-being of residents.

The research presented in the paper also emphasizes the need to support local culture and take into account the uniqueness of each city in planning the urban environment, as well as the importance of training and the transition to innovative approaches in urban space management [12].

## 4 Value-Oriented Approach

The cultural environment surrounding the citizen, the mentality of micro- and macro-communities, is formed on the basis of urban space and determines the leading social and individual values. Based on the theory of Sh. Schwartz can identify ten basic values that influence the formation of a reference lifestyle in the minds of city residents in an urban environment. Let's describe the relationship of basic values with elements of the urban environment, which can be objectively identified in the analysis of digital experience.

- The value of power associated with the presentation of a certain status will be reflected in the presentation of the attributes of wealth, authority, dominance. In relation to the analysis of the urban environment, this value will be realized through a demonstration of belonging to a number of urban social institutions and showing interest in objects of state power and management. Based on the analysis of this value, it is possible to evaluate the successful and unsuccessful elements of the image policy of the city administration, to identify attractive infrastructure facilities of the city.
- The value of achievement is associated with the presentation of social successes and competencies that will be presented in demonstrating belonging to certain professional and cultural circles. The analysis of such digital information posted by the residents of the city can help to assess the potential of the economic directions of the city's development, its labor resources in various fields.
- The values of hedonism and stimulation, related to the demonstration of pleasure, recreation and entertainment and can help in the analysis of the cultural and recreational resource of the city and directions in the development of entertainment infrastructure.
- The value of independence is associated with creative and research activity. This value can be analyzed through the study of scientific and creative urban communities and show the degree of realization of the scientific and technical potential of the city.
- The value of universalism is expressed in the understanding of the need to protect the well-being of the community and will be manifested in participation in social urban projects, volunteer and activist movements. This value indicates that residents support the development potential of a healthy society, the popularity and importance of social cooperation in society.
- The values of affiliation, traditional values associated with belonging to various social groups, can be assessed through the analysis of participation in local urban communities, the presence of individual symbols, rituals necessary to maintain a sense of belonging and stability. The analysis of this value can help to assess well-being in everyday interaction and life in individual urban locations, to reveal unfavorable elements of the environment.

– The need for security, as a basic component of the stability of the urban environment, can be assessed through the analysis of reviews and comments of residents of the city about different locations related to the description of social order, economic, environmental safety, mutual assistance, involvement of management structures in the organization of city life.

Through the value analysis of the digital image of the urban environment, it is possible to describe the social geography of the urban environment, identify the degree of development of human, technical and economic potential, determine the prospects for the development of a certain infrastructure, identify points of growth and development. The digital space provides a huge amount of open information that can be used for such analysis. Urban space includes many communication platforms implemented in both real and virtual environments, the value-oriented analysis of which is necessary to create effective socially successful management systems.

Additionally, a search was conducted in the Scopus database on the subject of the study, to review the methodology of value-oriented city management and development programs. It was possible to find separate directions described in [11–13]. The results of processing are illustrated in Fig. 3.

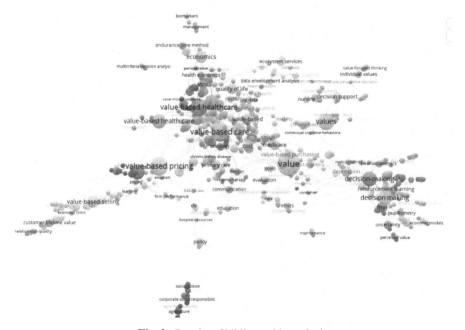

**Fig. 3.** Results of bibliographic analysis

## 5  Values and Social Networks

In the classical situation, to determine values, it is necessary to use a value questionnaire, for example, the Schwartz questionnaire. The Schwartz Value Questionnaire is a psychological diagnostic tool developed by psychologist Shalom Schwartz. The purpose of the questionnaire is to establish the personal values and orientations of the interviewee in various life situations. The questionnaire consists of about 57 questions to choose one of the two proposed options. Each question contains a number of ideals and values, from which you need to choose one that is closer to personal values and orientations. The answers to the questions help to set priorities in life values, such as self-realization, personal status, security, prosperity, harmony with the environment, etc. The analysis of the data obtained makes it possible to determine the basic value orientations of a person and her attitude to certain areas of life. The Schwartz value questionnaire is widely used both in research activities in psychology and sociology, and in applied activities, for example, in business to analyze the culture of an organization and to determine professional orientation.

This method allows you to accurately assess the basic values, however, it has a disadvantage - you need to answer 57 questions, the survey can take more than 30 min. It may be almost impossible or impractical to promptly interview a reliably significant sample of residents, which is why a new method is proposed in this paper - determining the values of residents through information in social networks.

However, in order to use such sources, it is necessary to conduct a validation that proves that it is possible to use social media data to determine values. To prove this hypothesis, an original method based on cyberpsychology was used in this work. It combined classical psychology with automated methods. The essence of the hypothesis is that there is a relationship between the real personality of a person with his profile in social networks and what the user writes.

The daily introduction of information technologies into our lives has changed our understanding of urban space, and most importantly has changed the experience of interaction of a city resident with the environment. Virtual space is mixed with physical space and is often replaced through a large number of visual images (Chen Feng, Hua-wei Xu). A resident of a modern city has the opportunity to "be present" in any corner of the city, any socio-cultural location, at any event in real time through social networks and media space. Such inclusiveness makes it possible to actively change the urban environment in order to realize their socio-psychological needs and creates a new complex form of urban space that needs to be studied and monitored.

To prove the hypothesis put forward, work was carried out in which the data after the survey of a real person was compared with the information that he publishes about himself on social networks. During the study, 3 stages of work were carried out:

- Psychodiagnostic survey of subjects using the Schwartz method from different urban communities to determine the main interests and needs that mediate interaction with the urban environment. Each respondent gave a link to their profile on the social network, as well as consent to the collection and processing of data.

- An automated analysis of the profiles of the subjects in social networks was carried out to identify the main value-semantic components of their information image, which is the basis for building communication.
- Identification of reliably significant relationships between the value-semantic attitudes of city residents, their needs for the development of infrastructure and the components of their profiles in the social network for the theoretical justification of value-oriented forecasting of infrastructure development needs.

Based on the data on the number of residents of St. Petersburg, the sample size for the survey was calculated - 330 respondents. The sample consisted of users aged 18 to 67 years (M = 31.12, SD = 11.54), 64% of whom (211) were women and 36% (119).

During the psychodiagnostic testing, the subjects gave links to their social networks. In the next step, we studied the profile of each user using automated methods. In this study, we analyzed only the main publicly available parameters.

As a result, a database of respondents was prepared to compare the collected information with the test results in order to identify significant relationships. For example, profile subscriptions, basic publicly available information, interests and other parameters were collected. All data has been processed and translated into binary code.

Using correlation analysis (Spearman correlation coefficient), we have identified the relationship between the needs of residents in infrastructure development. Infrastructure development, components of their profile in the social network and their personal characteristics that determine interaction with the urban environment (Fig. 4).

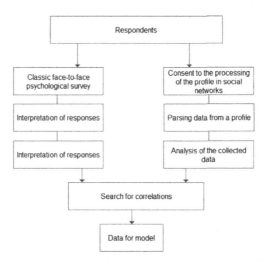

**Fig. 4.** A scheme for finding a correlation between a real person and a profile in a social network

Evidence has been obtained that social networks can serve as a source of information about the values of citizens. This information can be used to develop a model of citizens' values.

# 6   Data from Geoinformation Networks

At the previous stage, the possibility of using social network data was proved. Now it is necessary to determine which social networks can still be used.

As we found out, the Vkontakte profile and user comments sufficiently accurately describe the personality. It was proposed to supplement the set with two sources, Google Maps and Telegram messenger.

Google Maps is a mapping and navigation service developed by Google. With Google Maps, you can view maps of the globe at various scales, plan routes from one point to another, use the car navigation function, view photos and reviews of places on the map, as well as use geolocation-related functions.

Google Maps is used not only in the daily life of users, but also in business, to determine the location of companies and plan delivery routes or customer service. In addition, Google Maps can be used in tourism, education, scientific research and other industries.

In addition to routes, this service allows you to leave comments under every object you have visited, even under urban objects. It can be concluded that this is a kind of geoinformation social network.

For the current publication, it was decided to analyze reviews of parks and squares in St. Petersburg, to study communication practices and identify the values of residents. Recreational objects were collected by districts, there are 18 districts in the city, landscaping objects were selected for each of them using an internal Google Maps search, the words "park", "garden", "square", "alley", "forest", "field" were used for search, then each object was saved as a link to the object card in the system.

Further, with the help of an automated parser, reviews were collected for each park. During the analysis, we managed to collect a database of recreation facilities presented in the Google Maps service, the final database includes 291 objects of landscape design (parks, squares, alleys). More than 360000 reviews have been processed. The final database of reviews was depersonalized, only the text of the review and the date were saved.

Based on the results of collecting statistical information, an assessment of various communicative practices of city residents was carried out: the number of reviews of parks and squares, the average rating indicated by a city resident in geoinformation resources, and also calculated the landscaping index of districts, which is based on the ratio of the total area of urban areas. The area of green spaces, as well as the number of green spaces per 10 thousand is calculated.

It is worth noting that the rating of parks and squares is interrelated with the subjective assessment of safety, comfort and aesthetics of the environment and can serve as a communicative practice as an indicator of the overall quality of life of the population of the city.

Table 1 shows an example of the distribution of topics identified in Google Maps reviews.

**Table 1.** Number of reviews for different security categories

| Security category | % | Security category | % |
|---|---|---|---|
| Road and transport safety | 59,1 | Criminal security | 6,6 |
| Ensuring order | 21,2 | Road lighting | 3,3 |
| Aesthetic and environmental safety | 9,2 | Economic security | 0,3 |

The obtained result indicates that it is possible to monitor several values from the previously mentioned ones using geoinformation social networks.

## 7 Data from Messengers

Telegram is popular in both personal and professional spheres. It is used to communicate with friends and family, to work in the office and exchange documents, to create and promote channels and groups in social networks, as well as for mass mailing of messages and advertising. Tele-gram also supports an API that allows developers to create their own applications and bots based on the messenger. This functionality is used for various purposes, from games and entertainment to banking applications and bots for monitoring stock prices.

In this messenger, in addition to chats, it is possible to create channels in which the author can publish news or content, and subscribers can leave comments. In this paper, comments are of interest. This question has not been sufficiently studied yet, since comment parsing has been available relatively recently.

In the course of the study, an attempt was made to use user comments to identify needs and values. For this purpose, comments to popular city channels were uploaded using automated methods. Further, using clustering methods, the main topics were highlighted, which were discussed in the city Telegram channel.

The final database consisted of an array of comments from residents. Further, using machine learning methods, all messages were divided into need groups. Table 2 shows the processing results. We can say that we managed to get the distribution of basic needs, which are discussed in the neighboring city channels in Telegram.

**Table 2.** Table captions should be placed above the tables.

| Words highlighted during clustering | Quantity | % | Cluster |
|---|---|---|---|
| regime, fire, situation, operational, coronavirus, vaccination, control, restriction, spread, infection | 4469 | 10,3 | Safety |
| festival, sport, athlete, competition, team, game, sports, championship, guest, museum | 3287 | 7,5 | Leisure |
| construction, housing, house, object, emergency, apartment, gas, gasification, ruble, program | 3205 | 7,4 | Housing issue |
| road, street, kilometer, plot, landscaping, repair, work, road, yard, bridge | 3109 | 7,1 | Comfort of living |
| help, doctor, medical, hospital, patient, medic, healthcare, help, person, ambulance | 2727 | 6,3 | Health |
| school, building, kindergarten, new, renovation, garden, construction, build, facility, equipment | 2672 | 6,1 | Demographics |
| support, ruble, measure, payment, business, rate, income, family, loan, preferential | 2491 | 5,7 | Social protection |
| competition, guys, student, university, education, graduate, student, winner, youth, young | 2238 | 5,1 | Education |
| Other topics | 1284 | 44,6 | Other |

# 8 Depersonalization

All stages of the work go through fine-tuning the boundaries of the use of personal data. However, this issue was resolved at the very first step, when developing the database and the parser. It excludes the storage of information about the name, age and other important information, only the text of the review or comment is stored in the database. Additionally, a Python script has been developed that analyzes the collected array and deletes all proper names, phone numbers and email. This approach allows you to depersonalize and depersonalize data. Additionally, a study of the legislative framework was conducted to comply with all norms.

This script was implemented based on the Yargy parser and the Natasha library. Yargy parser is a library for extracting structured information from a natural language text based on rules. This library is used to perform operations such as extracting dates, names, addresses, organizations and other named entities from the text in Russian and English. Yargy works by generating Parser combinators from rules describing the structure of data in the text. It can be used in various natural language processing tasks, such as analyzing news articles, machine learning texts, or building business logic through text query processing.

The Natasha library is a set of tools for natural language processing. In particular, it allows lemmatization, morphological analysis, extraction of named entities and other operations with text. Natasha uses the pymorphy2 library for morphological analysis of words. The processing procedure takes place immediately after data collection, the deleted information is not duplicated anywhere.

The result justified the efforts, all the reviews remained depersonalized, firstly, we deleted all the contact information provided by the geoinformation network itself and at the second step, with the help of our script, we got rid of any mentions of personal data, thereby not violating the requirements.

## 9 Conclusions

The results obtained demonstrate that it is possible to use data from social networks for a value-oriented approach to managing city development programs. The data obtained cannot replace traditional planning methods, however, they can significantly supplement operational data for city management and solving strategic issues for the sustainable development of the city.

The chosen topic is socially significant in society, since technologies for creating a socio-psychological portrait of users will allow to assess the human capital of the state, and can also form the basis for the development of socio-spatial structures of the urban environment.

The use of new technologies and forecasting methods will improve the accuracy of the analysis of changes in the internal environment of urban space, forecasting the needs and needs of city residents, as well as the ability of the management system to adjust tasks and operational plans for changing the infrastructure to some new circumstances. The creation and use of predictive models based on social networks is one of the most promising areas for the creation and testing of new urban technologies.

The study of the socio-cultural and economic needs of residents of different districts of the city, which are represented in social networks, will allow us to characterize the needs of the city in infrastructure development at different levels of centralization, taking into account the spatial localization of people with different types of needs and requests, which in turn will allow us to implement one of the priority areas of urban development associated with improving the quality of the urban environment and ensuring the effectiveness of management and development of the urban environment.

This project is a practical and promising solution in poorly formalized areas of knowledge. In addition, the application of such a solution at the national level can be an example of the introduction of digital technologies and platform solutions in the areas of public administration, business and society.

**Acknowledgements.** This research is financially supported by the Russian Science Foundation, Agreement 17–71-30029 (https://rscf.ru/en/project/17-71-30029/), with co-financing of Bank Saint Petersburg.

## References

1. Yigitcanlar, T.: Smart cities: an effective urban development and management model? Aust. Plan. **52**(1), 27–34 (2015). https://doi.org/10.1080/07293682.2015.1019752

2. Van Oers, R., Pereira Roders, A.: Historic cities as model of sustainability. J. Cult. Herit. Manag. Sustain. Dev. **2**, 4–14 (2012)
3. Castells, M.: The Rise of the Network Society, 2nd edn. Blackwell Publishing, Oxford (2010)
4. Widodo, J.: Urban environment and human behaviour: learning from history and local wisdom. Soc. Behav. Sci. **42**, 6–11 (2012). https://doi.org/10.1016/j.sbspro.2012.04.161
5. Remm, T. Understanding the city through its semiotic spatialities. Sign Syst. Stud. **39**(2/4), 124 (2011). https://doi.org/10.12697/SSS.2011.39.2-4.06
6. Horlings, L.G.: Values in place: a value-oriented approach toward sustainable place-shaping. Reg. Stud. Reg. Sci. **2**, 257–274 (2014)
7. Barkovskaya, A.Yu., Nazarova, M.P.: Stress factors in the socio-cultural space of a modern big city. Izvestiya VolgSTU. **5**(132). 37–42 (2014)
8. Feng, C., Xu, H-W.: Urban public space context and cognitive psychology. Evolution in information environment. In: IOP Conference Series: Earth and Environmental Science, vol. 94, 2017. https://doi.org/10.1088/1755-1315/94/1/012046
9. Coleman, A.: Environmental Psychology and Urban Green Space: Supporting Place-Based Conservation in Philadelphia, PA (2014)
10. Karami, S., Ghafary, M., Fakhrayee, A.: Analyzing the correlation between urban spaces and place attachment. Evidence from: Narmak neighborhood in Tehran. Eur. Online J. Nat. Soc. Sci. **3**(4) (2014). https://core.ac.uk/download/pdf/230053339.pdf
11. Moore, M.H.: Creating Public Value: Strategic Management in Government, 480 p. Harvard University Press, Cambridge (1995)
12. Stocker, G.: Public value management: a new narrative for networked governance? Am. Rev. Public Adm. **36**(1), 41–57 (2006)
13. Parston, G., Goodman, J.: High-Performance Government Organizations: Principles for Creating Public Value (2008)
14. Mityagin, S.A., Gornova, G.V., Drozhzhin A.I., Sokol, A.A.: Value-oriented management in a smart city. Int. J. Open Inf. Technol. **9**(12) (2021)

# Short Papers

# OdeShell: An Interactive Tool and a Specific Domain Language to Develop Models Based on Ordinary Differential Equations

Rafael Sachetto Oliveira$^{(\boxtimes)}$ ⓘ and Carolina Ribeiro Xavier ⓘ

Universidade Federal de São João del-Rei, São João del-Rei, MG, Brazil
{sachetto,carolinaxavier}@ufsj.edu.br

**Abstract.** ODEs are a useful mathematical tool for modeling dynamic systems in different fields, such as physics, engineering, biology, and economics. They can provide insights into the behavior of complex systems over time. However, creating ODE models can be difficult and requires expertise in the subject matter and mathematical techniques. This paper presents the OdeShell, a command line interface that enables users to build and simulate ODE models while examining their behavior under diverse circumstances. OdeShell is a valuable addition to the ODE modeling domain, with the capability to ease the development of intricate models in various fields. The tool accommodates novice and proficient modelers, giving them a flexible and user-friendly environment to build and test ODE models. We elaborate on the principal features and functionality of OdeShell and demonstrate its utility in developing ODE models through small examples. Additionally, we discuss the ODE language, emphasizing its syntax and meaning.

**Keywords:** ODEs · interactive · shell

## 1 Introduction

Ordinary Differential Equations (ODEs) are a powerful mathematical tool for modeling dynamic systems in various fields, from physics and engineering to biology and economics [12]. Ordinary Differential Equation (ODE) models can capture complex systems' underlying mechanisms and behaviors, providing insights into their dynamics over time. However, developing ODE models can be challenging, requiring expertise in the subject matter and the mathematical techniques involved.

To address this challenge, we introduce OdeShell[1], an interactive tool and specific domain language for developing ODE models. OdeShell provides a command line interface (CLI) that allows users to construct and simulate ODE models and analyze their behavior under various conditions. The tool is designed to

---

[1] Available at https://github.com/rsachetto/odecompiler.

O. Gervasi et al. (Eds.): ICCSA 2023, LNCS 13957, pp. 385–392, 2023.
https://doi.org/10.1007/978-3-031-36808-0_25

support novice and expert modelers, providing a flexible and intuitive environment for developing and testing ODE models.

In this paper, we describe the key features and functionality of OdeShell and demonstrate its use in developing ODE models in small examples. We also describe the ODE language, highlighting its syntax and semantics. Overall, OdeShell represents a valuable contribution to the field of ODE modeling and has the potential to facilitate the development of complex models across several disciplines.

## 2    The ODE Language and the Source-to-Source Translator

ODE models can be implemented and solved using general-purpose programming languages like C/C++, Python, and Matlab. While these languages offer a high degree of flexibility and control over the model implementation, they often require significant manual coding and debugging efforts.

An alternative approach is describing ODE models using a definition language such as CellML [8]. CellML is an XML-based language that provides a standardized, machine-independent representation of mathematical models. By utilizing CellML, modelers can streamline the model development process, reduce the potential for errors, and enhance model reproducibility.

Once a model is defined in CellML, it can be translated into a general programming language using the CellML API or publicly available tools such as Agos[2] [2] or Myokit[3] [4]. These tools provide a convenient and efficient means of generating simulation code directly from the CellML model, allowing for rapid prototyping and efficient model testing.

### 2.1    ODE Development Language

The primary goal of our ODE representation language is to provide a clear and concise way to describe complex models. To achieve this, we have developed a syntax that focuses on the ODEs in the model but also allows for the use of *if* and *while* statements as well as function definitions. Our language is designed to be more approachable than CellML, while still being powerful as a general-purpose programming language. Researchers can easily communicate their findings and reproduce results by writing models in plain text using our language.

**Builtin Function.** All mathematical functions in the C math library[4] can be used with our ODE language. In addition, we have included four built-in utility functions: print(var), ode_get_value(ode_var, iteration), ode_get_time(ode_var, iteration), and ode_get_num_iterations(). These functions are intended for use within a particular function type called *endfn*, which will be explained in greater detail later in the text.

---

[2] Available at: https://github.com/FISIOCOMP-UFJF/agos.

[3] Available at: http://myokit.org.

[4] Available at: https://cplusplus.com/reference/cmath/.

**Examples.** Listing 1.1 (sir.ode) shows the implementation of the Susceptible, Infectious, or Recovered (SIR) model [1], described in Eq. 1, using the ODE language. The *ode* keyword is used to define an ordinary differential equation, and the ODE variable name on the left-hand side (LHS) needs to end with a ' character. For now, it is impossible to have mathematical expressions on the LHS; only the ODE variable is allowed. The *initial* keyword is used to set the initial condition of each defined ODE. Variables used in initial conditions must be marked as *global*. Global variables can be used anywhere in the code.

$$\begin{cases} \dfrac{dS}{dt} = -\beta SI \\ \dfrac{dI}{dt} = \beta SI - \gamma I \\ \dfrac{dR}{dt} = \gamma I \end{cases} \tag{1}$$

```
1 global n = 1000
2 global init_i = 3
3 beta = 0.4/n
4 gamma = 0.04
5 #Variables used in initial conditions need to be global
6 initial S = n - init_i
7 initial I = init_i
8 initial R = 0
9 #ODE'S
10 ode S' = -beta*S*I
11 ode I' = beta*S*I - gamma*I
12 ode R' = gamma*I
```

**Listing 1.1.** SIR model implemented using the ODE language (sir.ode).

We can see a more complex model in Listings 1.2 (common.ode) and 1.3 (hh.ode). In the code described in Listing 1.2, we define two functions: *stim* and *calc_E_Na*. In the current version, functions can have Boolean or numeric parameters, and their return values must be numeric (internally, the numeric values are represented in double precision). Listing 1.3 shows the implementation of the Hodgkin-Huxley model [7]. In line 1, we have the *import* keyword. With this statement, the user can import all functions of a file, *common.ode* in this example, and use them to define the model. In the current version, the ODE independent variable is always named *time*, starts from 0, and is global.

```
1 fn stim(t) {
2     if(t > 10 and t < 10.5) { return 20; }
3     return 0;
4 }
5 fn calc_E_Na(E_R) {
6     return E_R + 115.0
7 }
```

**Listing 1.2.** Functions used in the Hodgkin-Huxley model (common.ode).

```
 1 import  "common.ode"
 2 Cm    = 1.0
 3 E_R   = -75.0
 4 g_Na  = 120.0
 5 g_K   = 36.0
 6 g_L   = 0.3
 7 E_Na     = calc_E_Na(E_R)
 8 alpha_m  = ((-0.1)*(V + 50.0))/(exp((-(V + 50.0))/10.0) -
      1.0)
 9 beta_m   = 4.0*exp((-(V + 75.0))/18.0)
10 alpha_h  = 0.07*exp((-(V + 75.0))/20.0)
11 beta_h   = 1.0/(exp((-(V + 45.0))/10.0) + 1.0)
12 E_K      = E_R - 12.0
13 alpha_n  = ((-0.01)*(V+65.0))/(exp((-(V+65.0))/10.0)-1.0)
14 beta_n   = 0.125*exp((V+75.0)/80.0)
15 E_L      = E_R + 10.613
16 i_Na     = g_Na*pow(m,3.0)*h*(V - E_Na)
17 i_K      = g_K*pow(n, 4.0)*(V - E_K)
18 i_L      = g_L*(V - E_L)
19 #Initial conditions
20 initial V = -7.5e+01
21 initial m = 5.0e-02
22 initial h = 6.0e-01
23 initial n = 3.25e-01
24 #ODEs
25 ode V' = -(-stim(time)) + i_Na + i_K + i_L)/Cm
26 ode m' = alpha_m*(1.0-m) - beta_m*m
27 ode h' = alpha_h*(1.0-h) - beta_h*h
28 ode n' = alpha_n*(1.0-n) - beta_n*n
```

**Listing 1.3.** Hodgkin-Huxley model implemented using the ODE language. In this example we show the usage of imports and functions (hh.ode).

## 2.2   The Source-to-Source Translator

After defining a model using the ODE language, it is possible to generate a solver using the *odec* (ODE compiler) software. The *odec* is an almost complete compiler with lexical, syntactic, and semantic analysis that translates the source model to a C solver (a python solver is also planned for future development) that can be compiled and executed to solve the developed model. In the current version, it is possible to generate a solver using a linear multistep method with Backward Differentiation Formulas (provided by the CVODE library [5]) or an adaptive time step method [3] that is implemented with no external dependencies. The current version of the shell and odec is currently available only on Linux and needs the GCC compiler installed.

Using a domain-specific language instead of a markup language to develop a model has several advantages. Firstly, it simplifies the parsing of code and the creation of an abstract syntax tree, making it easier to translate the original code to a general-purpose language such as C or Python. Additionally, performing semantic and syntactic analysis of the code is more straightforward, providing a better means of discovering and correcting errors in the developed model than a description language, even with a visual inspection. In short, using a domain-specific language can lead to more efficient and accurate model development, with fewer errors and easier debugging.

The C solver can be generated from the SIR model code presented in Listing 1.1, using the command:

```
$ ./bin/odec -i sir.ode -o sir.c
```

If the solver was generated using the default adaptive time step method, the code will not have external dependencies, making it simple to compile using gcc:

```
$ gcc sir.c -o solver -lm
```

After the compilation, the solver can be executed, as described below:

```
$ ./solver 100 out.txt
```

where 100 is the simulation final time and *out.txt* is the output file (these are not fixed parameters, 100 and out.txt where only used as an example).

Listing 1.4 shows the first five lines of the outputted data after solving the sir model. The first line describes the order and the name of the variables, and the following lines are the value of each variable in each timestep.

```
1 #t, S, I, R
2 0.000000 997.000000 3.000000 0.000000
3 0.000001 996.999999 3.000001 0.000000
4 0.000002 996.988139 3.010671 0.001190
5 0.009915 996.976123 3.021482 0.002395
```

**Listing 1.4.** First five lines of the output file after solving the sir model.

# 3   The ODE Shell

The ODE Shell is an interactive command line interface (CLI) tool that can be used to solve, manipulate and analyze models developed using the ODE language presented before. The CLI tool was created to provide a flexible and intuitive environment for developing and testing ODE models, catering to novice and expert modelers.

## 3.1   Shell Commands

Several commands were implemented in the ODE shell to allow the developed models' manipulation, plotting, and solving. Following, we have an example usage of the ode shell, using as a model the *sir.ode* file (Listings 1.1):

```
$ /bin/ode_shell -w examples
Using qt as gnuplot terminal.
Current directory /odecompiler/examples
ode_shell> load sir
Model sir successfully loaded
ode_shell> solve 100
Model sir solved for 100.000000 steps.
ode_shell> plotvars
```

In the first line, we execute the ode_shell, passing the directory we want to be our "Work Directory" (-w option). After that, we can start writing commands to the shell. In this example, we first load the sir. model (the ode extension can be omitted), and then we solve the model for 100 steps using the *solve 100* command. After solving the model, we can plot all its variables over time using the *plotvars* command.

Figure 1 shows the output graph of the *plotvars* command as used in the example above. It is worth noting that all the plotting in the shell is performed using the Gnuplot software [10]. The *ode_shell* automatically checks if gnuplot is available in the user's machine and, if not, disables all plotting commands.

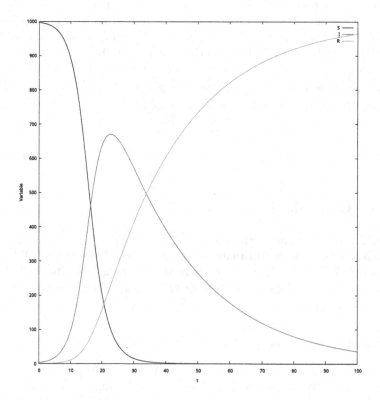

**Fig. 1.** Example output of the *plotvars* command for the sir model.

Table 1 list all the currently available commands in the ODE shell. The user can type 'help command', inside the shell, for more information about a specific command.

**Table 1.** Currently available commands for the ODE shell

| Available commands | | |
|---|---|---|
| cd | closeplot | converttoc |
| editmodel | getglobalvalue | getglobalvalues |
| getinitialvalue | getinitialvalues | getodevalue |
| getodevalues | getparamvalue | getparamvalues |
| getplotconfig | getruninfo | help |
| list | listruns | load |
| loadcmds | ls | odestolatex |
| plot | plottofile | plottoterm |
| plotvar | plotvars | printmodel |
| pwd | quit | replot |
| replottofile | replottoterm | replotvar |
| resetruns | savemodeloutput | saveplot |
| setautolreload | setcurrentmodel | setglobalreload |
| setglobalvalue | setinitialvalue | setodevalue |
| setparamvalue | setplotlegend | setplotx |
| setplotxlabel | setploty | setplotylabel |
| setshouldreload | solve | solveplot |
| unload | vars | |

# 4    Conclusions and Future Work

ODE models are a critical mathematical tool for understanding complex systems dynamics across various fields. However, developing ODE models can be challenging, requiring subject matter expertise and mathematical knowledge. In this paper, we presented OdeShell, an interactive tool, and specific domain language.

OdeShell is designed to support both novice and expert modelers. The described tool is an open-source project, freely available at https://github.com/rsachetto/odecompiler that provides a flexible and intuitive environment for constructing, simulating, and analyzing ODE models. By providing a streamlined and efficient means of generating simulation code, OdeShell has the potential to facilitate the development of complex models and enhance model reproducibility in a wide range of disciplines.

As for future work, the authors plan to incorporate additional analytical functionalities into the software, such as uncertainty quantification [9], sensitivity analysis [6], and stability analysis [11]. These complements would further enhance the capabilities of OdeShell and enable a more comprehensive analysis of ODE models.

# References

1. Anderson, R.M.: Discussion: the Kermack-McKendrick epidemic threshold theorem. Bull. Math. Biol. **53**, 1–32 (1991). https://doi.org/10.1007/BF02464422
2. Barbosa, C.B., et al.: A transformation tool for ODE based models. In: Alexandrov, V.N., van Albada, G.D., Sloot, P.M.A., Dongarra, J. (eds.) ICCS 2006. LNCS, vol. 3991, pp. 68–75. Springer, Heidelberg (2006). https://doi.org/10.1007/11758501_14
3. Campos, R.S., Lobosco, M., dos Santos, R.W.: Adaptive time step for cardiac myocyte models. Procedia Comput. Sci. **4**, 1092–1100 (2011)
4. Clerx, M., Collins, P., de Lange, E., Volders, P.G.: Myokit: a simple interface to cardiac cellular electrophysiology. Prog. Biophys. Mol. Biol. **120**(1), 100–114 (2016). https://doi.org/10.1016/j.pbiomolbio.2015.12.008. Recent Developments in Biophysics & Molecular Biology of Heart Rhythm
5. Cohen, S.D., Hindmarsh, A.C., Dubois, P.F.: CVODE, a stiff/nonstiff ODE solver in C. Comput. Phys. **10**(2), 138–143 (1996)
6. Dickinson, R.P., Gelinas, R.J.: Sensitivity analysis of ordinary differential equation systems-a direct method. J. Comput. Phys. **21**(2), 123–143 (1976)
7. Hodgkin, A.L., Huxley, A.F.: A quantitative description of membrane current and its application to conduction and excitation in nerve. J. Physiol. **117**(4), 500–544 (1952)
8. Miller, A.K., et al.: An overview of the CellML API and its implementation. BMC Bioinform. **11**(1), 1–12 (2010). https://doi.org/10.1186/1471-2105-11-178
9. Mitra, E.D., Hlavacek, W.S.: Parameter estimation and uncertainty quantification for systems biology models. Curr. Opin. Syst. Biol. **18**, 9–18 (2019)
10. Racine, J.: gnuplot 4.0: a portable interactive plotting utility (2006)
11. Roussel, M.R.: Stability analysis for ODEs. In: Nonlinear Dynamics: A Hands-on Introductory Survey. Morgan & Claypool Publishers (2019)
12. Teschl, G.: Ordinary Differential Equations and Dynamical Systems, vol. 140. American Mathematical Society (2012)

# Multiple Integer Divisions with an Invariant Dividend and Monotonically Increasing or Decreasing Divisors

Daisuke Takahashi[✉][iD]

Center for Computational Sciences, University of Tsukuba, 1-1-1 Tennodai, Tsukuba, Ibaraki 305-8577, Japan
daisuke@cs.tsukuba.ac.jp

**Abstract.** In this paper, we propose an algorithm for multiple integer divisions with an invariant dividend and monotonically increasing or decreasing divisors. In such multiple integer divisions, we show that if the dividend and divisors satisfy a certain condition, then if only one quotient is calculated by division first, the remaining quotients can be obtained by correcting the previously calculated quotients at most once. The proposed algorithm is up to approximately 1.90 and 1.85 times faster than the 64-bit unsigned integer division instruction of the Intel 64 architecture and Intel Short Vector Math Library (SVML) on the Intel Xeon Platinum 8368 processor, respectively.

**Keywords:** Multiple integer divisions · invariant dividend · approximate quotient

## 1 Introduction

Integer division is a widely used arithmetic operation, being included in many applications. In general, division is known to be slower than addition, subtraction, and multiplication. For this reason, algorithms have been proposed to perform division using only addition, subtraction, and multiplication. In particular, algorithms for division by invariant integers [3,5,8–10] and algorithms for integer division using reciprocals [1,13,14] have been proposed. Additionally, 32- and 64-bit integer division using double-precision floating-point arithmetic has been proposed [11].

In this paper, we consider multiple integer divisions when the dividend is invariant and the multiple divisors are monotonically increasing or decreasing. Such multiple integer divisions appear when converting an integer to Montgomery representations [12] for multiple moduli [15].

The remainder of this paper is organized as follows. Section 2 presents the proposed algorithm for multiple integer divisions with an invariant dividend and monotonically increasing or decreasing divisors. Section 3 presents the performance results. Finally, Sect. 4 presents concluding remarks.

O. Gervasi et al. (Eds.): ICCSA 2023, LNCS 13957, pp. 393–401, 2023.
https://doi.org/10.1007/978-3-031-36808-0_26

## 2   Proposed Algorithm

An unsigned integer division is defined by the quotient $q = \lfloor a/b \rfloor$ and the remainder $r = a - bq$ ($0 \le r < b$), where the dividend is $a$ and the divisor is $b$.

We consider multiple integer divisions when the dividend is invariant, and the multiple divisors are monotonically increasing or decreasing. In such multiple integer divisions, we show that if the dividend and divisors satisfy a certain condition, then if only one quotient is calculated by division first, the remaining quotients can be obtained by correcting the previously calculated quotients at most once.

**Theorem 1.** *Consider integers $a \ge 0$, $b > 0$, and $c \ge 0$. If $ca \le b(b + c)$, then*

$$\left\lfloor \frac{a}{b} \right\rfloor < \left\lfloor \frac{a}{b+c} \right\rfloor + 2. \tag{1}$$

*Proof.* For any real number $x$, $x - 1 < \lfloor x \rfloor \le x$ holds. Thus, we have

$$\frac{a}{b} - 1 < \left\lfloor \frac{a}{b} \right\rfloor \le \frac{a}{b}, \tag{2}$$

$$\frac{a}{b+c} + 1 < \left\lfloor \frac{a}{b+c} \right\rfloor + 2 \le \frac{a}{b+c} + 2. \tag{3}$$

From inequalities (2) and (3), the condition $a/b \le a/(b + c) + 1$ for inequality (1) to hold can be obtained as $ca \le b(b + c)$. $\qquad\square$

From Theorem 1, if $a$, $b$, and $c$ satisfy the condition $ca \le b(b + c)$, the quotient $\lfloor a/b \rfloor$ can be obtained by making at most one correction to the quotient $\lfloor a/(b + c) \rfloor$. Thus, Theorem 1 is applicable when the divisors are monotonically decreasing. When the divisors are monotonically increasing, the quotient can be obtained in the same way by reversing the order of the divisors.

Algorithm 1 shows the proposed algorithm for multiple integer divisions with an invariant dividend and monotonically increasing divisors. If it is known in advance that the condition of Theorem 1 is satisfied for the dividend $a$, the minimum divisor $b_0$, and the maximum difference $c$ between adjacent divisors, then multiple integer divisions can be efficiently calculated using Algorithm 1.

The first and second lines of Algorithm 1 calculate the quotient $q_{n-1}$ and remainder $r_{n-1}$, respectively, for the dividend $a$ and the divisor $b_{n-1}$. In line 4, the previously calculated quotient $q_{i+1}$ is used as the approximate quotient. In line 5, the remainder $r_i$ is obtained from the dividend $a$, the divisor $b_i$, and the quotient $q_i$. If the remainder $r_i$ is greater than or equal to the divisor $b_i$, then lines 7 and 8 correct the quotient $q_i$ and remainder $r_i$.

Algorithm 2 shows the proposed algorithm for multiple integer divisions with an invariant dividend and monotonically decreasing divisors. If it is known in advance that the condition of Theorem 1 is satisfied for the dividend $a$, the

---

**Algorithm 1.** Multiple integer divisions with an invariant dividend and monotonically increasing divisors

---

**Input:** $a \geq 0$, $b_0, b_1, \ldots, b_{n-1} > 0$, $b_i \leq b_{i+1}$ for $0 \leq i \leq n-2$, $ca \leq b_0(b_0 + c)$,
    where $c = \max(b_{i+1} - b_i)$ for $0 \leq i \leq n-2$
**Output:** $q_i = \lfloor a/b_i \rfloor$ for $0 \leq i \leq n-1$, $r_i = a \bmod b_i$ for $0 \leq i \leq n-1$
1: $q_{n-1} \leftarrow \lfloor a/b_{n-1} \rfloor$
2: $r_{n-1} \leftarrow a - b_{n-1}q_{n-1}$
3: **for** $i$ **from** $n-2$ **downto** 0 **do**
4:     $q_i \leftarrow q_{i+1}$
5:     $r_i \leftarrow a - b_iq_i$
6:     **if** $r_i \geq b_i$ **then**
7:         $q_i \leftarrow q_i + 1$
8:         $r_i \leftarrow r_i - b_i$.

---

**Algorithm 2.** Multiple integer divisions with an invariant dividend and monotonically decreasing divisors

---

**Input:** $a \geq 0$, $b_0, b_1, \ldots, b_{n-1} > 0$, $b_i \geq b_{i+1}$ for $0 \leq i \leq n-2$, $ca \leq b_{n-1}(b_{n-1} + c)$,
    where $c = \max(b_i - b_{i+1})$ for $0 \leq i \leq n-2$
**Output:** $q_i = \lfloor a/b_i \rfloor$ for $0 \leq i \leq n-1$, $r_i = a \bmod b_i$ for $0 \leq i \leq n-1$
1: $q_0 \leftarrow \lfloor a/b_0 \rfloor$
2: $r_0 \leftarrow a - b_0q_0$
3: **for** $i$ **from** 1 **to** $n-1$ **do**
4:     $q_i \leftarrow q_{i-1}$
5:     $r_i \leftarrow a - b_iq_i$
6:     **if** $r_i \geq b_i$ **then**
7:         $q_i \leftarrow q_i + 1$
8:         $r_i \leftarrow r_i - b_i$.

---

minimum divisor $b_{n-1}$, and the maximum difference $c$ between adjacent divisors, then multiple integer divisions can be efficiently calculated using Algorithm 2.

The first and second lines of Algorithm 2 calculate the quotient $q_0$ and remainder $r_0$, respectively, for the dividend $a$ and the divisor $b_0$. In line 4, the previously calculated quotient $q_{i-1}$ is used as the approximate quotient. In line 5, the remainder $r_i$ is obtained from the dividend $a$, the divisor $b_i$, and the quotient $q_i$. If the remainder $r_i$ is greater than or equal to the divisor $b_i$, then lines 7 and 8 correct the quotient $q_i$ and remainder $r_i$. In Algorithms 1 and 2, when the divisors $b_0, b_1, \ldots, b_{n-1}$ are an arithmetic progression, then $c$ is equal to the absolute value of the common difference.

In integer division, it is sometimes desirable to calculate only the quotient or remainder [2]. In such cases, Algorithms 1 and 2 can be modified to output only the desired result. Figures 1 and 2 show multiple 64-bit unsigned integer divisions with an invariant dividend and monotonically increasing and decreasing divisors, respectively.

We now consider vectorization of Algorithms 1 and 2. In Algorithms 1 and 2, the quotients are obtained by correcting only the previously calculated quotient and this process cannot be vectorized due to data dependency. However,

```
void divinc64(uint64_t *q, uint64_t *r, uint64_t a, uint64_t *b, int n)
/* Compute q[0:n] = floor(a / b[0:n]) and r[0:n] = a mod b[0:n].
   Requires a >= 0, b[0:n] > 0, b[i] <= b[i + 1] for 0 <= i <= n - 2
   and c * a <= b[0] * (b[0] + c),
   where c = max(b[i + 1] - b[i]) for 0 <= i <= n - 2. */
{
  int i;

  q[n - 1] = a / b[n - 1];
  r[n - 1] = a - b[n - 1] * q[n - 1];

  for (i = n - 2; i >= 0; i--) {
    q[i] = q[i + 1];
    r[i] = a - b[i] * q[i];
    if (r[i] >= b[i]) {
      q[i]++;
      r[i] -= b[i];
    }
  }
}
```

**Fig. 1.** Multiple 64-bit unsigned integer divisions with an invariant dividend and monotonically increasing divisors

```
void divdec64(uint64_t *q, uint64_t *r, uint64_t a, uint64_t *b, int n)
/* Compute q[0:n] = floor(a / b[0:n]) and r[0:n] = a mod b[0:n].
   Requires a >= 0, b[0:n] > 0, b[i] >= b[i + 1] for 0 <= i <= n - 2
   and c * a <= b[n - 1] * (b[n - 1] + c),
   where c = max(b[i] - b[i + 1]) for 0 <= i <= n - 2. */
{
  int i;

  q[0] = a / b[0];
  r[0] = a - b[0] * q[0];

  for (i = 1; i < n; i++) {
    q[i] = q[i - 1];
    r[i] = a - b[i] * q[i];
    if (r[i] >= b[i]) {
      q[i]++;
      r[i] -= b[i];
    }
  }
}
```

**Fig. 2.** Multiple 64-bit unsigned integer divisions with an invariant dividend and monotonically decreasing divisors

by simultaneously correcting multiple previously calculated quotients, this data dependency can be resolved, making it possible to vectorize the process. To do this, the previously calculated quotients for the divisors at multiples of the vector length are used as the approximate quotients. Thus, the value of $c$ in Algorithms 1 and 2 is the maximum difference between divisors at intervals of the vector length.

```
void vdivinc64(uint64_t *q, uint64_t *r, uint64_t a, uint64_t *b, int n)
/*  Compute q[0:n] = floor(a / b[0:n]) and r[0:n] = a mod b[0:n].
    Requires a >= 0, b[0:n] > 0, b[i] <= b[i + 1] for 0 <= i <= n - 2
    and c * a <= b[0] * (b[0] + c),
    where c = max(b[i + VLEN] - b[i]) for 0 <= i <= n - VLEN - 1. */
{
  int i, j;

  for (i = n - 1; i >= n - VLEN; i--) {
    q[i] = a / b[i];
    r[i] = a - b[i] * q[i];
  }

  for (j = n - VLEN - 1; j >= 0; j -= VLEN) {
    for (i = j; i >= j - VLEN + 1; i--) {
      q[i] = q[i + VLEN];
      r[i] = a - b[i] * q[i];
      if (r[i] >= b[i]) {
        q[i]++;
        r[i] -= b[i];
      }
    }
  }
}
```

**Fig. 3.** Vectorized multiple 64-bit unsigned integer divisions with an invariant dividend and monotonically increasing divisors

Figures 3 and 4 show vectorized multiple integer divisions with an invariant dividend and monotonically increasing and decreasing divisors, respectively. In these programs, the inner loop of the doubly nested loop can be vectorized. These programs assume that the number of divisors $n$ is divisible by the vector length VLEN. If $n$ is not divisible by VLEN, a remainder loop needs to be executed.

```
void vdivdec64(uint64_t *q, uint64_t *r, uint64_t a, uint64_t *b, int n)
/* Compute q[0:n] = floor(a / b[0:n]) and r[0:n] = a mod b[0:n].
   Requires a >= 0, b[0:n] > 0, b[i] >= b[i + 1] for 0 <= i <= n - 2
   and c * a <= b[n - 1] * (b[n - 1] + c),
   where c = max(b[i] - b[i + VLEN]) for 0 <= i <= n - VLEN - 1. */
{
  int i, j;

  for (i = 0; i < VLEN; i++) {
    q[i] = a / b[i];
    r[i] = a - b[i] * q[i];
  }

  for (j = VLEN; j < n; j += VLEN) {
    for (i = j; i < j + VLEN; i++) {
      q[i] = q[i - VLEN];
      r[i] = a - b[i] * q[i];
      if (r[i] >= b[i]) {
        q[i]++;
        r[i] -= b[i];
      }
    }
  }
}
```

**Fig. 4.** Vectorized multiple 64-bit unsigned integer divisions with an invariant dividend and monotonically decreasing divisors

## 3    Performance Results

For performance evaluation, we compared the execution times of multiple 64-bit unsigned integer divisions using the following four implementations:

1. Implementation using the 64-bit unsigned integer division instruction div of the Intel 64 architecture
2. Implementation of the proposed algorithm using the Intel 64 architecture instructions
3. Implementation using the _mm512_div_epu64() intrinsic function, which divides packed 64-bit unsigned integers in the Intel Short Vector Math Library (SVML) [6]
4. Implementation of the proposed algorithm using the Intel Advanced Vector Extensions 512 (AVX-512) instructions [7]

   The evaluation used the following settings. The batch size $n$ of 64-bit unsigned integer divisions varied from 128 to 1024. In these cases, the divisors, the quotients, and the remainders fit into the L1 cache. The dividend $a$ is set to be a random number in the range $[0, 2^{64} - 1]$. For the monotonically increasing divisors $b_i$ ($0 \leq i \leq n - 1$), $b_0$ is set to $\lfloor \sqrt{\text{VLEN} \times a} \rfloor + 1$, and $b_i = b_0 + i$. For the monotonically decreasing divisors $b_i$ ($0 \leq i \leq n - 1$), $b_{n-1}$ is set to $\lfloor \sqrt{\text{VLEN} \times a} \rfloor + 1$, and $b_{n-i-1} = b_{n-1} + i$, where the vector length VLEN is set to 8. Note that the dividend and divisors satisfy the condition of Theorem 1.

Each batch of 64-bit unsigned integer divisions was executed one million times. The number of 64-bit unsigned integer divisions per second (Mops) was calculated based on the average elapsed time.

The specifications of the platform are shown in Table 1. The Intel Xeon Platinum 8368 processor has 38 cores. However, we evaluated the performance on a single core and a single thread to focus on vectorization. The Intel C compiler (version 19.1.3.304) was used. The compiler options were icc -O3 -xCORE-AVX512 -qopt-zmm-usage=high. The compiler option -O3 specifies to optimize for maximum speed and enable more aggressive optimizations. The compiler option -xCORE-AVX512 specifies to optimize for Intel processors that support Intel AVX-512 instructions. The compiler option -qopt-zmm-usage=high specifies to generate zmm code without restrictions.

Table 2 shows the performance of multiple 64-bit unsigned integer divisions with an invariant dividend and monotonically increasing divisors. When the batch size $n$ is 1024, the proposed algorithm is approximately 1.49 and 1.76 times faster than the 64-bit unsigned integer division instruction of the Intel 64 architecture and Intel SVML on the Intel Xeon Platinum 8368 processor, respectively. The Ice Lake microarchitecture of the Intel Xeon Platinum 8368 processor requires significantly fewer cycles for the Intel 64 architecture integer division instruction div than previous Intel microarchitectures such as the Skylake microarchitecture [4], and so the difference in performance between the proposed algorithm and the 64-bit unsigned integer division instruction of the Intel 64 architecture is smaller on the Intel Xeon Platinum 8368 processor.

**Table 1.** Specifications of the platform

| Platform | Intel Xeon Platinum processor |
|---|---|
| Number of cores | 38 |
| Number of threads | 76 |
| CPU type | Intel Xeon Platinum 8368 Ice Lake 2.4 GHz |
| L1 cache (per core) | I-cache: 32 KB D-cache: 48 KB |
| L2 cache (per core) | 1.25 MB |
| L3 cache | 57 MB |
| Main memory | DDR4-3200 256 GB |
| Theoretical peak performance | 2.918 TFlops |
| OS | Linux 4.18.0-305.25.1.el8_4.x86_64 |

**Table 2.** Performance of multiple 64-bit unsigned integer divisions with an invariant dividend and monotonically increasing divisors (Mops)

| Batch size $n$ | Intel 64 | Proposed (Intel 64) | Intel SVML | Proposed (Intel AVX-512) |
|---|---|---|---|---|
| 128 | 336.622 | 507.979 | 600.133 | 1110.869 |
| 256 | 338.892 | 503.765 | 604.713 | 1069.585 |
| 512 | 339.121 | 505.398 | 603.699 | 1068.396 |
| 1024 | 338.809 | 505.617 | 604.131 | 1065.383 |

**Table 3.** Performance of multiple 64-bit unsigned integer divisions with an invariant dividend and monotonically decreasing divisors (Mops)

| Batch size $n$ | Intel 64 | Proposed (Intel 64) | Intel SVML | Proposed (Intel AVX-512) |
|---|---|---|---|---|
| 128 | 336.906 | 640.423 | 718.866 | 949.816 |
| 256 | 338.859 | 638.441 | 717.021 | 941.146 |
| 512 | 338.772 | 637.106 | 713.086 | 936.785 |
| 1024 | 338.666 | 637.954 | 703.699 | 933.340 |

Table 3 shows the performance of multiple 64-bit unsigned integer divisions with an invariant dividend and monotonically decreasing divisors. When the batch size $n$ is 1024, the proposed algorithm is approximately 1.88 and 1.33 times faster than the 64-bit unsigned integer division instruction of the Intel 64 architecture and Intel SVML on the Intel Xeon Platinum 8368 processor, respectively.

# 4    Conclusion

In this paper, we proposed an algorithm for multiple integer divisions with an invariant dividend and monotonically increasing or decreasing divisors. In such multiple integer divisions, we showed that if the dividend and divisors satisfy a certain condition, then if only one quotient is calculated by division first, the remaining quotients can be obtained by correcting the previously calculated quotients at most once. Performance results showed that the proposed algorithm is faster than the 64-bit unsigned integer division instruction of the Intel 64 architecture and Intel SVML.

**Acknowledgments.** This work was supported by JSPS KAKENHI Grant Number JP22K12045.

# References

1. Alverson, R.: Integer division using reciprocals. In: Proceedings of 10th IEEE Symposium on Computer Arithmetic (ARITH 1991), pp. 186–190 (1991)
2. Brent, R.P., Zimmermann, P.: Modern Computer Arithmetic. Cambridge University Press, Cambridge (2010)
3. Drane, T., Cheung, W.C., Constantinides, G.: Correctly rounded constant integer division via multiply-add. In: Proceedings of 2012 IEEE International Symposium on Circuits and Systems (ISCAS 2012), pp. 1243–1246 (2012)
4. Fog, A.: Instruction tables: lists of instruction latencies, throughputs and micro-operation breakdowns for Intel, AMD, and VIA CPUs (2022). https://www.agner.org/optimize/instruction_tables.pdf
5. Granlund, T., Montgomery, P.L.: Division by invariant integers using multiplication. In: Proceedings of ACM SIGPLAN Conference on Programming Language Design and Implementation (PLDI 1994), pp. 61–72 (1994)
6. Intel Corporation: Intel C++ compiler classic developer guide and reference (2021). https://www.intel.com/content/dam/develop/external/us/en/documents/cpp_compiler_classic.pdf
7. Intel Corporation: Intel 64 and IA-32 architectures software developer's manual, volume 1: Basic architecture (2022). https://cdrdv2-public.intel.com/671436/253665-sdm-vol-1.pdf
8. Jacobsohn, D.H.: A combinatoric division algorithm for fixed-integer divisors. IEEE Trans. Comput. **C-22**, 608–610 (1973)
9. Lemire, D., Bartlett, C., Kaser, O.: Integer division by constants: optimal bounds. Heliyon **7**, e07442 (2021)
10. Möller, N., Granlund, T.: Improved division by invariant integers. IEEE Trans. Comput. **60**, 165–175 (2011)
11. Monniaux, D., Pain, A.: Formally verified 32- and 64-bit integer division using double-precision floating-point arithmetic. In: Proceedings of 29th IEEE Symposium on Computer Arithmetic (ARITH 2022), pp. 128–132 (2022)
12. Montgomery, P.L.: Modular multiplication without trial division. Math. Comput. **44**, 519–521 (1985)
13. Robison, A.D.: N-bit unsigned division via n-bit multiply-add. In: Proceedings of 17th IEEE Symposium on Computer Arithmetic (ARITH 2005), pp. 131–139 (2005)
14. Rodeheffer, T.L.: Software integer division (2008). https://www.microsoft.com/en-us/research/wp-content/uploads/2008/08/tr-2008-141.pdf
15. Takahashi, D.: Computation of the 100 quadrillionth hexadecimal digit of $\pi$ on a cluster of Intel Xeon Phi processors. Parallel Comput. **75**, 1–10 (2018)

# Large Scale Study of Binary Galaxy Image Classification and the Impact of Image Augmentation Techniques

Tomas Mūžas[✉][iD], Andrius Vytautas Misiukas Misiūnas[iD], and Tadas Meškauskas[iD]

Institute of Computer Science, Faculty of Mathematics and Informatics, Vilnius University, Didlaukio 47, 08303 Vilnius, Lithuania
tomas.muzas@mif.stud.vu.lt

**Abstract.** Current galaxy classification studies are usually conducted on small, expert-classified datasets, constrained within a low redshift ($z$) range. Lower redshift implies better image quality – the lower the $z$ value, the closer the object is, thus more features and details can be observed. Additionally, various augmentation methods are used to further improve classification accuracy, however, there is a lack of studies measuring their impact on other metrics. Therefore, we study the impact of augmentation techniques using the largest dataset that covers a broad redshift range (315,942 galaxies, $0 < z \leqslant 0.28$). We provide comparable evidence that for binary galaxy image classification, common image augmentation techniques – rotation, zoom and flipping – increase accuracy and F1 score, unless the model is underfitting. The most significant increase was observed on the ResNet50 model, for which the accuracy increased from 93.53% to 95.21%, and the F1 score – from 88.66% to 91.82%. Additionally, combining the aforementioned techniques with random noise stabilises a model by significantly decreasing the spread of metrics – for ResNet50, the standard deviation of the F1 score decreased by more than 9 times.

**Keywords:** Galaxy morphology · GalaxyZoo · Image augmentation · Deep learning · Convolutional neural networks

## 1 Introduction

Based on their morphology (visual appearance), galaxies are grouped into three major categories – spiral, elliptical and irregular. Spiral galaxies have arms, which extend from the centre of the galaxy, while elliptical galaxies are round and smooth, with a continuously declining brightness distribution [3]. The galaxies that do not fit the aforementioned criteria are known as irregular.

It was shown that the morphological classification of the galaxy also correlates with its properties, such as star formation and merger history, gas accretion or nuclear activity [3]. Thus, it is important to classify galaxies to better understand their properties.

O. Gervasi et al. (Eds.): ICCSA 2023, LNCS 13957, pp. 402–412, 2023.
https://doi.org/10.1007/978-3-031-36808-0_27

The classification process can be automated by utilising machine learning. Studies have shown that convolutional neural networks (hereinafter CNNs) in particular excel at such task [2,4,8]. While the results achieved by other authors are great (over 95%) [5,8], or sometimes even near-perfect (over 98%) [2,4], the authors tend to carry out their experiments using datasets of varying size and image quality. Usually, a small, expert-classified dataset is taken (such as [4,5,8]), which implies a better image quality. Additionally, authors limit the range of the galaxy redshift (see Sect. 3.4 for comparison), which is another proxy to the image quality – the higher the redshift value, the less features of an object can be observed, making it more difficult to classify.

Moreover, the majority of the authors use image augmentation techniques to improve classification accuracy, though there is a lack of studies quantifiably and comparably evaluating whether those techniques have any meaningful impact on metrics other than accuracy.

Hence, in this paper, we combine data from two "citizen science" projects – Galaxy Zoo 1 and 2 (hereinafter GZ1 and GZ2) – to produce the largest dataset that covers a broad redshift range and consists only of reliably classified galaxies (see Sect. 3 for details). Using this dataset, we aim to provide comparable and reliable binary classification results of different CNN models, as well as measure the impact of currently used image augmentation techniques on various metrics. Furthermore, we introduce two novel, noise-based means of augmentation and study their impact in combination with other techniques.

We conclude that commonly used image augmentation techniques – rotation, horizontal and vertical flipping and zoom – do in fact increase accuracy and F1 score by a statistically significant amount. The most significant increase was observed on the ResNet50 model, for which the accuracy improved from 93.5% to 95.2% and the F1 score rose from 88.66% to 91.82%. However, single-class metrics – precision, recall and TNR – have improved by less than one standard deviation. Nonetheless, we also show that combining the aforementioned techniques with random noise allows reducing the standard deviation of metrics by up to 9 times – for the same ResNet50 model, the $\sigma$ of F1 reduced from 1.14 to 0.14, and $\sigma$ of precision reduced from 2.27 to 0.57.

## 2    Related Work

A significant amount of research has been conducted to accurately classify galaxies into spiral and elliptical with the help of various machine learning techniques. In particular, convolutional neural networks have produced better results compared to other machine learning methods such as decision trees, K-nearest neighbours or support vector machines [2,5,8,12]. This paper analyses galaxy classification into spiral and elliptical, as these are the main classes.

Some authors claim to have achieved near-perfect classification results in terms of binary classification. One example would be Barchi et al. [2], who managed to achieve 99.5% overall accuracy for the brightest galaxies from the GZ1 dataset, and 98.7% on a wider range of GZ1 galaxies. Similar results were achieved by Cavanagh et al. [4], who classified galaxies with 98% accuracy. Those results are closely followed by Jimenez et al. [8] scoring 96.43% accuracy and Cheng et al. achieving [5] 95.1%.

Another prominent feature of the aforementioned studies is that the majority of authors use image augmentation techniques to achieve better results. The most frequently used augmentations are rotating and flipping image both horizontally and vertically. Such transformations were used by [4–6,12]. Two additional noteworthy techniques are Gaussian noise used by Cheng et al. [5] and zoom utilised by [6,9,16].

However, there are several shortcomings in the aforementioned papers. The first one is that the accuracy results are not comparable to each other, as datasets of different sizes are used. Additionally, all authors use either expert-classified [4,8] or low-redshift galaxies, which implies better image quality (the dataset diversity in terms of redshift is discussed in detail in Sect. 3.4).

The second issue is that different verification metrics and methods are provided by the authors. With respect to verification methods, [2,8] use cross-validation and average the metrics across the folds, while [4,5] use training-validation split technique and take the best results. In terms of metrics, [2,4,5] provide additional metrics such as precision, recall or F1 score, while [8] use only accuracy as their key metric.

The third shortcoming concerns augmentation techniques. While multiple authors use image augmentation techniques, only Cheng et al. study its impact on the metrics [5]. Other authors simply present results with augmentations already applied. Hence, it is not known whether image augmentation has any significant impact on the metrics.

Therefore, the aim of this paper is twofold: to provide comparable baseline binary classification metrics (accuracy, precision, recall, TNR and F1) using a large, reliable and diverse dataset, and to study the impact of frequently used augmentation techniques. Two novel, noise-based augmentation techniques are studied as well.

## 3    Data

This section describes the process of combining GZ1 and GZ2 data into one large, reliable and diverse dataset.

### 3.1    Galaxy Zoo 1

GZ1 project provides classification for 667,944 galaxies, where each is assigned one of the three classes – spiral, elliptical or uncertain [11]. The final, author-proposed classification is based on the debiased votes – a galaxy is considered either spiral or elliptical only if the debiased vote fraction is above the threshold of 0.8, otherwise, the "uncertain" class is attributed.

Thus, all the galaxies that have an UNCERTAIN flag in the dataset were filtered out. There were no galaxies that have both SPIRAL and ELLIPTICAL flags. Therefore, only 252,415 GZ1 galaxies were considered reliable.

## 3.2 Galaxy Zoo 2

As for the GZ2 dataset, the distinction whether the galaxy is spiral or elliptical was done based on the first question, in which participants were asked whether the galaxy is smooth (elliptical), or has features or a disk (spiral). After the votes for each answer option were counted, they also underwent the debiasing process [15]. Based on the debiased vote fraction, two different flags are assigned independently only if the fraction for the particular answer option exceeds 0.8 - smooth_flag and features_or_disk_flag. Thus, only the galaxies that have either one of these flags are considered reliable.

However, it is important to note that some of the galaxies had both of those flags. In this paper, such galaxies were considered ambiguous and subsequently excluded. All entries that had a gz2_class value of "A" were considered artefacts (not galaxies) and were excluded as well. After applying all of the aforementioned criteria, 154,887 galaxies were kept.

## 3.3 Combined Dataset

The resulting datasets from Sects. 3.1 and 3.2 were merged by their SDSS object identifiers (OBJID for GZ1, dr7objid for GZ2). The GZ1 data was used as a base. This has left a total of 319,991 unique galaxies.

If a galaxy was present in both datasets, and the final classifications did not agree, it was considered ambiguous as well. 4,049 such galaxies were identified and subsequently removed. Therefore, the resulting combined dataset contained 315,942 unique, reliably classified and unambiguous galaxies (224,775 spiral (71%) and 91,167 elliptical (29%)). This dataset will be referred to as GZC throughout the paper.

## 3.4 Diversity in Terms of Redshift

To satisfy the criterion of diversity, galaxy redshift (denoted as $z$) was chosen as a proxy for image quality. Redshift is the decrease in frequency of the electromagnetic radiation (such as light) emitted by the galaxy as it travels throughout space [7]. This means that the further the galaxy is from the observer (in this case - the telescope), the greater the redshift, hence the fainter it gets, corresponding to poorer quality.

GZ2 project was constrained to contain galaxies within the redshift range of $0.0005 < z < 0.25$, while GZ1 did not impose any redshift restrictions. This lack of restrictions introduced outliers as well as expanded the redshift range of the dataset. Using the 3-$\sigma$ method, it was calculated that the galaxies outside of the range of $z \in (-0.01; 0.28)$ are outliers. Nonetheless, it was decided to keep all the initial galaxies, as they have been unambiguously classified by the GZ1 volunteers. As there were only 4 galaxies with negative $z$, it will be considered that the redshift range of the dataset is $0 < z \leqslant 0.28$.

The redshift range of the GZC dataset was compared to the ranges of other authors' datasets. The comparison of dataset ranges and sizes is visualised in the Table 1. It can be concluded that the GZC dataset not only is 3 times larger in terms of size, but also has the widest redshift range.

**Table 1.** Comparison of the dataset sizes of various authors that performed binary classification.

| Author | Size | Redshift range | Comment |
|---|---|---|---|
| Cheng et al. | 2,862 | $0 < z < 0.25$ | DES and GZ1 data |
| Cavanagh et al. | 14,304 | $0.01 < z < 0.1$ | Nair and Abraham dataset used |
| Jimenez et al. | 41,424 | $0.05 < z < 0.1$ | Bigger redshift range taken among MOSES and Longo subsets |
| Barchi et al. | 104,787 | $0.05 < z < 0.1$ | Size of GZ1 dataset used for binary classification. Redshift range not explicitly specified, largest stated range taken |
| This work | 315,942 | $0 < z \leqslant 0.28$ | Galaxies that have $z > 0.28$ are considered outliers, though still kept in the dataset |

### 3.5 Image Gathering Process

An image for each galaxy in the GZC dataset was generated using the SkyServer's ImgCutout service[1] [13] and SciServer script[2]. Each image had a dimension of $424 \times 424$ pixels, generated using the same parameters as described by GZ1 and GZ2 projects [11,15].

After that, a square of $212 \times 212$ pixels was cropped from the centre of the initial image, removing part of the background. Finally, the image was rescaled to $128 \times 128$ pixels and all the pixel values were normalised to be between 0 and 1 by diving them by 255.

## 4    Models and Their Modifications

In total, four different architectures were chosen to carry out the experiments. Three of them were used by other researchers to classify galaxies with high accuracy – ResNet50, used by Jimenez et al. [8], and Dieleman and C2 architectures, studied by Cavanagh et al. [4]. The fourth architecture was introduced by the authors of this paper to evaluate the effectiveness of augmentations on a model with significantly fewer parameters (approximately 100k), which would potentially underfit. The architecture itself is a simplification of the C2 and Dieleman models. It is visualised in Table 2 and will be referred to as the simplified model.

---

[1] Accessible at http://skyservice.pha.jhu.edu/DR7/ImgCutout/getjpeg.aspx.

[2] https://github.com/sciserver/SciScript-Python/blob/master/py3/SciServer/SkySe rver.py.

Table 2. Architecture of the simplified model.

| Convolution, 5x5, 64 channels, (*ReLU*) |
| --- |
| Max pool, 2x2 |
| Convolution, 5x5, 32 channels, (*ReLU*) |
| Max pool, 2x2 |
| Convolution, 5x5, 16 channels, (*ReLU*) |
| Dropout, probability - 0.5 |
| Flatten |
| Fully connected layer, 1 node (*Sigmoid*) |

Each architecture was modified in such a way that it accepts a batch of images of size $128 \times 128$, and produces an output of 1 node in the range of $(0, 1)$. Then, a threshold of 0.5 is applied – if the output value is strictly greater than 0.5, then the galaxy is treated as elliptical, spiral otherwise.

## 5    Training Process

### 5.1    Parameters and Process

In total, 5 experiments were carried out with each model using the GZC dataset – baseline (no augmentations applied), standard augmentations only (rotation, horizontal and vertical flips and zoom), and standard augmentations together with random, random centred, random background noises.

To ensure that all the results are as comparable and reliable as possible, fixed initial model weights were used for all experiments. Additionally, to eliminate any bias inherent in the dataset split selection, 10-fold cross-validation method was employed, and all the results were averaged.

Each experiment had exactly the same configuration – training batch size was 1024, test batch size was 16. Adam optimiser with parameters of learning rate of $10^{-4}$, $\beta_1 = 0.9, \beta_2 = 0.999, \epsilon = 1 \times 10^{-8}$ [10] was used to optimise the loss function of the binary cross-entropy. Each experiment was continued for maximum of 500 epochs, although if loss has not improved for 10 consecutive epochs, the training process was stopped early.

Some constrains were introduced by the fact that the model training was conducted on the tensor processing units (TPUs) provided by Google Collaboratory[3]. To ensure that all the dataset batches are full, two different approaches were used. For the training data, additional galaxies were sampled to complete the last batch. For the test data, such approach would skew the results, therefore it was decided to lower batch size to 16, and discard the last underfull batch. However, this was done only during the training process – after all the experiments were completed, the final results were reevaluated using the full test split. Only the aforementioned reevaluated results are presented in this paper.

---

[3] https://colab.research.google.com/.

## 5.2  Augmentation Techniques

For all the experiments, each augmentation technique had an independent probability of 0.5 to be applied on each image individually.

1. **Rotation.** This augmentation technique is widely used by multiple authors [4–6,9,12,16]. An image is rotated by $\{90, 180, 270\}$ degrees to avoid interpolation and introduction of new pixels.
2. **Horizontal and vertical flip.** Another highly utilised augmentation technique, used by [4,6,9,12,16]. This technique simply flips image pixels either horizontally or vertically.
3. **Zoom.** This technique, or its variations, were used by [6,9,16]. In this paper, 10 pixels are cropped from each side of an image. The resulting image is rescaled to the initial size of $128 \times 128$ pixels.
4. **Random noise.** This method is intended to simulate the noise that may be introduced by the observing telescope itself and was used by Cheng et al. [5]. As this is still an ongoing research, only a single noise amplitude of 0.2 was explored. To produce the noise, a random value between -0.2 and 0.2 is taken from a uniform distribution and applied to each pixel, in each channel, individually. The resulting value is clipped to the original range of 0 to 1.
5. **Random centre and background noises.** This novel technique aims to apply targeted noise only on a part of an image. The centre noise effect is achieved by first creating a Sersic surface brightness profile [14] using the Astropy library [1] with the following parameters: `amplitude` = 3, `r_eff` = 5, `n` = 1, and `ellip` = 0 (fully round). The generated values are then scaled between 0 and 1 using $log_{10}$ and 90-per-cent percentile interval scaling. The resulting profile is then multiplied with random noise (generated as mentioned above) and applied on the image. As for the background noise profile, the exact same process is repeated, except that the Sersic profile is inverted. Both noise profiles are visualised in Fig. 1.

# 6  Results and Discussion

This section outlines and compares the results of all the experiments. In this paper, five model performance metrics will be analysed – accuracy, precision (also known as true positive rate), recall, true negative rate (hereinafter TNR) and F1 score.

Accuracy, precision, recall and F1 were chosen as those metrics are quite often used by other authors [2,4–6], which would allow for better comparability of studies. Along with precision, which is also known as true positive rate, another metric is taken into account – true negative rate. This is the same metric as precision, except it measures model performance on the negative class (in this case spiral galaxies), instead of positive (elliptical galaxies). Having both of those metrics allows to evaluate model performance for both morphological classes.

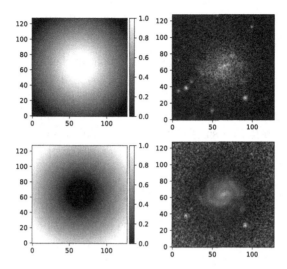

**Fig. 1.** A visualisation of the novel noise profiles. Top row depicts the Sersic profile and resulting centre noise, the bottom row – inverted Sersic profile and resulting background noise.

Throughout all the experiments, zoom, rotation and flipping were combined into a single group and will be referred to as the standard augmentations. The results of the experiments are visualised in Tables 3a–3e.

First of all, a few important observations can be made from Tables 3a and 3b. First of all, none of the metrics has improved for the simplified model. This is most likely due to the fact that the model is too simple and underfits as initially predicted. As for the C2, Dieleman and ResNet50 models, applying standard augmentations has improved average accuracy and F1 score by a statistically significant amount. However, other metrics had just a negligible improvement which falls within one standard deviation. Nonetheless, applying standard augmentations has helped the ResNet50 model to reduce the standard deviation of all 5 metrics by 2, or in the case of recall and F1 score, 4 times, thus stabilising the model. A similar effect can be observed in the C2 model, though the improvement is not as significant.

According to Tables 3c–3e, it is evident that there is no statistically significant difference between the experiments with only standard augmentations. It is worth mentioning that since this is an ongoing research, only one value of noise amplitude was explored. A wider variety of noise amplitudes should be considered in the future, which could potentially alter the results.

Nevertheless, even though the metrics have not improved, there is one important observation to be made in terms of the random noise profile. Using this technique, the ResNet50 model was stabilised even further, by once again halving $\sigma$ compared to standard augmentations alone.

**Table 3.** Average metrics of the experiments across 10 folds. Value in parentheses denotes standard deviation, all values are given in percentages.

(a) None of the augmentations applied.

| Model | Acc. ($\sigma$) | Precision ($\sigma$) | Recall ($\sigma$) | TNR ($\sigma$) | F1 ($\sigma$) |
|---|---|---|---|---|---|
| Simplified | 94.72 (0.24) | 90.15 (0.51) | 91.72 (0.63) | 96.62 (0.25) | 90.93 (0.41) |
| C2 | 94.71 (0.12) | 89.80 (1.18) | 92.19 (1.47) | 96.80 (0.56) | 90.96 (0.23) |
| Dieleman | 94.70 (0.12) | 89.68 (0.79) | 92.28 (0.93) | 96.83 (0.36) | 90.95 (0.21) |
| ResNet50 | 93.53 (0.48) | 89,54 (2.27) | 88.01 (3.93) | 95.21 (1.44) | 88.66 (1.14) |

(b) Standard augmentations only.

| Model | Acc. ($\sigma$) | Precision ($\sigma$) | Recall ($\sigma$) | TNR ($\sigma$) | F1 ($\sigma$) |
|---|---|---|---|---|---|
| Simplified | 94.56 (0.17) | 89.84 (0.61) | 91.52 (0.76) | 96.54 (0.29) | 90.67 (0.30) |
| C2 | 95.36 (0.14) | 90.73 (0.68) | 93.49 (0.95) | 97.33 (0.37) | 92.09 (0.26) |
| Dieleman | 95.42 (0.17) | 91.18 (0.81) | 93.17 (0.72) | 97.20 (0.28) | 92.16 (0.28) |
| ResNet50 | 95.21 (0.23) | 90.50 (1.11) | 93.21 (1.02) | 97.22 (0.39) | 91.82 (0.36) |

(c) Standard augmentations + random noise.

| Model | Acc. ($\sigma$) | Precision ($\sigma$) | Recall ($\sigma$) | TNR ($\sigma$) | F1 ($\sigma$) |
|---|---|---|---|---|---|
| Simplified | 94.47 (0.16) | 89.80 (0.52) | 91.21 (0.73) | 96.41 (0.28) | 90.49 (0.30) |
| C2 | 95.34 (0.10) | 90.73 (0.55) | 93.42 (0.54) | 97.30 (0.21) | 92.05 (0.16) |
| Dieleman | 95.31 (0.08) | 90.74 (0.46) | 93.28 (0.53) | 97.24 (0.20) | 91.99 (0.14) |
| ResNet50 | 95.38 (0.09) | 91.32 (0.57) | 92.80 (0.53) | 97.06 (0.20) | 92.05 (0.14) |

(d) Standard augmentations + centre noise.

| Model | Acc. ($\sigma$) | Precision ($\sigma$) | Recall ($\sigma$) | TNR ($\sigma$) | F1 ($\sigma$) |
|---|---|---|---|---|---|
| Simplified | 94.63 (0.20) | 89.76 (0.55) | 91.89 (0.34) | 96.68 (0.13) | 90.81 (0.32) |
| C2 | 95.29 (0.19) | 90.67 (0.51) | 93.27 (0.47) | 97.24 (0.19) | 91.95 (0.32) |
| Dieleman | 95.34 (0.13) | 91.04 (0.78) | 93.02 (1.06) | 97.15 (0.41) | 92.01 (0.26) |
| ResNet50 | 95.23 (0.28) | 90.75 (0.91) | 92.97 (1.07) | 97.12 (0.42) | 91.84 (0.49) |

(e) Standard augmentations + background noise.

| Model | Acc. ($\sigma$) | Precision ($\sigma$) | Recall ($\sigma$) | TNR ($\sigma$) | F1 ($\sigma$) |
|---|---|---|---|---|---|
| Simplified | 94.72 (0.23) | 89.93 (0.42) | 92.01 (0.84) | 96.73 (0.33) | 90.95 (0.42) |
| C2 | 95.39 (0.17) | 90.86 (0.60) | 93.43 (0.75) | 97.30 (0.29) | 92.12 (0.30) |
| Dieleman | 95.52 (0.11) | 91.44 (0.56) | 93.22 (0.43) | 97.23 (0.17) | 92.32 (0.17) |
| ResNet50 | 95.07 (0.37) | 90.33 (1.15) | 92.88 (0.98) | 97.08 (0.38) | 91.58 (0.61) |

To summarise, this study shows that standard augmentation techniques do in fact increase accuracy and F1 score. Additionally, standard augmentations, especially in combination with random noise, greatly improve model stability by decreasing $\sigma$ values across different runs.

Nonetheless, there was no statistically significant evidence that the metrics that represent single-class performance (namely precision, recall and TNR) improve with the use of augmentations. Moreover, neither background nor centre noise profiles had any significant impact on the metrics. Although those techniques might still prove useful with different noise amplitudes which are to be explored with future research.

It is crucial to emphasise that contrary to other similar studies, this research provides not only all of the most commonly used performance metrics, but also uses the largest dataset of only reliably classified galaxies that have a great diversity in terms of redshift values. Furthermore, the use of 10-fold cross-validation allows to remove the bias of dataset splits by exploring all split combinations. Thus, the aforementioned methods together make all the metrics reliable, comparable, and more representative of models' expected performance with larger amounts of data than the metrics provided by other authors.

## 7    Conclusions

By conducting multiple experiments using the largest dataset of reliably classified galaxies covering the range of $0 < z \leqslant 0.28$ and verifying results using 10-fold cross-validation and models of four different CNN architectures, we conclude that the usage of standard augmentation techniques (rotation, horizontal and vertical flip and zoom) improves accuracy and F1 score by a statistically significant amount. The most significant improvement was observed for the ResNet50 model, for which accuracy improved from 93.53% to 95.21%, and F1 score from 88.66% to 91.82%.

Moreover, adding the random noise profile greatly stabilises the performance of the model by reducing the spread of all the metrics across the folds. The most significant improvement was observed for the ResNet50 model – the standard deviation ($\sigma$) improved from the 2.27% to 0.57% for the precision metric, from 1.44% to 0.20% for the TNR score, and from 1.14% to 0.14% for the F1 score.

However, none of the augmentation techniques improve single-class metrics (precision, recall and TNR) by a statistically significant amount, nor have any effect if the model is underfitting (as in the case of the simplified model).

## References

1. Astropy Collaboration: The astropy project: sustaining and growing a community-oriented open-source project and the latest major release (v5.0) of the core package. Astrophys. J. **935**(2), 167 (2022). https://doi.org/10.3847/1538-4357/ac7c74
2. Barchi, P., et al.: Machine and deep learning applied to galaxy morphology - a comparative study. Astron. Comput. **30** (2020). https://doi.org/10.1016/j.ascom.2019.100334
3. Buta, R.J.: Planets, Stars and Stellar Systems: Volume 6: Extragalactic Astronomy and Cosmology. Springer, Netherlands (2013)

4. Cavanagh, M.K., Bekki, K., Groves, B.A.: Morphological classification of galaxies with deep learning: comparing 3-way and 4-way CNNs. Mon. Not. R. Astron. Soc. **506**(1), 659–676 (2021). https://doi.org/10.1093/mnras/stab1552

5. Cheng, T.Y., et al.: Optimizing automatic morphological classification of galaxies with machine learning and deep learning using Dark Energy Survey imaging. Mon. Not. R. Astron. Soc. **493**, 4209–4228 (2020). https://doi.org/10.1093/mnras/staa501

6. Dieleman, S., et al.: Rotation-invariant convolutional neural networks for galaxy morphology prediction. Mon. Not. R. Astron. Soc. **450**(2), 1441–1459 (2015). https://doi.org/10.1093/mnras/stv632

7. Gray, R., Dunning-Davies, J.: A review of redshift and its interpretation in cosmology and astrophysics. arXiv (2008)

8. Jiménez, M., et al.: Galaxy image classification based on citizen science data: a comparative study. IEEE Access **8**, 47232–47246 (2020). https://doi.org/10.1109/ACCESS.2020.2978804

9. Khalifa, N.E., et al.: Deep galaxy V2: robust deep convolutional neural networks for galaxy morphology classifications. In: 2018 International Conference on Computing Sciences and Engineering (ICCSE), pp. 1–6. IEEE (2018). https://doi.org/10.1109/ICCSE1.2018.8374210

10. Kingma, D., Ba, J.: Adam: a method for stochastic optimization. In: International Conference on Learning Representations (2014)

11. Lintott, C.J., et al.: Galaxy Zoo: morphologies derived from visual inspection of galaxies from the Sloan Digital Sky Survey. Mon. Not. R. Astron. Soc. **389**(3), 1179–1189 (2008). https://doi.org/10.1111/j.1365-2966.2008.13689.x

12. Mittal, A., Soorya, A., Nagrath, P., Hemanth, D.J.: Data augmentation based morphological classification of galaxies using deep convolutional neural network. Earth Sci. Inf. **13**(3), 601–617 (2019). https://doi.org/10.1007/s12145-019-00434-8

13. Nieto-Santisteban, M., Szalay, A., Gray, J.: ImgCutout, an engine of instantaneous astronomical discovery. In: Astronomical Data Analysis Software and Systems (ADASS) XIII, vol. 314, p. 666 (2004)

14. Sérsic, J.L.: Influence of the atmospheric and instrumental dispersion on the brightness distribution in a galaxy. Boletin de la Asociacion Argentina de Astronomia **6**, 41 (1963)

15. Willett, K.W., et al.: Galaxy Zoo 2: detailed morphological classifications for 304,122 galaxies from the Sloan Digital Sky Survey. Mon. Not. R. Astron. Soc. **435**(4), 2835–2860 (2013). https://doi.org/10.1093/mnras/stt1458

16. Zhu, X.-P., Dai, J.-M., Bian, C.-J., Chen, Yu., Chen, S., Hu, C.: Galaxy morphology classification with deep convolutional neural networks. Astrophys. Space Sci. **364**(4), 1–15 (2019). https://doi.org/10.1007/s10509-019-3540-1

# A Prediction Model of Pixel Shrinkage Failure Using Multi-physics in OLED Manufacturing Process

Byunggoo Jung[✉], Sunghwan Hong, Hyungkeon Cho, Yudeok Seo, and Sungchan Jo

Samsung Display, Yongin-Si, South Korea

**Abstract.** Recently, as the application range of high-end Organic Light Emitting Diodes (OLED) displays has expanded, the pixel area has become larger and panel architecture complexity has been raised to increase the lifespan and efficiency of the panel. At the same time, the remaining moisture in the organic material of the panel increases, and pixel shrinkage defects in which the pixel edge emission area is reduced by cathode oxidation due to moisture diffusion within the panel are increasing. Therefore time and cost are incurred in the process of design and manufacturing process enhancing to improve reliability of the display panel. In this study, we introduce an analysis model that can quantify pixel shrinkage and predict the occurrence of defects in advance. In order to make up for the shortcomings of existing Finite Element Method (FEM) and numerical analysis models, product design specifications were applied through layout-based 3D geometry, and the degree of curing according to the heat treatment conditions of organic materials was calculated and the physics of moisture diffusion between subsequent cleaning and oven process were also applied in the model. The degree of moisture absorption during the waiting time between processes, one of the main factors affecting defects was applied in connection with the curing rate of organic materials. In addition, the residual concentration after moisture diffusion in the final deposition process was quantified and matched with the actual shrinkage defect occurrence level to optimize design and process factors of the model. As a result of verification based on 20 evaluation models, the consistency of about 0.96 based on R2 was confirmed.

**Keywords:** OLED · Pixel Shrinkage · Remaining Moisture · Diffusion

## 1 Introduction

Recently, demand for OLED continues to grow rapidly in a wide range of areas from high-end smartphones to IT products such as laptops and tablet PCs as well as automobile and TV. In particular, OLED panel shipments for IT products were reached 15 million units in 2022. This is almost double as many as the previous year [1].

As the utilization of OLED increases in various devices, a high pixel area ratio is required to increase the lifespan of the panel, and the complexity of panel architecture is also increasing as high efficiency and new form factor technologies such as Under

© The Author(s), under exclusive license to Springer Nature Switzerland AG 2023
O. Gervasi et al. (Eds.): ICCSA 2023, LNCS 13957, pp. 413–422, 2023.
https://doi.org/10.1007/978-3-031-36808-0_28

Panel Camera (UPC) is applied. As a result, the residual moisture in the organic layers between processes increases due to the high-density metal wiring and pixel area. And it causes Pixel Shrinkage (P-SK) defects in which the light emitting area is reduced due to cathode oxidation, as shown in Fig. 2, and this leads to affect production yield and reliability [2].

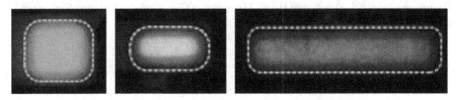

**Fig. 1.** Pixel Shrinkage defective image.

In addition to various efforts from design and process perspectives such as design revision and organic layer heat treatment reinforcement, numerical analysis model development activities are also being carried out for prediction of defects in advance. For example, as shown in Fig. 2, an analysis model and an index were developed to predict the residual moisture in the organic material according to the design specifications through the FEM model. Since process factors were not applied, the influence of process conditions cannot be predicted, so it can be used only for design verification.

In addition, another prediction model was developed through a mathematical model using both design and process factors, such as Eq. (1). It contains weights for design factors and organic layer heat treatment process factor. However, the omission of the panel structure and the waiting time between processes called Cooling Buffer (C/B), which are highly correlated with the occurrence of P-SK are not applied.

$$Index\#2 = pixel\ Area \times Organic\ Thickness \times$$
$$\sqrt{\frac{PXL\ Ratio}{Organic\ Open\ Ratio}} \times Process\ Index \qquad (1)$$

In this study, we would like to introduce the methodology and model for improving the previously developed P-SK prediction model. Moisture emission characteristics according to the design specifications were applied through panel architecture modeling. And the residual moisture concentration according to the moisture diffusion between processes was calculated by deriving the diffusion rate for each process condition through the Water Vapor Transmission Ratio (WVTR) characteristics of organic materials and the Arrhenius Equation. The curing rate of the materials between the organic layers heat treatment processes was calculated and applied to the moisture absorptivity in C/B process to derive the P-SK Index applying the design and process factors.

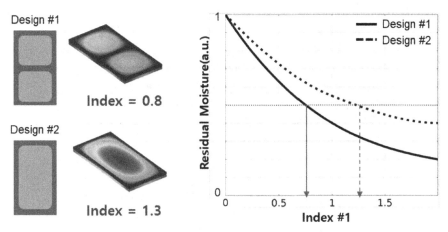

**Fig. 2.** Previously Developed Pixel Shrinkage Defect Prediction Model (Index #1)

## 2 Development of P-SK Quantification Analysis Model

### 2.1 Defect Mechanism

The main causes of pixel shrinkage defects have been identified through material analysis and various simulation evaluations. In the Backplane (BP) process, the organic layers go through processes such as coating, exposure, and development, and then material hardening and moisture emission are performed through a heat treatment process. In this process, as shown in Fig. 3(a), the metal wiring and the pixel layer which have a very slow diffusion rate compared to organic materials are arranged in a complex manner between the organic layers, serving as obstacles to block the path for moisture diffusion. After the heat treatment process, the remaining moisture in the organic layers which oxidizes the cathode layer by diffusion after encapsulation causes shrinkage defects in the pixel light emitting area.

### 2.2 Process Factor of P-SK

In addition to the design factors mentioned above, P-SK defects are affected by various process factors such as heat treatment of organic layers, cleaning, oven, and C/B time. First, in the heat treatment process, it is affected by the heating profile of the chamber and the duration of the process. The higher the temperature and the longer the time, the faster the diffusion rate and release of moisture, and the amount of moisture remaining in the organic film is reduced. Through this, by increasing the curing rate of the organic layers, it is possible to see the effect of reducing the amount of re-absorption of moisture in a subsequent moisture absorption-induced process such as C/B.

At the P-SK generation level according to the organic layer heat treatment conditions in Table 1, Treatment2 which is a relatively strong heat treatment condition compared to Treatment1, 270 °C/1 h was applied to different organic layers and the effect was compared. As a result of the evaluation, the largest amount of shrinkage was occurred in the condition consisting of only the Treatment1(#1), and a relatively low amount of

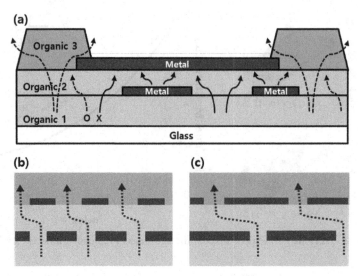

**Fig. 3.** (a) Mechanism of Pixel Shrinkage (P-SK). (b) P-SK non-occurring structure. (c) P-SK occurring structure

shrinkage occurred in the evaluation of #2 to #4 including the Treatment2, which is a strong heat treatment condition compared to Treatment1. According to this result, it can be seen that the effect is greatest when the application sequence of the strong heat Treatment2 process is applied to the last organic layer.

**Table 1.** Organic layer heat treatment process reinforcement evaluation result (Treatment1: 270 °C/1 h/Heating Profile1, treatment2: 270°C/2 h/Heating Profile2)

| Condition | Heat Treatment | | | P-SK(um) |
|-----------|------------|------------|------------|----------|
| | Organic1 | Organic2 | Organic3 | |
| #1 | Treatment1 | Treatment1 | Treatment1 | 1.5 |
| #2 | Treatment2 | Treatment1 | Treatment1 | 1.2 |
| #3 | Treatment1 | Treatment2 | Treatment1 | 1.4 |
| #4 | Treatment1 | Treatment1 | Treatment2 | 0.8 |

Through the results in Table 2, the correlation between C/B time and P-SK occurrence level can be confirmed. The split evaluation was conducted with the Treatment2 heat treatment conditions relatively weaker than the Treatment1, 250 °C/2 h and 270 °C/1 h respectively. As a result, despite the application of different heat treatment processes for each organic layer, no defects occurred in all conditions when C/B time was less than 0.1. But when C/B time increased to 0.3 or more, evaluation except for the strongest heat treatment condition (#1) shrinkage defects occurred in all of them, and it can be seen that the evaluation (#5) where Treatment2 is applied to the last organic layer is the most vulnerable condition. From this, it can be seen that C/B time is also closely related to the occurrence of shrinkage defects, and the difference in residual moisture and curing rate according to heat treatment conditions affects moisture absorption during C/B, resulting in different levels of shrinkage can be expected even at the same C/B time.

**Table 2.** P-SK occurrence level according to heat treatment conditions and C/B time (treatment1: 270 °C/1 h/Heating Profile1, treatment2: 250 °C/2 h/Heating Profile2)

| Condition | Heat treatment | | | | P-SK(um) | |
|---|---|---|---|---|---|---|
| | Organic1 | Organic2 | Organic3 | Organic4 | C/B Time | |
| | | | | | <0.1 | >0.3 |
| #1 | Treatment1 | Treatment1 | Treatment1 | Treatment1 | 0 | 0 |
| #2 | Treatment2 | Treatment1 | Treatment1 | Treatment1 | | 1.0 |
| #3 | Treatment1 | Treatment2 | Treatment1 | Treatment1 | | 1.2 |
| #4 | Treatment1 | Treatment1 | Treatment2 | Treatment1 | | 1.0 |
| #5 | Treatment1 | Treatment1 | Treatment1 | Treatment2 | | 1.4 |

## 2.3 Method

We built a multi-physics analysis model based on COMSOL S/W that can quantify shrinkage by applying the design factors identified above, curing of organic materials, and major process factors such as C/B time. As shown in Fig. 4, the entire analysis process proceeds in 5 steps, and consists of design layout-based geometry generation, hardening for each organic material, cleaning/oven, moisture absorption during C/B and moisture diffusion.

First, the 3D structural domain is completed by applying the design layout and the thickness of each material using software. Through this work, it is possible to improve the disadvantages of the existing design rule-based P-SK prediction model, such as Eq. (1) (Fig. 4).

Second, the curing rate according to the heat treatment process conditions for each organic layer is calculated. As shown in Fig. 5(a), through the curing rate evaluation data of organic materials, it can be seen that the curing rate of the material is highly sensitive to temperature increases (250 °C to 270 °C) compared to the increase in process time (60 min to 120 min).

Based on this, an analysis model that can calculate the curing rate of the material according to the process temperature and time was established using the two functions in Fig. 5(b) and (c).

After the heat treatment process, the inflow and diffusion of moisture generated during the cleaning and oven processes were implemented. In the analysis model, the inflow of water between washings was reflected as the initial water concentration in each organic layer domain using the analysis boundary condition. After that, in the oven

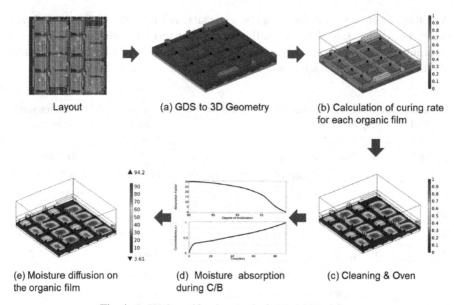

Layout    (a) GDS to 3D Geometry    (b) Calculation of curing rate for each organic film

(e) Moisture diffusion on the organic film    (d) Moisture absorption during C/B    (c) Cleaning & Oven

**Fig. 4.** P-SK Quantification Analysis Model Workflow

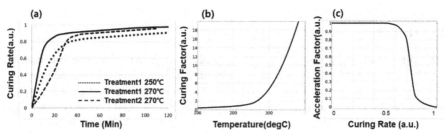

**Fig. 5.** (a) Curing rate analysis result for each process condition using evaluation data, (b) Material curing factor function according to process temperature, (c) Curing progress speed function according to curing rate

process, drying is performed for about several minutes at high temperature conditions. The analytical model for this process was implemented through Fick's 2nd Law Eq. (2) and the temperature-dependent diffusion Eq. (3) in the form of the Arrhenius Equation.

$$\frac{\partial C_i}{\partial t} = \nabla \cdot (D_i \nabla C_i) \tag{2}$$

$$D = D_0 \cdot exp\left(\frac{E_A}{RT}\right)_i \tag{3}$$

where $C_i$ are the concentrations of organic layers, $D_i$ are diffusion coefficient of each layer, $D_0$ is pre-exponential constant, $E_A$ is activation energy for diffusion, $R = 8.31(J/mol - K)$ is the gas constant, and T is temperature in Kelvin. As a result of the analysis, it can be seen that the residual moisture concentration at the bottom of the pixel electrode is high through the residual moisture concentration distribution in Fig. 6(a), and the change in the residual moisture concentration in the organic layers during the process time is confirmed as shown in (b). This pattern of change can appear differently through design factors such as pixel design and organic material thickness, oven temperature difference through the above Eq. (2) and (3), and increase or decrease of process time.

**(a)**                                    **(b)**

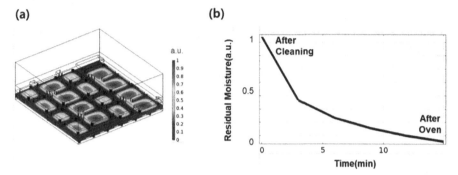

**Fig. 6.** (a) Distribution of residual moisture concentration in organic layers after Oven process. (b) Residual moisture concentration-time analysis result between cleaning and oven process.

Finally, the P-SK quantification analysis process which indexes the final amount of remaining moisture in the organic layers is completed based on the water inflow during C/B and the diffusion model to the outside air during the deposition process. After drying in the oven, the panel increases the moisture in the organic layers by the inflow of outside air during the waiting time at room temperature. In the analysis model, the process influence was applied by increasing the moisture in the organic layers of the analysis domain through the combination of the two functions in Fig. 7(a) and (b). As shown in the evaluation data previously introduced in Table 1 and 2, a difference in curing rate occurs depending on the heat treatment process conditions of organic layers, and the final curing rate affects the amount of moisture absorption during C/B.

**(a)**                **(b)**                **(c)**

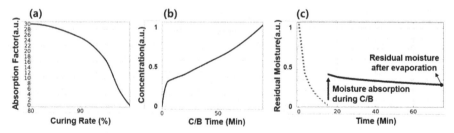

**Fig. 7.** Function to quantify organic material water inflow during C/B. (a) Moisture absorption – Curing rate. (b) Moisture concentration – C/B time (c) moisture content in organic materials between processes

**Table 3.** P-SK occurrence level according to heat treatment conditions and C/B time (treatment1: 270 °C/1 h/Heating Profile1, treatment2: 250 °C/45 min/Heating Profile2, treatment3: 270 °C/1 h/Heating Profile2, treatment4: 270 °C/2 h/Heating Profile1)

| Model | Heat Treatment | | | | P-SK (um) | | |
|---|---|---|---|---|---|---|---|
| | Organic1 | Organic2 | Organic3 | Organic4 | C/B | Measurement | Sim. |
| #1 | Treatment1 | Treatment1 | Treatment2 | - | 1.0 | 0 | 0 |
| | | | | | 2.0 | 0 | 0 |
| | | | | | 4.0 | 2.50 | 2.79 |
| | | | | | 6.0 | 4.50 | 4.53 |
| #2 | | | | | 1.0 | 1.80 | 1.97 |
| #3 | | | | | | 0 | 0 |
| #4 | | | | | | 0.40 | 0 |
| #5 | | | | | | 2.00 | 2.55 |
| #6 | | | | | | 1.50 | 2.06 |
| | | | Treatment1 | | | 0 | 0 |
| | | | Treatment3 | | | 0.50 | 0 |
| #7 | Treatment1 | | | | 0.3 | 0 | 0 |
| | | | | | 0.4 | 0 | 0 |
| | | | | | 0.6 | 1.58 | 2.30 |
| | | | | | 0.9 | 3.40 | 4.45 |
| | Treatment1 | | Treatment4 | | 0.3 | 0 | 0 |
| | | | | | 0.4 | 0.53 | 0.61 |
| | Treatment4 | | | | 0.5 | 1.78 | 1.78 |
| | | | | | 0.9 | 3.03 | 4.14 |
| | | | | | 0.4 | 0 | 0 |

This phenomenon was applied as a characteristic to the higher moisture absorption coefficient as the curing rate decreases, as shown in Fig. 7(a). And the amount of moisture absorption over time ($mol/m^3$) shows an increase in linear type after a rapid increase in the initial C/B time. These two functions were calibrated based on the heat treatment evaluation in Table 2 and the amount of P-SK occurred according to C/B time in #1 of Table 3. The amount of moisture absorbed during C/B through the multiplication of the two functions is added to the amount of residual moisture in the existing organic domains. The amount of moisture in the organic layers before the deposition process is defined in this way.

The final deposition process and P-SK quantification are completed through the moisture diffusion analysis to the outside air. Diffusion analysis proceeds through Fick's 2nd Law Diffusion Equation of Eq. (2) based on the diffusion coefficient calculated through Eq. (3) in the same way as the existing Oven process. After completion of the analysis, the residual moisture concentration $(mol/m^3)$ in the organic layers was indexed in units similar to the amount of P-SK generation (um) through post-processing.

## 2.4  Verification

To verify consistency, evaluation data for a total of 20 cases including models and process splits were obtained as shown in Table 3. The data is the result of measuring the degree of shrinkage of actual pixels after applying the heat treatment process and C/B time for each organic layer differently to evaluate the process impact.

As a result of analyzing and calculating the index using the P-SK analysis model introduced earlier, the consistency between the actual measurement and the index was confirmed to be about 0.98 based on R2 as shown in Fig. 8. In the future, the task of function calibration, which is applied to additional consistency verification and analysis through the expansion of evaluation models with accurate process conditions remains, and verification and evaluation will be conducted through model data to be developed later.

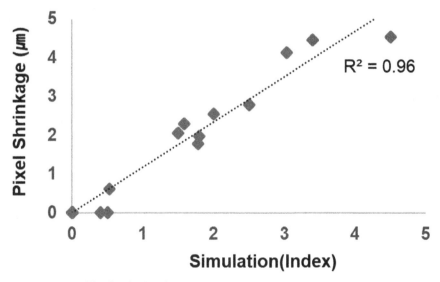

**Fig. 8.** Pixel Shrinkage Measurement - Index Consistency

## 3  Conclusions

In this study, we proposed an analysis model that can predict pixel shrinkage caused by the residual moisture in the organic layers according to the increase of pixel area and panel architecture complexity.

In order to improve the disadvantages of the previously developed FEM and numerical analysis models, design elements were applied through the creation of design layout-based 3D geometry. And the influence of process factors using evaluation data was reviewed and related physics were applied to the model.

As a result, the consistency based on 20 evaluation data was confirmed to be about 0.96 based on R2. Using this analysis model, it is possible to quickly predict the probability of defects and define optimal process conditions such as organic layers heat treatment conditions and C/B time in advance. It is judged that by establishing a process window for the P-SK of the model, it will be able to contribute to saving time and cost when developing a new model.

## References

1. Hi Investment & Securities. http://hkconsensus.hankyung.com/apps.analysis/analysis.dow npdf?report_idx=606687. Accessed 21 Mar 2023
2. Kwon, S.K.: OLED pixel shrinkage dependence with cathode influenced by thermal effect. IEEE Electr. Dev. Lett. **39**, 1536–1539 (2018)

# Wavelength Computation from RGB

Vaclav Skala[1(✉)] [iD], Tristan Claude Louis Bellot[1,2], and Xavier Berault[1,2]

[1] Department of Computer Science and Engineering, Faculty of Applied Sciences, University of West Bohemia, 301 00 Pilsen, Czech Republic
skala@kiv.zcu.cz
[2] University of Technology of Troyes, 10004 Troyes CEDEX, France
{tristan.bellot,xavier.berault}@utt.fr
https://www.vaclavskala.eu/

**Abstract.** Conversion RGB to wavelength is not a simple problem. This contribution describes a simple method for wavelength extraction for colors given by the RGB triplet. The method is simple and accurate, based on known RGB values of the rainbow. It also respects different saturation of a color.

**Keywords:** Color systems · RGB · wavelength · color conversion · image processing · computer vision · autonomous vehicles · physics

## 1 Introduction

There are many fields in which RGB images are used and processed, extracting important features in images, etc. Image processing techniques are based nearly exclusively on shadow processing and RGB image representation. It is well known that RGB does represent a fraction of natural colors contained in the rainbow spectrum [1–12].

Surprisingly, computation of a wavelength $\lambda$ of the color $c$ given in RGB is not simple if the accurate value is required. Mostly, the RGB values are converted to the HLS, resp. HSV or similar color system, and the wavelength is estimated from the HUE value, which is quite inaccurate. This contribution presents a precise method for computing the wavelength $\lambda$ based on re-sampling the spectral rainbow curve, i.e. the rainbow curve with 100% color saturation. The rainbow curve samples give the precision, Table 3. The preprocessing generates a look-up table for the whole interval of wavelengths independent of images. The run-time is based on very simple computation and extraction of the wavelength using the look-up table.

## 2 Color and Color Representation

The RGB values cover luminosity and chromaticity. It means that chromaticity is two-dimensional as it covers a wavelength and saturation of the given color.

Supported by the University of West Bohemia (UWB) - Institutional research.
T. C. L. Bellot and X. Berault—Students of the Erasmus ACG course at UWB.

O. Gervasi et al. (Eds.): ICCSA 2023, LNCS 13957, pp. 423–430, 2023.
https://doi.org/10.1007/978-3-031-36808-0_29

The wavelengths contained in white light are given in Fig. 1 using the reference wavelengths $\lambda_R = 780$[nm] for red, $\lambda_G = 546.1$[nm] for green and $\lambda_B = 435.8$[nm] for blue colors.[1] It can be seen, that the curve for the red color is partially negative. It means, that some colors of a rainbow are not represented within the RGB color model, as a color is represented by the RGB cube $[0, 1] \times [0, 1] \times [0, 1]$.

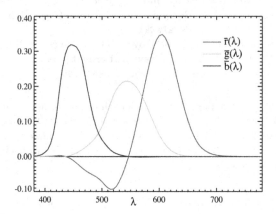

**Fig. 1.** RGB coefficients; courtesy WiKi [16]

To eliminate intensity, the RGB values are projected to a unitary plane $R + G + B = 1$ using Eq. 1. The chromaticity of a color is given by values $r$ and $g$ in the $r - g$ plane representing color saturation and wavelength together.

$$r = \frac{R}{R + G + B} \quad , \quad g = \frac{R}{R + G + B} \quad , \quad b = 1 - R - G \qquad (1)$$

After projecting to the unitary plane, colors form the area in Fig. 2 (pseudo-coloring was used). Colors in the $r < 0$ are not representable within the RGB system. The rainbow curve is labeled by color wavelengths with 100% color saturation. Figure 3 represents colors available within the RGB system and $E$ is the equal energy white light position, i.e. $(1/3, 1/3)$.

The line G-E is given as:

$$\mathbf{p}_{GE} = \mathbf{x}_G \wedge \mathbf{x}_E = \begin{vmatrix} \mathbf{i} & \mathbf{j} & \mathbf{k} \\ 0 & 1 & 1 \\ \frac{1}{3} & \frac{1}{3} & 1 \end{vmatrix} = [\frac{2}{3}, \frac{1}{3} : -\frac{1}{3}]^T$$

$$p_{GE} : \quad \frac{2}{3}x + \frac{1}{3}y - \frac{1}{3} = 0 \triangleq 2x + y - 1 = 0 \qquad (2)$$

where $\mathbf{x}_E = [1/3, 1/3 : 1]^T$ is the equal energy point position, $[0, 1 : 1]^T$ is the green color position and $\triangleq$ means projective equivalency.[2]

---

[1] The *RBG* spectral values for iso-energetic white color are specified in Table 3 [7].

[2] Details on projective geometric algebra use can be found in [12–14] and intersection computation in [15].

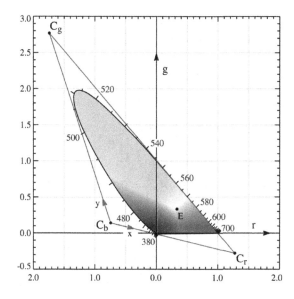

**Fig. 2.** Colors in RGB and XYZ coordinate systems; courtesy WiKi [16]

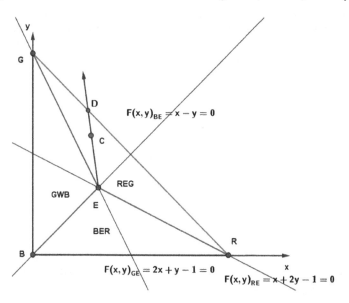

**Fig. 3.** RGB - color sectors

It should be noted that positions are given in homogeneous coordinates[3] of the white light, $\mathbf{x}_G = [0, 1 : 1]^T$ is a position of the pure green color, see Fig. 2.

---

[3] A value $(X, Y)$ in Euclidean space can be expressed as $[wx, wy : w]^T$ in the projective space & $w \neq 0$; $w = 1$ is used in this case [13].

The function $F(x, y)_{GE}$ forms a separation function, which is positive for colors in the Red(R)-White(E)-Green(G) sector of colors.

$$F(x, y)_{GE} = 2x + y - 1 \qquad (3)$$

The lines R-E and B-E are given similarly as:

$$\mathbf{p}_{RE} = \mathbf{x}_R \wedge \mathbf{x}_E = \begin{vmatrix} \mathbf{i} & \mathbf{j} & \mathbf{k} \\ 1 & 0 & 1 \\ \frac{1}{3} & \frac{1}{3} & 1 \end{vmatrix} = [-\frac{1}{3}, -\frac{2}{3} : \frac{1}{3}]^T$$

$$p_{RE} : \quad -\frac{1}{3}x - \frac{2}{3}y + \frac{1}{3} = 0 \triangleq x + 2y - 1 = 0 \qquad (4)$$

$$\mathbf{p}_{BE} = \mathbf{x}_B \wedge \mathbf{x}_E = \begin{vmatrix} \mathbf{i} & \mathbf{j} & \mathbf{k} \\ 0 & 0 & 1 \\ \frac{1}{3} & \frac{1}{3} & 1 \end{vmatrix} = [-\frac{1}{3}, \frac{1}{3} : 0]^T$$

$$p_{BE} : \quad -\frac{1}{3}x + \frac{1}{3}y = 0 \triangleq x - y = 0 \qquad (5)$$

where $\mathbf{x}_R = [1, 0 : 1]^T$, $\mathbf{x}_B = [0, 0 : 1]^T$ and $\mathbf{x}_E = [1/3, 1/3 : 1]^T$ are positions in homogeneous coordinates of the red, blue and white colors in the diagram Fig. 2. If the given color $C$ is in the $BER$ color sector, the color is not a spectral color, e.g. purple or brown colors are not present in a rainbow, and complementary wavelength is to be used. In the case of light, only the sectors $REG$ and $GEB$ are valid.

Therefore, if $F(x, y)_{GE} \geq 0$, the sector $REG$ is to be used, otherwise the sector $GEB$.

$$F(x, y)_{GE} \begin{cases} \geq 0 & \text{the sector REG is to be used} \\ < 0 & \text{the sector GEB is to be used} \end{cases}$$

Now, edges of the sectors have to be labeled by the relevant wavelength $\lambda$.

## 3   Wavelength Computation

In the case of the sector $REG$, the wavelength of the color RGB is determined as the intersection $D$ of a ray $\mathbf{p}_{EC}$ from the point $E$ passing the point representing the color $C$ with the edge of the relevant color sector, i.e. $\mathbf{p}_{RG}$. The intersection point $\mathbf{x}_D$ is given as:

$$\mathbf{p}_{EC} = \mathbf{x}_E \wedge \mathbf{x}_C \quad , \quad \mathbf{p}_{RG} = [1, 1 : -1]^T$$

$$\mathbf{x}_D = \mathbf{p}_{RG} \wedge \mathbf{p}_{EC} = [x_D, y_D : w_D]^T \triangleq (\frac{x_D}{w_D}, \frac{y_D}{w_D}) \qquad (6)$$

It should be noted, that lines representing the triangle edges are constant, i.e. $\mathbf{p}_{RG} = [1, 1 : -1]^T$, $\mathbf{p}_{GB} = [1, 0 : 0]^T$ and $\mathbf{p}_{BR} = [0, 1 : 0]^T$.

Similarly, in the case of the sector $GEB$. The intersection point $\mathbf{x}_D$ is given as:

$$\mathbf{p}_{EC} = \mathbf{x}_E \wedge \mathbf{x}_C \quad , \quad \mathbf{p}_{GB} = [1, 0 : 0]^T$$
$$\mathbf{x}_D = \mathbf{p}_{GB} \wedge \mathbf{p}_{EC} = [x_D, y_D : w_D]^T \triangleq (\frac{x_D}{w_D}, \frac{y_D}{w_D}) \tag{7}$$

In the actual implementation, the code should be optimized as general formulations are used.

The RGB values of the spectrum given in Table 3 have to be recomputed and relevant wavelengths on $\mathbf{p}_{RG}$ and $\mathbf{p}_{GB}$ are obtained. In the case of $REG$ sector projection to the $x$-axis is made, while in the case of $GEB$ sector projection to the $y$-axis is made.

Now, the relevant points on the $x$-axis and $y$-axis have wavelengths projected from the spectral curve. As the distance between consecutive wavelengths in Table 3 is $5[nm]$ the axes $x$ and $y$ can be finely uniformly re-sampled and relevant wavelengths can be linearly interpolated. It means, that if a color $C = (r, g)$ is given, relevant position of the point $D$ is to be computed and the $r$, resp. $g$ value is index to a table with the wavelengths using a scaling factor $\xi$

$$index = \lfloor \xi * r \rfloor \text{ , resp. } index = \lfloor \xi * g + k \rfloor \tag{8}$$

where $\xi$ is a scaling (re-sampling) factor[4], e.g. $\xi = 100$, $k = \xi + 1$ is the index of the first row in the table with the interpolated wavelengths for the $y$-axis. It should be noted that $r \in [0, 1]$ $g \in [0, 1]$.

**Table 1.** Example of wavelength reconstructed

Original image                Pseudo-colored wavelengths

---

[4] $\xi = 100$ means 100 sub-intervals on the $x$, resp. $y$ axis.

## 4    Experimental Results

The presented approach of the wavelength reconstruction from acquired RGB images are proving, that wavelength can be determined as described above. Table 1 presents wavelengths using a gray, i.e. it is pseudo-colored, and Table 2 presents saturation and histogram of wavelengths.

**Table 2.** Example of saturation reconstructed, and wavelength histogram.

 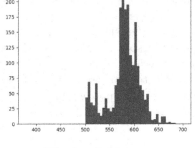

Saturation                          Wavelength histogram

## 5    Conclusions

A precise methods for RGB conversion to the wavelength is presented. It consist of a look-up table generation, which is constant for all images and can be generated once forever. The run-time is simple as it needs only simple linear interpolation and actual wavelength extraction using the look-up table. The run-time is fast and convenient for processing of large images. The expected applications can be seen within image processing, computer vision. Standard techniques used in image processing, e.g. edge detection, feature detection etc., using the wavelength instead of grey, resp. RGB will be explored in future work. In future, XYZ color system will be explored as it eliminates negative $r, g, b$ and values, but not appearing in captured images using RGB representation.[5]

**Acknowledgments.** The author thanks to colleagues and colleagues at the Shandong University(Jinan) China, and University of West Bohemia (Pilsen) for their critical comments. Thanks belong also to anonymous reviewers, as their comments and hints helped to improve this paper significantly.

---

[5] (Responsibilities: Skala, V.: theory, algorithm design, algorithm implementation design, manuscript preparation; Bellot, T.C.L., Berault, X.: implementation and experimental verification).

# RGB Trichromatic Coefficients

To avoid numerical instability in Eq. 1 $r = 0.00001$ was set for $\lambda = 780$[nm].

**Table 3.** RGB spectral trichromatic values.

| $\lambda$ | $r$ | $g$ | $b$ | $\lambda$ | $r$ | $g$ | $b$ |
|---|---|---|---|---|---|---|---|
| 380 | 0,00003 | −0,00001 | 0,00117 | 580 | 0,24526 | 0,13610 | −0,00108 |
| 385 | 0,00005 | −0,00002 | 0,00189 | 585 | 0,27989 | 0,11686 | −0,00093 |
| 390 | 0,00010 | −0,00004 | 0,00359 | 590 | 0,30928 | 0,09754 | −0,00079 |
| 395 | 0,00017 | −0,00007 | 0,00647 | 595 | 0,33184 | 0,07909 | −0,00063 |
| 400 | 0,00030 | −0,00014 | 0,01214 | 600 | 0,34429 | 0,06246 | −0,00049 |
| 405 | 0,00047 | −0,00022 | 0,01969 | 605 | 0,34756 | 0,04776 | −0,00038 |
| 410 | 0,00084 | −0,00014 | 0,03707 | 610 | 0,33971 | 0,03557 | −0,00030 |
| 415 | 0,00139 | −0,00070 | 0,06637 | 615 | 0,32265 | 0,02583 | −0,00022 |
| 420 | 0,00211 | −0,00110 | 0,11541 | 620 | 0,29708 | 0,01828 | −0,00015 |
| 425 | 0,00266 | −0,00143 | 0,18575 | 625 | 0,26348 | 0,01253 | −0,00011 |
| 430 | 0,00218 | −0,00119 | 0,24769 | 630 | 0,22677 | 0,00833 | −0,00008 |
| 435 | 0,00036 | −0,00021 | 0,29012 | 635 | 0,19233 | 0,00537 | −0,00005 |
| 440 | −0,00261 | 0,00149 | 0,31228 | 640 | 0,15968 | 0,00334 | −0,00003 |
| 445 | −0,00673 | 0,00379 | 0,31860 | 645 | 0,12905 | 0,00199 | −0,00002 |
| 450 | −0,01213 | 0,00678 | 0,31670 | 650 | 0,10167 | 0,00116 | −0,00001 |
| 455 | −0,01874 | 0,01046 | 0,31166 | 655 | 0,07857 | 0,00066 | −0,00001 |
| 460 | −0,02608 | 0,01485 | 0,29821 | 660 | 0,05932 | 0,00037 | 0,00000 |
| 465 | −0,03324 | 0,01977 | 0,27295 | 665 | 0,04366 | 0,00021 | 0,00000 |
| 470 | −0,03933 | 0,02538 | 0,22991 | 670 | 0,03149 | 0,00011 | 0,00000 |
| 475 | −0,04471 | 0,03183 | 0,18592 | 675 | 0,02294 | 0,00006 | 0,00000 |
| 480 | −0,04939 | 0,03914 | 0,14494 | 680 | 0,01687 | 0,00003 | 0,00000 |
| 485 | −0,05364 | 0,04713 | 0,10968 | 685 | 0,01187 | 0,00001 | 0,00000 |
| 490 | −0,05814 | 0,05689 | 0,08257 | 690 | 0,00819 | 0,00000 | 0,00000 |
| 495 | −0,06414 | 0,06948 | 0,06246 | 695 | 0,00572 | 0,00000 | 0,00000 |
| 500 | −0,07173 | 0,08536 | 0,04776 | 700 | 0,00410 | 0,00000 | 0,00000 |
| 505 | −0,08120 | 0,10593 | 0,03688 | 705 | 0,00291 | 0,00000 | 0,00000 |
| 510 | −0,08901 | 0,12860 | 0,02698 | 710 | 0,00210 | 0,00000 | 0,00000 |
| 515 | −0,09356 | 0,15262 | 0,01842 | 715 | 0,00148 | 0,00000 | 0,00000 |
| 520 | −0,09264 | 0,17468 | 0,01221 | 720 | 0,00105 | 0,00000 | 0,00000 |
| 525 | −0,08473 | 0,19113 | 0,00830 | 725 | 0,00074 | 0,00000 | 0,00000 |
| 530 | −0,07101 | 0,20317 | 0,00549 | 730 | 0,00052 | 0,00000 | 0,00000 |
| 535 | −0,05316 | 0,21083 | 0,00320 | 735 | 0,00036 | 0,00000 | 0,00000 |
| 540 | −0,03152 | 0,21466 | 0,00146 | 740 | 0,00025 | 0,00000 | 0,00000 |
| 545 | −0,00613 | 0,21487 | 0,00023 | 745 | 0,00017 | 0,00000 | 0,00000 |
| 550 | 0,02279 | 0,21178 | −0,00058 | 750 | 0,00012 | 0,00000 | 0,00000 |
| 555 | 0,05514 | 0,20588 | −0,00105 | 755 | 0,00008 | 0,00000 | 0,00000 |
| 560 | 0,09060 | 0,19702 | −0,00130 | 760 | 0,00006 | 0,00000 | 0,00000 |
| 565 | 0,12840 | 0,18522 | −0,00138 | 765 | 0,00004 | 0,00000 | 0,00000 |
| 570 | 0,16768 | 0,17087 | −0,00135 | 770 | 0,00003 | 0,00000 | 0,00000 |
| 575 | 0,20715 | 0,15429 | −0,00123 | 775 | 0,00001 | 0,00000 | 0,00000 |
| 580 | 0,24526 | 0,13610 | −0,00108 | 780 | 0,00000 | 0,00000 | 0,00000 |

# References

1. Burger, W., Burge, M.J.: Digital Image Processing: An Algorithmic Introduction Using Java, 2nd edn. Springer, London (2016). https://doi.org/10.1007/978-1-4471-6684-9
2. Faugeras, O., Luong, Q.-T., Papadopoulou, T.: The Geometry of Multiple Images: The Laws That Govern The Formation of Images of A Scene and Some of Their Applications. MIT Press, Cambridge (2001)
3. Giorgianni, E.J., Madden, T.E.: Digital Color Management: Encoding Solutions. Addison-Wesley Longman Publishing Co., Inc., Boston (1998)
4. Gonzalez, R.C., Woods, R.E.: Digital Image Processing, 3rd edn. Prentice-Hall Inc., Hoboken (2006)
5. Hall, R.: Illumination and Color in Computer Generated Imagery. Springer, Heidelberg (1988). https://doi.org/10.1007/978-1-4612-3526-2
6. Hoffmann, M.: Digital signal processing mathematics. CAS - CERN Accelerator School: Course on Digital Signal Processing (2008)
7. Hornak, P.: Svetelna technika (Lighting technology). Alfa, Slovakia (1989)
8. Hrdina, J., Vašík, P., Matoušek, R., Návrat, A.: Geometric algebras for uniform colour spaces. Math. Methods Appl. Sci. 41(11), 4117–4130 (2018)
9. Jackson, R., MacDonald, L., Freeman, K.: Computer Generated Color: A Practical Guide to Presentation and Display. Wiley, Hoboken (1994)
10. Nassau, K. (ed.): Color for Science, Art and Technology, 1st edn. North Holland, Amsterdam (1998)
11. Ohta, N., Robertson, A.R.: Colorimetry: Fundamentals and Applications. Wiley, Hoboken (2006)
12. Skala, V.: Length, area and volume computation in homogeneous coordinates. Int. J. Image Graph. 6(4), 625–639 (2006)
13. Skala, V.: Barycentric coordinates computation in homogeneous coordinates. Comput. Graph. 32(1), 120–127 (2008)
14. Skala, V.: Intersection computation in projective space using homogeneous coordinates. Int. J. Image Graph. 8(4), 615–628 (2008)
15. Skala, V.: A brief survey of clipping and intersection algorithms with a list of references. Informatica 34(1), 169–198 (2023)
16. Wikipedia contributors. CIE 1931 color space – Wikipedia, the free encyclopedia (2023). Accessed 9 Feb 2023

# A Close-Up on the AI Radiologist Software

Ayman Al-Kababji[1]([✉])(ID), Faycal Bensaali[1](ID), and Sarada Prasad Dakua[2](ID)

[1] College of Engineering, Qatar University, Doha, Qatar
{aa1405810,f.bensaali}@qu.edu.qa
[2] Department of Surgery, Hamad Medical Corporation, Doha, Qatar
SDakua@hamad.qa

**Abstract.** Proper computer-assisted detection (CADe) based on machine learning (ML) is a hot research topic in healthcare. Thousands of studies are published yearly focusing on enhancing the performance of ML-based models, but few tackle the challenge of deploying them efficiently. This paper focuses on designing an effective graphical user interface (GUI) tool, AI Radiologist, that clinicians can use during pre-operative planning to segment different liver tissues (parenchyma, tumors, and vessels). The tool employs convolutional neural networks (ConvNets) for liver tissue segmentation. This helps increase the success rate of any operation through meticulous pre-planning that allows surgeons to prepare well and plan for worst-case scenarios that might occur during surgery. AI Radiologist, an offline system application, utilizes three ConvNet models trained to segment all liver tissues. We use the PyQt5 Python module for the GUI to create a single-page application. The output of the AI Radiologist application is the liver, tumors, and vessels 2D slices and the 3D interpolation in .obj and .mtl format. The 3D interpolation can be visualized as a 3D liver object on any 3D-friendly software or 3D printed. Creating the AI Radiologist provides clinicians with a user-friendly GUI tool for liver tissues' segmentation and 3D interpolation, employing state-of-the-art models for all tissues' segmentation processes. Clinicians can select the volume(s) and the pre-trained models, and the AI Radiologist will take care of the rest.

**Keywords:** computer-assisted detection (CADe) systems · artificial intelligence · one-page application · liver tissues segmentation · graphical user interface (GUI)

## 1 Background

Two million tragic deaths worldwide are credited to hepatic-related diseases annually [5]. 50% of these deaths are caused by complications following liver

This publication was made possible by an Award [GSRA6-2-0521-19034] from Qatar National Research Fund (a member of Qatar Foundation). The contents herein are solely the responsibility of the authors. Moreover, the HPC resources and services used in this work were provided by the Research Computing group in Texas A&M University at Qatar. Research Computing is funded by the Qatar Foundation for Education, Science, and Community Development (http://www.qf.org.qa).

O. Gervasi et al. (Eds.): ICCSA 2023, LNCS 13957, pp. 431–440, 2023.
https://doi.org/10.1007/978-3-031-36808-0_30

cirrhosis, while the other half are due to hepatitis and hepatocellular carcinoma (HCC) [5]. Moreover, it is a hub for metastasis originating from neighboring organs such as the colon, rectum, pancreas, stomach, esophagus, breasts, lungs, etc. [18]. Since tumors can originate from the liver or adjacent organs, the liver and its lesions are always analyzed in primary tumor staging [11], as the screening for liver-related diseases can reduce mortality [13]. Early detection and accurate delineation of hepatic tumors can dramatically help clinicians decide on more appropriate treatment plans.

Researchers usually offer interactivity within their applications (desktop/web) to give users the ability to control the application's flow or enhance the algorithms' segmentation. In [4], a desktop application, goes by the name CardiovasculaR Integrated Modelling and SimulatiON (CRIMSON), is created to provide a customizable, potent, and user-friendly system for performing 3D and reduced-order computational hemodynamic studies. Another well-known framework is the interactive learning and segmentation toolkit (ilastik) developed by [6]. It provides interactivity for application-domain experts to train classical machine learning (ML)-based biomedical image analysis tools for nuclei segmentation through their graphical user interface (GUI). This survey will not be complete without mentioning the famous ITK-SNAP application [21]. It is a classic for interactive segmentation and visualization tools for medical images.

In the case of [3], trainable WEKA segmentation (TWS), where WEKA stands for Waikato environment for knowledge analysis, is a pixel classification tool with a versatile pool of applications such as boundary detection, object detection and localization, and semantic segmentation for objects under a microscope.

On the other hand, the following studies have standalone applications, but they also deploy ML, ConvNets, and deep learning algorithms to tackle different challenges. In [12], an automated web-based application employing the famous U-Net as the deep learning model is utilized for spine segmentation. In [7], a web application named BreastScreening focuses on supplying AI-assisted techniques in the breast cancer classification challenge. In [16], FeAture Explorer (FAE) is a GUI created to allow researchers to develop classical supervised ML models, along with preprocessing techniques that are engineered to enhance their performance.

Some surveyed studies incorporate virtual reality (VR) technologies into the medical field for various applications. In [10], a collaborative VR environment is implemented, using Unity, Virtual Environment Toolkit (VRTK), and Photon frameworks, to assist surgeons in a remote or co-located environment in liver tumors surgery planning.

In the case of [9,20], the end goal is slightly different from the other surveyed literature in terms of the target audience. Chen et al. [9] create DeepLNAnno, which we assume stands for "Deep Lung Nodules Annotation" to discover and annotate lung nodules. It is deployed semi-automatically utilizing a simple 3D ConvNet, trained over adenocarcinoma and benign nodules, that annotates the nodules on unannotated CT images. Consequently, it produces reference images for human annotators, especially since they are Ph.D. candidates, not expert radiologists. The nature of the framework used to build the GUI is not disclosed.

In [20], RadCloud integrates the algorithmic aspect of ML, deep learning, and radiomics analysis functions over medical image processing with the data management one. The end-users for this platform are the researchers and scientists aiming to build better and enhanced tools to tackle different medical challenges. Their strategy is to host ML and deep learning applications and services on a cloud, providing low-cost, easy-to-use, and remotely-accessible data storage and sharing system. Some radiomics-related challenges investigate organs like the liver, breasts, kidneys, lungs, and rectum. They offer functionalities from automatic feature extraction, ML and ConvNets training, validation and testing, and hyperparameters tuning, providing scientists with an easy user experience (UX) for non-programmers.

One common theme that can be distinguished from all the surveyed studies is that they want to reduce the inconvenience that non-programmers and clinicians endure when creating/deploying statistical, ML, or deep learning models on various applications. This is exactly the aim of creating our artificially intelligent (AI) Radiologist tool for the liver tissues segmentation challenge. What we uniquely do in this paper is that we first built a tool to segment all the liver tissues from end to end in a sequential manner. Moreover, even though it is currently targeted for the liver, the software can be slightly modified to be used as is with any other organ where the organ needs to be segmented first, and the tumors and vessels within are also desired to be segmented. Lastly, we also avoid user interaction and do not presume significant pre-existing knowledge/experience to allow easier deployment to the extent that the user can figure out the mechanics of the application without any significant help.

This paper mainly focuses on developing the AI Radiologist system application but briefly mentions the implementation aspect of the deep learning technique. From this aspect, we highlight the significance of our work portrayed by Fig. 1. AI Radiologist allows clinicians to precisely segment the liver tissues (parenchyma, tumors, and vessels), followed by a 3D object creation using the segmented tissues. We create a highly intuitive tool such that the AI Radiologist system's learning curve is minimal and very efficient. The AI Radiologist system takes as an input a CT scan in "neuroimaging informatics technology initiative (NIfTI)" format, and the output is the generated masks for each tissue (NIfTI), along with the 3D liver object (.obj and .mtl). The reason for choosing the .obj and .mtl is because they can include multiple objects and are the file types used by 3D printers for multi-object printing. The main contributions presented in this paper can be summarized as follows:

- We present AI Radiologist, an AI-powered offline desktop application with pre-trained models for the liver segmentation tissues challenge. It offers extremely powerful computations but with minimal user interactivity and expertise.
- It extensively elaborates on the methodology of creating multi-tissued objects, which are conveniently the output of our AI Radiologist system, where they can be immediately 3D printed.

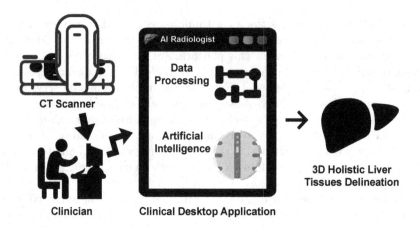

**Fig. 1.** AI Radiologist operation diagram.

The remainder of this paper is organized as follows. Section 2 describes the methodology followed to create the AI Radiologist application. Section 3 showcases the developed AI Radiologist application, and finally, we conclude the paper in Sect. 4.

## 2 Methodology

It is worth pointing out that the schema of our system to tackle the liver tissues segmentation always begins with the first ConvNet tackling the liver segmentation task. Then, its output is multiplied by the original CT slices to keep the liver's voxels and remove other voxels considered as background. Then, the CT slices, with liver voxels only, are fed into the tumors and vessels ConvNets in parallel to generate these tissues' masks. Lastly, the output of the three ConvNets is then combined and interpolated to create the 3D object of the liver, ready to be visualized or even printed.

### 2.1 Utilized Dataset and ConvNet

This paper aims to segment the liver parenchyma, tumors, and vessels; a complete dataset containing the manual segmentation for all three tissues is a must. The conducted review study in [2] shows that the dataset qualifying for this role is the medical segmentation decathlon challenge: task 8 hepatic vessel (MSDC-T8) dataset. It contains 443 contrast-enhanced (CE)-CT scans of varying voxels' dimensions between 0.58 and 0.97 mm for the intra-slice dimensions, while the inter-slice dimension varies between 0.8 and 8 mm. The number of slices varies between 24 and 251 slices. The liver ground-truth labels are provided in [17], while the tumors and vessels manual masks are provided by the challenge organizers in [15]. The liver masks are publicly available for the 443 records; however, the tumors and vessels masks are known for 303 only.

For the ML model, the U-Net ConvNet is utilized. It is worth mentioning that the size of the filters ($f$) is 3 (i.e., $3 \times 3$), with padding ($p$) being 1 and stride ($s$) being 1 are both applied to maintain the width and height of the convoluted layers so the outputs from the encoder side can be easily patched to the equivalent ones in the decoder side, without applying any cropping.

## 2.2   AI Radiologist Desktop Application

This subsection delves into the GUI design of the desktop application's schema and the framework used to create it. The application is designed in mind that it must be easy to use, intuitive, and with a high-quality UX.

Figure 2 shows the preliminary design of the AI Radiologist application. Users should be able to select the records they intend to segment by pressing the "Search Records" button. Once pressed, a pop-up window appears, allowing them to select multiple records to segment sequentially. Once the records have been selected, a table that shows the CT records' metadata is shown. The clinicians can examine the different information, such as the voxels' dimensions and the number of slices; the displayed metadata can be customized further based on the clinicians' needs. Following that, the ConvNets, that were trained on segmenting the liver's tissues can be selected by pressing the "Select ConvNets" button, which will pop up another window. Once selected, users can segment the tissues consecutively by pressing the "Segment Records". The achieved progress is displayed via a progress bar within the application and a status text message to allow for a better UX.

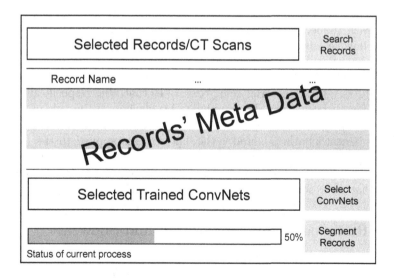

**Fig. 2.** Preliminary design of the AI Radiologist desktop application.

## 2.3   3D Construction and Printing

After creating the three ConvNets designed to segment the parenchyma, tumors, and vessels, creating a 3D object model of the liver's essential tissues has become attainable. We use "The Marching Cubes" algorithm [19] to interpolate the 2D cross-sectional slices into their 3D counterpart. It is deemed suitable as our focus is on the AI Radiologist system part implemented on the CT scans. However, we group the objects in a single .obj and .mtl file on Python from scratch.

Firstly, the three tissues' masks are loaded into the script after being generated by the designated ConvNets, via the nibabel Python library. Then, the 3D Lewiner interpolation using "The Marching Cubes" algorithm is used to create the 3D object of each tissue (the .obj file). It is worth noting that four mandatory types of parameters are mentioned in the .obj file, namely, the vertex (v), the vertex texture (vt), the vertex normal (vn), and the face (f).

The (v)s define the coordinates of vertices in the XYZ 3D space. On the other hand, the (vt)s and (vn)s are not as important, but the (vt)s aid in making the 3D object more realistic by mapping a pre-defined texture map on the faces, and the (vn)s aid in specifying the direction of the normal vector [8]. Lastly, the (f)s combine the three above components in the following order as shown by Eq. (1):

$$ f \quad v_1[/vt_1][/vn_1] \quad v_2[/vt_2][/vn_2] \quad v_3[/vt_3][/vn_3] \quad \cdots \quad v_x[/vt_x][/vn_x] \quad (1) $$

where $x$ is the number of vertices designated for each face f, as it can have as many vertices as needed.

The square brackets [ ] in Eq. (1) indicate that these values are optional. Moreover, because the scikit-image library generates vertices for triangular faces, three vertices are needed to build each face. Once the .obj file has been created for each tissue, the statement "mtllib <material_filename>.mtl" is added, enabling linkage with the .mtl file. The linking allows importing the defined texture and color onto different surfaces. Moreover, the statement "usemtl <tissue_material>" precedes the faces of an object in that file, allowing any software to assign the material color/texture to that object specifically. Lastly, .obj files for all tissues are then combined by placing all the (v)s of each .obj at the beginning, followed by all the (vt)s beneath the (v)s, and followed by the (vn)s beneath both (v)s and (vt)s. The same is applied to the (f)s; however, because more (v)s, (vt)s, and (vn)s have been added within the same file, the $2^{nd}, 3^{rd}, 4^{th}, \cdots, x^{th}$ vertices for the (f)s have to account for the number of vertices that are reserved for the preceding objects.

## 3   AI Radiologist Implementation and Showcase

We mention the trained ConvNets here in this paper to provide readers with context regarding what was used; however, more details about the development of models can be found in [1]. The focus is their employment within the AI Radiologist described within the following subsection.

This section outlines the next steps after creating the three ConvNet models developed to segment the three tissues (liver parenchyma, tumors, and vessels). We specifically use the PyQt5 framework to build the desktop application [14], available in Python. Figure 3 shows the main display that end-users get prompted with when they launch the application. The application is called "AI Radiologist" and has a liver icon for a logo.

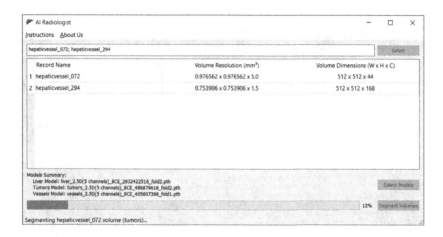

**Fig. 3.** Showing the progress in volumes processing.

When end-users press the "Select" button, a prompt pop-up window appears, enabling them to select multiple CT scans (saved as NIfTI format). Once CT scans are selected, a table shows the records' metadata for the end-user to observe. Moreover, the user must choose the PyTorch models trained to segment the liver, tumors, and vessels. Once selected, the application is ready to perform the segmentation.

Once the "Segment Volumes" button is pressed, the heavy-backend processes commence. Volumes undergo the same preprocessing techniques applied during the models' training phase. They are all done in real-time and efficiently, especially when using graphical processing units (GPU). We avoid using the main thread for heavy computations since it is responsible for all the GUI interactions. Hence, they are delegated to other subthreads. Figure 3 shows the effect of selecting multiple volumes for delineation and the chosen models to perform the segmentation process. Moreover, it shows the progress made by the application via the progress bar and the status bar.

The liver.nii.gz, tumors.nii.gz, and vessels.nii.gz have the segmented tissues in separate files for easier access, such that any medical software can open these masks, such as the ITK-SNAP software. Following that, the 3D interpolation process for the three generated masks commences. The resulting masks and the 3D object are placed in a folder holding the same name as the segmented volume within the same directory.

Moreover, the "complete_model.obj" file is created with all the vertices and faces needed to visualize the volume in 3D form. Lastly, the .mtl file adds color to different tissues to easily differentiate between them. Exporting both the .obj file and the .mtl file is the best option for multi-colored 3D printing [8]. The 3D interpolated liver volumes can be immediately put into a 3D printer; however, in the absence of such 3D printers, the 3D object can still be visualized using any 3D compatible software as seen in Fig. 4.

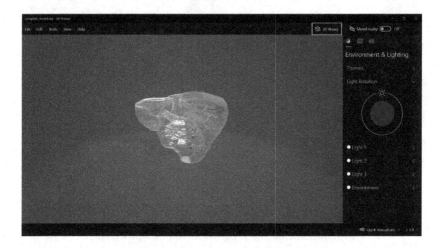

**Fig. 4.** Opening 3D interpolated object on 3D Paint software in Windows 10.

## 4    Conclusions and Future Directions

To conclude, by creating the AI Radiologist, we provide clinicians with an end-to-end user-friendly GUI tool for liver tissues segmentation that enables them to segment and 3D interpolate multiple records sequentially for medical analysis, with minimal possible human intervention. We are also employing state-of-the-art models for all tissue segmentation processes. All they need to do is select the volume(s), and select the models, and they will have to wait approximately a minute or two for each volume to be completed. It is worth re-iterating that volumes are done sequentially, meaning that the doctors can look into the first processed volume while waiting for the remaining ones.

In the future, we aim to enhance the AI Radiologist by adding the following features: i) Make it compatible with files that are of DICOM extension similar to the support we have for NIfTI files format; ii) Further enhance the segmentation results for both tumors and vessels tissues; and iii) Further develop the AI Radiologist to segment other tissues within the body such as lungs, pancreas, heart, and others. However, this requires available ConvNets trained over those tissues as well.

# References

1. Al-Kababji, A., Bensaali, F., Dakua, S.P.: Scheduling techniques for liver segmentation: ReduceLRonPlateau vs OneCycleLR. In: Bennour, A., Ensari, T., Kessentini, Y., Eom, S. (eds.) Intelligent Systems and Pattern Recognition, pp. 204–212. Springer, Cham (2022). https://doi.org/10.1007/978-3-031-08277-1_17

2. Al-Kababji, A., Bensaali, F., Dakua, S.P., Himeur, Y.: Automated liver tissues delineation techniques: a systematic survey on machine learning current trends and future orientations. Eng. Appl. Artif. Intell. **117**, 105532 (2023)

3. Arganda-Carreras, I., et al.: Trainable weka segmentation: a machine learning tool for microscopy pixel classification. Bioinformatics **33**(15), 2424–2426 (2017). https://doi.org/10.1093/bioinformatics/btx180

4. Arthurs, C.J., et al.: CRIMSON: an open-source software framework for cardiovascular integrated modelling and simulation. PLoS Comput. Biol. **17**(5), 1–21 (2021). https://doi.org/10.1371/journal.pcbi.1008881

5. Asrani, S.K., Devarbhavi, H., Eaton, J., Kamath, P.S.: Burden of liver diseases in the world. J. Hepatol. **70**(1), 151–171 (2019). https://doi.org/10.1016/j.jhep.2018.09.014

6. Berg, S., et al.: Ilastik: interactive machine learning for (bio)image analysis. Nat. Methods **16**(12), 1226–1232 (2019). https://doi.org/10.1038/s41592-019-0582-9

7. Calisto, F.M., Santiago, C., Nunes, N., Nascimento, J.C.: Introduction of human-centric AI assistant to aid radiologists for multimodal breast image classification. Int. J. Hum. Comput. Stud. **150**, 102607 (2021). https://doi.org/10.1016/j.ijhcs.2021.102607

8. Chakravorty, D.: OBJ File Format - Simply Explained — All3DP (2021). https://all3dp.com/1/obj-file-format-3d-printing-cad/

9. Chen, S., Guo, J., Wang, C., Xu, X., Yi, Z., Li, W.: DeepLNAnno: a web-based lung nodules annotating system for CT images. J. Med. Syst. **43**(7), 1–9 (2019). https://doi.org/10.1007/s10916-019-1258-9

10. Chheang, V., et al.: A collaborative virtual reality environment for liver surgery planning. Comput. Graph. **99**, 234–246 (2021). https://doi.org/10.1016/j.cag.2021.07.009

11. Christ, P.F., et al.: Automatic Liver and Tumor Segmentation of CT and MRI Volumes using Cascaded Fully Convolutional Neural Networks (2017)

12. Kim, Y.J., Ganbold, B., Kim, K.G.: Web-based spine segmentation using deep learning in computed tomography images. Healthc. Inf. Res. **26**(1), 61–67 (2020). https://doi.org/10.4258/hir.2020.26.1.61

13. Nasiri, N., Foruzan, A.H., Chen, Y.W.: Integration of a knowledge-based constraint into generative models with applications in semi-automatic segmentation of liver tumors. Biomed. Signal Process. Control **57**, 101725 (2020). https://doi.org/10.1016/j.bspc.2019.101725. https://www.sciencedirect.com/science/article/pii/S1746809419303064

14. Phil Thompson: PyQt5 PyPI (2021). https://pypi.org/project/PyQt5/

15. Simpson, A.L., et al.: A large annotated medical image dataset for the development and evaluation of segmentation algorithms. arXiv preprint arXiv:1902.09063 (2019)

16. Song, Y., et al.: FeAture Explorer (FAE): a tool for developing and comparing radiomics models. PLoS ONE **15**, 1–10 (2020). https://doi.org/10.1371/journal.pone.0237587

17. Tian, J., Liu, L., Shi, Z., Xu, F.: Automatic couinaud segmentation from CT volumes on liver using GLC-UNet. In: Suk, H.-I., Liu, M., Yan, P., Lian, C. (eds.) MLMI 2019. LNCS, vol. 11861, pp. 274–282. Springer, Cham (2019). https://doi.org/10.1007/978-3-030-32692-0_32

18. UCSF Department of Surgery: Liver Metastases (2020). https://surgery.ucsf.edu/conditions-procedures/liver-metastases.aspx

19. van der Walt, S., et al.: scikit-image: image processing in Python. PeerJ **2**, e453 (2014). https://doi.org/10.7717/peerj.453

20. Yayuan, G., et al.: RadCloud-an artificial intelligence-based research platform integrating machine learning-based radiomics, deep learning, and data management. J. Artif. Intell. Med. Sci. **2**(1–2), 97 (2021). https://doi.org/10.2991/jaims.d.210617.001

21. Yushkevich, P.A., et al.: User-guided segmentation of multi-modality medical imaging datasets with ITK-SNAP. Neuroinformatics **17**(1), 83–102 (2018). https://doi.org/10.1007/s12021-018-9385-x

# Thematic Modeling of Professional Communication Practices of Helping Specialists

A. B. Uglova[1] ⓘ, I. M. Bogdanovskaya[1] ⓘ, and B. A. Nizomutdinov[2](✉) ⓘ

[1] Institute of Psychology, The Herzen State Pedagogical University of Russia, Saint Petersburg, Russia
anna.uglova@list.ru, ibogdanovs@herzen.spb.ru
[2] Institute of Design and Urban Studies, ITMO University, Saint Petersburg, Russia
boris@itmo.ru

**Abstract.** The paper examines the content and structure of professional communicative practices of helping specialists in digital professional communities, and also identifies psychological influence techniques used to manage interaction with the audience. A platform with profiles of psychologists offering their services was selected for the study. With the help of parsing methods, all the specialists' questionnaires were saved. Further, thematic modeling was carried out using LDA methods. 10 main topics and 55 unique terms describing the content of the professional discourse of helping specialists were identified. As a result, the components of the communicative strategy of using digital resources were evaluated: the presence of professional vocabulary, basic terminology, descriptions of transformational techniques, the presence of a product image, an image of the result, a description of the target audience, the presence of suggestive manipulative technologies. The model of monitoring the professional digital community as a whole, the possibilities of the platform for implementing elements of the communicative strategy of specialists were also described..

**Keywords:** parsing · data collection · mathematical modeling · psychology · specialists

## 1 Introduction

At a fundamental level, in the era of the fourth industrial revolution, there are issues of changing the healthcare system, the possibility of introducing cyber-physical systems into the care system, and the impact of digitalization on the quality of psychologists' work. It becomes important to study information technologies that are used to connect helping specialists with clients, as well as to transfer knowledge and psychological online help [1].

Within the framework of the UNESCO initiative related to the modernization of the health saving system, an important stage in rethinking the system of psychological assistance is the problem of analysis, evaluation and design of constructive communication practices in a virtual environment.

© The Author(s), under exclusive license to Springer Nature Switzerland AG 2023
O. Gervasi et al. (Eds.): ICCSA 2023, LNCS 13957, pp. 441–452, 2023.
https://doi.org/10.1007/978-3-031-36808-0_31

The relevance of the study of communication practices in a virtual environment is associated with the need to organize a successful dialogue between specialists and clients. The search for a helping specialist requires a high informational and psychological culture from the user. The client's choice is determined by the information that the assisting specialist presents on the web and popular information trends that are created by the digital professional community as a whole. The success of the interaction will depend on how well the user will understand the communication strategies and tactics of specialists [2].

In our study, we define professional communication practices as a complex multi-dimensional process of establishing and developing contacts generated by the needs of people's joint life activity in a virtual environment [3].

Communication practices in a virtual environment include: 1) communication actors, as well as technical objects and socio-cultural artifacts (computer intellectual agents, content, etc.), 2) are associated with the search and exchange of information, ensuring the social community of communicants while preserving their individuality, 3) function in accordance with the rules of a particular network community and 4) are mediated by a number of principles of digital media [4].

To improve information and psychological literacy, it is important to study the leading communicative practices of helping specialists in the digital environment [5].

Communication practices in digital media have a number of features that distinguish them from traditional social practices. These include virtuality, textual character, inter-activity, hypertextuality, uncertainty of spatial and temporal localization, creativity [6]. At the same time, communication practices in the virtual space include such character-istics of digital media as: programmability (the ability to make changes to the mode of communication using technical means), modularity (the ability to work with individual elements of a web page, the use of links, etc.), automation (standardization of many func-tions and elements of communication), variability (the ability to create multiple copies of a single object, which will be modified somewhat if desired by the user), hyperme-dia (the presence of non-text elements in hypertext), scalability (the ability to choose a simplified or full version of the site), periodic updating, transcoding (mutual projection of the communication process in the cultural and computer, technological layers) [7].

Since these characteristics add a sense of engagement and personal communication to communication, they are able to increase customer loyalty and reduce the criticality of his attitude to the information consumed [8]. For this reason, specific cyber risks appear, which are important to study for the organization of constructive Internet interaction [9].

An additional aspect of the relevance of the study of communicative practices in the virtual space is their, in many cases, openness and accessibility for observation. For this reason, cyberspace is currently one of the main platforms for the study of man. Mastering communicative practices in a virtual environment, the user learns and generates new values, norms and patterns of behavior, forms a system of actions that allow adequately perceiving and transmitting information to achieve both individually significant and group goals [10]. These features allow us to consider communicative practices in the virtual space, including as a methodological basis for studying social phenomena and processes.

In connection with the above, we would like to present 2 research questions.

RQ1. What is the specificity of the content and structure of professional communication practices of helping specialists in digital professional communities?

RQ2. What methods of psychological influence are used to manage interaction with the audience?

Currently, for online search of psychologists and psychotherapists in Russia, either specialized specialist recruitment services or websites for posting profiles of freelance specialists are mainly used. The choice to study the B17 platform was due to the fact that at the moment it is one of the oldest and most popular services for posting questionnaires of specialists of helping professions.

## 2  Data Collection

As previously noted, in our work we studied information about psychologists and helping specialists through a resume on the B17 Website. This is a social network that allows users to create personal profiles, write blog posts, share photos and videos, and communicate with other users on the topic of psychology. The website features a variety of topics including relationships, lifestyle, entertainment, and self-expression. The name of the Site "B17" comes from the phrase "be yourself at 17", which reflects the site's emphasis on self-expression and individuality. The website also has a forum where users can discuss various topics and ask for advice from other users, as well as a messaging system for private communication between users. We studied only the open part - the profiles of specialists, that is, only the information that users themselves openly publish about themselves.

The parsing method was used to collect the data. Data parsing is the process of extracting information from structured or unstructured data, which may be different in format and source. With the help of parsing, you can automatically extract and process information from various sources, such as web pages, databases, document files, etc.

Various methods and technologies are used for parsing, including regular expressions, machine learning algorithms, as well as special programming tools and libraries. The result of parsing can be data in a format that is convenient for further use for various purposes.

The surest way is to collect data through the API. An API (Application Programming Interface) is a set of instructions and data structures that programmers can use to create applications. The API provides a standardized way to interact between different applications, allowing them to exchange information and functionality. Interaction with the API can be carried out via communication protocols, such as HTTP or TCP/IP. As a rule, APIs are used to access functions and services of remote systems or external resources, for example, databases, calendars, social networks, online stores, etc. We examined the B17 site for the presence of an API, and did not find such an interface. Therefore, it was decided to use data parsing methods using a crawler.

A crawler for parsing (also called a web scraper or web spider) is a program that automatically crawls websites, extracts the necessary information and saves it in a convenient format, for example, in a database or file. The crawler starts working from a certain start page, and then follows links to other pages (depending on the set rules and logic), extracts the page content, processes it and saves it in the appropriate format. The crawler is used to automate the extraction of information from websites, which speeds up and simplifies the processing of a large amount of data.

However, it should be remembered that the use of crawlers may violate the rules of use of sites (depending on the specific case), therefore, in order to use a crawler, it is necessary to comply with the rules of a particular website and legislation. We have studied the terms of use of this website and found no contradictions. It is also worth noting that we used all the collected data only for scientific research, we do not use this data for commercial purposes.

All the collected data were additionally depersonalized. For this task, we conducted a depersonalization stage of the data. Depersonalization is the process of deleting or replacing personal data that can identify an individual in order to protect privacy and confidentiality. The depersonalization procedure allows you to hide or replace sensitive information, while preserving the value of the data for analysis and other purposes.

All collected information was preprocessed to remove any proper names. To solve this problem, a script was written using the Natasha library. Natasha is a free library for natural language processing (NLP) for texts developed in Python. It has an open source code and is used for analyzing texts in natural Russian. As a result, all the collected data were depersonalized and did not contain contacts, names and surnames. All this was necessary to comply with the legislation on the processing of personal data.

The Phython language was chosen for writing the parser - it is widely used for writing parsers due to its rich libraries and ease of use. Additionally, 2 libraries were used - Selenium and Scrapy. Python Selenium is a Python library that allows you to automate web browsers using WebDriver. Selenium also allows you to record and replay actions in the browser, which can greatly simplify the process of testing web applications or automating routine actions.

Python Scrapy is a Python framework for collecting data from websites. It provides a powerful set of tools for automatic data extraction, tracking changes on pages and automating work with websites. Scrapy makes it easy to create and manage web scrapers using Python. It provides a set of convenient and flexible tools for data extraction and processing, including multithreading, proxy support, monitoring changes on pages and other functions.

Scrapy provides automatic page navigation, interactive form processing, AJAX parsing and other functions for working with complex websites. In addition, it has a large number of additional functions, such as searching for elements on the page, using cookies and managing browser windows. This makes it one of the most popular tools for automating web browsers. The general scheme of work is shown in Fig. 1.

The result of data collection was the MySQL database. The following parameters are stored in the database:

- Specialty
- City
- Number of publications
- Number of reviews
- Number of examples of consultations
- Number of trainings
- Number of online consultations

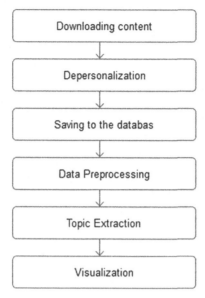

**Fig. 1.** General scheme of data collection and processing

- Full text description of the specialist

The final database contains 2224 records. As a result, we managed to collect a database of psychologists from the largest cities for further processing.

## 3  Data Processing

The next step was data processing. In our work, we have carried out intelligent data processing for the descriptions of psychologists that are published in profiles. To identify the main areas in which specialists work. To solve this problem, we conducted thematic modeling based on full-text descriptions of specialists. 10 main topics were identified.

Orange Text Mining software was selected for data processing. It is a free Python tool used to analyze text data. It provides a set of tools that facilitate the analysis of a large volume of text data, including text classification, clustering, visualization, keyword extraction, and others. It has a rich set of tools that allow you to analyze texts, starting from the basic analysis of the frequency of words and ending with the combination of various machine learning methods for the classification and clustering of texts. Another interesting feature of Orange Text Mining is the ability to visualize text data. It provides tools that allow you to create visualizations, such as a tag cloud, heat maps, a graph using the TSNE method, and others [11]. One of the most useful features of Orange Text Mining is the ability to extract keywords. It contains a set of tools that allow you to process text documents and extract keywords that can help in analyzing text data. In general, Orange Text Mining is a powerful and flexible tool for text data analysis, which can be used for both small and large projects in various fields, such as marketing, science and technology related to text data analysis.

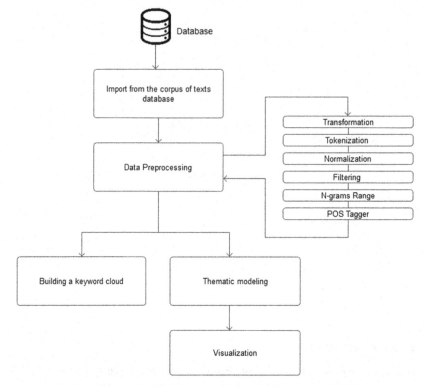

**Fig. 2.** General text processing scheme for thematic modeling

The general scheme of thematic modeling is shown in Fig. 2.

In our work, we used the following tools for text processing:

- Preliminary preparation of the text. Text preprocessing breaks your text into smaller units (tokens), filters them, starts normalization (stemming, lemmatization), creates n-grams and marks tokens with part-of-speech labels. Additionally, a dictionary with negative words was prepared to remove unnecessary information, such as emojis and other information.
- Building a keyword cloud. Word Cloud displays tokens in the corpus, their size indicates the frequency of a word in the corpus or the average number of words in a packet when the functions of the word packet are at the widget input. The words are listed in the widget by their frequency (weight). The widget outputs documents containing the selected tokens from word cloud.
- Thematic modeling. Thematic modeling identifies abstract topics in the corpus based on groups of words found in each document and their corresponding frequency. A document usually contains several topics in different proportions, so the widget also reports the weight of topics for each document. Thematic modeling can be carried

out using various methods. Using a hidden Dirichlet distribution, hidden semantic indexing, or a hierarchical Dirichlet process.

Among the methods of thematic modeling, many researchers still use LDA, a generative model that observes the frequency of words in the corpus and iteratively builds a thematic model for a given number of topics [12]. We settled on the LDA method, because in our context it showed the optimal result.

For thematic modeling in Orange Text Mining, the Gensim library is used. Gensim is an open source library for unsupervised thematic modeling, document indexing, similarity search and other natural language processing functions using modern statistical machine learning. The result of the processing were 10 topics described by keywords, as well as the possibility of visualization. Each cluster was interpreted by our team, the results of cluster processing are given in the next chapter.

## 4  Results

Professional communication practices are being transformed in the digital environment, acquiring new functions and forms. However, the structure of the communicative strategy remains classical, which allows us to evaluate the main components of the content: why the material is published, what the professional wants to say about himself, to whom the self-presentation is addressed, how the final result of the work is seen, what vocabulary and forms of speech are used, how grammatical forms are used that can affect the process of perception and understanding of information by the reader (potential client).

At the first stage, we conducted a semantic analysis of the uploaded information and identified 55 unique terms describing the content of the professional discourse of helping specialists (Table 1).

Assessing the content of the professional digital discourse of helping specialists, we can say that they use a wide range of vocabulary that has both direct and intentional meaning.

The general psychological vocabulary is widely used to indicate that a specialist belongs to a certain professional group. It is worth noting the presence of both medical and psychological terminology, which indicates the presence of specialists of different profiles in the community.

The basic directions of psychotherapy and counseling, a wide range of approaches and techniques that are used for treatment, improvement of mental health and personal development in individual work with a client are described. As a result of the analysis, the basic areas of work were identified: psychoanalytic approach, gestalt therapy, cognitive behavioral therapy. As well as the most popular methods of work: positive psychotherapy, Hellinger placement, art therapy, AST (acceptance and commitment therapy).

The communication strategy also provides a description of the main object of the work - the image of a psychological request. The request to a psychologist is primarily related to the problems faced by clients (the sphere of communication, self-realization, health, etc.). The creation and presentation of a certain "standard" request affects the process of reflection and sets a trend in self-understanding among customers. Specialists primarily appeal to the spheres of relationships, work, and education. Separately, it is

**Table 1.** The content of the professional discourse of helping specialists

General psychological vocabulary

| Therapy | Psychotherapy | Consultation | Example |
|---|---|---|---|
| Psychology | Counseling | Help | Course |
| Transfer | Psychotherapeutic | Medical | Scheme |

**Basic directions of psychotherapy and counseling**

| Gestalt | CBT (Cognitive Behavioral Approach | Psychoanalytic | ACT (Acceptance and commitment therapy) |
|---|---|---|---|
| Psychoanalysis | Positive Psychotherapy | Arrangements by Hellinger | Art Therapy |

**The image of a psychological request**

| Situation | Condition | Case | Problem |
|---|---|---|---|
| Life | Relationship | Work | Education |
| Speech | Speech | Difficulty | Weight loss |

**Image of the result**

| Success | Happy | | |
|---|---|---|---|

**Psychological transformation techniques**

| Mental changes | Emotional changes | Positive changes | |
|---|---|---|---|
| Responsibility | Development | Acceptance | |

**Target audience**

| Children | Child | Client | |
|---|---|---|---|

**Intention of commitment (commission)**

| Be Able | To Want | To Do | |
|---|---|---|---|
| Find | To Know | Work out | |

worth noting the popularity of the topics of weight loss and speech development as basic psychological trends.

A place is given to the description of the idealized image of the result (happiness and success). The image of the result as a mental picture of what we want to achieve is a visualization of the desired result. In this case, the desired result is described quite abstractly, which on the one hand makes it possible to attract more customers, and on the other hand creates conflicting expectations in relation to specialists.

The description of specialists presents psychological transformational techniques for achieving results, which are designed to help change behavior, thinking or emotional state, achieve personal growth, as well as overcome various problems and conflicts. The greatest emphasis is on the techniques of taking responsibility therapy, which is associated with the leading areas of therapy. Suggestive intentional statements (commissives) are also actively used: I can, want, do, find, know, try, encouraging active actions of clients.

The target audience that experts plan to interest is described rather sparingly. There is a separate emphasis on working with children. Adults are not described in a differentiated way, messages are shared, without personal addressing, which reduces the effectiveness of communication.

At the second stage, using thematic modeling, we evaluated the structure of the communicative strategy of helping specialists (Table 2).

**Table 2.** Structure of the communication strategy of helping specialists

| Clusters | Tags |
|---|---|
| Attributes of medical psychology, psychotherapy | Psychotherapy, psychology, psychotherapy, positive, psychotherapeutic, medical, positive, education, clinical, center |
| Cognitive behavioral therapy of taking responsibility | Cognitively, acceptance, client, transference, AST, case, responsibility, therapy |
| Cognitive-behavioral approach to working with weight loss | CBT, course, condition, success, cognitive, psychotherapy, therapy, scheme, weight loss, gestalt |
| Gestalt therapy of child-parent relations | Example, gestalt, counseling, children, psychology, emotionally, work, psychotherapy, therapy, relationships |
| Techniques and tasks of gestalt therapy | Happiness, games, find, you know, work, do, gestalt, life |
| Techniques and tasks of art therapy | Life, relationships, therapy, art, problems, situations, stage, help, development, want |
| Psychoanalytic work with children | Psychoanalysis, psychotherapy, psychoanalytic, psychoanalytic, work, children, counseling, psychotherapy, psychoanalysis, psychology |
| Integrative approach in working with the sphere of relations | Gestalt, help, relationships, CBT, min, therapy, consultation |
| Positive psychotherapy and Hellinger placement | Dynamic, example, placement, positive, consultation, psychotherapy, psychotherapeutic, mental |
| The technique of the Hellinger method of arrangements | Speech, speech, speech, speech, a, can, difficulties, various, constellations |

Based on the results of the structural analysis, it is possible to identify the main topics and describe the problems with which specialists are ready to work in various directions. For example, it is proposed to work with the topic of weight loss within the framework of a cognitive-behavioral approach, and with children, specialists offer therapy within the framework of psychodynamic and gestalt approaches. It can also be noted that the psychodynamic direction, including art therapy, psychoanalysis, the method of placement, positive psychotherapy, is the most popular and is most represented in professional discourse. With the help of thematic modeling, it is also possible to evaluate the structuring of the description of individual directions, the inclusion of the user's image, the targeting of self-presentation, the description of techniques and the result.

As a result of the analysis, the following constructive and destructive characteristics of professional communication on digital platforms can be described:

- targeted openness, which is characterized by the absence of a clearly defined audience and focus on the description of the problem field;
- genre diffuseness associated with the combination of often contradictory directions of assistance in one message;
- idealization of the image of the result of the work, forming unrealistic expectations of the audience;
- the use of suggestive statements (commis-sives) to encourage the audience to communicate.

The leading characteristics of professional psychological discourse indicate the integration of its types as professional-practical and advertising-commercial, which correlates with the main objectives of such platforms, but may contradict the ethical principles of helping specialists, which needs further study.

At the same time, the communication strategies of specialists in the professional community are mediated by such characteristics of digital media as the ability to work with individual elements of a web page, the use of links, standardization of many functions and elements of communication, hypermedia (the presence of non-text elements in hypertext), periodic updating, etc. Thus, with the help of thematic modeling, it is possible to evaluate not only the work of individual specialists, but also to monitor the professional digital community as a whole. Based on the results of the analysis, it can be said that the digital platform under study is focused on the presentation of the following elements of the communication strategy:

- Analysis of the goals and objectives of psychological assistance, through an active description of the issues;
- Self-presentation of professional achievements and skills of specialists.

However, almost no attention is paid to the description of the target audience and segmentation of consumers of services to improve targeted communication. Also, a clearer description of the result of work can become a point of development, in order to increase the understanding of customers of what they can get as a result of work and increase the desire to cover current needs with the help of the services offered.

Discussion.

The results obtained allow us to conclude that we have received answers to the research questions posed. There is a specificity of the content and structure of professional communicative practices of helping specialists in digital professional communities:

- the community of helping specialists has absorbed the basic properties of virtual communities associated with hypertextuality (the use of multimodal messages, the intersection of social networks, the use of different information channels, etc.), targeted openness, crowdsourcing, the absence of geographical boundaries, etc.
- the virtual community has retained offline functions: the possibility of self-presentation, exchange of professional information, etc.
- the virtual community has created new properties of the professional environment of psychologists: genre diffuseness, changing the ethical norms of self-presentation of services, expanding the space for communication with patients, creating new conditions for seeking psychological help.

These conclusions correlate with the results of research by Wu H. et al., which indicate that in online interaction, clients show more trust in psychologists than in offline interaction, based on the assessment of the resource and the community as a whole [13]. We can say that the question of the ethics and usefulness of such communities for customers remains open and needs further research.

## 5   Conclusions

In conclusion, I would like to say that with the help of thematic modeling, it is possible to assess the content and structure of the areas of work of the helping specialists. It also became possible to evaluate the communicative strategy of using digital resources: the presence of professional vocabulary, basic terminology, descriptions of transformational techniques, the presence of a product image, an image of the result, a description of the target audience, the presence of suggestive manipulative technologies. This model can be used to evaluate various professional communities.

Also, with the help of thematic modeling, it is possible to evaluate not only the work of individual specialists, but also to monitor the professional digital community as a whole, the capabilities of the platform for the implementation of all elements of the communicative strategy.

In the continuation of this study, we plan to study the regional specifics of professional communication of helping specialists to refine the monitoring model taking into account socio-demographic and territorial specifics.

The advantage of this method is that it can be scaled for any platform containing specialist questionnaires. In our study, we studied one site, however, the parser can be configured to collect information from other sites, and collect data. Further thematic analysis will not require refinement and the same algorithm will be used.

## 6   Conclusions

The research was carried out at the expense of the grant of the Russian Science Foundation No. 22–78-10047, https://rscf.ru/project/22-78-10047 / "Constructive and destructive communicative practices of specialists of helping professions in digital media".

# References

1. Wu, H., Dan, J., Evans, R.: Building patient confidence in psychologists in online mental health communities. Data Sci. Manage. **5**(1), 21–27 (2022)
2. Heather, H.J.: Dialogic communication in the context of healthcare: a case study of Kaiser Permanente practice in social networks. Overv. Publ. Relat. **40**(5), 856–858 (2014). https://doi.org/10.1016/j.pubrev.2014.07.007
3. Warren, M.: "Just spoke to …": The types and directionality of intertextuality in professional discourse. English Specific Purp. **32**(1), 12–24 (2013). https://doi.org/10.1016/j.esp.2012.07.001
4. Radkevich A.L.: Social Internet practices as an object of sociological analysis. Knowledge. Understanding. Skill: information humanitarian portal. Sociology. № 3 (2009). http://www.zpu-journal.ru/e-zpu/2009/3/Radkevich
5. Karasne, R., Al-Azzam, S., Muflikh, S., Suda, O., Khawamde, S., Khader, Y.: The influence of the media on the formation of knowledge, awareness of risks and communication practices in connection with the COVID-19 pandemic among pharmacists. Res. Field Soc. Admin. Pharm. **17**(1), 1897–1902 (2021). https://doi.org/10.1016/j.sapharm.2020.04.027
6. Marres, N.: Digital Sociology. Rethinking the social. Research, p. 232p. Polity Books, Cambridge (2017)
7. Manovich L. The Language of New Media, 400 p. Moscow (2018)
8. Rose, S., Fandel, D., Dibley, A.: Information exchange is the name of the game: a study of the role of communication practices in social networks in relations with B2B clients in the natural sciences industry. Ind. Mark. Manage. **93**, 52–62 (2021)
9. Bogdanovskaya, I.M., Koroleva, N.N., Uglova, A.B., Petrova, Y.: The role of personal characteristics in the formation of problematic Internet use among high school students. Prosp. Sci. Educ. **54**(6), 271–284 (2021). https://doi.org/10.32744/pse.2021.6.18
10. Zotov V.V., Lysenko V.A.: Communicative practices as a theoretical construct of the study of society. Theory and practice of social development. No.3 (2010). https://cyberleninka.ru/article/n/kommunikativnye-praktiki-kak-teoreticheskiy-konstrukt-izucheniya-obschestva. Accessed 20 Mar 2023
11. Lamba, M., Madhusudhan, M.: Tools and techniques for text mining and visualization. In: Lamba, M., Madhusudhan, M. (eds.) Text Mining for Information Professionals: An Uncharted Territory, pp. 295–318. Springer International Publishing, Cham (2022). https://doi.org/10.1007/978-3-030-85085-2_10
12. Sievert, C., Shirley, K.E.: LDAvis: a method for visualizing and interpreting topics. In: Proceedings of the Workshop on Interactive Language Learning, Visualization, and Interfaces, pp. 63–70, Baltimore, Maryland, USA (2014)
13. Wu, H., Deng, Z., Evans, R.: Building patients' trust in psychologists in online mental health communities. Data Sci. Manage. **5**(1), 21–27 (2022)
14. Jiang, Y., Hu, C., Xiao, T., Zhang, C., Zhu, J.: Improved differentiable architecture search for language modeling and named entity recognition. In: Proceedings of the 2019 Conference on Empirical Methods in Natural Language Processing and the 9th International Joint Conference on Natural Language Processing (EMNLP-IJCNLP), pp. 3585–3590 (2019). https://doi.org/10.18653/v1/D19-1367
15. Dieng, A.B., Ruiz, F.J.R., Blei, D.M.: Topic modeling in embedding space. Trans. Assoc. Comput. Linguist. **8**, 439–453 (2020). https://doi.org/10.1162/tacl_a_00325
16. Wolf, T., Debut, L., Sanh, V.: Transformers: state-of-the-art natural language processing. In: Proceedings of the 2020 Conference on Empirical Methods in Natural Language Processing: System Demonstrations, pp. 38–45 (2020). https://aclanthology.org/2020.emnlp-demos.6
17. Hwang, C.L., Lai, Y.J., Liu, T.Y.: A new approach for multiple objective decision making. Comput. Oper. Res. **20**(8), 889–899 (1993). https://doi.org/10.1016/0305-0548(93)90109-v

# Mobility Networks as a Predictor of Socioeconomic Status in Urban Systems

Devashish Khulbe[1]([✉]) [ID], Alexander Belyi[1] [ID], Ondřej Mikeš[2] [ID],
and Stanislav Sobolevsky[1,3,4] [ID]

[1] Department of Mathematics and Statistics, Faculty of Science, Masaryk University,
Kotlarska 2, 611 37 Brno, Czech Republic
dk3596@nyu.edu
[2] RECETOX, Masaryk University, Kamenice 753/5, 625 00 Brno, Czech Republic
[3] Center for Urban Science and Progress, New York University, 370 Jay Street,
Brooklyn, NY 11201, USA
[4] Institute of Law and Technology, Faculty of Law, Masaryk University, Veveri 70,
611 80 Brno, Czech Republic

**Abstract.** Modeling socioeconomic dynamics has always been an area of focus for urban scientists and policymakers, who aim to better understand and predict the well-being of local neighborhoods. Such models can inform decision-makers early on about expected neighborhood performance under normal conditions, as well as in response to considered interventions before official statistical data is collected. While features such as population and job density, employment characteristics, and other neighborhood variables have been studied and evaluated extensively, research on using the underlying networks of human interactions and urban structures is less common in modeling techniques. We propose using the structure of the local urban mobility network (weighted by commute flows among a city's geographical units) as a signature of the neighborhood and as a source of features to model its socioeconomic quantities. The network structure is quantified through node embedding generated using a graph neural network representation learning model. In the proof-of-concept task of modeling the location's median income and housing profile in two different cities, such network structure features provide a noticeable performance advantage compared to using only the other available social features. This work can thus inform researchers and stakeholders about the utility of mobility network structure in a complex urban system for modeling various quantities of interest.

**Keywords:** Mobility networks · socioeconomic modeling · Network representations · Graph Neural Networks

## 1 Introduction

Networks are an integral part of any urban system, with many intra-city dynamics that can be perceived as a structure of interconnected entities. Urban researchers

© The Author(s), under exclusive license to Springer Nature Switzerland AG 2023
O. Gervasi et al. (Eds.): ICCSA 2023, LNCS 13957, pp. 453–461, 2023.
https://doi.org/10.1007/978-3-031-36808-0_32

have recognized the utility of network structures and topology to measure relationships and understand the organization of cities. Networks from the perspective of social, geographical, political, and cultural domains have been well established in the context of cities [1]. Their scales, structures, and development over time have informed urban studies in understanding complex city characteristics. Inter-city networks have also been an area of focus, with research informing broader policies like polycentric urban development [2] and long-term economic investments [2,3] in large urban regions. Local neighborhood characteristics like median income, employment rate, housing prices, etc., are some of the many variables that help urban scientists develop a "profile" of an area. These socioeconomic indicators help understand the local health of a neighborhood. Studying the evolution of economic health over time is particularly useful to policymakers with regard to decisions like investments, development potential, energy consumption, and migration trends within a large city [4–6]. Socioeconomic modeling has been studied extensively at both the individual and neighborhood levels. Contextual socioeconomic features such as population density, job density, ethnic profile, etc., are well established as indicators of a larger population standard of living [7]. In smaller urban areas where consistent official data could be hard to obtain, features like bank card transactions have been used to predict regional economic indices [8]. More recently, researchers employed aggregate mobility indicators for socioeconomic modelling [9]. Spatial variables like natural amenities, public parks, etc., have also been used in modeling [10] to understand the impact of physical geography. In the context of networks, these external variables have also been studied in conjunction with road network topology to model and understand traffic capacity in urban regions [11]. However, interactions among entities is not a common feature that is incorporated in modeling, even though relationships between a given neighborhood and other parts of a city could be an important aspect of measuring economic health. Traditional machine learning modeling approaches are limited by the inability to properly define a feature space for a region within a larger interconnected network. With the development and proven applicability of methods like Graph Neural Networks, there is a potential to leverage their power in urban contexts.

Large-scale mobility data has been used to study complex city dynamics while measuring the resilience of cities [12], although the network structure itself is not considered here to model socioeconomic performance indicators. Researchers have proposed using multitude of digital and physical variables like mobile app records, taxi and bike trips, and geo-tagged social media data as a measure of urban mobility [13]. Data-driven research has also emphasized modeling and studying dependencies among external features like 311 service requests data [14], showing the importance of local neighborhood context in modeling. Using social media networks, metrics like centrality and average clustering coefficient have also been used as features to model economic growth in neighborhoods as a result of government investments [15]. These methods rely on combining external node variables with pre-defined network metrics as input features rather than being able to learn the network representations of the whole urban area. Urban street networks using geo-located Twitter data have also been used to study public spaces and evaluate their success [16], indicating that granular networks are useful in the analysis of sophisticated urban geographies. Networks based on twitter metadata have also proved to be useful in delineating urban neighborhoods [17]. However, social media-based networks are not the best proxy for urban interactions, as they may exclude large populations based on age and location. Dynamic mobility data may help decision-makers assess the distribution and/or dynamics of the socioeconomic performance across the city based on the available urban mobility data in nearly real-time, without having to wait for years until Census and/or other official statistics reflecting such performance gets collected or updated. Figure 1 illustrates the idea outline with New York City's mobility among zip-code neighborhoods.

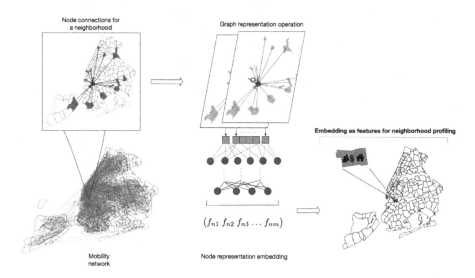

**Fig. 1.** Structure of the locations' mobility network as a characteristic of its socioeconomic performance - an illustration for NYC

## 2    Data and Methodology

### 2.1    Network Representation

The general idea behind constructing representations of a network is to capture the connectivity and topology through some transformations, which produces a representation feature set (embedding). With respect to a given node, a node embedding thus represents each node as a vector in a low dimensional space. In this regard, many techniques have been used in graphs to generate embedding, with graph-based applications such as node classification, node clustering, node retrieval/recommendation, link prediction, etc. [18]. However, in many of the applications, the stability and robustness of the embedding become important. Techniques such as node2vec are found to be susceptible to sources of noise, stochastic effects, or specific parameter choices [19,20]. At the same time, GNN (and some variations) based embedding has shown promising results in generating stable and robust embedding [21,22]. We consider two techniques to produce node representations:

1. *Personalized PageRank (PPR),* which quantifies the significance of all nodes with respect to the given node. Formally, PPR embedding of a source node is the stationary probability distribution of a Markov chain that, with probability $\alpha$, randomly transitions following the link structure of the network, and with probability $1 - \alpha$ teleports to a source node [23,24]. For a given node $s$ in a weighted directed graph $G(V, E)$ with adjacency matrix $A$, we normalize neighboring edges by the total of edge weights among $s$ and its connections to obtain a stochastic transition matrix $P$. The teleport probabilities are thus proportional to the relative "activity" between the origin and destination node.

2. *Graph Neural Network (GNN) based embedding,* which quantifies the node embedding as the series of network convolutions of certain initial embedding (e.g. one-hot encoding) of the interconnected nodes [25]. The goal is to learn a node function within the graph that preserves important structural properties of the network, such as local connectivity and symmetry. The formula for computing GNN embedding typically involves several iterations of message passing between nodes in the graph, which allows for the incorporation of local and global information. The message passing at the node level can be formulated as

$$h_i^k = \sigma(W_{self}^k h_i^{k-1} + W_{neigh}^k \frac{1}{|\mathcal{N}(i)|} \sum_{j \in \mathcal{N}(i)} h_j^{k-1} + b^k) \tag{1}$$

where $h_i^k$ represents the embedding of node $i$ at iteration $k$, $\mathcal{N}(i)$ represents the set of neighboring nodes of $i$, $W^k$ and $b^k$ are learnable weight and bias parameters at iteration $k$, and $\sigma$ is a non-linear activation function such as ReLU or sigmoid. By repeating this message passing process, GNN embedding can capture increasingly complex relationships and structures in the graph. Many GNNs can also be succinctly defined using graph-level equations. In the case of a basic GNN, we can write the graph-level definition of the model as follows:

$$H^k = \sigma(H^{k-1}W_{self}^k + AH^{k-1}W_{neigh}^k + B^k) \tag{2}$$

where $H^k \in R^{V \times d}$ denotes the matrix of node representations at layer $k$ in the GNN (with each node corresponding to a row in the matrix), $B^k$ is the matrix of bias vectors $b^k$, and A is the normalized graph adjacency matrix. $H^k$ is usually a lower dimensional matrix that encodes the network representations through the GNN framework. Embedding is thus learned as a part of the network representation task, where the goal is to reconstruct the original network edges.

## 2.2    Experiment Setup

We consider the mobility network as a directed graph $G(V, E)$, where the nodes $V$ represent the geographical regions in a city and edges $E \subseteq V \times V$ are weighted by the mobility values between nodes. The graph adjacency matrix is therefore populated by the mobility values among the nodes, which then serve as the input to generate node representations. While PPR embedding is represented by a vector of probabilities for each node, GNN-based node representation is a $d$ dimensional vector, where dimensionality is configured as part of representation learning of the mobility network. The output matrix (embedding) is then used as node features, with each vector corresponding to a node in the mobility network. Data from two cities are considered:

**New York City, USA.** To represent NYC mobility, we consider job flows obtained from The Longitudinal Employer-Household Dynamics (LEHD), a U.S. census bureau program [26]. U.S. Census also provides other neighborhood variables. The median income is considered as the target feature representing the socioeconomic profile of a node. We aggregate the mobility and median income on the zip-code level to get 173 nodes with significant mobility and socioeconomic information. For baseline models, we use population density and job density as contextual neighborhood features.

**Brno, Czechia.** Brno is the second largest city in Czechia, with a population of around 700,000 people in its metropolitan area. The city is an important cultural and administrative center and the largest city in the Moravia region of Czechia. Mobility information for Brno is retrieved from the commute information from T-mobile cell-phone-based location data. The data is provided as hourly aggregated values among 48 unique districts in the city. We further aggregate the commute flows over 14 available days to weight the network with districts as nodes. With economic characteristics like income not easily available for Brno, we consider housing profile as a measure of a district's economic status. The percentage of single-family houses in districts is taken as the target feature. Furthermore, the employment rate is used as input to train baseline models.

The embeddings and node features thus serve as inputs to the supervised learning models. Three approaches are considered – Regularized Linear model (Lasso), Random Forests, and a Vanilla Neural Network (VNN). These models are tuned to find the optimal hyperparameters for the modeling task.

## 3    Results

### 3.1    Network Embedding vs. Contextual Node Features

Table 1 presents out-of-sample results using various input features with the three models considered. The evaluation of model performance is done based on Root

**Table 1.** Out-of-sample RMSE values with supervised learning based on different model inputs

|  | NYC | | | Brno | | |
|---|---|---|---|---|---|---|
|  | Node features | PPR | GNN | Node features | PPR | GNN |
| Lasso | 0.92 | 0.78 | 0.54 | 1.41 | 0.74 | 0.45 |
| RF | 0.63 | 0.59 | 0.42 | 1.06 | 0.68 | 0.42 |
| VNN | 0.63 | 0.47 | 0.40 | 1.01 | 0.60 | 0.42 |

Mean Squared Error (RMSE) values across a range of features, including contextual node features and network embeddings derived from PPR and GNN techniques. The input features are used individually to train the models, allowing for a comparison of the modeling capability of embeddings over neighborhood variables. The results show that both node embedding approaches, PPR and GNN, outperform external node features considered individually. In particular, the GNN embedding of mobility network nodes has the best results overall, with the highest out-of-sample performance in both cities. The use of contextual node features is also useful, although to a lesser extent than the network embedding. This suggests that mobility embedding alone is effective in capturing complex relationships between nodes and the larger interactions in a city. Additionally, we also notice that model fitting on Brno data is somewhat unstable with noticeable variance on the validation set RMSE values. Whereas the results for NYC are much more stable, highlighting the differences in data and network sizes between the cities. Nevertheless, the better performance with embeddings for both cities shows the importance of mobility in socioeconomic profiling.

Although the target features for NYC and Brno are different, they represent important aspects of an urban neighborhood. While median income is directly a measure of economic health, housing type could be a proxy for complex social dynamics, including poverty, transport accessibility, etc. Local neighborhood features could be an important signal for these characteristics. Thus, the superior performance of mobility embedding over node features is significant since node features do not capture the intricacies of the network structure and interactions between nodes.

## 3.2   Discussion

We investigate the utility of mobility networks over two very different cities. NYC and Brno differ vastly in scale, geography, economy, and demographics. Nevertheless, results show that mobility network embedding proves to have significant modeling capability for the socioeconomic profiling of neighborhoods in both cities. GNN-based embedding is particularly promising in this regard, with the potential to improve the accuracy of various network modeling applications. The inherent difference in scale and lack of consistent socioeconomic features between the two cities could be a potential reason for somewhat unstable results for Brno. Brno's mobility network is much smaller, with data available among 48 districts. This potentially is an issue for supervised modeling, with not enough data samples to optimize model parameters. More granular data could help to stabilize the models. In general, data augmentation techniques could be explored for fixing data scarcity issues in smaller cities. There is a broader scope to evaluate the impact of other urban networks, such as social media, in urban profiling. While we have focused on median income and housing profile as the target features, there is room to investigate the methodology in other socioeconomic variables of interest, such as unemployment, poverty rate, education, etc.

## 4    Conclusion

Diverse networks, which can represent dynamic relationships among entities in urban systems, have proven to be quite useful for researchers. However, using their representations in modeling complex urban quantities is not commonplace. With interactions among individuals or urban entities becoming increasingly intense in the modern world, the importance of networks in urban modeling becomes more relevant. Applications such as link prediction, node classification, etc., can thus be extended in urban contexts, in which GNN-based methods have already proven to be useful. We demonstrate their ability to model the socioeconomic characteristics of urban geographies. While mobility is an essential aspect of any city's function, we show that its network structure representations can be useful estimators for urban modeling tasks, as demonstrated in the case of modeling the average income of urban locations. Additionally, there is potential for other urban networks, such as traffic networks, social media, etc., also to inform urban models.

Our broader work aims to find the most efficient way of incorporating the network structure with other available neighborhood local contextual features to determine the maximum modeling capability. We also aim to experiment more with supervised learning, and non-linear network representation approaches to fine-tune and improve the models. Overall, our work can inform scientists and stakeholders to study and model complex urban systems from the perspective of a city's real-time networks while also leveraging the utility of local geographical contexts.

**Acknowledgements.** This research was supported by the MUNI Award in Science and Humanities (MASH Belarus) of the Grant Agency of Masaryk University under the Digital City project (MUNI/J/0008/2021). The work of Stanislav Sobolevsky was also partially supported by ERDF "CyberSecurity, CyberCrime and Critical Information Infrastructures Center of Excellence" (No. $CZ.02.1.01/0.0/0.0/16\_019/0000822$).

# References

1. Pflieger, G., Rozenblat, C.: Introduction. Urban networks and network theory: the city as the connector of multiple networks. Urban Stud. **47**(13), 2723–2735 (2010)
2. Liu, X., Derudder, B., Wu, K.: Measuring polycentric urban development in China: an intercity transportation network perspective. Reg. Stud. **50**(8), 1302–1315 (2016)
3. Glaeser, E.L., Ponzetto, G.A., Zou, Y.: Urban networks: connecting markets, people, and ideas. Pap. Reg. Sci. **95**(1), 17–59 (2016)
4. Townsend, A.M.: Smart Cities: Big Data, Civic Hackers, and the Quest for a New Utopia. W. W. Norton & Company, New York (2013)
5. Borjas, G.J.: Economic theory and international migration. Int. Migr. Rev. **23**(3), 457–485 (1989)
6. Swan, L.G., Ugursal, V.I.: Modeling of end-use energy consumption in the residential sector: a review of modeling techniques. Renew. Sustain. Energy Rev. **13**(8), 1819–1835 (2009)
7. Wen, M., Browning, C.R., Cagney, K.A.: Poverty, affluence, and income inequality: neighborhood economic structure and its implications for health. Soc. Sci. Med. **57**(5), 843–860 (2003)
8. Sobolevsky, S., Massaro, E., Bojic, I., Arias, J.M., Ratti, C.: Predicting regional economic indices using big data of individual bank card transactions. In: 2017 IEEE International Conference on Big Data (Big Data), Boston, MA, USA, pp. 1313–1318 (2017). https://doi.org/10.1109/BigData.2017.8258061
9. Xu, Y., Belyi, A., Bojic, I., Ratti, C.: Human mobility and socioeconomic status: analysis of Singapore and Boston. Comput. Environ. Urban Syst. **72**, 51–67 (2018)
10. Lee, S., Lin, J.: Natural amenities, neighbourhood dynamics, and persistence in the spatial distribution of income. Rev. Econ. Stud. **85**(1), 663–694 (2018)
11. Loder, A., Ambühl, L., Menendez, M., et al.: Understanding traffic capacity of urban networks. Sci. Rep. **9**, 16283 (2019). https://doi.org/10.1038/s41598-019-51539-5
12. Yabe, T., Rao, P.S.C., Ukkusuri, S.V.: Resilience of interdependent urban sociophysical systems using large-scale mobility data: modeling recovery dynamics. Sustain. Cities Soc. **75**, 103237 (2021). https://doi.org/10.1016/j.scs.2021.103237
13. Zhu, E., Khan, M., Kats, P., Bamne, S.S., Sobolevsky, S.: Digital urban sensing: a multi-layered approach. arXiv preprint arXiv:1809.01280 (2018)
14. Wang, L., Qian, C., Kats, P., Kontokosta, C., Sobolevsky, S.: Structure of 311 service requests as a signature of urban location. PLoS ONE **12**(10), e0186314 (2017). https://doi.org/10.1371/journal.pone.0186314
15. Zhou, X., Hristova, D., Noulas, A., Mascolo, C., Sklar, M.: Cultural investment and urban socioeconomic development: a geosocial network approach. R. Soc. Open Sci. **4**(9), 170413 (2017). https://doi.org/10.1098/rsos.170413
16. Agryzkov, T., Martí, P., Nolasco-Cirugeda, A., Serrano-Estrada, L., Tortosa, L., Vicent, J.F.: Analysing successful public spaces in an urban street network using data from the social networks Foursquare and Twitter. Appl. Netw. Sci. **1**(1), 1–15 (2016). https://doi.org/10.1007/s41109-016-0014-z
17. Sobolevsky, S., Kats, P., Malinchik, S., Hoffman, M., Kettler, B., Kontokosta, C.: Twitter Connections Shaping New York City (2018). https://doi.org/10.24251/HICSS.2018.127
18. Cai, H., Zheng, V.W., Chang, K.C.-C.: A comprehensive survey of graph embedding: problems, techniques, and applications. IEEE Trans. Knowl. Data Eng. **30**(9), 1616–1637 (2018). https://doi.org/10.1109/TKDE.2018.2807452

19. Hacker, C., Rieck, B.: On the Surprising Behaviour of node2vec. arXiv preprint arXiv:2206.08252 (2022)
20. Schumacher, T., Wolf, H., Ritzert, M., Lemmerich, F., Grohe, M., Strohmaier, M.: The effects of randomness on the stability of node embeddings. In: Kamp, M., et al. (eds.) ECML PKDD 2021. CCIS, vol. 1524, pp. 197–215. Springer, Cham (2021). https://doi.org/10.1007/978-3-030-93736-2_16
21. Gallicchio, C., Micheli, A.: Fast and deep graph neural networks. In: Proceedings of the AAAI Conference on Artificial Intelligence, vol. 34, no. 04, pp. 3898–3905 (2020)
22. Agarwal, C., Lakkaraju, H., Zitnik, M.: Towards a unified framework for fair and stable graph representation learning. In: Uncertainty in Artificial Intelligence, pp. 2114–2124. PMLR (2021)
23. Page, L., Brin, S., Motwani, R., Winograd, T.: The PageRank citation ranking: bringing order to the web. Stanford infolab (1999)
24. Gleich, D.F.: PageRank beyond the web. SIAM Rev. **57**(3), 321–363 (2015). https://doi.org/10.1137/140976649
25. Kipf, T.N., Welling, M.: Semi-supervised classification with graph convolutional network. In: International Conference on Learning Representations (2017). https://openreview.net/forum?id=SJU4ayYgl
26. United States Census Bureau: Longitudinal Employer-Household Dynamics (2021). https://lehd.ces.census.gov/. Accessed 16 Mar 2023

# Forecasting in Shipments: Comparison of Machine Learning Regression Algorithms on Industrial Applications for Supply Chain

Nunzio Carissimo[1], Raffaele D'Ambrosio[2], Milena Guzzo[1], Sabino Labarile[1], and Carmela Scalone[2([⊠])]

[1] Code Architects, Via Campania, 1-3, 70029 Santeramo in Colle (Bari), Italy
{ncarissimo,mguzzo,slabarile}@codearchitects.com
[2] Department of Information Engineering and Information Science and Mathematics, University of L'Aquila, L'Aquila, Italy
{raffaele.dambrosio,carmela.scalone}@univaq.it

**Abstract.** Supply chains are very complex systems and their correct and efficient management represents a fundamental challenge, in which the practical needs of the corporate world can find answers together with the advanced skills of the academic world. This paper fits exactly in this area. In particular, starting from a project by the company Code Architects, we will illustrate how it is possible to make forecasts on shipments with machine learning tools, which can support business decisions.

**Keywords:** Supply Chain · Forecasting · Random Forest

## 1 Introduction

A supply chain is an entire network of producing and delivering a commodity or a service. It includes all the stages, from the very beginning of the source of the raw materials to the final delivery to customers. Since it involves all the aspects of the production process, such as, materials, informations, human resources and activities, the study and management of the supply chain are as important as it is complex for its correct functioning, see [19] and reference therein. This is also the reason why supply chain management is applied at different levels, with respect to multiple aspects and involves different technical figures. The present work is an example of interaction between academic and industrial cooperation. This is a key point, since, it is fundamental to understand the scopes and the targets from the industrial point of view, while it is decidedly more correct that the modeling, experimental and commentary phase of the results be taken care of by the academic component. The aim of this paper is to provide an analysis, comparing the behaviour of different machine learning algorithms, of an industrial case of study provided by Code Architects company. As pointed out in other works, see [4] and reference therein, it ideally should be interesting

O. Gervasi et al. (Eds.): ICCSA 2023, LNCS 13957, pp. 462–470, 2023.
https://doi.org/10.1007/978-3-031-36808-0_33

to involve in the study the whole supply chain, but, in the majority of the cases this is very difficult to do, due to several reasons, including convergence of business interests, sharing informations, complexity of large scale supply chain, etc. We focus on the part of the supply chain regarding the delivery of the final products to the end-users. In particular, we aim to select an efficient forecasting approach with respect to two fundamental aspects: days of delay in delivery and customer demand. These are typical problems in industrial applications, see for instance [9,20,22]. The products involved in the supply chain delivery step, are from food industry, therefore it appears clear that the delay issue is particularly crucial, not only for customer satisfaction, which is always a variable in play, but also for correct planning that avoids the deterioration of the goods as much as possible. Similar problems are presented in the works [13,14] and [18]. Forecasting, therefore, has an important role in preventing critical situations that have occurred in the past. Another fundamental point is related to the prevision of the demand from the customers.

Forecasting informations on the future demand, i.e. the quantities of commodities ordered, is useful in terms of organization of the stocks, in particular to help in preventing the Bullwhip Effect, i.e. the phenomenon for which small fluctuations in demand at the retail level provokes progressively larger fluctuations in demand at the wholesale, distributor, manufacturer and raw material supplier levels. See [2,8,12], for a deepening on the Bullwhip effect. It is important to highlight that these considerations, both as regards the forecasts of the ordered quantities and as regards possible delays, also have a significant repercussion from an environmental point of view. As anticipated above, since the industrial project concerns food products subject to perishability, an organized and efficient delivery system avoids unnecessary waste. It is well known that these issues are of great actuality and importance.

We proceed with our analysis assuming our forecasting considerations based on the previous data in the delivery process. We consider three different Machine Learning Regression algorithms, basing our choices on the related literature, see [20,22] for instance.

The paper is organized as follows: in Sect. 2, we describe the composition of the data available for our analysis; in Sect. 3 we provide the motivations and brief descriptions of the choosen algorithms. Section 4 is dedicated to the experimental details and results.

## 2   Data

The dataset used, is made up of 180520 rows, each of which represent a shipment. To be more precise, for each shipment (row) we have the following informations:

1. **Customer Id**: an identification number associated to the customer;
2. **Customer Zipcode**: takes into account the distance for shipping;
3. **Product Id**: an identification number associated to the product;
4. **Product Quantity**: the ordered product units;

5. **Product Price**;
6. **Benefit per order**: net income derived from the shipment;
7. **Late Risk**: a binary variable associated to the shipment;
8. **Scheduled days for shipment**;
9. **Real days for shipment**.

The data related to Product Price and Benefict per order are real numbers. The remaining data associated to the other variables are integers. In particular, the Late Risk is binary: 1 is associated to a shipment for which there is a high risk associated to the delay (connected to the particularly high perishability), 0 otherwise. Based on the available data, we are interested in providing an efficient Machine Learning approach able to predict two crucial target variables: real days for shipment and quantities of product ordered. The prevision on the real days for shipment is important to prevent delay situations, comparing real and scheduled days. Preventing delays is important both because we work with perishable food products and for full customer satisfaction. Similarly, forecasting quantities is crucial for efficiently organizing the shipments and prevent the bullwhip effect. Being able to manage shipments in a harmonious way in terms of requests is therefore fundamental for all the correct functioning of the supply chain, and to have an algorithm of machine learning that supports the decisions turns out very profitable.

## 3  Machine Learning Algorithms

The ability of Machine Learning of learn complex relations among data, just using the data, i.e. without any other preliminary and sometimes expensive information (data distributions for instance) is extremely convenient. However, it is well known that, the quality of training dataset is a crucial factor to reach accurate results. In general, Machine Learning algorithms need large volume of data, for better processing and modeling results. This is the reason why, they are widely used in big data analysis. We aim to understand the applicability of Machine Learning models in delay and demand forecasting for our industrial case of study. With the awareness that there is no absolute algorithm better than others, but that the result depends on considerations relating to the company, the market, the product and the availability and structure of the dataset, we analyze and comment on the behavior of different Regression Algorithms, which are suited for our problems. In fact, these are Supervised Learning algorithms, to make predictions and Regression is a process of finding the correlations between dependent and independent variables. In other words, the problem of regression is to find a function that approximates mapping from an input domain to real numbers on the basis of a training sample. In our case, we have as dependent variables quantity/days for shipment and as independent the remaining ones. The model is trained on the "past data", and once the training is completed, it can easily predict the "future data". We compare the following Regression Algorithms:

1. **Support Vector Regression - Linear Kernel**
2. **Gradient Boosting Regression**
3. **Random Forest Regression**

This choice is due to the fact that Gradient Boosting and Random Forest have proved very efficient on problems similar to our. Linear Regression is a classical algorithm and it is interesting to test it and compare. There are several works in litaìerature based on the comparison of algorithms, see [11,16,22]. Now we propose a brief explanation for all the considered algorithms.

### 3.1   Random Forest

As we will see in the next Section, Random Forest is particularly important for our analysis, therefore we are pleased to provide a brief introduction following [5] and [21], which are optimal references for a deepening on this algorithm. Random forests is a supervised machine learning algorithm made up by a combination of tree predictors. The final prediction is made by averaging the predictions of each decision tree. The averaging makes a Random Forest better than a single Decision Tree, in terms of accuracy and reduction of overfitting. As observed in [22], Random Forest is a very convenient and easy to use algorithm, because of default hyper-parameters often produce a good prediction result.

As suggested by the name, a Random Forest is a tree-based ensemble with each tree depending on a collection of random variables. More precisely, for a $p$-dimensional random vector $X = (X_1, ..., X_p)^T$ representing the real-valued input or predictor variables and a random variable $y$ representing the real-valued response, we assume an unknown joint distribution $P_{XY}(X, Y)$. The goal is to find a prediction function $f(X)$ for predicting $Y$. The prediction function is determined by a loss function $L(Y, f(X))$ and defined to minimize the expected value of the loss $\mathbb{E}_{XY} L(Y, f(X))$ where the subscripts denote expectation with respect to the joint distribution of $X$ and $Y$. Intuitively, $L(Y, f(X))$ is a measure of how close $f(X)$ is to $Y$; it penalizes values of $f(X)$ that are a far from $Y$. Typical choices of $L$ are squared error loss

$$L(Y, f(X)) = (Y - f(X))^2$$

for regression. It is known that, minimizing $\mathbb{E}_{XY} L(Y, f(X))$ for squared error loss gives the conditional expectation

$$f(x) = \mathbb{E}_{XY}(Y|X = x)$$

otherwise known as the regression function. Ensembles construct $f$ in terms of a collection of so-called "base learners" $h_1(x), ..., h_J(x)$ and these base learners are combined to give the "ensemble predictor" $f(x)$. In regression, the base learners are averaged

$$f(x) = \frac{1}{J} \sum_{j=1}^{J} h_j(x).$$

In Random Forests the $j$-th base learner is a tree denoted $h_j(X, \Theta_j)$, where $\Theta_j$ is a collection of random variables and the $\Theta_j$'s are independent for $j = 1, .., J$. This is the basic idea of Random Forest, but there are several ways to realize this algorithm. The main feature is a good knowledge of the type of trees used as base learners. See also [3, 21] for further informations and descriptions of the Random Forest algorithm.

## 3.2   Gradient Boosting

In Machine Learning setting, "Boosting" is referred to a combination of multiple simple models into a single composite model. This is also the reason why boosting is called additive model, since simple models (also called weak learners) are added one at a time, while keeping existing trees in the model unchanged. This combination of more and more simple models makes the complete finalmode a stronger predictor. The term "gradient" in "gradient boosting" refers to the fact that the algorithm uses gradient descent to minimize the loss. The function consists of a random output or response variable $y$, and a set of random input variables $X = x_1, .., x_n$. Given a training sample, the aim is to find a function, $F(X)$ that maps $X$ to $y$, such that the loss function is minimized. Gradient Boosting is an efficient Machine Learning algorithm and a greedy additive strategy.

It is an iterative procedure in which, at each step, the residuals of the previous step are fitted, employing a Bass learning model. Gradient Boosting is highly considered and used in scientific literature, see [11, 22].

## 3.3   Support Vector Regression - Linear Kernel

Support Vector Regression is a supervised machine learning algorithm, used to predict discrete values. The main features related to Support Vector Regression are:

1. **Kernel**: the function used to map a lower dimensional data into a higher dimensional data. We consider a linear kernel.
2. **Hyper Plane**: the line to predict the continuous value or target value.
3. **Boundary line**: there are two lines other than Hyper Plane which creates a margin. The support vectors can be on the Boundary lines or outside it. This boundary line separates the two classes.
4. **Support vectors**: this are the data points closest to the boundary. The considered distance of the points is minimum or least.

In Support Vector Regression, the best fit line is the hyperplane that has the maximum number of points. In simple regression, the idea is to minimize the error rate while in Support Vector Regression the idea is to fit the error inside a certain threshold, say $\varepsilon$, which means, work of Support Vector Regression is to approximate the best value within a given margin called $\varepsilon$ - tube. The best fit line is the line hyperplane that has maximum number of points. We refer to [1, 6, 10] and reference therein, for further explanations on the Support Vector Regression algorithms.

# 4    Experimental Setting and Results

We analyze the data-types, dimensions, and missing values in the dataset. We have scaled the variables so that they are normalized with 0 mean and with a standard deviation equal to 1. To do that, we use the MinMaxScaler function in sklearn in Python. We have split the train data-set into a train and a validation data-set using the function train_test_split in Python. We consider the 80% of the dataset as train set (i.e. 144416 data rows). The remaining 20% are used as test set for validation.

## 4.1    Performance Estimation

Let us denote by $\{y\}_{i=1,..n}$ the true variables and by $\{\hat{y}\}_{i=1,..n}$ the predicted variables. For comparing and evaluating the performances of the algorithms we use the following measures:

$$\text{MSE} = \frac{\sum_{i=1}^{n}(y_i - \hat{y}_i)^2}{n}$$

$$\text{MAE} = \frac{\sum_{i=1}^{n}|y_i - \hat{y}_i|}{n}$$

$$R^2 = 1 - \frac{\sum_{i=1}^{n}(y_i - \hat{y}_i)^2}{\sum_{i=1}^{n}(y_i - \overline{y})^2}$$

where $\overline{y} = \frac{1}{n}\sum_{i=1}^{n} y_i$.

The mean square error (MSE) is a risk metric corresponding to the expected value of the squared (quadratic) error or loss. The mean absolute error (MAE) is the risk metric corresponding to the expected value of the absolute error loss or 1-norm loss. We compute the previous errors by using the Python functions mean_absolute_error and mean_absolute_error. $R^2$ si called coefficient of determination and it is computed by the Python function r2_score. $R^2$ represents the proportion of variance (of $y$) that has been explained by the independent variables in the model. It is an indicator of goodness of fit and therefore a measure of how well unseen samples are likely to be predicted by the model, through the proportion of explained variance. It ranges over interval 0 and 1. Best possible score is 1 and it can be negative (because the model can be arbitrarily worse).

## 4.2    Experimental Results

This section is dedicated to show and comment the experimental results. All instances are implemented in Python 3.6.2. All the learning and modeling processes are run on a PC with a 3.5 GHz Intel CoreTM i7-4770 processor and 16 GB RAM. We refer to Python library Scikit-learn, [15]. It should be pointed out that each algorithm has run five times and the outcomes are presented in Tables 1 and 2 are the average values. The metrics of performance are computed with respect to the test set. In Table 1, the results regarding the prediction of demand commodities quantities are reported. We can see that Random Forest and Gradient Boosting have very good performances, with respect all the metrics. Anyway Random Forest show the best performace with respect all the parameters, confirming to be an accurate and stable algorithms. In this case, the Support Vector Regression does not show a good behaviour; in particular the determination coefficient is negative.

In Table 2, we provide the results for prediction of the three choosen Algorithms of the real days for shipping. In this case, Random Forest is not as excellent as in the previous case. However, we get a coefficient of determination equal to 0.8 which makes the algorithm absolutely good. Again Gradient Boosting is slightly below the results of Random Forest, while Support Vector Linear Regression shows very modest accuracy.

**Table 1.** Experimental results of the listed Algorithms for quantity forecasting.

| Algorithms | MSE | MAE | $R^2$ |
|---|---|---|---|
| Random Forest | 0.0595 | 0.053 | 0.97 |
| Gradient Boosting | 0.1724 | 0.053 | 0.92 |
| Support Vector Regression | 2.2072 | 1.068 | −0.05 |

**Table 2.** Experimental results of the listed Algorithms for real days for shipment forecasting.

| Algorithms | MSE | MAE | $R^2$ |
|---|---|---|---|
| Random Forest | 0.5578 | 0.546 | 0.8 |
| Gradient Boosting | 0.5874 | 0.546 | 0.78 |
| Support Vector Regression | 1.0388 | 0.721 | 0.61 |

## 5    Conclusion

Demand forecasting is one of the most vital tasks in supply chain management and also a prerequisite of meeting customers' needs. We can comment on the results obtained by saying that evidently the dataset used is well structured for forecasting demand by the Random Forest algorithm. With less excellent performances, we are able to obtain a good feedback also on the real delivery times, in order to act in advance and avoid delays. This is particularly important for industrial data related to perishable foods. This paper may be seen as a good example of joint academic and industrial research, since a practical industrial issue found a satisfactory answer in the advanced tools of the academic world.

Further data informations may stimulate projects involving classification or cluster algorithms to understand customers behaviour and provide recommendation systems, starting from suited numerica analysis methods (as [7,17]). This may be subject for future research.

**Acknowledgements.** The authors thank the project PON "Ricerca Innovazione" 2014-2020 (PON) risorse FSE-REACT EU - DM 10 agosto 2021, n. 1062.

R. D'Ambrosio and C. Scalone are supported by GNCS-INDAM project and PRIN2017-MIUR project 2017JYCLSF "Structure preserving approximation of evolutionary problems".

This paper is part of the project: **OR.F.E.O.- ORchestrator For Enterprise Omniplatform** Decreto n r.0001497 del 11/03/2020, Progetto n. F/190189/00/X44 Fondo per la Crescita Sostenibile - Sportello "FABBRICA INTELLIGENTE" PON I&C 2014-2020, di cui al D.M. 5 marzo 2018 Capo III.

# References

1. Awad, M., Khanna, R.: Support vector regression. In: Efficient Learning Machines. Apress, Berkeley (2015). https://doi.org/10.1007/978-1-4302-5990-9_4
2. Bhattacharya, R., Bandyopadhyay, S.: A review of the causes of bullwhip effect in a supply chain. Int. J. Adv. Manuf. Technol. **54**, 1245–1261 (2011)
3. Breiman, L.: Random forests. Mach. Learn. **45**, 5–32 (2001)
4. Carbonneau, R., Laframboise, K., Vahidov, R.: Application of machine learning techniques for supply chain demand forecasting. Eur. J. Oper. Res. **1843**, 1140–1154 (2008)
5. Cutler, A., Cutler, D.R., Stevens, J.R.: Random forests. In: Zhang, C., Ma, Y.Q. (eds.) Ensemble Machine Learning, pp. 157–175. Springer, New York (2012). https://doi.org/10.1007/978-1-4419-9326-7_5
6. David Sánchez, A.V.: Advanced support vector machines and kernel methods. Neurocomputing **55**(1–2), 5–20 (2003)
7. Guglielmi, N., Scalone, C.: An efficient method for non-negative low-rank completion. Adv. Comput. Math. **46**(2), 1–25 (2020). https://doi.org/10.1007/s10444-020-09779-x
8. Fransoo, J.C., Wouters, M.J.F.: Measuring the bullwhip effect in the supply chain. Supply Chain Manag. **5**(2), 78–89 (200)
9. Keung, K.L., Lee, C.K.M., Yiu, Y.H.: A machine learning predictive model for shipment delay and demand forecasting for warehouses and sales data. In: 2021 IEEE International Conference on Industrial Engineering and Engineering Management (IEEM) (2021). https://doi.org/10.1109/IEEM50564.2021.9672946
10. Kavitha, S., Varuna, S., Ramya, R.: A comparative analysis on linear regression and support vector regression. In: 2016 Online International Conference on Green Engineering and Technologies (IC-GET) (2016). https://doi.org/10.1109/GET.2016.7916627
11. Islam, S., Amin, S.H.: Prediction of probable backorder scenarios in the supply chain using distributed random forest and gradient boosting machine learning techniques. J. Big Data **7**(1), 1–22 (2020). https://doi.org/10.1186/s40537-020-00345-2
12. Lee, H.L., Padmanabhan, V., Whang, S.: The bullwhip effect in supply chains. Sloan Manag. Rev. **38**(3), 93–102 (1997)

13. Lin, Q., Zhao, Q., Lev, B.: Cold chain transportation decision in the vaccine supply chain. Eur. J. Oper. Res. **283**(1), 182–195 (2020)
14. Mercier, S., Uysal, I.: Neural network models for predicting perishable food temperatures along the supply chain. Biosys. Eng. **171**, 91–100 (2018)
15. Pedregosa, F., et al.: Scikit-learn: machine Learning in Python. J. Mach. Learn. Res. **12**, 2825–2830 (2011)
16. Raczko, E., Zagajewski, B.: Comparison of support vector machine, random forest and neural network classifiers for tree species classification on airborne hyperspectral APEX images. Eur. J. Remote Sens. **50**(1), 144–154 (2017)
17. Scalone, C., Guglielmi, N.: A gradient system for low rank matrix completion. Axioms **7**(3), 51 (2018)
18. Siddh, M.M., Soni, G., Jain, R.: Perishable food supply chain quality (PFSCQ): a structured review and implications for future research. J. Adv. Manag. Res. **12**(3), 292–313 (2015)
19. Stadtler H.: Supply chain management - an overview. In: Stadtler, H., Kilger, C. (eds) Supply Chain Management and Advanced Planning, pp. 9–36. Springer, Heidelberg (2008). https://doi.org/10.1007/978-3-540-74512-9_2
20. Vairagade, N., Logofatu, D., Leon, F., Muharemi, F.: Demand forecasting using random forest and artificial neural network for supply chain management. In: Nguyen, N.T., Chbeir, R., Exposito, E., Aniorté, P., Trawiński, B. (eds.) ICCCI 2019. LNCS (LNAI), vol. 11683, pp. 328–339. Springer, Cham (2019). https://doi.org/10.1007/978-3-030-28377-3_27
21. Zhang, C., Ma, Y.: Ensemble Machine Learning: Methods and Applications. Springer, New York (2012). https://doi.org/10.1007/978-1-4419-9326-7
22. Zohdi, M., Rafiee, M., Kayvanfar, V., Salamiraad, A.: Demand forecasting based machine learning algorithms on customer information: an applied approach. Int. J. Inf. Technol. **14**(4), 1937–1947 (2022)

# An Unseen Features-Enriched Lifelong Machine Learning Framework

Nesar Ahmad Wasi$^{(\boxtimes)}$ and Muhammad Abulaish

Department of Computer Science, South Asian University, New Delhi 110068, India
nesarahmadwasi17@gmail.com, abulaish@sau.ac.in

**Abstract.** The dialect of a machine learning model is comprised of the features encountered during training. Nonetheless, as time passes, a deployed machine learning model may encounter certain features for the first time. In conventional machine learning approaches, newly observed features are typically discarded during testing data sample preprocessing. In lifelong machine learning, newly observed features may have appeared in the feature space of previously learned tasks; consequently, the knowledge associated with those features present in the knowledge base is incorporated to handle these features. However, there may be some features that have yet to appear in the knowledge base; lifelong machine learning also discards such features. Features that were not seen before are called *unseen features*. In this paper, we propose an enhanced lifelong machine learning framework for handling *unseen features* during the testing phase that incorporates *relative knowledge*. To extract *relative knowledge*, we retrieve semantically similar features using a language model. In addition, semantically similar features are examined in the knowledge base, and the knowledge of those present in the knowledge base is incorporated in order to deal with *unseen features*. Experiments conducted on the Amazon review dataset indicate that the proposed method outperforms three baselines and is competitive with state-of-the-art methods.

**Keywords:** Unseen Features · Lifelong Machine Learning · Continual Learning

## 1 Introduction

Data diversity is essential to generalize an unseen data sample using a machine learning model. The benefit of data diversity is that it enables the machine learning model to learn an accurate representation of the task's features. Lifelong Machine Learning (LML) is a process of continuous learning that retains knowledge acquired from previous learning tasks and uses this knowledge to learn incoming tasks. LML has a knowledge base that typically includes features that the model may not have seen for the current task, but there is a high likelihood that these features have appeared in previous tasks. Therefore, knowledge from the knowledge base is utilized to handle the unseen feature. However, there

© The Author(s), under exclusive license to Springer Nature Switzerland AG 2023
O. Gervasi et al. (Eds.): ICCSA 2023, LNCS 13957, pp. 471–481, 2023.
https://doi.org/10.1007/978-3-031-36808-0_34

may be unseen features that neither the model nor the knowledge base has covered; such features are typically discarded during the preprocessing phase of the testing data sample. Because unseen features lack associated knowledge, it is difficult to incorporate them during classification.

In this paper, an unseen features-enriched lifelong machine learning (ULML) framework is proposed to address the problem of unseen features utilizing relative knowledge. We propose two methods for extracting *relative knowledge*: a synonym-based approach and a language model-based approach. In the synonym-based approach, the external dictionary's synonyms are extracted to extract *relative knowledge* for the unseen feature. The extracted synonyms are explored in the knowledge base, and the average weight associated with those features that are present in the knowledge base is assigned to the unseen feature. To handle unseen features in the language model-based approach, we identify semantically similar features to the unseen feature present in the language model itself [16].

This paper extends the approach proposed by [4] to the ULML framework. The method proposed in [4] extends Naïve Bayes to the LML setting. As regularization terms, two types of knowledge, namely domain-level and document-level knowledge, are incorporated. The training phase of our approach is identical to the one proposed by [4]. During the testing phase, however, unseen features are implemented based on *relative knowledge*. We have conducted extensive experiments on the Amazon review dataset. We compared the performance of the proposed approach to three baselines and one state-of-the-art method. Extensive empirical tests indicate that the proposed approach is better than three baseline methods and is comparable to the state-of-the-art method.

The rest of the paper is organized as follows. In Sect. 2, we have discussed related works. In Sect. 3, the proposed ULML framework is discussed. In Sect. 4, we discuss the experimental setup and results of the proposed approach. We also present performance, comparative analysis, and limitations of the proposed approach in Sect. 4. Finally, we conclude the paper in Sect. 5.

## 2    Related Works

The concept of Lifelong Machine Learning (LML) was first proposed by [21]. Though the concept of LML is similar to learning paradigms such as Transfer Learning (TL) [14], Multi-Task Learning (MTL) [27], and Online Learning [8], however, the core difference is that the knowledge transfer is not continues in the aforementioned paradigms. Thereafter, [20] used the idea of LML to formulate a binary classification problem for concept learning. [19] proposed an LML approach to extend the concept of MTL to the lifelong setting.

The approach proposed by [4] extended Naïve Bayes to the LML framework and utilized stochastic gradient descent to optimize domain-dependent and domain-independent knowledge in the Naïve Bayes. Further, they applied their approach to the sentiment classification task. Further, [24] proposed an LML approach to handle the difference between opinion and aspect words in

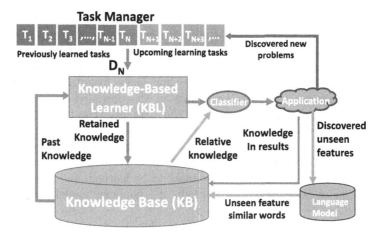

**Fig. 1.** The overall workflow of the unseen features enriched lifelong machine learning framework

an aspect-based sentiment classification task. In [22], the authors extended the work of [4] and proposed an LML approach for the sentiment classification task that can transfer knowledge to the future and previously learned tasks. In [23], a Bayes-enhanced deep learning approach is proposed that uses the generative parameters of Naïve Bayes to learn knowledge used in attention networks. Further, [23]'s approach is used for the task of sentiment classification.

In [10], the authors proposed a neural network-based continual learning approach for sentiment classification that is able to transfer knowledge learned from the previous tasks to the current task as well as it is able to enhance the performance of those tasks that are previously learned by incorporating knowledge learned from the current task. In [7], an iterative pruning approach is utilized for pruning the unwanted parameters in a deep learning network. By using pruning, it is able to free up space that can later be used to learn new tasks. They also adopted an uncertainty regularization based on the Bayesian framework while updating the weights associated with the previously learned tasks, which as a result, facilitate the learning in previously learned tasks to have positive knowledge transfer.

The significant difference between our approach and all aforementioned approaches is in utilizing unseen features. The idea of unseen features was first proposed by [25]. To the best of our knowledge, we are the first to incorporate unseen features in lifelong machine learning.

## 3   Unseen Features Enriched Lifelong Machine Learning Framework (ULML)

In this section, we propose a lifelong machine learning (LML) framework in which unseen features that appear for the first time during the testing phase are utilized. LML is a continuous learning paradigm that aims to mimic how human beings learn. In the LML paradigm, a machine learning model has faced $n-1$ tasks; when it faces $n^{th}$ task, it can leverage the knowledge learned from the previous $n-1$ tasks. An approach is called an LML approach if it is able to continuously learn, store, and extract new knowledge from the task it faces [3].

Figure 1 presents the overall workflow of the proposed framework. Starting from assigning Task $T_N$ along with the data $D_N$, the task is assigned to the knowledge-based learner to learn new knowledge from data $D_n$ and utilize knowledge in the knowledge base to train the classifier. The classifier is deployed to the retrospective application area. In LML, it can identify new problems, which can further be assigned as new tasks to be learned, and discover unseen features that can be learned with the help of a language model and knowledge base.

From Fig. 1, it can be observed that the ULML framework has four main components, namely, Task Manager (TM), Knowledge-Based-Learner (KBL), Knowledge Base (KB), and Language Model. TM manages the arrival of incoming tasks as well as manages the tasks previously learned by KBL. KBL learns and mines knowledge from the training data of the incoming tasks and stores the results in KB. When the classifier is employed in the application area, it may face some features that are not present in the features space of KB. For each unseen feature, the most similar features are extracted from language model. The extracted features are looked at in the KB to get knowledge of similar features from KB. Further, the average of the similar features found in KB is computed and assigned to the unseen feature, and the knowledge is termed as *relative knowledge*.

In this paper, we extend the approach proposed by [4] to the ULML framework. In the approach presented by [4], the Naïve Bayes is extended to the lifelong machine learning setting. Naïve Bayes is a probabilistic generative model [13] that uses Bayes Rule [1]. Bayes theorem was first applied to text classification by [12].

$$c_{pred} = \operatorname*{argmax}_{c_k \in C} P(c_k|d) \tag{1}$$

In Naïve Bayes, in order to classify a document $d$ to the corresponding class label $c \in C$, Eq. (1) is used. In Eq. (1), each document $d$ can also be represented using set of features $f_1, f_2, f_3, \cdots, f_n$. The base for Naïve Bayes is the Bayes theorem, which calculates the conditional probability of each feature given class $c_k$.

$$P(f|c_k) = \frac{F_{c_k,f} + \lambda}{\sum_{v=1}^{|V|} F_{c_k,f_v} + \lambda|V|} \tag{2}$$

In Eq. (2), $F_{c_k,f}$ is the frequency of feature $f_i$ appeared in class $c_k$. The main parameter of Naïve Bayes is $F_{c_k,f}$. $\lambda$ is the smoothing parameter. $|V|$ denotes the number of features present in the vocabulary. In Naïve Bayes, each feature $f_i$ in a document $d$ is assumed to be independent of each other. The Naïve Bayes classifier for a document $d$ is defined as (3).

$$P(c_p|d) = \frac{P(c_p)\prod_{f_i \in |V|} P(f_i|c)}{\sum_{b=1}^{2} P(c_b)\prod_{f_i \in |V|} P(f_i|c)} \tag{3}$$

For correct classification of the document $d$ in a binary classification setting, the $P(c_p|d) = 1$ and $P(c_q|d) = 0$, where $c_p$ is the label of the positive class, and $c_q$ is the label of the negative class.

$$\underset{c_k \in C}{\operatorname{argmax}} P(c_p|d) - P(c_q|d) \tag{4}$$

In order to solve the optimization problem in Eq. (4), Stochastic Gradient Descent (SGD) is used. SGD updates the expected frequency of feature $f_i$. To differentiate the expected frequency from the actual frequency of the feature $f_i$, i.e., $F_{c_k,f}$, the expected frequency of feature $f_i$ is denoted by $X_{c_k,f}$. The starting point for SGD is $F_{c_k,f}^t + F_{c_k,f}^{KB}$, where $F_{c_k,f}^t$ is the frequency of feature $f$ in target domain $t$, and $F_{c_k,f}^{KB}$ is the frequency of feature $f$ in KB.

During the training phase of the proposed approach, two types of knowledge – domain-dependent and domain-level knowledge are incorporated in the form of regularization terms. For both types of knowledge, two vocabularies, $V_t$, and $V_{KB}$ are constructed for both types of knowledge. Domain-dependent knowledge ensures that features appear in $V_t$ are those features that are highly reliable in the target domain, i.e., $\frac{P(f_i|+)}{P(f_i|-)} \geq \sigma$ or $\frac{P(f_i|-)}{P(f_i|+)} \geq \sigma$, number of documents is denoted by $\sigma$.

$$\frac{1}{2} \sum_{f \in V_t} \left( \left(X_{+,f} - F_{+,f}^t\right)^2 + \left(X_{-,f} - F_{-,f}^t\right)^2 \right) \tag{5}$$

Features that appeared in more number of previous tasks/domains compared to those features that are highly specific to some domains are more reliable. Domain frequency of each feature is recorded, and a list of features is constructed for those features that appear in a substantial number of domains, i.e., $R_{+,f}^{KB} \geq \tau$ or $R_{-,f}^{KB} \geq \tau$, the $\tau$ denoted number of domains. $V_d$ denotes the list of domain-level knowledge.

$$\begin{aligned} &\tfrac{1}{2}\alpha \sum_{f \in V_d} \left( \left(X_{+,f} - M_f \times \left(F_{+,f}^t + F_{+,f}^{KB}\right)\right)^2 \right. \\ &\left. + \left(X_{-,f} - M_f \times \left(F_{-,f}^t + F_{-,f}^{KB}\right)\right)^2 \right) \end{aligned} \tag{6}$$

In Eq. (6), $M_f$ is equal to $R_{+,f}^{KB} / \left(R_{+,f}^{KB} + R_{-,f}^{KB}\right)$. Equations (5) and (6) are incorporated along with Eq. (4) as penalty terms to leverage document-level and domain-level knowledge. Further, SGD is employed to train the machine learning model.

---

**Algorithm 1:** ULML for a document $d_p$ of target domain in testing phase.

---

**Input**  : Document $d_p$ having features $\{f_1, f_2, \ldots, f_n\}$, $\mathcal{F}_{kb}$ vocabulary of
features of all domains, parametric weight $X_{\pm, f_i}$ of all features.

**Output:** Predicted sentiment label of the document $d_p$.

1  **for** *each feature $f_i \in d_p$* **do**
2      **if** *$f_i$ belongs to $\mathcal{F}_{kb}$* **then**
3         $F_{+, f_i} \leftarrow X_{+, f_i}$
4         $F_{-, f_i} \leftarrow X_{-, f_i}$
5      **else**
6         $F_{+, f_i} \leftarrow \hat{P}(f_i|+)$              #Equation (8)
7         $F_{-, f_i} \leftarrow \hat{P}(f_i|-)$              #Equation (8)
8      **end**
9  **end**
10 **return** $\text{argmax}_{c_k \in \{+,-\}} P(c_k|d_p)$              #Equation (1)

---

## 3.1  Relative Knowledge Extraction

During the testing phase, when document $d_p = \{f_1, f_2, f_3, \ldots, f_{|d_p|}\}$ is fed to a classifier to predict its class label, there may exist some features which are not present in the features space of all previously learned domains as well as features space of the target domain stored in the knowledge base, i.e.,

$$\mathcal{F}_u = \forall f_i \notin \mathcal{F}_{kb} \quad where, \ 1 \le i \le |d_p| \tag{7}$$

In Eq. (7), $\mathcal{F}_{kb}$ denotes features space of the knowledge base, and $\mathcal{F}_u$ denotes unseen features. In order to detect $\mathcal{F}_u$, Eq. (7), is used. As $\mathcal{F}_u$ are those features that the classier has not seen before and do not carry direct knowledge with them; therefore, it is hard to utilize. In order to utilize such features, language models, such as Word2Vec [11], GloVe [16], BERT [6], Fastext [9], ELMO [17], XLNet [26], GPT [18] can be instrumental. Language models can be used to extract relative knowledge of $\mathcal{F}_u$ features, as language models are vector-spaced representations of words that preserve contexts and semantics.

To extract relative knowledge associated with the features identified as unseen features $\mathcal{F}_u$, those features that are semantically similar to the unseen feature are extracted from the language model. Because language models are high-dimensional vector representations, a multi-dimensional data structure is used to index all features present in the language model. K-dimensional tree [2], is used as the multi-dimensional data structure. In order to extract semantically similar features for the unseen feature, the nearest neighbor approach [5] is used. Further, the extracted features denoted by $\mathcal{S}_u$ are looked in KB, i.e., $\exists \mathcal{S}_u \in KB$. The list of semantically similar features discovered in KB is denoted by $\mathcal{R}_u$.

The average weight associated with features $\mathcal{R}_u$ is calculated and assigned to the unseen feature using Eq. (8).

$$\hat{P}(F_u|c_k) = \frac{\sum_{r=1}^{|\mathcal{R}_u|} P(\mathcal{R}_u^r|c_k)}{|\mathcal{R}_u|} \tag{8}$$

Algorithm 1 presents the procedure of ULML to handle unseen features during the testing phase. In Algorithm 1, in order to detect the polarity of the document $d_p$ during the testing phase, we need $\mathcal{F}_{kb}$, i.e., the vocabulary of features that appeared in all previous domains to check whether the feature $f_i \in d_p$ is an unseen feature. If feature $f_i$ already appears in previous domains, the parametric weight $X_{\pm,f_i}$ is assigned to the feature $f_i$. Else $f_i$ will be assigned relative knowledge extract using Eq. (8).

# 4    Experimental Setup and Results

In order to perform experiments, we use the same dataset[1] as used in the work of [4]. This dataset contains reviews from 20 different types of products. It is extracted from Amazon.com. This dataset has 1000 reviews for each type of product. Each review present in the dataset is labeled as *positive, negative,* or *neutral.* Those reviews with a rating greater than 3 are labeled as *positive.* Those reviews with a rating less than 3 are labeled as *negative,* and those reviews with a rating of exactly 3 are labeled as *neutral.* As the setting of the problem is a binary classification problem, the neutral reviews are discarded from the experiments. The complete statistics of the dataset are presented in Table 1. As per Table 1, the dataset is skewed towards the positive class. Therefore, the minority class is the negative class which is very hard to classify.

In each domain, we randomly partition data into train and test partitions, and the ratio of both train and test in each domain is set to $80\% : 20\%$, respectively. We have used the 5-fold cross-validation strategy for performance evaluation. In our experiments, we have used uni-gram features. In order to handle negation words, we followed [15]'s approach. To handle negation during the pre-processing phase, we prefix the token *"Not_"* to each word that appears after a logical negation word, i.e., *n't, not, no,* and *never* in the document until the next punctuation mark appears. We have used the default parameters for all baselines or as specified in the original paper. In order to extract relative knowledge in ULML-G, we have used the pre-trained GloVe [16] language model. We extract the top 35 similar features from the language model. We experimented with different numbers of top similar features. We got the best results with the top 35. In ULML-S, we have used the synonyms of the unseen feature. To extract synonyms, we have used *GroupDocs.search*[2] API. Further, knowledge associated with those synonyms that appeared in the knowledge base is incorporated as relative knowledge.

---

[1] https://www.cs.uic.edu/~zchen/downloads/ACL2015-Chen-Datasets.zip.
[2] https://docs.groupdocs.com/search/java/synonym-search.

**Table 1.** The proportion of negative instances in each domain of the dataset.

| Domain | Proportion | Domain | Proportion |
|---|---|---|---|
| Alarm Clock | 30.51 | Baby | 16.45 |
| Bag | 11.97 | Cable Modem | 12.53 |
| Dumbbell | 16.04 | Flashlight | 11.69 |
| Gloves | 19.50 | GPS | 13.76 |
| Graphics Card | 14.58 | Headphone | 20.99 |
| Home Theater System | 28.84 | Jewelry | 12.21 |
| Keyboard | 22.66 | Magazine Subscriptions | 26.88 |
| Movies TV | 10.86 | Projector | 20.24 |
| Rice Cooker | 18.64 | Sandal | 12.11 |
| Vacuum | 22.07 | Video Games | 20.93 |

**Table 2.** F1-Score: Performance evaluation results of the proposed approach and all baselines to identify the negative (minority) class which is harder to identify.

| Domain | NB-S | NB-T | NB-ST | LSC | ULML-S | ULML-G |
|---|---|---|---|---|---|---|
| Alarm Clock | 45.722 | 64.71 | 64.71 | 78.56 | 79.48 | 78.45 |
| Baby | 39.34 | 46.51 | 41.03 | 62.76 | 61.95 | 62.47 |
| Bag | 34.29 | 62.22 | 63.16 | 66.28 | 66.26 | 66.59 |
| Gloves | 30.30 | 57.14 | 57.78 | 74.54 | 50.70 | 74.66 |
| Headphone | 52.27 | 56.66 | 52.78 | 66.14 | 65.93 | 65.48 |
| Home Theater System | 76.09 | 71.73 | 82.00 | 81.64 | 81.73 | 81.27 |
| Magazine Subscriptions | 48.65 | 79.23 | 64.71 | 67.95 | 67.98 | 69.05 |
| Projector | 65.57 | 61.54 | 71.43 | 74.63 | 74.08 | 74.06 |
| Rice Cooker | 60.71 | 69.84 | 69.84 | 69.82 | 69.82 | 69.60 |
| Sandal | 50.00 | 45.16 | 50.00 | 54.01 | 53.75 | 53.75 |
| Average over top 10 domains | 50.29 | 61.47 | 61.74 | 69.63 | 67.17 | 69.54 |

## 4.1  Performance and Comparative Analysis

In order to evaluate the performance of the proposed approach, we compare it with three variants of Naïve Bayes (NB) and one state-of-the-art approach, i.e., lifelong learning for sentiment classification (LSC) [4]. While performing experiments, each domain is considered the target domain, while the rest 19 domains are considered non-target domains. As NB is a classification approach that works on a single domain at once, it is fed with three types of data to have a fair comparison. *NB-S* is trained using data from non-target domains. *NB-T* is a traditional supervised learning model. *NB-ST* is trained using data from both target and non-target domains. All the above approaches are tested using data from the target domain. *LSC* is the state-of-the-art approach that we used as our primary baseline. *NB-T* do not use data from other domains(tasks); therefore, it can be regarded as a non-lifelong machine learning approach. Since *NB-S* and *NB-ST* incorporate data from other domains (tasks), these approaches can be regarded as basic lifelong machine learning approaches.

From Table 2, it can be observed that in *NB-ST*, simply incorporating data from other domains during training is an advantageous task. In Table 2, it can be seen that *NB-S* and *NB-T* are inferior to *NB-ST*. However, *NB-ST* is inferior to our proposed approaches, i.e., *ULML-G* and *ULML-S*. In *ULML-G*, we have used the knowledge extracted from the language model for the unseen feature. In *ULML-S*, we have used the knowledge extracted from synonyms of unseen features present in KB. In both proposed approaches (ULML-G and ULML-S), when we used relative knowledge associated with the unseen feature from GloVe, it performed better compared to the synonym-based approach. The prime reason that the proposed approach is not able to get competitive results in some domains compared to the state-of-the-art approach is the lack of correct relative knowledge in the knowledge base. Because unseen words appear for the first time during the testing phase, therefore, are very hard to handle.

### 4.2  Limitations

When a machine-learning model is deployed in an application domain, a testing data sample cannot be directly fed to the machine-learning model (trained model) for prediction. To prepare the testing sample for the trained model, it must go through a preprocessing phase. A testing data sample may contain features that the model has never seen before (traditionally, the unseen features are discarded during this phase); our approach is able to extract relative knowledge with the assistance of a language model and knowledge base, allowing us to incorporate the unseen features. As these features emerge for the first time, a lack of accurate knowledge can hinder prediction. Suppose there are insufficient semantically similar features to an unseen feature in the knowledge base. In that case, the relative knowledge assigned to the unseen feature will be incorrect and detrimental to the classification task. A further limitation of the proposed method is that we discard unseen features absent from the language model. However, such features can be managed more efficiently. We believe that addressing the aforementioned issue is beyond the scope of this paper because it involves the concept of the language model's out-of-vocabulary problem.

## 5  Conclusion

In this paper, we proposed a framework for lifelong machine learning that incorporates features that emerge for the first time when a machine learning model is deployed. First, unseen features are identified by comparing the features space of the incoming document to the features space of tasks contained within the knowledge base. We proposed two approaches, ULML-S and ULML-G, for handling unseen features. In ULML-S, we have utilized knowledge associated with synonyms of unseen features. In ULML-G, similar words are retrieved from the language model for an unseen feature. In addition, knowledge associated with similar words is extracted from the knowledge base. The retrieved knowledge is assigned to the unseen features. We conducted exhaustive experiments on the Amazon review dataset. We compared the performance of the proposed method to three baselines and one state-of-the-art method. The performance evaluation results indicate that the proposed method outperforms the three baseline methods and is competitive with the state-of-the-art method.

# References

1. Bayes, T.: An essay towards solving a problem in the doctrine of chances. Philos. Trans. R. Soc. Lond. (53), 370–418 (1763)
2. Bentley, J.L.: Multidimensional binary search trees used for associative searching. Commun. ACM **18**(9), 509–517 (1975). https://doi.org/10.1145/361002.361007
3. Chen, Z., Liu, B.: Lifelong Machine Learning, 2nd edn. Morgan & Claypool Publishers, San Rafael (2018)
4. Chen, Z., Ma, N., Liu, B.: Lifelong learning for sentiment classification. In: Proceedings of the 53rd Annual Meeting of the Association for Computational Linguistics and the 7th International Joint Conference on Natural Language Processing (Volume 2: Short Papers, Beijing, China), pp. 750–756. Association for Computational Linguistics (2015). https://doi.org/10.3115/v1/P15-2123
5. Cover, T.: Estimation by the nearest neighbor rule. IEEE Trans. Inf. Theory **14**(1), 50–55 (1968). https://doi.org/10.1109/TIT.1968.1054098
6. Devlin, J., Chang, M., Lee, K., Toutanova, K.: BERT: pre-training of deep bidirectional transformers for language understanding. In: Proceedings of the 2019 Conference of the North American Chapter of the Association for Computational Linguistics: Human Language Technologies, NAACL-HLT, Minneapolis, MN, USA, 2–7 June, pp. 4171–4186. Association for Computational Linguistics (2019). https://doi.org/10.18653/v1/n19-1423
7. Geng, B., Yang, M., Yuan, F., Wang, S., Ao, X., Xu, R.: Iterative network pruning with uncertainty regularization for lifelong sentiment classification. In: Proceedings of the 44th International ACM SIGIR Conference on Research and Development in Information Retrieval, SIGIR 2021, pp. 1229–1238. Association for Computing Machinery, New York (2021). https://doi.org/10.1145/3404835.3462902
8. Hoi, S.C., Sahoo, D., Lu, J., Zhao, P.: Online learning: a comprehensive survey. Neurocomputing **459**, 249–289 (2021). https://doi.org/10.1016/j.neucom.2021.04.112
9. Joulin, A., Grave, E., Bojanowski, P., Douze, M., Jégou, H., Mikolov, T.: Fasttext.zip: compressing text classification models. CoRR abs/1612.03651 (2016). https://doi.org/10.48550/arXiv.1612.03651
10. Ke, Z., Liu, B., Wang, H., Shu, L.: Continual learning with knowledge transfer for sentiment classification. In: Hutter, F., Kersting, K., Lijffijt, J., Valera, I. (eds.) ECML PKDD 2020. LNCS (LNAI), vol. 12459, pp. 683–698. Springer, Cham (2021). https://doi.org/10.1007/978-3-030-67664-3_41
11. Mikolov, T., Chen, K., Corrado, G., Dean, J.: Efficient estimation of word representations in vector space. In: Proceedings of the 1st International Conference on Learning Representations, ICLR, Scottsdale, Arizona, USA, 2–4 May, Workshop Track Proceedings (2013). https://doi.org/10.48550/arXiv.1301.3781
12. Mosteller, F., Wallace, D.L.: The Federalist: Inference and Disputed Authorship. Addison-Wesley, Boston (1964)

13. Nigam, K., McCallum, A., Thrun, S., Mitchell, T.: Learning to classify text from labeled and unlabeled documents. In: Proceedings of the 15th AAAI Conference on Artificial Intelligence, pp. 792–799. AAAI Press (1998). https://doi.org/10.5555/295240.295806

14. Pan, S.J., Yang, Q.: A survey on transfer learning. IEEE Trans. Knowl. Data Eng. **22**(10), 1345–1359 (2010). https://doi.org/10.1109/TKDE.2009.191

15. Pang, B., Lee, L., Vaithyanathan, S.: Thumbs up? Sentiment classification using machine learning techniques. In: Proceedings of the 7th Conference on Empirical Methods in Natural Language Processing (EMNLP), pp. 79–86. Association for Computational Linguistics (2002). https://doi.org/10.3115/1118693.1118704

16. Pennington, J., Socher, R., Manning, C.D.: GloVe: global vectors for word representation. In: Proceedings of the 2014 Conference on Empirical Methods in Natural Language Processing, EMNLP 2014, 25–29 October 2014, Doha, Qatar, pp. 1532–1543. ACL (2014). https://doi.org/10.3115/v1/D14-1162

17. Peters, M.E., et al.: Deep contextualized word representations. In: Proceedings of the 2018 Conference of the North American Chapter of the Association for Computational Linguistics: Human Language Technologies, Volume 1 (Long Papers), New Orleans, Louisiana, pp. 2227–2237. Association for Computational Linguistics (2018). https://doi.org/10.18653/v1/N18-1202

18. Radford, A., Narasimhan, K., Salimans, T., Sutskever, I.: Improving language understanding by generative pre-training (2018)

19. Ruvolo, P., Eaton, E.: Ella: an efficient lifelong learning algorithm. In: Proceedings of the 30th International Conference on Machine Learning, pp. 507–515. JMLR.org (2013)

20. Thrun, S.: Is learning the n-th thing any easier than learning the first? In: Proceedings of the Conference on Advances in Neural Information Processing Systems, pp. 640–646. The MIT Press (1996)

21. Thrun, S., Mitchell, T.M.: Lifelong robot learning. Robot. Auton. Syst. **15**(1), 25–46 (1995)

22. Wang, H., Liu, B., Wang, S., Ma, N., Yang, Y.: Forward and backward knowledge transfer for sentiment classification. In: Proceedings of The 11th Asian Conference on Machine Learning, ACML, pp. 457–472. PMLR (2019). https://doi.org/10.48550/arXiv.1906.0350

23. Wang, H., Wang, S., Mazumder, S., Liu, B., Yang, Y., Li, T.: Bayes-enhanced lifelong attention networks for sentiment classification. In: Proceedings of the 28th International Conference on Computational Linguistics, pp. 580–591. International Committee on Computational Linguistics (2020). https://doi.org/10.18653/v1/2020.coling-main.50

24. Wang, S., Zhou, M., Mazumder, S., Liu, B., Chang, Y.: Disentangling aspect and opinion words in target-based sentiment analysis using lifelong learning. CoRR abs/1802.05818, pp. 1–7 (2018). https://doi.org/10.48550/arXiv.1802.05818

25. Wasi, N.A., Abulaish, M.: An unseen features enhanced text classification approach. In: The Prodings of the International Joint Conference on Neural Networks (IJCNN), Queensland, Australia, p. 8 (2023)

26. Yang, Z., Dai, Z., Yang, Y., Carbonell, J., Salakhutdinov, R.R., Le, Q.V.: Xlnet: generalized autoregressive pretraining for language understanding. In: Proceedings of the 32th Advances in Neural Information Processing Systems, vol. 32. Curran Associates, Inc. (2019). https://doi.org/10.5555/3454287.3454804

27. Zhang, Y., Yang, Q.: A survey on multi-task learning. IEEE Trans. Knowl. Data Eng. **34**(12), 5586–5609 (2022). https://doi.org/10.1109/TKDE.2021.3070203

# Urban Zoning Using Intraday Mobile Phone-Based Commuter Patterns in the City of Brno

Yuri Bogomolov[1](✉)(iD), Alexander Belyi[1](iD), Ondřej Mikeš[2](iD),
and Stanislav Sobolevsky[1,3,4](iD)

[1] Department of Mathematics and Statistics, Faculty of Science, Masaryk University,
Kotlarska 2, 611 37 Brno, Czech Republic
bogomoloviura@gmail.com , ss9872@nyu.edu
[2] RECETOX, Masaryk University, Kamenice 753/5, 625 00 Brno, Czech Republic
[3] Center for Urban Science and Progress, New York University, 370 Jay Street,
Brooklyn, NY 11201, USA
[4] Institute of Law and Technology, Faculty of Law, Masaryk University, Veveri 70,
611 80 Brno, Czech Republic

**Abstract.** The emergence of information and mobile technology has had a profound impact on modern life, altering the manner in which individuals communicate, access information, entertain themselves, and conduct business. This development has created new opportunities for researchers to access datasets that were not accessible to prior generations of scholars. Historically, studies of urban commuting have relied on census data, which portrays commute patterns as a static number that are updated every few years. However, over the last two decades, the advent of mobile phone datasets has facilitated new research avenues. This study employs mobile phone mobility data to define a signature of urban districts within the Czech city of Brno, utilizing it for the purpose of urban zoning. The proposed signatures provide a tangible classification of neighborhoods with potential applications in urban and transportation planning. This approach is demonstrated using mobile data of 13 thousand inhabitants of Brno and can be applied to other cities wherever similar data is available.

**Keywords:** Intraday commute patterns · Urban commute · City delineation · Urban zoning · Mobile phone mobility data

## 1 Introduction

Understanding commute patterns is crucial for city planning, as it can inform decisions on transportation infrastructure, public transport services, and urban development. Existing models are used to predict commute flows based on the spatial structure of cities [1].

The four-step transportation model [7] is a widely used approach for analyzing and forecasting transportation patterns in urban areas. The model consists of four sequential steps: trip generation, trip distribution, mode choice, and trip assignment. After trips are generated based on the population and household data the model matches trip origins with destinations based on commute patterns.

The gravity model [21] is often used to model commute patterns because it provides a simple yet effective way to estimate the volume of traffic between two locations based on distance and attractiveness. In the context of commuting, the gravity model assumes that the volume of traffic ($T_{ij}$) between two locations ($i$ and $j$) is proportional to the product of their attractiveness ($P_i$, $P_j$) and inversely proportional to some increasing function $f(d)$ of the trip distance or travel time:

$$T_{ij} \propto \frac{P_i P_j}{f(d)} \qquad (1)$$

In 2012, Simini et al. proposed the radiation model [11], which accounts attractiveness of neighboring nodes to model commute flows between locations $i$ and $j$. But the commute is still considered a static flow by the model. In 2021, Schlapfer et al. proposed the universal visitation law of human mobility [10] to describe visit frequencies. However, none of these models cover the time component of the commute, which is crucial to address traffic congestion during peak hours. While existing models focus on the commute flow and frequency, understanding intraday commute patterns is important for city planning for several reasons:

**Infrastructure Planning:** Intraday commute patterns help city planners to identify the areas where traffic congestion is most common and determine the necessary infrastructure improvements to alleviate traffic flow. For instance, if there is heavy traffic congestion during the morning rush hour, city planners can determine if it is caused by too few lanes, too few exits, or a bottleneck that requires additional infrastructure.

**Public Transport Planning:** Knowing intraday commute patterns is crucial for planning and improving public transport services. City planners can identify areas with high passenger demand and optimize routes and schedules accordingly. This can help reduce waiting times and improve passenger comfort and convenience, encouraging more people to use public transportation.

**Parking Management:** Understanding intraday commute patterns helps city planners to optimize parking facilities in areas with high traffic volumes. By analyzing parking utilization patterns, city planners can determine the optimal number of parking spaces required and adjust the pricing structure to encourage carpooling, cycling, or using public transportation.

**Environmental Impact:** Intraday commute patterns can provide insights into the environmental impact of transportation on a city. By identifying areas with high traffic congestion, city planners can implement measures such as low-emission zones, carpooling or bike-sharing programs, and promote sustainable transport options. For example, the negative health impact of congested traffics flows could be reduced if the peak traffic hours do not overlap with the drop-off and pick-up time in neighboring schools.

The lack of hourly datasets limits the research of intraday commute patterns. Previous attempts covered only narrow mobility flows like bicycle commuting in Melbourne [12] or taxi trips in New York City [4]. The mobile phone data was successfully used to study the city structure based on the population density [15], mobility patterns [19,20] and their relation to socioeconomic status [17,18], urban park catchment areas [5], and changes in the average distance between individuals [6].

Defining city and district boundaries is known to be a challenge [2,3]. Previous attempts to define district signatures and use them for district clustering were based on the municipal request datasets [14], financial activities [13], and mobile call records [8,9,16]. However, all these events are generated only in case of particular activities and therefore have limited coverage. Also, the resulting clusters did not reflect the mobility and transportation needs of inhabitants.

In this paper, we propose to use the mobile origin-destination commute data to build district mobility signatures based on the hourly commute patterns and then use these signatures to group districts into areas with similar temporal patterns. Mobile flow data can be collected for any modern city, which makes the proposed approach generally applicable, while the district signatures provide insights into mobility patterns and transportation needs.

The following sections of the paper describe the input dataset, data processing, and aggregation steps. Then we share our findings and the follow-up experiments. Finally, we discuss the results and provide a conclusion, including recommendations on how our findings may be used for urban and transportation planning.

## 2    Materials and Methods

### 2.1    Data

Our research is based on the origin-destination commute dataset provided by a mobile phone company. The dataset provides hourly origin-destination flows for 48 districts of Brno, the second-largest city in the Czech Republic, with a population of about 380,000 inhabitants. We had access to aggregated commute data that covered one full week in October 2019.

There are two types of mobile phone datasets: active and passive. Active datasets are based on records of certain actions, like phone calls or text messages. Every phone communicates with the mobile phone network at least every 30 min, and these communications allow for capturing passive datasets. Active datasets are very useful for studying the interaction graph between people, while passive datasets provide better coverage to study mobility or population density. Our research is based on the passive mobile phone dataset.

In modern cities, people tend to carry their mobile phones for the whole day, and the dataset above provides unique insights into general mobility flows. We aggregated all outgoing trips for all districts for a given hour. As a result, every Brno district was represented by a vector with 168 (7 days × 24 h) outflow numbers. Due to the differences in population between districts, we normalized

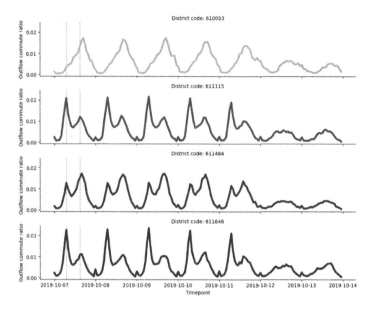

**Fig. 1.** Hourly commute outflow ratios for four Brno districts. The first five days of data represent weekdays, while the last two days represent weekends. The vertical lines highlight commute spikes, corresponding to 8 am and 4 pm on weekdays.

commute vectors by the total amount of outflow. Therefore every vector component represented what ratio of total outflow was observed in a given hour.

The normalized vectors had clear weekday and weekend patterns (see Fig. 1). Some timelines had a surprising outflow spike around midnight, but after further investigation, this behavior was attributed as an artifact of data collection: the input dataset was provided in daily files, and any trip that spanned across midnight was recorded as a trip that ended at midnight.

We noticed a few repeating patterns across city districts. Some districts had very similar outflow vectors that followed the same pattern (see the second and the fourth plot in Fig. 1), while overall, patterns had significant differences. The initial investigation showed some correlation between commute pattern similarity and district location: e.g., the districts in the city center followed a similar pattern. To study the common patterns holistically, we decided to reduce dimensionality and cluster the outflow vectors.

## 2.2 Principal Component Analysis and Clustering

We used PCA (Principal Component Analysis) to reduce the dimensionality of vectors. Table 1 gives a summary of PCA performance based on the number of components. Using just two components explains more than 73% of cumulative variance, and we observe smaller incremental improvements for each additional component.

Putting two-dimensional vectors for all districts on a single plot helped to identify patterns of city districts. The similarity of commute vectors for related districts gave us the idea to use commute vectors as a district signature.

**Table 1.** Cumulative variance of 168-component outflow commute vectors based on the number of PCA components.

| Number of components | Cumulative variance explained by the components |
|----------------------|------------------------------------------------|
| 1                    | 59.34%                                         |
| 2                    | 73.87%                                         |
| 3                    | 78.67%                                         |
| 4                    | 82.81%                                         |
| 5                    | 85.26%                                         |

We considered clustering two types of vectors:

1. The original 168-component outflow vectors.
2. 2-component PCA vectors.

Using the original vectors helps to preserve all the information from the vectors. At the same time, the vector components are highly correlated due to the repeating patterns within day boundaries (e.g., mobility tends to reduce during nighttime) and over the week due to the repeating weekday patterns and weekend patterns.

To mitigate the correlation and focus on the orthogonal components, we clustered 2-component PCA feature vectors. Using the elbow method, we decided to move forward with 3 clusters. The clustering output is presented in Fig. 2.

## 3 Results

While the district signature does not contain any information about the spatial structure, we received a spatially cohesive separation of the city center, residential area, and the mixed zone in between. The outflow profile of the residential cluster has a clear spike in the morning when people go to work. The city center outflow spikes in the evening. And mixed areas in between have traces of both patterns. Also we discovered that the sum of all outflow vectors is consistent with the intraday bicycle volumes in Melbourne [12].

The overall picture matches our intuition: remote city districts followed one pattern, while the city center districts followed a different pattern. However, the resulting clusters have some asymmetry: the northern part of the city has commute patterns similar to the city center. At the same time, the southern and northwestern borders of the city do not belong to the residential cluster.

After additional research, we found that both irregularities match the industrial zones of the city (see Fig. 3). A large number of industry workers commuting

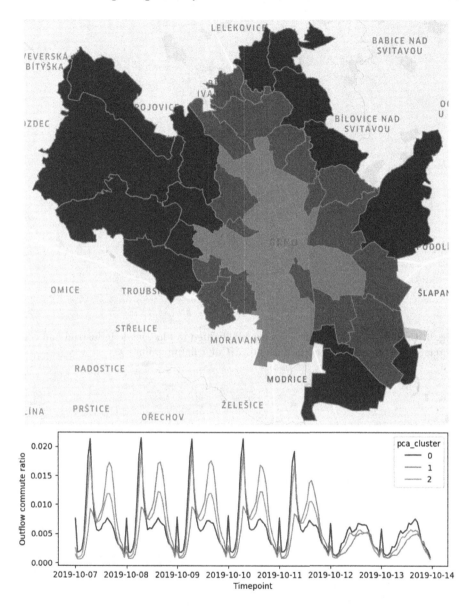

**Fig. 2.** The top figure demonstrates three city clusters, while the bottom figure shows aggregated hourly outflow commute profile for each cluster. The blue cluster corresponds to residential areas, the orange one covers the city center and business districts, while the green cluster has a combination of both. (Color figure online)

from work increases the afternoon spike, while a limited number of residential properties reduces the commute outflow in the morning.

In addition to the visual inspection of urban zones, we performed a quantitative comparison of clusters based on Brno Census data. We observed a 200%–300%

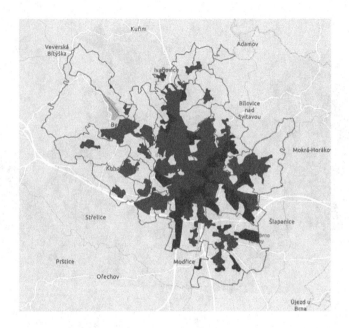

**Fig. 3.** Brno city zones: urban zones are highlighted in blue, while industrial and commercial zones are highlighted in dark grey. (Color figure online)

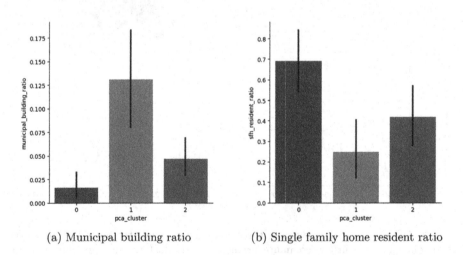

(a) Municipal building ratio    (b) Single family home resident ratio

**Fig. 4.** Comparison of the building structure between the identified zones based on commute patterns. The ratio of a) municipal building and b) single-family homes residents among all the buildings/residents within each zone, and 95% confidence intervals showing the variation of those percentages across the locations within the zone

difference in the municipal home ratio (the number of municipal buildings in a cluster divided by the total number of buildings) and the single-family home resident ratio (the proportion of cluster residents living in single-family homes) between the clusters (see Fig. 4). Furthermore, we performed statistical t-tests to compare mean municipal home ratios for all pairs of clusters. The comparison of the residential and mixed clusters yielded a p-value of 3%, while the other two pairs had a p-value below 1%. These results show a statistically significant difference between the clusters.

## 4    Conclusion and Discussion

To summarize, we identified strong patterns in the urban mobility outflow vectors and proposed using them as a district signature. Characterizing urban locations with their commute timeline allows the delineation of city zones with similar mobility behavior. We found a relationship between the resulting clusters and the ratio of municipal buildings (including libraries, schools, and city administration) and single-family home residents. While this fact is insufficient to establish the causal relation, we plan to conduct further research that will help us better understand the connection between the socioeconomic features of districts and their commute clusters.

Using the mobility signatures to delineate city districts provides great insights into mobility needs and can be directly used for transportation planning and land use classification. At the same time, the relationship between the municipal building and commute patterns contributes new information for city planners.

We proposed an approach leveraging mobility data from mobile phones to define unique signatures of urban locations and apply them to urban zoning. The proposed approach can be applied to any city where a similar input dataset can be collected. Relying only on the mobility data makes the signatures uniform for any country (in contrast to financial or municipal records), while comprehensive dataset coverage enables capturing general commute patterns (counter to taxi or biking datasets).

## References

1. Barthélemy, M.: Spatial networks. Phys. Rep. **499**(1–3), 1–101 (2011)
2. Bettencourt, L.M.: The origins of scaling in cities. Science **340**(6139), 1438–1441 (2013)
3. Bettencourt, L.M., Lobo, J., Strumsky, D., West, G.B.: Urban scaling and its deviations: revealing the structure of wealth, innovation and crime across cities. PLoS ONE **5**(11), e13541 (2010)
4. Buchholz, N.: Spatial equilibrium, search frictions and efficient regulation in the taxi industry. Working paper, Technical report (2015)
5. Guan, C., Song, J., Keith, M., Akiyama, Y., Shibasaki, R., Sato, T.: Delineating urban park catchment areas using mobile phone data: a case study of Tokyo. Comput. Environ. Urban Syst. **81**, 101474 (2020)

6. Louail, T., et al.: From mobile phone data to the spatial structure of cities. Sci. Rep. **4**(1), 1–12 (2014)
7. McNally, M.G.: The four-step model. In: Handbook of transport modelling. Emerald Group Publishing Limited (2007)
8. Pei, T., Sobolevsky, S., Ratti, C., Shaw, S.L., Li, T., Zhou, C.: A new insight into land use classification based on aggregated mobile phone data. Int. J. Geogr. Inf. Sci. **28**(9), 1988–2007 (2014)
9. Ratti, C., et al.: Redrawing the map of great Britain from a network of human interactions. PLoS ONE **5**(12), e14248 (2010)
10. Schläpfer, M., et al.: The universal visitation law of human mobility. Nature **593**(7860), 522–527 (2021)
11. Simini, F., González, M.C., Maritan, A., Barabási, A.L.: A universal model for mobility and migration patterns. Nature **484**(7392), 96–100 (2012)
12. Smith, M.S., Kauermann, G.: Bicycle commuting in Melbourne during the 2000s energy crisis: a semiparametric analysis of intraday volumes. Transp. Res. Part B: Methodol. **45**(10), 1846–1862 (2011)
13. Sobolevsky, S., Sitko, I., Des Combes, R.T., Hawelka, B., Arias, J.M., Ratti, C.: Money on the move: big data of bank card transactions as the new proxy for human mobility patterns and regional delineation. the case of residents and foreign visitors in Spain. In: 2014 IEEE International Congress on Big Data, pp. 136–143. IEEE (2014)
14. Wang, L., Qian, C., Kats, P., Kontokosta, C., Sobolevsky, S.: Structure of 311 service requests as a signature of urban location. PLoS ONE **12**(10), e0186314 (2017)
15. Xinyi, N., Liang, D., Xiaodong, S.: Understanding urban spatial structure of shanghai central city based on mobile phone data. China City Plann. Rev. **24**(3) (2015)
16. Xu, Y., Belyi, A., Bojic, I., Ratti, C.: How friends share urban space: an exploratory spatiotemporal analysis using mobile phone data. Trans. GIS **21**(3), 468–487 (2017). https://doi.org/10.1111/tgis.12285
17. Xu, Y., Belyi, A., Bojic, I., Ratti, C.: Human mobility and socioeconomic status: analysis of Singapore and Boston. Comput. Environ. Urban Syst. **72**, 51–67 (2018). https://doi.org/10.1016/j.compenvurbsys.2018.04.001
18. Xu, Y., Belyi, A., Santi, P., Ratti, C.: Quantifying segregation in an integrated urban physical-social space. J. R. Soc. Interface **16**(160), 20190536 (2019). https://doi.org/10.1098/rsif.2019.0536
19. Yu, Q., Li, W., Yang, D., Zhang, H.: Mobile phone data in urban commuting: a network community detection-based framework to unveil the spatial structure of commuting demand. J. Adv. Transp. **2020**, 1–15 (2020)
20. Zhang, B., Zhong, C., Gao, Q., Shabrina, Z., Tu, W.: Delineating urban functional zones using mobile phone data: a case study of cross-boundary integration in Shenzhen-Dongguan-Huizhou area. Comput. Environ. Urban Syst. **98**, 101872 (2022)
21. Zipf, G.K.: The P 1 P 2/D hypothesis: on the intercity movement of persons. Am. Sociol. Rev. **11**(6), 677–686 (1946)

# Management Qualification and Responsible Management in Local Government

Martin Hronec[1]([✉]), Štefan Hronec[1], Janka Beresecká[2], Veronika Svetlíková[3], and Veronika Dobiášová[4]

[1] Faculty of Economics, Matej Bel University in Banska Bystrica, Tajovského 10, 975 90 Banská Bystrica, Slovak Republic
{martin.hronec,stefan.hronec}@umb.sk

[2] Faculty of European Studies and Regional Development, Institute of Regional Studies and Rural Development, Slovak University of Agriculture in Nitra, Trieda Andreja Hlinku 609, 949 01 Nitra-Chrenová, Slovak Republic
janka.beresecka@uniag.sk

[3] Faculty of Civil Engineering, Technical University of Ostrava, Ludvíka Podéště 1875/17, 708 00 Ostrava-Poruba, Czech Republic
veronika.svetlikova@vsb.cz

[4] Faculty of Philosophy, Constantine the Philosopher University in Nitra, Tr. A. Hlinku 1, 949 01 Nitra, Slovak Republic

**Abstract.** The scientific objective of the study is to identify the qualification prerequisites of local government management as an element of the economic and social pillar of socially responsible action, based on the analysis of theoretical approaches to socially responsible action in the public sector and secondary research in the environment of local governments. The aim was to identify the real impact of education on selected indicators of economic performance of local government - an element of the economic pillar of social responsibility. The subject of the scientific study is the education (theoretical as well as practical component) of the statutory as well as local government councillors and their impact on selected economic indicators of local government performance such as long-term and short-term liabilities, capital expenditures, non-current assets, liquidity, current account balance, investment intensity, the size of the municipality's net assets per capita, economic performance as well as the overall financial health of the local government. The subject was also an examination of the impact of education, as an element of the social pillar of social responsibility, on another, economic pillar of social responsibility - efficient and responsible management.

**Keywords:** Efficiency · Management · Qualifications · Education

## 1 Introduction

Nowadays, more and more organisations are applying the principles of social responsibility to ensure sustainable development in economic, social and environmental terms. Corporate social responsibility is a relatively new concept for the public sector in terms of

O. Gervasi et al. (Eds.): ICCSA 2023, LNCS 13957, pp. 491–515, 2023.
https://doi.org/10.1007/978-3-031-36808-0_36

transparent and effective management of public sector organisations. Most private sector organisations consciously and voluntarily apply the principles of social responsibility to ensure sustainable development. Public sector organisations do not consciously and deliberately apply the principles of social responsibility, but still behave responsibly. This follows from the legislation of the Slovak Republic, as all public sector organisations manage public budgets, their performance is subject to public scrutiny and decision-making is by public choice. Therefore, public sector organisations are obliged to behave in an economically, socially and environmentally responsible manner towards all stakeholders. In recent years, socially responsible behaviour has become an increasingly debated topic and a growing number of organisations are applying the principles of socially responsible behaviour.

The scientific objective of the study is to identify the qualification prerequisites of local government management as an element of the economic and social pillar of socially responsible action, as well as the real impact of education on selected indicators of economic performance of local government - an element of the economic pillar of social responsibility, based on the analysis of theoretical approaches and secondary research. The output of the scientific study is to summarize the mutual influences of both pillars, where qualification prerequisites and required competences would contribute or influence the efficiency and good responsible management of local government. This includes the standards and structure of knowledge and skills that management should possess and which positively influence the efficient and socially responsible management of local government.

The subject of the scientific study is the education (theoretical as well as practical component) of the statutory as well as local government councillors and their impact on selected economic indicators of local government management such as long-term and short-term liabilities, capital expenditures, non-current assets, liquidity, current account balance, investment intensity, the size of the municipality's net assets per capita, economic performance as well as the overall financial health of the local government. The subject was also an examination of the impact of education, as an element of the social pillar of social responsibility, on another, economic pillar of social responsibility - efficient and responsible management.

## 2   The Economic Benefits of Social Responsibility in Local Government

Conducting organisations in accordance with the principles of responsible behaviour brings a range of benefits to the organisation, particularly in non-financial terms. Just as tangible assets are important to an organisation, so are intangible assets such as human capital, brand equity, reputation and trust and partnership. Economic benefits are the biggest motivating factors for organisations and we will therefore focus on the economic aspect of corporate social responsibility.

The essence of the concept under study is the pursuit of meeting new expectations, which increases the cost of operations. Changing wider social, political and environmental conditions make the effect of social responsibility on an organisation's financial performance difficult to measure accurately. In the long term, organisations are unlikely to suffer harm by choosing to embed CSR practices into their operations [2]. The benefits to organisations by stakeholder group are shown in Table 1.

**Table 1.** Benefits of socially responsible behaviour

| Interested group | Benefits for the organisation |
| --- | --- |
| General public | - additional access to capital,<br>- increasing attractiveness to potential investors,<br>- reducing risk management costs,<br>- increased transparency,<br>- protection from costly litigation |
| Employees | - Improving company culture,<br>- loyal employees,<br>- reduced employee turnover,<br>- improvement of the organisation's position on the job market |
| Customers | - reputation building,<br>- differentiating yourself from the competition,<br>- increasing competitive advantage,<br>- increase socially and environmentally conscious customers |
| Suppliers | - oboznamovanie sa s víziou a zámermi,<br>- budovanie dobrej povesti v dodávateľskom reťazci,<br>- vyššia efektívnosť dodávateľského reťazca |
| Competition | - respect from competitors |
| Community/MVO | - good reputation in the community |
| State | - reduced monitoring by the state,<br>- avoidance of sanctions by the state,<br>- relaxation of legal measures,<br>- possibility to bid for public tenders |

Source: own elaboration

From the point of view of the general public, one of the most important benefits of the concept under review is better state access to foreign capital. The fact that socially responsible organisations and states are benefiting from increased investor interest is also demonstrated by some stock market indices (Dow Jones Sustainability Index, FTSE4Good and Domini 400 Social Index: an index of 400 large companies that meet the criteria for CSR), which have started to take into account social responsibility criteria. According to Hlaváček [9], it is natural that investments in socially responsible funds are less risky for investors because investors' risk aversion places such high demands on the profitability of risky projects that it ultimately means 'cutting them off' from viable financial resources. Hence investors' interest in states and organisations that respect social responsibility and banks' interest in lending to them, which is a positive feedback loop, as lower interest rates on loans provide an additional comparative advantage compared to other businesses.

In relation to the general public, the authors Kašparová, Majdúchová and Trnková [11, 14, 22] mention additional benefits of implementing this concept: greater attractiveness for investors (socially responsible investing), greater transparency, stronger credibility of the state itself and of public organisations, and the long-term sustainability of the organisation.

The economic benefits in interaction with employees are primarily based on increased employee loyalty [7, 13], which is linked to the ability to attract and retain not only quality but also top-quality employees. Based on the aforementioned benefits and research that have proven the causality of the application of corporate social responsibility in interaction with employees and the attractiveness of the organization for potential employees [5, 7] we can argue that the application of this concept in practice not only reduces employee turnover, but also increases the overall position of the organization in the market of employment opportunities.

The benefits accruing to businesses from interacting with customers may take the form of increased profits, greater customer loyalty, increased trust, positive brand attitudes, present an opportunity to avoid negative publicity [13] or may increase social awareness and environmental awareness of conscious customers, enable new markets to be developed, positively influence customer loyalty and facilitate purchasing decisions [12].

Current trends in responsible supply chain practices highlight the assumption of responsibility by large, multinational enterprises for the environmental and labour practices of their suppliers [1]. Based on the above, organisations should choose their suppliers not only according to their economic situation, but also taking into account social and environmental practices. Thus, if an organisation is to be part of a socially responsible supply chain, it must take into account the economic, social, environmental and ethical criteria against which the organisation evaluates its suppliers or is itself evaluated in the supplier-supplier relationship. The economic benefits accruing to the organisation in its interaction with suppliers can themselves be comprehensively characterised as reputational improvements in supplier-supplier relationships.

One of the most frequently cited economic benefits is the acquisition of competitive advantage [4, 9, 11, 15, 22]. Mohtsham and Arshad [17] consider the source of competitive advantage to be the organisation's social capital and the reputation that the organisation acquires; according to Porter and Kramer [20], the competitive advantage in the context of applying the concept under study arises for organisations mainly from the implementation of social and environmental practices in the strategic management of the organisation and from differentiating themselves from competitors. Another source of competitive advantage is considered to be improving the reputation of the organisation in the local community [4] and building a relationship of trust with the organisation's environment [9].

Other economic benefits take the form of mitigation of legal measures, e.g. direct financial savings associated with environmental [9, 23] and social practices.

In relation to the aforementioned economic benefits accruing to organisations from the application of social responsibility in practice, a number of studies have been conducted which confirm [9, 10, 14] or do not confirm the causality of good financial performance and the implementation of responsible activities in practice [2, 8, 16].

According to Hlaváček [9], the cause of increased profitability is that responsible business reduces the so-called implicit costs associated with current and future business, e.g., the costs of future environmental damage remediation and the costs of future litigation. Most of the research touching on the concept under investigation is carried out by its proponents. This fact may affect not only the interpretation of the results but also the formulation of the questions. As a counterargument, it presents the problem on the basis of which conclusions are formulated in terms of the causality of social responsibility and improvement of the economic status of the organization. The author stresses that the causality can also be reversed. Only organisations that are (e.g. due to their dominant market position) in a strong economic position can afford to be socially responsible. Therefore, the survey results can be interpreted as meaning that above-average economic performance is not a consequence but a condition for the application of social responsibility.

Since their establishment in 1990, cities and municipalities have proved their viability through their local government bodies and are a fundamental pillar of democracy in Slovakia as well as in other EU countries and around the world. Since its inception, local government has had a legislative basis for functioning according to self-governing principles. It is exposed to various external and internal influences which exert great distorting pressures and which must be faced by the governing bodies of towns and municipalities (e.g. the mayor/mayor, town or municipal council, employees of the town or municipal authority, budgetary organisations, etc.). As an organization, local government most integrates and can effectively use the management systems of public administration, business entities, as well as civil organizations (e.g., non-profit organizations). Local government is a branch of public administration, so its "good or bad" decisions, as well as the "quality or poor quality" of its services, directly affect the residents (families) who live and work in the municipality.

Local government has cross-cutting competences in its performance. Typical examples of specific services are services and activities in the field of management, economic support and municipal development. These areas also belong to the least specified competences in the field of legislation [19]. In spite of these facts, among the important tasks of local government are the competences related to the involvement at different levels of government in the promotion of economic growth and employment generation in their territory. Here, certain elements of social responsibility can already be discerned. This is an area that is only loosely assigned to a certain level of local government. Local authorities have taken and are taking a number of initiatives to strengthen rural development or even to improve the position of specific towns and villages on the international market (in terms of attracting investment, the economy, trade development, tourism or even the promotion of industrial production, etc.).

The scope of the competences to be provided remains an important issue. In Slovakia, out of 2890 towns and municipalities, 2478 have up to 2000 inhabitants, which, in terms of human resources, qualifications, efficiency and cost-effectiveness, requires new approaches in the management of financial, material and human resources, as well as in the provision of public and other services, with an orientation towards inter-community cooperation.

How to make and streamline decisions at political level, i.e. in local councils as well as in municipal and municipal authorities, and thus improve their position in terms of social responsibility, requires continuous training and education, according to the needs of the municipality concerned. In order to be able to cope with negative influences and various socio-economic challenges, local government needs highly qualified professionals, managers and well-prepared local politicians who are future-oriented and who can set policy in the interests of the citizens and the municipality, i.e. in the spirit of social responsibility. At the same time, they will be able to set objectives and define the various strategies for achieving the objectives set. At present and in the future, the most important role in the life of local government is played by the human factor, i.e. elected and appointed representatives, local government employees and the citizens themselves. Their success or failure is reflected in their skills, abilities and knowledge, which are oriented towards the effective and efficient use of all resources (all material, technical, financial and especially human resources that can be mobilised to achieve the set objectives) and information, including various social and economic tools and methods in the management and provision of the activities of the city or municipality. It is the human resources, headed by the statutory authority, that have the responsibility to be able to respond flexibly to the constantly changing conditions in the socio-economic sphere and need to take the right decisions even in difficult conditions, so as to consider the short, medium and long-term impact on the lives of its inhabitants. At the same time, they are subject to the instruments of the social pillar of social responsibility. In order to raise awareness, increase the credibility of local government and enable citizens to get involved in public affairs, it is essential to systematically develop the quality of human resources and the social capital of local government.

Due to the rapid pace of urban growth, various crises and the scarcity of assets, the need for competent workers is increasing dramatically every year. There is a need to build capacities, introduce optimal ways of managing and developing settlements with the help of promoting new approaches, methods and techniques. All this must be done in accordance with the principles of sustainability.

An important part of the competence of local government officials (but also other VS organizations) is the introduction of performance information into the budget. The purpose is to improve the control of expenditures as well as overall performance management. Local government elected officials, in particular city statutes, councillors and municipal/local government staff, are the holders of competence and accountability for the best possible delivery of public services and effective performance and management [18].

By efficiency of local government officials we refer to the trade-off between the cost of resources - financial, material and especially human resources and the potential predictive advantages and benefits. It is part of the economic pillar of social accountability. Good management also includes good financial planning, which requires comprehensive systems thinking to ensure that good results are sustained in the future. It requires competences related to adapting local government legislation to the dynamics and multi-causal internal and external relations (as well as markets) of the municipality. Economic, demographic, legislative, socio-cultural, political-legal, technological, environmental and internal management practices are at work. At the same time, good management includes the competence and experience of the people in charge, who monitor, create and influence financial indicators and thus the fiscal health of the municipality. Last but not least, competencies must also be adapted to the factor of time or to the time period - historical, current, evolving i.e. future [16].

As in the private sector, city and town planners and management face a variety of influences in their management. In addition, they are influenced by factors that are absent in the private sector, notably citizen control, public opinion, public interest and others. It is the participatory decision-making in local governments, the so-called public choice, that connects two markets, namely the political and the economic market, i.e. the public and the private market [21].

## 3 Efficient Management of Municipalities and the Ethics of Public Resources

The management of cities and municipalities is based on the management of public resources and assets of cities and municipalities. It is important that municipal leaders make information available on the direction the municipality is taking. At the same time, they should publicly present a management report, i.e., regularly inform the public about the results of the management and spending of the municipality's approved budget.

The management of local government should be expected by the public to provide transparent and comprehensible information on the efficiency of the management of the city or municipality and to act in accordance with the ethical principles of public life in terms of social responsibility.

The means of implementing the principles of social responsibility are qualifications and qualifications. The qualifications of local government management should be closely linked not only to economic indicators, but also to the dimension and principles of public administration ethics. The question of implementing ethics in the functioning of public administration is a topical and relevant issue that is worth addressing. It concerns the impact of qualifications and competences on the efficiency of the management of towns and municipalities, but also of the entire public administration in Slovakia.

In the last decade, when examining the causes of economic, fiscal and monetary crises, it is possible to identify moral and ethical problems not only in the business sector, but also in the public sector. European Union funds and state subsidy funds, the purpose of which was and is to promote socio-economic development, in various areas are often the subject of corrupt behaviour at various levels and sectors. The balance between productive capacity and production will not be maintained without moral and ethical values that are integral to the concept of social responsibility [6]. Currently, business and public sector organizations often focus in practice on unilateral benefit, profit or egoism (e.g. unilateral contracts for subsidies and loans, where nobody accepts the interests of the recipient of the subsidy and loan in case of various problems; lengthy court processes where the injured party is more persecuted than the one who caused the damage; various organizations, cities and municipalities as well as the citizen do not assert their rights due to complicated bureaucratic procedures and unclear interpretation of legislation; unenforceability of rights at different levels of state or local government, etc.).

## 4  The Impact of Education on the Efficient Management of Local Governments

Social responsibility and the ethical management it entails are of growing importance in public administration. As a result, the ethical implications of governance are taken into account while respecting legality and efficiency. We need to learn from historical mistakes and we need to devote ourselves more to learning and quality, which will ensure quality of life for future generations. By employing the right people and managers, who can be trained with the content of developing ethical values and gradually improved, public administration organisations, including local government, will achieve greater efficiency. However, in order to ensure its sustainability, it is important to continuously evaluate and then continuously improve it according to social and economic indicators, including environmental indicators (NB: this is also a principle of social responsibility).

Moral and ethical behaviour is a key attribute of any successful company, its sustainability and competitiveness. This is also true for smaller parts of society, such as towns and cities. It is therefore necessary to start with local authorities or local governments and then to introduce changes throughout society through public administration structures. Since social accountability begins and ends with the quality of human resources, our research has focused on examining two fundamental aspects - education and its impact on the performance of local government. We hypothesise that as the level of education and practical experience (qualifications) increases, the level of social accountability in local government will also increase. This may be reflected in responsible management and the achievement of good parameters of individual economic indicators.

The research of the above relations was carried out on a sample of 251 municipalities in the Slovak Republic. The data were analysed in aggregate for the sample, as well as selectively according to the size of the municipalities and by regional distribution. The following table presents the test of representativeness for the purpose of the regression model of the relationship between the education of the statutory body and selected aggregate indicators of the economic pillar of social responsibility. The representativeness test showed a virtually ideal distribution (0.999) and thus we can generalize the results to the whole of Slovakia (Tables 2 and 3).

**Table 2.** Representativeness test by size groups of towns and villages

|  | Researched | Number expected | Difference |
|---|---|---|---|
| 1 to 250 | 47 | 44,9 | 2,1 |
| 2 from 251 to 499 | 54 | 54,7 | -0,7 |
| 3 from 500 to 999 | 66 | 66,0 | 0,0 |
| 4 from 1000 to 1 999 | 47 | 48,9 | -1,9 |
| 5 from 2000 to 2 999 | 14 | 14,8 | -0,8 |
| 6 from 3000 to 9 999 | 14 | 13,8 | 0,2 |
| 7 from 10 000 to 99 999 | 9 | 7,8 | 1,2 |
| Total | 251 |  |  |

Source: SPSS

**Table 3.** Statistical test of representativeness by size groups of towns and villages

|  | size group |
|---|---|
| Chi-Square | $,420^a$ |
| df | 6 |
| Asymp. Sig. | 0,999 |

Source: SPSS

Another test of representativeness was carried out on the conditions of the distribution of the research sample according to their location in individual regions of Slovakia. In this case, too, the sample distribution was almost ideal (0.999). The total number of participating municipalities was 251 (Tables 4 and 5).

**Table 4.** Representativeness test by region

|  | Researched | Number expected | Difference |
|---|---|---|---|
| 1 Bratislava Region | 9 | 7,5 | 1,5 |
| 2 Trnava Region | 22 | 21,6 | 0,4 |
| 3 Trenčin Region | 25 | 23,6 | 1,4 |
| 4 Nitra Region | 29 | 30,4 | -1,4 |
| 5 Žilina Region | 26 | 26,9 | -0,9 |
| 6 Banská Bystrica Region | 44 | 44,4 | -0,4 |
| 7 Prešov Region | 56 | 57,0 | -1,0 |
| 8 Košice Region | 40 | 39,7 | 0,3 |
| Total | 251 |  |  |

Source: SPSS

**Table 5.** Statistical test of representativeness by region

|  | Region |
|---|---|
| Chi-Square | ,492[a] |
| df | 7 |
| Asymp. Sig. | 0,999 |

Source: SPSS

The first test of the correlations was to examine the relationships and associations of municipality size and elected officials by education. We assumed that the larger the municipality, the more socially responsible the residents would be and there would be a clear greater tendency to elect representatives with more education. This dependence was confirmed only in the case of the relationship between the size of the local government and the number of university-educated deputies. In the case of the statutory mayor, the relationship was moderate, a straight linear (Table 6).

**Table 6.** Pearson correlation by population and education indicators

|  |  | F_Number of inhabitants as of 1.1. | G_Štat. | I_Pos-VŠ-3 | J_Pos-SŠ-2 |
|---|---|---|---|---|---|
| F_Number of inhabitants as of 1.1. | Pearson Correlation | 1 | ,248[**] | ,857[**] | −0,005 |
|  | Sig. (2-tailed) |  | 0,000 | 0,000 | 0,940 |
|  | N | 251 | 250 | 251 | 251 |

Source: SPSS
**Correlation is significant at the 0.01 level (2-tailed)
*Correlation is significant at the 0.05 level (2-tailed)

There is a weak to moderate direct correlation between the population of a municipality and the education of the statutory officer. Thus, the higher the number of inhabitants of the municipality, the higher the level of education (this shows a weak to moderate tendency of dependence). Thus, there is a strong direct correlation between the number of inhabitants of a municipality and the number of deputies with higher education.

There is a weak inverse relationship between the population of a community and the overall financial health of the community. The higher the number of inhabitants, the lower the value of the indicator of financial health, etc. (Table 7).

The following table presents the relationship between the educational attainment of a statutory officer and selected economic indicators. These are the mutual influences of the social and economic pillars of social responsibility. From an overall perspective (251 municipalities without more detailed characteristics in terms of size and regions), we can speak of a direct moderate dependence. The above relationships show a higher activity

**Table 7.** Pearson correlation by population and economic indicators

|  |  | F_Number of inhabitants as of 1.1. | R_total debt | V_investment intensity | Z_overall financial health |
|---|---|---|---|---|---|
| F_Number of inhabitants as of 1.1. | Pearson Correlation | 1 | ,148[*] | −0,026 | −,154[*] |
|  | Sig. (2-tailed) |  | 0,019 | 0,685 | 0,014 |
|  | N | 251 | 251 | 251 | 251 |

Source: SPSS
**Correlation is significant at the 0.01 level (2-tailed)
*Correlation is significant at the 0.05 level (2-tailed)

of educated mayors in the field of modernization of local governments. This is associated with higher capital expenditures and long-term commitments linked to borrowing (Table 8).

**Table 8.** Correlation between statutory education and economic indicators A

|  |  | G_Štat. | M_ capital expenditure | O_ financial accounts | P_ long-term liabilities |
|---|---|---|---|---|---|
| G_Štat. | Correl. Coefficient | 1,000 | ,357[**] | ,336[**] | ,279[**] |
|  | Sig. (2-tailed) |  | 0,000 | 0,000 | 0,000 |
|  | N | 250 | 250 | 250 | 250 |

Source: SPSS

The following table presents the relationship between educational attainment and total debt, investment intensity and overall financial health of the local government. The correlations were not significant (Table 9).

**Table 9.** Correlation between statutory education and economic indicators B

|  |  | G_Štat. | R_total debt | V_investment intensity | Z_overall financial health |
|---|---|---|---|---|---|
| G_Štat. | Correl. Coefficient | 1,000 | −0,013 | 0,057 | 0,053 |
|  | Sig. (2-tailed) |  | 0,841 | 0,374 | 0,404 |
|  | N | 250 | 250 | 250 | 250 |

Source: SPSS

Similarly insignificant relationships have been demonstrated for MPs with university degrees. Neither in the case of debt service nor in the case of investment intensity was the dependence confirmed (Table 10).

**Table 10.** Pearson correlation by number of MPs with tertiary education and economic indicators A

|  |  | I_Pos-VŠ-3 | S_debt service | V_investment intensity |
|---|---|---|---|---|
| I_Pos-VŠ-3 | Pearson Correlation | 1 | 0,034 | −0,043 |
|  | Sig. (2-tailed) |  | 0,588 | 0,499 |
|  | N | 251 | 251 | 251 |

Source: SPSS

In this case, no relationships have been demonstrated either with the economic outturn and the overall financial health of the municipality (Table 11).

**Table 11.** Pearson correlation by number of MPs with tertiary education and economic indicators B

|  |  | I_Pos-VŠ-3 | Y_economic result per capita | Z_overall financial health |
|---|---|---|---|---|
| I_Pos-VŠ-3 | Pearson Correlation | 1 | 0,048 | −0,091 |
|  | Sig. (2-tailed) |  | 0,447 | 0,149 |
|  | N | 251 | 251 | 251 |

Source: SPSS

The relationships of high school-educated MPs and economic indicators were not confirmed. Neither in the case of debt service nor in the case of investment intensity does a higher share of MPs with a secondary education in the Chamber of Deputies have an impact (Table 12).

**Table 12.** Pearson correlation by number of MPs with tertiary education and economic indicators

|  |  | J_Pos-SŠ-2 | S_debt service | V_investment intensity |
|---|---|---|---|---|
| J_Pos-SŠ-2 | Pearson Correlation | 1 | −0,001 | −0,114 |
|  | Sig. (2-tailed) |  | 0,989 | 0,071 |
|  | N | 251 | 251 | 251 |

Source: SPSS

Where a moderate relationship was demonstrated, regression analysis was also performed. The regression model showed that if the level of education increases by 1 unit (from secondary to tertiary or primary to secondary), the amount of capital expenditure increases by an average of € 273049 (Table 13).

**Table 13.** Regression analysis between statutory education and capital expenditure

| Model | | Unstandardized Coefficients | | Standardized Coefficients | t | Sig. |
|---|---|---|---|---|---|---|
| | | B | Std. Error | Beta | | |
| | (Constant) | -387602,746 | 144538,886 | | -2,682 | 0,008 |
| | G_Štat. | 237049,541 | 56956,300 | | 0,256 | 4,162 | 0,000 |
| a. závislá premennná: M_kapitalove vydavky | | | | | | |

Source: SPSS

Another regression model showed that if education increases by one level, the value of financial accounts increases by an average of €337592 (this is a statistical average, not a lump-sum value for each municipality) (Table 14).

**Table 14.** Regression analysis between statutory education and financial accounts

| Model | | Unstandardized Coefficients | | Standardized Coefficients | t | Sig. |
|---|---|---|---|---|---|---|
| | | B | Std. Error | Beta | | |
| | (Constant) | -553565,834 | 194041,188 | | -2,853 | 0,005 |
| | G_Štat. | 337592,827 | 76462,940 | | 0,270 | 4,415 | 0,000 |
| a. závislá premennná: O_financne ucty | | | | | | |

Source: SPSS

Similar increases are expected for education and long-term liabilities. In terms of the whole research sample, mayors with higher education have a higher propensity to go into debt (due to capital investments) (Table 15).

**Table 15.** Regression analysis between statutory education and long-term liabilities

| Model | | Unstandardized Coefficients | | Standardized Coefficients | t | Sig. |
|---|---|---|---|---|---|---|
| | | B | Std. Error | Beta | | |
| | (Constant) | -522061,679 | 224621,024 | | -2,324 | 0,021 |
| | G_Štat. | 311544,890 | 88513,083 | | 0,218 | 3,520 | 0,001 |
| a. dependent variable: P_long-term liabilities | | | | | | |

Source: SPSS

The following table presents an analysis of the dependencies of selected indicators of education of the management of local governments in the size group up to 250 inhabitants and economic indicators. In the case of educational focus (divided into economic/legal/technical and other humanities, possibly without higher education), a moderately strong direct linear dependence was shown for capital expenditure. This means that higher capital expenditures are spent in municipalities with mayors with other humanities education. This means that mayors are more socially responsible, and have a greater propensity to make long-term investments than to consume. In other cases, the dependence was insignificant. The positive effect of university education was demonstrated in the case of the number of members in the municipal council. A moderate to strong dependence was found for the amount of capital expenditure, financial accounts and long-term liabilities, which are mainly related to loans taken for the construction of civic infrastructure (Table 16).

**Table 16.** Dependency analysis of management education and selected economic indicators in municipalities with population up to 250 inhabitants. A

| municipalities up to 250 inhabitants | capital expenditure | non-current assets | financial accounts | long-term liabilities | immediate liquidity | total debt | debt service |
|---|---|---|---|---|---|---|---|
| Focus of education | 0,2748 | 0,0837 | -0,1000 | -0,0596 | -0,0340 | -0,1210 | -0,0724 |
| Education of the statutory officer | 0,1714 | 0,1541 | -0,0250 | -0,0839 | -0,0170 | 0,1626 | 0,2803 |
| Percentage of university-educated MEPs | 0,3455 | 0,3021 | 0,4767 | 0,3127 | 0,1507 | 0,2052 | 0,0333 |
| Percentage of MEPs with a secondary education | -0,0542 | 0,2804 | 0,0580 | 0,1193 | 0,1292 | 0,1044 | -0,1025 |

Source: own elaboration

A moderately strong dependence was shown for educational focus and investment intensity, where the propensity to invest is expected to be lower as the number of statisticians with economics, technical and legal education increases, compared to the group of other humanities disciplines. The investment intensity indicator was also significant in relation to the amount of education attained by the statutory. An inverse linear relationship was demonstrated for the proportion of secondary-educated MPs and net worth per capita as well as economic output per capita. There is an inverse relationship, the higher the number of MPs with this level of education, the lower the net wealth as well as the per capita economic result (Table 17).

In the group of municipalities from 251 to 500 inhabitants, only a slight dependence was found for 4 indicators. Rather, economic legal and technical education has a positive impact on immediate liquidity. The correlation coefficient reached the value of − 0.23. A moderate dependence was proved in the case of the share of university educated

**Table 17.** Analysis of the relationship between management education and selected economic indicators in municipalities with up to 250 inhabitants. B

| municipalities up to 250 inhabitants | payables 60 days past due | current account balance | investment intensity | basic balance per capita | net worth per capita | economic result per capita | overall financial health |
|---|---|---|---|---|---|---|---|
| Focus of education | - | 0,0588 | 0,3843 | -0,3503 | -0,0462 | -0,1587 | 0,2009 |
| Education of the statutory officer | - | 0,1095 | 0,2528 | -0,1919 | 0,0936 | 0,2267 | 0,1777 |
| Percentage of university-educated MEPs | - | -0,1975 | -0,0909 | -0,1563 | 0,2275 | 0,1614 | 0,1677 |
| Percentage of MEPs with a secondary education | - | 0,0367 | -0,1184 | 0,0495 | -0,2893 | -0,2962 | 0,0442 |

Source: own elaboration

deputies and the total debt of the municipality. This is related to the caution and responsibility of university-educated MPs, who evaluate the risks of debt more and behave more conservatively when taking loans and borrowing (Table 18).

**Table 18.** Dependency analysis of management education and selected economic indicators in municipalities with 251 to 500 inhabitants. A

| From 251 to 500 inhabitants | capital expenditure | non-current assets | financial accounts | long-term liabilities | immediate liquidity | total debt | debt service |
|---|---|---|---|---|---|---|---|
| Focus of education | -0,0782 | 0,0208 | -0,1584 | -0,0365 | -0,2302 | 0,0682 | 0,1013 |
| Education of the statutory officer | 0,1928 | 0,1209 | -0,0173 | -0,0679 | -0,1870 | 0,0385 | 0,0317 |
| Percentage of university-educated MEPs | -0,0291 | 0,1779 | 0,1238 | -0,1890 | -0,0309 | -0,2644 | -0,0671 |
| Percentage of MEPs with a secondary education | 0,0651 | 0,0697 | -0,1919 | 0,1980 | -0,0455 | 0,2209 | 0,1915 |

Source: own elaboration

A moderately strong direct linear relationship was also shown for the educational attainment of the statutory and the basic per capita balance. A moderately strong inverse linear dependence was also demonstrated for the focus of education and the overall financial health of the local government. In this case, better financial health is found in municipalities with 251 to 500 inhabitants, where the elected mayor with an economics or law degree is in office. In the other cases, the interdependence between the variables is not confirmed (Table 19).

**Table 19.** Dependency analysis of management education and selected economic indicators in municipalities with 251 to 500 inhabitants. B

| From 251 to 500 inhabitants | payables 60 days past due | current account balance | investm ent intensity | basic balance per capita | net worth per capita | economic result per capita | overall financial health |
|---|---|---|---|---|---|---|---|
| Focus of education | -0,0786 | - 0,0712 | - 0,0038 | 0,0039 | - 0,0192 | - 0,0064 | - 0,3361 |
| Education of the statutory officer | -0,0912 | 0,04 45 | - 0,2298 | 0,2872 | 0,14 05 | 0,2293 | - 0,0616 |
| Percentage of university-educated MEPs | 0,0947 | 0,03 57 | - 0,0589 | 0,0724 | 0,20 44 | - 0,0993 | - 0,0495 |
| Percentage of MEPs with a secondary education | -0,1658 | 0,13 60 | 0,18 48 | -0,1625 | - 0,0099 | - 0,0063 | 0,0583 |

Source: own elaboration

The next group is the municipalities in the size group from 501 to 1000 inhabitants. In this case as well, not many relationships and correlations have been proven. In the case of education focus, an inverse linear relationship with financial accounts was proven. A more positive situation was observed in the case of municipalities where the mayors have an economic-legal or technical university education. In this group of municipalities, a correlation was also found for the proportion of deputies with a secondary education and total debt (a different situation from the previous group) (Table 20).

**Table 20.** Dependency analysis of management education and selected economic indicators in municipalities from 501 to 1000 inhabitants. A

| From 501 to 1000 inhabitants | capital expenditure | non-current assets | financial accounts | long-term liabilities | immediate liquidity | total debt | debt service |
|---|---|---|---|---|---|---|---|
| Focus of education | 0,0467 | 0,087 5 | -0,2462 | - 0,1561 | - 0,1462 | - 0,0496 | 0,0789 |
| Education of the statutory officer | 0,0573 | - 0,0056 | -0,0881 | - 0,1299 | 0,0426 | - 0,1196 | 0,1263 |
| Percentage of university-educated MEPs | 0,1888 | - 0,0351 | 0,0282 | 0,1810 | - 0,0610 | 0,205 0 | 0,21 53 |
| Percentage of MEPs with a secondary education | -0,1321 | 0,045 8 | 0,0716 | - 0,1059 | 0,0670 | - 0,2391 | - 0,2207 |

Source: own elaboration

For education focus, a moderately strong direct linear relationship was found between education focus and liabilities after 60 days of maturity. A stronger slope was observed for non-economic education (Table 21).

**Table 21.** Dependency analysis of management education and selected economic indicators in municipalities from 501 to 1000 inhabitants. B

| From 501 to 1000 inhabitants | payables 60 days past due | current account balance | investment intensity | basic balance per capita | net worth per capita | economic result per capita | overall financial health |
|---|---|---|---|---|---|---|---|
| Focus of education | 0,2517 | -0,1136 | 0,2080 | -0,1427 | 0,1435 | -0,0184 | -0,0367 |
| Education of the statutory officer | 0,1884 | -0,0313 | 0,0843 | -0,0190 | 0,0512 | 0,0941 | 0,1033 |
| Percentage of university-educated MEPs | -0,0958 | 0,2208 | 0,1756 | -0,1306 | -0,0748 | 0,1007 | 0,1247 |
| Percentage of MEPs with a secondary education | 0,0667 | -0,1835 | -0,1424 | 0,1145 | 0,0473 | -0,0567 | -0,0653 |

Source: own elaboration

In the group of municipalities from 1,001 to 2,000 inhabitants, the correlation was proved for long-term liabilities, liquidity, total debt and liabilities 60 days past due. Long-term liabilities grew mainly in municipalities with mayors with non-economic education (lower accountability was demonstrated). Conversely, in these municipalities, on average, immediate liquidity declined at the same time. There was also a moderately strong inverse linear relationship for statutory education and immediate liquidity as well as total debt. Since a simultaneous dependence with capital expenditures was not demonstrated, this can be considered a negative phenomenon (Table 22).

**Table 22.** Dependency analysis of management education and selected economic indicators in villages with 1001 to 2000 inhabitants. A

| From 1001 to 2000 inhabitants | capital expenditure | non-current assets | financial accounts | long-term liabilities | immediate liquidity | total debt | debt service |
|---|---|---|---|---|---|---|---|
| Focus of education | -0,2059 | 0,0426 | -0,1025 | 0,3313 | -0,2967 | -0,0472 | 0,2089 |
| Education of the statutory officer | -0,0964 | -0,0199 | -0,0136 | 0,1785 | -0,2382 | -0,3615 | 0,0044 |
| Percentage of university-educated MEPs | 0,0369 | -0,0951 | 0,2255 | 0,1305 | 0,1228 | -0,0452 | 0,0024 |
| Percentage of MEPs with a secondary education | 0,0212 | 0,0351 | -0,1273 | -0,1212 | -0,1931 | -0,0302 | -0,0926 |

Source: own elaboration

Both direct and indirect dependence has been demonstrated for the relationship between Members' education and liabilities with more than 60 days of maturity. It is precisely the higher proportion of Members with a university degree that was found to be more prone to default. The situation was reversed for municipalities with a higher proportion of secondary-educated Members (Table 23).

**Table 23.** Dependency analysis of management education and selected economic indicators in municipalities with 1001 to 2000 inhabitants. B

| From 1001 to 2000 inhabitants | payables 60 days past due | current account balance | investment intensity | basic balance per capita | net worth per capita | economic result per capita | overall financial health |
|---|---|---|---|---|---|---|---|
| Focus of education | 0,13 93 | - 0,1501 | - 0,2150 | 0,15 52 | 0,0183 | - 0,1524 | -0,0111 |
| Education of the statutory officer | 0,11 28 | - 0,0706 | - 0,1295 | 0,12 59 | - 0,0024 | - 0,1507 | 0,1091 |
| Percentage of university-educated MEPs | 0,33 68 | 0,01 93 | - 0,1101 | 0,17 24 | - 0,0796 | 0,0044 | -0,1174 |
| Percentage of MEPs with a secondary education | - 0,2873 | 0,00 19 | 0,1686 | - 0,1853 | - 0,0002 | 0,0702 | 0,0932 |

Source: own elaboration

In municipalities with a population greater than 2,000, incomparably more interrelationships were found than in small municipalities. In municipalities with populations between 2001 and 3000, municipalities with non-economically educated mayors had better performance in financial accounts, long-term liabilities as well as immediate liquidity. Economically educated mayors performed better on debt service. In a positive sense, higher education affected the level of capital expenditures as well as financial accounts. Conversely, municipal indebtedness as well as the associated debt service declined with increasing educational attainment. In this size group, a positive relationship (direct linear relationship) was found between the proportion of university educated councillors and the level of capital expenditure, non-current assets as well as financial accounts. The opposite was true for the higher proportion of secondary-educated Members (Table 24).

**Table 24.** Dependency analysis of management education and selected economic indicators in municipalities from 2001 to 3000 inhabitants. A

| From 2001 to 3000 inhabitants | capital expenditure | non-current assets | financial accounts | long-term liabilities | immediate liquidity | total debt | debt service |
|---|---|---|---|---|---|---|---|
| Focus of education | 0,0449 | -0,2772 | 0,51 38 | 0,2489 | 0,5203 | 0,03 66 | -0,2404 |
| Education of the statutory officer | 0,3321 | -0,0708 | 0,25 93 | -0,0432 | 0,1412 | -0,3572 | -0,4609 |
| Percentage of university-educated MEPs | 0,3281 | 0,3719 | 0,26 99 | -0,0291 | -0,0277 | -0,0144 | -0,0786 |
| Percentage of MEPs with a secondary education | -0,2985 | -0,3930 | -0,2295 | 0,0352 | 0,0793 | -0,0456 | 0,0670 |

Source: own elaboration

For the other economic indicators, in the case of the educational orientation of the statutory officer, a positive strong dependence was observed in the group of non-economically oriented educational backgrounds. Balance sheet indicators increased for this group, but so did the per capita economic result and overall financial health. The current account balance, investment intensity, and overall financial health economic indicators also grew with the level of educational attainment.

A direct linear relationship was demonstrated for higher numbers of Members with a university degree and net worth per capita. An inverse linear relationship was found for a higher proportion of MPs with a secondary education (Table 25).

**Table 25.** Dependency analysis of management education and selected economic indicators in municipalities from 2001 to 3000 inhabitants. B

| From 2001 to 3000 inhabitants | payables 60 days past due | current account balance | investment intensity | basic balance per capita | net worth per capita | economic result per capita | overall financial health |
|---|---|---|---|---|---|---|---|
| Focus of education | - | 0,67 36 | 0,2287 | 0,3097 | -0,1069 | 0,5915 | 0,6427 |
| Education of the statutory officer | - | 0,31 26 | 0,4210 | 0,0146 | -0,0583 | 0,3605 | 0,4519 |
| Percentage of university-educated MEPs | - | 0,13 92 | 0,1101 | 0,0533 | 0,2846 | 0,1176 | 0,0484 |
| Percentage of MEPs with a secondary education | - | -0,0840 | -0,0835 | -0,0441 | -0,2987 | -0,0563 | 0,0323 |

Source: own elaboration

As the size of local governments increased, the number of direct and indirect correlations to education indicators also increased. The largest number of correlations was demonstrated for indicators and educational attainment. In this case, rather in a negative direction. Higher education of the statutory meant lower capital expenditure, as well as lower values of the financial accounts indicator, higher long-term liabilities, lower immediate liquidity, as well as higher debt service. For deputies with a higher proportion of college educated, capital expenditures, financial accounts as well as long-term liabilities also increased. The opposite relationships were shown for municipalities with a higher proportion of MPs with a secondary education (lower capital expenditure but also lower long-term liabilities) (Table 26).

**Table 26.** Dependency analysis of management education and selected economic indicators in villages from 3001 to 10000 inhabitants. A

| From 3001 to 10000 inhabitants | capital expenditure | non-current assets | financial accounts | long-term liabilities | immediate liquidity | total debt | debt service |
|---|---|---|---|---|---|---|---|
| Focus of education | -0,0783 | 0,2749 | 0,0181 | - 0,0075 | - 0,0504 | 0,1753 | 0,0974 |
| Education of the statutory officer | -0,2354 | 0,0905 | - 0,3927 | 0,2911 | - 0,2759 | 0,2070 | 0,3060 |
| Percentage of university-educated MEPs | 0,4716 | 0,1972 | 0,2592 | 0,5796 | - 0,0745 | - 0,0729 | 0,2282 |
| Percentage of MEPs with a secondary education | -0,3902 | -0,1020 | - 0,2214 | - 0,4767 | - 0,0179 | 0,1664 | - 0,1337 |

Source: own elaboration

A moderate dependence was found for the educational orientation for the intensity of investment (a greater tendency for mayors/mayors with economic, legal and technical backgrounds). Liabilities after 60 days of maturity were equally more common in municipalities with non-economics-oriented mayors. In municipalities with a higher share of councillors with secondary education, the intensity of investment declines (Table 27).

**Table 27.** Dependency analysis of management education and selected economic indicators in municipalities from 3001 to 10000 inhabitants. B

| From 3001 to 10000 inhabitants | payables 60 days past due | current account balance | investment intensity | basic balance per capita | net worth per capita | economic result per capita | overall financial health |
|---|---|---|---|---|---|---|---|
| Focus of education | - 0,3420 | 0,0849 | - 0,2338 | 0,2941 | 0,0149 | 0,121 2 | 0,10 79 |
| Education of the statutory officer | 0,1434 | - 0,1353 | - 0,3028 | 0,0756 | 0,1874 | - 0,1382 | - 0,2562 |
| Percentage of university-educated MEPs | 0,0290 | 0,0802 | 0,2247 | -0,0878 | - 0,1747 | - 0,1654 | 0,00 01 |
| Percentage of MEPs with a secondary education | - 0,1392 | - 0,0869 | - 0,3080 | 0,1757 | 0,1277 | 0,117 1 | - 0,0076 |

Source: own elaboration

The largest number of relationships was demonstrated for the group of largest municipalities. When focusing on education, lower total debt as well as debt service was observed for statutory bodies with economics and law and technical education. A similar relationship was evidenced for non-current assets. A very strong direct linear relationship was shown between the proportion of university educated MPs and the level of capital expenditure, financial accounts and immediate liquidity. An inverse linear dependence was proved in the case of a higher proportion of high school educated MPs and financial accounts or immediate liquidity (up to $-0.9187$). A negative relationship (statistically positive) was demonstrated in relation to long-term liabilities, total debt and debt service (Table 28).

**Table 28.** Dependency analysis of management education and selected economic indicators in villages with population between 10001 and 50000 inhabitants. A

| From 10001 to 50000 inhabitants | capital expenditure | non-current assets | financial accounts | long-term liabilities | immediate liquidity | total debt | debt service |
|---|---|---|---|---|---|---|---|
| Focus of education | 0,1801 | - 0,5062 | 0,25 65 | - 0,1244 | 0,1665 | - 0,2996 | -0,5600 |
| Education of the statutory officer | 0,5844 | 0,05 41 | 0,89 54 | - 0,1818 | 0,2467 | 0,0238 | -0,0343 |
| Percentage of university-educated MEPs | 0,1867 | 0,22 51 | - 0,5844 | 0,7892 | - 0,9187 | 0,7667 | 0,5732 |

Source: own elaboration

To the disadvantage of non-economically educated statisticians, the dependencies in relation to the current account balance, the basic balance per capita as well as the net worth per capita come out. Similar relationships were also shown for the higher proportion of university-educated MPs (non-economic majors were more likely to be represented in the research sample) (Table 29).

**Table 29.** Dependency analysis of management education and selected economic indicators in municipalities from 10001 to 50000 inhabitants. A

| From 10001 to 50000 inhabitants | payables 60 days past due | current account balance | investment intensity | basic balance per capita | net worth per capita | economic result per capita | overall financial health |
|---|---|---|---|---|---|---|---|
| Focus of education | - | -0,6874 | -0,1564 | -0,2581 | -0,3238 | 0,2544 | -0,0059 |
| Education of the statutory officer | - | -0,2901 | 0,0440 | -0,2713 | -0,6457 | -0,1602 | -0,1834 |
| Percentage of university-educated MEPs | - | 0,7002 | 0,6819 | -0,2856 | 0,0596 | 0,3281 | -0,4065 |

Source: own elaboration

For secondary-educated MPs, a positive correlation was found for the current account, investment intensity as well as per capita economic output. For the first two, the tightness of the relationship was strong. An inverse relationship was shown for the basic balance per capita and overall financial health.

As the analysis shows, education is not a universal tool for increasing the management parameters in local governments, but in many cases it has a positive impact on the achievement of good results. From the partial results of the causal analysis, it is possible to confirm the relationship between educational attainment and a positive propensity for social responsibility. Education as a result of training, qualification as a combination of education and acquired practical experience is a prerequisite for a more comprehensive implementation of the principles of social responsibility not only in the economic sphere, but also in all other spheres that do not have a direct economic effect and cannot be expressed in monetary units.

## 5   Conclusions and Discussion

The human resources of the public administration are formed on the basis of democratic elections (according to the constitution, qualifications are not important), by appointment, where selection criteria are often related to qualifications and experience, less to the ability to be creative, imaginative and to see risks or to solve real problems for the benefit of the citizen, i.e. the client.

Education, training and, consequently, qualification are a continuous process and therefore one of the basic human activities. Qualifications and competences are the result of the educational process, which has two basic components - theoretical and practical. The theoretical one includes the attainment of a degree as official evidence of the completion of education in the formal education system and the completion of education in the non-formal education system. The practical includes acquired work experience.

The scientific aim of the scientific monograph was: On the basis of the analysis of theoretical approaches, primary research and secondary research to identify the qualification prerequisites of local government management, as an element of the economic and social pillar of socially responsible action, as well as the real impact of education on selected indicators of economic performance of local government - an element of the economic pillar of social responsibility. The output of the scientific monograph was to summarize the mutual influences of both pillars, where qualification prerequisites and required competences would contribute or influence the efficiency and good responsible management of the municipality. Included are the standards and structure of knowledge and skills that management should possess and that positively influence the efficient and socially responsible management of a municipality.

Competencies related to the process of leadership, resource management (material, financial, human, strategy), service delivery, partnership building, communication with partners, processes related to change management, risk management, project management, etc. are relatively invisible. Similarly, the evaluation of performance, results and activities such as customer or employee satisfaction. Also, performance growth, stagnation or decline in performance is often invisible in local government organizations unless it is regularly monitored. Similarly, gaps in the skills and competencies of the statutory, management as well as staff are invisible, or simply a lack of intrinsic motivation and personal approach.

Challenges for the future also lie in how these tools can be used in practice by statutory officers and members, and whether they underestimate the value of education and available management tools in improving the efficiency and management of local government. Social responsibility, including environmental protection, the use of new technologies and innovation, is an area that respondents rated as having a low impact on the efficiency of management in a city or municipality. However, it is a dichotomous phenomenon, in terms of assessing the short-term and long-term impact on management. When evaluating the electoral period, it is obvious that statutory and local government management focuses on visible results, including efficient management, which are expressed in numerical values. It is for this reason, therefore, that environmental protection, the purchase of new technologies, appear to a lesser extent in the answers. As an example; in the long term, new technologies can reduce the energy intensity of buildings, can make the education of a new generation more efficient, or can contribute to sustainable economic results at the local level as well as to a more efficient municipal economy. Education itself brings benefits in the long term and the effect of education is not immediately visible. In cities and municipalities, leaders see the value in education not only in relation to themselves, but also to their co-workers. The research also confirmed that longer-term statutory and management staff were more able to focus on leadership and strategic planning due to their competencies, as they highlighted this area as a top priority. Management effectiveness is much more tangible after a minimum of 2 terms or more (e.g. 8–12 years), but systematic evaluation and change in the socio-economic environment requires constant adaptation to different influences, which they can manage due to their economic and financial competencies, in budgeting and cash management, which was also highlighted by the respondents in the evaluation. Efficiency is directly measurable and visible in raising external funds and in grants which the research sample of statutory and management staff confirmed in the first rank. Importantly, in doing so, they highlighted prior qualifications and competencies.

**Acknowledgements.** This study has been supported by the Research and Development Agency under Contract No. APVV-21-0363.

# References

1. Andersen, M., Skjoett-Larsen, T.: Corporate social responsibility in global supply chains. Supply Chain Manag. Int. J. **14**(2), 75–86 (2009)
2. Alexander, J.G., Buchholz, R.A.: Corporate social responsibility and stock market performance. Acad. Manag. J. **21**, 479–486 (1978)
3. Bateman, T.: Zamyslenie sa nad Spoločenskou zodpovednosťou podnikov (2008). http://www.partnerstva.sk/buxus/docs. Accessed 22 Mar 2023
4. Bussard, A., Marček, E., Markuš, M., Bunčák, M.: Spoločensky zodpovedné podnikanie. Nadácia Integra, Nadácia Pontis, PANET (2005)
5. Carrol, A.B., Buchholtz, A.K.: Ethics, Sustainability and Stakeholder Management. Business and Society Cengage Learning (2012)
6. Covey, S.R.: 7 návykov skutočne efektívnych ľudí; Zásady rozvoja osobnosti, ktoré zmenia váš život. Tešínska tiskárna (2010)
7. Greening, D.W., Turban, D.B.: Corporate social performance as a competitive advantage in attracting a quality workforce. Bus. Soc. **39**(3), 254–280 (2000)
8. Guerard, J.B.: Additional evidence on the cost of being socially responsible in investing. J. Investing Winter **6**(4), 31–36 (1997)
9. Hlaváček, J., Hlaváček, M.: Za jakých podmínek je pro firmu lukrativním společensky zodpovědné chování? (2007). http://ies.fsv.cuni.cz/sci/publication. Accessed 11 Feb 2023
10. Hopkins, M., Cowe, R.: Corporate social responsibility: is there a business case? J. Appl. Acconut. Res. (2003)
11. Kašparová, J.: Výhody zapojení se do CSR aktivít (2006). http://www.csr-online.cz/. Accessed 19 Feb 2023
12. Lee, C.G.: Education and economic growth: further empirical evidence. Eur. J. Econ. Finance Adm. Sci. **23**(8), 161–169 (2010)
13. Maignan, I., Ferrel, O.C.: Corporate citizenship as a marketing instrument: concepts, evidence and research directions. Eur. J. Mark. **35**(3/4), 457–484 (2001)
14. Majdúchová, H.: Spoločenská zodpovednosť podnikov – teoretické vymedzenie a praktická aplikácia v podmienkach slovenskej ekonomiky. Svět práce a kvalita živoa v globalizované ekonomice, pp. 136–144 (2007)
15. Majdúchová, J.: Súčasné možnosti aplikácie spoločenskej zodpovednosti v podmienkach manažmetnu firiem na Slovensku. Aktuálne manažérske trendy v teórii a praxi – vedecký monografický zborník, pp. 89–94 (2008)

16. McWilliams, A., Siegel, D.: Corporate social responsibility and financial performance: correlation or misspecifacation? Strateg. Manag. J. **21**, 603–609 (2000)
17. Mohtsham, M.S., Arshad, F.: Corporate social responsibility as a source of competitive advantage: the mediating role of social capital and reputational capital. J. Database Mark. Cust. Strategy Manag. **19**, 219–232 (2012). https://doi.org/10.1057/dbm.2012.19
18. OECD: Education at aglance (2007). http://www.oecd.org/document/21/0,3746,en_215 71361_33915056_35203221_1_1_1_1,00.html. Accessed 18 Jan 2023
19. Parrado, S.: Support for Improvement in Governance and Management, Assignig competence and functions to local self-government in four EU memebers states: SIGMA, Comparative revue by Parrado S. (2005). http://www.sigmaweb.org/publications/40987105.pdf. Accessed 10 Feb 2023
20. Porter, M.E., Kramer, M.R.: Strategy & society: the link between competitive advantage and corporate social responsibility. Harv. Bus. Rev. **84**, 78–85 (2006)
21. Potůček, M., et al.: Veřejná politika. Slon Sociologické nakladatelství (2005)
22. Trnková, J.: Spoločenská odpovědnost firem – Kompletní pruvodce témata a závěry z pruskumu v ČR. Business Leaders Forum (2004)
23. Zelený, J.: Spoločenská zodpovednosť organizácií ako platforma kreovania a implementácie systémov environmentálneho riadenia II. koncepty a modely. Fakulta prírodných vied UMB (2007)

# The Issue of Small Municipalities - The Possibility of Applying the Principles of Socially Responsible Management

Janka Beresecká[1], Jana Hroncová Vicianová[2], Štefan Hronec[2(✉)],
and Radovan Lapuník[2]

[1] Faculty of European Studies and Regional Development, Institute of Regional Studies and Rural Development, Slovak University of Agriculture in Nitra, Trieda Andreja Hlinku 609, 949 01 Nitra-Chrenová, Slovak Republic
janka.beresecka@uniag.sk

[2] Faculty of Economics, Matej Bel University in Banska Bystrica, Tajovského 10, 975 90 Banská Bystrica, Slovak Republic
{jana.hroncovavicianova,stefan.hronec,radovan.lapunik}@umb.sk

**Abstract.** The problem of efficient and socially responsible management of small municipalities is a discussed topic in many countries of the world. Applying the concept of social responsibility in the management of self-government strengthens the image, increases transparency and contributes to the interest of citizens in governance in self-government. The aim of the paper is to analyze the problems of small municipalities in Slovakia and abroad, and to propose partial solutions mainly in the economic and administrative area based on the principles of social responsibility, inter-municipal cooperation and possible positive impacts on management due to economies of scale. As small municipalities are unable to take advantage of the effects of economies of scale, certain activities (mainly municipal administration) are more expensive than larger ones. However, before the idea of merging municipalities is approached, it is first necessary to apply tools that will enable municipalities to perform certain activities cheaper, faster, or of better quality. The essence of these tools must be based on mutual cooperation, specialization, joint use of human, material, and financial resources and subsequent use of the effects that such cooperation brings (including marketing - improving the image of the community, improving communication channels, benchmarking, etc.).

**Keywords:** Social Responsibility · Management · Small Communities · Efficiency · Communication · Image · Non-Profit Marketing

## 1 Introduction

At present, the public pressure to prove the results of the implemented activities of individual public administration bodies and especially self-government, which is closest to their consumers in terms of the provision of public services, is growing. Individual self-governments with their activities influence three pillars - economic, social, and

O. Gervasi et al. (Eds.): ICCSA 2023, LNCS 13957, pp. 516–540, 2023.
https://doi.org/10.1007/978-3-031-36808-0_37

environmental. Applying the concept of social responsibility in the management of self-government strengthens its image, increases transparency and contributes to the interest of citizens in governance in self-government. The advantage of applying the concept is also the strengthening of the responsibility of local authorities towards the population. The concept of social responsibility assigns an important role to self-government. In the theory of stakeholder management, it proves to be the key entity that defines the local legislative framework, creates conditions for the performance of business and non-governmental activities, which is reflected in new job creation. The philosophy of the concept of social responsibility in the environment of self-government bodies is based on the assumption that no office exists only in economic contexts, but affects the whole environment (community, social situation of employees, civil servants, citizens). The relationship is reciprocal, as stakeholders influence the success of the office. In this respect, the concept of social responsibility also plays an important marketing role. The office's commitment in terms of the triple-bottom-line method can be demonstrated as follows: improving the quality of public services provided in self-government, improving the ability to demonstrate self-government results, active self-government approach to public interests, greater transparency of self-government decision-making, involvement of all actors affected credibility of self-government and increasing the competence of self-government employees [17]. In this context, solutions to the problems faced, in particular, by smaller municipalities need to be sought. As small municipalities do not have enough opportunities to obtain sufficient budgetary resources, the systematic development of the territory is considerably limited. A large part of the budget is spent by small municipalities on the administration itself (in some cases they reach up to 60–70%). However, it is not possible to talk about inefficiency, but rather about an economic fact, which can be influenced by appropriate solutions. At the beginning of the scientific study, the authors of the paper deal with the identification of the main problems of small municipalities and only then the authors propose solutions that could improve the conditions of their functioning in terms of the principles of corporate social responsibility.

The municipality is a local institution that produces or manages most of the public services needed to meet the requirements of a modern lifestyle, and is also the central administrator of the technical infrastructure needed to develop the local business community. Both of these general tasks create significant problems, especially for small municipalities. Good performance of these tasks requires appropriate economic strength, which small municipalities do not have [20].

For many small and underfunded municipalities, current impacts such as immigration, demographic change, and a shrinking tax base which undermines general capacity, are highly problematic. The problem of size and peripherality poses an urgent challenge and raises the question of what small municipalities can do to be active participants in regional policy and development [8].

The issue of the size of municipalities has been widely discussed for decades not only in many European countries, but also overseas (USA, Canada). It also became the subject of discussion in the states of the former "Eastern block" after the social changes in 1989. In evaluating it in terms of use of experience, it is necessary to take into account a different starting situation in the long-term democratic conditions of Western Europe and overseas, in countries where for many decades decentralized public administration was put in place, and the situation in countries still undergoing the reform process. The issue of settlement structure and its relationship to governance is addressed by many scientific institutes. Several studies have argued in favor of consolidating the territorial structure, while others have argued in favor of maintaining a fragmented settlement. The arguments in favor of consolidating the settlement structure place particular emphasis on the efficiency of the provision of the providing services, while the arguments in favor of maintaining a fragmented settlement structure focus more on democratizing their performance. There is no clear answer to the question of which solution is better. As this is primarily a matter of a political reform and the decision-making depends on the elected representatives of the citizens at the central level, it is important what values and the degree of decentralization they prefer and what their support is among the population. From the research into the issue so far, especially in the "western" states, it has been concluded (not only by experts, but also by politicians), that the consolidated settlement structure, i.e. larger municipalities, is able to assume a greater range of powers and responsibilities; with adequate funding, of course. This view (especially from politicians) is not entirely true in the countries of Central and Eastern Europe [14].

However, this does not mean that small municipalities should be rehabilitated, as they, by their very economic nature, do not achieve the same economic results as large municipalities. As small municipalities are unable to take advantage of the effects of economies of scale, certain activities (mainly municipal administration) are more expensive than large ones. Before approaching the idea of merging municipalities (many of which often have more than 500–700 years' tradition), it is first necessary to apply tools that will allow municipalities to carry out certain activities cheaper, faster, and better. The essence of these tools must be based on mutual cooperation, specialization, joint use of human, material, and financial resources and the subsequent use of the effects that such cooperation brings.

The issue of mergers or cooperation is discussed from an economic, political, administrative point of view in almost all states. They are often put in an extreme position: either - or, where in fact, these are co-operative, non-exclusive processes, with the common goal of increasing efficiency and effectiveness. Even in the case of a merger decision, municipalities will be merged in some areas for economic, competitive or other reasons and forced to cooperate. Examples are various forms of cooperation in regions and agglomerations in Europe with a population exceeding several million (London, Stockholm, Rotterdam, Copenhagen, Berlin, Stuttgart, Zurich, …). In the case of merging municipalities, the positives include a more suitable organization, clearer structure, the possibility of greater professionalism, and unified management, and it is not necessary to reach an agreement individually with all municipalities. The risks most often contain the actual implementation of the merger and the internal resistance that can be expected from residents and local politicians [14].

## 2 The Issue of Small Municipalities

Internal and cross border working migration causing outflow of population [14], the overburdening of small communities and insufficient staff capacity create management problems and demands for tougher prioritization (Reingewertz, 2012; Slack - Bird, 2013). Further studies in this area are needed to provide convincing arguments for each of the options - merger or cooperation. The approach of this cooperation may in some respects have the potential to achieve similar results as a merger, but maintains the territorial structure of local autonomy and retains a voluntary and flexible choice of territorial and functional context for joint efforts. In Sweden, an alternative in terms of asymmetric division of responsibilities between municipalities has also been generally discussed [16]. However, the conclusions presented in the Statskontoret report are that such a distinction between responsibilities between municipalities is not appropriate to address their problems and challenges [23].

In some respects, small and large communities do not differ much from each other. Both need a comprehensive, integrated approach and need to use their existing assets. However, a small village does not mean small problems, and compared to large areas, the problems of the small are surprisingly complex. From challenges in the field of economic development and analytical needs to complex issues of land use and transport. They also often suffer from chronic unemployment. Another problem is the lack of resources and expertise to support and implement change. Successful small communities have developed a number of alternative approaches through the use of limited resources and cooperation with surrounding communities, as well as the creation of non-profit associations, business networks, programs for cyclists and consortia, and economic development organizations [15].

Most often, the size of municipalities is related to the economic aspects of their activities: the efficiency of administration (which is extremely difficult to measure in the municipal environment), the need to provide increasingly differentiated demand for services, creating optimal conditions for local development, or state-building aspects associated with the gradual liquidation of the foundations of the administrative, centralist type of state and its transformation into a state of multilevel democratic governance. In this context, less is said about the need to respond to global change, reflected in transnational cohesion policy documents, and the resulting responsibility of local and regional politicians to respond to them [14].

In any effort to increase efficiency through mergers (so far unproven), various concerns arise within the groups involved. On one hand, there is a concern about the loss of the identity of the municipality and the position of the leader deciding on the development of the municipality, and about the lack of understanding of the need for mergers by citizens and the associated complexity of working with the inhabitants of the municipality. There is also a lack of a factual and financial motive that would convince the municipality and citizens of the benefits of the merger process and open government support for such a form of consolidation, which would initiate discussion in professional circles and the general public [1].

Abroad, the carried out research focuses mainly on strong centers and their economic results. Research in the US typically focuses on cities such as Vancouver, BC, Portland, OR, New York, or Charleston, SC. However, a lot can also be learned by looking at the functioning of local governments on a smaller scale. The authors [15] focused on small municipalities. Experience in small municipalities has clearly confirmed that two basic and broad principles of revitalization are equally applicable to small communities and large ones: the need for a comprehensive approach to revitalization and the need to focus on using existing assets. However, there is a need to focus on three other topics that demonstrate these principles and deserve attention: comprehensive economic development is a challenge for many small communities, and job creation, especially in rural areas, which is a chronic and seemingly unsolvable problem. Small communities often lack the resources and wide range of experts to initiate and manage large-scale economic change [15].

In the Nordic countries, the issue of small municipalities was solved by merging. This process had its greatest impact especially in the 1970s. The restructuring of self-government has become topical again in countries such as Denmark, Norway, Sweden, Iceland, and the Faroe Islands. Even the largest municipalities within these countries would be considered small in other parts of Scandinavia (with the exception of the Icelandic capital Reykjavik). Municipalities are subject to common development trends, such as decentralization, outsourcing, privatization, etc. The problems of smaller municipalities in these countries are usually exacerbated by problematic geographical structures - high mountains and sometimes greater distances in Iceland, the decentralized island structure of the Faroe Islands. In addition, smaller municipalities find it difficult to compete with larger, typically more centrally located municipalities. This is due to the problem of "poorer infrastructure" and specific "backward" developments in the primary sphere of industry or commerce. The smaller the municipality, the more problematic it is to resist negative exogenous influences and cope with their consequences [8].

The results of small municipalities' perception of their problems are summarized in the following tables. From the point of view of the size of municipalities, the most intense perception of problems are in municipalities with less than 250 inhabitants in the area of demography, insufficient income of the municipality, and insufficient coverage in the quality of the road network (Table 1).

In the case of municipalities with a population of more than 10,000, problems were observed in the area of income and communications. The lack of income was most intensively perceived in municipalities in the size group from 2000 to 10000 inhabitants.

**Table 1.** Perception of problems by local government leaders according to the size of local governments

|  | Less than 250 inh | 250–999 | 1000–1999 | 2000–10000 | More than 10000 |
|---|---|---|---|---|---|
| Demographic development | 52 | 34 | 31 | 30 | |
| Insufficient income of the municipality | 34 | 53 | 42 | 68 | 49 |
| Road communications | 31 | 36 | | 21 | 44 |
| Economic development | 23 | 33 | 27 | | 22 |
| Lack of entrepreneurial spirit | 21 | 16 | 18 | | |
| Rental housing market | | | 28 | 21 | |
| Overview of population preferences | | | | 22 | |
| Pre - primary and primary education | | | | | 25 |
| Air Transport | | | | | 22 |
| Senior care | | | | | 22 |

# 3 Socially Responsible Management - An Integrated Approach to Cooperation

New governance innovations demonstrate the overcoming of traditional public organizations and the creation of collaborative production systems that build on new sources of funding, materials, and human energy and redistribute the right to define and assess the values of what is produced [14].

The main task of new forms of cooperation between municipalities must be to provide highly professional, quality service for self-governments, which are part of it. Along with increasing the quality of processes and decision documents, it is subsequently possible to achieve the desired savings (analyzed in another section - economies of scale). To achieve this goal, it is necessary to provide a qualified workforce that will systematically work on its improvement and increase its own professional, communicative, and economic as well as managerial competencies.

In addition to its mission, each (small and large) municipality should introduce responsible behavior in order to contribute to sustainable development in its own economic, social, and environmental factors that affect local, national, and international society. This may include the organization's approach and involvement in quality of life, environmental protection, protection of global resources, equal employment opportunities, ethical behavior, involvement in societal development and local development. The main role of social responsibility explains the will of the municipality to integrate social and environmental aspects into the consideration of its own decisions, but also the ability to respond to the effects of its own decisions and activities on society and the environment. Social responsibility should be an integral part of the municipality's strategy. Strategic objectives should be verified from the point of view of social responsibility in order to avoid unintended consequences.

The municipality, which works on its own social responsibility, strives to improve its own reputation and image towards all citizens as a whole, improve its own ability to attract and retain its employees, and maintain motivation and commitment of its employees and improve its relations with companies, other public organizations, media, suppliers, citizens/customers and the company in which it operates [25]. The table shows the main purpose of each of the public sector tasks (Table 2).

**Table 2.** The role of public administration in the field of CSR

| The role of the public sector | Main purpose |
|---|---|
| Self-government organizations as a user of social responsibility activities implemented by the private sector | - Self-government organizations as one of the target groups to which the activities<br>- Self-government organizations assist a private entity with the definition of public services to which it should direct its CSR activities. Established visions and strategies for the use of the concept of CSR |
| Self-government as a supporter and disseminator of the concept of social responsibility | - Promotion of the concept of CSR to various target groups<br>- Recognition and appreciation of socially responsible companies and their partners in the field of CSR<br>- Strengthening the transparency and credibility of the CSR concept<br>- Adoption of a standard for CSR<br>- Cooperation with other countries in the field of CSR<br>- Support for research and education in the field of CSR<br>- Support CSR initiatives and deepen dialogue between all stakeholders |
| Self-government organizations as an entity actively applying the concept of social responsibility | - The elf-government organization accepts and declares its social responsibility, is aware of the impact of its activities on the local, national and global level |

The main goal of the social responsibility of self-government is to ensure long-term sustainable development of the territory in which it operates. The public sector is one of the largest sectors in any country. Its policy significantly influences the development of the territory. Greater efficiency, accountability and transparency are just as important as in the private sector, and therefore the public sector must be reliable [11].

At present, the public pressure to prove the results of implemented public administration activities is growing. Outside the business environment, the area of public administration is an important one. The concept of socially responsible conduct is also applied in public administration. Public authorities influence three pillars - economic, social and environmental. The application of the concept of social responsibility in public administration strengthens the image of public administration, increases transparency, and contributes to the interest of citizens in governance in public administration. The advantage of applying the concept is also the strengthening of the responsibility of public administration bodies towards the population [17].

The issue of sustainable development of local governments and their responsibility was addressed at Local Governments for Sustainability (ICLEI). They identified the introduction of new tools and mechanisms supporting the principles of sustainable development based on the four pillars of sustainable development (economic, environmental, social and security) as a starting point. One of the possibilities is the very concept of social responsibility, which integrates the aforementioned areas. In the conditions of local governments, it must be based on the principle of cooperation. In Australia, ICLEI has launched a program to explore the Triple-bottom-line issues in local government. They have developed a range of support services for building local capacity in reporting, planning, and decision-making. The program has later expanded to Canada. The use of the Triple-bottom-line method enables the development of local governments in terms of sustainability [14].

Effective cooperation of municipalities on the principle of the concept of social responsibility in the territory leads to synergetic effects. It is an effect of joint action (synergy) of several elements, which is usually greater or qualitatively better than a simple sum of effects from the separate action of individual elements. Only cooperation that is not an end in itself and that leads to improvements in a number of related areas leads to synergy effects. It is necessary to distinguish between the fulfillment of quantitative goals (length of built roads, construction of accommodation capacities, creation of new jobs, economic savings) and fulfillment of qualitative goals (improvement of conditions for tourism - improvement of provided services, provision of necessary tourism infrastructure, etc.). The development of qualitative characteristics (intensive development) of the municipality usually brings a greater synergistic effect than the development of quantitative characteristics (extensive development) of the territory [14].

Economic effects (falling under the economic pillar of the concept) are usually the main (but not the only) aspect to start cooperation. In particular, it is appropriate to promote the projects for which it is found that their implementation could achieve a higher economic benefit compared to other commonly used procedures. When joining forces with other entities, the cooperating entities will achieve the so-called economies of scale if this method of securing public goods would lead to higher economic efficiency. Economies of scale are effects that entities achieve internally, e.g. production technology or thanks to the simultaneous work on several similar projects. The premise is that each of the subjects will do what they do best. "Activities requiring specific expertise should be carried out by entities that are able to perform them as efficiently as possible" [6].

In terms of specific expertise, higher efficiency can be achieved thanks to the management and organizational techniques of the private sector. In addition to this ability, subjects must be motivated to behave correctly, i.e. in the case of an entrepreneur, not seeking to increase their profitability excessively at the expense of public budgets. For example, in particular, the system of fixed payments from the municipal budget to the business entity providing public services contributes to the fact that the operator tries to achieve savings, tries to prevent losses, etc. [5].

Collaboration can generate spatial overlap. In other words, it can have unintended consequences for nearby communities. This basically means that other municipalities are inspired to start similar cooperation or join the current grouping. A closely related term is a political overlap. It refers to the phenomenon in which political leaders change their expectations and political activities in order to address new challenges and opportunities they face. As a result, political leaders may be more supportive of further integration [24].

There are three perspectives at each level of the cooperation concept:

a) better cost-effectiveness in self-government;
b) safer services for the population; and;
c) the introduction of service innovations.

More cost-effective and reliable public service delivery is important for sustainable development and for meeting the goals of the concept of social responsibility. It is a challenge to seek the efforts of partnerships with neighboring municipalities to share costs, services, and capabilities. The basic premise is that there is closeness between potential partners in other dimensions as well. In addition, in order to be able to use the full support capacity of the public sector above the level of the original municipality, adaptation to the sector as well as to regional policies at national and EU level needs to be addressed. Traditionally, the strongest support instruments operate at the national level in the form of laws, rules, and a system of redistribution of tax collection. Instruments at EU level are important, where the Structural Funds are available for regional development projects and the EU Leader for Rural Development. These resources provide opportunities to take initiatives leading to both - the development and strengthening of different types of infrastructure [24].

## 4     Economies of Scale – A Possible Path to a Socially Responsible Management of Small Municipalities

The analytical part of the scientific study focuses on exploring the possibilities of achieving better economic results of small municipalities through cooperation and joint sharing of resources between them. According to research results, effective cooperation can bring economies of scale and a more socially responsible approach to the use of public resources. We conducted primary and secondary research on a representative set of local governments in Slovakia, which in terms of the number of employees, fall under small to medium-sized organizations. Municipalities and cities were both represented in the sample. The sample was determined on the basis of two criteria, which are size, determined on the basis of the number of inhabitants, and the location, determined on the basis of the spatial distribution within the regions of the Slovak Republic. The authors of the paper determined the sample for the needs of research into possible effects of cooperation through quota selection. The percentage of local governments in the sample does not fully correspond to the percentage of size categories and the spatial distribution of local governments in the population. For this reason, the authors verified the representativeness of the sample using the $\chi 2$ quadrant of the wellness offit test.

To identify economies of scale, research was carried out on a sample of 236 local governments in Slovakia, with a separate group consisting of cities from 20,000 inhabitants to 90,000 inhabitants. From the point of view of individual regions, the representation was relatively even (Table 3 and Fig. 1).

**Table 3.** Research sample of local governments by region

| Region | number of self-governments |
| --- | --- |
| Banská Bystrica region | 31 |
| Bratislava region | 29 |
| Košice region | 25 |
| Nitra region | 27 |
| Prešov region | 24 |
| Trenčín region | 27 |
| Trnava region | 27 |
| Žilina region | 25 |
| Above 20000 - | 21 |
| Total | 236 |

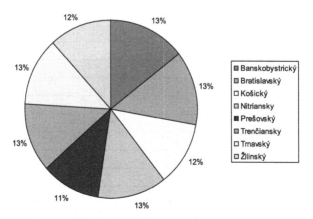

**Fig. 1.** Research sample by region

However, in the case of economies of scale, it is necessary to consider the optimal size of the cooperating unit. Increasing the size above a certain level will lead to an increase in average costs. These are also evidenced by surveys, where unit expenditures 01.1.1 per capita decline, especially in small municipalities, but gradually, with increasing population, the decline slows down until there is a renewed (albeit slight) growth (Fig. 2).

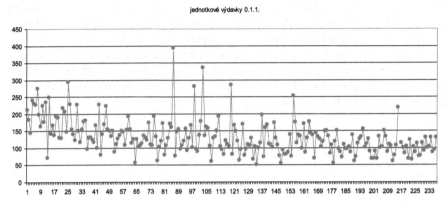

**Fig. 2.** Development of unit expenditures per capita of the surveyed municipalities in comparison with population growth.

This is due to the fact that as the offices grow, so does their administrative complexity. The increased number of municipalities involved in joint offices may result in discontinuous changes in management, as well as the need to recruit additional administrative staff who may not be overburdened (20.1.2020, https://corporatefinanceinstitute.com/resources/knowledge/economics/economies-of-scale/).

Correlation analysis confirmed the direct linear relationship between unit expenditures 01.1.1 per capita and the size of self-government. Stronger dependence is due to a smaller sample, where there are larger differences between the smallest and largest municipality/city. The least dependence was proved in the self-governments of the Bratislava region, on the contrary the largest in the Žilina region (Fig. 3).

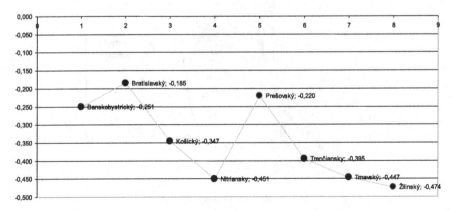

**Fig. 3.** Correlation coefficients of local governments by individual regions.

Economies of scale are also evidenced by an analysis of the share of expenditure 01.1.1. On the total current expenditures of local governments. The highest share was recorded in the smallest municipalities, which is natural, as the volume of implemented competencies in other areas is smaller than in larger municipalities. From a certain size of local governments (approx. 1,500 inhabitants), the expenditure ratio has stabilized. The total share stabilized in the range of 10–20%. This means that the effect of economies of scale is lost from a certain size. The appropriate size of the cooperating unit will determine when it is no longer economically advantageous to increase the number of municipalities as management costs increase, as will the complexity of the system and, last but not least, the availability of the cooperating unit for residents of participating municipalities (Fig. 4).

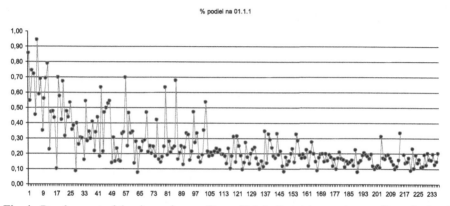

**Fig. 4.** Development of the share of expenditures 01.1.1. On total current expenditures by local government and population

Regression, correlation analysis, and analysis of average unit expenditures of individual size groups of local governments proved that the most suitable size with the highest economies of scale are municipalities with a size of 2000 to 5000 inhabitants and units from 10000 to 20000 inhabitants. In the group 5001 to 10000, there is even an increase in unit expenditure per capita. The following graphs present the development of expenditures (current) 01.1.1 in the monitored municipalities and the growth rate of the population in the research sample (Fig. 5).

The course of the increase has a similar shape; with the increase in the number of inhabitants, the volume of expenditures also increases 01.1.1 (COFOG). However, for local governments with more than 10,000 and more significantly over 20,000 inhabitants, the increase is quite inconsistent. The size of expenditures does not increase evenly with the growth of the population. On the other hand, expenditure growth has a more moderate trend than population growth (Fig. 6).

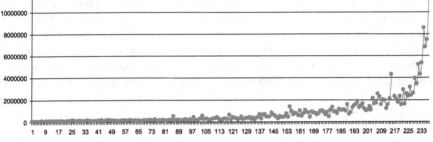

**Fig. 5.** Research sample by expenditure growth 01.1.1.

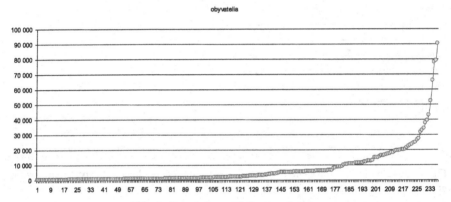

**Fig. 6.** Research sample by population

This also proves that the optimal size of the cooperating unit should be in the range of up to 20,000 inhabitants.

The highest savings can be achieved (not only on the basis of regression analysis) in municipalities with less than 1,000 inhabitants. The results of the analysis showed a medium-strong indirect linear dependence with a regression coefficient of −0.108, which means that when the population is increased by 1 unit, unit expenditures 01.1.1. Will be reduced by 10 cents. In the case of a municipality of 500 inhabitants, these expenses will decrease by merging within the joint office with other self-governments, e.g. with 1000 inhabitants by 50 €, which represents an annual saving of 25000 €. The p-value expresses statistical significance and its value must be less than 0.05. In this case, we can say that the regression model is statistically significant (Table 4).

**Table 4.** Results of the analysis for local governments up to 1000 inhabitants

| Regression Statistics | |
|---|---|
| Multiple R | 0,474 |
| R Square | 0,224 |
| Adjusted R Square | 0,212 |
| Standard Error | 43,109 |
| Observations | 63,000 |

| ANOVA | df | SS | MS | F | Signific ance F |
|---|---|---|---|---|---|
| Regression | 1 | 32785,734 | 32785,734 | 17,642 | 9E-05 |
| Residual | 61 | 113361,197 | 1858,380 | | |
| Total | 62 | 146146,931 | | | |

| | Coeffici ents | Stand ard Error | t Stat | P-value | Lower 95% | Upper 95% | Lower 95,0% | Upper 95,0% |
|---|---|---|---|---|---|---|---|---|
| Intercept | 229,793 | 16,516 | 13,913 | 0,00000 | 196,767 | 262,818 | 196,767 | 262,818 |
| X Variable 1 | -0,108 | 0,026 | -4,200 | 0,00009 | -0,160 | -0,057 | -0,160 | -0,057 |

Economies of scale were also proved by a regression model in a group of municipalities with less than 2,000 inhabitants. The dependence between the variables as well as the possible economies of scale are smaller in this group. Nevertheless, a positive influence of increasing the size of the unit (joint office) can be confirmed (Table 5).

**Table 5.** Results of the analysis for local governments up to 2000 inhabitants

| Regression Statistics | |
|---|---|
| Multiple R | 0,270 |
| R Square | 0,073 |
| Adjusted R Square | 0,064 |
| Standard Error | 54,972 |
| Observations | 108,000 |

| ANOVA | df | SS | MS | F | Signific ance F |
|---|---|---|---|---|---|
| Regression | 1 | 25196,015 | 25196,015 | 8,338 | 5E-03 |
| Residual | 106 | 320319,810 | 3021,885 | | |
| Total | 107 | 345515,825 | | | |

| | Coeffici ents | Stand ard Error | t Stat | P-value | Lower 95% | Upper 95% | Lower 95,0% | Upper 95,0% |
|---|---|---|---|---|---|---|---|---|
| Intercept | 186,177 | 12,579 | 14,801 | 0,00000 | 161,239 | 211,116 | 161,239 | 211,116 |
| Population | -0,037 | 0,013 | -2,888 | 0,00471 | -0,062 | -0,012 | -0,062 | -0,012 |

In the group from 2001 to 5000 inhabitants, a weak indirect linear dependence was proved. Although economies of scale were proven, also other factors also affect values (per capita expenditure) (Table 6).

**Table 6.** Results of the analysis for local governments from 2001 to 5000 inhabitants

| Regression Statistics | |
|---|---|
| Multiple R | 0,027 |
| R Square | 0,001 |
| Adjusted R Square | -0,029 |
| Standard Error | 46,391 |
| Observations | 36,000 |

| ANOVA | | | | | |
|---|---|---|---|---|---|
| | df | SS | MS | F | Signific ance F |
| Regressi on | 1 | 55,177 | 55,177 | 0,026 | 9E-01 |
| Residual | 34 | 73171,550 | 2152,104 | | |
| Total | 35 | 73226,727 | | | |

| | Coefficie nts | Stand ard Error | t Stat | P-value | Lower 95% | Upper 95% | Lower 95,0% | Upper 95,0% |
|---|---|---|---|---|---|---|---|---|
| Intercept | 126,969 | 29,655 | 4,282 | 0,00014 | 66,703 | 187,236 | 66,703 | 187,236 |
| Population | -0,002 | 0,010 | -0,160 | 0,87373 | -0,022 | 0,018 | -0,022 | 0,018 |

In the group from 5001 to 10000, similarly to the group from 2001 to 5000 inhabitants, a weak indirect linear dependence was proved. The regression coefficient reached a negative value and thus savings can be achieved by increasing the number of inhabitants (adding more municipalities) (Table 7).

**Table 7.** Results of the analysis for municipalities from 5001 to 10000 inhabitants

| Regression Statistics | |
|---|---|
| Multiple R | 0,077 |
| R Square | 0,006 |
| Adjusted R Square | -0,023 |
| Standard Error | 39,898 |
| Observations | 37,000 |

| ANOVA | | | | | |
|---|---|---|---|---|---|
| | df | SS | MS | F | Signific ance F |
| Regressi on | 1 | 328,718 | 328,718 | 0,206 | 7E-01 |
| Residual | 35 | 55715,224 | 1591,864 | | |
| Total | 36 | 56043,942 | | | |

| | Coeffici ents | Stand ard Error | t Stat | P- value | Lower 95% | Upper 95% | Lower 95,0% | Upper 95,0% |
|---|---|---|---|---|---|---|---|---|
| Intercept | 135,639 | 36,027 | 3,765 | 0,00061 | 62,500 | 208,778 | 62,500 | 208,778 |
| Population | -0,003 | 0,006 | -0,454 | 0,65233 | -0,014 | 0,009 | -0,014 | 0,009 |

In the case of the two largest groups of municipalities, regression analysis showed the opposite effect. With an increasing population, COFOG 01.1.1. Unit expenditures should increase slightly. This means that the optimal size of the cooperating unit is determined somewhere within this interval (10,001 to 20,000 inhabitants) (Table 8).

**Table 8.** Results of the analysis for municipalities from 10001 to 20000 inhabitants

| Regression Statistics | | | | | | | | |
|---|---|---|---|---|---|---|---|---|
| Multiple R | 0,160 | | | | | | | |
| R Square | 0,026 | | | | | | | |
| Adjusted R Square | -0,005 | | | | | | | |
| Standard Error | 32,182 | | | | | | | |
| Observations | 34,000 | | | | | | | |

| ANOVA | | | | | | |
|---|---|---|---|---|---|---|
| | | df | SS | MS | F | Significance F |
| Regression | | 1 | 871,436 | 871,436 | 0,841 | 4E-01 |
| Residual | | 32 | 33140,892 | 1035,653 | | |
| Total | | 33 | 34012,328 | | | |

| | Coefficients | Standard Error | t Stat | P-value | Lower 95% | Upper 95% | Lower 95,0% | Upper 95,0% |
|---|---|---|---|---|---|---|---|---|
| Intercept | 82,131 | 25,257 | 3,252 | 0,00270 | 30,685 | 133,578 | 30,685 | 133,578 |
| Population | 0,002 | 0,002 | 0,917 | 0,36585 | -0,002 | 0,005 | -0,002 | 0,005 |

The last group of municipalities were municipalities with more than 20,000 inhabitants. According to descriptive statistics, similarly to the previous case, unit expenditure per capita should increase with increasing population. It follows that it is not economically advantageous for cities with more than 20,000 inhabitants to enter the shared system of providing administrative services, as the average expenditure per capita is increasing. On the other hand, since small municipalities have high unit expenditures, the connection with larger municipalities will be beneficial for them (Table 9).

**Table 9.** Results of the analysis for local governments from 20001 inhabitants

| Regression Statistics | | | | | | | | |
|---|---|---|---|---|---|---|---|---|
| Multiple R | 0,292 | | | | | | | |
| R Square | 0,086 | | | | | | | |
| Adjusted R Square | 0,037 | | | | | | | |
| Standard Error | 19,835 | | | | | | | |
| Observations | 21,000 | | | | | | | |

| ANOVA | | | | | | |
|---|---|---|---|---|---|---|
| | | df | SS | MS | F | Significance F |
| Regression | | 1 | 698,930 | 698,930 | 1,776 | 2E-01 |
| Residual | | 19 | 7475,195 | 393,431 | | |
| Total | | 20 | 8174,124 | | | |

| | Coefficients | Standard Error | t Stat | P-value | Lower 95% | Upper 95% | Lower 95,0% | Upper 95,0% |
|---|---|---|---|---|---|---|---|---|
| Intercept | 88,970 | 9,117 | 9,758 | 0,00000 | 69,887 | 108,053 | 69,887 | 108,053 |
| Population | 0,00027 | 0,000 | 1,333 | 0,19834 | 0,000 | 0,001 | 0,000 | 0,001 |

The following table presents a summary of the results of the analysis. Regression coefficients point to high savings reserves, especially in the smallest municipalities, and gradually, as the theories of economies of scale present, decrease with increasing units, eventually reaching negative values (Table 10 and Fig. 7).

**Table 10.** Development of regression coefficients by size groups

| Size of municipality | A | P - value |
|---|---|---|
| 1000 | −0,1082 | 0,000090 |
| 1001–2000 | −0,0368 | 0,004710 |
| 2001–5000 | −0,0016 | 0,873700 |
| 5001–10000 | −0,0026 | 0,652233 |
| 10001–20000 | 0,0016 | 0,365849 |
| 20001 | 0,0003 | 0,198344 |

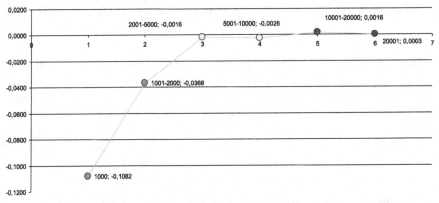

**Fig. 7.** Development of the regression coefficient (savings) by size groups of local governments

The following table presents the possible economies of scale for model communities and their potential growth into higher size groups (Table 11).

**Table 11.** Total savings/additional expenses when the population in the group increased by 1000 (impact for individual model municipalities)

| Size of municipality | 1000 | 1001–2000 | 2001–5000 | 5001–10000 | 10001–20000 | 20001 |
|---|---|---|---|---|---|---|
| Municipality/regr. Coefficient | −0,1082 | −0,0368 | −0,0016 | −0,0026 | 0,0016 | 0,0003 |
| 500 inhabitants | −54100 | −18400 | −800 | −1300 | 800 | 150 |
| 1500 inhabitants | | −55200 | −2400 | −3900 | 2400 | 450 |
| 2500 inhabitants | | | −4000 | −6500 | 4000 | 750 |
| 6000 inhabitants | | | | −15600 | 9600 | 1800 |
| 15000 inhabitants | | | | | 24000 | 4500 |
| 30000 inhabitants | | | | | | 9000 |

According to the regression analysis, it would be possible to achieve economies of scale only with a joint office of up to 10,000 inhabitants. From this size on, unit expenditures would gradually increase. In this case, however, it is not the cumulative revenues from the range, only the revenues for a given size group. This means that it would still be advantageous for the smallest municipalities to be a participant in such a joint office, but they would not maximize the achievable economies of scale. Another, more realistic view of economies of scale is the weighted average unit expenditure per capita (01.1.1). The following table presents unit expenditures per capita of current expenditures 01.1.1. Average expenditures were adjusted on the basis of weights (number of inhabitants of individual municipalities) (Table 12).

**Table 12.** Average expenditures per capita (01.1.1). In individual size groups and their weighted average

|  | Up to 1000 | 1001–2000 | 2001–5000 | 5001–10000 | 10001–20000 | 20000–90000 |
|---|---|---|---|---|---|---|
| Average | 166,00 | 138,00 | 122,00 | 120,00 | 105,00 | 99,00 |
| Weighted average | 157,00 | 131,00 | 110,00 | 114,00 | 103,00 | 102,70 |

Based on the obtained data, potential savings in individual model municipalities were recalculated. The total unit expenditure would e.g. for a municipality with 500 inhabitants, which would be part of a joint office with a total size of up to 20,000 inhabitants, their current expenses 01.1.1. Would be at a height of approx. € 51,500, the total savings would be approx. 27 thousand € (Table 13).

It follows from the above that effectively the highest savings would be achieved by local governments in cooperation with a size of 10,000 to 20,000 inhabitants, but also smaller units from 2,000 to 5,000 inhabitants. Within the scope of economies of scale according to average values, it would be economically worthwhile for local governments to increase the size above 20,000 inhabitants, but the savings would not offset the disadvantages associated with higher distribution and decision-making costs. In this case, the expenses on the part of the population associated with the availability of the office (taking over more and more remote municipalities) would also increase.

The analysis of economies of scale has shown that the appropriate tools can be used to solve, at least in part, the problems faced by small municipalities. The way is effective cooperation, which would not endanger the sovereignty of small municipalities, but would allow to take advantage of economies of scale, specialization, and the increase of the quality of services provided as a result of this cooperation. The unit, which would be created on the basis of cooperation agreements, should be an unequivocally independent legal entity, a service center without regulatory competence towards cooperating municipalities. The principles of operation of this institution must be based on the principles of the concept of social responsibility, in the context of positive PR, image, communication and non-profit marketing.

**Table 13.** Total cumulated unit expenditure 01.1.1 and total savings/additional expenditure for each size class

| Expenses | 1000 | 1001-2000 | 2001-5000 | 5001-10000 | 10001-20000 | 20001 |
|---|---|---|---|---|---|---|
| Municipality / weighted averageexpenses | 157,0 | 131,0 | 110,0 | 114,0 | 103,0 | 102,7 |
| 500 inhab. | 78500 | 65500 | 55000 | 57000 | 51500 | 51350 |
| 1500 inhab. | | 196500 | 165000 | 171000 | 154500 | 154050 |
| 2500 inhab. | | | 275000 | 285000 | 257500 | 256750 |
| 6000 inhab. | | | | 684000 | 618000 | 616200 |
| 15000 inhab. | | | | | 1545000 | 1540500 |
| 30000 inhab. | | | | | | 3081000 |
| Savings | 1000 | 1001-2000 | 2001-5000 | 5001-10000 | 10001-20000 | 20001 |
| 500 inhab. | | -13000 | -23500 | -21500 | -27000 | -27150 |
| 1500 inhab. | | | -31500 | -25500 | -42000 | -42450 |
| 2500 inhab. | | | | 10000 | -17500 | -18250 |
| 6000 inhab. | | | | | -66000 | -67800 |
| 15000 inhab. | | | | | | -4500 |
| 30000 inhab. | | | | | | |

## 5  Conclusion

Not only in the V4 countries, but in all European countries, there are major changes in the structure of urbanization in the cities and municipalities themselves. They take place in the context of new patterns of social and economic relations. Social, economic, ecological and political problems are increasing, which results in changes in the processes of local government management. Local governments are elected by the people, but economic interests are increasingly dependent on financial organizations and industrial enterprises, which are not politically responsible for the operation and development of the government itself. Small municipalities with 2,000 to 3,000 inhabitants in Slovakia create rural settlements, and it is essential that they respond to the problems of the future, but also to opportunities by cooperating at local and regional levels. Traditional general policies and institutions appear to be ineffective and unable to achieve the goals that guide these new groupings and organizations. With the increased mobility of the population, the very relations between the population and the territory have become very dynamic.

This scientific study does not provide clear guidance for solving the problem of small communities, but provides a good orientation or direction which local governments can go when cooperating, and what possibilities they have in reducing the costs of their activities and increasing their social responsibility. The new model of cooperation should be based on the principles of the concept of social responsibility, communication, and good experience that participants have with each other. The main goal is to use all the effects that this cooperation can bring (especially in terms of socially responsible management). However, the basis for solving all problems are well-equipped human resources that can effectively use the possible synergetic effects of inter-municipal cooperation.

Inter-municipal cooperation exists in many countries, regardless of the nature of the settlement-administrative system and the extent of its fragmentation. It can be found both in countries with a large number of small municipalities and in systems that have undergone recent municipalisation (e.g. Belgium, Germany), but also in countries with large local government units (Great Britain). Of particular importance is the cooperation of municipalities in Germany, where they solved the problems of small municipalities in two ways: by introducing self-governing districts, union municipalities and local administrative units (the original municipalities remain preserved in terms of their legal personality, the most demanding administrative agendas are performed by one municipality). The second solution (a similar model is recommended for the use of the effects of economies of scale in the conditions of Slovakia) is the building of associations to perform selected, usually individual tasks that exceed the capabilities of the municipality (special purpose association, contractual community, municipal labor community and various regional associations). In France, a wide range of different forms of cooperation has emerged between local authorities, with the aim of overcoming the disadvantages of the fragmentation of the public administration system. French municipalities thus have the opportunity to join various single - and multi - purpose associations, called syndicates. In Austria, municipalities are creating so-called communities of municipalities, which do not have their own legal personality, but have a broad focus on several activities (e.g. joint municipal office, operation of a computer network, fire protection equipment, joint collection of local taxes and fees, etc.). According to the law, the federal state can also create a so-called association with compulsory participation of municipalities (e.g. for the performance of tasks under the Social Assistance Act). In addition, Austrian municipalities form associations, and the sovereignty of such associated municipalities must not be endangered by law. The sovereignty of associated municipalities is also reflected in the fact that each of these municipalities must be represented in the bodies of the association. The activities of associated municipalities are usually focused on the joint performance of only one task. Another model is introduced, for example, in Lower Saxony, where municipalities with a population of less than 400 are mandatory to merge, while in such common municipality, there can be a maximum of 10 original municipalities and its population should not exceed 7,000 inhabitants [21]. This model is not preferred, although it is possible to apply certain proven principles.

One of the ways to preserve local democratic traditions within the merged units is the so-called decentralized governance neighborhood councils with specific responsibilities. Such solutions can be found in both Sweden and Finland. Katajamäki and Mariussen [12] reported on how this concept was assessed for the merged community. However, a decision was later taken in Umeå, where these neighborhood councils were dissolved. Such "Councils" in the context of Umeå included competence issues concerning schools, young people, leisure, culture, libraries, families, the elderly and services for the disabled. Another alternative that took place in Sweden was the possibility of cooperating across city borders in the form of a federation of local government (in Swedish "Kommunalförbund") to address certain responsibilities. The task of such an organizational framework was to create a body responsible for matters mutually agreed between the municipalities. Today, we can find about 90 such organizations throughout Sweden, which indicates a weak interest in this type of cooperation solution. A similar concept ("samkommun" or joint municipal councils) exists in Finland and is much more widespread. The main reasons for the existence of these councils are that the number of small municipalities is much larger than in Sweden [24].

The Västerbotten region and the subregion Region 8 is characterized by a large number of small municipalities. Addressing local cooperation provides incentives to develop common policy support tools and proposals for central government and the EU. Voluntary access to cooperation across regions and the flexibility of partners provide good opportunities. If the results are negative, it is relatively easy to review the cooperation (unless long-term contracts have been established). In addition to internal experience, active external search for "best practices" may be important. The cross-border dimension of such voluntary cooperation is based on identity in terms of feelings of belonging and lasting ties between the inhabitants of each municipality. According to a survey in northern Sweden, trust in local politicians depends on feelings and closeness in a broad social context [23].

Improving the management of small municipalities on the principle of social responsibility through intergovernmental cooperation provides, from the point of view of self-government, the possibility of maintaining autonomy and gradually building cooperation with other municipalities that are interested. However, the risks are a high degree of compliance required, costing problems, and price conflicts. Every change requires intensive communication and the search for consensus. Sometimes, it can be an endless process [2]. From the point of view of the state, the political identity of the municipalities is preserved in voluntary cooperation and unpopular interventions in the structure of municipalities and their autonomy are not necessary. Based on the experience of Bavaria, where in the 1970s municipalities were merged on the basis of a central decision; at present, such a decision would be difficult to implement politically. The advantage is that cooperation can take place only in selected areas and in solving selected problems [22]. However, the disadvantage is that with increasing cooperation, there is a risk (especially in connection with cooperation in many areas) that the influence of administrative staff increases and the possibility of control by elected representatives and citizens decreases [9].

All the mentioned solutions and experiences of individual states are based on the joint (shared) provision of public services. The basic and common element of all these solutions is the use of positive effects from the joint provision of services.

The problem of co-operation of municipal self-governments, connected with the creation of institutions and bodies of an inter-municipal nature, is undoubtedly a complex, multidimensional and sensitive issue concerning individual self-governing communities. This is evidenced by the experience of several European countries, where the process, which is also called municipalization, has already taken place. A municipality with 5,000 to 10,000 inhabitants was considered effective in most countries (but not in the conditions of Slovakia). However, it should be emphasized that due to the specific conditions of individual states (especially the settlement structure), it is not possible to determine the universal optimal size of the lowest level of self-government [7], which is a municipality or commune [10]. Based on the authors' research, it has been shown that more responsible economies of scale can be achieved with a unit of 2,000 to 5,000 inhabitants and 10,000 to 20,000 inhabitants.

Increasing the size above this level can lead to an increase in average costs. Regression, correlation analysis and analysis of average unit expenditures of individual size groups of local governments proved that the most suitable size with the highest economies of scale are the aforementioned municipalities of two groups. In the group 5001 to 10000, there is even an increase in unit expenditure per capita. Joining municipalities on the basis of cooperation alone does not have to bring economic effects. Modern approaches to the management of public administration bodies and especially new forms of cooperation and the principles applied in them are reflected in 3 basic models of public service provision. The new units must be built on a combination of these three models (Table 14).

The beginning of the 21st century in the system of providing public services by municipalities brought a transition from the principle of competition between public, private and third sectors to the principle of cooperation between these sectors in order to meet public needs by providing the public with active citizen participation. The basic principles of social responsibility in the provision of public services lie in the gradual transition from traditional / internal approaches to the provision of public services to alternative approaches based on partnership and cooperation with the active participation of a group of municipalities, but also the citizen in the service process. These principles are among the basic principles of social responsibility. In this context, the tasks within the partnership between local governments are divided so that the strengths of the partners are maximized, and the risks arising from their weaknesses are eliminated in the interest of more effective provision of quality public services.

**Table 14.** Approaches to process control in cooperating units

| | Bureaucratic approach | New Public Management | New Public Governance |
|---|---|---|---|
| Primary theoretical foundations | Political theory | Economic theory | Democratic theory |
| Rationality, related models of human behavior prevail | Political rationality, "administrative man" | Economic rationality "economic man", own interests | Strategic rationality, multi-rationality (political, economic, organizational) |
| Public interest | Politically defined and legally expressed | Expressed by grouping individual interests | The result of a dialogue on shared values |
| Who are civil servants responsible for? | Client and voter | Customer | Citizen |
| The role of government | Order (design and implementation of a policy focused on a single politically defined goal) | Manage and act as a catalyst for market power) | Serve-help (negotiate interests between citizens and community groups, create shared values) |
| Mechanisms for achieving goals | Through government organizations. | Through private organizations and NGOs | Forming coalitions of public, non-governmental and private agencies to meet shared needs. |
| Approach to responsibility | Hierarchical - administrators are accountable to democratically elected political leaders. | Market-driven - accumulation of individual interests with results for a wide group of customers | Multilateral civil servants accountable to the law, the values of society, political norms, standards and the interests of citizens. |
| Powers of officials | Limited powers | Broad, meet business goals | Powers limited and responsible |
| Assumed organizational structure | A bureaucratic organization marked by top-down management | Decentralized public institutions | Collaborative structure, external and internal cooperation |
| Assumed motivational basis of civil servants / providers | Plat, výhody | Entrepreneurial spirit, ideology of reducing government | Public service, desire to contribute to society |

The basic motive for the joint and socially responsible provision of services must be the improvement of processes for the benefit of users of municipal and municipal services. This will then be reflected in areas such as: performance growth in public services - a joint cooperating unit producing public services collects payments for the production of services if the services produced meet set standards, leading to pressure to increase performance, growth in quality of public services - citizens consider the quality of services provided within the partnership to be higher than in the case of traditional approaches to the provision of services with the application of an internal form of service provision. Furthermore, it is the generation of additional revenues - in the system of alternative provision of public services, the provision of services to citizens may charge, so citizens participate in direct payments to bear the costs of service, reducing demands on public budgets, decrease operating costs (economies of scale) – it can be assumed that cooperation within a joint unit will bring a reduction in costs to a greater extent than an individual municipality, which will be reflected in reduced demands with regard to public budget expenditures. Another advantage is the growth of the quality of management in the public sector - the partnership between the created unit and individual governments, and the need for communication and cooperation within this relationship will be positively reflected in the form of knowledge transfers and "best practices" and more effective risk management - adequate distribution of risk and competencies to influence key factors among the participating partners will lead to more efficient management and contribute to better results of mutual cooperation between the created unit and individual self-governments [14].

**Acknowledgements.** This study has been supported by the Research and Development Agency under Contract No. APVV-21-0363.

# References

1. Belajová, A., Hamalová, M., Matúšová, S.: The principle of partnership in current concepts of regional policy. Vedecké State **1**, 21–31 (2012)
2. Bogumil, J., Kuhlmann, S.: Impacts of decentralization: the French experience in a comparative perspective. Fr. Polit. **8**, 166–189 (2010). https://doi.org/10.1057/fp.2010.5
3. Principles of Good Administration In the Member States of the European Union (2005). http://www.statskontoret.se/globalassets/publikationer/2000-2005-english/200504.pdf. Accessed 10 Nov 2022
4. Čukan, J., et al.: Závery z mapovania a hodnotenia kultúrneho potenciálu Slovákov v Rumunsku. Kontexty kultúry a turizmu 9–15 (2020)
5. Dragoun, M.: The economic efficiency of the intermunicipal cooperation and its forms in the Euroregion "TATRY". Bankovní institut vysoká škola Praha (2005)
6. Galvasová, I., et al.: Cooperation of municipalities as a factor of development. Georgetown (2007)
7. Hampl, M., Müller, J.: Společenská transformace a regionální diferenciace Česka: příklad vývoje rozmístění pracovních míst a obyvatelstva. Geografie **3**, 211–230 (2011)
8. Hovgaard, G., Eythórsson, T.G., Fellman, K.: Future Challenges to Small Municipalities. The Cases of Iceland, Faroe Islands and Åland Islands, Nordregio (2004)

9.  Hulst, R., Montfort, A.: A matter of scale - the accomplishment of scale advantages by Dutch housing corporations. https://www.rikkoolma.com/files/A-Matter-of-Scale.pdf. Accessed 03 Aug 2022
10. Ištok, R., Klamár, R.: Geografické aspekty vytvárania spoločných obecných úradov v kontexte mikroregionálnej medziobecnej spolupráce. Acta Facultatis Rerum Naturalium Universitatis Comenianae, Geographica Supplementum **3**, 221–228 (2004)
11. Jaďuďová, J., Repa, M.: Social responsibility in the environment of public administration and self-government. In: Trends in Business, pp. 14–20 (2011)
12. Katajamàki, H., Mariussen, A.: Transnational learning in local governance: two lessons from Finland. In: Learning Transnational Learning, pp. 363–374 (2013)
13. Linhartova, V.: Modern concepts of public sector governance. In: Stejskal, J., et al. (eds.) Theory and Practice of Public Services. Wolters Kluwer (2017)
14. Mihályi, G.: Kvalifikačné predpoklady manažmentu miestnej samosprávy a ich vplyv na efektívnosť hospodárenia. EF UMB (2019)
15. Milder, D.N., Dane, D.A.: Some Thoughts on the Economic Revitalization of Small Town Downtowns (2013). http://www.ecdevjournal.com/en/News/index.aspx?newsId=acaba33d-Oe15-4994-b899-eacd1c6d8d21!. Accessed 01 Dec 2020
16. Statskontoret, S.: Myndigheternas spamhantering: en vägledning kring rättsliga frågor. Statskontoret (2005)
17. Pavlík, M., Bělčík, M., et al.: Social responsibility of the organization. Grada Publishing (2010)
18. Reingewertz, Y.: Do municipal amalgamations work? Evidence from municipalities in Israel. J. Econ. **72**(2–3), 240–251 (2012)
19. Slack, E., Bird, E.: Merging Municipalities: Is Bigger Better? EconPapers, University of Toronto, Institute on Municipal Finance and Governance (2013)
20. Storper, M.: The Regional World. Territorial Development in a Global Economy. Guilford Press (1997)
21. Tichý, D.: The right way is cooperation of municipalities. Current problems of fiscal decentralization in Slovakia (III). Public Administration 13 (2003)
22. Trhlíková, Z.: Problems of managing the property of the municipality through the establishment of legal entities - case study of the city of Napajedla. Masaryk University (2018)
23. Westin, L., Öhrn, I., Danielson, E.: Residents' experiences of encounters with relatives and significant persons: a hermeneutic study. Nurs. Health Sci. **14**(4), 495–500 (2012)
24. Wiberg, U., Limani, I.: Intermunicipal cooperation: a smart alternative for small municipalities? Scand. J. Public Adm. **1**, 63–82 (2015)
25. Zlepšovanie organizácií verejnej správy, príručka Model CAF. Resource Centre, European Institute of Public Administration, EIPA (2013). http://www.unms.sk/swift_data/source/dok umenty/kvalita/2014/caf/Prirucka_CAF_2013.pdf. Accessed 22 Mar 2023

# Author Index

O. Gervasi et al. (Eds.): ICCSA 2023, LNCS 13957, pp. 541–544, 2023.
https://doi.org/10.1007/978-3-031-36808-0

Printed in the United States
by Baker & Taylor Publisher Services